LITERACY

ASSESSMENT AND INTERVENTION

FOR THE ELEMENTARY CLASSROOM

Beverly A. DeVries

SOUTHERN NAZARENE UNIVERSITY

Holcomb Hathaway, Publishers
Scottsdale, Arizona

Library of Congress Cataloging-in-Publication Data

DeVries, Beverly A.
    Literacy assessment and intervention for the elementary classroom / Beverly A. DeVries.
        p.   cm.
    Includes bibliographical references and index.
    ISBN 1-890871-53-2
    1. Reading (Elementary)   2. Reading (Elementary)—Ability testing.   3. Literacy.   I. Title.
    LB1573.D445 2004
    372.48—dc22

                        2003022297

To my husband, Merlyn, who is always there for me.

Poetry credits for page 87: "My Family of Dinosaurs," copyright © 1998 by Helen
Ksypka. Reprinted from *Miles of Smiles* with permission from Meadowbrook Press. •
"Kangaroos," copyright © 1998 by Kenn Nesbitt. Reprinted from *Miles of Smiles*
with permission from Meadowbrook Press. • "Dainty Dottie Dee," text copyright
© 1998 by Jack Prelutsky. Used by permission of HarperCollins Publishers. •
"Fishes' Evening Song," copyright © 1966 by Dahlov Ipcar from the book
Whisperings and Other Things published by Alfred A. Knopf, Inc. Reprinted by
permission of McIntosh and Otis, Inc.

Holcomb Hathaway, Publishers, Inc.
6207 North Cattletrack Road
Scottsdale, Arizona 85250
(480) 991-7881
www.hh-pub.com

10   9   8   7   6   5   4

ISBN 1-890871-53-2

Printed in the United States of America

CONTENTS

CHAPTER 4
Tutoring   62

CHAPTER 5
Phonemic Awareness   80

CHAPTER 6
Phonics   106

CHAPTER 7
Word Identification   128

CHAPTER 8
Vocabulary Building   150

CHAPTER 9
Comprehension of Narrative Text   172

CHAPTER 10
Comprehension of Informational Text   204

CHAPTER 11
Fluency   244

CHAPTER 12
Writing   268

APPENDIX C
Assessment Devices 348

APPENDIX D
Instructional Materials 409

PREFACE

"If children could work on literacy tasks most of the time at a level of success, we would have solved the biggest problem in learning to read."

DON HOLDAWAY

In today's world, the importance of literacy cannot be over emphasized. Elementary students who struggle with reading and writing and other aspects of literacy require and deserve more instructional time than other students. The purpose of this text is to help you recognize and assess particular problems and provide effective interventions to help struggling students. It is intended for use by undergraduates majoring in elementary education, for graduate students as they tutor, for classroom teachers as they work with struggling readers and writers, for reading specialists who provide staff development for their districts, and for coordinators of volunteer community tutoring programs.

The many aspects of literacy are interconnected—writing supports the growth of reading ability and reading supports writing ability. As a teacher, you will encounter many different types of literacy problems. Some students may struggle with word identification, comprehension, or fluency, while others may need help in understanding letter–sound relationships, writing narrative text, or spelling. This book focuses on the major areas of literacy identified in the No Child Left Behind Act signed by President George W. Bush in January 2002; these are phonemic awareness, phonics, word identification, comprehension (of both narrative and expository text), vocabulary, fluency, and writing, which includes spelling.

Nine chapters of this text are devoted to these major areas of literacy. These nine chapters offer a four-part approach to their topics:

Research. Each chapter begins with a discussion of research studies and a review of the various theories related to the particular literacy skill.

Assessment. Next, chapters discuss possible assessment instruments for diagnosing and assessing problems and growth in these areas.

Intervention. Third, the chapters present a wide variety of activities and strategies in detail, since different students benefit from different approaches. Many of the activities in these sections call for students to read fiction and non-fiction books that interest them.

Technology. Finally, each of these chapters also includes a section on how teachers can use technology to increase students' skills in these areas.

I believe that comprehension is the primary purpose of reading and that the other areas are skills to aid comprehension. In order to comprehend texts, readers need to automatically identify thousands of words and quickly analyze unknown words. They need to understand the meanings of words in context. They must be fluent and have a good reading rate in order for reading to be enjoyable. Thus, two chapters of this book are devoted to comprehension—one focuses on comprehension of narrative texts and the other on comprehension of expository texts. These chapters are separate because narrative and expository texts are organized differently. Readers must use different strategies to comprehend, analyze, and evaluate these different types of texts.

In order to become more effective teachers, undergraduate students, graduate students, and practicing educators should reflect on personal experiences that inform their teaching philosophy. Literacy educators need to understand the qualities of effective teachers and the traits of skilled and unskilled readers and writers. Chapters 1 and 2 offer an opportunity to reflect on the experiences and opinions that may affect interaction with students and the ability to understand particular literacy problems. Chapter 3 discusses formal and informal assessment. It reviews the various types of standardized tests and explains how to administer an informal reading inventory, a miscue analysis, running records, cloze/maze tests, and checklists and rubrics that are based on state standards. Chapter 4 describes four different tutoring programs that have proven to be successful. A sample tutoring session, based on all four of these programs, is included. Throughout the text, I emphasize the importance of teachers partnering with students' parents or caregivers. In Chapter 14, I discuss types of parental behavior and how teachers can work effectively with all parents.

ACKNOWLEDGMENTS

I am grateful to David Yellin, my mentor from Oklahoma State University, for teaching me that reading is a sociopsycholinguistic process, for reviewing the manuscript, and for offering constructive critique. His encouragement throughout the writing of this text was an inspiration. Thanks to Jo Dorhout, who shared her expertise on computer software available for developing reading skills. Also, special thanks to my colleague Betty Lou Thompson, who encouraged me as she continued to inquire about the progress of the manuscript.

I also wish to thank the following individuals, who reviewed this book in manuscript stage and offered suggestions for its improvement: Diane Allen, University of North Texas; Carol Bunch, Hannibal-LaGrange College; Donna Harkins, State University of West Georgia; Charlene Hildebrand, University of Nebraska at Kearney; G. Peter Ienatsch, University of Texas of the Permian Basin; Kouider Mokhtari, Oklahoma State University; Timothy Rasinski, Kent State University; Elizabeth Rowell, Rhode Island College; and Martha Sheppard-Mahaffey, Tarleton State University. I appreciate their constructive comments, and the book is better as a result of their help.

LITERACY

ASSESSMENT AND INTERVENTION

FOR THE ELEMENTARY CLASSROOM

FORMING A PERSONAL PHILOSOPHY ABOUT LITERACY ASSESSMENT AND INTERVENTION

Learning is not attained by chance, it must be sought for with ardor and attended to with diligence.

ABIGAIL ADAMS

Scenario

Mr. Hugo is excited to sign his first teaching contract the week after his May graduation. He has been hired to teach second grade, the grade he has always dreamed of teaching. Throughout the summer, he organizes his classroom, designs thematic units, creates learning centers, and collects books for his classroom. When school starts, he feels prepared to begin teaching. However, all his planning does not prepare him for the challenges posed by the wide range of academic abilities in his class.

The greatest differences are in the reading abilities of the various students. Some students are reading above grade level. For example, Lori is independently reading the *Little House on the Prairie* series, and Matt can navigate his way on the Internet as he learns about sea creatures. Other students can barely read first-grade material, while some students can read words but do not comprehend passages. When he discusses some of his concerns about student reading levels with his colleagues, each one has the perfect "fix." Without questioning the purpose of any of the suggested teaching strategies, he tries one technique after another, only to find that none of them works.

By fall break in mid-October, Mr. Hugo is frustrated because he knows he is not challenging the strong readers and is not giving struggling readers what they need. During the break, he takes time to reflect on his reading instruction. It becomes clear to him that he is merely introducing instructional strategies without knowing why he has selected them. As he reflects, he remembers a phrase that one of his professors continually repeated: "Teach the child, not a method!" He knows this issue is at the core of his frustration—he is trying multiple instructional strategies without focusing on the students. He makes a plan that before winter break, he will carefully assess each struggling student's oral reading by administering a running record and the Woodcock Mastery Reading Test. He then will analyze each student's strengths and weaknesses and set up classroom reading time as a reading workshop. During the workshop, he will focus on individual students and begin teaching at each student's instructional level of reading. When possible, he will group students with similar strengths and needs in order to teach them instructional and/or metacognitive strategies for processing texts. He will group advanced readers into literature circles to study a particular author or genre. His goal is for all students to become independent readers.

INTRODUCTION

Mr. Hugo is wise to take time to reflect on his practices. It is important for all teachers to reflect on their teaching, and this chapter is designed to give you that opportunity. First, you will have the chance to reflect on personal literacy experiences that may influence your philosophy about teaching literacy. In addition, you will be encouraged to reflect on your views of reading and reading instruction. I will review two reading models to aid you in focusing on your view of reading instruction. Finally, I will examine the use of computers in building literacy.

THE IMPORTANCE OF LITERACY

For many of us, reading is an enjoyable and easy experience. Reading realistic fiction can make us laugh, cry, or empathize with the protagonist. Reading a mystery can make us bite our nails or draw the blinds. Reading realistic novels about people in other parts of the world can help us to appreciate other cultures. In addition to bringing relaxation and pleasure, reading is also a necessary skill for productive citizens in today's global society. Each day we are bombarded with printed material that we must be able to read in order to function: warning signs on medication and household cleaning products, disclaimers on television commercials, information on computer screens, preparation directions on microwave dinners, nutritional information on packaged foods, road signs, application forms, instructional manuals, and the list goes on. The more advanced our society becomes, the higher the reading level becomes for these everyday reading activities. Figure 1.1 lists the reading grade levels needed for various tasks. From this information, it is obvious that children must become proficient readers in order to perform daily tasks. Classroom teachers need to be prepared to teach reading and to detect students who struggle to make sense of print.

Readers not only need to read at an advanced level for everyday tasks, they also must be able to read with discernment. The Internet holds a wide array of information. Responsible readers must analyze the source and synthesize the information with prior knowledge and other sources so that they can evaluate the "information" presented. Writing is another aspect of literacy that many people enjoy. Some enjoy writing poems and songs to express their beliefs and feelings. Others enjoy writing stories of suspense, adventure, or romance. Many adults and children write as a form of therapy; as they journal, they express their true feelings. Others keep diaries to document important events in their lives.

Writing, however, is also an important skill that is needed in today's society. Children need to become fluent in expressing their ideas and feelings. At a very young age, it is important that children understand that writing is a means of communication and that the most important aspect of writing is the message. As they learn to communicate, they need to understand the importance of using standard spelling and grammatical conventions so that the reader will understand the intended message. Children also need to learn how to write for different audiences and for different purposes. All the skills associated with writing must begin to be developed in the early grades.

Former President Bill Clinton and President George W. Bush emphasized the importance of literacy in our global society when they signed into

FIGURE 1.1 Reading levels of daily reading materials.

Help wanted ads	6th–7th grade
Front-page newspaper stories	9th–12th grade
Information on medication	10th grade
Directions on frozen dinners	8th grade
Directions on 1040 income tax forms	9th–10th grade
Articles in romance, TV, and movie magazines	8th grade
Life insurance policies	12th grade

Source: McCormick, S. (1999). *Instructing students who have literacy problems* (3rd ed.). Upper Saddle River, NJ: Merrill.

law acts that affect literacy instruction across the United States. In 1997 Clinton signed The America Reads Challenge Act, which mandated that all students would be reading at grade level by the end of the third grade and inaugurated many new community-based tutorial programs. More recently, President Bush signed the No Child Left Behind Act of 2001, which requires that all students through the eighth grade progress in the following six area of reading: phonemic awareness, phonics, spelling and writing, fluency, text comprehension, and vocabulary. Schools need to document student growth in these six areas if they are to receive federal funds.

Elementary and middle school teachers face great challenges and are frequently pressured by principals and school districts to achieve higher student performance. They cannot merely try a number of instructional strategies, hoping one will "do the trick." Instead, they should aid every student in becoming a proficient reader. To do this, teachers need to understand the reading process. They must know how to assess reading problems, how to match interventions to particular problems, how to teach students to use reading strategies effectively, and how to reflect on the effectiveness of their own pedagogic practices.

FORMING ONE'S PHILOSOPHY

It is important that teachers have a personal teaching philosophy. They need to understand how children learn and which factors affect student learning. Elementary and middle school teachers should also have a specific literacy philosophy. They must understand the reading and writing processes, types of problems, methods of assessment, and appropriate instructional strategies to strengthen their students' literacy. For example, Ms. Rea's philosophy of reading instruction is that reading is learning to read words correctly. She believes that the root of all reading problems is the failure to pronounce words. She assesses her students by having them read word lists, and she spends many hours each week teaching them phonics rules. Mr. Garcia has a contrasting philosophy. He believes that reading involves bringing one's background knowledge to the reading event in order to understand or comprehend the passage. He understands that there are many reasons why readers do not comprehend texts; therefore, he assesses what readers do while reading a passage that is at their instructional level. Mr. Garcia draws

from a wide array of instructional strategies to help readers become proficient readers. Both of these teachers have a philosophy of reading instruction, and both assess students and provide strategies based on their philosophies. You may want to reflect on which of the two philosophies is closest to yours. Your philosophy may be completely different from both Ms. Rea's and Mr. Garcia's.

A teacher's philosophy evolves from many experiences: professional readings, class lectures, class discussions, and previous school experiences that may include effective and ineffective teachers. Beginning teachers frequently teach reading and writing in the manner in which they were taught, even when they are familiar with research and theories that suggest more effective ways to teach literacy. For example, if teachers have learned to read in small groups arranged by ability or in "Round Robin" reading circles (in which students take turns reading short sections of a text), they will usually feel most comfortable with those same techniques when they begin teaching. If, however, teachers have taken the time to reflect and develop a literacy philosophy, they, like Mr. Hugo, will be able to formulate a more comprehensive, coherent approach to teaching reading, as well as writing, speaking, and listening.

Reflection on Previous Literacy Experiences

To formulate a personal literacy philosophy, you should reflect on your own learning experiences since these experiences will influence your thinking. Figure 1.2 provides an opportunity for you to reflect on previous literacy experiences, beginning with early childhood and continuing to present literacy habits.

Reflection on Literacy Instruction

Teachers' experiences in elementary, middle, and high school impact their teaching philosophies. Preservice teachers' college experiences—reading books and articles about reading and writing theory and practice, and discussing educational practices with classroom teachers, peers, and parents—also inform their philosophies about how to teach reading and writing and help struggling students. There are many differing, strong opinions on the topic of literacy instruction. These include the six beliefs presented in Figure 1.3, which Allington and Walmsley identify as "conventional wisdom" in their book *No Quick Fix* (1995). As you read, mark each statement True or False according to your present beliefs about literacy instruction.

FIGURE 1.2 Personal reflection of literacy experiences.

1. **Preschool experiences**

   a. Describe your literacy experiences with your parents. Did your parents read to you every day? At a particular time? In a particular (favorite) place?

   b. What type of texts did your parents read to you? Stories? Non-fiction books? Magazines such as *Jack and Jill*?

   c. Did you listen to recorded stories or songs?

   d. Did you watch and discuss educational television shows such as *Sesame Street*?

   e. Did you go regularly to the public library? Did you get to choose your own books?

   f. Did you "read" to your parents? Did they "correct" you when you misread?

   g. Did you have opportunities to write and draw?

   h. Did you have access to a computer for playing games or reading interactive books?

2. **Elementary school experiences**

   a. What were some of your favorite books in elementary school? Who were your favorite authors?

   b. What were some of your favorite writing experiences?

   c. Did you learn in reading groups based on ability? What were they called?

   d. Did your teacher immediately correct students' reading errors?

   e. Were slower readers assigned extra worksheets to help them?

   f. Did struggling readers go to another room for special assistance?

   g. When writing, were you encouraged to sound out words or to look them up in a dictionary?

   h. Did all your words have to be spelled correctly before you handed your paper in to your teacher?

   i. Did you use basal readers? Do you recall any of your favorite stories?

   j. Did you get to read fiction or non-fiction books of your choice?

   k. What type of poetry did you read?

   l. Did you do any drama activities?

   m. Did you have a DEAR (Drop Everything And Read) or SSR (Sustained Silent Reading) program?

   n. Did you have a school-wide literacy program (e.g., the Pizza Hut Reading program)?

   o. What computer activities did your teachers assign?

3. **Middle school experiences**

   a. What were some of your favorite books in middle school? Who were your favorite authors?

   b. Were you assigned reading materials or did you get to choose them?

   c. Did you have a regular time for reading instruction?

   d. Did struggling readers receive extra assistance?

   e. Were you allowed to choose topics for your compositions or were they assigned?

   f. Did you take vocabulary and spelling tests included in special spelling/vocabulary books?

   g. Did you write a composition once and receive a grade, or did your teacher work with you to improve your work?

   h. What were you told to do when you did not know how to spell a word?

   i. Did you read and write poetry in class?

   j. What computer activities did you do?

4. **High school experiences**

   a. How did your reading experiences differ from those in middle school?

   b. What was your favorite book? Who was your favorite author?

5. **Current habits**

   a. What types of writing (e.g., grocery lists, poetry, songs, stories, letters) do you do voluntarily?

   b. Do you enjoy writing assignments in your classes?

   c. Do you consider yourself a good writer?

   d. Describe your writing process. (Do you begin on the computer? On lined paper? Do you keep everything you write or scrap passages you do not like?)

   e. Name a book that you read purely for pleasure during the past month.

   f. Name your favorite section of the newspaper.

   g. Do you consider yourself a good reader? Why or why not?

   h. How do you read a textbook with many new concepts that are difficult to understand?

   i. Do you read a novel differently from a textbook?

   j. Name one book that has made a difference in your life and explain why.

   k. Name a book you would recommend to your colleagues or classmates because you consider it a "must-read." Explain why you would recommend it.

   l. Explain how you feel when you are asked to give a presentation in class.

   m. Describe the type of group to whom you feel most comfortable presenting.

   n. How would you rate your technology skills?

FIGURE 1.3   Six beliefs about literacy instruction.

TRUE OR FALSE   1. It is not possible for all children to achieve literacy at the same pace as their peers.

TRUE OR FALSE   2. It is possible for educators to measure children's literacy aptitude.

TRUE OR FALSE   3. The best setting for children to learn to read is in a homogeneous group.

TRUE OR FALSE   4. Children learn to read through a hierarchy of increasingly complex skills.

TRUE OR FALSE   5. Children who struggle with reading need instruction in specific skills that is given at a slower pace.

TRUE OR FALSE   6. Struggling readers need to be instructed by specially trained reading teachers.

Source: R. Allington & S. Walmsley (Eds.) (1995). *No Quick Fix: Rethinking Literacy Programs in America's Elementary Schools.* New York: Teachers College Press.

How many of the statements in Figure 1.3 did you mark as true? Allington and Walmsley (1995) argue that all of the statements are false and that literacy instruction will not improve until all teachers change their thinking. They refute these statements of "conventional wisdom" as follows:

Belief 1: Allington and Walmsley believe that all children can become literate at the pace of their peers. They encourage teachers to recognize that individual reading differences are not indicators of how much students *can* learn, but rather "how much intensive instruction will be needed to accelerate their literacy development and move them alongside their peers" (Allington & Walmsley, 1995, p. 6).

Belief 2: Educators cannot measure a reader's literacy aptitude because readiness assessments only reflect the student's previous literacy experiences. Some parents have the time and money to provide rich language experiences for their children; they can take their children on field trips and give them a broad range of cultural experiences. These parents can provide tutorial help if they observe their children having problems with language development or reading. Obviously, children whose parents do not have the means to provide such experiences will not have equivalent literacy skills when they enter kindergarten and first grade.

Belief 3: Allington and Walmsley argue that using only a homogeneous grouping of struggling readers creates an atmosphere of failure because these readers hear no fluent reading from peers; they only hear other struggling readers.

Belief 4: Researchers never have been able to verify the existence of a specific set of skills that new readers must master in a specific sequence even though

many basal readers have attempted to describe the scope and sequence of such skills.

Belief 5: Children who are struggling do not need slower-paced but rather accelerated instruction in specific areas that will benefit them. It is important that students who do not have rich literacy experiences outside of school be provided many different language experiences in the early grades.

Belief 6: Allington and Walmsley suggest that instead of hiring specialized reading teachers, school districts should use the same funds to make all their classroom teachers reading experts. All teachers in all grades should know how to work with specific reading problems and ESL students.

You should take time to reflect on Allington and Walmsley's interpretation of these six beliefs and discuss them with elementary teachers and peers.

Reflections on Assessing Reading Problems

Proficient and struggling readers constantly make reading miscues (errors). Not all miscues, however, are "bad" (Goodman, Watson, & Burke, 1996) because they do not hinder comprehension. Some miscues indicate that the reader is reading for meaning instead of merely pronouncing words correctly. When assessing children's reading, teachers need to be able to discern which miscues do and do not hinder comprehension. Please explore your own philosophy of correcting miscues by deciding if the following miscues should be corrected or ignored.

1. The student reads very fast and makes many substitutions; for example, *home* for *house* and *steps* for *stairs.*

2. The reader never responds to commas or periods; she reads right through them.

3. The student reads very smoothly, but cannot summarize or retell what he has read.

4. When reading word lists, the reader reverses the spellings of many words, such as *was* for *saw* and *top* for *pot*.

5. The student reads "um" for *them*, "dent" for *didn't*, and "kin" for *can*.

6. When reading dialogue, the reader omits phrases such as "Mother replied" and "said George."

Which statements caused you concern? Would you correct all the errors or would you ignore all of them? Now continue reading to discover how reading researchers would respond.

There is no reason to correct the readers described in statements 1, 4, 5, and 6; however, teachers will want to aid readers such as those depicted in statements 2 and 3 for the following reasons (Goodman, Watson, & Burke, 1996):

- The first and sixth statements depict fluent, proficient readers who are reading for meaning and are less concerned about reading each word correctly.

- The first and sixth statements indicate that the readers' eyes are moving ahead of their voices; they are constructing meaning cognitively, even though they make substitutions and omissions.

- The reader described in the second statement may have comprehension problems if she omits punctuation, which helps determine the meaning of any passage. For example, the only difference between the following two sentences is a comma: "Mary, read the book" and "Mary read the book." Note the difference in the meanings of the two sentences.

- Statement 3 depicts a reader who can decode words without hesitation, but who does not read for comprehension. This should be a great concern for teachers because the purpose of reading is to grasp meaning.

- The fourth statement illustrates a common reading error. I have found that when reading lists, students may misread such words in isolation and yet will not misread them in a passage. If the same problem persists when reading a passage, comprehension obviously breaks down.

- The reader in statement 5 is simply pronouncing words according to her dialect; there is no need for alarm when that occurs.

Chapter 3 will discuss in detail how to assess miscues, separating those that hinder comprehension from those that do not.

Personal Philosophy of Intervention and Instruction for Struggling Readers

The DeFord Theoretical Orientation to Reading Profile is designed for teachers to reflect on their personal views of reading and reading instruction. Before reading any further, you are encouraged to complete the DeFord Theoretical Orientation to Reading Profile (TORP) found in Figure 1.4. The abbreviation SA means "strongly agree"; SD means "strongly disagree." There are no "right" or "wrong" answers. After completing the inventory, discuss your responses with your peers. When disagreement arises, explain your reasoning for your response. You can also share the TORP with a practicing teacher who you consider to be an effective reading teacher. After each of you complete the inventory, you can discuss your responses.

To score the inventory in Figure 1.4, different sets of responses need to be added separately. First, add your responses from numbers 1, 2, 3, 6, 8, 9, 10, 12, 13, 14, 16, 19, 20, 21, 22, 24, 25, and 28. If the sum of these responses is low (18–45), you view reading as a set of skills. You probably also believe that students must be taught phonics and other skills in order to read complete passages. Second, add your responses from numbers 4, 5, 7, 11, 15, 17, 18, 23, 26, and 27. If the sum of these responses is low (10–25), you view reading as a holistic event. You would likely teach skills using stories that students have read and enjoyed. If your scores were midrange and not low or high on these sets, you probably have not given much thought to how you would teach and assess reading.

It is clear that opposing points of view are presented in the DeFord Inventory. For example, statement 5 is in direct contrast to statement 20, and statement 6 is in direct contrast to 15. If you strongly agree that early reading materials should be written in natural language (statement 5), you will strongly disagree that early reading materials should have controlled vocabulary (statement 20).

Learning Theories Related to Literacy Assessment and Instruction

While exploring how children learn to read and write, it is prudent also to consider the learning theories you have been studying in your other education courses. The following are some important learning theories that relate to literacy assessment and instruction.

Constructivist Theory

All students make sense of new learning situations by linking what they know with what they are learning. Through accommodation and assimilation, they build

FIGURE 1.4   DeFord Theoretical Orientation to Reading Profile.

SA = strongly agree, SD = strongly disagree.

SA . . . SD

1. A child needs to be able to verbalize the rules of phonics in order to ensure proficiency in processing new words.   1 2 (3) 4 5

2. An increase in reading errors is usually related to a decrease in comprehension.   1 2 (3) 4 5

3. Dividing words into syllables according to rules is a helpful instructional practice for reading new words.   (1) 2 3 4 5

4. Fluency and expression are necessary components of reading that indicate good comprehension.   1 2 3 4 (5)

5. Materials for early reading should be written in natural language without concern for short, simple words and sentences.   1 2 (3) 4 5

6. When children do not know a word, they should be instructed to sound out its parts.   1 2 (3) 4 5

7. It is good practice to allow children to edit a text into their own dialect when they are learning to read.   1 (2) 3 4 5

8. The use of a glossary or dictionary is necessary for determining the meaning and pronunciation of new words.   1 2 3 4 (5)

9. Reversals (e.g., saying "saw" for "was") are significant problems in the teaching of reading.   1 2 (3) 4 5

10. It is good practice to correct a child as soon as she makes an oral reading mistake.   1 2 (3) 4 5

11. It is important for a word to be repeated a number of times after it has been introduced to ensure that it will become a part of sight vocabulary.   1 2 3 (4) 5

12. Paying close attention to punctuation marks is necessary to understanding story content.   (1) 2 3 4 5

13. The repetition of words and phrases is a sign of an ineffective reader.   1 2 3 (4) 5

14. Being able to label words according to grammatical function (nouns, verbs, etc.) is useful in proficient reading.   1 (2) 3 4 5

SA . . . SD

15. When encountering an unknown word, the reader should be encouraged to guess abut its meaning and go on.   1 (2) 3 4 5

16. Young readers need to be introduced to the root forms of words (*run, long*) before they are asked to read inflected forms (*running, longest*).   1 2 3 (4) 5

17. It is necessary for a child to know the letters of the alphabet in order to learn to read.   1 2 (3) 4 5

18. Flashcard drills with sight words is an unnecessary form of practice in reading instruction.   1 2 (3) 4 5

19. The ability to use accent patterns in multi-syllable words (*pho' to graph, pho to' gra phy,* and *pho to gra' phic*) should be developed as part of reading instruction.   1 2 3 4 (5)

20. Controlling text through consistent spelling patterns ("The fat cat ran back. The fat cat sat on a hat.") is an effective means of learning to read.   1 (2) 3 4 5

21. Formal instruction in reading is necessary to ensure the adequate development of all the skills used in reading.   1 2 (3) 4 5

22. Phonics analysis is the most important form of analysis used when encountering new words.   1 2 3 (4) 5

23. Children's initial experiences with print should focus on meaning more than precise graphic representation.   1 (2) 3 4 5

24. Word shapes (word configuration) should be taught to aid in word recognition.   1 2 (3) 4 5

25. It is important to teach skills in relation to other skills.   (1) 2 3 4 5

26. If a child says "house" for the written word *home*, this response should be left uncorrected.   1 (2) 3 4 5

27. It is not necessary to introduce new words before they appear in the reading text.   1 2 (3) 4 5

28. Some problems in reading are caused by readers dropping the inflectional endings from words (e.g., jump*s*, jump*ed*).   1 2 (3) 4 5

on their prior knowledge (Piaget & Inhelder, 1969). To facilitate this learning process, teachers provide authentic learning experiences for students, help them build connections, and provide background knowledge for students who have not yet acquired it. As proficient readers construct meaning, they activate prior knowledge and select necessary strategies to complete the task. With struggling readers, teachers need to build their background knowledge and explicitly teach strategies until they become proficient readers.

Zone of Proximal Development

Students construct meaning and validate new information and processes through interaction with someone who already knows the information and processes (Vygotsky, 1962). Vygotsky uses the phrase "zone of proximal development" to represent "the distance between the [child's] actual development as determined by independent problem solving and the level of potential development as determined through problem solving under adult guidance or in collaboration with more capable peers" (1978, p. 86). Further, he argues that "what the child can do in cooperation today he can do alone tomorrow" (1962, p. 104). His ideas suggest that teachers can play a key role in students' learning by providing the necessary scaffolding—providing support until students are able to work independently.

Hierarchy of Human Needs

Psychologists suggest that all humans have a wide variety of needs, some that are essential for survival and others that are necessary for psychological well-being. Maslow (1987) proposes that humans have the following basic needs:

1. Physiological: Need for oxygen, water, food, shelter, and so on.
2. Safety: Need for security in one's present environment.
3. Love and belonging: Need to be accepted by others.
4. Esteem: Need to feel good about oneself and to know that one has the respect of others.
5. Self-actualization: Need to know that one has fulfilled one's potential.

Maslow contends that the most basic needs must be satisfied before addressing the other needs. For example, many schools now provide free or reduced breakfasts and lunches because children cannot concentrate if they are hungry. State Departments of Education are also concerned about the safety of their students. For example, most states now have laws that require all visitors to sign in at school entrances and wear badges so that administrators can monitor who visits classrooms. Many schools also have on file a list of caregivers and others who may check each student out of the building and with whom they may leave after school. Many classroom teachers emphasize the importance of having every child experience a sense of belonging in the "classroom family." Effective teachers also seek ways to build self-esteem by making sure all students experience some measure of success. They know that each student has different abilities; they know the strengths and weaknesses of their students and provide specialized instruction accordingly. Successful teachers also help students recognize their abilities and provide appropriate praise when they fulfill their potential.

Working with Diverse Learners

Another aspect of teaching on which you should reflect is how to work with the diverse abilities and cultures you will have in your classroom. How will you teach reading and writing to students who do not speak English? How will you teach reading and writing to an autistic child? How will you challenge a student who has been identified as gifted, but struggles with reading and writing? How will you work with students who have learning disabilities? Finally, how will you work with students who are not motivated to learn to read or write? Not all these questions will be answered directly in this text. However, as you continue your study of education and learn about the special needs of children, you should be considering how you would teach literacy to each child.

Among those who study literacy practices and theories, and their impact on diverse populations, there is often disagreement about which is the "best" way to ensure that *all* students learn to read. Some researchers and educators advocate part-to-whole methods, while others advocate whole-to-part. It is important to remember that no one method is right for all readers. Remember, teachers teach children, not methods! It is important for teachers, however, to understand as much they can about different reading models.

READING MODELS

There are many points of view on how children learn to read. These perspectives can be grouped into two major reading models: the part-to-whole approach, often called the skills or phonics approach, and the whole-to-part approach, often referred to as the sociopsycholinguistic approach (Weaver, 2002). Teachers' philosophies about how children learn to read shapes the way they assess and assist struggling readers.

Part-to-Whole Model

The part-to-whole model emphasizes the importance of students first learning letter names and sounds, followed by simple words that are easily decoded and then reading stories that consist of these easily decoded words (Adams, 1990; Chall, 1983; Grossen, 1997; Stanovich, 1991; Vellutino, 1991). Phonics concepts are taught in isolation. The part-to-whole model represents three approaches to teaching reading—phonics approach, linguistic approach, and sight word approach.

Phonics Approach

The **phonics approach** emphasizes learning the names of each letter of the alphabet and the various sounds associated with the letters (e.g., the short and long vowel sounds, the two sounds of *c* and *g*). Blends (*cl, br, gr,* etc.), vowel digraphs (*oa* as in *road* and *ea* as in *sea*), consonant digraphs (*ck* as in *back* and *ch* as in *cheese*), and diphthongs (*oi* as in *oil, oy* as in *toy,* and *au* as in *caught*) are also studied out of their linguistic context. In phonics programs, students learn phonic rules along with the exceptions to these rules.

There are many commercial phonics programs that differ in their approaches; in general, however, phonics lessons are systematic and explicitly taught. Teachers' manuals for these programs are usually scripted; they indicate exactly what teachers are to say and which student responses are correct. Students are instructed in one concept at a time and complete worksheets based on that concept. Mastery in one concept is expected before students proceed to the next concept. Skills are often taught in isolation and teachers frequently do not integrate them with the texts used during shared reading.

Most commercial phonics programs are based on the analytical phonics approach or the synthesis phonics approach. In the **analytical phonics approach,** the entire word is presented to the students, and students are instructed to sound out each letter of the word. For example, the word *cat* is presented as a whole word; then it is broken down into its parts: /c/ + /a/ + /t/. In the **synthetic phonics approach,** children learn words by adding each sound onto that which follows. For the word *cat,* the teacher first presents the letter *c* and has the children say the /k/ sound. Then the teacher adds the letter *a,* and the children say the short /a/ sound and then say /ka/. Finally, the teacher presents the letter *t* with the children first saying the /t/ sound and then stringing the three letters together to say *cat.*

Some commercial phonics programs introduce letters in pairs of voiced and unvoiced sets (e.g., *b* with *p,* and *d* with *t*). Other commercial programs differ in their approach by presenting first the letters that are distinctly different from the others, such as *l, m,* and *n.* In commercial phonics approaches, the first stories read by students have limited vocabularies, which include only words that are easy to decode according to phonics rules they have just learned. These stories are often stilted. If the lesson emphasizes the CVC pattern with the short /a/ sound, the "story" will have sentences such as "Jan sat on Sam's hat."

Often readers who are struggling with reading are given a heavy dose of phonics and/or instruction word identification (Weaver, 2002). Phonics-oriented teachers reason that struggling readers need to understand the simplest linguistic units (the sound of letters) before they can progress to single words and later to sentences that are composed of words that are easy to decode. Their students often spend their "reading" time doing worksheets instead of actually reading.

Linguistic Approach

In the **linguistic approach,** another part-to-whole approach, the emphasis is on seeing patterns in words. Proponents of this approach believe that it is easier for children to learn words when they focus on two distinctive parts of each word (the onset and rime) instead of on individual letter sounds. **Onset** is "the part of the syllable that precedes the vowel." **Rime** is "the vowel and any consonants that follow it in a syllable" (Savage, 2001, p. 21). For example, in the word *three,* the *ee* is the rime and the *thr* is the onset. Onset and rime are also called **phonograms, word patterns,** or **word families** (Savage, 2001). The rime is taught first, and then children add onsets to create different words. For example, students learn the rime *at,* and then add the /s/ to create *sat,* /h/ to create *hat,* and so on, until they know *fat, bat, cat, mat, pat, Nat,* and *rat.* Simple "stories" are then created from each word family. An example of a linguistic story might be: "Pat sat on a flat hat. Cat sat on a flat hat." The Bob series is an example of the linguistic approach. There are many trade books that also use word families. For example, Dr. Seuss's *Green Eggs and Ham* (1960) uses many words from the *am* family, and *The Cat in the Hat* (1957) uses words from the *at* family.

Sight Word Approach

In the **sight word approach,** children are first taught the words that will appear in a story they are about to read. The once popular *Dick and Jane* series is an example of the sight word approach. In this approach, students memorize lists of words through the use of flash cards. The goal is for children to automatically recognize large sets of words. With the sight word approach, struggling readers spend much of their "reading" time memorizing flashcards.

Whole-to-Part Model

The second major model is the whole-to-part model. Some of the proponents of this model are Kenneth Goodman (1996), Yetta Goodman (1996), and Constance Weaver (2002). Teachers who use this model begin reading instruction with a shared book experience. A **shared book experience** begins with teachers reading and enjoying a story with the children. With young children, teachers often use a big book so that the students can follow along as teachers read and point to the words. The initial emphasis is on enjoying the plot, the characters, and the language of the story, and relating the story to their lives. During repeated readings, children begin to chime in on the parts of the story they know, such as the repeated phrases or refrains. Later, the teacher and students discover and discuss rhyming words, word endings, new vocabulary, and mechanics such as periods. For example, after multiple readings of Lorinda Bryan Cauley's (1992) *Clap Your Hands*, a book with many rhyming words, students are guided to discover words that rime (words that end in same letters, such as *sand* and *land*). After they find *down*, *clown*, and *frown*, they discover with the teacher that these words end in *own*. Later, they find other rhyming words such as *toes* and *nose* and discover that they rhyme even though they do not end with the same letters. Children become aware of letter sounds as they talk about words in the stories that they are reading with the teacher.

Teachers using the whole-to-part method often appreciate the importance of phonics instruction and plan stories that they can use to teach a specific letter sound or word family. The phonics instruction in the whole-to-part model is also explicit, systematic, and extensive; however, these teachers tend to avoid separate commercial phonics programs. Instead, they teach phonics concepts children need, using books that they enjoy (Cunningham, 2001).

Struggling readers in the whole-to-part programs receive the same type of instruction through individual tutoring. Teachers and struggling readers spend their tutoring time reading authentic texts, and then working on the "parts" that students need help with. As teachers work with struggling readers, they carefully plan the instruction, building on concepts students already know and helping them discover new language patterns and strategies to aid comprehension (Cunningham, 2001).

Figure 1.5 indicates how part-to-whole phonics and whole-to-part phonics are alike and different.

The whole-to-part approach to reading instruction has been criticized in recent years. Critics say that students do not learn decoding skills. However, proponents of the whole-to-part approach do know that decoding is one of the skills that proficient readers use as they comprehend texts. In the whole-to-part approach, these skills are learned from books that students are reading with the teacher and not from separate phonics programs.

Sixty years of research indicates that the whole-to-part approach does work for many proficient students and struggling readers (Daniels, Zemelman, & Bizar, 1999; Moustafa, 1996; Thompson, 1971; Weaver, Gillmeister-Krause, & Veno-Zogby, 1996).

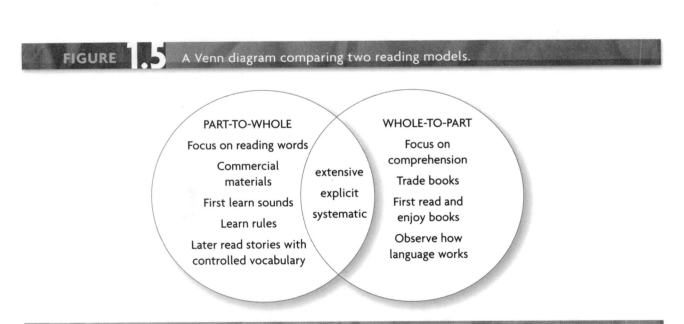

FIGURE 1.5 A Venn diagram comparing two reading models.

PART-TO-WHOLE

Focus on reading words

Commercial materials

First learn sounds

Learn rules

Later read stories with controlled vocabulary

extensive
explicit
systematic

WHOLE-TO-PART

Focus on comprehension

Trade books

First read and enjoy books

Observe how language works

Research comparing the two approaches can be traced in Constance Weaver's book *Creating Support for Effective Literacy Education.*

Which Method Is Best?

As a pre-service teacher, you may wonder which method is the best way to teach reading. No method is *the best one.* Beginning teachers who are formulating their philosophies of reading instruction must understand that teachers teach children; they do not teach methods or materials (Allington, 2001). Teachers must always consider the needs of the individual student and the student's learning style. Some children need to isolate small "parts" in order to understand the "whole," while other children are only confused by many small parts; they need to first understand the whole in order to see the parts (Carbo, 1996c). As Duffy and Hoffman (1999) point out, "[t]here is no 'perfect method' for teaching reading to all children . . . the answer is not in the method but in the teacher" (p. 10).

If teachers are so vital to the reading process, it is important for us to examine the qualities of effective teachers.

EFFECTIVE TEACHERS

Each one of us can remember good and bad teachers. Most of us can list a number of qualities our good teachers possessed. Some of the list may include descriptions such as *fair, consistent, sense of humor, made learning fun, organized, knowledgeable, caring, did not waste time,* and *even tempered.* Peart and Campbell (1999) find that effective teachers possess four critical characteristics: (1) good interpersonal skills, (2) the ability to communicate subject matter well through good instructional methods, (3) the ability to motivate students, and (4) an indifference to ethnicity in their treatment and expectations of students. Effective teachers also continuously assess students' literacy abilities and adjust their instruction based on this assessment (International Reading Association, 2000).

Wray, Medwell, Fox, and Poulson (2000) were commissioned by the Teacher Training Agency to study more- and less-effective teachers. The team found that in general effective teachers set time limits for sub-tasks within larger tasks so that students learn time management skills. This practice is likely to be useful when teachers are working with students who are struggling, because these students frequently need help managing their time.

TECHNOLOGY

Technology is a helpful tool for developing students' literacy skills. Teachers must use technology effectively, however, and use programs that help students become independent readers and writers. New reading and writing software is marketed every day. New programs are also being developed to aid assessment and for developing portfolios. It is important that teachers continuously review new software and learn to use it to enhance literacy in the classroom.

The National Reading Panel (2000) reports the following conclusions from studies that examined technology in literacy instruction:

1. Word processing supports the reading–writing connection.
2. Word processing supports process writing.
3. Technology supports students' motivation to read and write.

Hawisher and Selfe (1999) also find that technology positively affects (1) writing fluency, (2) the quality of student writing, (3) how much students write, and (4) students' social interaction while writing.

It is essential that teachers instruct students how to operate software. When students know how to use features of the keyboard and various programs, they save time.

Computers should be used for more than drills and "busy" work. Instead, teachers can use technology "to strengthen students' interpretative, analytical, and problem solving skills (Galin & Latchaw, 1998, p. 10). As students gather information from many new sources, they need to critically evaluate those sources (Rafferty, 1999). Who authored the passage and why? What points of view and values are presented? Did the author present a biased perspective?

Throughout this text we will review various software programs that focus on particular aspects of reading and writing.

CONCLUDING THOUGHTS

This chapter has given you the opportunity to reflect on past literacy experiences, on reading models, and on reading practices. Effective teachers constantly examine how they impact student learning, and they continuously study the effective use of technology to enhance literacy skills. Teachers must formulate and revise their own opinions regarding reading instruction, assessment, and remediation through research and working with children.

THE LITERACY EVENT

The great aim
of education is
not knowledge
but action.

HERBERT SPENCER

Scenario

Mr. Green is a principal in Westbrook Elementary, a building with five first-grade classrooms. At the end of his first year, he noted that every student in Ms. Bass's room was reading at or above grade level. The other first-grade classrooms did not achieve the same level of success. Mr. Green speculated that Ms. Bass had been assigned above-average students at the beginning of the year, but school records indicated that was not the case. He also discovered that for the past 14 years, Ms. Bass's students always read at or above grade level by the end of the year. At the beginning of his second year, Mr. Green decided to observe Ms. Bass in order to understand what makes her an exemplary reading teacher. He compiled the following list of all the activities he observed in Ms. Bass's room during the year:

1. Eighty-five percent of the day, Ms. Bass engages students in reading or writing activities.

2. She reads to the class at least four times a day for at least ten minutes each session. Sometimes she reads funny or tender stories. At other times, she uses reading to introduce students to science concepts through discussion of Eric Carle's books and other concepts books. Patricia Polacco's *Meteor!* (1987) and Darleen Bailey-Beard's *Twister* (1999) introduce the students to some of nature's wild phenomenon. Students learn about the world around them by listening to books that feature many different cultures. For example, after reading Mem Fox's *Possum Magic* (1983), Ms. Bass and the students located Australia on the globe. They learned about opossums and food products from Australia. She displayed samples of Minties, Vegemite, pavlova, and Lamington. She selects a broad range of books in order to introduce the students to the world beyond their own community.

3. She uses Guided Reading (see the Guided Reading activity in Chapter 7) so that students are reading books at their particular instructional level and learning new reading strategies. She always gives explicit instructions on one or two concepts to each reading group.

4. One half-hour each day is set aside for a "free read." During this time, children read books

selected from book bins that are at their "easy" reading level. They may also choose wordless books to "read" (see Appendix A.4 for a list).

5. When she sings with the children—and she engages them in a *lot* of singing—she keeps the words in sentence pockets so that she can point to the words as they sing. Some favorites in her class are "Follow the Yellow Brick Road," "Supercalifragilisticexpialidocious," "Zip-a-dee-doo-dah," "A Spoonful of Sugar," and "Frère Jacques." She often chooses songs with fun, colorful words to call attention to their sounds. Another class favorite is "Do Re Mi." Ms. Bass introduces the students to this song in order to also teach them to read notes on a musical staff. They learn to identify intervals as they read the notes.

6. As soon as students can count to five, she allows them to "buy" candies of various sizes with corresponding price tags (e.g., "one cent" tags for small pieces, "two cents" tags for bigger pieces, "three cents" tags for the largest pieces, "four cents" tags for two pieces of small candy, and "five cents" tags for two pieces of two-cent candies). She gives each student a nickel of play money at the beginning of each week and students can buy candy at designated times. As they learn larger numbers, she offers different treats. Ms. Bass explains to Mr. Green how students read tags and learn about money at the same time.

7. Every day she reads a poem from a flip chart, pointing to words as she reads. The poems are from Jack Prelutsky's and Shel Silverstein's collections, Jill Bennett's *Noisy Poems* (1987), and from various anthologies of children's poetry. (See Appendix A.3 for a list of poetry anthologies for children.)

8. Each day she reads a riddle from a flip chart and has students write their answer on a piece of paper along with their name. The following day, she reveals the winner(s). Her students love this! She explains that riddles elicit higher level thinking skills. So far, the most difficult riddle for the children was the following: "What can go up the chimney down, but cannot go down the chimney up?"

9. Each day she reserves time for storytelling. She often tells stories she loved as a child. Ms. Bass does not merely *tell* the stories—she entertains her students by *acting out* the narratives. She usually invites the students to act out parts with her. For example, when telling Jan Brett's *The Mitten* (1989), Ms. Bass encourages the children to enact the parts of the different animals snuggling into the mitten. When she tells Tomie dePaola's *Strega Nona* (1997), the students enjoy singing Strega Nona's song, eating the imaginary spaghetti, and pretending that their stomachs are growing larger and larger.

10. Most days, as a treat, she tells her own stories—always composed on the spot. Her stories always begin with "Once upon a time—a long, long, long, *very* long time ago . . . " or "Come with me on a magic carpet ride . . . ." The students know that if the carpet she describes is black, the story's setting is night. If the carpet is red, they are headed for danger, such as a stormy sea. If the carpet is green, they are entering a forest. If the carpet is blue, they are off in space. Yellow carpets always take them on a humorous journey. Ms. Bass explains that she uses this time to introduce students to new words. For example, she might tell a humorous story about a ragamuffin. By the end of the story, the students know the word's meaning and enjoy saying the word. Ms. Bass writes the word on the word wall and encourages children to write their own stories about a ragamuffin. Examples of other fascinating words with interesting sounds that she introduces are *lackadaisical, bamboozle, pandemonium,* and *zingiberaceous.*

11. At the end of every day, the students write a note to take home to their parents or caregivers.

12. Children listen to books on tape.

13. Students use computers to read books on CD-ROMs.

14. Often students retell stories through puppet shows or skits.

15. Each student has a buddy from the fifth grade with whom they read. The buddies come twice a week for 15 to 20 minutes.

16. Each day, students read in pairs; the pairs change every week.

17. Ms. Bass's room is filled with language games that can be played independently, with a partner, or in a small group. She uses community volunteers to play with the small groups. She gives the community volunteers extensive training on reading strategies that they can teach children.

18. Ms. Bass embraces an inclusive learning process; therefore, she has a reading specialist visit the class to aid any child that needs extra help.

19. Ms. Bass offers personal tutoring three evenings a week after school for the few students who need it. She gives them explicit instruction in decoding and encoding words. The school district does not have a Reading Recovery Program, but Ms. Bass has read many of Marie Clay's books and articles about good tutoring sessions and running records.

20. Each day, Ms. Bass and the children do interactive writing.

21. Each day students write in their journals. At the beginning of the year, many children's journals include pictures, but as the year progresses, the students do more writing than drawing.

22. Every day, Ms. Bass and her students have fun with language!

INTRODUCTION

Ms. Bass is an effective teacher. She focuses on literacy activities that both she and the students enjoy. When the students do independent reading, they read materials at their "easy" reading level so that they can be successful. She also understands that young children need to hear and experience language that will help them grow. She provides scaffolding for her students consistent with Lev Vygotsky's (1962) theory of the zone of proximal development; all children learn by first doing the activity alongside someone who is proficient in the skill. Ms. Bass also is knowledgeable about different learning styles—visual, auditory, tactile, and kinesthetic. She uses a wide variety of learning environments—large group, small group, pairs, and individual—and she invites other adults to share in the students' learning. Each time students are engaged in a reading activity, Ms. Bass and many teachers like her understand that five essential components must come together—teacher, student, text, context, and task. This chapter examines each of these five components of a literacy event.

TEACHERS

Much has been written about effective teachers in general and effective literacy teachers in particular (Darling-Hammond, 1999; Duffy, 1997; McGill-Franzen, 2000; Wray, Medwell, Fox, & Poulson, 2000). Chapter 1 highlighted some general traits of effective teachers. This section focuses on effective literacy teachers.

Effective teachers are an essential element in the reading event. They are more influential in the learning process than any curriculum or strategy (Allington, 2002). After a decade of observing exemplary elementary classroom teachers, Allington concludes that "enhanced reading proficiency rests largely on the capacity of classroom teachers to provide expert, exemplary reading instruction—instruction that cannot be packaged or regurgitated from a common script because it is responsive to children's needs" (p. 740). He reports that all effective literacy teachers he studied provide the following:

1. Time: students are engaged in reading or writing authentic passages; they are not spending time filling out worksheets.

2. Text: students read texts that interest them and that they can successfully read.

3. Teaching: teachers do more than assign and assess; they spend time demonstrating and modeling strategies that students need to make them successful readers and writers.

4. Talk: teachers foster students' communication skills by posing higher level thinking questions; they permit students to ask questions and to discuss ideas with their peers.

5. Tasks: students have a choice of tasks that require them to integrate reading, writing, thinking, speaking, and listening.

6. Testing: teachers grade process as well as product through the use of rubrics.

Effective teachers of literacy provide maximum opportunity for students to learn. They do not waste time with "classroom chores" nor do they waste time during transitions. They use this time to teach or for demonstrating and modeling. Effective teachers do not explain a concept, assign a worksheet, and sit at a desk correcting papers; instead they monitor and respond to children as they read and write.

Effective teachers of literacy also match the task to the ability of the students. When reading independently, students read materials at their "easy" reading level; when they work with the teacher, they read materials at their instructional level.

Effective teachers of literacy carefully use a combination of whole class, small group, and individual instruction. They permit students to teach and learn from each other. They also use community volunteers whom they train to assist students as they read and write. These volunteers teach strategies and play language games to reinforce literacy skills. Effective teachers also spend a lot of time reading aloud. Reading aloud offers many benefits to struggling readers:

1. They listen to books that are too hard for them to read by themselves.
2. They are introduced to new vocabulary.
3. They build comprehension skills.
4. They encounter new authors and new styles of writing.
5. They develop creative thinking skills by visualizing scenes from the books.

Jim Trelease (1996) suggests that "Every time we read to a child, we're sending a pleasure message to the child's brain, conditioning him/her to associate books and print with pleasure" (p. 57). Struggling readers usually do not find reading fun because they have to work so hard at it. When teachers read to them something of interest, however, their attitude toward reading begins to change and they start to associate books with pleasure.

Effective teachers also know the importance of independent reading in the development of literacy (Krashen, 1993). Too often, struggling readers are given worksheets that emphasize only one skill (e.g., circling the words that have a long *i* sound). If students can do the task, they obviously can read the word in isolation; so why give them the busy work? What struggling readers need is time to read and view books, magazines, or computer programs that interest them. Their interest in a particular topic will keep them on task and help them realize the importance of reading.

Effective teachers understand the importance of having a large selection of books that represent the different reading levels in the classroom and the various interests of the students. They understand that some reluctant readers are only interested in books when they can learn something from them; they prefer concept books instead of storybooks. Classroom teachers can use the public library and school library to keep changing the selection of books in the classroom. A wide range of books must be given to proficient and struggling readers for their free reading.

Effective reading teachers consider the impact of family on literacy development. They develop and implement programs that enlist the school community and families in reading instruction. This process will be discussed in detail in Chapter 14.

Effective teachers understand that "literacy is no longer simply about learning to read in a print-text format" (Rafferty, 1999, p. 22). Information and communication technologies permeate our society; therefore, it is essential that teachers understand how technology affects literacy instruction.

Effective teachers also place "great emphasis on children's knowledge of the purposes and functions of reading and writing" (Wray & Medwell, 2001, p. 1). They engage children in reading and writing for authentic purposes—to learn, to inform, for enjoyment and entertainment, for expressing opinions, for clarifying ideas. Figure 2.1 lists common traits of effective literacy teachers and the activities they offer.

STUDENTS

The last trait of effective teachers listed in Figure 2.1 is "Understand the uniqueness of each student." Each student is uniquely different from any other student! That is what makes teaching so enjoyable and challenging. Teachers encounter enormous and differing challenges each year. For example, the National Center for Education Statistics reported that more than 75 percent of all fourth graders and eighth graders scored below the reading proficiency level for their grade (U.S. Department of Education, 1998). The Individuals with Disabilities Education Act (IDEA) states that regular classrooms are the most appropriate placement for all students, even students with disabilities.

Students arrive at school with many types of differences and it is prudent for teachers to learn as much as possible about each student. Students differ (1) in their background knowledge of subjects and in how they integrate new information; (2) in literacy knowledge; (3) in how they make sense of print; (4) in learning styles; and (5) in different types of intelligences.

FIGURE 2.1   Traits and activities of effective literacy teachers.

EFFECTIVE TEACHERS . . .

1. Teach letter sounds using big books.

2. Model sound activities.

3. Stress the importance of writing for an audience beyond the teacher.

4. Engage in interactive writing with students.

5. Avoid published materials for handwriting practice; instead, they have students copy favorite poems.

6. Use whole texts for teaching concepts, instead of worksheets.

7. Teach the parts of speech through poetry study and composition.

8. Teach specific language features in the wider context of writing activities.

9. Teach fast paced lessons.

10. Use large blocks of time (as much as 90 minutes) for literacy activities.

11. Respond to and provide feedback on students' assignments while they work.

12. Set time limits for tasks.

13. Model writing extensively through the use of flip charts, posters, and blackboards.

14. Demonstrate and explain the thought process behind reading or writing.

15. Model how to write dialogue.

16. Teach students how and when to skim and scan.

17. Model expressive reading.

18. Emphasize rhyme and word patterns through the study of poems.

19. Emphasize good diction by studying authors' word choices.

20. Use a wide range of higher-level thinking questions and ask students to provide reasons for their answers.

21. Hold students responsible by requiring them to submit a report of the work they accomplish in each literacy time block.

22. Teach metacognitive strategies.

23. Understand that no single strategy works best for all students.

24. Demonstrate to students when and where to use a particular strategy.

25. Instruct students to monitor their own performance.

26. Engage and challenge all students in constructing new knowledge.

27. Make modifications in instruction and materials as needed.

28. Provide explicit instructions for use with authentic reading and writing activities.

29. Understand the uniqueness of each student.

Sources: Wray, D., Medwell, J., Fox, R., & Poulson, L. (2000). The teaching practices of effective teachers of literacy. *Educational Review, 52*(1), 75–85. Schmidt, R., Rozendal, M., & Greenman, G. (2002). Reading instruction in the inclusion classroom. *Remedial and Special Education 23*(3), 130–141. Rankin-Erickson, J. & Pressley, M. (2000). A survey of instructional practices of special educational teachers nominated as effective teachers of literacy. *Learning Disabilities Research and Practice 15*(4), 206–226.

Knowledge of General information

Many students come to school with a wide array of experiences beyond their families and local communities. They have experienced trips to zoos, museums, fire stations, mountains, oceans, rural areas, cities, and other places of interest. During these trips, they have discussed the sights and sounds of each place with their parents or other adults. These students have a rich aural and oral vocabulary, which enhances their literacy skills. Research has demonstrated that students' prior knowledge does aid them as they construct meaning through literacy activities (Cooper, 2000; Smith, 1965). Other students lack these experiences and, as a result, often lack specific vocabulary and background knowledge related to many topics studied in school. Effective teachers understand that they need to either activate or provide background knowledge, depending on the needs of individual students. They also understand that some students may rely too much on background knowledge when they read. Teachers need to help all students learn how to synthesize new information with prior knowledge.

Literacy Knowledge

Before you read this section, you should have a clear understanding of three terms—skills, strategies, and metacognition—used in this section and throughout the text. **Skills** refer to one's ability to perform a task. **Strategies** are plans or methods used to accomplish a task. Finally, **metacognition** is the ability to explain what and how one knows. For example, all golfers playing in a PGA tournament possess skills. They have the skills to drive a ball straight down the fairway, to chip a ball onto the green, and to putt a ball into the cup. All of these are skills. In addition, players have particular strategies they use to perform each step. They have a particular stance, depending on the position of the hole; a particular swing, based on the number of yards to the pin; and a particular chip, depending on the slope and conditions of the green. Golfers may have been taught these strategies by another pro, but in order for them to become skilled golfers, they needed to practice different strategies and decide which ones work for them. Metacognition is both the thought process a golfer uses as he decides which swing, chip, and putt to use and his ability to explain why he chose them. The same three capacities apply to readers.

Skills

Students' background with books greatly affects their literacy development. Some students enter kindergarten with rich language backgrounds and advanced literacy skills because their parents or other adults have read to them and discussed stories and informational books. These children understand the conceptual organization of printed material in English. They know that books should be read from top to bottom and left to right. They can find where a book begins and ends, and understand the difference between letters and words. They know that some books convey good stories and other books provide interesting information about various topics. Many of these students have had experiences "writing" notes to parents and enter kindergarten knowing letter names and the formation of the letters of the alphabet.

Other students, however, may not have these skills because they have had limited reading experiences with adults. They do not understand narrative form or that one reads top to bottom and left to right. They have little knowledge of letters and words, and they have a limited vocabulary. Teachers are challenged when students with these different skill levels are in the same class. The students with limited literacy experience will need guidance to become skilled readers. It is the teacher's responsibility to understand the strengths and weaknesses of each reader's literacy skills.

Strategies

Reading strategies should be taught explicitly. The purpose of teaching these strategies is to help students become more proficient readers when they read by themselves. There are three types of reading strategies—strategies to use *before* reading, strategies to use *while* reading, and strategies to use *after* reading.

Effective teachers teach strategies to use before reading to activate students' prior knowledge. Other strategies improve students' comprehension and reading skills while they read, and some strategies help students after they read to analyze, reflect on, or to remember what they read (Walker, 2000). Effective teachers provide strategies for all three parts of a reading event. These strategies will be discussed in Chapters 9 and 10.

When a teacher teaches a strategy, he must explicitly teach the steps of the strategy, model it, and then have the students practice it under supervision. For example, during reading, students need to know what to do when they encounter an unknown word. A teacher might instruct them to do the following:

1. Skip the word and read to the end of the sentence.
2. Look at the picture for clues.

3. Think of a word that would make sense in context.

4. Check to see if the letters of that word correspond to those of the word in the passage.

5. If the letters do not correspond, think of a different word that fits the context.

For example, in the book *The Wobbly Tooth*, from the Oxford Reading Tree Series, the teacher comes to the word *humungous*. She models the strategy above by first skipping over this difficult word and reading to the end of the sentence. She then comments, "The picture looks like the girl has a big smile," and asks, "Would *big* make sense here?" As she reads the sentence with the word *big*, she agrees with the students that *big* makes sense; however, *big* begins with a *b* and the word in the book begins with an *h*. "Hmm, let me think," she says. "What word means *big*, but begins with an *h*? Do any of you children know of a word?" One student exclaims, "Humungous! My brother always says he wants a humungous hamburger!" The teacher then checks to see if the letter and sounds correspond by spelling out *humungous* on the whiteboard and comparing it to the word in the text. "Yes," she says, "the word is *humungous*." She then continues reading.

The next few times that students encounter an unknown word, the teacher reminds the students of this strategy and has them practice its steps. The goal is for the students to automatically use the strategy when they read by themselves.

Teaching appropriate strategies is demanding for teachers because they must constantly assess students as they read, demonstrate the appropriate steps, and teach students how and when to use them. They can teach reading strategies to large groups, small groups, or to individuals. Effective teachers teach reading strategies when the students need them, in the context of authentic reading or writing activities (Allington, 2002; Fountas & Pinnell, 1996; Rankin-Erickson & Pressley, 2000; Schmidt, Rozendal, & Greenman, 2002; Stahl & Kuhn, 1995; Weaver, 1994a).

Metacognition

Poor readers lack metacognitive strategies. Metacognition involve a person's awareness of his or her own thinking and the conscious efforts to monitor this awareness. Effective teachers not only teach appropriate reading strategies, but also teach metacognitive techniques that help students decide how and when to employ such (Schmidt, Rozendal, & Greenman, 2002).

One way to enhance students' metacognition is for a teacher to use a "think-aloud" to demonstrate her metacognitive process as she monitors her own reading. For example, when reading a passage on Abraham Lincoln, she might comment, "It says here that Abe Lincoln had very little schooling by the time he was 16. That doesn't seem right. It seems like he should have had more schooling by that age in order to be president. I need to reread to see how old Lincoln actually was when he began schooling to confirm the fact that he did not have much schooling before 16." The teacher then invites the students to read; when they encounter an unknown or puzzling fact, she asks them what they need to do and guides them through the process. Students use metacognitive strategies when they independently monitor their reading processes and comprehension.

Language Systems Readers Use

Readers use four cueing systems—syntactic, semantic, graphophonic, and pragmatic—as they make sense of written text. **Syntax** refers to the grammar of sentences. In English, most words in sentences must appear in a particular order. "Mary had a little lamb" is acceptable, while "Had little a lamb Mary" is not. Very young children learn the accepted syntax when they begin to talk. **Semantic** refers to the meaning of words and sentences. For example, a writer conveys two very different ideas with the following two sentences: "I went to visit England" and "I went to conquer England." The change of one word makes the meaning of the two sentences drastically different. The third, **graphophonic** cueing system refers to letter–sound relationships. When students do not produce the correct vowel sounds, they can easily mix-up words (e.g., *dig* can become *dog*, *cut* can become *cat*, and *bag* can become *big*). Obviously students who misread *dog* for *dig* will misunderstand the meaning of the sentence. The fourth, **pragmatic** cueing system refers to the context of the passage. Some texts, such as emails to friends, are less formal than others, such as business letters. Reading teachers need to understand what language systems students use when they read (Clay, 1993; Pinnell, 1989; Walker, 2000). Some students use syntax clues to figure out unknown words. Syntax involves the study of grammar—the rules by which sentences are formed and ordered. Students who use syntactic clues recognize when a sentence does not "sound" right based on their knowledge of the common sentence patterns in English. Other readers use context clues; they recognize from the surrounding words, phrases, sentences, or paragraphs that a sentence does not make sense. Still other students use visual clues; they recognize the difference between *frog* and *toad* because the *frog* begins with an /f/ sound while *toad* begins with a /t/ sound. Once teachers understand which clues students use, they can demonstrate how to use the other clues. Proficient readers can explain what language systems and strategies they use when the reading process breaks down.

Learning Styles

Every child has a preferred approach to learning situations, often referred to as a learning style. Studies indicate that there is a strong relationship between academic achievement and individual learning styles; instruction based on the student's learning style builds on the student's strengths (Carbo, 1983, 1996b; Gadt-Johnson & Price, 2000). A series of over 120 studies suggest that "when academic underachievers were taught new and difficult (for them) content through instructional approaches that responded to their learning styles strengths, they achieved statistically higher standardized achievement test scores than they did when the approach was dissonant from their style" (Dunn, Denig, & Lovelace, 2001, p. 10).

The following are five factors that affect learning styles (Carbo, Dunn, & Dunn, 1986):

1. Environmental preferences—sound, light, temperature, and design of the classroom.
2. Physiological preferences—time (morning or afternoon); food and water intake; kinesthetic (learning through body movement) and/or tactile (learning through touching and manipulating).
3. Emotional preferences—motivation (intrinsic or extrinsic), structured versus flexible classroom, responsible and persistent versus casual.
4. Sociological preferences—pairs or larger groups; competitive versus individual learning.
5. Processing inclinations—global versus analytical; right brain versus left brain; visual and/or auditory.

Effective teachers understand the range of factors that affect learning styles. Not all students learn best in a quiet classroom. Some need soft music or the sounds of other students around them. These students are often uncomfortable with a quiet environment. Some may even say, "It's too quiet in here; I can't think." Other students are annoyed by the slightest bit of noise or movement and cannot concentrate. For this reason, you should provide reading carrels for students who need a quiet atmosphere, and tape recorders and headphones for other students who concentrate best while listening to soft music.

Some students need extrinsic rewards in order to stay on task. A reading chart that marks their progress or a trinket from the classroom's "treasure chest" may be necessary to motivate some students to read. Other students do not need such rewards and do not take the time to record books on the chart or to take a prize from the chest. You should recognize these different needs and not expect the same behavior from all children.

Some students prefer to work with an adult or peer in order to stay on task. Other students prefer to read and write by themselves. Some students need to be munching a snack or sipping water in order to stay on task; other students do not need either. Some teachers have a classroom policy that students may have a snack whenever they want if they do not distract other students.

These learning styles can be found across many cultures; no cultural group has one specific learning style (Dunn, Denig, & Lovelace, 2001). However, those gifted in a particular area (e.g., music, mathematics, or linguistics) may have similar learning styles. Two opposing learning styles that frequently affect reading instruction are the analytical and the global style of learning (Carbo, 1996b).

Students process academic information analytically, globally, or using a combination of styles. Global readers tend to be visual and tactile learners, while analytical readers tend to be auditory. Analytic learners usually prefer brightly lit rooms and quiet, formal surroundings, with no snack or breaks; global learners prefer softly lit rooms, casual environments, music, and periodic breaks with snacks (Dunn, Denig, & Lovelace, 2001).

Analytic readers are auditory learners and process information in logical, sequential steps. Since phonics programs are logical and sequential, analytic readers often learn to read best when first presented with phonics and then proceed to whole text with decodable words. Global processing is accomplished when students are first presented with an overview of the information and then taught to analyze the parts. Global readers tend to learn best if they first read stories and then learn skills in the context of the narratives (Carbo, 1996c). Poor readers usually have an approach that is more global than analytical (Carbo, 1996b). It is important to note that both analytical and global readers need to read whole text and need explicit phonics and word study (Stahl & Kuhn, 1995). They just need them presented in a different order. For this reason, homogeneous groupings of students with similar learning styles may enhance instruction.

Multiple Intelligences

Another contemporary theory of interest to teachers is Howard Gardner's theory of multiple intelligences (1983, 1993). This theory overlaps in some ways with learning styles theory, but the two have one major difference. Learning styles theory focuses on *how* materials are taught, while multiple intelligences theory concerns *what* is taught (Dunn, Denig, & Lovelace, 2001). For example, Joey, a third grader with musical ability, stays on task when background music is played. When he is asked to retell a story, he likes to make up a jingle about the plot. Juan, another boy in the same class, learns best when manipulating objects and has the ability to create intricate models. When Juan is asked to retell a story, he likes to retell it by creating a diorama. Teachers must learn as much as possible about the unique talents (abilities) and learning styles of students, and then cater lessons and learning environments to fit the students' needs.

Gardner's multiple intelligences theory states that all humans possess nine different intelligences; however, one tends to be dominant in each person. Figure 2.2 lists the nine intelligences with a brief description of each.

Gardner did not develop multiple intelligences as an educational theory; however, many educators have written curricula based on the theory of multiple intelligences. I contend that teachers teach children, not curricula, and that the more teachers understand the uniqueness of individuals, the better they can aid students as they develop literacy abilities. Therefore, it is helpful for teachers to know about multiple intelligences as a means to better understand the differences among learners. For example, students with a dominant musical intelligence may be able to clap back complex syncopated rhythms after hearing them only once. Students with a dominant spatial intelligence may be able to relate ideas through drawing and graphing. Students who have a dominant interpersonal intelligence may be able to provide effective organization for various group activities because they understand which personalities work well together.

TEXT

The third element of the reading event is the text. Each reader encounters three levels of difficulty in texts:

Independent Reading Level

When reading independently, a student reads a passage with 95 to 100 percent accuracy. This means that in a passage of 100 words, the reader makes five or fewer errors and has a comprehension level of 90 percent or better. The reader can read these passages at an appropriate rate, with correct phrasing, and with expression that conveys the meaning of the passage.

Instructional Reading Level

When reading at an instructional level, a student reads a passage with 90 to 95 percent accuracy and with a comprehension level of 60 percent or better. This means that in a 100-word passage, the reader makes no more than 10 errors. At the instructional level, the reader can comprehend most of the unknown words quickly and accurately.

FIGURE 2.2 Howard Gardner's multiple intelligences.

1. Linguistic: Ability to use and manipulate languages.
2. Logical–Mathematical: Ability to understand causes and effects, to calculate easily, and to think abstractly.
3. Spatial: Ability to represent the spatial world in one's mind.
4. Kinesthetic: Ability to use one's body.
5. Musical: Ability to hear rhythms and melodies.
6. Intrapersonal: Ability to understand oneself.
7. Interpersonal: Ability to interact with and understand others.
8. Naturalistic: Ability to discriminate among the parts of nature.
9. Existential: Ability to understand philosophies and theories.

Frustration Reading Level

At this level, a student reads a passage with less than 90 percent accuracy and a comprehension level of 50 percent or less. This means that in a 100-word passage, he makes more than 10 errors. If the passage is at his frustration level, he cannot comprehend unknown words quickly. He begins to read at a slow pace, reading words instead of phrases.

Selecting Appropriate Texts

When reading independently, students should work with texts they can read easily and successfully. To become independent, proficient readers, they must spend an enormous amount of time reading books successfully. Children become motivated to read when they read easy material that interests them (Allington, 2001; Carbo, 1997; Clay, 1993; Fountas & Pinnell, 1996). When working with a teacher or other adult, students need to be challenged with a text at their instructional reading level, which means that the text offers a minimum of new words and concepts (Fountas & Pinnell, 1996). Frustration level texts are discouraging to children and adults.

Effective teachers give students a wide array of reading materials. They expose students to historical fiction, biography, mysteries, folklores, science fiction, and poetry. They also use reading materials other than books such as magazines, the Internet, and other nontraditional texts. All these materials need to be at the student's easy reading level for independent reading and at instructional level when students are working with teachers or paraprofessionals (Allington, Johnston, & Day, 2002).

When selecting reading materials for students, you should follow these criteria for both easy and instructional reading texts:

1. Select books that bring students enjoyment and meaning.
2. Choose books that are interesting for the particular readers.
3. Be certain books present accurate information.
4. Choose books with accurate and diverse multicultural representations.
5. Use books from a range of genres (e.g., poetry, stories, drama, and nonfiction exposition).
6. Use many books at each reading level.
7. Choose books with high quality illustrations.
8. Choose books with complimentary texts and illustrations.
9. Select books of a length appropriate for the desired reading level.
10. Use instructional reading–level books that are challenging, but not discouraging.
11. Include easy reading–level books to build fluency.
12. Use easy reading–level books to allow readers to build comprehension rather than focusing on deciphering words.

Many publishers now publish books with fine gradient texts for teachers to use for instructional purposes (Fountas & Pinnell, 1996, 1999a, 2001). The level of instructional books is determined using the following criteria:

1. *Length and number of words in the book.*
2. *Size and layout of the print.* First levels have a larger print size with the text on the same part of each page.
3. *Vocabulary and concepts.* First levels begin with vocabulary and concepts found in children's oral language.
4. *Language structure.* First levels begin with phrases and continue to simple sentences.
5. *Text structure and genre.* First levels have a single incident or concept.
6. *Predictability and pattern of language.* First level follows a single linguistic pattern.
7. *Illustration support.* The illustrations in the first level thoroughly support the text.

Reading recovery (see Chapter 4), a tutoring program used in more than 6,000 U.S. school districts, and guided reading, a small-group reading program (see Chapter 7), use gradient or "leveled" books. "Leveled" books are different from "grade-leveled" books in that the shift in difficulty between the levels in the former is very minute. Reading recovery books have a finer gradient than the books used for guided reading.

Fountas and Pinnell (1996) have leveled guided reading books from levels A to Z. The following discussion gives some brief examples of the characteristics of some of these levels, but readers should refer to the Fountas and Pinnell text *Guided Reading: Good First Teaching for All Children* (1996) for more in-depth descriptions of levels and examples of books that fit these levels.

According to this system of leveling, Level A books are short and simple and demonstrate a "direct correspondence between the text and the pictures" (p. 117). Pages typically contain only one to four lines of text on a page, and the words are spaced far enough apart so that readers can point to the words as they read the text. As other examples, in Level F books, the placement of the text may vary, the print tends to be proportionately smaller, and the stories have plots with a beginning, middle, and end. Level J signifies short chapter books, which still include pictures but offer a wider range of literacy language. Level L books represent a significant shift in reading material, including chapter books with few illustrations, more complex characterization, and more-involved plots. In Level L, word spacing is narrower, which makes reading more challenging to many students. According to Fountas and Pinnell, one example of a Level L book is *Cam Jansen and the Mystery of the Monster Movie* by David Adler. Level P books (e.g., Jean Fritz's *George Washington's Breakfast* and Eloise Greenfield's *Rosa Parks*) are longer chapter books that require more than more sitting to complete, requiring readers to recall what was read in the previous sitting. Levels Q through Z offer challenging vocabulary and still more complex plots and characterization. Readers need to use many strategies to comprehend the text. As an example of a Level Q book, Fountas and Pinnell cite Dick King-Smith's *Babe the Gallant Pig*, and as a Level Z book, *The Hobbit* by J.R.R. Tolkien.

According to Fountas & Pinnell (1999), kindergarten students are expected to read Levels A and B by the end of the school year. First graders are expected to independently read through Level I by the end of the school year. Second graders are expected to read through Level L, while third graders are expected to read through Level O. Fourth graders are expected to master Level T by the end of the year, and by the end of the fifth grade, students should master Level W. Finally, sixth graders are expected to master Level Z books by the end of the year.

Publishers use a range of codes for leveling. Each book listed in Figure 2.3 includes an extended list of books from many publishers. All books are categorized according to guided reading guidelines. Figure 2.4 lists publishers of leveled books used in reading recovery and guided reading.

FIGURE 2.3   Guided reading book lists.

Fountas, I. C. & Pinnell, G. S. (1996). *Guided Reading: Good first teaching for all children.* Portsmouth, NH: Heinemann.

Fountas, I. C. & Pinnell, G. S. (1999). *Matching books to readers: Using leveled books in Guided Reading, K–3.* Portsmouth, NH: Heinemann.

Fountas, I. C. & Pinnell, G. S. (2001). *Guiding readers and writers, Grades 3–6: Teaching comprehension, genre, and content literacy.* Portsmouth, NH: Heinemann.

Schulman, M. B. & Payne, C. D. (2000). *Guided Reading: Making it work.* New York: Scholastic.

FIGURE 2.4   Publishers of leveled books.

Celebration Press, www.celebrationpress.com

Creative Teaching Press, www.creativeteaching.com

Education Insights, www.edin.com

Houghton Mifflin, www.eduplace.com

Newbridge Educational Publishing, www.newbridgeonline.com

Rigby, www.rigby.com

Scholastic Inc., www.sadlier-oxford.com

Scott Foresman, www.sf.aw.com

Sundance, www.sundancepub.com

Wright Group, www.wrightgroup.com

FIGURE 2.5   Websites for locating books for given grade levels.

1. Touchstone Applied Science (www.tasaliteracy.com) offers computer software for over 12,500 textbooks and trade books, rated by difficulty.

2. Scholastic Reading Counts (www.readingcounts.com) offers access to 25,000 titles, rated by difficulty.

3. Advantage Learning Systems (www.renlearn.com) offers access to 22,000 trade book titles. This is Accelerated Reader's website. Accelerated Reader is a program that levels books by grade level and provides quizzes for students to take on the computer. The computer program administers the grades and quizzes and determines the "points" students earn. Points are based on students' grade level, the number of correct answers on the quiz, and the level of the book.

Figure 2.5 lists websites that identify the *grade levels* for many trade books. Grade leveling (e.g., 1.4 = first grade, fourth month; 3.6 = third grade, sixth month) is not the same as the gradient levels used in reading recovery and guided reading.

The grade level of most trade books can be found by accessing one of the websites found in Figure 2.5; however, occasionally you may select a book that is not listed on one of these sites. In such cases, one of a number of readabilities formulas (e.g., Dale-Chall, Flesch, Spache, and Fry) can be used to determine the grade level of a trade or textbook. The extended readability graph developed by Edward Fry (2002) is easy to use on texts over 100 words and is intended for grades 1 to 17.

The Fry Readability formula gives teachers an *estimate* (plus or minus one year) of the readability of the text. Teachers must remember that all readability formulas yield a mere approximation of the book's grade level. However, an estimate is better than no information (Allington, 2001). Many textbooks intended for a particular grade are often written at a higher grade level. It is helpful for teachers to recognize when a textbook is too difficult for most students to read independently. Figure 2.6 includes a sample passage, the Fry Readability graph, and directions for estimating the reading level of a text. The best way to understand how the formula works is to choose an elementary science or social studies textbook and a trade book with narrative text, and then calculate the reading level of each, using the Fry Readability formula.

Readability software programs are also available. *Reading Calculations*, available for both PC and Mac computers, includes nine readability formulas, including Fry. With this program, teachers can type the passage into a text file or merely cut-and-paste it. The computer then calculates the reading level of the passage.

CONTEXT

The *context* of the reading event is the entire classroom climate. It includes teacher and student beliefs, type of literary event or interaction, student groupings, and other factors. Teachers' beliefs about teaching and learning are essential for creating an effective learning environment. Teachers who believe all students can be successful focus on students' strengths instead of their weaknesses. They provide unison reading for all students so that struggling readers can be a part of fluent reading experiences. They permit students to practice short poems or passages before they read in front of their classmates. They effectively use readers theater, giving long, difficult passages to fluent readers and short, repetitive passages to struggling readers. With these three types of reading experience, all readers achieve success in front of their peers.

Effective teachers understand the social aspect of literacy. Students need time to expand their ideas through discussion with peers. From those discussions they encounter different points of view and new ideas. Through discussions, students often connect the information or narrative to some aspect of their personal lives. Effective

FIGURE 2.6 Applying the Fry Readability Formula.

DIRECTIONS

1. Identify three 100-word passages in the book. The three passages should be from the beginning, middle, and end of the book.

2. Count the number of syllables in each passage and find the average number of syllables of the three passages. For example, the sample passage has 145 syllables.

3. Count the number of sentences, estimating length of the fraction of the last sentence to the nearest one-tenth. For example, the sample passage has eight complete sentences. The 100th word of the passage is the 6th word of the 9th sentence, which is not the end of the sentence. To find the fraction of the last sentence in the passage, count the number of words in the 9th sentence through the 100th word; this is the numerator. Then count all the words through the end of the sentence; this is the denominator. Find the fraction and change it to a decimal. There are 16 words in the 9th sentence and the 100th word is the 6th word of the sentence. Convert the fraction 6/16 to the nearest tenth (6/16 = .375 or .4). The total number of sentences for this passage would be 8.4 sentences.

After finding the number of sentences in each 100-word passage, find the average number for the three passages.

4. On the Fry Readability Graph, plot the average number of syllables and the average number of sentences for the three passages to get the estimated reading level of the book.

SAMPLE PASSAGE

(Sample Passage from Boyle, D. (1998). *Coral reef hideaway: The story of a clown anemonefish.* New York: Scholastic.)

3   1   1 1   1 1 1   1 1   1   1   2   1 1 1
Percula's mate cleans the rock. If they get the chance, some wrasses will eat the

5   1 1   1 1 1   2   2   1 1 1   1   3
anemonefish eggs when they are laid. Before twilight the rock is clean. Percula's

1   1   1   1   4   1   1 2   1   1   1   1 1
mate rests near the anemone mouth as darkness falls. Now sharks, jacks and

4   1   2 1   3   1   2   1 1 1   1   3
barracudas swarm around the shadowy reef, snapping up blue tangs and parrotfish

1 1   1   1 1 1 1   2   2   3   1 1   1 1 1
that have stayed too long in their daytime waters. Percula and her mate are safe in

1   4   1 1 2   1   1   2 2 1   2   1   1   1
the anemone. As the nearly full moon rises over the lagoon, the reef's night

2   1   1   2   1   3   1 1 2   2   1
creatures emerge. Like thousands of miniature stars, the coral itself blooms.

3   1   3   1 1   2
Squirrelfish and soldierfish leave the sheltered (100th word) crevices and hunt
along the bottom for worms and crabs.

(1) 100 words
(2) syllables = 126
(3) sentences = 8½

NOTE:

1. Scores falling in the gray areas of the graph are invalid. If this occurs, another sample must be taken.

2. A word is defined as a group of symbols with a space on either side. Acronyms (IRA), dates (2004), initials (J.), titles (Jr.), and symbols (&) each count as one word.

3. With numerals, acronyms, initials, titles, and symbols, each symbol within them is one syllable. For example, 2004 = 4 syllables; IRA = 3 syllables; J. = 1 syllable.

FIGURE 2.6 Continued.

Graph for estimating readability—extended
by Edward Fry

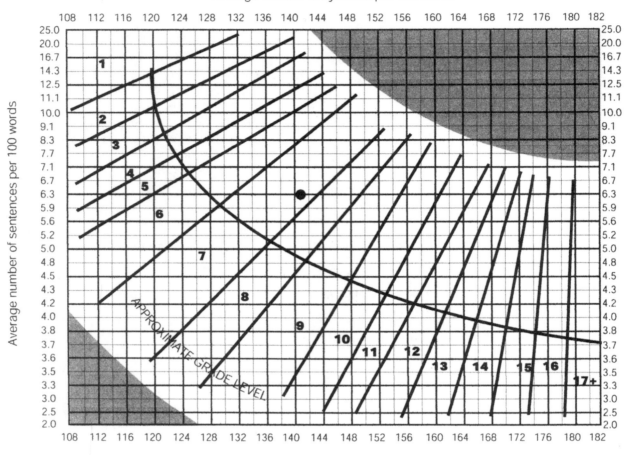

Directions: Randomly select three passages of 100 words each from a book or an article. Plot the average number of syllables and average number of sentences per 100 words on graph to determine the grade level of the material. Choose more passages per book if great variability is observed and conclude that the book has uneven readability. Few books will fall in gray area but when they do grade level scores are invalid.

Count proper nouns, numerals, and initialization as words. Count a syllable for each symbol. For example, "1945" is 1 word and 4 syllables and "IRA" is 1 word and 3 syllables.

Example:	Syllables	Sentences
First hundred words	124	6.6
Second hundred words	141	5.5
Third hundred words	158	6.8
Average	141	6.3

Readability seventh grade (see dot plotted on graph)

Source: Fry, Edward B. (2002). Readability versus leveling. *The Reading Teacher, 56*(3), 286–291.

teachers use discussions instead of simple questions to get the students engaged in higher level thinking activities.

Effective teachers create classrooms where there are frequent, sustained, and consistent opportunities for literary discussion (Schmidt, Rozendal, & Greenman, 2002). They use a wide array of class groupings, including homogeneous and heterogeneous small groups. They frequently change groupings. They shift heterogeneous groups so that struggling readers can listen to many different fluent readers and so that students have opportunity to discuss stories and expository texts with many different thinkers. Teachers change homogeneous groups based on the need. Teachers use homogenous groups so they can teach a skill that all the students in that group need. These groups change frequently, because students' needs are constantly changing. One small homogeneous group setting is guided reading (see Chapter 7).

TASK

Allington (2002) reports that effective literacy teachers have children reading or writing 50 percent of the school day! Many effective teachers assign large blocks of time to literacy activities, usually 90 minutes. This reading block includes all types of interesting and authentic tasks—independent reading, reading along with tapes or CD-ROMs, paired reading, or guided reading. Students do not complete meaningless worksheets; instead they read a variety of books—stories, mysteries, poems, plays, expository texts, and so on. Reading extends beyond books; they also read computer screens, children's magazines, newspapers, other students' stories, and posters. Not all students read the same text at the same time.

Teachers need to foster higher level thinking tasks through discussions that include teacher–student as well as student–student exchanges. In the discussions, teachers should ask higher level thinking questions that have no simple "correct" answer. This permits students to think and express themselves logically. It also encourage students to question the authors and ask questions to improve their comprehension.

Teachers should also personalize tasks by responding to students' interests, needs, strengths, and weaknesses (Allington, Johnston, & Day, 2002). Teachers should exercise control over tasks that the students need to accomplish, but they should give students the opportunity to choose from many texts to accomplish them. For example, if a struggling reader needs to work on improving fluency, the teacher might provide ten selections of easy reading material from which the student can choose one or two to practice fluency.

Teachers should engage students in longer tasks that integrate reading, writing, thinking, and listening. They should give students opportunities to choose from a suggested list of activities. They should make sure all tasks are meaningful and challenging enough so all students are developing and refining their literacy skills.

Teachers also need to understand that all students need time for silent reading. Silent reading and oral reading make different demands on students. During oral reading, students must pronounce words correctly, read with expression, and comprehend. During silent reading, young children must remain focused.

Students should master the task of skimming, abandoning, and scanning. When selecting a book for independent reading, students must learn how to skim the first page and the illustrations to see if they find the book interesting. Students should know that proficient readers can often abandon books that are not interesting or are too difficult for them. When selecting a book, students should understand that if they miss one word in ten then the book is probably too difficult for them to read independently. Students need to learn to scan for particular pieces of information. They need to scan for capital letters if they are trying to locate the name of a person or other proper noun, and to scan for numerals if they are locating dates.

During small group reading instruction, it is important that teachers set up the class space and time so that students not working in the small group can work independently, with a tutor (see Chapter 4), or with a volunteer (see Chapter 12). During this time, teachers can concentrate on the needs of the students in the small group without interruption from other students. Some literacy tasks the students can do independently follow (Fountas & Pinnell, 1996):

1. Read self-selected books; write in reading journal and logbook.

2. Listen to books on tape and respond to questions, with or without a partner.

3. Read in pairs.

4. Read from poem box and draw a picture based on the poem.

5. Read books on CD-ROM.

6. Buddy reading (see Chapter 4).

7. Practice roles for readers theatre.

8. Read riddles on bulletin board and write answers.

9. Read books the class has written together.

10. "Tape, Check, Chart" to increase reading fluency and rate. (See Chapter 11 and Appendix D.22.)

11. "Tape, Time, Chart: to increase reading rate. (See Chapter 11 and Appendix D.23.)

CONCLUDING THOUGHTS

Reading is a complex skill. As with any skill, it requires a lot of practice in order to perfect it. It is the teacher's responsibility to provide a setting where all students can be successful. Teachers need to consider (1) their own effectiveness, (2) the uniqueness of each student, (3) multifaceted strategies that will fit readers' needs, (4) appropriate use of a variety of texts, (5) the context of the reading event, and (6) meaningful and appropriate tasks. To be effective, teachers also need an understanding (1) of the reading process, (2) of various assessment instruments, and (3) of how and when to teach reading strategies so students will know how and when to use them independently. All teachers should remember to have fun with language so that their literary passion will be infectious.

ASSESSMENT

I hear, and I forget. I see, and I remember.
I do, and I understand.

CHINESE PROVERB

Scenario

Miss Wilson, who is in her first year as a second-grade teacher, has seven students who struggle with reading, but she has only a general understanding of their problems. She knows that Juan and Julie, who are both repeating second grade, struggle with many simple one-syllable words. Shawna reads at a very slow rate and cannot summarize what she reads. Jennifer skips words if she does not know them. For unknown words, Scott and Jeremy substitute totally different words that make no sense. Mike turns up his nose any time reading or writing is mentioned.

Miss Wilson, who firmly believes that reading is important to a child's success in school and in life, is determined to help these seven students. She knows that the school has standardized test scores on file for all her students. These tests scores record the students' reading level and some information about general areas in which they are weak. However, Miss Wilson recognizes that if she is to give these seven students the specific help that they need, she needs to administer different types of tests that will help her understand how each child attempts to make sense of print. Miss Wilson decides to administer selected informal reading tests.

INTRODUCTION

Without knowing it, Miss Wilson is taking the first step in the assessment of reading problems: she is observing students in order to understand what assessment instruments would help her identify specific reading strategies that her seven readers lack. There are many tests from which Miss Wilson could choose. The Buros Institute publication, *Reading* (2002), lists 102 different reading assessments that measure reading competencies and attitudes toward reading. The list includes reading inventories, reading achievement and aptitude tests, reading comprehension tests, reading decoding tests, and oral reading tests.

The purpose of this chapter is not to debate the pros and cons of testing, but rather (1) to define some terms associated with assessment, (2) to explain the differences among achievement tests, criterion-referenced tests, and diagnostic tests, (3) to describe the characteristics of standardized tests, (4) to list some of the commonly used standardized tests, and (5) to discuss in detail how to administer and score the various informal assessments that teachers use to identify literacy problems. The focus of this chapter will be on informal assessment because these tests can be beneficial to classroom teachers as they identify students' strengths and weakness and make plans for instruction.

DEFINING ASSESSMENT

Assessment is the "process of gathering data in order to better understand the strengths and weaknesses of student learning, as by observation, testing, interviews, etc." (Harris & Hodges, 1995, p. 12). There are two basic types of assessment, formal and informal. Formal assessments involve standardized tests that are given under controlled conditions so that groups with similar backgrounds can be compared. Informal assessments do not use standardized tests; they involve observations with anecdotal records, checklists, rubrics, portfolios, informal reading inventories, running records, and miscue analysis. Figure 3.1 illustrates the hierarchy of the various types of assessments.

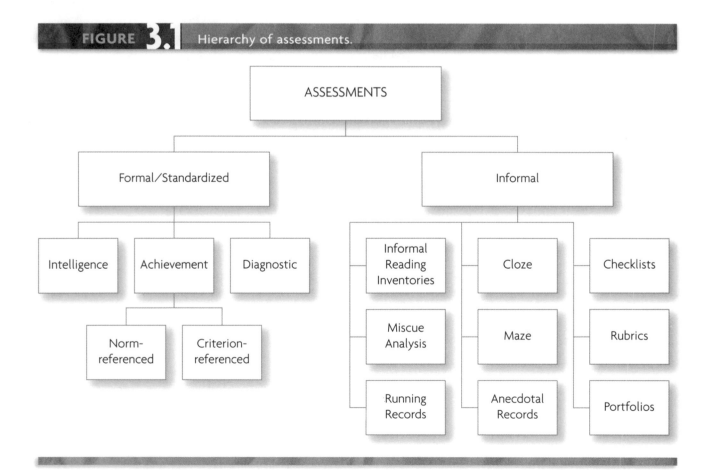

FIGURE 3.1 Hierarchy of assessments.

FORMAL/STANDARDIZED ASSESSMENT INSTRUMENTS

As shown in Figure 3.1 there are three types of standardized tests: intelligence, achievement, and diagnostic. Most schools administer standardized tests, and classroom teachers who suspect a student has a reading problem should use the student's standardized test score as a starting point for recommending individual reading tests.

Standardized tests have advantages and disadvantages. Two advantages of standardized tests are (1) they can indicate if an individual student needs additional screening, and (2) the tests have been designed for validity and reliability. *Validity* means that the test measures what it claims to measure; *reliability* means that it does so on a consistent basis.

There are a number of disadvantages to standardized tests. First, since many questions are in a multiple-choice format, the score may not be accurate because the student can guess at the answers. Second, students may be able to answer some questions without comprehending the passage. This is especially true for literal questions, which use the exact language of the passage. Consider the following scenario as an example. The passage the student reads includes the following sentence: "A favorite main dish in Louisiana is gumbo, a type of soup." One of the multiple choice questions that follows the short passage is: "Gumbo is a type of (A) bread, (B) fish, (C) soup, (D) none of the above." Students may deduce that they merely need to find the word *gumbo* in the passage and follow the word to complete the answer.

Individual and Group Intelligence Tests

Intelligence tests are used to determine the scholastic aptitude of students. It is important for classroom teachers to understand students' potential; however, teachers must remember that some students with low IQ scores do not struggle with reading, while some students with high IQ scores do struggle with reading (Barry, 1998). Intelligence test scores must be used with great caution because scores may differ depending on students' exposure to schooling and other cultural experiences.

Group intelligence tests are administered to a group or class of children by the classroom teacher who closely follows the script found in the testing manual. The classroom teacher does not score these tests, but can interpret the scores if instructed. One example of a group intelligence test given by the classroom teacher is the California Test of Mental Maturity. Since most students do not perform as well on group tests as they do on individual tests (Miller, 1988), most intelligence tests used in school are individual tests.

School psychologists or guidance counselors administer individual intelligence tests because of the complexity of administering and scoring the tests. Two examples of individual intelligence tests are the Stanford-Binet Intelligence Scale and the Wechsler Intelligence Scale for Children–Revised (WISC–R).

The Wechsler Intelligence Scale for Children–Revised (WISC–R)

The Wechsler Intelligence Scale for Children–Revised (WISC–R) is designed for children from ages five to fifteen. Older students take the Wechsler Adult Intelligence Scale (WAIS). The WISC–R gives a verbal intelligence quotient (IQ), a performance IQ, and a full-scale or overall IQ. The Verbal Scale includes the sub-tests (1) general information, (2) comprehension, (3) arithmetic, (4) similarities, (5) vocabulary, and (6) digit span, which tests the individual's ability to recite digits forward and backward. The Performance Scale includes sub-tests (1) picture completion—finding the missing part of a picture, (2) picture arrangement—or sequencing, (3) block design—a task that resembles a jigsaw puzzle, (4) object assembly—a timed assembly activity, (5) coding—which involves making associations, and (6) mazes—finding one's way through a maze.

Stanford-Binet Intelligence Scale

The Stanford-Binet Intelligence Scale, appropriate for individuals aged two through adulthood, provides an estimate of the individual's mental age. This test is not very helpful for diagnostic purposes because there is only one performance score; the sub-tests are not scored separately. However, if a teacher suspects that a child is not capable of a particular task, this test score may affirm or refute the teacher's suspicion.

Even though classroom teachers do not administer the WISC–R and the Stanford-Binet Intelligence Scale, it is advantageous for them to understand the various tasks the student is asked to perform so that they can better grasp what each score represents.

Peabody Picture Vocabulary Test–Revised

The Peabody Picture Vocabulary Test–Revised is an individual intelligence test that assesses a student's receptive vocabulary, based on life experience. It is for grades Pre-K through 12. Any teacher with some instruction can administer the test. The teacher names one of the four pictures on the page, and the student points to the correct picture. Like any multiple-choice test, the child can guess; however, since the test is administered to individuals, a teacher can mark the response as an incorrect response if a student guessed at the answer. This test is not considered to be an accurate measure of the individual's intelligence (Harris & Hodges, 1995). However, it does provide information about a student's oral vocabulary.

Slosson Intelligence Test for Children and Adults (SIT)

The Slosson Intelligence Test for Children and Adults measures the overall mental ability of both children and adults, but has no sub-test scores. Through training, a teacher can learn how to estimate the student's vocabulary, auditory memory, and general knowledge by closely observing the pattern of the student's correct responses. The test is a set of ten graded-word lists. The score is based on the student's ability to pronounce words at different levels of difficulty. Students must be able to pronounce the word in five seconds. From the raw score, the teacher can obtain the reading level by using a table that is attached to the test.

Achievement Tests

Achievement tests measure the current level of a student's performance in a variety of areas, including reading, language arts, mathematics, science, and social studies. Each of these main areas has sub-tests;

for example, the reading tests may include comprehension, vocabulary, phonics, and so on. There are two different types of standardized achievement tests—norm-referenced and criterion-referenced. All of these tests assess students' achievement and are given under standardized conditions; however, the goal is different in each of these tests.

Norm-Referenced Tests

Norm-referenced tests are assessment instruments that have been developed by publishers, who administer them to a large population of students from different geographic locations and socioeconomic backgrounds in order to develop norms. The norms are the average scores of the large population of students in each age group and grade level that take the test. That average score then becomes the "measuring stick" or norm to compare the performance of students who take the tests to the performance of those students in the norm group. A norm-referenced test permits teachers to compare the results of their students to a similar group of students that were used in the standardization sample.

The scores of achievement tests that are norm-referenced provide a comparison of each child's achievement level to national norms. Scores are reported in the form of grade equivalent scores, stanine scores, percentile ranks, and standard scores. It is important for teachers to communicate to parents the test scores and to accurately interpret the scores to parents. Figure 3.2 provides an explanation of the different types of scores.

Figure 3.3 has a list of standardized, norm-referenced achievement tests with their reading sub-tests.

Norm-referenced tests include a battery of subject tests, including reading, mathematics, social

---

FIGURE 3.2 Types of standardized test scores.

Grade equivalent scores reflect the median raw score for a grade level. For example, a raw score of 126 with a grade equivalent of 6.4, indicates that the students used in setting the norm, whose median raw score was 126, were in the sixth grade, fourth month.

A **percentile ranking** compares the student to other students her age. For example, if Jane has a percentile rank of 65 percent, it indicates that 35 percent of all students Jane's age had better scores than Jane, while 64 percent had worse scores than Jane.

Stanine scores are much like percentiles; however, the stanine scores range from one through nine. Stanine scores are more general than percentile scores. Scores of four through six are average scores. For example, if Joe has a stanine of six, it indicates that his score is average when compared to all students at his same grade level who were used for establishing the norm. To find a stanine score for a particular test, the teacher needs to calculate the overall score and use the test's chart to convert the raw score into a stanine score. If the tests are graded by a testing company, the stanine score is given.

FIGURE 3.3   Standardized norm-referenced achievement tests.

1. Iowa Test of Basic Skills (Grades K–8).

   Sub-tests: vocabulary, comprehension, listening, word attack, spelling, study skills.

2. Stanford Achievement Tests–Ninth Edition (Grades K–13).

3. Gates-MacGinitie Reading Tests (Grades K–12).

   Sub-tests: vocabulary and comprehension.

4. Metropolitan Achievement Tests–Reading (Grades K–12).

   Sub-tests: primer = listening for sounds; primary = word knowledge, word analysis; grades 1–12 = vocabulary and comprehension, spelling.

5. Comprehension Test of Basic Skills, U and V (Grades K–12).

   Sub-tests: vocabulary, comprehension, word attack.

6. California Achievement Tests–Reading (Grades K–9).

   Sub-tests: vocabulary, comprehension, listening, spelling.

---

studies, and science. The reading section has sub-tests that often include word identification, vocabulary, comprehension, reading rate, and study skills.

Criterion-Referenced Tests

Criterion-referenced tests assess the point at which the student has achieved mastery; these tests do not compare a student to other students with similar backgrounds. Criterion-referenced tests enable teachers to compare a student's performance to a predetermined goal. They help teachers determine whether a student has met the goal or criteria and compare a student's performance to standards considered appropriate for mastery in a particular area. For example, these tests can assess an individual's degree of competency on specific reading sub-skills. One advantage of these tests is that they can aid teachers in identifying particular areas of student weakness. Teachers can then plan instruction based on the students' needs. Teachers need to realize, however, that sub-tests divide reading into fragments instead of approaching reading as a holistic process.

All of the following criterion-referenced tests have many sub-tests, including reading.

1. Comprehensive Test of Basic Skills: Reading, Expanded Edition (Grades K–12).

   Sub-tests: comprehension, word identification.

2. Phonics Criterion Test (Grades 1–3).

   Sub-tests: consonants, short vowels, long vowels, digraphs, schwa sounds, controlled *r*, diphthongs, consonant blends.

3. Prescriptive Reading Performance Test (Grades 1–12), a group test.

   Sub-tests: phonic analysis, structural analysis, translation, and literal, interpretive, and critical comprehension.

The Reading First Legislation of 2001, also known as the No Child Left Behind Act (PL 107–110), has prompted state departments of education to design criterion-referenced tests that are aligned with their state standards (also called benchmarks or competencies in some states). Each state must develop its own standards for each subject area. Language arts standards include speaking, listening, viewing, visually representing, reading, and writing. Under each of these main standards are subheadings that address the areas of reading, writing, and the other components of the language arts. For example, one Oklahoma standard under first-grade reading is Phonics/Decoding, and one subheading under that standard states that the student will use consonant sounds in the beginning, medial, and final positions to decode unknown words.

In order for school districts to qualify for Title I funding, they must document student growth in the following six areas of literacy: phonemic awareness, systematic phonics, spelling and writing, fluency, text comprehension, and vocabulary. One way to document student growth is through the administration of state-designed criterion-referenced tests at the beginning of the school year and again at the end of the year. Each state designs tests that reflect their state standards. Throughout the year, teachers can then use checklists and/or rubrics, based on the state standards, to monitor growth patterns. (See Checklists and Rubrics sections in this chapter.)

Diagnostic Tests

Diagnostic tests are standardized but they differ from achievement tests. Diagnostic tests aim to determine a student's strengths and weaknesses. In most school districts, primary students who score one year below grade level on achievement tests and intermediate students who score two or more years below grade level on achievement tests are given diagnostic tests.

Diagnostic reading tests include many sub-tests that cover a wide range of skills—visual and auditory discrimination, phonics skills, sound blending, word recognition, structural analysis, syllabication, scanning, skimming, contextual analysis, vocabulary, and comprehension. All these sub-tests indicate a student's strengths and weaknesses, but none of these sub-tests identify the causes for the weaknesses.

As with all tests, there are advantages and disadvantages to diagnostic tests (Calkins, Montgomery, Santman, & Falk, 1998). Some advantages are (1) they are standardized so they are more valid and reliable than running records, miscue analyses, maze tests, and cloze tests, (2) they identify the reading level of the student, (3) most are normed tests so they can be used to compare a student to others with similar characteristics, and (4) they identify a student's weaknesses. Some disadvantages to diagnostic tests are (1) they need to be administered and scored by trained teachers, (2) the individual tests are time consuming to administer, (3) the tests may discriminate based on cultural differences, (4) some tests use nonsense words to evaluate a student's word identification skills, which may frustrate younger students, and (5) they are timed, which requires students to perform on-demand (Murphy, 1995).

Diagnostic tests are either group tests or individual tests. All group tests can also be administered for individuals. Even though classroom teachers do not administer the tests, they should be familiar enough with the sub-tests of the reading diagnostic tests to understand the tasks the students must perform.

Individual Diagnostic Tests

Oral reading tests. Oral reading tests are individual tests used to assess a reader's rate, accuracy, fluency, and comprehension. They are usually reserved for a struggling reader because of the time it takes to administer them. The oral tests are graded passages that range from first through eighth grade levels. The student begins reading passages until she reaches a ceiling level, which is called her frustration reading level. As the student reads, the teacher checks the oral errors, which include substitutions, mispronunciations, omissions, insertions, repetitions, and hesitations. As a teacher administers these tests, he learns about the specific types of errors a student makes and what she does when she reaches an unknown word. The teacher also notes the reader's expression and prosody, two aspects of fluency.

Two oral reading tests commonly used are the Gilmore Oral Reading Test, which evaluates the reader's accuracy, comprehension, and rate, and the Gray Oral Reading Test, which evaluates accuracy and comprehension, but not rate. A classroom teacher can easily be trained to administer and score these two tests; however, because they are individually administered, they are time consuming.

Other individual diagnostic tests. The following is a list of other diagnostic tests:

1. Woodcock Reading Mastery Test (Grades 1–12).
   Sub-tests: letter identification, word attack skills (with nonsense words), word comprehension (analogies), and passage comprehension. This test is easy for classroom teachers to administer and score.

2. Durrell Analysis of Reading Difficulties–Third Edition (Grades K–6).
   Sub-tests: pre-reading phonics inventories, auditory analysis of words and word elements, visual memory of words, pronunciation of word elements, listening, vocabulary, and spelling.

3. Gates-McKillop-Horowitz Tests (Grades K–6).
   Sub-tests: auditory discrimination, phonics analysis, structural analysis, vocabulary, and spelling.

4. Diagnostic Reading Scales (Grades 1–7).
   Sub-tests: twelve sub-tests on phonics analysis, word identification, oral reading, and silent reading.

5. Sipay Word Analysis Test.
   All sub-tests evaluate word identification or phonics analysis skills.

6. *Follow Me* and *No Shoes*: Concepts about Print (Ages 5–7).
   Examine readers' basic knowledge of print.

Group Diagnostic Tests

The following is a list of group diagnostic tests:

1. Stanford Diagnostic Reading Test; Red Level, Green Level, Brown Level, and Blue Level. (Levels range from primary grades through high school.)
   Sub-tests: auditory vocabulary, auditory discrimination, phonetic analysis, structural analysis, and comprehension.

2. Iowa Silent Reading Test (Grades 6–adult).
   Sub-tests: comprehension, vocabulary, reading efficiency, work–study skills.

3. Nelson-Denny Reading Test (Grades 9–adult).
   Sub-tests: vocabulary, comprehension, rate.

INFORMAL ASSESSMENT INSTRUMENTS

Informal assessments are assessment practices that are not standardized or normed. They are not used to compare one student to another. Rather, they are designed for the following purposes:

1. To understand what an individual student can do as a reader and writer.
2. To diagnose reading problems.
3. To check the reading level of a student.
4. To analyze which cueing systems students use when making sense of print.
5. To understand a student's interests and attitudes toward reading and writing so that they can find materials that interest the student.
6. To monitor growth.
7. To give a student an opportunity to reflect on reading and writing accomplishments.
8. To give a student an opportunity to set realistic goals.
9. To help a teacher plan for instruction.

Authentic assessment is a relevant issue to discuss in relation to informal assessment. Authentic assessment measures literacy behavior in real-life situations (e.g., in the community or workplace). For example, an authentic assessment may measure a child's ability to read and comprehend the directions when constructing a model airplane. "Authentic assessment practices . . . hold enormous potential for changing what and how we teach and how children come to be readers and writers" (Allington & Cunningham, cited in Fountas & Pinnell, 1996, p. 89).

Commonly used types of informal tests are informal reading inventories (IRIs), running records, cloze tests, maze tests, anecdotal records, checklists, rubrics, portfolios, interest and attitude surveys, and student self-assessments. All of these informal assessment instruments aid a teacher as she gains insight into her students' reading and writing processes. Informal assessment instruments differ "significantly from all other commonly used diagnostic and evaluative instruments in that the resulting analysis of reading proficiency is qualitative as well as quantitative" (Goodman, Watson, & Burke, 1987, p. 4).

Since the classroom teacher is the first person to detect that a student is struggling with reading, it is advantageous for a classroom teacher to administer and score the informal reading tests so she can observe the reader as he makes sense of print.

Informal Reading Inventories (IRIs)

Informal reading inventories (IRIs) are individual tests given by a classroom teacher. They generally include lists of leveled words or sentences and sets of graded reading passages with accompanying questions. Commercial IRI passages range from 50 to 250 words, depending on the grade level; thus, they do not take a long time to administer. The passages, together with the retelling of main points and/or questions, measure the readers' comprehension and recall ability. Most commercial IRIs have three equivalent passages for each grade, accompanied by graded word lists. Two passages are narrative text and the third passage is expository text. This permits a teacher to use one of the narrative passages to test oral reading comprehension and the other narrative passage for silent reading comprehension.

The comprehension score is based on the reader's retelling. In the retelling, students should include an account of *who, what, where, when, why,* and *how.* A teacher can listen to the retelling to determine how many of these six items were included in the retelling and then calculate the comprehension score. For example, if Joey recounted only *who* and *what* in his retelling of the story "The Pumpkin Man for Piney Creek" (by Darleen Bailey-Beard, 1995), his comprehension score would be 33 percent. This indicates that this story is at Joey's frustration reading level. A set of sample scoring criteria from the Ekwall/Shanker Reading Inventory is found in Figure 3.4. They define the three reading levels for retelling.

FIGURE 3.4 Reading comprehension chart based on retelling.

Independent Reading Level	=	90% or better
Instructional Reading Level	=	60–89%
Frustration Reading Level	=	60% or less

Source: J. Shanker & E. Ekwall (2000). *Ekwall/Shanker Reading Inventory* (4th ed.). Boston: Allyn & Bacon.

Appendix A.1 features a list of commercial IRIs. Commercial IRIs also include forms for a teacher to use when administering a miscue analysis, which will be discussed in the next section.

Miscue Analysis

Miscue analysis, designed by Yetta Goodman and Carolyn Burke (1972), is based on Kenneth Goodman's Taxonomy of Reading Miscues (1969). Kenneth Goodman developed this taxonomy "by analyzing the degree to which unexpected responses or *miscues* change, disrupt, or enhance the meaning of a written text" (Goodman, Watson, & Burke, 1987, p. 5). Kenneth Goodman used the word *miscues* instead of *errors* in order "to eliminate the pejorative connotations of words such as *error* and *mistake* and to underscore the belief that all reading is cued by language and personal experience and is not simply random, uncontrolled behavior" (Goodman, Watson, & Burke, 1987, p. 5). In analyzing miscues, teachers ask the following questions:

1. Does the miscue fit the sentence semantically (i.e., in its meaning)?
2. Does the miscue resemble the spelling of the word in the text?
3. Does the miscue resemble the sound of the word in the text?
4. Does the miscue fit the sentence syntactically? (Does it sound like a sentence?)
5. Does the miscue cause a grammatical transformation (e.g., plural to singular or past tense to present tense)?
6. What strategy does the reader use to self-correct?

When analyzing miscues, a teacher also focuses on what type(s) of miscues—substitutions, mispronunciations, repetitions or insertions, and omissions—the reader makes.

Substitutions. There are many different types of substitutions. Sometimes a substitution is a word that does not "look like" the written word, but it may mean nearly the same thing as the word in the text. For example, a student may read *frog* for the word *toad.* This type of substitution may occur if the student uses picture clues to help with unknown words; in this case the student is reading for meaning. Other times, substitutions may not "look like" or mean anything like the original word. An example of this type of substitution would be if the student reads *cookie* for the word *catalog.* Obviously, when this occurs the student is not reading for meaning. A third type of substitution is a rever-

sal. The text may read "Dad said" but the student reads "said Dad." Obviously, the meaning remains intact when readers reverse these two words.

Mispronunciations. Mispronunciations often reflect a student's dialect. For example, the student may pronounce *specific* as *pecific*, or *spaghetti* as *pashetti* or *breakfast* as *breafest.* Mispronunciations caused by dialects are not considered miscues (Goodman & Burke, 1972). Other times, a student's mispronunciations may result from accenting the wrong syllable. For example, "He will record his voice" becomes "He will record [accent on first syllable so it sounds like the noun form] his voice."

Repetitions/insertions. Repetitions are words that the student repeats, while insertions are words the student adds to a text. The text may read, "The fisherman was hungry after his long day of fishing" and the student reads, "The fisherman was *very* hungry after his long *long* day of fishing." Many times the reader is reading for meaning and is adding words for effect. Insertions of this type are miscues; however, they do not disrupt meaning.

Omissions. Omissions are words that the student drops from the text. Sometimes the student may not know the word and merely skips it; obviously these types of omissions disrupt meaning. Other types of omissions may involve omitting commas and end marks. These omissions also hinder comprehension. One type of omission that does not always hinder comprehension is the skipping of explanatory words in dialogue. For example, in the following sentence the student may omit *asked Dad:* "Will you," asked Dad, "please mow the lawn for me?" This type of miscue indicates a proficient reader (Goodman & Burke, 1972).

The unified set of conventions used for miscue analysis is found in Figure 3.5.

A teacher can administer a miscue analysis using any text; however, as stated previously, commercial IRIs include reading passages and grids for administering a miscue analysis. Some advantages of using commercial miscue analyses are (1) they have graded passages for both narrative and expository texts, (2) they have graded word lists, and (3) they provide the passage from which the students read and a prepared script with a grid for the teacher's use. There is one drawback to the commercial miscue analyses—the short passages do not have the elements of a good story or a well-developed expository text. Weaver (2002) found that students make fewer miscues after reading approximately 200 words because they become familiar with the vocabulary and style of the author. A teacher who wants to use

FIGURE 3.5 Conventions used for miscue analysis.

1. Substitutions: Write substituted word above actual word.

    frog
    The toad leaped down the path.

2. Mispronunciations: Write mispronounced word above actual word.

    countent
    I was content with my B on the test.

3. Omission: Circle omitted word.

    Jane walked into the (huge) store.

4. Insertion: Use caret to show point of insertion; write word above.

    new
    I want to go to the ∧ movies.

5. Repetition: Underline repeated words.

    <u>Dan's pet is a</u> monkey.

6. Long pauses: Use "P" to show where pause occurred.

    Molly wants a new P dollhouse.

7. Self-corrections: Use symbol and underlining as shown.

    ⓒ
    Molly wants a (new) doll.

8. Sounding-out words: Write out approximate version of sounded-out word.

    A–All–Al–i–ga–tors
    Alligators live in swamps.

---

longer passages than the commercial tests and wants to carefully analyze the reading process of their struggling students can prepare a miscue analysis on a story using the following steps:

1. Select an interesting story that has all the elements of good literature and is at least 600 words in length. The story must be challenging to the reader, but not so difficult as to cause frustration.
2. Prepare the script, using the blank form found in Appendix C.1.
3. Prepare a number of questions, based on setting, character, and main events of the story.
4. Prepare a quiet "reading station" with a copy of the passage from which the student reads (it can be the original text or a photocopied script) and a tape recorder.
5. Instruct the student to start by silently reading the story.
6. Ask the student to retell the story. Makes note of the prepared questions that are answered in the retelling.
7. Have the student read the story orally into the tape recorder. Inform the student that you will *not* help her. She must try to figure out the words or skip them and go on.

8. Ask the student to retell the story again. Take notes on the prepared questions the reader answered in this retelling. (This step is included to help teachers determine whether students' comprehension increases with oral reading.)
9. Dismiss the student and listen to the taped story, marking the miscues on the prepared grid. For example, if the miscue is an omission, mark an X in the "Omission" column. If the miscue makes sense grammatically, mark an X in the "Syntax acceptable" column. If the miscue disrupts meaning, mark an X in the last column.
10. Total the number of miscues in each column, making note of which type of miscue the student most often makes.
11. Calculate the total number of miscues that disrupt meaning and summarize the reading and retelling.
12. Decide which reading strategy to teach the student first, in order to increase the student's reading comprehension.

Figure 3.6 is a short example of a fourth-grade student's reading of *The Mitten*, by Jan Brett (1989).

To obtain the quantitative score, the teacher calculates the number of words read correctly (words

FIGURE **3.6**　Grid for miscue analysis.

TEXT	substitution	mispronun-ciation	insertion	omission	repeats	self-correction	syntax acceptable	meaning disrupted
upon a time Once/there was a boy named			✓				X	
(sc) *went* Nicki who \wanted his new		✓				X		
of mittens made from wool	✓						X	
as white as snow.								
grandma At first, his grandmother,	✓						X	
who Baba,\did not want to knit			✓				X	
white mittens. "If you								
it drop one in the snow,"	✓						X	
(she warned) "you'll				✓			X	
(never) find it. But				✓				X
Nicki wanted (snow-				✓				X
first (white) mittens, and finally		✓						X
Baba made them. After								
she finished she said,								
"When you come home,								
TOTAL MISCUES:	3	2	2	3		1	6	3

Notes: Three miscues disrupted meaning.

Source: Text from Jan Brett (1989), *The Mitten*. New York: Scholastic.

that do not disrupt meaning). The quantitative score is calculated using the following steps:

1. Count the number of words in the passage.
2. Count the number of miscues that disrupted meaning.
3. Subtract the number of miscues that disrupted meaning from the total number of words in the passage.
4. Divide the number of words read correctly by the total number of words in the passage.
5. Multiply quotient by 100 to get the percentage of the reading score.
6. Use the Reading Level Chart, found in Figure 3.7, to determine the reading level of that passage for the student.

For example, if Joey reads a passage of 500 words and makes 30 miscues that disrupt meaning, he reads 470 words correctly. To calculate the score, divide 470 by 500 and multiply by 100 to get 94 percent. Joey scores a 94 percent on the oral reading, which means the passage is at Joey's instructional level. This passage would be an appropriate passage to use when teaching Joey some new reading strategies. The criteria for the three reading levels are found in Figure 3.7.

Finding the quantitative score of a miscue analysis may help a teacher determine the instructional level of a reader. However, the main purpose of a miscue analysis is to evaluate a reader's miscues "based on the degree to which the miscue disrupts the meaning of the written material" (Goodman, 1972/1997, p. 534). It is important for a teacher to assess a reader's strategies when encountering unknown words or those he uses to correct a miscue. This qualitative analysis of miscues "provides specific information regarding readers' strengths and weaknesses, which can be used to plan a personalized reading program" (Goodman, 1972/1997, p. 534).

Retrospective Miscue Analysis

Retrospective miscue analysis, designed by Yetta Goodman and Ann Marek (1996), follows all the steps of a miscue analysis with additional steps following the taped oral reading of a passage. After analyzing the miscues, the teacher finds a portion of the written passage that has a number of miscues that are representative of the reader's miscues in general. The teacher then cues the tape to that portion of the passage and asks the student to listen to his reading while following the script. The purpose is to determine if the student can locate his miscues—omissions, insertions, and so on—and articulate what type of miscue it was. The teacher and student then discuss the miscues and the ways the student can improve his reading. The teacher records this second session on a second tape recorder in order to analyze that session. Retrospective miscue analysis is more than assessment; it becomes a powerful instructional tool when the student listens for his errors and attempts to understand if the error disrupted the intended message. When he listens to his reading, he also determines if he read at an appro-

priate rate and if he made the same type of errors throughout the passage. (Goodman & Marek, 1996).

Running Records

Running records, designed by Marie Clay (1993), are another type of informal assessment. The purpose of the running record is to give a teacher the opportunity to observe, score, and interpret a student's reading behaviors. As the name suggests, this tool is a running record of the student's oral reading. The running record has three steps:

1. Record the student's oral reading through check marks and other conventions.
2. Examine each error and determine which of the three cueing systems—syntactic, semantic, or graphophonic—the student used when making the errors.
3. Determine if the passage is at the student's independent, instructional, or frustration reading level.

Unlike the miscue analysis, a running record does not require the teacher to use a tape recorder or a prepared script. The only instruments the teacher needs are a copy of a book from which the student reads, a pen or pencil, and a blank sheet of paper. In a running record, all words read incorrectly are called errors, not miscues.

The running record's goal also differs from that of the miscue analysis. In the miscue analysis, the end result is to determine if the miscue disrupts the intended meaning of the text and if the student comprehended what was read. The objective of the running record is (1) to determine a student's instructional level, (2) to analyze cues used and cues neglected during oral reading, (3) to analyze the student's strategic processing of a text through the teacher's interpretation of the strategies used during oral reading, and (4) to use the results to plan for individual instruction.

FIGURE 3.7 Reading level chart based on correct word identification.

Independent Reading Level	=	99%
Instructional Reading Level	=	90–98%
Frustration Reading Level	=	Below 90%

Scores set by the International Reading Association. *Source:* T. Harris and R. Hodges (1995). *The literacy dictionary: The vocabulary of reading and writing.* Newark, DE: International Reading Association.

Quantitative Analysis of Running Records

The marking conventions used for the quantitative analysis of running records are somewhat different from the conventions used in a miscue analysis. The teacher makes a check mark (✓) for each word the student reads correctly. Figure 3.8 lists all the conventions used to record a reader's oral reading, with examples. Each error is recorded above the word that appears in the text with a horizontal line separating the two words. In order for the teacher to relate the running record to the text, he makes the check marks on the record in the same pattern as the words on the page. For example, if the first page of the passage has three lines, with five words on each line, the teacher makes five check marks (if the student reads all words correctly) on three different lines. To keep track of page numbers, the teacher draws a line across the page for every new page and records the page number in the left column.

When scoring a running record, a teacher calculates the errors in the following manner:

1. Substitutions, omissions, insertions, and "tolds" each count as one error.
2. Multiple attempts count only as one error.
3. Self-corrections do *not* count as errors.
4. Repeats are *not* errors.

The percentage of correct words read correctly is calculated by (1) subtracting the number of errors from the total number of words in the reading, (2) dividing that remainder by the number of words in the passage, and (3) multiplying the answer by 100. For example, a passage has 200 words, and Jodi has 20 errors.

$$200 - 20 = 180$$
$$180 \div 200 = .9$$
$$.9 \times 100 = 90\%$$

Jodi reads 90 percent of the words correctly. Figure 3.9 provides a conversion table for a running record, and Figure 3.10 lists the reading level for the percentage of words read correctly. The passage that Jodi reads is at her instructional level.

Qualitative Analysis of Running Records

The quantitative analysis of a running record identifies the reading level of the passage for a particular student, while the qualitative analysis determines which of the three cueing systems the student uses when encountering an unknown word and whether she self-corrects and monitors her reading. The quantitative analysis lets the teacher know if the

---

FIGURE 3.8 Running record conventions.

Correct reading	= ✓ ✓ ✓	
Omission (one error)	= Child / text	— / very
Insertion (one error)	= Child / text	very / —
Repeats (no error)	= R (one repeat), R2 (two repeats)	R2 / The house
Self-corrections (no error)	= misread sc / text	want/went / went
Appeal	= — |A / Text |	"What's that word?" / hurricane
Teacher told (one error)	= —┼ / Text ┤ T	long pause ┤ / hurricane ┤ (teacher gives word)

Try that again [TTA]: one error for the entire confusion (if a reader jumps a line or really gets confused).

FIGURE 3.9 Conversion table for running records.

EASY READING LEVEL:		INSTRUCTIONAL READING LEVEL:		DIFFICULT READING LEVEL:	
Error Rate	Percentage (%) Accuracy Rate	Error Rate	Percentage (%) Accuracy Rate	Error Rate	Percentage (%) Accuracy Rate
1:200	99.5	1:17	94	1:9	89
1:100	99	1:14	93	1:8	87.5
1:50	98	1:12.5	92	1:7	85.5
1:35	97	1:11.75	91	1:6	83
1:25	96	1:10	90	1:5	80
1:20	95			1:4	75
				1:3	66
				1:2	50

Source: Adapted from Schulman, M. & Payne, C. (2000). *Guided reading: Making it work.* New York: Scholastic.

reading material was too easy, too hard, or perfect for the instructional purpose, while the qualitative analysis helps a teacher in deciding which reading strategies to teach the student. In the qualitative analysis, the teacher decides with each error which cueing system—semantic, syntactic, or graphophonic—the student used while making each error.

Semantic system. If the student uses the semantic cueing system, the word read in error will make sense in the sentence and the passage. The question the teacher asks is, "Does this error make sense in the sentence and passage? Is the meaning the same?" If a student reads *house* instead of *home* in the following sentence, the meaning would remain almost exactly the same: "We moved to a new home last fall."

Syntactic system. If the student uses the syntactic system, the word read in error will sound correct in the sentence. The question the teacher asks is, "Does that sound right in the sentence?" The student uses the syntactic cueing system if he reads, "I got a valentine *for* my grandmother" instead of "I got a valentine *from* my grandmother." The reader changes the meaning of the sentence; however, the error fits the sentence structure.

Visual or graphophonic. If the student uses the graphophonic system, the word read in error will resemble the word in the text. The error may share the same initial letter as the word in the text or it may share other letters of the word in the text. The question the teacher asks is, "Does the error look like the word in the text?" For example, if Jodi reads *cap* instead of *cape*, she is using the visual cueing system.

When determining which cueing system the student is using, the teacher asks these three questions: "Does it make sense?" "Does it sound right?" and "Does it look right?" During instructional time, the teacher will instruct the reader to ask these three questions when encountering unknown words. It is important to note that when administering a running record, a teacher focuses on the specific cueing system that the reader uses.

The teacher uses the acronym MSV (Meaning, Structure, Visual) to represent the three cueing systems. Notice on the right side of the scoring sheet, found in Figure 3.11, there are four columns, marked E, SC, E, and SC. In the first E column, the teacher records the number of errors the reader made in each line. In the first SC column, the teacher records the number of self-corrections the reader made in each line. In the second E column, the teacher writes an

FIGURE 3.10 Reading levels for percentage of words read correctly.

95–100% = Easy level

90–94% = Instructional level

Below 90% = Frustration level

MSV for each error the reader made in each column. If a reader made three errors in one line, the teacher writes three MSVs on that line and circles the cueing system the reader used for each error. Many times, the reader uses more than one cueing system for each error; then the teacher circles each letter that represents a cueing system that the reader used. In the second SC column, the teacher writes an MSV for each self-correction and circles the cueing systems the reader used for each self-correction. Figure 3.11 is a sample record for a student's reading of *Jesse Bear, What Will You Wear?* (1986) by Nancy White Carlstrom. The story's original text is written out in the left column.

Once a teacher determines which strategies students use when they reach an unknown word, he can use his findings during instruction. For example, when Jodi read *Jesse Bear, What Will You Wear?* (Figure 3.11), she used visual cues to self-correct. With two of the three self-corrections, she sounded out the word. During instructional time, the teacher should work with Jodi to develop strategies that will help her use the other cueing systems that she does not currently use.

As previously stated, running records can be taken on any sheet of paper. However, for beginning teachers and tutors, the blank form found in Appendix C.2 may be helpful. The top of the form includes spaces for the reader's name, the name of the story, the quantitative score, and some general notes about the reading.

Cloze Test

The cloze test is another type of informal reading assessment. The purpose of the cloze test is twofold—for informal assessment and for instruction. When it is used for assessment, the cloze test helps a teacher to (1) understand how readers use context and background knowledge to figure out unknown words, and (2) determine if a particular text is too easy or too difficult for a particular reader. A teacher can also use cloze tests during instruction to show a student how to use context clues and background knowledge when she encounters unknown words. A cloze passage can be taken from

---

FIGURE 3.11 Running record of *Jesse Bear, What Will You Wear?* by Nancy White Carlstrom.

TEXT	RUNNING RECORD	Number		System Used	
		E	SC	E	SC
PAGE					
1. Jesse Bear, what will you wear?	✓ ✓ ✓ ✓ ✓ ✓	O	O		
What will you wear in the morning?	✓ ✓ ✓ ✓ ✓ ✓ noon/morning	I	O	(M)(S) V	
2. My shirt of red	✓ skirt/shirt ✓ ✓	I	O	(M)(S)(V)	
Pulled over my head	p – p/pulled ✓ ✓ ✓	I	O	M S (V)	
Over my head in the morning.	✓ ✓ ✓ ✓ ✓ noon|sc/morning	O	I		M S (V)
3. I'll wear my pants	✓ we/wear ✓ p – p|sc/pants	I	I	M S (V)	M S (V)
My pants that dance	✓ ✓ ✓ d – da|sc/dance		I		M S (V)
My pants that dance in the morning.	✓ ✓ ✓ ✓ ✓ ✓				

M = meaning (semantic system); S = structure (syntactic system); V = visual (visual/graphophonic system); E = errors; SC = self-corrections

---

any text. The length of the passage is 125 to 500 words, depending on the grade level of the reader. To construct a cloze test, delete every fifth word in the passage, while keeping the first and last lines intact. To calculate the reader's score, divide the total number of correct suggestions for missing words by the total number of blanks. For example, if there are 100 missing words and the student has 80 correct responses, the student's final score would be 80 percent.

The most valid scoring system for diagnostic purposes is to accept only the exact word (Ruddell, 1964). When using the cloze test for instructional purposes, synonyms are acceptable (Gillet & Temple, 2000). When determining the reading level, the following scale is used:

Individual reading level = 60–100%

Instructional reading level = 40–59%

Frustration reading level = Below 40%

Later chapters will discuss in detail and provide examples of how to use cloze tests in instruction.

Figure 3.12 is a short example of a cloze test from Chapter One of *Little Men: Life at Plumfield with Jo's Boys* by Louisa May Alcott (1913). Since the reader has only 12 correct responses, which is approximately 46 percent, the passage is at the reader's instructional level. Since most of the responses make sense, the teacher can conclude that the reader reads for meaning and will be able to read and comprehend the passage with some instructional help. If the teacher observes the student while she

FIGURE 3.12   Sample cloze test.

CHAPTER 1

"Please, sir, is this Plumfield?" asked a ragged boy of the man who opened the great gate at which the omnibus left him.

"Yes; who sent you?"

"__1__ [*Hello*] Laurence. I have got __2__ [*a*] letter for the lady."

"__3__ [*All*] right; go up to __4__ [*the*] house and give it __5__ [*to*] her; she'll see to __6__ [*it*], little chap."

The man __7__ [*talked*] pleasantly, and the boy __8__ [*walked*] on, feeling much cheered __9__ [*by*] the words. Through the __10__ [*new*] spring rain that fell __11__ [*on*] sprouting grass and budding __12__ [*flowers*], Nat saw a large __13__ [*green*] house before him—a __14__ [*big*] house, with an old-fashioned __15__ [*porch*], with wide steps, and lights __16__ [*on*] in many windows. Neither __17__ [*curtains*] nor shutters hid the __18__ [*shiny*] glimmer; and, pausing a __19__ [*second*] before he rang, Nat __20__ [*saw*] many little shadows dancing __21__ [*on*] the walls, heard the __22__ [*cheerful*] hum of young voices, __23__ [*and*] felt that it was __24__ [*just*] possible that the light __25__ [*and*] warmth and comfort within __26__ [*would*] be for a homeless "little chap" like him.

"I hope the lady will see to me," he thought; and gave a timid rap with the great bronze knocker, which was a jovial griffin's head.

ANSWERS:

1. Mr.	2. a	3. All	4. the	5. to	6. you
7. spoke	8. went	9. by	10. soft	11. on	12. trees
13. square	14. hospitable-looking	15. porch	16. shining	17. curtains	18. cheerful
19. moment	20. saw	21. on	22. pleasant	23. and	24. hardly
25. and	26. could				

Source: Excerpt from *Little Men: Life at Plumfield with Jo's Boys,* by Louisa M. Alcott. Copyright © 1913, Little, Brown, & Co.

reads, the teacher will be able to detect what strategies she uses to complete the test. Does the reader read to the end of the sentence to figure out the missing word? Does she read past the sentence to figure out the missing word? Based on the observation, the teacher can introduce the reading strategies that the student did not use.

Maze Test

The maze test is much like the cloze test, in purpose and construction. The purpose is to give *younger* students an opportunity to demonstrate what context clues and background knowledge they use when they encounter unknown words. Like the cloze test, the maze test can be used for diagnostic and for instructional purposes. To construct a maze test, again delete every fifth word while keeping the first and last sentences intact. However, instead of every fifth word being replaced with a blank, students are given three choices. One choice is correct, one fits the sentence's syntax, and the third choice does not

fit the sentence in any way. Figure 3.13 has a short example from Paula Danziger's (2001) *A is for Amber: It's Justin Time, Amber Brown.* The maze test is best used if the teacher observes the student while she completes it. Then the teacher can note if the student rereads sentences, reads beyond the word choice, or reads beyond the sentence to figure out the word.

Anecdotal Records

Anecdotal records are notes a teacher makes as she observes behaviors in students. Anecdotal records follow no criteria or standards; they are merely observations teachers make about a student's habits, attitudes, or abilities. For one student, a teacher may record changes in attitude, while for another student, all the anecdotal notes may be about changes in the reading strategies that the child uses. The notes can be taken in a number of ways. Some teachers keep anecdotal records in a file folder for each student to record changes in behavior or perfor-

---

FIGURE 3.13   Maze test for *A Is for Amber: It's Justin Time, Amber Brown* by Paula Danziger

I, Amber Brown,
am one very excited six-year,
364-day-old kid.
I am so excited
      1.   2.
(which, that, too) I am dancing with (your, two, my) toy gorilla.
            3.
He is (a, that, for) two-year,
364-day-old gorilla.
      4.   5.
I (have, got, by) him on my fourth (school, built, birthday).
                        6.
Tomorrow, July 7, is our (fun, birthday, bottle).
                  7.
Last year I was (seven, five, six) on July 7.
            8.   9.
Next year (I, we, too) will be eight on (August 3, birthday, July 7).
This year I will be seven on July 7. (p. 5)

ANSWERS:

1. that	2. my	3. a	4. got	5. birthday
6. birthday	7. six	8. I	9. July 7	

mance. Some teachers will use a three-ring note-book. Other teachers use the computer to keep these notes. Each teacher should select a method that is compatible with her organizational style. Anecdotal records should begin at the beginning of the year and continue throughout the year.

Two examples of teachers who use anecdotal records are Mr. Jackson, a first-grade teacher, and Mr. Green, a second-grade teacher. At the beginning of the year Mr. Jackson notes that Ali is shy and appears to have negative feelings about reading. As you read the anecdotal records for Ali in Figure 3.14, note how Mr. Jackson detects the problem that hinders Ali from becoming engaged in the reading

activities. Figure 3.15 displays Mr. Green's notes as he observes Rosa, whose native language is Spanish. His notes are based on Rosa's reading habits. Mr. Green records the instructional strategies he uses to help Rosa become a more proficient reader. Notice that Mr. Green's notes are quite detailed. Not all anecdotal records need to be so thorough.

Checklists

The purpose of checklists is for a teacher to observe students' literacy habits periodically throughout the year. A checklist is a list of traits that a teacher

---

FIGURE 3.14 Mr. Jackson's anecdotal record.

STUDENT: Ali   GRADE: 1st

DATE:	COMMENTS
9–10	Ali readily went to the back of the group rug during shared book reading when other children pushed her. During the reading of the story, she did not pay attention and offered no comments to the class discussion.
9–12	Ali sat right in the middle of the horseshoe table during guided reading, facing me. She pointed to each word as we read in unison. She contributed to group discussion. She appears to have a speech impediment.
9–13	During guided reading, she sat at the end of the horseshoe table, next to me. She did not follow along with her finger. She did not read in unison with group and gave no comments during discussion.
9–17	During shared reading, she sat right in front of me and chimed in on "Catch me if you can." She added comments during discussion. She definitely has a speech problem. I referred her to Miss Wilson, the speech teacher.
9–18	Miss Wilson reported that Ali has a hearing problem. She called her mother. Ali reads lips.
9–19	During guided reading, Ali sat directly in front of me so she could hear and read my lips. She participated in unison reading and discussion. She told me she gets to go to the hospital to get her ears fixed.
9–24	Ali had tubes put into her ears.
10–1	During guided reading, she sat at the end of the table and participated. She told me she can hear now!
10–2	During shared reading, she sat at the back of the rug and chimed in and discussed questions with the group.

FIGURE 3.15 Mr. Green's anecdotal records.

STUDENT: Rosa GRADE: 2nd

DATE:	COMMENTS
9-10	When she orally read to me <u>Grandma's Bicycle,</u> she read words, not phrases. She skips over all words that she does not know. She could not retell the story. When asked the purpose of reading, she said, "To read words correctly." I taught her to read to the end of the sentence to see what word would make sense. She chose a Spanish word.
9-11	I took the first and second pages of <u>Grandma's Bicycle,</u> and deleted words that may be unknown to her. I reminded her to read to the end of the sentence. Then I instructed her to see if the word "looked right." (She can "sound out" words quite well.) With my guidance, she was able to do the first page. I observed her as she did the second page. She got all but one word.
9-12	Rosa read <u>Grandma's Bicycle</u> into the tape recorder. I did a miscue analysis and found that she read words instead of phrases because she did not want to skip words. Her miscues were Spanish substitutions for English words.
9-13	Did a retrospective miscue analysis (RMA) with Rosa. She enjoyed listening to herself read <u>Grandma's Bicycle.</u> As she pointed to each word, she noticed words that she read in Spanish. At the end she said, "I don't sound like you do when you read." I asked her what she meant. She said, "It is not smooth." After modeling how I read phrases, I gave her the tape recorder and asked her to read and reread only the first page of the book, until she thought she was "smooth." After her fifth time, she thought she was good.
9-14	I listened to all five recordings with her, and found that she did improve in fluency. She wanted to read the second page until it was "smooth." After she practiced, I listened to the second page to make sure she had no miscues.

expects students to display by the end of the school year, with a column to indicate whether the behavior is or is not observed. The teacher dates each observation in order to document student changes. Many times the checklist lists the traits with a column to mark "yes" if the trait is observed or "no" the trait is not observed. Sometimes different symbols will be used to show consistency of a trait (e.g., a plus sign means "always observed," a check means "sometimes observed," and a zero means "seldom observed"). Other times, symbols are used to indicate degrees of mastery of a trait (e.g., a plus sign means "target," a check means "acceptable," and a zero means "unacceptable").

The objective with a checklist is three-fold: (1) to assist a teacher as he observes a student's behavior or performance, (2) to assist a teacher as he plans for instruction, and (3) "to compare evidence of behavior over time and thus help determine student progress" (Cooper & Kiger, 2001, p. 31). To design a checklist, a teacher includes a list of competencies—often based on national or state standards or benchmarks—that all students are expected to attain by the end of the school year. The checklist may be used at the end of each quarter so that the teacher can analyze which students are meeting the standards and which students need more instructional time and practice.

Figure 3.16 reproduces a standard from the Oklahoma Core Curriculum Guide. To illustrate the simple procedure of designing a checklist based on such state standards, Figure 3.17 shows a partial checklist that includes the main language arts standards for the second grade in Oklahoma. The Oklahoma Standards are called the Priority Academic Student Skills (PASS). The partial checklist was completed after the first grading period. The teacher could see which students were progressing and which ones needed extra help. The complete checklist is located in Appendix C.3.

This particular checklist gives the date and the names of the students. The plus sign (+) indicates that the student performs the task all the time, an X indicates that the student performs the task sometimes, and a zero (0) means that the student does not perform the task. As you can tell, this type of assessment also provides a general assessment of the class. From this assessment, the teacher can readily note which standards no one in the class has met and thus need to be addressed during instruction.

Another checklist, based on the National Standards for the English Language Arts, established by the National Council of Teachers of English (NCTE)

and the International Reading Association (IRA) in 1996 is provided in Appendix C.4. This checklist is more specific than the one in Figure 3.17 because it is for one student and records the context in which the behavior was observed. This type of checklist can be used to show a student and his caregivers how he is progressing to meet the national standards. Checklists that do not include the context are more subjective and serve as general guidelines for teachers.

The Literacy Habits checklists in Appendix C (C.5–C.9) are intended for teachers to use for emergent readers through proficient readers. Each one is a separate checklist, but a teacher may need to use two consecutive checklists to get accurate records of what she observes in students. Later chapters will discuss other checklists for assessing specific aspects of literacy.

Rubrics

A rubric "describes the knowledge and skills a particular project or performance demonstrates, based on specific criteria for quality work" (Fiderer, 1999, p. 5). Rubrics, like checklists, list competencies that students are expected to have mastered; however,

---

FIGURE 3.16   Standard 5: Comprehension/critical literacy.

The student will interact with the words and concepts in a text to construct an appropriate meaning.

1. Literal understanding
   a. Read and comprehend both fiction and nonfiction that is appropriately designed for the second half of second grade.
   b. Use prereading strategies to preview, activate prior knowledge, make predictions, use picture clues, and establish the purpose for reading (e.g., graphic organizers).
   c. Ask and respond to questions to aid comprehension about important elements of fiction and nonfiction.

2. Inferences and Interpretation
   a. Make inferences about events, characters, and ideas in fictional texts by connecting knowledge and experience to the story.
   b. Support interpretations or conclusions with examples taken from the text.

3. Summary and Generalization
   a. Retell or act out narrative text by identifying story elements and sequencing the events.
   b. Produce oral or written summaries of text selections by discussing who, what, when, where, why, and how to identify the main idea and significant supporting details of text.

4. Analysis and Evaluation
   a. Identify cause/effect relationships in text.
   b. Make comparisons and draw conclusions based on what is read.
   c. Describe character traits, changes and relationships.

5. Monitoring and Correction Strategies—Integrate the use of semantics, syntax, and graphophonic cues to gain meaning from the text.

Source: Oklahoma State Department of Education (revised 2002). *A core curriculum for our children's future: Priority academic student skills (PASS).* Oklahoma City: Oklahoma State Dept. of Education.

FIGURE 3.17 Checklist for second grade, based on PASS.

TEACHER Mr. Reinhart   DATE Jan.

+ = always   X = sometimes   O = seldom/never

STANDARD	Hannah	Kent	Marc	Reed	Zack	Vanessa	Austin	Lauren	Adam	Merrick	Ryan	Emily	Rachel	Jacob	Chrystie	Miranda	Juanita	Riley
1. Read and comprehend fiction, suitable for grade level.	+	X	X	+	+	X	O	O	+	+	+	X	X	+	+	+	X	O
2. Read and comprehend non-fiction, suitable for grade level.	X	O	X	+	+	O	O	O	+	X	+	X	O	+	+	+	O	O
3. Uses prereading strategies to preview and make predictions.	+	O	X	+	O	O	O	O	O	X	+	O	O	O	+	+	O	O
4. Uses picture clues and graphic organizers as prereading strategies.	X	O	O	+	O	O	O	O	O	O	+	O	O	O	+	+	O	O

unlike checklists, rubrics are *scoring guides* for particular assignments or for particular evaluation periods within the school year. Most rubrics describe three or four levels of achievement or performance. Each level gives a detailed explanation of the degree of mastery and/or a numerical score. Often the same rubric is used for similar assignments that the teacher gives throughout the year so the rubric can show student growth in a particular area. The rubric in Figure 3.18, used at the end of each grading period, gives a detailed explanation of degrees of mastery. Like many rubrics, this one is based on a state standard, in this case the Oklahoma Priority Academic Student Skills (PASS), Standard 5 for the second grade. The standard is printed in Figure 3.16.

The rubric in Figure 3.18 closely reflects the state standard. Using the rubric will help the teacher focus on each item in the standard. Note that on the rubric that the target degree of mastery (5 points) corresponds to meeting the state standard; the other two degrees of mastery—acceptable (3 points) and unacceptable (1 point)—represent the degree to which the student has met the standard.

If the teacher uses the same rubric each quarter, she can document each student's progress in reading comprehension. If the entire class is weak in one or two areas, she can readily tell which part of the standard she needs to emphasize with the class. From the rubric, she will also be able to identify the weaknesses of individual students.

Figure 3.18 shows Victor's rubric at the end of the first grading period. After reviewing Victor's portfolios, running records, and miscue analyses for the first nine weeks, his teacher was able to complete the rubric. The teacher's comments at the end of the rubric are a summary of its contents. Obviously, at the end of the first grading period, no second grader would have reached the target degree of mastery in each part of Standard 5; therefore, Victor will not score a 42 percent for the grading period. Rather, the percentage helps Victor's teacher mark his growth from one grading period to the next. Some teachers may choose not to assign a number to degrees of mastery.

Different rubrics for different subjects can be accessed at http://Rubistar.4teachers.org. The rubrics at this site fall into eight main categories—oral projects, research/writing, work skills, multimedia, science, math, music, and art. There are rubrics in English, Spanish, and Dutch. The user can modify the rubrics to fit the particular assignment.

Portfolios

Portfolios are collections of students' work from the school year. They are useful tools to organize materials, to document growth, and to display exemplary work. Portfolios can be file folders, three-ring binders, or electronic files. At the beginning of each

FIGURE 3.18 Rubric for reading comprehension based on standard 5 of the Oklahoma PASS.

SECOND GRADE

STUDENT: _Victor_   GRADING PERIOD ①2 3 4   TOTAL SCORE: 23 / 55

LEVEL OF MASTERY

TRAIT	TARGET (5 POINTS)	ACCEPTABLE (3 POINTS)	UNACCEPTABLE (1 POINT)
1. Grade Appropriate Material	Reads & comprehends fiction and nonfiction at the assigned grade & month. ___	Reads & comprehends fiction & nonfiction at two or three months below grade level. _X_	Reads & comprehends fiction & nonfiction at more than three months below grade level. ___
2. Prereading Strategies	Always uses prereading strategies to preview, activate prior knowledge, make predictions, use picture clues, & establish the purpose for reading. ___	Sometimes uses prereading strategies to preview, activate prior knowledge, make predictions, use picture clues, & establish the purpose for reading. _X_	Seldom uses prereading strategies to preview, activate prior knowledge, make predictions, use picture clues, & establish the purpose for reading. ___
3. Questioning	Always asks & responds to questions to aid comprehension about important elements of fiction & nonfiction. ___	Sometimes asks & responds to questions to aid comprehension about important elements of fiction & nonfiction. ___	Seldom asks & responds to questions to aid comprehension about important elements of fiction. _X_
4. Inference & Interpretation	Always makes inferences about events, characters, & ideas in fictional texts by connecting prior knowledge to story. ___	Sometimes makes inferences about events, characters, & ideas in fictional texts by connecting prior knowledge to story. ___	Seldom makes inferences about events, characters, & ideas in fictional texts by connecting prior knowledge to story. _X_
5. Gives Examples	Always supports interpretations or conclusions with examples from the text. ___	Sometimes supports interpretations or conclusions with examples from the text. ___	Seldom supports interpretations or conclusions with examples from the text. _X_
6. Retells	Always retells or acts out narrative by correctly sequencing the events. ___	Retells or acts out narrative with some events out of order. _X_	Retells or acts out narrative with most events out of order. ___
7. Summarizes	Always produces oral or written summaries of text by discussing _who, what, when, where, why,_ and _how_ to identify the main idea and significant supporting details. ___	Sometimes produces oral or written summaries of text by discussing _who, what, when, where, why,_ and _how_ to identify the main idea and significant supporting details. _X_	Seldom produces oral or written summaries of text by discussing _who, what, when, where, why,_ and _how_ to identify the main idea and significant supporting details. ___
8. Cause/Effect	Always identifies cause/effect relationships. ___	Sometimes identifies cause/effect relationships. ___	Seldom identifies cause/effect relationships. _X_
9. Comparisons	Always makes comparisons & draws conclusions. ___	Sometimes makes comparisons & draws conclusions.	Seldom makes comparisons & draws conclusions. _X_
10. Descriptions	Always describes character traits, changes, & relationships. ___	Sometimes describes character traits, changes, & relationships. _X_	Seldom describes character traits, changes, & relationships. ___
11. Monitoring	Always integrates the use of semantic, syntactic, & graphophonic cues to gain meaning. ___	Sometimes integrates the use of semantic, syntactic, & graphophonic cues to gain meaning. ___	Seldom integrates the use of semantic, syntactic, & graphophonic cues to gain meaning. _X_

TEACHER COMMENTS:

Victor's strength is his ability to retell most of a story in order and list main events. He enjoys talking about characters. He uses graphophonic cues most of the time and sometimes uses syntax. Victor struggles w/expository text. He needs one-on-one attention while reading expository text that is at his instructional level.

portfolio, it is helpful to have a log to record the title of the composition or passage read, and the date it was completed. Figure 3.19 is a partial reading log for Becky, a first-grade student. There are three types of portfolios—working portfolios, best-work portfolios, and growth portfolios.

Working Portfolios

Working portfolios organize a student's project in process. For example, a working portfolio for reading may contain the tape that the student is using to increase reading expression, rate, or fluency. On this tape, the student will tape over previous practices. If a student is writing a research report, the working portfolio may contain the following: pre-writing graphic organizers; notes taken from sources; list of sources; the first draft with all other drafts, including revisions; the editing copy; and the final copy. After the teacher has assessed and discussed the process and end result of the project, the final copy of the composition, poem, or report is placed in the growth portfolio.

Growth Portfolios

Teachers usually have one growth portfolio for reading, one for writing, and another for math or other subjects. The growth portfolio contains all the final copies of the student's work along with the scoring rubrics.

Growth portfolios, because they contain samples of a student's work over time, are valuable assessment tools. Growth portfolios can provide the assessment materials from which teachers and students can document growth in particular areas of reading and writing. For example, a growth portfolio may include an audiotape of the student's monthly reading. With each reading, the teacher includes a miscue analysis, a running record and/or anecdotal records, as well as checklists and rubrics for assessing the student's read-

ing ability. The teacher then uses the audiotape (1) to discuss reading strengths and weaknesses with students and parents, (2) to plan for future instruction, and (3) to encourage readers' abilities.

Teachers can share the growth portfolios during parent–teacher conferences. The portfolio will indicate what particular literacy skills the students are developing or need to develop. It will also help the teacher and caregiver identify the areas in which the child may need extra help. For example, if a second-grade student cannot retell a story in the correct sequence by the end of the third grading period, the teacher and caregiver know that they need to give the child opportunities to develop that skill. Portfolios are tools to encourage the caregiver and the child about the child's growth.

Best-Work Portfolio

If the student believes that an item represents his best work, he will place a copy of it in his best-work portfolio. The best-work writing portfolio may contain poems, stories, reports, newspaper articles, and so on. The compositions that are placed in the best-work portfolio have a self-assessment sheet, which explains why the student believes this is his best work. The best-work reading portfolio may include selections from the student's favorite stories, poems, and other passages. The student reviews each selection and chooses to keep it as a "favorite" story, poem, or passage.

Electronic Portfolios

The contents of an electronic portfolio are usually the same as the file folder and three-ring binders; however, the contents are saved for electronic presentation. The electronic portfolio contains scanned forms, student writings, audiotapes of students' readings, digital photographs, and videos. The material is saved on a CD or a disk with a large capacity. Teach-

---

FIGURE 3.19 Sample reading log.

READING LOG FOR BECKY

TITLE/LEVEL	DATE RECORDED
1. The Hungry Kitten/D	9/9
2. I can Swim/D	9/12
3. I Live in a House/D	9/16
4. Nana's Sweet Potato Pie/E	9/19
5. Over the Marble Mountain/E	9/25

ers or students who use electronic portfolios need to be able to use equipment such as scanners, digital cameras, video cameras, and portfolio software.

One flexible software program is the *Scholastic Electronic Portfolio.* The program permits the teacher to store text, record a student's readings, and to make slide shows and videos. The program comes with a detailed manual for teachers. At present, the software is available only for Macintosh.

Another software program that can be used in primary and middle school is *The Portfolio Assessment Kit,* produced by Super School Software. This program is also designed for Macintosh, but can be transferred to Windows. Student writing can easily be stored and viewed with this program. Teachers can also scan forms such as rubrics, checklists, logs, and anecdotal records that can be shared with caregivers during conferences. All these records can be viewed on the screen and the teacher can print out any report the caregiver may want to keep. A third software program, useful

to elementary and middle school teachers, is *The Portfolio Builder for PowerPoint,* produced by Visions-Technology in Education. This program is available for Windows and Macintosh. This program permits users to create graphics, sound, video, and, of course, texts.

It is important for you to study the capabilities of new software programs before you make a purchase. You should consider these questions: (1) What do I want to accomplish with the program? (2) Is it complicated and time-consuming to operate? (3) Can students readily learn how to use it?

PERSONAL INTEREST SURVEYS

If you understand each student's interests, you can provide more effective reading and writing opportunities. Figure 3.20 is a personal interest survey for

FIGURE 3.20 Personal interest survey.

MY FAVORITES!
By Grey

Foods: pizza, grandpa's waffles

Snacks: apples, grapes

Hunt for bugs

Swim by grandpa's house

Sleep over by grandpa's house

Read: about snakes, bugs, wild animals

Don't like to write!

I am a star at ___Roller blades___.
I like to ___read___ alone.
I like to ___swim___ with friends.
I like to ___ride bike___ with my family.
My favorite things to do on Saturday and Sunday are ___roller blade in the park with grandpa___.

young students. It is best for the teacher to be the scribe for the student so he will express what he really likes, without having to worry about spelling or grammar. You should feel free to extend the interest inventory if the student expresses interest in things not listed on the survey. For example, the interest survey in Figure 3.20 suggests that Grey enjoys spending time with his grandpa. His teacher can then look for stories about grandparents, such as Tomie dePaola's *Tom*.

Personal Interest Surveys can also help you focus on areas of study that interest older students. Some students may enjoy reading informational books or magazines, but dislike funny stories. Other students may dislike informational books but enjoy mysteries or other puzzle-like materials. Older students should complete the surveys themselves to ensure honest responses. If they give their responses verbally to you, they may not give honest responses because they think there is a "correct" answer. After students complete the surveys, you can use them to find materials that interest the students. Figure 3.21 contains a partially completed example of a Personal Interest Survey for older students; Appendix C.10 contains the full survey.

ATTITUDE SURVEYS

It is pertinent that teachers understand their students' attitudes. Some readers and writers are quite happy when someone else reads to or writes for them, but they dislike reading aloud or writing of any kind. When students have strong dislikes for reading and/or writing, you should attempt to understand why. Students may dislike reading and/or writing because they find it boring or too hard, or they are afraid of failure. You need to help students change these negative attitudes so that they will not avoid these crucial activities. Once you understand what reading and writing events a student dislikes and why, you can help the student build a more positive attitude.

Appendixes C.11–C.15 include Reading and Writing Attitude Surveys for primary and older students. The scoring sheet found in Appendix C.13 can be used for the primary reading and the primary writing attitude surveys. The pre- and post-test scores are recorded on this one sheet. To score these attitude surveys, the teacher gives four points for each happy character circled, three points for each somewhat happy character circled, two points for each neutral character circled, and one point for each unhappy character circled. The higher the score, the more interest the student has in reading or writing.

"Collecting data about students is an empty exercise unless the information is used to plan instruction" (McKenna & Kear, 1990, p. 627). With any attitude survey, the quantitative score is not as important as the information the student shares about each statement. A score of 20 indicates that a student does not have a positive attitude toward any kind of writing, while a score of 80 indicates that a student does have a positive attitude. However, as Miss Hendricks discovers in a discussion with one of her students, the student only circled the happy character because it was friendlier than the others. It is important that after the survey, the teacher takes time to discuss each item. The discussion may indicate that the student likes to write about himself or his pets, but dislikes composing letters to authors, thank you notes, poems, or riddles.

FIGURE 3.21 Personal interest survey.

NAME: LaVonda   GRADE: 6   QUARTER: 1st

List more than one item for each category if you have more interests. Explain why you gave each response. For example, why do you enjoy researching (*your favorite topic*) on the Internet?

1. My favorite subject(s) in school are _music and art because I like to sing and draw_.
2. My least favorite subject in school is _science because it is hard_.
3. My favorite topic to research on the Internet is _art galleries to learn about them_.
4. My favorite topic to study in science is _weather because it is interesting_.
5. My favorite foreign country to study is _Italy because I would like to go there_.

It is also important to remember that attitude surveys do not indicate the sources of poor attitudes nor do they give suggestions about instructional techniques that will change them (McKenna & Kear, 1990).

These surveys are effective pre- and post-tests. After a student is tutored by a teacher, paraprofessional, or adult volunteer, the surveys will hopefully reflect a change in attitude.

LITERACY SELF-PERCEPTION SCALES

Self-perception scales are designed to provide a picture of how students feel about themselves as readers and writers. The Reader Self-Perception Scale (RSPS) (Henk & Melnick, 1995) and the Writer Self-Perception Scale (WSPS) (Bottomley, Henk, & Melnick, 1998) have been validated systematically. If teachers are conducting experimental studies and need validated assessment instruments, these surveys can be used. For your convenience, the two surveys with the directions for administrating, scoring, and interpreting them are found in Appendices C.16 and C.17.

STUDENT SELF-ASSESSMENT

Assessment by a teacher is important; however, self-assessment by students can increase their self-esteem and motivation to read and write.

Book Logs

Logging the books that they read and indicating their likes and dislikes is something that helps students see themselves as having a voice in the reading process. These logs also help them see if they prefer one genre over another or one author over another. The log in Figure 3.22 (also found in Appendix C.18) is for primary students to record their reading habits. At the end of a grading period they can check how many books they read and can note their favorite authors and illustrators. Even young children have a preference for certain authors and illustrators over others. They can simply circle the face that fits their attitude toward the book. Figure 3.23 (also found in Appendix C.19) has a similar log form for more advanced readers. They also record the genre and how long it took them to read each book. In the "comment" column, they can indicate if they recommended the book to others or if they liked a particular character. This column is not intended to be used as a "book report."

Skill Logs

When students log what particular skills they learn during conferencing, they have a record of reading strategies and skills they can return to when they struggle with a passage. For younger students, you can record what you taught the student during a teacher–student conference. Older students can record what they learned in the conference with the teacher, with a peer, or by themselves.

It is advantageous for students to record things that they have learned to do as readers and writers. When they forget how to approach a task, they can

---

FIGURE 3.22 Book log for primary school student.

RECORD OF BOOKS _____*Chao*_____ READ   GRADE: __2__

Circle the face that best shows how you feel about the book.

BOOK	AUTHOR/ILLUSTRATOR	COMMENTS
The Little Red Hen Makes Pizza	Philemon Sturges/Amy Walrod	☺ ☺ ☹
Gumbrella	Barry Root	☺ ☺ ☹
26 Fairmount Avenue	Tomie dePaola	☺ ☺ ☹
Here We All Are	Tomie dePaola	☺ ☺ ☹
Fables from Aesop	Tom Lynch	☺ ☺ ☹

FIGURE 3.23 Book log for older student.

BOOKS THAT _____ Kalee _____ READ   GRADE: _5_   QUARTER ① 2 3 4

BOOK	AUTHOR	GENRE	DATE STARTED/ ENDED	COMMENTS
Mister and Me	Kimberly Willis Holt	Realistic fiction	8/24–8/26	Very easy reading. My mom is dating too and I know how Jolene felt.
Choosing Up Sides	John Ritter	Realistic fiction	9/1–9/5	I recommended this to Jack because his dad is a preacher.
Don't You Know There's a War On?	Avi	Realistic/ Historical fiction	9/10–9/12	It was so funny! I loved it!
Graveyard Girl	Anna Myers	Historical fiction	9/13–9/14	Loved it! But it was so sad! I cried.

My favorite book I read this quarter was ___Mister and Me___

because ___my mom is dating again and I treat my mom badly too.___

look back at their log. It also gives them a record of what they have learned over a period of time. These sheets are also helpful during home–school conferences, to show caregivers what a child has learned. Logs also let students list information about different genres and authors. The form in Figure 3.24 is a sample form for a second-grade reader. The form in Figure 3.25 is designed for older students to record details they have learned about genres and authors.

Reflection Logs

Students should be taught to think about their reading habits. At the end of each quarter, a form such as that used with Sheila in Figure 3.26 can be used to generate students' thoughts. A blank form is provided in Appendix C.20. In the primary grades, the teacher confers with each student and writes as the student responds to each statement. Older students are given time to first write their responses and then confer with the teacher about their responses. Forms such as "My Thoughts about My Reading" challenge students to become life-long reflective readers. Profi-

cient readers reflect on aspects of books they liked or disliked. They also attempt to understand why they prefer certain books to others.

Accomplishment and Goal-Setting Logs

After students reflect on their reading habits and understand what they like and dislike, they need to set goals for themselves. Setting personal reading and writing goals gives students a voice in their literacy development. With the teacher's guidance, students should set realistic goals and then reflect on what they need to do in order to accomplish them. For younger children, the teacher can fill out the form with students, while older students can fill out the form and then discuss it with the teacher. When students set their own goals, they feel empowered and are more likely to work for the goal than if they have no voice in the decision-making process. You should encourage your students to reach their goals by periodically checking their goal list with them throughout the grading period. Figure 3.27 is a form that Ms. Walker uses with her sixth-grade students to record

FIGURE 3.24 Skills list for primary school student.

FOR QUARTER 1 ② 3 4

Things that _____Syndee_____ learned to do as a reader.

1. Stop at the periods (.)
2. Point to every word as I read it.
3. Raise my voice with questions (?)
4. Get excited when I see !
5. Read to the end of the sentence when I come to a word I don't know. Then ask, "What word would make sense?" Also look at pictures.

FIGURE 3.25 Skills list for older student.

FOR QUARTER 1 2 ③ 4

Things that _____Hayley_____ learned about literature and authors.

1. Sometimes authors don't use explanatory words.
2. Authors can use flashbacks like movies do.
3. Authors use first person—you only know what that person thinks.
4. Authors use some real information in fiction.
5. Stories are interesting when authors use dialect.

FIGURE 3.26 Reflection log.

MY THOUGHTS ABOUT READING

NAME _____Sheila_____   GRADE: _6_   QUARTER ① 2 3 4

1. The informational books I read were about _____Composers and their compositions._____
2. The novels I read were mostly (realistic, historical, biographies, autobiographies, mysteries, science fiction, fantasy, folktales).
3. My favorite author is _____Avi._____
4. The best book I read was _____Don't You Know There's a War Going On?_____
5. When I dislike a book, _____I put it back on the book shelf._____
6. My favorite place to read is _____on my bed._____
7. My reading habits at home are: _____I always read before I go to bed._____
8. I do not enjoy reading books _____that are science fiction._____
9. The book I recommended to my friends was _____Don't You Know There's a War Going On?_____
10. After I read a book, I like to _____talk about it with Megan._____

FIGURE 3.27   Accomplishment and goal-setting log.

ACCOMPLISHMENTS AND GOALS FOR READING

NAME _____India_____   GRADE: __5__   QUARTER ① 2 3 4

ACCOMPLISHMENTS	GOALS	WAYS TO ACHIEVE GOALS
I read 2 chapter books. Both—realistic fiction. I re-read almost all the poems from <u>A Light In the Attic.</u>	Read at least 3 books—historical fiction.	Read at least 30 minutes each night and 1 hour on Sat. and Sun. Don't read books that are too hard for me. Read a book that someone else recommends so I know it's good.

TEACHER'S COMMENTS: _____

Student's Signature _____

Teacher's Signature _____

their accomplishments and goals. It is clear that India has been working on becoming a faster reader so she can read more books and she knows what she needs to do in order to accomplish that goal.

CONCLUDING THOUGHTS

There are all types of reading assessment instruments, both formal and informal. Formal tests are standardized, which means they are given under the same standard conditions. Formal tests include intelligence, achievement, and diagnostic tests. Achievement tests measure the achievement level of the student and can be either norm-referenced or criterion-referenced. Norm-referenced tests compare the performance of a student to the group on which the test was standardized. Criterion-referenced tests measure a particular skill that the student is expected to have mastered. Diagnostic tests have many sub-tests that assess a student's strengths and weaknesses in particular areas.

Teachers use informal assessment instruments (1) to diagnose reading problems, (2) to check the reading level of a student, (3) to analyze which cueing systems students use when making sense of print, (4) to understand student attitudes toward reading and writing and help identify materials that interest them, (5) to monitor student growth, (6) to provide opportunities for students to reflect reading and writing accomplishments, (7) to help students set realistic goals, and (8) to develop plans for instruction. Both formal and informal tests are useful to teachers in the measurement of students' reading and writing skills. Formal test scores indicate general abilities in various areas of literacy. Informal tests, administered by classroom teachers, permit those teachers to observe students' behaviors while they make sense of print.

Rubrics, checklists, and anecdotal records serve as indicators of certain aspects of students' growth that cannot be measured on a test. Throughout this chapter and other chapters in this text, I have included checklists and rubrics for specific types of reading and writing activities. All the checklists, rubrics, surveys, and logs are designed to help you assess the entire reading process, which encompasses students' skills, attitudes, and interests. When teachers diligently assess the entire reading process, they can truly *teach the student, and not a method!* All the checklists and rubrics in this text are only provided as suggestions. You should create your own checklists and rubrics that fit your curriculum and your students' needs.

TUTORING

*Education's
purpose is to
replace an empty
mind with an
open one.*

MALCOLM FORBES

Scenario

Mrs. Hughes has been teaching first grade for 14 years in a small rural community. Every year she encounters some struggling readers, but never so many that she cannot give them proper help. However, last year, a new industry brought many more families to her community. This has caused her class to increase from 15 to 23 students; with that increase, the number of struggling readers has also grown. Mrs. Hughes finds she no longer has enough time or energy to meet individual reading needs. Her principal encourages her to ask parents to volunteer to read with the children.

The response is great! However, after a year, Mrs. Hughes realizes that the help the parents are providing is very haphazard. It is not the volunteers' fault, but her own, because she has failed to give them adequate direction. She has been overwhelmed trying to find interesting activities for the volunteers and has not had time to develop activities that cater to individual needs. She knows the volunteers are frustrated by tutoring different students each session and by having to learn new activities while they work with the child. The most frustrating result for everyone is that after the first year, there is little improvement in students' reading scores. Mrs. Hughes knows she has to implement a system for working with volunteers.

During the following summer, Mrs. Hughes reads journal articles and attends a conference about successful volunteer tutoring programs. She takes ideas from the various programs and designs her own system. At the beginning of the year, she trains the volunteers in one day of intensive instruction, based on the Book Buddies Tutoring Program (Johnston, Invernizzi, & Juel, 1998). She explains that they will be working with the same two students throughout the semester. Each session will be 45 minutes long. She will provide a folder with the lesson plan and all necessary materials. She stresses the importance of the volunteers being prompt and faithful. She also teaches them how to proceed through each lesson and gives them specific strategies to use when students struggle with word identification or comprehension.

At the end of the year, she is happy with the structured sessions; her volunteers enjoy the work because they see progress in the children. Finally, her struggling readers show improvement in their reading scores.

INTRODUCTION

In the last decade, two national initiatives have made reading a priority in elementary education. As discussed in Chapter 1, the America Reads Challenge Act of 1997 states that all children will be able to read at grade level by the end of third grade; the No Child Left Behind Act of 2001 states that in order for schools to qualify for Title I funding, they need to document student growth in the following six areas of reading: phonemic awareness, systematic phonics, spelling and writing, fluency, text comprehension, and vocabulary. Obviously, the challenge is great for classroom teachers and administrators. Teachers recognize that many students need one-on-one or small group instruction in order to meet the goals of these two initiatives.

This need for more individualized instruction frequently motivates educators and researchers to design tutoring programs. The tutors used in these programs range from certified teachers to community volunteers, from peers to older students. Four nationally known tutoring programs with a good success rate are Reading Recovery, Success for All, The Howard Street Tutoring Program, and Book Buddies.

This chapter focuses on (1) the benefits and drawbacks of tutoring, (2) different types of tutoring programs, (3) successful tutoring programs, (4) guidelines for tutors, and (5) planning and conducting a tutoring session.

BENEFITS OF TUTORING

Tutoring is one-on-one instruction. Struggling readers benefit from being tutored. First, because instruction is based on the individual needs of the student, instant feedback is provided to the struggling reader (Chambers, Abrami, McWhaw, & Therrien, 2001; Clay, 1985; Johnston, Invernizzi, & Juel, 1998; Nunnery, Ross, Smith, Slavin, Hunter, & Stubbs, 1999; Pinnell, 1989). Because it is tailored to the individual student, "tutoring is one of the most effective forms of instruction" (Wasik, 1997, 1998). Most tutoring programs target students in the primary grades because it has been documented that children who are not reading by the third grade have higher chances of dropping out before graduating from high school (Chambers, Abrami, McWhaw, & Therrien, 2001).

There is one negative factor in tutoring; it is costly for school districts. One-on-one tutoring programs drain school districts' budgets, especially when they use certified teachers as tutors. In tutoring, a teacher works with one child at a time instead of 20 to 30 students. Even though certified teachers are more effective than uncertified tutors (Allington, 2001; Clay, 1985; Johnston, Invernizzi, & Juel, 1998), many school districts seek volunteers for tutoring to save money. Volunteers often include retired community members, college students, business leaders, and parents. These volunteers can be effective tutors, particularly if a certified teacher trains them (Johnston, Invernizzi, & Juel, 1998).

There are many benefits to using volunteer tutors. Besides reducing the cost of tutoring, volunteers also become more involved in their school, less critical of teachers, and more supportive when school bond issues arise. Since volunteers usually tutor for only one or two hours a day, they often have more energy than certified teachers—who often tutor for half the day and teach during the other half. This schedule can lead to fatigue and decrease the quality of tutoring (Chambers, Abrami, McWhaw, & Therrien, 2001).

TYPES OF TUTORS

Tutors can be categorized into six different types: (1) certified teachers, (2) trained volunteers, (3) reading coaches, (4) cross-age, (5) peer-to-peer, and (6) computer-assisted.

Certified Teachers

The school or district reading specialist usually trains certified teachers. Tutoring done by certified teachers is the best for the student because such teachers are able to diagnose reading problems, to assess the learning style of readers, and to match specific strategies with specific literacy problems (Allington, 2001; Clay, 1993; Johnston, Invernizzi, & Juel, 1998; Wasik, 1997). However, as mentioned before, hiring certified teachers is very expensive, and they often get tutoring fatigue because they frequently tutor one student after another for half a day. Working with struggling readers for long periods of time is taxing because tutors must constantly assess what a child does as he makes sense of a passage. Many struggling readers do not enjoy reading and this means that their tutors must maintain a positive tone and a fast pace. Good tutors also need to be alert to seize the "teachable moment" by selecting instructional strategies that hold the tutee's interest and that are tailored to individual needs and learning styles.

Trained Volunteers

Using trained volunteers as tutors has also proven to be a successful approach (Wasik, 1998, 1999). In this situation, a certified reading specialist is responsible for training the volunteer tutors. Good training includes information about how children learn to read and how to assess their reading problems, as well as how to help children decode words, learn sight words, and comprehend different types of text. The training also includes instruction on how to match specific reading strategies with specific reading problems.

After volunteers complete the initial training, they are supervised by the same reading specialist as they tutor. The reading specialist assesses the students, develops the lesson plans, organizes instructional materials, and provides feedback to the tutors. When volunteers have questions or problems, the reading specialist is on hand to assist them.

These trained volunteers usually tutor a couple of times a week for no more than an hour or two at a time. This schedule keeps them from becoming fatigued. Each tutoring session is usually 30 to 45 minutes in duration and should include the following four components, which are common to successful tutoring programs:

1. Rereading familiar texts. This gives the tutee opportunities to improve fluency, automaticity, and comprehension while experiencing success and gaining confidence.

2. Working with word analysis. These activities help the student to focus on the orthographic structure of words. They recognize patterns within words, listen for all the sounds, and link sound sequences with letters. The activities can include spelling words with magnetic letters, word sort, and syllable segmentation.

3. Writing activities in which the student composes a passage. Most passages are only one or two sentences long. While the student composes, the tutor helps the tutee listen for letter–sound relationships and recognize spelling patterns.

4. Reading new stories on the student's instructional level. The tutor creates interest in the story by providing background information and/or by looking through the pictures. New vocabulary words are introduced and discussed while they read the passage. During this time, the tutor teaches reading strategies.

To maintain a steady pace during a tutoring session, each activity is allotted a certain amount of time. The steady pace helps the tutor and the child to stay on task. If volunteer tutors are going to impact student literacy during these sessions, there are guidelines that must be followed (Wasik, 1997). Figure 4.1 lists the major guidelines for successful tutoring sessions.

Reading Coaches

Reading coaches are also volunteers from the community; however, they do not receive intensive training. Many times these volunteers are retired persons who

FIGURE 4.1 Guidelines for volunteer tutors.

1. Tutors need to be trained by certified reading teachers.
2. Tutors need ongoing training and feedback.
3. The child should work with the same tutor in each session.
4. Tutors must be reliable and punctual.
5. A certified teacher should be present during the tutoring sessions to answer questions and provide input.
6. Tutoring sessions need to be structured.
7. Tutors should use high-quality instructional materials.
8. The reading specialist needs to assess the tutee on a regular basis.
9. The instruction in the tutoring session must coordinate with classroom instruction.

Sources: Allington, R. (2001). *What really matters for struggling readers: Designing research-based programs.* New York: Longman. Invernizzi, M., Rosemary, C., Juel, C., & Richard, H. (1997). At-risk readers and community volunteers: A three-year perspective. *Scientific Studies of Reading, 1*(3), 277–300. Wasik, B. (1998). Using volunteers as reading tutors: Guidelines for successful practice. *The Reading Teacher, 51*(7), 562–571.

are interested in helping young children succeed, or business leaders who do not have time for formal training, but understand the importance of reading in any job. Since coaches read to children, they need some minimal training from a reading specialist about effective reading techniques with children. First, they need to know how to model fluent, expressive reading so that the story comes alive for the listener. To train coaches, reading specialists demonstrate expressive reading and "echo reading" (in which the tutee repeats the phrase or short sentence the coach has just read, using the same rate and intonation). Later the coaches read to each other so they are comfortable reading with expression. Since children are introduced to new vocabulary words as they listen to stories, coaches should learn how to prompt tutees to make guesses about the meaning of new words using picture clues and context clues. For example, when a tutee comes to an unknown word, he should be encouraged to read to the end of the sentence and ask, "Does the picture tell me what the word is? What word makes sense? Does that word sound right? Does it look right?" Reading coaches also need to be trained to encourage tutees to predict what will happen next in a story and how to discuss books without making the discussion seem like a quiz.

For example, the following are two strategies that coaches can use to help tutees make predictions. The first strategy involves looking at and discussing the cover illustration. The coach asks, "What do you think this book is about?" The tutee makes predictions based on the illustration. In the second strategy, the coach and tutee preview the book by looking at and discussing all the pictures. While they discuss the pictures, the coach uses words that

are found in the text. For example, while previewing the book *The Koalas,* from the Literacy 2000 Satellite series, the tutee may see a picture and predict that the koala is "sleeping." While discussing how the koala is hanging in the tree, the coach uses the word *resting,* the word used in the text.

Discussions with tutees should evoke higher level thinking skills that "require children to elaborate on concepts" (Wasik, 1999, p. 655). During training, coaches need to be taught the difference between lower level questions that have the answer written on the page and higher level questions that have no simple right or wrong answers. When asking higher level thinking questions, the coaches need to understand the importance of having the child explain answers because sometimes children's answers appear to be incorrect until they give their reasoning. Coaches also need to encourage children to ask questions as they read stories and concept books.

During their tutoring sessions, reading coaches do not diagnose reading problems nor do they provide instruction; however, they are important as they support a child's literacy development. Reading coaches' main goal is to provide enrichment experiences without emphasizing the diagnostic and intervention aspects of reading events (Wasik, 1999). They accomplish this goal by supporting children as they read and by modeling good fluent reading. Research indicates that reading to children is positively related to children's reading success (Morrow, 1997; National Research Council, 1998). As reading coaches spend time listening to tutees read, they also teach tutees new words. They encourage tutees to work on expression, fluency, and rate by reading easy books. When a tutee reads a book that is at his or her instructional level, the coach and the tutee can read in unison so that the tutee does not struggle with unknown words. If possible, coaches should tape a tutee's reading and then listen to the tape with him or her, pointing out areas of improvement. This procedure permits children to evaluate their own reading. Coaches provide encouragement and give struggling readers a chance to read without fear of being ridiculed by classmates.

Throughout this text, there are many game-like activities that build reading and writing skills. Reading coaches can conduct these activities with tutees to make reading a more enjoyable experience for tutees. Reading specialists should explain how these activities build literacy skills so that the coaches understand their importance in helping a child learn to read.

Figure 4.2 lists the differences between a trained volunteer and a reading coach.

Cross-Age Tutors

Cross-age tutors are older students who tutor younger struggling readers. The tutors are often struggling middle school or high school students. These older students benefit from tutoring younger children for a number of reasons: (1) older students get to read material that is at their easy or instructional level, which helps them gain fluency, (2) they have an authentic reason for reading and for learning reading strategies, (3) they have a chance to integrate writing with reading, (4) they have an opportunity to discuss texts, and (5) they plan instruction for their tutees, which facilitates their own retention, comprehension, and metacognition (Cohen, 1986; Fisher, 2001; Thrope & Wood, 2000). Fisher (2001) found that

when less proficient middle school students tutor first and second graders, both the middle school and elementary students' reading improved. Jacobson, Thrope, Fisher, Lapp, Frey, and Flood (2001) reported the following results when less proficient middle school readers tutored struggling third graders:

1. Cross-age tutoring improved the reading comprehension of the middle school students.
2. The middle school students' attitude toward reading improved.
3. Picture books and wordless books were useful texts for middle school struggling readers.
4. Rereading of texts improved comprehension for both the middle school students and the third graders.
5. The middle school students "owned" the reading comprehension strategies that they taught because they had to teach the strategy to someone else. They used the learned strategy in their other reading assignments.
6. The attitudes and reading ability of the third graders improved.

In order for cross-age tutoring to be helpful, the middle school and high school students need to learn how to use the reading strategies they will teach to the younger children. The secondary school teacher first teaches a strategy or lesson to her students; then these students practice teaching the strategy to their peers. Finally, the older students teach the strategy or lesson to younger struggling readers. As in all tutoring, a consistent format is used in cross-age tutoring sessions. Jacobson et al. (2001) suggest the following format:

FIGURE 4.2   Differences between trained volunteers and reading coaches.

TRAINED VOLUNTEERS	READING COACHES
1. Play a central role in instruction.	1. Provide one-on-one literacy experiences for children.
2. Teach reading and writing strategies.	2. Support children's literacy learning.
3. Evaluate children's weaknesses and strengths.	3. Model good reading so children can appreciate the rich language of books.
4. Monitor how children acquire information.	4. Listen to children read.
5. Know how to assess reading problems.	5. Do not diagnose or assess children.
6. Have expert knowledge of subject matter.	6. Do not provide specific interventions.
7. Have knowledge of effective methods of communicating knowledge to children.	7. Read with children and discuss passages.
8. Focus on teaching children to read and write.	8. Encourage children in their literacy development.

Source: Adapted from Wasik, Barbara A. (1999, March). Teaching Reading: Reading coaches: An alternative to reading tutors. *The Reading Teacher, 52*(6), 653–656. Copyright © 1999 by the International Reading Association.

Day 1. The middle school or high school teacher teaches the lesson to the middle or high school students.

Day 2. Middle school or high school students teach the lesson to each other.

Days 3 and 4. Older students teach the lesson to four different third-grade struggling readers (two on Day 3 and two on Day 4).

Day 5. Tutors discuss their experiences with their teacher and each other.

Cross-age tutoring is a useful tool for elementary classroom teachers who do not have time to spend 30 minutes a day with each struggling reader. It also saves time for the middle school and high school teachers because on days 3 and 4, when one group of their students is tutoring younger children, they have time to devote to the remaining students.

Peer-to-Peer Tutoring

Peer-to-peer tutoring occurs when students who have mastered a particular reading skill or strategy teach it to a less proficient reader. The main objective of peer-to-peer tutoring is to increase and improve fluency and comprehension. Both unison reading (a number of students reading in unison) and shared reading (one student reads one page while a second student reads the next, and so on) permit the struggling readers to hear fluent reading. Secondary objectives of peer-to-peer tutoring are (1) to provide a pleasurable reading atmosphere, (2) to teach positive social interaction, and (3) to give proficient readers an opportunity to teach reading strategies. In order to accomplish the main objective, teachers need to train children how to read in unison at a pace that struggling readers can match and yet maintain reading fluency. In shared reading, the peer tutor and tutee can read alternating sentences or pages. To help tutees increase comprehension of texts, teachers should train peer tutors to discuss favorite characters and favorite passages. Casual discussions aid comprehension. Consider the following discussion between Evette and Sara, two first-grade readers, as they read *I Remember*, from the 2000 Literacy Satellite series. Evette is a more advanced reader than Sara and is considered the tutor.

Evette [viewing the cover]: What do you think is happening?

Sara: The girl's grandma is reading a bedtime story to the girl.

Evette: Do you have a grandma?

Sara: Yes, and I go sleep at her house every Friday night and I get to sleep in the bed that momma slept in when she was a little girl. Mamma's bed has a blanket on it like this one.

Evette: That's a quilt.

Sara: Why is it called a quilt?

Evette: Because all the pieces are different pictures and they are sewn together.

Sara (turning the page, pointing to the sewing machine): What's that thing?

Evette: That's a sewing machine. Her grandma is sewing all the pieces together. My momma has a pincushion like that (pointing to the pincushion).

Sara: My grandma sews with a needle and thread.

The two continue discussing the book's pictures before they read it. This is a strategy that the girls' teacher taught them in guided reading groups.

For the atmosphere to be pleasurable, teachers need to demonstrate how peer tutors should share a book, point at words, and assist tutees with unknown words. Tutors need to learn how to offer pleasant greetings and partings and how to be positive when the tutee struggles with unfamiliar words. Notice what happens as Logan, a first grader, reads page seven in *Shadows* (also from the 2000 Literacy Satellite series) to Nathan, the more advanced reader.

Logan [reading]: So I made a (pause as he looks at the shadow of the picture and the smaller picture of a monster) dragon.

Nathan: That picture does look like a dragon and this little picture looks like a mean green dragon. But does this word (pointing to *monster*), look like dr . . . ag . . . on? (drawing out the sounds of the word)

Logan: Dr . . . dr—dr is a /d/ sound.

Nathan: Yeah, that's right. Let's look at this word (pointing to *monster*). Is that a *d*?

Logan: No, it's an *m*.

Nathan: What other word means the same thing as dragon, but begins with an *m*?

Logan: (pause) *Monster*?

Nathan: *Monster* begins with an *m*. What other sounds are in *monster*?

Logan: M . . . o . . . n . . . s . . . t . . . r. (Nathan writes the letters on a piece of paper as Logan gives each letter.)

Nathan: Let's see if this word looks like the one in the book.

Logan (matching the letter): Yes, but this one in the book has an *e* in it.

Nathan: That's right. Now read this page again.

Logan: So I made a monster (reads in scary voice).

Nathan: I like that scary voice.

Logan (turning the page): Shadows don't (pause) *s . . . s*

Nathan (covering up the *s*): What's this word?

Logan: *Care.*

Nathan: Now put the /s/ sound before *care*.

Logan: *. . . scare* me. Shadows don't scare *me!* (emphasis)

Nathan: Great job! I like your expression.

Peer tutors need to learn how they can encourage the tutee without being condescending. The peer tutor should also learn the five-second wait time before giving the word. Notice that Nathan, in reading with Logan, gives him this wait time and encourages Logan by saying, "Yes, that looks like *dragon*." Nathan also attempts to activate Logan's prior knowledge about scary creatures—monsters. When Logan gives only the initial sound for *scare*, Nathan isolates the part of the word that he thinks Logan knows. He gives appropriate praise when he says, "Great job! I like your expression." It is obvious that Nathan has been taught instructional strategies (such as activating prior knowledge) and that the teacher has modeled the positive responses that he gives to Logan.

Peer tutors also need to be trained in teaching reading strategies. If peer tutors understand how they themselves decode words and use context clues this will aid them as they read with their tutees. When working with proficient readers, teachers should discuss with the tutors what they do when they come to unfamiliar words or when they do not understand the material. This discussion is important because proficient readers usually do not think about their practices. When proficient readers understand when and why they use certain strategies, they can then teach those strategies to tutees. For example, after Nathan and Logan completed *Shadows* and started the activity on the last page, Nathan returned to page 7, and asked Logan to explain what he did to read the word *monster*. Their discussion follows.

Logan: I first looked to see if *dragon* started with the same letter as the word in the book. Then I thought of a word that begins with an *m* and means the same as *dragon*. Then I told you how to spell *monster*, but I spelled it wrong. Then I checked if the word on the paper was the same as the one in the book.

Nathan: That's right. (Then he repeats the steps.) First see if the word begins with the same letter, think of a word that means the same, spell that word, check if it's right. What did you do when you weren't sure about the word *scare*?

Logan: You covered up the *s* and asked me what word was left. Then I put the /s/ sound in front of *care* to get *scare*.

Nathan: That's right. Wow! Today you read a book using your scary voice. I liked that. You also learned two ways to help you read words that you don't know. I think we get to work together again on Wednesday. Have a great day!

Logan: Thanks! You have a great day too!

Teachers should make sure that peer-to-peer tutoring sessions are a part of the weekly schedule and that lessons are well-structured. Teachers should also make sure that they periodically provide feedback to the tutors. One successful peer-to-peer tutoring program, Books and Buddies (Kreuger & Braun, 1998/1999), uses the weekly schedule found in Figure 4.3.

Peer-to-peer tutoring is successful and effective for both the tutors and the tutees. It not only develops literacy skills in both students, but also increases social skills and self-esteem (Labbo & Teale, 1990; Maheady, Harper, & Mallette, 1991). Peer-to-peer tutoring is also an effective practice for students who are English-language learners (Kreuger & Braun, 1998/1999) and students with a mild to moderate disability in a self-contained classroom (Butler, 1999).

Computer-Assisted Tutoring

The computer can serve as a tutor in itself or it can be used as a tool in tutoring sessions. If the tutees use tutorial software programs by themselves, teachers need to first provide instruction. Students should spend their computer time on developing literacy skills and not trying to figure out how a program works. Reading specialists should also train tutors how to use tutorial programs effectively with their students.

Effective computer programs should meet the following criteria. They should be (1) motivational, (2) self-monitoring, (3) skill reinforcing, and (4) self-pacing. These programs should also be able to record and analyze students' progress. The best programs also suggest reading strategies students can use based on their performance. There is a wide variety of computer programs designed to reinforce literacy skills. Some programs build fluency, comprehension, and/or word attack skills. Some computer programs focus on writing skills, while others connect reading and writing. Appendix A.6 contains a list of skills with appropriate software programs. Many interactive books are available on CD-ROMs. As children listen to a story on the computer or read it on-screen, they increase their fluency and build vocabulary. Appendix A.7 has a list of interactive books on CD-ROM.

Reading CAT is a computer-assisted tutoring program that can be used by the classroom teacher, tutor, and tutee. The teacher shares with the tutor the mate-

FIGURE **4.3**   Books and Buddies weekly schedule.

MONDAY

1. They exchange friendly greetings.
2. (five minutes) Tutor dictates spelling words to tutee while the latter writes and names the letters.
3. Tutor chooses a book to read.
4. Tutee and tutor discuss a favorite part of the book.
5. Tutor and tutee compliment each other's contributions to the exercise.
6. They exchange pleasant partings.

TUESDAY

1. Tutor and tutee discuss what each did well on Monday.
2. (five minutes) Tutor dictates spelling words to tutee while the latter writes and names the letters.
3. (ten minutes) They choose and play a game that emphasizes spelling (e.g., how many words they can spell using the letters in *Thanksgiving*).
4. They read in unison or share-read a story that the teacher has chosen.
5. Tutor makes observations about tutee's reading.
6. They exchange pleasant partings.

WEDNESDAY

1. They exchange greetings.
2. Tutor reads a letter from the tutee. The letter is an assignment (e.g., write a letter containing three words that you learned to spell on Monday).
3. (five minutes) Tutor dictates spelling words to tutee while the latter writes and says the letters.
4. Tutee selects a book to read.
5. Tutor and tutee ask each other questions about the book.

6. They find four words to add to the spelling list. The teacher indicates the characteristics of the words (e.g., words with long /a/ sound).
7. Tutor offers a positive comment about the tutee's behavior.
8. They exchange pleasant partings.

THURSDAY

1. They exchange greetings.
2. Tutee writes two sentences, each sentence includes two spelling words.
3. Tutee reads his or her letter to tutor, assigned as homework.
4. Tutor selects and reads a book with tutee.
5. Tutor asks tutee to name characters, describe the setting, and retell the plot.
6. Tutor compliments tutee on these responses.
7. They exchange pleasant partings.

FRIDAY

1. Tutee and tutor complete the following sentence for each other: "I like the way you . . . ."
2. Tutor dictates spelling words to tutee. They cross off the words from the list that the tutee spelled correctly every day that week.
3. Tutee chooses a book to read with tutor.
4. The tutee and tutor compose a new ending for the story.
5. Tutee identifies the most important part of the story and explains why.
6. They exchange pleasant partings for the week.

Source: Adapted from Kreuger, Elizabeth & Braun, Brenda. (1998/99, Dec./Jan.). Books and buddies: Peers tutoring peers. *The Reading Teacher,* 52(4), 410–417. Copyright © 1998/99 by the International Reading Association.

rials that the child is using in the classroom. For example, if the student is reading *Betty Doll* by Patricia Polacco, the tutor uses that book to record the tutee's miscues into the reading CAT, and the computer program then offers reading strategies for the student to use, such as breaking longer words into single syllables. The tutee can select from various strategies to assist in building word identification skills. This program also models how to sound out words by blending phonemes. Students receive immediate feedback on whether they have decoded the word correctly.

SUCCESSFUL TUTORING PROGRAMS

There are many successful tutoring programs. The four programs highlighted in this section have a documented record of student growth. All four programs have been evaluated in comparison with control groups; when the programs are executed correctly, the tutees have demonstrated gains in reading ability.

Reading Recovery

Reading Recovery is a program used in over 6,000 schools in the United States (Wasik, 1998). It was developed in New Zealand as an early intervention and remediation program for first graders having extreme difficulty in learning to read and write (Clay, 1985; Fountas & Pinnell, 1996). The tutoring is a pullout program—a program that uses certified teachers who tutor one child for 30 minutes each day. The goal of Reading Recovery is to help struggling readers to read at grade level as soon as possible, usually within 15 to 22 weeks. The child is then either tested out of the program because she is at the reading level of her class or she is referred for long-term tutoring, such as a program supported by Title I. The program uses certified teachers who are trained by certified Reading Recovery instructors. The program is effective (Pinnell, 1989; Wasik, 1997), but expensive due to the specialized training, the staff of certified teachers, and the use of leveled books. The recommended books are organized into fine gradients, labeled 1 through 20 for first graders. (See discussion in Chapter 2.) Some publishers of Reading Recovery books include Sundance, Rigby, Newbridge, and AKG Educational Services. Figure 4.4 lists the addresses of these publishers.

Reading Recovery tutorial sessions are scheduled every day for 30 minutes. Each session has the following structure:

1. Student rereads two or more familiar books on easy reading level to experience success.
2. Student rereads a book (on instructional level) that was introduced in the previous session. Tutor keeps a running record of this reading to analyze and assess growth.
3. Tutor gives isolated word study instruction, often using plastic letters on a magnetic board.
4. Student writes a short story, focusing on writing for meaning and on listening for the sounds in words. Stories are only one or two sentences long. Tutor uses sound boxes to aid student in letter–sound recognition.
5. Tutor writes the story on a sentence strip and cuts it so that words are on separate pieces. Tutee must arrange the words to construct the sentence. The tutor puts the pieces in a plastic bag, writes the sentence on the bag so that the student can take it home and practice putting the pieces back together.
6. Tutor introduces a new book on the student's instructional level, and the student attempts to read the new book, which becomes text used for the running record the following day.

Howard Street Tutoring

The Howard Street Tutoring Program was developed in Chicago as an after-school program to help struggling second- and third-grade readers. The tutors are community volunteers who are trained by a reading specialist. It has many of the same components as the Reading Recovery Program; however, the format is somewhat different. Each 45-minute session follows this sequence:

1. Contextual reading at the student's instructional level (18 minutes).
2. Word study (10 minutes).
3. Easy reading (10 minutes).
4. Tutor reads to the child (7 minutes).

The Howard Street Tutoring Manual: Teaching At-Risk Readers in the Primary Grades (1999) by Darrell Morris has assessment instruments, word lists, word study activities, and book lists. This tutoring program has had documented success (Morris, Shaw, & Perney, 1990).

FIGURE 4.4   Publishers of Reading Recovery books.

Sundance
Department 0502
P.O. Box 1326
Littleton, MA 01460
www.sundancepub.com

AKG Educational Services, Inc.
5609-2A Fishers Lane
Rockville, MD 20852

Newbridge
Department 0502
P. O. Box 1270
Littleton, MA 01460
www.newbridgeonline.com

Rigby
P.O. Box 797
Crystal Lake, IL 60039-0797
www.rigby.com

Success for All

Success for All, developed by Robert Slavin, is based (1) on the premise that all children must succeed at reading in the early grades and (2) on the principles of immediate and intensive intervention (Nunnery et al., 1999).

Success for All is more than a tutoring program. It is a language arts program for all students in the first through third grades. It includes a systematic reading program, a tutoring program, professional development for teachers and tutors, and a family support program. The 90-minute reading program emphasizes storytelling, story retelling, auditory discrimination, sound blending, phonics, and vocabulary building. The tutoring program is a pullout program for students who are reading below grade level. The tutors are trained certified teachers. The professional development program is a three-day training that takes place before school begins, with follow-up training throughout the school year. The family support program (1) provides parenting classes, (2) assists families whose children are experiencing personal or health problems, and (3) encourages families to become involved in the school.

In 1996, Slavin and his colleagues evaluated the impact of Success for All in the schools that had implemented the program. They found (1) that students improved in reading ability relative to comparable counterparts in other schools, (2) the daily attendance rate improved in the Success for All schools, and (3) fewer students had to be placed in special education programs. The program's 20-minute tutoring sessions are structured according to the following format:

1. Rereading familiar easy books (5 to 7 minutes).
2. Working with letter sounds and words in isolation (2 minutes).
3. Writing (5 to 7 minutes).
4. Reading new stories (5 to 7 minutes).

Book Buddies

Book Buddies, developed by Charlottesville City School, The University of Virginia, and the community of Charlottesville, Virginia, is a tutoring program for first- and second-grade struggling readers. Many of its components are based on the Reading Recovery and The Howard Street Tutoring Programs. It is a pullout program with tutors who are community volunteers, trained and supervised by a reading specialist. The reading specialist assesses the students and prepares lessons. The students are tutored for 45 minutes, twice a week, for 20 weeks. The schedule for emergent readers and for early readers varies slightly. Figure 4.5 gives the format for the program's two sessions.

Students in the Book Buddies program showed improved scores on the Iowa Tests of Basic Skills (Johnston, Invernizzi, & Juel, 1998).

PLANNING AND CONDUCTING THE TUTORING SESSION

Regardless of whether tutors are implementing one of the programs discussed in the previous section, they need to plan each tutoring session. This does not mean that they should never deviate from the lesson plan to seize teachable moments. Whenever possible, a reading specialist or other trained tutor should observe tutoring sessions to provide feedback for the tutor.

Lesson Plans for Tutoring Sessions

Each tutoring session should be based on a lesson plan to ensure that it is directed toward a particular goal and that the activities planned for the session help the child meet that goal. Figure 4.6 presents a completed form for a sample tutoring session and

---

FIGURE 4.5 Book Buddies tutoring sessions.

EMERGENT READERS' SESSIONS

1. Rereading familiar texts (10 to 15 minutes).
2. Word study (10 to 12 minutes).
3. Writing (5 to 10 minutes).
4. Learning to read new text (10 to 15 minutes).

EARLY READERS' SESSIONS

1. Reading familiar or easy material (5 to 10 minutes).
2. Reading and writing (20 to 30 minutes).
3. Word study and phonics (5 to 10 minutes).
4. Revisiting a favorite book (5 minutes).

Source: Johnston, F., Invernizzi, M., & Juel, C. (1998). *Book Buddies: Guidelines for volunteer tutors of emergent and early readers.* New York: The Guilford Press.

FIGURE 4.6   Lesson plan for tutoring.

LESSON PLAN

TUTOR: Terri   DATE: 9-23

TUTEE: Marie   GRADE: 2

Easy Reading Objective: Marie will read <u>Bear's Cave</u> with 95% accuracy.

Rereading of Last Session's Book Objective: When Marie rereads <u>Wobbly Tooth,</u> she will learn to pause when she comes to a period.

Word Study Objective: Marie will create a list of at least five words that have the /oo/ sound, as in <u>tooth.</u>

Writing Objective: Marie will compose two sentences about pulling a loose tooth, spelling all words correctly.

Reading of Instructional Material Objective: When reading <u>Grandma's Bicycle,</u> Marie will use picture clues to determine unknown words.

LESSON PLAN	PLANNED ACTIVITY	TIME	REFLECTION
Easy Reading	Book: <u>Bear's Cave</u>	8 min.	Marie read with 97% accuracy. She only struggled with "growled."
Rereading	Book: <u>Wobbly Tooth</u>	7 min.	She self-corrected 85% of errors. On the running record, she used visual cues more than reading for meaning.
Word Study	Materials: Dry-erase board, magnetic letters	10 min.	Her list: food, moon, broom, loose, noon. She also created a list of "oo" words that do not rhyme with <u>loose tooth:</u> book, look, cook. She liked the dry erase board better than the magnetic letters.
Writing	Materials: Her tutoring journal	10 min.	Marie wrote 3 sen.: My dad pulls my tooth. It hurts (we used sound boxes for this word) when my dad pulls my tooth. I have six new tooths. (I explained that the plural form of tooth is teeth.)
New Reading	Book: Grandma's Bicycle	10 min.	She read with only 80% accuracy. She reads too fast. She needs to slow down. She told me fast reading is good reading. She liked the funny story. Her grandma rides a bicycle too.

Appendix D.1 includes a blank form. The lesson plan includes (1) written objectives for each area of the tutoring session, (2) the sequence of the lesson, (3) needed materials, and (4) reflection on each area of the lesson.

Written objectives. As tutors define objectives for each area of the lesson, they need to reflect on the tutee's past accomplishments, current progress, and future goals. Like all objectives, these should state what the child is expected to do with a targeted degree of accuracy. Figure 4.7 provides sample objectives for each area of the lesson. At the beginning of the school year, the tutor may write simple objectives that reflect the level of accuracy that is intended for easy reading and instructional reading. For example, for easy reading he may write, "Marie will read *I Paint* with 95% accuracy." However, as the year progresses and the tutor understands the unique needs of the tutee, he should set more specific goals that will challenge the tutee. For example, if the tutee is an inexpressive reader, he may write, "Marie will raise her voice at the end of each question in *I Went Walking, What Did I See?*"

Sequence of the lesson. As stated previously, the four successful programs reviewed in this chapter follow a consistent format. The five major components—reading easy material, rereading a book to keep a running record, word study, writing, and new reading—are all used in the sample lesson plan that is provided in this chapter.

It has been documented that effective tutorial programs designate a specific time for each activity (Clay, 1985; Jacobson, Thrope, Fisher, Lapp, Frey, & Flood, 2001; Johnston, Invernizzi, & Juel, 1998; Pinnell, 1998; Wasik, 1998, 1999). For this reason, tutoring sessions should include the following elements:

1. 45-minute sessions, at least twice a week.
2. Consistent format:
   a. Ten minutes for easy read.
   b. Five minutes to reread the material introduced in the previous session. (Tutor keeps a running record during this reading.)
   c. Ten minutes for word study.
   d. Five to ten minutes for writing.
   e. Ten to fifteen minutes introducing and reading new material at the tutee's instructional level.

The purpose of the easy reading is to build the tutee's reading confidence, rate, fluency, and expression. Many struggling readers read word-for-word, with no expression, and at a slow rate, and need to hear themselves read fluently to make a story exciting. These first ten minutes are a time for struggling readers to experience success! During the rereading

---

FIGURE 4.7 Sample objectives.

EASY READING OBJECTIVES:

Sally will read *I Paint* with 95% accuracy.

When George reads *Grandma's Bicycle*, he will observe 95% of the periods with a pause.

When Juan reads *Do Whacky Do*, he will appropriately inflect his voice at the phrase, "Do Whacky Do."

REREADING OF LAST SESSION'S BOOK OBJECTIVES:

Lee will read *Bear's Cave* with 90% accuracy.

When Jon reads *Bear's Cave*, he will self-correct 80% of his errors.

WORD STUDY OBJECTIVES:

Roberto will identify 90% of the "an" family words when he plays Wordo.

Emily will correctly push and say, with 95% accuracy, the letters of these three-letter words: *hop, pup, dad, map.*

WRITING OBJECTIVES:

Heather will write the following sentence with 95% accuracy: "I like to jump rope and play ball." (Early in the semester, children can write anything about their personal lives; this is an example of such a sentence.)

Ben will compose a sentence of at least six words with 95% accuracy.

READING NEW MATERIAL OBJECTIVES:

When Virginia comes to an unknown word in *Sea Animals*, she will read to the end of the sentence to understand the context.

When reading *Making a Cake*, Marie will use picture clues to determine unknown words.

of the previous session's material, the tutor should keep a running record in order to analyze the percentage of words read correctly and what cueing systems the reader uses with materials at the instructional level. Chapter 3 provides detailed instructions on taking and analyzing running records. Appendix C.2 includes a blank form to use for a running record and Figure 3.9 provides a conversion table for quick analysis of the percentage of words read correctly. An easy text for students is one in which they make less than 1 error for every 20 words read. If students read with 99 percent accuracy, they make only 1 error for every 100 words read.

Appropriate materials. Because a tutoring session should be fast-paced, the tutor needs all necessary books and supplies at her fingertips. The list presented in the lesson plan (Figure 4.6) includes all the materials that will be needed: books, whiteboards, magnetic letters, letter stamps, salt or sand trays for writing, pencils, paper, and sentence strips. Before a session, tutors should make sure they have the materials on the list. This will ensure that no tutoring time is wasted in a search for materials.

Reflection on the lesson. An essential part of teaching is reflecting on every lesson taught. The lesson-plan form, shown in Figure 4.6, gives the tutor an opportunity to reflect on each aspect of the lesson. Effective tutors should reflect on what the child did well, the child's improvement from previous lessons, and how the child's attitude has changed. For example, in the easy reading section, the tutor should note if the goal was reached and how the tutee responded to the story. If some specific skill was taught, such as reading to the end of the sentence to figure out an unknown word, this should be noted in the reflection. If a running record was kept during the repeated reading, the tutor should note the degree of accuracy and what cueing system the tutee used. If a goal in word study or writing was not met, the tutor should reflect on why the student failed to reach the goal. Sometimes, the tutee's fatigue may be the reason. These reflections should be honest and accurate so that the tutor can plan more effectively for the next tutoring session. When pre-service teachers serve as tutors, the professor can observe the session and help the tutor understand the tutee's responses.

Getting Started

The first tutoring session should be a time for the tutor and tutee to become acquainted.

Session One

During the first session, it is important to establish a comfortable rapport and to learn about each other's interests. The activity in Figure 4.8 encourages such a discussion. First they can complete the activity, discussing the tutee's interests, and then they can complete one for the tutor. Tutees who are at least emergent writers can "share the pen" with the tutor as they fill out the form. Tutees should be encouraged to write what they can and the tutor should complete each thought. Sharing the pen gives the tutor some idea of the tutee's writing ability.

Making a collage of "favorites" is also a good icebreaker. Using old magazines, the tutee and tutor can cut out "their favorites" and glue them on a piece of construction paper. They can exchange collages at the end of the session. Creating collages gives tutor and tutee time for informal discussion of their personal interests.

During the first session, it is also important that the tutor has a number of books on hand to read to the tutee. By having a number of books available, the tutee can choose the book he would most like the tutor to read. This gives the tutee a feeling of ownership in the reading process. Books with repetitive text permit the tutee to chime in on familiar phrases. For young children, books like *It Looked Like Spilt Milk* (Shaw, 1947) and *Brown Bear, Brown Bear* (Martin, 1983) are easy enough for them to chime in on the repetitive lines. *Jump, Frog, Jump* (Kalan, 1981) and *"Not Now!" Said the Cow* (Oppenheim, 1989) are good for beginning readers, while *Shoes from Grandpa* (Fox, 1989) and *The Napping House* (Wood, 1964) are suitable for older struggling readers. Appendix A.5 has a list of books with repetitive text.

Session Two

After the first session, the tutor should have some idea of what books would be an easy read for the tutee. The tutor should have four or five easy reading books from which the tutee can choose to read. It is important that the tutor chooses books easy enough for the tutee to experience success. During the second session, the tutor can administer one of the Reading Attitude and Writing Attitude Surveys, found in Appendices C.11–15. Understanding the tutee's attitudes helps the tutor understand what specific aspects of reading and writing the tutee does or does not enjoy. Often a tutee may enjoy being read to but does not enjoy reading in front of peers due to embarrassment about being a "poor" reader. If this is the case, the tutor can assure the tutee that they will be reading together where no

FIGURE **4.8**   Interest activity.

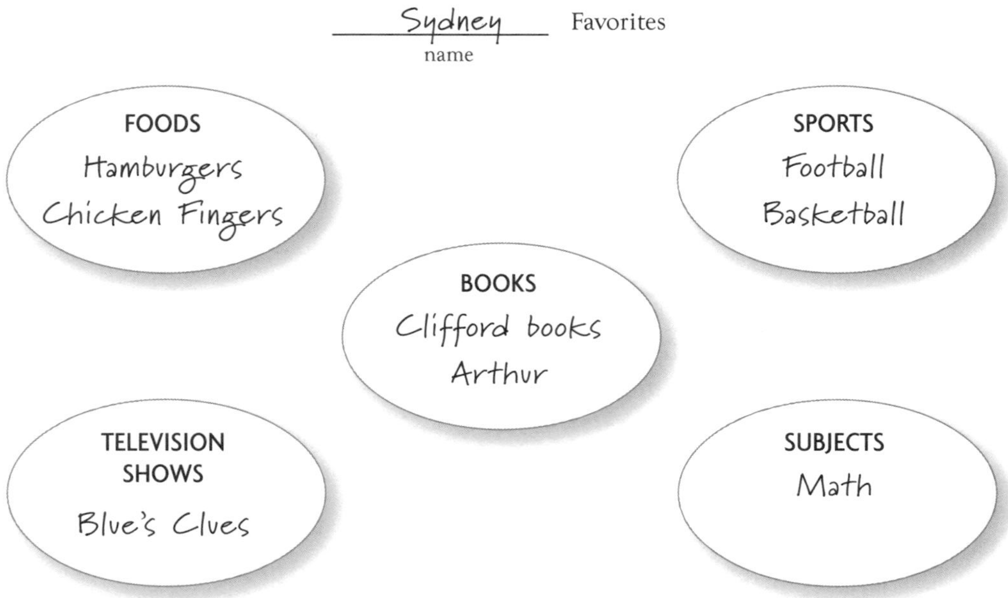

Sydney   Favorites
_____
name

FOODS
Hamburgers
Chicken Fingers

SPORTS
Football
Basketball

BOOKS
Clifford books
Arthur

TELEVISION
SHOWS
Blue's Clues

SUBJECTS
Math

one else can hear them. The Attitude Survey may also reveal that the tutee prefers expository text over stories. By completing the Writing Attitude Survey, the tutor may realize that the tutee thinks writing is synonymous with composing long stories. To correct this misunderstanding, the tutor can have the tutee compose short lists or sentences, and thereby demonstrate that writing can also be about creating lists of favorite things to do or eat. This session ends with the tutor reading a book to the tutee. Again, the book should be a repetitive text so that the tutee can join in. During the reading, the tutor models fluent, expressive reading.

Session Three

During this session, the tutor begins to assess the tutee's reading and writing ability. If the student is an emergent reader, the tutor should assess the student's knowledge of letter names and sounds by using a chart such as the one in Appendix C.25. If the student is a beginning reader, the tutor should assess the child's knowledge of letter recognition, sight words, phonics, and word and passage comprehension by administering the Woodcock Tests (see Chapter 3). Administering a miscue analysis gives the tutor an opportunity to analyze the type of miscues the beginning reader makes most frequently. Administering the Bear, Invernizzi, Templeton, and Johnston Qualitative Spelling Inventory (2000)

will aid the tutor in assessing the tutee's spelling ability. (See Chapter 13 and Appendix C.40 for further information.) Assessment is an ongoing process, but it must begin early so that the tutor can plan lessons to meet the needs of the tutee.

Intervening with the Tutee During Reading

During tutoring sessions, tutors are always "scaffolding" struggling readers as they tackle materials with challenging new words. Simply telling the children the word does not teach them a strategy and telling them to "sound it out" may not constitute clear direction for struggling readers. Tutors can give a number of responses when readers come to unfamiliar words or when they give incorrect responses. Figure 4.9 lists appropriate responses for different circumstances.

Throughout the chapters in this text, I have included instructional strategies to develop phonemic awareness, word identification, comprehension, vocabulary, and so on. Many of these activities are suitable for use in tutoring sessions. For example the games found in the Intervention sections of the Phonemic Awareness and Word Identification chapters are intended to be played by a struggling reader paired with an adult.

It is also helpful for the tutor to log all the reading strategies a child learns and all the books read to and by the child. If tutors log the strategies

FIGURE **4.9** Helping tutees tackle challenging words.

When a reader gets stuck on a word, always wait five seconds before intervening!

When readers lose their place or skip words:

- Have them point to each word.

When readers stop because they do not know the word:

- Have them read to the end of the sentence and ask them what would make sense.
- Have them look at the picture for clues.
- Have them read the sentence with what they think the word is and ask if that word makes sense.
- Have them check their first response with the spelling of the written word and ask them if that looks like the written word.
- If their response is incorrect, provide the correct word and ask them to read the sentence with that word to see if it makes sense.
- If there is a part of the word they know (e.g., *am* in *ham*), cover with your finger the part they do not know and ask them to read the part they do. Then ask them to try again.

When readers read incorrect words:

- Read the sentence to the students as they have just read it and ask them if it makes sense.
- Ask them if their response matches the printed word.
- Help them find familiar elements in the printed word.
- Have them reread the sentence with the new word and ask them if that makes sense.

When readers self-correct:

- Ask them how they knew that the first response was incorrect.
- Ask them how they figured out the correct word.
- Compliment them on using the strategy!

When readers do not pause for periods:

- Read the passage back to the students and ask them if it sounds correct.
- Have them point to periods in the same manner as they point to words.

Adapted from Johnston, F., Invernizzi, M., & Juel, C. (1998). *Book buddies: Guidelines for volunteer tutors of emergent and early readers.* New York: The Guilford Press.

taught, they can refer back to the log sheet and remind the tutee of each strategy learned. This will help the tutee understand that they should apply these strategies in new situations. These logs can also be shared with classroom teachers so that they understand the strategies the tutee has mastered with the tutor. The classroom teacher then can remind the student of the strategy by asking, "What did you learn to do with your tutor when you come to an unknown word?" Many young children do not automatically transfer information from one setting to another. The log of learned strategies will help connect the tutoring session to the classroom.

Figures 4.10 and 4.11 contain completed log sheets. Appendices D.2 and D.3 contain blank forms.

CONCLUDING THOUGHTS

If educators are going to realize the goals set by the America Reads Challenge Act of 1997 and the No Child Left Behind Act of 2001, they must tap the resources of their communities by drawing on volunteer tutors. If these tutors are to be effective, they must be trained and supervised by reading specialists. The programs they implement need to be appropriately structured and make use of appropriate materials. Teachers must remember the goal of all of tutoring is to help struggling readers and writers to become literate. All tutoring sessions must be interesting and worthwhile for the tutee.

FIGURE 4.10 Log sheet for strategies.

Strategies Taught to: **Marie**   By: **Terri**

DURING EASY READ

Read phrases instead of words.
Slow down.
Raise voice with questions.
Pause for periods.
Change voice with different speakers.

DURING WORD STUDY

Words that rhyme with cat.
Learn the first 20 words of Dolch list.
Words that rhyme with sound.
Words that rhyme with Sam.
Learn 21–40 words of Dolch list.
How to add "ing" to verbs.
How to separate the onset from the rime in word families (looking for small parts within words).
How to segment sounds when writing new words.
Worked with homonyms: hear/here, dear/deer, two/too/to, four/for.

DURING WRITING

Put spaces between words.
Stop for periods.
Begin sentences with capital letters.
Make sure all sentences are complete (they make sense).
Do not connect all ideas with "and."
Capitalize people's names.
Use question marks with questions.

DURING NEW BOOK

How to read to end of sentence when encountering new words.
How to find smaller parts within one-syllable words.
How to use picture clues when encountering unknown words.
How to look at pictures to predict what will happen next.
How to fill in a story map.
How to do a cluster of facts learned in book.

FIGURE 4.11 Log sheet for books.

BOOKS READ DURING TUTORING

Tutor: **Chan**   Tutee: **Jackson**

BOOKS READ BY TUTOR	DATE	BOOKS READ BY TUTEE	DATE
The Remarkable Farkle McBride (J. Lithgow)	12–1	Noses (E)	12–1
Too Much Noise (A. McGovern)	12–1	Koalas (E)	12–1
If You Take a Mouse to the Movies (L. Numeroff)	12–2	Nesta (E)	12–2
Shoes from Grandpa (M. Fox)	12–2	Dragonflies (E)	12–2
The Snow Tree (C. Repchuk)	12–3	What's Inside (F)	12–3
Too Much Noise (A. McGovern)	12–3	Bruno's Birthday (E)	12–3
The Napping House (A. Wood)	12–4	Mr. Wind (F)	12–4
Seven Candles for Kwanzaa (M. Pinkney)	12–4	Frog's Lunch (F)	12–4

PHONEMIC AWARENESS

*Education is what survives after what has
been learned has been forgotten.*

B. F. SKINNER

Scenario

During small group language activities, Ms. Applegate, a kindergarten teacher, notices that E. J. gives incorrect responses when asked to name objects that began with /m/. Other children are calling out words such as *money, monkey, milk,* and *mom,* with occasional incorrect responses like *nose* and *nails.* E. J., however, responds with words such as *car, dog,* and *cat,* which do not begin with anything like the /m/ sound. When Ms. Applegate proceeds to the next activity, rhyming words, she finds that E. J. cannot supply rhyming words for words such as *ball* or *hat.* During the last language activity, Ms. Applegate observes that E. J. cannot clap the syllables of his name with the other children.

Since E. J. at times acts silly to get attention, Ms. Applegate wants to know if he really lacks awareness of the sounds in words or if he is just having one of his "get attention" episodes. During center time, she asks E. J. if he will play a game with her. He readily agrees, happy for the special attention. Ms. Applegate places a generic game board with 15 spaces from "start" to "finish" on the table. (See the sample board game below, "Over the River and Through the Woods.") The "game" is for E. J. to say a word that begins with the same sound that Ms. Applegate pronounces. If he gets the word correct he can move his piece to the next space.

Over the River and Through the Woods

Since E. J. cannot provide any correct responses to match the sounds in Ms. Applegate's three words—*cake, mommy,* and *lake*—she realizes that E. J. lacks phonemic awareness. Accordingly, she chooses some activities for her paraprofessional to conduct with E. J. See the Intervention section at the end of this chapter for some of the activities that Ms. Applegate could choose for E. J.

INTRODUCTION

Booth (1999) argues that children should discover the joy of language while engaging in linguistic play through a wide spectrum of activities such as listening to the rhythm and rhymes in songs, poems, jump rope jingles, riddles, jokes, tongue twisters, and stories. Young children become aware of different and similar sounds within words by enjoying the alliteration, rhyme, rhythm, and onomatopoeia found in songs, nursery rhymes, poems, and children's books. It is the teacher's responsibility to provide opportunities for children to experience joy in using the English language. One way to fulfill this responsibility is to encourage children to enjoy and play with language as they sing, chant, and read.

During the 1980s and 1990s much was written about phonemic awareness. In this chapter, a number of different topics surrounding phonemic awareness will be discussed: (1) the definition of phonemic awareness, (2) the seven dimensions of phonemic awareness, (3) activities teachers can use to introduce children to the wonderful sounds of our language, (4) the controversy surrounding phonemic awareness, (5) types of phonemic awareness assessments, and (6) activities that can be used to help children become sensitive to the sounds within words.

As an adult who has spent hours reading and writing, you may think phonemic awareness is a simple skill for younger children to develop. However, as you read this chapter, take time to reflect on the intricate characteristics of phonemic awareness so you may be able to assess why some young children struggle with written language.

DEFINITION

According to the International Reading Association and the National Association for the Education of Young Children (1998), **phonemic awareness** is "a child's understanding and conscious awareness that speech is composed of identifiable units, such as spoken words, syllables, and sounds" (p. 4). Yopp and Yopp (2000) elaborate on this definition by characterizing phonemic awareness as "the ability to generate and recognize rhyming words, to count syllables, to separate the beginning of a word from its ending (e.g., the *st* from the *op* in *stop*), and to identify each of the phonemes in a word" (p. 30). Phonemic awareness is not the same concept as **phonics,** which is the understanding that letters represent certain sound(s). Phonemic awareness tasks are aural and oral, while phonics focuses on written letters and the aural process. Children do not need to know letter names or sounds in order to merely *hear* the sounds in a word. However, if children do know the letter names, teachers can facilitate their learning by highlighting the letters in their instruction.

DIMENSIONS OF PHONEMIC AWARENESS

According to Adams (1990), Blevins (1997) and Yopp and Yopp (2000), there are various dimensions to phonemic awareness; nevertheless, it is important to note that "there is no research to suggest that there is an exact sequence of acquisition of specific sounds" (Cunningham, Cunningham, Hoffman, & Yopp, 1998, p. 3). The following are seven dimensions of phonemic awareness:

1. Ability to hear syllables within a word.
2. Ability to hear initial letter sounds or recognize alliteration.
3. Ability to hear rime and rhyme.
4. Ability to distinguish oddity (which word in a list begins with an initial sound that is different from other words in the list).
5. Ability to blend sounds together orally to make a word.
6. Ability to segment words orally.
7. Ability to manipulate sounds orally to create new words.

1. *The ability to hear syllables within a word.* To assess children's ability to hear syllables, teachers can first have children clap one-syllable words or names (e.g., Jim, Jane, Kim), and then progress to two-, three-, and four-syllable words (e.g., Ste-ven, Gin-ger, Kim-ber-ly, In-di-a, Ok-la-ho-ma).

2. *The ability to hear initial letter sounds or recognize alliteration.* This includes listing words like those Ms. Applegate was asking her students to list. Most children enjoy adding to a list of words that begin with the same sound. For example, the teacher may say, "*Sally sells seashells* all begin with the /s/ sound. What other words, children, can you think of that begin with the /s/ sound?" The children that have phonemic awareness will respond with such words as *silly, summer,* and *sun.*

3. *The ability to hear rime and rhyme.* Rime and rhyme concepts are often confused with one another. Words with rime end with the same letters (e.g., *sit, hit, fit*), while words with rhyme do not necessarily share the same ending letters (e.g., great/late or bear/care). Words with rime have two parts—onset, the consonant or consonant blend at the beginning of the word, and rime, the ending letters that are shared by other (riming) words. For example, in the words *cat* and *bat,* the *c* and the *b* are the onsets and the *at* in each of the words is the rime. Words with the same rimes are often referred to as "word families." Both rime and rhyme are concepts that may be difficult for some children to hear. To introduce rime, the teacher should first read one of the many books that emphasize rime, such as *Pigs Aplenty, Pigs Galore* by David McPhail (1993), as well as *Carrot/Parrot* (1991) and *Mitten/Kitten* (1991) by Jerome Martin. To introduce rhyme, the teacher can also choose from a wide array of books. (See Appendix A.5 for a list of books that include rime and rhyme.) After enjoying a book such as *Pigs Aplenty, Pigs Galore,* the teacher can then ask the children to listen for repeated words with the same rimes (such as *mop* or *sings* in McPhail's book), and the various rhyming words in other books. Like many authors, Guarino (1989) emphasizes both rime and rhyme in her book. The following example is from *Is Your Mama a Llama?*

> "Is your m*ama* a ll*ama*?" I asked my friend Clyde. (rime)

> "No, she is not," is how Clyde rep*lied*. (rhyme)

4. *The ability to distinguish oddity.* Children's ability to identify the words that begin with a different

sound from the other words in a list that the teacher pronounces is their ability to distinguish oddity. For example, the teacher might pronounce *man, money,* and *cat* and ask the children to listen and identify which word begins with the different sound.

5. *The ability to blend sounds together orally to make a word.* For this dimension, the teacher should again first work with onset and rime because they are larger units of sound and children are able to control larger units of sound before smaller units or phonemes—which are the smallest units of sound (Blevins, 1997; Yopp & Yopp, 2000). When working with blending, the teacher says the first sound (the onset) of a word (e.g., /s/) and has the children repeat it. Then she says the rime (e.g., *at*), and asks the children to say the rime. She then asks them to blend the two parts into one word. The teacher may wish to work with one word family (e.g., the *at* family) before going on to another family. Appendix B.3 has a list of word families commonly used in instruction.

Another aspect of the fifth phonemic awareness dimension is children's ability to blend individual sounds to form a word. With this task, the teacher begins with three-letter words that have the consonant-vowel-consonant (CVC) pattern, such as *big, fun, bat,* and so on. (Notice that these words are members of word families; at present, however, the teacher is working with individual letters and not the onset, rime, or rhyme.) The teacher articulates each sound separately, asks the child to repeat each sound, and then asks her to blend the three sounds together to form a word. An example of such an activity would be the following exchange:

TEACHER: /s /

STUDENT: /s /

TEACHER: /a /

STUDENT /a /

TEACHER: /t /

STUDENT: /t /

TEACHER: Now blend all three sounds together.

STUDENT: *sat*

If children already know the names of the letters and the sounds of some of the letters, Ransom, Santa, Williams, and Farstrup (1999) recommend that the teacher work with magnetic letters because this helps children's visual and auditory processes. If children do not know letter names, the teacher can simply emphasize the sounds within the words. Blending may be difficult for some children because this task involves working with language in an unnatural form, a form in which they have not heard words spoken (Smith, 1999). The section on

the controversy surrounding phonemic awareness later in this chapter will explain in greater detail why this task is difficult for many students.

6. *Ability to segment words orally.* Segmenting is different from blending. In blending, the task is to put sounds *together* to make a word *before* hearing the entire word. In segmenting, however, the task is to pull sounds apart *after* hearing the entire word. In segmenting, the teacher says the entire word—for example, *man*—and asks the children to say all three sounds that are in the word. An example of such an exercise is the following:

> TEACHER: I'm going to say a word that has three sounds in it. I want you to tell me the three sounds you hear. For example, in *cat,* I hear /c /, /a /, and /t/. Now I want you to tell me which three sounds you hear in *man.*
>
> STUDENT: /m/ . . . /a/ . . . /n/.

7. *The ability to manipulate sounds orally to create new words.* This task can be difficult for some children because they must again focus on small parts of a word (Smith, 1999). **Manipulating** sounds can be either the task of substituting one sound for another or deleting a sound from a given word. **Substituting** is the act of replacing one sound for another sound in a word. For example, in substitution, the teacher says the word *Sam,* asks children to put an /h/ sound in place of the /s/ sound, and then asks them to pronounce the new word (*ham*). **Deleting** is the act of removing a sound from a word to create a new word. The sound can be either an initial or an ending sound. One example of deleting is to first pronounce the word *beat* and then omit the /t/ sound to get *be.* Another example is to pronounce the word *beat* and then omit the /b/ sound to get *eat.*

According to Blevins (1997), children should master the first three of the seven dimensions of phonemic awareness by the end of kindergarten and the last four dimensions by the end of first grade. This does not mean, however, that one dimension needs to be mastered before working with the next.

INTRODUCING CHILDREN TO THE WONDERFUL SOUNDS OF OUR LANGUAGE

Jongsma (2000) points out that the building materials and tools of the English language are the eight parts of speech—adjective, adverbs, verbs, pronouns, conjunction, prepositions, nouns, and interjections—which are themselves filled with many wonderful sounds that add color and luster to our speech. She believes that a teacher must help students develop an acute ear for the sounds within words. One way to develop an acute ear for word sounds is through language play. Teachers can engage children in language play through songs, nursery rhymes, poems, jump rope jingles, riddles, jokes, tongue twisters, and stories because they are filled with words and phrases that emphasize the sound and rhythm of our language. These words and phrases may fall into one of the following categories:

- alliteration (sentences or phrases that begin with same letter sound; e.g., *Silly Sally shines sea shells*).
- ssonance (sentences or phrases that have ___ vowel sounds; e.g., *Aunt Bea flees when sh___s*).
- onomatopoeia (words that sound like their meaning ___ *crackle, pop*).
- nonsens___ (made up words e.g., *jabberwocky*).

Language learning begins with oral language; children first hear and speak words that they will later learn to read and write. Children of all ages, beginning with the very young, should have many opportunities to orally play with language—to enjoy the sounds of words through alliteration (*Peter Piper picked a peck of pickled peppers*), rhymes (*Humpty Dumpty sat on a wall / Humpty Dumpty had a great fall*), and onomatopoeia (*Snap, Crackle, Pop!*) before they are asked to analyze words (Booth, 1999; Smith 1999). Because language learning occurs when teachers engage children in language play (Cunningham, Cunningham, Hoffman, & Yopp, 1998; Foorman, Novy, Francis, & Liberman, 1991; Taylor, Pressley, & Pearson, 2000), there should be many different opportunities for students to engage in play-based aural and oral language activities.

Songs

Some language activities can include singing, since many songs are filled with alliteration and rhyme. A teacher should be familiar with many songs that emphasize the sounds within words. Words and phrases such as "fid-dle-ee-fee," "chimney chuck, chummy chuck," and "swishy, swashy" in the delightful "Barnyard Song" (adapted by Glazer, 1973) delight young children. "Hush, Little Baby" (traditional) gives children the opportunity to make up their own rhyming verses after they are familiar with the first few verses. After singing the following (seventh) verse of "Hush, Little Baby," a teacher can

make up her own verse (something like the eighth verse given below), and then invite the children to make up their verses.

7TH VERSE:

If that dog named Rover don't bark,
Papa's gonna buy you a horse and cart.

8TH VERSE:

If that horse and cart won't run,
Papa's gonna buy you the golden sun.

There are many books of children's songs. *Wee Sing: Children's Songs and Fingerplays* (1979) by Pamela Conn Beall and Susan Hogan Nipp includes 73 classic children's songs with finger play directions and an audio tape (in case a teacher does not feel comfortable leading children in singing). Tom Glazer's *Eye Winker, Tom Tinker, Chin Chopper* (1973) is a collection of 50 musical finger plays with piano arrangements, guitar chords, and detailed directions for the finger plays. *Children's Favorites*, an audiotape produced by Music Little People (1987) also has a wide selection of songs for young children. Hilda Jackman's *Sing Me a Story! Tell Me a Song!* (1999) includes creative curriculum activities with many songs for young children. This book's songs are grouped into thematic units.

Nursery Rhymes and Poems

Children's first introduction to poetry is often through nursery rhymes, recited by a caregiver. A teacher should continue to model the joy of hearing the sounds, feeling the rhythms, and grasping the stories found in nursery rhymes. Every nursery rhyme abounds with wonderful rhythm, rhyme, and onomatopoeia. Think of the musical sounds in the words "Hickory, Dickory, Dock." The rhythm of the three words is triplet, triplet, quarter note, with an accent on the beginning of each word. To assist children in feeling the rhythm, a teacher can add actions, such as the following:

"Hick" (right hand up) "ory" (right hand down)

"Dick" (left hand up) "ory" (left hand down)

"Dock" (both hands up in a *v*-shape and then down again)

"The mouse ran up the clock" (run fingers up the imaginary clock)

"The clock" (draw a circle with finger) "struck one" (hold up index finger)

"The mouse ran down" (run fingers down the imaginary clock)

"Hick" (right hand up) "ory" (right hand down)

"Dick" (left hand up) "ory" (left hand down)

"Dock" (both hands up in a *v*-shape)

Another favorite nursery rhyme that has evoked many different types of characters and story lines is the wonderful rhythmic rhyme of "Humpty Dumpty." Again, body actions can help the children feel the beat of the syllables.

"Hump" (bounce once so the accent and syllable can be felt) "ty"

"Dump" (bounce once) "ty"

"Sat" (crouch in a sitting position) "on a wall."

"Hump" (bounce once) "ty"

"Dump" (bounce once) "ty"

"Had a great fall." (fall down)

"All the King's horses,"

"And all the King's men,"

"Couldn't put Humpty together again." (stay sprawled out)

Iona Opie, in the forward to *My Very First Mother Goose* (1996), suggests that Mother Goose nursery rhymes are "jollifications that cheer parents as well as children" (unpaged). She goes on to say that Mother Goose is "astonishing, beautiful, capricious, dancy, eccentric, funny, goluptious, haphazard, intertwingled, joyous, kindly, loving, melodious, naughty, outrageous, pomsidillious, querimonious, romantic, silly, tremendous, unexpected, vertiginous, wonderful, x-citing, yo-heave-ho-ish, and zany" (unpaged). You should approach the nursery rhymes with that jolly spirit! The following selections, all found in *My Very First Mother Goose*, demonstrate the joyful language of nursery rhymes:

- "Down By the Station," with words and phrases such as *puffer-billies; puff, puff; peep, peep.*
- "Cackle, cackle, Mother Goose," with rhyming words such as: *goose/loose* and *fellow/pillow.*
- "To Market to Market," with such words as *jiggety-jig.*
- "Horsie, Horsie," with words such as *clipity-clop, swish, giddy-up.*
- "From Wibbleton to Wobbelton." The repetition of the two words in the title makes it a tongue twister.

Another enjoyable aspect of nursery rhymes and poetry occurs when an author emphasizes the sounds of words as spoken by children. Sometimes these sounds are much different from the way the word is usually spoken. One poem that focuses on how a child might speak with a loose tooth is George Ulrich's poem "My tooth Ith Loothe" (1995):

My tooth ith looth! My tooth ith loothe.

I can't go to thcool, that 'th my excuthe.

I wath fine latht night when I went to bed

But today it'th hanging by a thread!

(p. 6)

You can continue to use poems with older children. Again, you should read the poems aloud, emphasizing the rhythm and engaging the children in the sounds of the words and rhymes. In many of Jack Prelutsky's *Zoo Doings: Animal Poems* (1983), he uses words that are enjoyable to hear and even more fun to roll off the tongue. "Yickity-yackity yickity-yak, the yak has a scriffily, scraffily back!" begins one delightful poem about a yak. Later in the same poem, Prelutsky uses the phrase, "Sniggildy-snaggildy, sniggildy-snag." Children can have fun with these words and even change the beginning consonant to form a new tongue twister. Try changing the *y* in "yickity-yackity yickity-yak" to *j* or *l* or *s*, and the *scr* in "scriffily, scraffily" to a *tw* or *th*. You should model these transformations to help children become aware of the sounds within words.

"The Giggling Gaggling Gaggle of Geese," in Prelutsky (1983), uses the title phrase ten times in a short five-verse poem. The words are as noisy as the geese and twist the tongue if the reader attempts to read it with speed. Again, you might change the beginning sound of "giggling, gaggling gaggle of geese" to a *ch* and say it fast!

Many poems use onomatopoeia, which naturally emphasizes the sounds of words. *Noisy Poems*, collected by Jill Bennett (1987), has many delightful poems that emphasize the noisy sounds of our language. It is important that you visibly take pleasure in the alliteration, assonance, onomatopoeia, rhyme, and rhythm as you read these poems. You can model how these sounds evoke laughter and other emotions by substituting different initial sounds for some words and by emphasizing how sounds create different moods. The following few lines of "Jazz-Man," from *Noisy Poems*, demonstrate how the poet Eleanor Farjeon uses onomatopoeia:

Crash and

　　Clang!

Bash and Bang!

And up in the road the Jazz-Man sprang . . .

. . . Toot and

　　Tingle!

Hoot and

　　Jingle!

Oh, what a clatter! How the tunes all mingle!

(unpaged)

Also included in *Noisy Poems* is Dahlov Ipcar's delightful poem "Fishes' Evening Song." The use of onomatopoeia, alliteration, rhythm, and rhyme help the reader feel the fish's gentle movement through the water:

> Flip, flop,
>
> Flip, flap,
>
> Slip, slap,
>
> Lip, lap:
>
> Water sounds;
>
> Soothing sounds.
>
> (unpaged)

Poets also play with language by coining names and words to indicate the characteristics of people. One such poem is Helen Ksypka's "My Family of Dinosaurs," in *Miles of Smiles: Kids Pick the Funniest Poems, Book #3* (1998) edited by Bruce Lansky:

> My sister, finkasaurus,
>
> is a tattletaling skrew.
>
> My brother, Slobasarus,
>
> doesn't quite know how to chew.
>
> My mother, rushasaurus,
>
> Finds it hard to be on time.
>
> (p. 85)

To emphasize how the name of the person fits the personality, you might change the poem to read: "My mother, flowerasaurus / Grows flowers of every kind." Or "My mother, jogasarus / Jogs both day and night." After you model some of these improvisations, children should be encouraged to add their own.

Kenn Nesbitt's "Kangaroos," also from Lansky (1998), contains more coined words:

> If a person has four babies
>
> You would call them all quadruplets.
>
> If a kangaroo does likewise,
>
> Should you call them Kangaruplets?
>
> (p. 89)

Many poems are written in **couplets,** two lines that rhyme. It is easy for children to hear the rhymes in couplets. An easy way to introduce children to couplets is to use the nonsense poem "Mr. Backward" by Douglas Florian, in Lansky (1998). You can read six lines and then engage the students by stopping and permitting them to insert a word that rhymes. It does not matter if the word is different from the original word used in the poem because the poem is full of nonsense.

> Mr. Backward lives in town
>
> He never wakes up; he always wakes down.

> He eats dessert before his meal.
>
> His plastic plants and flowers are real.
>
> He takes a bath inside his sink
>
> And cleans his clothes with purple ____ (ink).
>
> (p. 98)

By permitting the students to fill in the blank, you can engage them in language play and emphasize rhyme in an enjoyable manner.

Another great poem to engage children with language play is "Dainty Dottie Dee," by Jack Prelutsky, also found in Lansky (1998). This poem has alliteration, rhyme, onomatopoeia, and some great vocabulary:

> There's no one as immaculate
>
> as dainty Dottie Dee,
>
> who clearly is the cleanest
>
> that a human being can be,
>
> no sooner does she waken
>
> than she hoses down her bed,
>
> then hurries to the kitchen,
>
> and disinfects the _____ (bread).
>
> (p. 102)

Again, you should permit the students to supply the missing word to keep them fully engaged. You might also play with the clicking, squeaky, clean-sounding words that Prelutsky uses to show how clean Dottie Dee really is. Some clicking, squeaky sounds are the /c/ and /t/ in *immaculate*, /t/ in *dainty*, /d/ and /t/ in *Dottie*, /d/ in *Dee*, /c/ in *clearly*, and /c/ and /t/ in *cleanest*. You should emphasize these sounds as you read the poem.

A list of poetry books and Mother Goose books can be found in Appendix A.3.

Jump Rope Jingles

Jump rope jingles (or chants) are also full of rhythm and rhyme. Obviously, they cater to kinesthetic learners because the children jump in rhythm with the syllables. Straight jumping, in which young children can participate, requires children to jump once for every beat or syllable. Jump rope jingles also lend themselves to the addition of more rhyming verses by the children. A good example of this is the following jingle, which is found in Joanna Cole's *Anna Banana: 101 Jump-Rope Rhymes* (1989):

> I went upstairs to make my bed.
>
> I made a mistake and bumped my head.
>
> I went downstairs to milk my cow.
>
> I made a mistake and milked the sow.

I went in the kitchen to bake a pie.

I made a mistake and baked a fly.

(p. 17)

You can model adding to the jingle with lines such as the following:

I went to the closet to get my hat.

I made a mistake and stepped on the cat.

or

I went to town to buy a wig.

I made a mistake and ate a pig.

Another jingle, also in Cole's book, that lends itself to adding rhyming verses is "Standing on the Corner":

Standing on the corner,

Chewing bubble gum,

Along came a beggar

And asked me for some.

(p. 17)

Again, you can model additions to the jingle with verses such as the following:

Standing by the wall,

Playing with the ball,

Waiting for my uncle

To take me to the mall.

With all of the jump rope jingles, it is important to have fun with the jingles and with improvising verses. This activity should take place in a safe environment and children should feel comfortable adding their own verses. In a safe environment, the teacher and the children should accept all student suggestions. You should even accept nonsense words, realizing that nonsense words are a part of many jingles.

Tongue Twisters

Tongue twisters are a natural way to introduce children to alliteration. Not all the words in a twister need to begin with the same initial sound, but most of them should so that one hears the repeated sounds. An example of alliteration in a tongue twister is, "Peter Piper picked a peck of pickled peppers." When playing with tongue twisters, you should emphasize the repeated initial sounds so that children will develop an ear for words that begin with the same sound.

Some challenging tongue twisters are found in *Ready . . . Set . . . Read!* (1990) compiled by J. Cole and S. Calmenson. One of these tongue twisters is

"Fran fried five flat fishes," (p. 124). With this tongue twister, a teacher can extend the activity by adding to the sentence. "Fancy, frilly Fran fried five flat fishes on Friday." Another tongue twister found in the same book that allows teachers and children to add words is, "Sue saw sheep in shoes" (p. 125). Add the following words and attempt to say it really fast. "Silly Sally and sad Sue saw sheep in shoes and snakes in sneakers." After sharing tongue twisters with children, you should encourage children to make their own and share them with other children.

Children's Literature

You can also engage children in language play by reading books that use rhyme, alliteration, and onomatopoeia. While reading these books, it is again your responsibility to play with the language so the children become engaged and focus on the sounds within words. Listening to these sounds should be an everyday activity for children when adults read to them. You should *not* become concerned if at first children do not hear all the intricate sounds of a particular passage. Language experiences should remain positive, so children will look forward to working with more texts. Phonemic awareness will develop over time as children are exposed to and engaged in diverse language experiences (Cunningham, Cunningham, Hoffman, & Yopp, 1998).

Many of Dr. Seuss' books are filled with humor and rhymes, with the story line often taking second place to the wonderful sounds of the text. *Green Eggs and Ham* (1960) is filled with rhymes. Notice that the rhymes are all couplets so the children can easily hear them.

I do not like them in a box.

I do not like them with a fox.

I will not eat them in a house.

I do not like them with a mouse.

I do not like them here or there.

I do not like them anywhere!

The more you read the story and encourage the children to participate, the more fun the children should have as the words roll off their tongues. You can always permit children to add their own verses, such as the following:

I do not like them in the mall.

I do not like them with y'all. (In a nice Southern accent!)

or

I do not like them on a log.

I do not like them with a frog.

or

I do not like them in a tree.

I do not like them with a bee!

Some authors use couplets in stories in which the primary emphasis is on plot; the rhyme adds to the tone of the story. Jez Alborough, in *It's the Bear* (1994), uses couplets that enhance the tone of a wonderful adventure about a mother with her child in a forest:

"A bear?" said Mom. "That's silly, dear!

We don't get great big bears around here.

There's just you and me and your teddy, Freddie.

Now let's all get the picnic ready."

Jill Sardegna, in *The Roly-Poly Spider* (1994), also uses couplets and dialogue to tell a delightful story about a spider:

The roly-poly spider once spun a sticky web,

Spun a sticky chair,

Two couches and a bed.

"Come visit me," she cried.

"I'm as lonely as can be."

But the roly-poly spider was hungry too—

You'll see.

Instead of using couplets, Irma Joyce, in *Never Talk to Strangers* (1967), uses three lines of rhyme before the repeated line of "never talk to strangers":

If you are hanging from a trapeze

And up sneaks a camel with bony knees

Remember this rule, if you please—

Never talk to strangers.

Some other books with rhyme, alliteration, and other language play are listed in Appendix A.5.

Many authors use more elements than rhyme to add mood to the story. Some use onomatopoeia, alliteration, and assonance, which add a range of sounds and moods to a story. A favorite board book of my young children is *Miss Spider's New Car* (1999) by David Kirk. The verbs and interjections are filled with onomatopoeia, which are written in all capitals printed in bright colors. Here are a couple of sample lines:

It mustn't SCREECH (written in bright orange) or GROWL (written in blue) or WHINE! (written in green)

CHA-HISS! (written in orange) This speedster's charged with steam.

VA-ROOM! (written in bright pink) Slow down, I'm going to scream!

When reading to children, you can have fun exaggerating the sounds of a car.

Eve Bunting's *In the Haunted House* (1990) uses couplets with alliteration, assonance, and the carefully chosen words to provide the scary setting of the story:

There's a coffin-shaped tub, claw-footed and deep

and in it's a vampire who smiles in his sleep.

Ghosts swim in the hallway

Three witches appear

Bats hang by their feet

From the cracked chandelier . . . .

At the basin a werewolf is washing his snout

Sucking in water and spouting it out.

When you read this story, you should emphasize the alliteration and assonance and discuss with the students how the sounds of the words add to the story's scary mood. For example, you might emphasize the clicking /k/ and /t/ sounds in *coffin-shaped*, *tub*, and *claw-footed* to mimic the eerie sounds of the haunted house. (Notice how one can emphasize the /h/ sound in haunted house to echo the hollow sounds of the house!) You can add a devious mood to the story by drawing out the long /i/ sound in *vampire* and *smiles*. Forming one's mouth into a wide smile on the long /i/ also adds to the mood. In the next setting of the story, the alliteration of the /w/ in *werewolf washing* might evoke a feeling of fear or woe, and the /s/ sound in *washing, sucking*, and *spouting* suggests the hissing of the werewolf. Playing with language helps the students to become conscious of sounds within words and to realize that the sounds of words in a story or poem help set the mood, just like the illustrations do.

In *Zin! Zin! Zin! A Violin* (1995), Lloyd Moss uses couplets, alliteration, and onomatopoeia to introduce orchestral and musical terms to young readers. Notice the light, high-pitched, flute-like sounds in the following passage:

Flute, that sends our soul a-shiver,

Flute, that slender, silver sliver.

A place among the set it picks

To make a young sextet—that's six.

In many books, characters' names also have magical or musical sounds. Younger children can enjoy the rhyming names of the different characters in Joan Powers' *Henny Penny* (1988): *Cocky Locky, Ducky Lucky, Turkey Lurkey, Foxy Loxy,* and *Goosey Loosey.* You can substitute other sounds to make your own names, such as *Turkey Murkey* or *Ducky Mucky.* The more you manipulate word sounds while reading stories, the more the students will become aware of the sounds in language.

Jan Brett, in *Berlioz the Bear* (1991), also uses the sounds within words and names to suggest the sounds of the musical instruments played by the characters. Notice the /z/ sounds of the bass as the story begins:

> Zum. Zum buzz. Zum. Zum. Buzz. Berlioz had been practicing for weeks, and now just when the orchestra was going to play in the village square for a gala ball, a strange buzz was coming from his double bass.

Need any more be said about the wonderful language in children's songs, chants, poems, tongue twisters, riddles, and stories? It is a teacher's responsibility to read with expression and to play with word sounds. Drawing attention to the sounds within words while taking pleasure in reading poems, riddles, stories, and other texts is the best means to develop children's phonemic awareness. This kind of language play should take place in small groups or with individual students who lack a rich language background. Most of the activities that I have described can be conducted with children who have had a narrower range of language experiences at home. These children will need extra one-on-one experience with an adult who really engages them while they play with language.

THE CONTROVERSY SURROUNDING PHONEMIC AWARENESS

In recent years, there have been a number of controversies surrounding phonemic awareness, which involve the following questions: (1) Can and should phonemic awareness be taught? If yes, under what circumstances? (2) Is phonemic awareness necessary for students to become proficient readers? (3) Do children benefit from intense, explicit instruction? (4) If not through intense, explicit instruction, how do children become aware of the phonemes within words?

The issues concerning phonemic awareness are presented here so you can begin to formulate your own opinions on these topics. Ultimately, your opinion should be based on research and on experience working with many children of different ages, backgrounds, and cultures. When working with the children, ask yourself some of the following questions to help you develop your opinions:

1. How often has this child been read to by an adult?

2. How engaged in the reading process is this child when someone reads to him?

3. Do the child's parents or caregivers "play" with word sounds as they read to him?

4. Is the child a native English speaker?

5. Does the child have hearing problems?

6. Does the child have any speech impediments?

7. If the child is a reader, does he have a sense of the individual sounds within a word when he reads and writes?

As an informed educator, you must be open to understanding many points of view and should only consolidate your opinions about controversial issues *after* you have examined the relevant research and worked with many types of readers. To help you begin to think about the questions surrounding phonemic awareness, the next sections will discuss some of the differing perspectives about these issues.

Can and should phonemic awareness be taught?
This question has many opposing answers. Cunningham (1990) and Bryne and Fielding-Barnsley (1991) contend that phonemic awareness can be taught to children as young as five. Foorman, Novy, Francis, and Liberman (1991) agree that it should be taught to young children but insist that emphasizing sounds within words should come *after* children know letter names and some sounds. Wagner and Torgesen (1987) and Ehri (1994) believe that children learn phonemic awareness "as a consequence of learning to read" (p. 4). Smith (1999) believes that phonemic awareness cannot be taught to such young children because when detecting individual sounds within words, a child must combine two linguistic abilities: (1) the ability to abstract an individual sound from spoken language and (2) the ability to compare that sound with a beginning sound of another word. This combination is called "decentration," a characteristic of the concrete operational stage of learning that many 5- and 6-year-olds have not yet developed.

According to Smith (1999), teaching phonemic awareness is also difficult because of a process called co-articulation, which happens in ordinary speech. **Co-articulation** is the articulation of all the sounds within a syllable simultaneously with the articulation of the initial sound. For example, in the sentence: "The cat ate the big fat rat," each single-syllable word has one pulse of sound. Say the sentence. As you articulated the /k/ in *cat*, you were also articulating the /a/ and the /t/. To better understand co-articulation, do the following experiment in front of a mirror. Say *cat* and then *cost*. Notice the different shape of your mouth at the beginning of each word. With the word *cat*, your mouth has a smile-like shape when you begin to articulate the word; while with the word *cost*, your mouth has a round shape when you begin to articulate the word. Smith argues that words are inextricably combined; therefore, one "cannot separate the sounds from a word that has been uttered" (p. 153).

Is phonemic awareness necessary for students to become proficient readers? Blevins (1997) and IRA/NAEYC (1998) argue that children *must* become aware that words are made up of distinct different sounds if they are to become proficient readers and writers. Cunningham, Cunningham, Hoffman, and Yopp (1998) suggest that phonemic awareness is necessary, but not sufficient for producing good readers. They contend that "the precise relation between phonemic awareness abilities and reading acquisition remains under investigation" (p. 4). Cunningham (1990), Yopp and Yopp (2000), Blevins (1997), and IRA/NAEYC (1998), indicate that when children approach new, unfamiliar words, the only way they can read them is to understand that words are individual sounds and that every word is different. Otherwise, each new word must become a sight word, a word they automatically identify. They also suggest that in order to write, children must understand that words are composed of individual sounds. These writers do not conclude that children need to master all the phonemic awareness dimensions before they begin to read; they only need to detect beginning sounds in order to learn initial letter–sound relationships.

Many elementary teachers believe that instruction in phonemic awareness is important for reading achievement. These teachers specifically emphasize the importance of the following elements of phonemic awareness:

1. A child must understand that a word is a series of speech sounds.
2. A child must be able to isolate a sound in a word.
3. A child must be able to blend individual sounds to form a word.
4. A child must be able to substitute sounds in a word to produce new words.
5. A child must be able to recognize common rhymes.
6. A child must be able to recognize syllables within words.

Ransom, Santa, Williams, and Farstrup (1999) also argue that proficient readers need to understand how phonemes—the sounds of spoken language—are connected to the printed word.

Do children benefit from intense, explicit instruction? Again the answers present opposing points of view. Smith (1999) believes phonemic awareness instruction is an educational hazard. Smith claims that teaching children to listen to individual sounds within words is impossible because such sounds are inextricably combined with each other. He states that one cannot separate the sounds from a word that has been uttered any more than one "can extract the ingredients from a cake that has been baked" (p. 153), and that there is "no more need to identify and classify individual letter sounds in order to understand written words than we need to identify and classify eyes, noses, and mouths before we recognize faces" (p. 151). Smith feels so strongly about phonemic awareness that he calls is it "a spurious concept" (p. 150).

In opposition to this view, the IRA/NAEYC (1998) suggest that literacy does not develop naturally, and that careful instruction in phonemic awareness is necessary for students to become literate. Cunningham, Cunningham, Hoffman, and Yopp (1998) conclude that different children need different amounts and forms of phonemic awareness instruction. They find that some children benefit when teachers combine print with phonemic awareness instruction; while other children benefit when teachers engage them in oral language experiences such as nursery rhymes, songs, chants, and other language play. The key for success is that a teacher engages the child while manipulating sounds within words. Cunningham et al. conclude: "instruction with print with explicit attention to sound structure in spoken words is the best vehicle toward [language] growth" (p. 3).

To date, there is no longitudinal study that supports the effectiveness of intense, sustained activities that focus on phonemic awareness. However, the National Reading Panel conducted a quantitative meta-analysis evaluating the effects of phonemic awareness on learning to read and spell. The following is a summary of the results (Ehri, Numes, Willows, Schuster, Yaghoub-Zadeh, & Shanahan, 2001):

1. Instruction in phonemic awareness does impact children's awareness of sounds in letters.
2. Instruction in phonemic awareness does impact children's reading comprehension and decoding.
3. Instruction in phonemic awareness does impact normal children's spelling, but not the spelling of readers with a disability.

4. Instruction in phonemic awareness is more effective when taught with letter names.

5. Instruction in phonemic awareness is more effective when only one or two skills are taught in a session, instead of multiple skills.

6. Instruction in phonemic awareness is more effective when conducted in small groups, rather than individually or in classroom settings.

If not through intense, explicit instruction, how do children become aware of phonemes within words? Most researchers and educators would agree that when children are actively engaged and involved while participating in literacy activities, they become aware of the sounds within words (Cunningham, Cunningham, Hoffman, & Yopp, 1998; IRA/NAEYC, 1998; Taylor, Pressley, & Pearson, 2000). These activities include linguistic awareness games (like those found in the last section of this chapter), nursery rhymes, poems, songs, rhythmic activities like jump rope jingles, and stories that use rhyme and onomatopoeia. Because phonemic awareness develops over time and through sustained exposure, it is important to give children many opportunities to develop it every day. Cunningham et al. (1998) found that an estimated 80 percent of children will develop phonemic awareness by the middle of first grade. The other 20 percent will benefit from one-on-one language activities with an adult who actively engages the child in play with word sounds. These types of activities are found in the Intervention section of this chapter.

ASSESSMENT

Assessing a Child's Level of Phonemic Awareness

The first step in assessing phonemic awareness occurs during the careful "kid watching" that takes place during small-group language activities. For example, in the chapter's opening scenario, Ms. Applegate noticed when she was working with small groups that E. J. did not have the ability to clap the syllables of names or to recognize words that had the same beginning sounds. After making this observation, Ms. Applegate decided to assess E. J. individually, using commercial and informal assessment instruments. The following are some commercial phonemic awareness assessments avail-

able to teachers, based on the seven dimensions of phonemic awareness:

1. Lindamood-Bell Auditory Conceptualization Test (1979). Hingham, MA: Teaching Resources Corporation.

2. Test of Phonological Awareness (TOPA) (1994). Austin, TX: Pro-Ed.

3. Scholastic Phonemic Awareness Assessment (1997). New York: Scholastic.

4. Yopp–Singer Test of Phonemic Awareness, which can be found in "A test for assessing phonemic awareness in young children," (1995), *The Reading Teacher*, 49(1) 20–29.

One easy informal phonemic assessment device is the Quick Phonemic Awareness Assessment Device (Cecil, 2003; see Appendix C.21). Appendices C.22 and C.23 have two assessments, one as a pre-test before one-on-one time with the student, and the other as a post-test after some individualized time has been spent with the student. Five correct responses for each task indicate that the child has mastered the skill. Three or four correct responses indicate that the child is developing the skill and only one or two correct responses indicate that the child has difficulty with the tasks. Remember, this is only an *informal* assessment to give you some indication of children's knowledge about the individual sounds within words. Not all seven of these dimensions need to be mastered before children can read, nor does a teacher need to assess all students. The assessment only needs to be administered to children who would benefit from the assessment and the strategies. The assessment only measures children's capacity for hearing small units of sound within words. In addition, a teacher can easily make his or her own informal assessment by having students complete activities based on each of the seven dimensions.

Since the No Child Left Behind Act requires schools to document growth in phonemic awareness, it is also prudent for primary teachers to have a class checklist based on the seven dimensions of phonemic awareness. Using this checklist, the teacher can monitor class growth in each area during each grading period. She can use the checklist to form small groups based on the children's strengths and weaknesses. The checklist in Figure 5.1 reflects results at the end of the first quarter. As shown in this figure, Reed is competent in all seven dimensions, Erin and Stacey are weak in all areas, and most of the students cannot manipulate sounds or delete an ending sound. A blank checklist is provided in Appendix C.24.

 **FIGURE 5.1**   Checklist for phonemic awareness based on the seven dimensions, primary grades.

TEACHER *Jones*   DATE *9–15*

+ = always   X = sometimes   O = seldom/never

DIMENSION   **STUDENTS**

Dimension	Cooper	Cy	Reed	Melinda	Jami	Scott	Rebecca	Tim	David	Erin	Marie	Lori	Stacey	Terri	Aubree	Alea	Darci	Janelle
1. Ability to hear syllables within words.	X	+	+	X	+	X	+	X	+	O	+	+	O	+	+	X	+	+
2. Ability to hear initial sounds or recognize alliteration.	X	+	+	X	+	X	+	X	+	O	+	+	O	X	+	X	+	+
3. Ability to hear rhyming words.	X	+	+	X	+	X	+	X	X	O	+	X	O	X	+	X	X	+
4. Ability to distinguish oddity.	X	O	+	O	X	O	X	O	X	O	+	X	O	O	X	O	X	+
5. Ability to blend words orally.	O	O	+	O	X	O	X	O	X	O	X	X	O	O	X	O	X	X
6. Ability to segment words. * Drop beginning sound * Drop ending sound	O	O	+	O	O	O	O	O	O	O	O	O	O	O	O	O	O	O
7. Ability to manipulate sounds orally to create new words.	O	O	+	O	O	O	O	O	O	O	O	O	O	O	O	O	O	O

Assessing a Child's Growth in Phonemic Awareness

After a semester of reading to children in small groups, with an emphasis on listening to the sounds of our language, and after introducing them to language activities, most children will show signs of growth in phonemic awareness. To assess growth, you can use one of the assessment instruments listed above or you can use the post-test informal assessment instrument found in Appendix C.23. The scoring on the post-test is the same as the pre-test. To document the phonemic awareness growth of the class, you should make use of a Phonemic Awareness checklist found in this chapter or design one that fits your needs.

Intervention

STRATEGIES & ACTIVITIES

The following section includes a number of activities that correspond to the seven dimensions of phonemic awareness. You may believe that it is not necessary for students to develop all seven dimensions. However, you may find that some students, especially those who are inattentive in a large group, may benefit from some of these language activities, especially when done with an adult in a small group or individually, which gives them more intensive exposure to language sounds (IRA/NAEYC, 1998; Taylor, Pressley, & Pearson, 2000). Many children will become aware of the sounds of the English language through game-like activities and through sustained exposure to singing and rhymes. When engaging in these activities, you should remember that games are a part of child-hood play and are meant for enjoyment and entertainment, not direct instruction. Therefore, the emphasis should *not* be on *teaching* phonemic awareness, but rather on *playing* with language in an enjoyable, relaxed manner. Some instructions for the activities are written for small groups; however, all can be modified and used with individuals. Conversely, the activities that are written for individuals can be modified for small groups.

Activities Emphasizing Syllables

When you begin engaging children in activities that focus on the sounds within words, you should begin with syllables, which are generally a larger part of a word than a single sound. During small group work, you may observe some children are having a difficult time clapping out the syllables in their names or participating in other "syllable" activities. If you administer the Pre-Assessment for Phonemic Awareness instrument and find that the child cannot complete the first task (clapping out syllables), you can engage the child in one of the following activities that emphasize listening to syllables. For these activities, some children benefit from a tutoring setting where the teacher focuses only on them.

CLAPPING SYLLABLES TO FAMILIAR SONGS AND RHYMES

(GRADES K–2)

After children know the following songs and rhymes, have the children clap their hands or slap their knees for each syllable. All of the following rhymes can be found in *My Very First Mother Goose* (1996) edited by Iona Opie and illustrated by Rosemary Wells.

- "Jack and Jill Went up the Hill." (Most words have one syllable.)
- "Little Boy Blue, Come Blow Your Horn." (Most words have one syllable.)
- "Hey Diddle, Diddle." (Many two-syllable words.)
- "Humpty Dumpty." (Many one- and two-syllable words.)
- "Down at the Station, Early in the Morning." (A great combination of one- and two-syllable words.)

CLAPPING SYLLABLES TO MULTI-SYLLABLE WORDS

(GRADES 3–6)

Older students also need to hear syllables within words as they attempt to analyze multi-syllable words and write them. One activity to do with an older student is to find multi-syllable words in poems that you read together. You say the multi-syllable word and the student taps his fingers as he repeats the word. For example, *streptococcus* is a fun word in "My Brother Doesn't Like to Share," in Bruce Lansky (2000). You say the word and the student taps as he pronounces *strep-to-coc-cus*.

LET'S MAKE MUSIC

(GRADES K–1)

After the child knows and can sing the following songs by heart, give her a rhythm instrument and have her beat each syllable as she sings. The instruments should be those that produce a distinct beat, such as rhythm sticks, drums, triangles, and sand blocks. Any type of shaking instruments, such as maracas, are not as good because the beat is not distinct. All of the following songs can be found in Pamela Beall and Susan Nipp's *Wee Sing* (1979) songbook:

"The Eentsy Weensty Spider"   "This Old Man"
"Rain, Rain Go Away!"   "Teddy Bear"
"Twinkle, Twinkle, Little Star"   "Bingo Was His Name-o"

POP-BEAD SYLLABLES

ACTIVITY

(GRADES K–1)

Using the large Pop Beads found in many toy stores, dictate words to the child and have him put pieces together according to the number of syllables that are in the words. It is best to begin with two-syllable words, then progress to three- and four-syllable words. This can also be done in a small group by using each child's name as the words.

HOW MANY SYLLABLES IN THE ZOO?

ACTIVITY

(GRADES K–1)

Using the game board and picture cards found in Appendix D.6, have the child draw a picture card from the pile. The child says the word and claps the number of syllables. If the child claps the correct number, he can move the same number of spaces on the game board. If the child does not clap the number of syllables correctly, he must move back that number of spaces. You may need to help the child with any unfamiliar animals.

Activities Emphasizing Initial Sounds

Listening for initial sounds in words is best developed when a teacher models writing during Morning Message and other writing experiences (Bear et al., 2004). However, if a child cannot distinguish the difference between sounds when most of his peers can, or if he cannot tell which two words begin with the same sound (task #2 on the Pre-Assessment Phonemic Awareness instrument), he may benefit from engaging in the following activities with the teacher or another adult.

SOUND BOXES

ACTIVITY

(GRADES K–5)

Sound boxes, developed by Elkonin (1973), are used to demonstrate how words are made up of smaller pieces. When working with sound boxes, it is best to begin with three-letter words with the consonant-vowel-consonant (CVC) pattern.

1. To make the sound box, take a large piece of construction paper. Fold up the bottom to make a pocket by stapling the ends. (See Figure 5.2.) You should use colored pieces of paper to represent the sounds. Each different sound should be represented with a different color, but the same color does not always have to match a particular sound.

2. Place three different colored slips of paper in the pocket, one over "Beginning," one over "Middle," and one over "End." Since the focus is on sounds and not letter names, it is not necessary to put the letters on the slips of paper.

3. After sharing a song, poem, or book with rimes, select one word with the CVC pattern (e.g., *sun*). Bear et al. (2004) suggest singing the following song to the tune of "Are You Sleeping, Brother John?"

   Beginning, middle, end; beginning, middle, end.

   Where is the sound? Where is the sound?

   Where's the ssss in sun? Where's the ssss in sun?

   Let's find out. Let's find out.

   (p. 123)

FIGURE 5.2   Sound boxes.

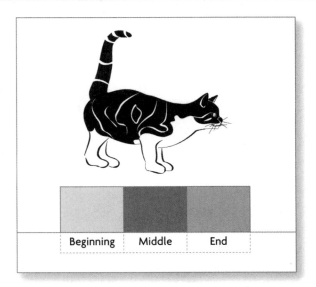

Beginning   Middle   End

Source: Cecil, N. (2003). *Striking a balance: Best practices for early literacy,* 2nd Ed. Scottsdale, AZ: Holcomb Hathaway.

4. After singing this verse, the child selects the position of the sound by selecting the first card. This activity can also be used when listening for final consonant sounds. The third line of the song is changed to the ending letter sound.

ACTIVITY

(GRADES K–3)

ALPHABET BOOKLETS

1. Give the child an old magazine and have the child find three or four pictures that begin with a designated consonant.
2. Have the child tear or cut out the picture and glue it onto a 3 × 5 index card.
3. Put the letter on an index card and use it as a cover for the booklet.
4. Make a booklet for each consonant by using a comb to secure the booklet. (See Figure 5.3 for an example.)

ACTIVITY

(GRADES K–1)

REMEMBER THE BEGINNING SOUND!

This activity is played like the popular Memory or Concentration game.

1. The picture cards (see Appendix D.7) are placed on the table or floor, face down.
2. The teacher and child take turns turning over two cards at a time. The player says the words on the cards; if the two words begin with the same sound, the player must isolate the beginning sound by saying it.
3. If the player recognizes that the words do begin with the same sound, the player keeps the two cards.
4. If the player does not pick up two cards that begin with the same sound or if the player does not recognize that the words begin with the same sound, the player turns the cards back over in their places.

FIGURE 5.3   Sample alphabet booklet.

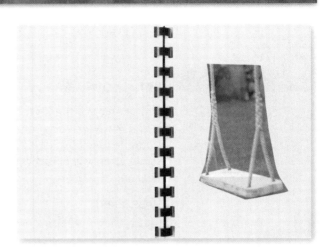

5. The objective is for the players to collect as many cards as possible. It is suggested that the game first begin with cards of two different letters and then proceeds to cards with three and four different letters. See Appendix D.7 for materials for this activity.

INITIAL SOUND BINGO

(GRADES K–2)

Make copies of the Bingo cards provided in Appendix D.8 on stock paper and laminate them. More than one set can be made if a large group is going to play. Call out words from the following list. Each participant puts a marker on any word that begins with the same letter sound. Participants try to get five in a row, in a vertical, horizontal, or diagonal line.

WORD LIST:

basket	kick	tip	doughnut	potato
cards	love	very	farmer	rooster
dad	move	want	game	Santa
first	no	yell	jelly	telephone
go	pick	zip	lace	water
hard	rise	bump	mom	yellow
jump	stand	camel	nice	zap

Note to teacher: Since the game focuses on initial sounds, you must accept a child's response if she confuses the c and k words.

TOSS THE CUBE

(GRADES K–2)

Using cubes like those found in Appendix D.9, students toss a cube, say the sound the letter makes, and name one word that begins with that sound.

GO FISH

(GRADES K–1)

For kinesthetic learners in the semi-phonemic stage, Go Fish reinforces initial sounds of words. First, attach pictures of objects known to students to fish that have a magnetic strip on their backs. Place the fish on a large piece of blue butcher paper. Have the students use the fishing pole (a stick attached to a piece of string, with a magnet as a hook) to fish for a word. Students should then say the initial sound and name the first letter of the word. Appendix D.10 has templates of fish for each letter of the alphabet.

TONGUE TWISTERS

(GRADES 2–6)

Some older students have a difficult time distinguishing words that have the same initial sound. One appropriate activity for these students is to share tongue twisters with a teacher. The focus should be on saying them, not writing them. Most older students are familiar with "She sells seashells down by the seashore." You can improvise a tongue twister based on your name and then invite the student to create one based on his name or any other word. The focus is on hearing initial sounds, not identifying the letter names. For example, you might improvise, "Cute Katie Cauthrin couldn't cut carrot cake."

Activities Emphasizing Rhymes

Many children have a difficult time hearing rhymes. A teacher who is a good "kid-watcher" will be able to detect which children have a difficult time identifying rhyming words as she reads poems and stories. These children will either not respond or will give incorrect responses. They often cannot complete the third task on the Pre-Assessment for Phonemic Awareness instrument. The following activities emphasize rhyme.

LISTENING TO RHYME IN POETRY

ACTIVITY

(GRADES 1-6)

One useful activity for any age student who cannot hear rhyme is for you to read an age-appropriate poem to the student and ask him to listen for rhyming words. For example, in the first two lines of "The Poet-Tree" in Bagert (1997), there are three different words that have rhyme—*tree, knee, me.* "Good Models," another poem in Bagert (1997), is appropriate for older students because he makes references to Elizabeth Browning, Emily Dickinson, and Walt Whitman. The poem includes these rhymes: *frowning/Browning, change/strange, weird/beard,* and *rule/school.*

HUMPTY DUMPTY BOARD GAME

ACTIVITY

(GRADES K-1)

After reading and enjoying the nursery rhyme "Humpty Dumpty," assemble the game board provided in Appendix D.11 and follow the directions below.

DIRECTIONS FOR HUMPTY DUMPTY:

- The game is for two participants.
- Turn all Humpty Dumpty halves upside down.
- Assign one side of the board to each participant.
- Decide which participant begins first.
- The first participant picks up a Humpty Dumpty half, pronounces the word, and checks to see if there is a half on her side of the wall that rhymes with it. If the participant has a rhyming picture and can correctly match it with its half on her side of the board game, she receives another turn. If she does not have a match or cannot identify the matching piece, her half is again turned upside down and put back in the playing pack.
- The objective for players is to get all the matches on their side of the wall.

CLOWNING AROUND WITH RHYMING WORDS

ACTIVITY

(GRADES K-2)

Using the picture word cards in Appendix D.7 from the "Remember the Beginning Sound" activity, lay out the pictures for the following words:

dog	pig	boat	fan	king
ham	bat	cow	coat	sun
cat	fish	duck	nose	
cake	ball	goat	hand	
top	fox	box	frog	

The child picks up the card and names the picture. The child then must name any word that rhymes with the picture; for example, if the child picks the picture of the **pig,** the child can say any word that rhymes with *pig,* such as *big* or *fig.* With each correct response, add one section of the clown (as shown in Figure 5.4) until the entire clown is drawn.

FIGURE 5.4 Steps for clown drawings.

Activity Emphasizing Oddity

When a teacher plays with language, she may ask the children to listen as she pronounces three words. Two words will begin with the same sound and one word will begin with a different sound (e.g., *milk, mom, table*). The children are to tell her which word is different. Some children may have a difficult time with this because they do not focus on the initial sound of a word; they listen to the entire word. Students who listen to the entire word may think that all the words are different. These students need to have some one-on-one time with the teacher so that the teacher can emphasize the beginning sounds of the two words that share the same initial sound and then point out the beginning sound of the word that begins with a different sound. The following activity may make the task easier because the child is working with manipulatives.

ODD-CARD OUT!

ACTIVITY

(GRADES 1–3)

Using the picture cards from "Remember the Beginning Sound" (Appendix D.7), place three cards in front of the student. Two picture cards begin with the same initial sound, and the other card is the "odd" picture card. The student must pick out the picture card that does *not* begin with the same initial sound as the other two picture cards.

    An example of the first game may be the following. Place the following three picture cards in front of the student: *fish, boat,* and *bat.* The student must pick out the *fish* card as the "odd" card. The teacher can work with any particular sounds that give the student trouble.

Activities Emphasizing Blending

Blending is a skill that is needed when children begin to decode and encode unknown words. Most children will learn to blend onsets with rime as the teacher plays with language in small groups. However, some children have difficulty blending because when decoding words, they often look for smaller parts within a word and then put the parts together. These children often struggle to complete the fifth task on the Pre-Assessment for Phonemic Awareness. The following activities emphasize blending.

ONSET AND RIME BLENDING CARD GAME

ACTIVITY

(GRADES 1–3)

Use the picture cards listed below. The actual cards are provided in Appendix D.7 (the cards from "Remember the Beginning Sounds"). Place three cards in front of the student; for example, the cards with pictures of the *fish, cat,* and *hat.* Then say the onset "plus" the rime for one of the card names. For example, say, "I see a /k/ plus *at.*" The student must pick up the *cat* card and say the word. Continue the activity by placing a new card with the *fish* and *hat* cards; for example, the *bed* card.

PICTURE CARDS TO USE:

ball	fish	jar	pig	socks
bat	frog	king	pan	sink
bed	fan	key	pail	top
bag	fork	log	pen	vest
box	fin	lock	pin	vase
bee	gate	map	ring	well
cat	goat	mouse	rat	web
cake	hand	nest	rake	wig
cup	hat	net	rug	wing
dog	ham	nose	sun	

BLENDING INDIVIDUAL SOUNDS CARD GAME

ACTIVITY

(GRADES 1–3)

Use the picture cards named below, and included in Appendix D.7 (the cards from "Remember the Beginning Sound"). Draw two cards and place them in front of the student. For example, the two cards may be the pictures of the *bell* and the *bat.* Ask, "Which picture is /b/ plus /a/ plus /t/?" (saying each sound separately, but not distorting the sounds). The student must say the word and select the correct card.

PICTURE CARDS TO USE:

ball (/b/ + /a/ + /l/)	coat	ham	nose	sun
bat	dog	jug	pipe	top
boat (/b/ + /o/ + /t/)	duck	jet	pig	tub
bell	dime	kite	pan	tie
bed	fan	key	pen	web
bag	fin	log	pin	wig
box	five	lock	rat	zoo
bee	gate	map	rake	
cat	goat	moon	rug	
cake	gum	nut	rope	
cup	hat	net	road	

Activity Emphasizing Segmenting

Being able to segment sounds within words can be an important skill needed as children write. As they write, they pronounce the entire word, and then segment the sounds as they write each letter. As you engage children with language activities in small groups, you may find that some children cannot detect individual sounds in words. You can administer the Pre-Assessment on Phonemic Awareness instrument to determine if a child has difficulty segmenting. If the child cannot complete the sixth task, he may benefit from the following activity.

ACTIVITY

(GRADES 1–3)

SEGMENTING INDIVIDUAL SOUNDS (CARD GAME)

Use the same picture cards from Appendix D.7 (listed for use in the "Remember the Beginning Sound" activity). For this activity, the student draws a card from the deck. The student must segment each sound of the word. For example, if he draws the picture card of the pig, he must say, "/p/ plus /i/ plus /g/."

Later, the teacher and the student can reverse roles; the teacher draws the card and says each individual sound. The student must determine if the teacher is correct. The teacher may want to make some errors to see if the student recognizes them.

Activities Emphasizing Deleting

Most children will be able to delete sounds as they participate in small group activities with the teacher. One activity you can do is to use the sound box described earlier in this section and three-letter words in which the rime is a word by itself (e.g., hit, fan, sat, Sam). Place a "word" (three different colors of paper) in the sound box and review with the small group the sound for each slip of paper (e.g., first slip: /b/ sound, second slip: short /a/ sound, and third slip: /t/ sound). Then, remove the first slip of paper (the /b/ sound) and ask the group to pronounce the new word. As you conduct this activity in the small group, you should be watching closely for children who do not understand the concept. For the children who struggle with the activity, you can conduct this activity and the next with individual students and the third activity with a small group.

ACTIVITY

(GRADES K–1)

POP OFF THE BEADS!

Some children will need one-on-one help in order to delete sounds from words. First, perform the activity using different colored pop beads. Each bead represents one sound within a word. If the child can do the activity using manipulatives, you can also conduct the activity orally.

If the word has three sounds, give the student three connected pop beads. Say to the student, "I'm going to say a word and ask you to take off one sound from the word. I want you to first say the entire word, and then I want you pop off a bead and say the new word. For example, here are three pop beads. The three beads are the word *bat*. The first red bead is the /b/, the middle yellow bead is the short /a/ sound, and the last green bead is the /t/. Now I am going to take off the /b/ bead, and I have the word *at*. Now, I am going to let you do it." You can use any three-letter words from the following lists. When the child is comfortable working with three-letter words, you can add one bead and work with four-letter words.

SET #1	SET # 2	SET # 3
Late; take off /l/	Harm; take off /h/	Bin; take off /b/
Meat; take of /m/	Burn; take off /b/	Send; take off /s/
Ball; take off /b/	Cup; take off /k/	Hand; take off /h/
Bat; take off /b/	Chair; take off /ch/	Ledge; take off /l/
Ham; take off /h/	Fear; take off /f/	Wax; take off /w/
Bake; take off /b/	Bus; take off /b/	Pant; take off /p/
Bill; take off /b/	Nod; take off /n/	Mask; take off /m/
Sit; take off /s/	Link; take off /l/	Cash; take off /k/
Boar; take off /b/	Ditch; take off /d/	Dan; take off /d/
Cart; take off /k/	His; take off /h/	Fact; take off /f/

You can make more sets by using the rimes from the list and adding new onsets.

CHILDREN AND SOUNDS

ACTIVITY

(GRADES K–1)

This activity is good for kinesthetic learners.

1. Choose a three-letter word, such as *bat, sit,* or *ham,* and assign one letter sound to each child. For example, Carolyn is the /b/ sound, Victor is the short /a/ sound, and Juan is the /t/ sound.

2. Line up the three children in a row in the correct order: *b a t.*

3. Ask them the following set of questions.
   - What sound is Carolyn?
   - What sound is Victor?
   - What sound is Juan?
   - What word do the three sounds make?
   - Now let's have Carolyn sit down.
   - What word do Victor and Juan make?
   - Now let's have Carolyn stand back up. What word do we have now?

This activity can be done with any word in which one letter can be deleted to form another word (e.g., *sand, ball, Jill, sit, meat*). Words such as *right* and *sound,* of course, do not work.

Activities Emphasizing Manipulating

Learning to manipulate sounds within words aids children when they later need to find patterns within words to decode unknown words and spell new ones.

Manipulating activities can be done in small groups. The following small group activity uses the sound box, discussed earlier in this chapter.

1. Assign a sound to each of the three slips of paper in the pocket (e.g., /f/ + /a/ + /n/), and pronounce the word with the students.
2. Remove the first slip of paper, the /f/ sound, replace it with another colored slip of paper, and call it the hard /c/ sound.
3. Ask the children what word the three sounds make. Take out the "c" slip of paper, replace it with yet another colored slip, and call it the /m/ sound. Have the children name the new word.

If some students cannot correctly respond and if they cannot complete the eighth task on the Pre-Assessment for Phonemic Awareness instrument, you can use the sound boxes with individual children and/or do the following activity.

ACTIVITY

MOVING THE TILES

(GRADES 1–4)

1. Cut seven 2 × 2 tiles from seven different colors of poster board. You can laminate the pieces so they can be used over a period of time.
2. Begin the activity by laying out tiles of three different colors in front of the child (e.g., blue, red, and yellow). Assign a letter sound to blue (e.g., the /b/ sound), another sound to the red tile (e.g., the short /a/ sound), and a third sound to the third tile (e.g., the /t/ sound).
3. Ask the child to say the word that the tiles make.
4. Remove the blue tile and replace it with a white tile, calling it the /f/ sound. Again the child is to pronounce the new word. You can first do this activity with three tiles and later add the fourth tile to form four-letter words.

The following are lists of suggested words. Note that the child is to replace the initial sound of each of the words in the list with the sound of the letter that is on top of the list.

S	M	B	P	H
pat	late	late (bait)	sat	sat
pit	neat	meat	meat	pit
neat	ball	call	ball (Paul)	meat
ham	bat	sat	bat	Sam
boar	bake	cake	ham	late
bake	fan	fill	bill	neat
ring	cart	sit	sit	ball
round	night	soar	cart	cart (heart)
right	round	turn	cup	fill
		pear	bear	farm
		wig	wig	fair
		site		night (height)

O ne CD-ROM that has a program that emphasizes phonemic awareness is *Kidspiration.* The program "Initial Me" is found in the "Reading and Writing" area. In this program, students place the initial of their first name in one box and the initial of their last name in another box. They then draw symbols with those beginning sounds to the appropriate box. This program is appropriate for students in kindergarten through the second grade. As with all computer programs, it is important that you demonstrate how the program works and closely monitor students until they can work the program by themselves.

The following Internet resources may be helpful to you as you help students build phonemic awareness:

www.readinglady.com

www.readwritethink.org

TECHNOLOGY

P honemic awareness is the oral ability to distinguish sounds and syllables within words. Children who have this ability can distinguish initial sounds, determine how many sounds are in a word, manipulate sounds to create new words, delete sounds from a word to create a new word, and determine the number of syllables within a word. Most researchers and educators would agree that proficient readers and writers need these skills; however, there is controversy as to how teachers should facilitate children's growth. Some educators believe that children must receive explicit instruction in phonemic awareness, while others believe that teaching phonemic awareness breaks language into too many parts, which makes language difficult for children.

It is important that you learn as much as you can about phonemic awareness and learn to listen to the wonderful sounds in our English language. Then, as you work with children, you can instill in them the fun of listening to and manipulating sounds in words.

CONCLUDING THOUGHTS

PHONICS

Education costs money, but then so does ignorance.

SIR MOSER CLAUS

Scenario

Kelli, an undergraduate elementary education major, is enrolled in a reading course in which she is required to tutor a struggling elementary school student. Brian, her tutee, is a first grader. Kelli has been apprehensive about this assignment because she has never before worked with a struggling reader.

During parts of the Woodcock Reading Mastery Test, Brian demonstrates that he knows all the names of the letters that are written in manuscript form, but he does not recognize many sight words and had no understanding of how to "sound out" the nonsense words in the third sub-test. When Kelli asks him to read *Who Is the Beast?* (1990) by Keith Baker, he cannot match letters to sounds when he comes to words such as *swing, stripes,* and *tracks*— all unknown words for him. Kelli realizes that if she is going to help Brian, she will first need to understand how to help him with letter–sound relationships. Kelli's mentor teacher gives her the titles of three books to help her: *Phonics from A to Z* (1998) by Willey Blevins, *Phonics They Use: Words for Reading and Writing* (2000) by Patricia Cunningham, and *Phonics for Teachers: Self-instruction, Methods and Activities* (1999) by J. Lloyd Eldredge. She finds all three to be helpful in different ways.

INTRODUCTION

In order to qualify for federal funds, school districts must demonstrate student growth in phonics, as well as phonemic awareness, spelling/writing, fluency, text comprehension, and vocabulary. The National Reading Panel subgroup, that provided much of the background research for the act, examined systematic phonics instruction. They conclude "that systematic phonics instruction makes a bigger contribution to children's growth in reading than nonsystematic alternative programs or no phonics. Effects last beyond the period of training" (International Reading Association, 2003, p. 1).

Systematic phonics instruction is teaching phonics in a planned sequence. There are five approaches to teaching phonics systematically:

1. *Analytic phonics.* Students first see the word and then pronounce it by analyzing the letter–sound relationship of each letter. For example, the students are given the word *hat.* They pronounce the word by first saying the sound of each letter in left-to-right sequence; that is, /h/ + the short /a/ + the /t/, and then they pronounce the word *hat.*

2. *Synthetic phonics.* Students convert letters into sounds and then blend the sounds to form a word. In the synthetic approach, the students do not first see the word.

3. *Phonics-through-spelling.* In this approach, students transform sounds into letters as they write; thus, they are engaged in many writing activities.

4. *Analogy phonics.* Students use parts of already-known words to identify unknown words.

5. *Phonics in context.* Students use sound–letter correspondences along with context cues to identify unknown words. In this last approach, students rely on their knowledge of letter–sound relationships and their knowledge about patterns in words.

Reading researchers and educators agree that phonics is important for readers as they attempt to understand how the sounds of language create words (Bear & Templeton, 1998; Cunningham, 2000; Fountas & Pinnell, 1999; Moustafa & Maldonado-Colon, 1999). The big question that teachers face is "What is the most effective way to help children as they learn the letter–sound relationships?"

That and other questions that surround phonics instruction will be addressed in this chapter.

Other key issues addressed in this chapter are (1) what teachers need to know about phonics, (2) how students learn phonics, (3) how to teach phonics, (4) types of phonics assessment, (5) effective strategies for teaching phonics, and (6) computer programs that reinforce phonics.

Since all elementary teachers work with struggling readers sometime during their teaching career, they need to know and understand some basic phonics terms. Terms associated with phonics are listed in the box "Phonics Glossary at a Glance."

WHAT TEACHERS NEED TO KNOW

In 1995, Louisa Moats surveyed teachers' backgrounds in linguistics. She found that about 50 percent of the surveyed teachers could benefit from additional training in linguistics, especially in phonics. Moats found that if teachers had a basic understanding of linguistics, they could better help struggling readers in the following ways:

- Interpret and respond to readers' errors.
- Provide clear and simple examples for decoding and spelling.
- Organize and sequence instruction.
- Explain spelling patterns.
- Integrate language instruction.

As a teacher, remember that students become confused by educational jargon—e.g., terms such as *consonant blends, clusters, diagraphs,* and *diphthongs* (Cunningham, 2000). Therefore, much of the information in this section is designed to help you grasp a better understanding of phonics, but the terms and "rules" are not intended to be taught to struggling readers. That would only confuse them.

Graphophonic System

The **graphophonic system** is the relationship between the letters and their sounds. A **phoneme** is the smallest unit of speech sound (e.g., /l/, /m/, /b/, /sh/, /ch/, and so on). A **grapheme** is the written representation of the phoneme. A grapheme can be one letter or a cluster of letters. For example, in the word *wish*, there are four letters, three phonemes (/w/, /i/, and /sh/), and three graphemes (*w, i,* and *sh*). The cluster /sh/ makes one distinct sound. Our English alphabet is complicated because some letters have more than one sound. For example, each vowel has more than one sound. Each

PHONICS GLOSSARY AT A GLANCE

Accent: The vocal emphasis applied to syllables in words. In *ac-cent*, the first syllable *ac* is accented.

Affix: Meaning units (prefixes and suffixes) that are added to root or base words.

Analytic phonics: An inductive approach to analyzing a word. The whole word is first read, then each letter sound is analyzed to determine the pronunciation of the word.

Base: Also called the root part of the word. The part to which affixes are added.

Blend: Two or three consonants with closely related but separate sounds. Also called consonant clusters. (Two examples: /br/, /fl/.)

Closed syllable: Syllable that ends with a consonant sound. (Example: first syllable of *but-ter*.)

Cluster: See **blend.**

Compound word: Two words joined together to form a new word. (Example: *butterfly*.)

Consonants: The letters *b, c, d, f, g, h, j, k, l, m, n, p, q, r, s, t, v, w, x, y, z.*

Consonant cluster: Two connecting consonants that when blended together make a unique sound:

/br/ as in *brick*	/cr/ as in *crib*
/dr/ as in *drink*	/fr/ as in *frog*
/gr/ as in *grape*	/pr/ as in *prize*
/tr/ as in *tree*	/bl/ as in *block*
/cl/ as in *clock*	/fl/ as in *flag*
/gl/ as in *glue*	/pl/ as in *plane*
/sl/ as in *slime*	/sc/ as in *scar*
/sk/ as in *skate*	/sm/ as in *small*
/sn/ as in *snail*	/sp/ as in *spoon*
/st/ as in *star* and *mist*	and *crisp*
/scr/ as in *screen*	/sw/ as in *swan*
/str/ as in *stream*	/squ/ as in *squirrel*
/spl/ as in *splash*	/spr/ as in *spring*
/nt/ as in *ant*	/thr/ as in *throne*
/rd/ as in *card*	/pt/ as in *slept*
/sk/ as in *ask*	/rk/ as in *park*

Consonant digraphs: Two connecting consonant that make one sound:

/sh/ as in *sheep*
/th/ (voiced) as in *the*
/th/ (voiceless) as in *third*
/ch/ as in *cheese*

/zh/ as in *pleasure*
/wh/ as in *wheel*
/ng/ as in *ring*

Decoding: The process of identifying words by attaching appropriate sounds to corresponding letters or letter sequences.

Digraph: Two letters that represent one sound. (Examples: /ch/ in *church*, and /oa/ in *road*.)

Diphthong: Two connecting vowels that make a distinct sound, unlike either of the two vowels:

/ou/ as in *cloud*	/ow/ as in *now*
/oi/ as in *oil*	/oy/ as in *boy*
/au/ as in *caught*	/aw/ as in *lawn*

Encoding: The process of attaching appropriate letters to sounds when writing.

Fricative consonants: When pronounced, they cause friction in the mouth (/f/, /v/, /th/, /z/, /s/, /zh/, /sh/).

Grapheme: Unit of writing that represents a phoneme.

Nasal consonants: When pronounced, the air is forced through the nose (/n/, /m/, /ng/).

Onset: The part of a word that precedes the vowel. (Examples: *p* in *pat* and *str* in *street*.)

Open syllable: Syllable that ends in a vowel sound. (Example: *ba* in *ba-by*.)

Phoneme: The smallest unit of sound. (Example: *fly* has three phonemes, /f/, /l/, and /y/.)

Phonetics: Study of speech sounds and the way these sounds are made.

Phonics: A way of teaching reading and spelling that stresses symbol–sound relationships.

Phonemic awareness: Awareness that spoken language consists of a sequence of phonemes.

Phonogram: The vowel and any letter that follows the beginning consonant. (Example: *am* in *Sam*.) Words that share the same phonograms are often called word families.

Plosive consonants: When pronounced, these consonants produce a burst of air (/b/, /p/, /d/, /t/, /k/, and /g/ as in *gate*).

Rhyme: Sound elements that consist of the same sound combination. (Examples: *fly* and *by*, *fox* and *socks*.)

(continued)

PHONICS GLOSSARY AT A GLANCE, CONTINUED

R-controlled vowel: When the letter *r* follows a vowel and alters the vowel sound. (Examples: *art, term, girl, fort, burp.*)

Rime: The vowel and any letter that follows the beginning consonant. (Example: *am* in *Sam.*) Also called phonogram.

Schwa: Vowel sound that is articulated with the tongue in a neutral position. (Examples: /a/ in *a-gree,* /e/ in *chil-dren,* /i/ in *e-dit,* /o/ in *ed-i-tor,* /u/ in *un-load.*)

Short vowel: Vowel sounds that occur in words like *hat, men, fit, hop, but.*

Silent letters: Letters that make no sound. (Example: *k* in *knit.*)

Syllable: Combination of phonemes that creates larger sound units within words. All syllables have a vowel sound. (Example: *clut-ter* has two syllables.)

Synthetic phonics: Stringing isolated letter sounds together to create words. (Example: /c/ + /a/ + /t/ = cat.)

Vowels: These letters of the alphabet: *a, e, i, o, u* and sometimes *y* and *w.*

Vowel digraph: Two connecting vowels that make one sound. Examples:

ai as in *mail*	*ee* as in *see*
ea as in *ear*	*oa* as in *road*
ay as in *day*	*ey* as in *they*
ie as in *die*	*ei* as in *receive* or *eight*

Whole word approach: Learning new words by memorizing the entire word.

---

vowel has a long sound, a short sound, a schwa sound (a vowel sound that is articulated with the tongue in a neutral position, e.g., *a* in *a-gree,* and *e* in *chil-dren*), and a controlled *r* sound (the letter *r* follows a vowel and alters the vowel sound, e.g., *art* and *term*). Sometimes more than one letter represents the same sound. The /k/ sound can be represented by a *k* (*kite*) or a *c* (*cake*), and sometimes the *k* is silent (*know*).

There is a disagreement among linguists on the actual number of phonemes in the English language. The disagreement stems from distinct dialects, accents, and individual speech patterns. Figure 6.1 lists the 44 phonemes on which most linguists agree.

English Spelling Patterns

English is "a complex system that is basically phonetic, but also relies upon patterns and meaning to provide an optimal system" (Johnston, 2001b).

Vowels

The five letters known as vowels (*a, e, i, o, u*) represent nineteen different phonemes. This makes vowels troublesome for struggling readers because every time they see a vowel, they need to determine which sound the vowel makes. Notice what happens to the sound of *o* as a different letter is added to *ho.*

hoe	hop	hoop	house
hope	hour	horse	hook
hoist	how		

It has at least nine distinct sounds. For this reason, synthetic phonics (teaching new words by adding one sound on to the next) may not be the best way to teach phonics.

The letter *y* is also used as a vowel when it appears at the end of a syllable or word. It usually has the long /i/ sound at the end of a syllable (*cycle*) or a one-syllable word (*by, fly*), and usually has the long /e/ sound at the end of a polysyllabic word (*funny, silly*). The letter *w* is also a vowel when it is used with another vowel (*low, now, flew, raw*).

Vowel sounds can be written many different ways. Figure 6.2 has the possible spellings of the long vowel sounds and vowel diphthongs.

When working with students who are English language learners, it is helpful to understand how vowels are articulated in the mouth. Teachers can demonstrate the positions by first saying these long vowel words in this order—*beet, bait, bite, boat, boot*—in which the articulation is from front to back. When teachers talk about articulation of vowels, they also need to "describe the shape of the mouth, the openness of the jaw, and position of the tongue" (Bear et al., 2004, p. 145). After demonstrating the position of the long vowels, teachers can demonstrate short vowels by pronouncing these words in this order—*bit, bet, bat, but, bah.* Note the short /o/ is represented with

FIGURE 6.1   The 44 most common phonemes.

VOWEL SOUNDS

/a/	cat	/ā/	game	/ə/	aloft	/ô/	all
/e/	bed	/ē/	see	/ōō/	spoon	/û/	bird
/i/	it	/ī/	I	/ŏŏ/	look		
/o/	odd	/ō/	hole	/ou/	m		
/u/	under	/ū/	use	/oi/	toy		

CONSONANT SOUNDS

/b/	boy	/k/	key	/s/	sun	
/d/	dad	/l/	log	/t/	tent
/f/	fish	/m/	man	/v/	vest
/g/	game	/n/	nose	/w/	wagon
/h/	hat	/p/	pipe	/y/	yellow
/j/	judge	/r/	rake	/z/	zipper

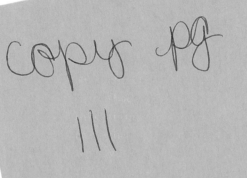

Source: Adapted from Blevins, W. (2001). *Teaching phonics and word study in the intermediate grades.* Ne...

FIGURE 6.2   Various spellings for long vowels and diphthongs.

LONG /A/ SOUND

a – came
ue – bouquet
ay – say
ey – they
ai – rain
ei – eight

LONG /E/ SOUND

e – be
ee – see
ea – eat
ey – key
ei – receive
ie – chief

LONG /I/ SOUND

i – bite
ey – geyser
ight – sight
ie – lie
ei – seismic

LONG /O/ SOUND

o – hope
oa – road
ow – know

LONG /U/ SOUND

u – use
ew – flew

DIPHTHONG /OI/ SOUND

oi – oil
oy – boy

DIPHTHONG /OU/ SOUND

ow – how
ou – house

VARIANT /OO/ SOUND

oo – food
ui – fruit

VARIANT /OO/ SOUND

oo – foot

VARIANT /O/ SOUND

au – haul
aw – saw

an *ah*. The diagram in Figure 6.3 depicts where the vowels are articulated in the mouth.

Vowel diphthongs are two vowels placed together to create a sound different from either of the two vowels. When pronouncing a diphthong, the mouth changes positions as the sound is pro-duced. Two common diphthongs are /oi/, spelled *oi* (*oil*) or *oy* (*boy*), and /ou/, spelled *ou* (*count*) and *ow* (*cow*). Also classified as diphthongs are the long *i*, pronounced /ie/, and the long *u*, pronounced /yoo/. Many Southerners make many of their vowels diphthongs; thus, the Southern drawl. Appendix

FIGURE 6.3   Articulation of vowel sounds.

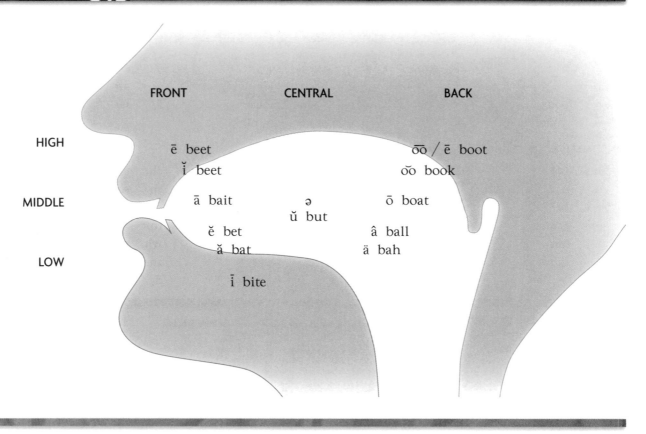

	FRONT	CENTRAL	BACK
HIGH	ē beet ĭ beet		o͞o / ē boot o͝o book
MIDDLE	ā bait ě bet ă bat	ə ŭ but	ō boat â ball ä bah
LOW	ī bite		

Source: Words their way: Word study for phonics, vocabulary, and spelling instruction (3rd ed.). by Bear/Invernizzi/Templeton/Johnston, © 2004. Reprinted by permission of Pearson Education, Inc., Upper Saddle River, NJ.

B.1 includes common diphthongs with an example and utility of each.

Vowel digraphs are two vowels placed together, but only the long sound of one of the vowels is heard. Many children are taught the chant: "When two vowels go a walking, the first one does the talking." Weaver (2002) views this chant as not very helpful to readers because there are so many exceptions to its rule. Appendix B.1 lists common digraphs with an example and the utility of each. The struggling reader should be familiar with the different possibilities and try them to see which one works or sounds best. When *r* follows a vowel, the vowel takes on an r-controlled sound. All five vowels can be controlled by the *r* (*care, fern, girl, corn, turn*).

Three other variant vowels are (1) /oo/ (*food*), (2) /oo/ (*book*), and (3) /o/, (spelled *a* as in *all*, *au* as in *author*, or *aw* as in *draw*). According to Blevins (2001), there are some generalizations about vowels that are helpful to struggling readers:

1. If a single vowel is followed by one or two consonants, it usually is short (*cat, cent, hop, cut*).

2. If the letter *a* comes before *l*, *u*, or *w*, it usually has the /o/ sound (*ball, caught, crawl*).

3. In the vowel digraphs *ai, ay, ee,* and *oa,* the first vowel is long (*bait, day, bee, road*).

4. The y usually represents the long /i/ sound in one-syllable words (*by, fly*).

5. The y usually represents the long /e/ sound at the end of a two-or-more syllable word (*happy, merry, sensibly*).

6. Some vowel spellings are used to distinguish word meanings (*meat–meet, red–read, beet–beat*).

7. In the word pattern (VCe) the *e* is often silent (*give, gave, have*).

Consonants

Many struggling readers and ESL students have a difficult time distinguishing consonant sounds because they do not know the proper mouth position when they say the sound. It is helpful for teachers to understand the position of the mouth and tongue as each sound is produced so they can help students who are struggling with correct pronunciation and spelling of words. Appendix B.2 provides detailed information about each consonant of the alphabet. This information is not intended for elementary students to memorize or recite, but rather for teachers to consult as they aid struggling readers. The better teachers understand the English language, the more help they can offer struggling readers and ESL readers as they make sense of print.

Consonant clusters, two connecting consonants that make a unique sound, may be troublesome to struggling readers because these readers attempt to pronounce each sound separately. Teachers need to help these readers recognize consonant clusters as distinct sounds. The same is true of **consonant digraphs,** which are two connecting consonants with one sound (e.g., *ck* in *truck*). Children need to recognize these digraphs as having one sound, instead of two distinct sounds.

Teachers working with struggling readers must also be aware of **allophones,** which are the slight variance of each phoneme. All allophones are caused by co-articulation. For example, in the words *most* and *mum*, the /m/ has a more distinct nasal sound in *mum* than in *most*. This is caused by the mouth positioning itself for the letter after the /m/.

Blevins (1998) found the following nine consonant generalizations to have 95 to 100 percent utility. This information may also aid teachers working with struggling readers.

1. Only one consonant is heard when two of the same consonants are side by side (*merry, ladder*).
2. C has the /k/ sound when it is followed by *a* or *o* (*cat, cot*).
3. C has the /s/ sound when followed by *e* or *i* or *y* (*cent, city, cycle*).
4. The digraph *ch* is usually pronounced /ch/, not /sh/ (*chair, chocolate*).
5. When *c* and *h* appear next to each other, they always are a digraph.
6. When a word ends in *ck*, it produces the /k/ sound (*buck, shock*).
7. When *ght* appear together, the *gh* is always silent (*light, might*).
8. When *kn* appears at the beginning of a word, the *k* is always silent (*knee, know*).
9. When *wr* appears at the beginning of a word, the *w* is always silent (*write, wren*).

Spelling Patterns of Words

Because the English language relies upon regular patterns of letters, it is advantageous for teachers to be familiar with these patterns in order to help readers discover them (Bear, Invernizzi, Templeton, & Johnston, 2000; Cunningham, 2000; Fountas & Pinnell, 1999b). Figure 6.4 lists 37 high-frequency spelling patterns.

HOW STUDENTS LEARN PHONICS

English spelling has three layers: alphabetic, pattern, and meaning. Alphabetic refers to spelling words letter by letter from left to right. Pattern refers to understanding the major patterns of letters: CVC (*hat*), CVe (*hate*), CVVC (*road*), and so on. Meaning refers to different spellings for the different forms of words, for example, *music* and *musical*. Children learn about these three layers as they decode (read) and encode (write) words in meaningful activities.

Decoding Words

The human brain detects patterns (Bear & Templeton, 1998; Cunningham, 2000). Therefore, young readers learn new words more easily by analyzing

---

FIGURE 6.4 High-frequency spelling patterns.

ack	(black)	ail	(pail)	ain	(train)	ake	(cake)	ale	(whale)	ame	(game)
an	(pan)	ank	(bank)	ap	(cap)	ash	(trash)	at	(cat)	ate	(skate)
aw	(claw)	ay	(tray)	eat	(meat)	ell	(shell)	est	(nest)	ice	(rice)
de	(bride)	ick	(brick)	ight	(night)	ill	(hill)	in	(pin)	ine	(nine)
ing	(king)	ink	(pink)	ip	(ship)	it	(hit)	ock	(sock)	oke	(Coke)
op	(mop)	ore	(store)	ot	(hot)	uck	(truck)	ug	(bug)		
ump	(jump)	unk	(skunk)								

onset and rime than by attempting to make letter–phoneme correspondences. For example, it is easier for young readers to read *Sam*, *ham*, and *jam* when they recognize the rime *am* and add the onsets *s*, *h*, and *j*. When the rimes become longer than two letters, it is even easier for children because they see two parts instead of four or five. Take the *ound* rime in *found*, *sound*, *round*, and *mound* as an example. *Ound* is rather complicated to sound out as individual letters; however, if students know *ound* as one sound, they merely add the onsets—*f*, *s*, *r*, and *m*—to create the four words.

Young readers also use analogies to pronounce unknown words (Moustafa & Maldonado-Colon, 1999). For example, if beginning readers know that the letter *m* makes the /m/ sound in *mom*, they know they need to make the /m/ sound when they see the word *milk* for the first time.

Students learn to read by focusing on onset, rime, and the initial letter, and by considering the length of words (Cunningham, 2000). Emerging readers can recognize their classmates' names by looking at initial letters; when two names begin with the same letter, they can identify which name sounds longer. For example, they know that when they pronounce *Jill*, it is shorter than when they pronounce *Jeremy*. Therefore, when they see *Jill* and *Jeremy* in print, they can determine which word is *Jill* and which one is *Jeremy*.

Students learn decoding skills when the skills are introduced, taught, practiced, and reinforced within a context that is meaningful to them (Cunningham, 2000; Dahl & Scharer, 2000; Hiebert, 1999; Kane, 1999). When a teacher reads a text that interests students, they see "real" words at work and not nonsense words. When reading, you can help students discover simple examples of the various phonics concepts. Hiebert (1999) found that "[p]honics instruction disconnected from texts that children read contributes little to children's use of phonics strategies in recognizing words" (p. 556).

Encoding Words

As students write their own texts, they learn to listen to the sounds within words when they break up words to encode them. They also learn (1) to read/write from left to right, (2) to read/write from top to bottom, and (3) that words have spaces between them. Again, in this process students should write meaningful texts, not strings of nonsense words. This does not mean that all their words will be spelled correctly. They will make approximations of correct spellings as they develop writing skills. Students who are encouraged to listen to the sounds and make approximations as they write become better decoders when they read (Cunningham, 2000).

Teacher Modeling

Another way students learn phonics is by observing teachers model and talk about their writing. As teachers write the morning message, they should talk about the initial sounds, ending sounds, and the patterns within words. Effective teachers choose texts that use rhyme. For example, Miss Synder might choose Ludwig Bemelmans's *Madeline and the Gypsies* (1986) to emphasize the word families for words such as *side*, *land*, *bring*, *went*, and so on. After the class reads the book, Miss Synder writes these words one at a time on the board or flip chart and asks the children to think of other words that rhyme with each word from the text. As Miss Synder writes, she spells out the words and points out how these rhyming words all have the same letters at the end of them. She can also demonstrate how some words rhyme even though they do not have the same endings. For example, in the same story, Bemelmans uses the following rhyming words: *more/door*, *blue/new*, *girls/curls*, *bread/bed*, and so on. After returning to the book, Miss Synder writes *more* on the board or flip chart and asks the children to recall all the words they heard in this book that rhyme with *more*. After writing these words she can discuss the different spellings with her students. Her students learn about rhyme through this type of guided discovery and discussion.

PRINCIPLES OF PHONICS INSTRUCTION

Four key principles underlie phonics instruction:

1. Phonics instruction is based on what students know (Piaget & Inhelder, 1969).
2. Phonics instruction must be explicit, systematic, and extensive (National Institute of Child Health and Human Development, 2000).
3. Appropriate texts must be used.
4. Phonics instruction must be embedded in meaningful contexts (Bear & Templeton, 1998; Cunningham, 2000; Dahl & Scharer, 2000; Hiebert, 1999; Johnston, 2001; Kane, 1999; Moustafa & Maldonado-Colon, 1999; Wagstaff, 1997/1998).

Principle One: Phonics Instruction Is Based on What Students Know

When teaching any concept, effective teachers assess what students already know and build on that knowledge. Phonics instruction must take the same approach; teachers should begin with what students know. But how do teachers assess what students already know? During shared reading, interactive writing, and all other literacy activities, effective teachers closely observe ("kidwatch") what the students know about words. (See the informal assessment section of this chapter.)

Once teachers have a basic idea of students' literacy knowledge, they should homogeneously group students in order to provide appropriate instruction for each group. The instruction for the homogeneous group should be embedded in a meaningful context. Teachers need to carefully select texts that permit students to examine both known words and new words appropriate for their specific developmental writing stage. As students examine text, the teacher should encourage them to make generalizations about groups of words. Teachers can subtly guide students to discover the "phonic rule" behind the generalization.

Principle Two: Phonics Instruction Is Systematic, Explicit, and Extensive

Once teachers understand what students in the homogeneous groups already know and what skills they need to develop next, they can select books appropriate to teach these skills. When students discover words in the text that conform to a particular phonics concept, teachers can assist students in creating a word list that reflects that concept. Then teachers should choose more books with words that demonstrate the concept and guide students as they discover these words. Teachers should explicitly focus on the same concept until the students fully understand it. If some members of the homogeneous group grasp the idea faster than the others, the students should be regrouped so that those who need more time to work on the concept will receive it, while the others will move on to discover more phonics concepts. The time to discuss phonics concepts or "rules" with students is only after they understand the concept and can make generalizations for themselves (Bear & Templeton, 1998; Kane, 1999). The following are some phonics concepts involving one-syllable words that you can guide your students to discover:

1. Initial consonant or consonant blend sounds.
2. Onset and rime words (also called word families or phonograms).
3. Word patterns in one-syllable words:
   CVC (short vowel sounds; e.g., *pup, fit*)
   CVCe (long vowel with silent *e*; e.g., *time, cute*)
   CVVC (vowel digraphs within words; e.g., *road, beet*)
   CVV (words with two vowels and long sound; e.g., *toe, say*)

Principle Three: Phonics Instruction Needs Appropriate Texts

"At the earliest stages of reading acquisition—particularly with students who are first introduced to book reading in school—careful attention needs to be paid to the text of instruction" (Hiebert, 1999, p. 555). For example, books used during shared reading events should meet the following criteria:

- Include predictable text.
- Have a smaller amount of text on each page.
- Use large illustrations that support the text.
- Are appealing to children.
- Are conceptually appropriate (books that teachers can use to develop a concept, such as the topic for a unit, author study, or illustrator study).

In addition, reading researchers have found that during shared reading, it is effective to use authentic children's literature with (1) predictable text, (2) text that uses phonograms, and (3) text that includes rhyming words (Cunningham, 2000; Fountas & Pinnell, 1996; Hiebert, 1999; Kane, 1999).

1. *Predictable text.* Children enjoy stories with predictable text like *The Teeny Tiny Woman* (1986) by Jane O'Conner and *Hattie and the Fox* (1987) by Mem Fox. Students chime in as soon as they know words and refrains. Appendix A.5 lists books with predictable text patterns.
2. *Phonograms.* Books that emphasize phonograms (rimes following onsets) help students see patterns within words. As teachers read and discuss stories, they help students discover words that have the same letter patterns. Bill Martin, Jr. has written many books highlighting phonograms. Appendix A.5 lists many other books.
3. *Rhyming words.* Books with rhyming texts also draw attention to the sounds in words. When words rhyme they do not necessarily share the same letter pattern, as phonograms must (thus, *socks* and *fox* are rhyming words with different rimes). Teachers should draw attention to the difference between phonograms and words that rhyme. Appendix A.5 lists books that have alliteration, phonograms, and rhymes.

There is no research basis for the exclusive use of decodable texts (i.e., texts written with words that closely follow phonetic rules or with words from one word family; for example, "Dan can fan Nan") for beginning reading instruction (Cunningham, 2000).

Principle Four: Phonics Instruction Occurs in Meaningful Contexts

Reading, writing, listening, and speaking activities that focus on meaningful tasks create meaningful contexts. As mentioned before, you should carefully select texts that children enjoy, have predictable patterns, and use words that can be used to teach phonics concepts. Cunningham (2000) suggests the following steps when using meaningful context to teach phonics:

1. Choose a book with predictable text that both the teacher and students will enjoy.
2. First read and enjoy the book!
3. Act out the story or put on puppet shows. (Acting caters to kinesthetic learners and develops oral language skills.)
4. Have students discuss what they notice about words. (For example, ask "Which ones begin with same letter?")
5. Play word games based on the story.
6. Add words from story to the word walls.
7. Find rhyming words and words that end with the same spellings.
8. Have students write creative extensions of books that use predictable patterns. (For example, "I went walking. What did I see? I saw _____ looking at me.)

After rereading favorite predictable texts, you can ask students to point to words that begin with certain sounds and then ask them to help create a list of words that begin with that same sound. You can also give students words on index cards and ask them to match them with words in the text.

Students also learn much about phonics when they write meaningful messages (Bear & Templeton, 1998; Cunningham, 2000; Savage, 2001). They learn to break up words and listen for all the sounds when they write notes to friends, stories, log observations from experiments, and riddles. Effective teachers model "stretching out words" as they write morning messages and involve students in interactive writing. You should be aware that students are less likely to listen for sounds in words when performing rote exercises like copying words correctly. In Chapter 12 we will discuss writing skills in greater detail.

ASSESSMENT

Informal Assessment

The best type of phonics assessment is conducted in natural settings as you observe students making sense of letter–sound relationships as they read and write. However, if you want to record growth throughout the school year, you can choose from a number of informal assessment instruments: checklists, surveys, word sorts, rubrics, running records, miscue analyses, and inventories.

Checklists

The Checklist of Known Letter Names and Sounds, found in Appendix C.25, is a checklist to assess a student's knowledge of letter names, letter sounds, and words with these sounds. The student reads from the Master Card, while the teacher records the responses on the Checklist. The student is asked (1) the names of the uppercase letters, (2) the names of the lowercase letters, (3) the names of the script letters, if appropriate, (4) the sound of each letter, (5) a word that begins with that sound, and (6) a word that ends with that sound. Figure 6.5 is the checklist that Ms. McGee uses to assess Dustin's knowledge at the beginning of the year. She will use the checklist to record Dustin's growth throughout the school year. Two copies (one typeset and one in cursive) of the Master Card of Letter Names and Sounds, along with the score sheet are located in Appendix C.25.

As a teacher, you should be familiar with your state's standards, also called benchmarks, gateways, and competencies, and design appropriate rubrics and checklists so that you can follow the growth of your students. The partial checklist in Figure 6.6 is based on Texas's first-grade Standard 1.7: Reading/letter–sound relationships, which states: "The student uses letter–sound knowledge to decode written language" (Texas Education Agency, 1997, p. B-29). Mr. Francis, a first-grade teacher, uses this checklist to help him assess and monitor the growth of his students. At the beginning of the school year, he notes that many of his students know the letter names and understand that words are composed of letters that represent sounds; however, only a few of his students know the letter–sound relationships of consonants and no student knows the relationship for the short vowel sound. The complete checklist, based on the entire Texas First-Grade Standard 1.7 is located in Appendix C.27.

FIGURE 6.5   Sample checklist of known letter names and sounds for the beginning of the year.

STUDENT: Dustin   DATE: 8–27–04

LETTER	UPPERCASE NAME	LOWERCASE NAME	SCRIPT NAME	SOUND	WORD WITH INITIAL SOUND	WORD WITH ENDING SOUND
K	✓	✓				
N	✓					
E	✓					
J	✓	✓				
A	✓					
T	✓	✓				
B	✓			✓	✓	
S	✓	✓		✓	✓	

FIGURE 6.6   Letter–sound relationships checklist, first grade.

TEACHER M. Francis   PERIOD 1 ② 3 4

+ = always   X = sometimes   O = seldom/never   8–27–04
(Beginning of school)

SUB-STANDARD	Eric	Leah	Coby	Vanessa	Jocelyn	Hayden	Blake	Erin	Lindsay	Lesley	Cole	Shona	Ryan	Shannon	Casey	Warren	Brooke	Marsh
1. Names and identifies each letter.	+	+	+	+	+	+	X	X	+	+	+	+	+	+	X	+	X	+
2. Understands that written words are composed of letters that represent sounds.	+	+	+	+	+	+	X	X	+	+	+	+	+	+	X	+	X	+
3. Identifies letter–sound relationship for all consonants.	+	O	X	X	X	O	O	O	+	X	X	X	X	O	O	X	O	+
4. Identifies letter–sound relationship for short vowels.	O	O	O	O	O	O	O	O	O	O	O	O	O	O	O	O	O	O

Surveys

The Phonics Mastery Survey (Cecil, 2003) is an informal instrument for assessing various phonics elements. It assesses a student's ability to recognize (1) consonant sounds, (2) rhyming words, (3) consonant digraphs, (4) long vowel sounds, (5) words with CVC patterns, (6) consonant blends, (7) other vowel sounds, and (8) syllables in words. The scoring sheet and answer sheet for this survey can be found in Appendix C.26.

Word Sorts

Having a student perform a word sort task is another way to informally assess phonics skills. When you want to informally assess a student's ability to sort words by initial or ending sounds, use picture cards so that the student cannot look at the letters. When the student cannot see the words, you can determine if the student knows letter–sound relationships. Give the student pictures beginning with two, three, or four different letters, identify the letters for her, and ask her to sort the picture cards according to the initial letters. As a pre-test, you may choose letters that have not been formally introduced; for a post-test, you may choose letters that have been explicitly taught. Appendix D.7 contains a set of picture cards.

Informal Reading Inventories

The informal reading inventory, running record, and miscue analysis are excellent devices to assess a student's ability to attack unknown words. As the student reads an unfamiliar text, you can observe what cueing systems the reader uses and what types of miscues she makes. Although these informal assessments take time to administer and analyze, they provide valuable information about students' phonics skills. (See Chapter 3 for more discussion of these devices.)

Qualitative Spelling Inventories One and Two

The Bear, Invernizzi, Templeton, and Johnston (2000) Qualitative Spelling Inventories One and Two assess students' capacity for encoding letter sounds. The inventories indicate what students know about letter sounds as they write words. Chapter 13 describes the inventory and Appendix C.40 includes the two lists.

Formal Assessment

A number of standardized tests include phonics sub-tests; however, many of these tests use nonsense word lists. Remember that nonsense words are often confusing for struggling readers because even their correct response is not a real word. Figure 6.7 lists standardized tests with phonics sub-tests. Chapter 3 includes detailed descriptions of many of these tests.

FIGURE 6.7 Standardized tests with phonics sub-tests.

1. Iowa Test of Basic Skills
2. Stanford Achievement Tests–Ninth Edition
3. Metropolitan Achievement Test–Reading
4. Comprehension Test of Basic Skills, U and V
5. Phonics Criterion Test
6. Prescriptive Reading Performance Test
7. Stanford Diagnostic Reading Test–Red Level, Green Level
8. Woodcock Reading Mastery Test
9. Durrell Analysis of Reading Difficulties–Third Edition
10. Gates–McKillop–Horowitz Tests
11. Diagnostic Reading Scales
12. Sipay Word Analysis Test

Intervention

STRATEGIES & ACTIVITIES

It has been documented that students most effectively learn about letter–sound relationships and patterns within words when they read and discuss books that interest them and when they engage in other meaningful literacy tasks. As they work with small groups and individual students, teachers and tutors should remember the four principles of phonics instruction: (1) instruction must be based on what the student knows, (2) instruction must be systematic, explicit, and extensive (beginning with initial consonant sounds, onset and rime, and word patterns), (3) instruction must use appropriate texts, and (4) instruction must occur in a meaningful context. Therefore, the following intervention activities should be based on books that children have enjoyed and on words that they have encountered in print.

Instruction must always be based on the child's needs. The following activities are systematic—starting with initial consonant sounds, moving to onset and rime, and finally working with word patterns. However, if the child has no trouble with initial consonant sounds but does struggle with onset and rime, the teacher or tutor should emphasize activities that focus on onset and rime. Children can engage in many of these activities with a teacher, a volunteer tutor, an older book buddy, or a peer (see Chapter 4).

Activities Emphasizing Initial Consonant Sounds

If in a large or small group setting, you notice that a child cannot name three or four words that begin with the same sound, you can engage the child in one of the following activities in a tutoring setting. A volunteer tutor who understands the purpose of these activities can also work with the child. You should not merely engage the child in the activity, but also assess why the child has a difficult time distinguishing initial sounds. You may determine that the child has an auditory problem instead of merely needing more exposure to specific language activities. You will find that most young children who cannot distinguish initial sounds lack certain linguistic experiences; they only need time with an adult to develop the skill.

The following activities focus on listening to the initial sounds of words.

WORD SORTING WITH PICTURES

As beginning readers, students need practice in relating letters to their sounds. One activity that emphasizes letter–sound relationships is word sorting with picture cards.

ACTIVITY

(GRADES K–1)

1. Place two different magnet letters on the desk.
2. Have the student sort pictures according to the initial letter sounds using the picture cards found in Appendix D.7. At first you should lay out two magnetic letters and their corresponding cards and later shift to three or four letters with their corresponding cards.
3. If a student continues to confuse two letter sounds (e.g., the /d/ and /t/ sounds), work with just those two letters. Later you can ask the student to sort the pictures according to the ending sounds of words; be sure to set out the appropriate magnet letters for the ending sounds.

LISTEN FOR THE INITIAL CONSONANT BLENDS

ACTIVITY

(GRADES 1–3)

1. Using the picture cards and game board in Appendix D.12, turn all picture cards upside down in a pile. Decide which person should begin.
2. First person picks up a picture card, pronounces the word for the picture, and correctly places the picture on the consonant blend space that corresponds to the initial consonant blend of the word.
3. If the person cannot place a card on the correct consonant blend space, the card is placed on the bottom of the pile.

Note: The goal is for students to fill all the consonant blend spaces.

ACTIVITY

WORD WALLS

(GRADES 1–2) You can create one word wall for all the letters of the alphabet. Using a poster board or butcher paper, write all the letters of the alphabet on it and add words that children want to remember or will use in writing or reading. In a tutoring setting, write the letters of the alphabet in order on slips of paper, place them in a file folder, and have the tutee add words that he wants to remember below the appropriate letters.

ACTIVITY

PERSONALIZED WORD FAMILY DICTIONARY

(GRADES 1–5) A personalized dictionary should be arranged with two major sections. The first section has one page reserved for each letter of the alphabet. The second section has a page reserved for each of the following common word families: *ack, age, ake, an, am, at, ight, ound, all, it, in, ill, ig, ell, ed, ead, ot, op, og, ad, ap.* On top of each page there is either a letter in upper- and lowercases, or the name of a word family. See Figure 6.8 for an example.

FIGURE 6.8 Personalized dictionary.

Aa	ack (back)
after	lack
about	Jack
around	sack
alligator	smack

ACTIVITY

ALLITERATION

(GRADES 1–5) In this activity, either you or the student can do the writing.

1. Share some familiar tongue twister such as the following: *Sally sells seashells down by the seashore,* or *Peter Piper picked a peck of pickled peppers.*
2. Then share some of your own original tongue twisters; they can be based on the child's name.
3. Ask what sound the child hears at the beginning of the words.

   Some of these sentences can result in amusing tongue twisters that also help the student with articulation. The following sentences are examples.

   Happy, hungry Harry has hundreds of hamburgers.

   Brave Beverly Beaver blew blue bubbles.

ACTIVITY

DOMINOES

(GRADES 2–4) This activity of picture dominoes is designed so struggling readers focus not only on the initial sounds but also the ending sounds of words. Using the domino cards from Appendix D.13, participants match the ending consonant sound (not the letter) of one domino with the initial sound of the next word. For example, if one person lays out the *cat* domino, the next person must lay down a domino picture that begins with a /t/ sound. Teachers should either play the game with the students or observe as they play. Through observation, teachers can determine which letter sounds are troublesome for students.

Activities Emphasizing Onset and Rime

Often a teacher will observe a child "sounding out" phonograms letter-by-letter, instead of recognizing the pattern within the phonograms. For example, the child may read this passage in the following manner: "Mike put his h-h-a-a-n-n-d *hand* in the s-s-a-a-n-n-d *sand*." This child would benefit from tutoring sessions with some of the activities presented in this section, which emphasize the recognition of onset and rime. Helping a child recognize onset and rime will help him quickly recognize a large bank of words. It is helpful for a young reader if the teacher begins with books that have word families with two letters in the rime (e.g., the *an, at am, up,* or *op* families), because the reader only needs to recognize those two letters. Later, the teacher can choose books that have word families with more letters in the rime; for example, the *ound* and *ight* families.

WORD FAMILY WORD WALLS

ACTIVITY
(GRADES 1–3)

A separate word wall can be used for all phonograms that students discover in books. Word walls with phonograms draw students' attention to patterns within words. Appendix B.3 lists common phonograms. Figure 6.9 has a sample word wall.

FIGURE 6.9   Phonogram word wall.

at	all	an	and
bat	ball	ban	band
cat	call	can	sand
fat	fall	fan	land

FLIP BOOKS

ACTIVITY
(GRADES 1–2)

Often struggling readers do not see the common rime within word families. Teachers should show them how the rime is a common factor in the entire "family" and how the onset changes the words. Explicit instruction in word families encourages readers to look for known parts within words. Again, the word families should be taken from a book that has been read in a tutoring session or small group. For example, after reading Dr. Seuss's *The Cat in the Hat,* you can construct a Flip Book of all the *at* words.

1. To construct a Flip Book using sentence strips, neatly print *hat* on a strip and cut the word off the sentence strip.

FIGURE **6.10**   Sample flip books.

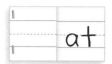 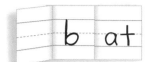 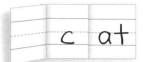 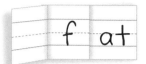

2. Using the rest of the sentence strip, write the letters—*b, c, f, h, m, p, r, s, v.*

3. Then cut them up and staple them on top of the *h* of *hat.* Since *at* is a word, the top sheet should be blank.

See Figure 6.10 for an example. Using *The Cat in the Hat,* a Flip Book can also be made for the *ump* family. The letters *h, c, gr, d, j, l, p, r, st, th* should be on the flips. Since *ump* is not a word, the top flip needs a letter. See Figure 6.10.

ACTIVITY

(GRADES 2–5)

WORD FAMILY CONCENTRATION

Concentration teaches students to focus and remember. Cards can be based on any book that the struggling reader enjoys. You should work with the student to decide which words she wants to learn and remember. Make two 2-inch by 2-inch cards of the same word. If the book has phonograms, the teacher can make the activity more challenging by having the student match phonograms (e.g., the *hat* card with the *cat* card). You should engage in the activity with the student in order to understand what letter sounds or words are troubling her. Appendix D.14 contains two examples. The first example, based on Nancy Shaw's *Sheep Out to Eat* (1992), is built on a number of different word families. The second example is built on other homophones. It is not recommended that you use all the cards in each activity.

ACTIVITY

(GRADES 2–5)

WHERE ARE THE MISSING LETTERS?

To connect writing with reading while focusing on sounds within words, you can write phrases or sentences from books that emphasize word families and rhymes. All the books used should be those you have already shared with the student. You can write a phrase or sentence and omit key letters. Appendix A.5 has a list of books with word families and rhymes. The following is an example from Yvonne Hooker's *One Green Frog* (1981):

Three lazy jellyfish,

Floating on the s __ __.

Along came a whale

And took them home for t __ __.

Five slithery snails.

They never need to p __ __ __.

For when a snail goes out,

He takes his house upon his b __ __ __.

Activities Emphasizing Word Patterns

No matter how explicitly you demonstrate word patterns, some children still will not recognize them. You can easily identify these children by closely observing what they do when they approach an unknown word. Often they will sound out unknown words letter-by-letter. Other children, who have learned to recognize word families, may tend to believe that all words will have onset and rime. You can easily identify these children by again observing them while they read. When these children approach an unknown word, they will often sound out the first letter and then attempt to put all the other letters together. For example, they will attempt to sound out *hope* as *h- op.* Children who continue to sound out words letter-by-letter or attempt to read all words as phonograms will benefit from some individualized sessions working on word patterns.

The following activities are designed to help a child see patterns within words. The first pattern, consonant–vowel–consonant (CVC), is also found in many phonograms. However, the emphasis is now on the short vowel sound that is found in most CVC words. Some exceptions to this pattern that a child may notice are words like *cow, how, few, sew,* and so on.

SHORT VOWEL BINGO

You can play short vowel bingo with readers who struggle with short vowel sounds.

(GRADES 1–3)

1. Duplicate the bingo cards found in Appendix D.15.
2. Write a list of 25 words with short vowel sounds on the board.
3. Instruct the students to write the list of words anywhere on their bingo card. They should put no word on the Free Space.
4. Write the words on index cards, draw one from the stock, and read the word aloud.
5. Have the students place a marker on the word.

The goal is for a child to fill five spaces in a row, vertically, horizontally, or diagonally. If you laminate the cards before students write on them, the cards can be used for many different bingo games. (You may want to use erasable pens or pencils.) The following word list is from Kristen Hall's *A Bad, Bad Day* (1995) and Rex Schneider's *That's Not All!* (1993). Both are books for beginning readers.

bad	dad	bed	hit	what	can
bus	got	not	that	bug	rug
has	pet	let	hen	pen	den
cat	rat	dog	hog	bat	hat
pig	wig	run	fun		

THE MAGICAL E!

The following activity builds on the CVC pattern and introduces the CVCe pattern. Using the following cards, have the child first pronounce the short-vowel word on the card. Then have the child move the "e" card after the word and pronounce the new word, which has a long vowel sound. You should choose only words that are familiar to the child.

(GRADES 1–3)

hug	cut	gag	rag	rat	mat

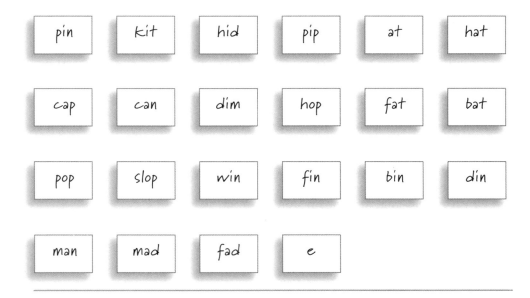

Activities Emphasizing Sounds Within Words

Children should learn to recognize long, short, controlled-r, and schwa vowels as well as the subtle differences between /b/ and /p/, /m/ and /n/, /f/ and /v/, and /t/ and /d/ sounds. As you observe children read, you may notice that some children, when they approach unknown words, do not know if a vowel sound is long, short, schwa, or controlled by the letter r. Other children may consistently write a *t* when the correct letter is a *d*, or a *p* instead of a *b*. These children will benefit from tutoring sessions that feature some of the following intervention activities.

ACTIVITY

(GRADES 1–3)

LISTEN TO THE VOWEL SOUNDS

1. Using the picture cards and game board in Appendix D.16, turn all cards upside down in a pile.
2. Decide which person should begin.
3. The first person picks up a picture card, pronounces the word for the picture, listens to the medial vowel sound, and matches the picture with the correct vowel space.
4. If the person cannot place the card on the correct vowel space, the card is placed on the bottom of the pile.

Note: The goal is for students to fill all the vowel spaces.

ACTIVITY

(GRADES 1–5)

COLLECTING VOWEL SOUNDS WITH DIFFERENT SPELLINGS

This activity will help a child understand that vowel sounds have different spellings (e.g., the long /a/ sound can be spelled *a, ue, ay, ey, ai,* or *ei*). Have the child find words in the texts he is reading that use different spellings to represent the same letter sounds. One way to have a child collect the words is by giving him one 4 × 6 index card for each specified vowel sound. For example, you might begin with all the spellings of the long /a/. A sample of a long /a/ card follows.

```
                        Long /a/ Sound

   ey words       ay words       a words       ai words
     they           day           came          rain
     grey           say           gave          main
                    play          made          pain
                                  mane


                    ve words       ei words
                    bouquet        eight
                    croquet
```

WORD SORTING WITH WORDS

ACTIVITY
(GRADES 1–5)

In addition to word sorts with pictures, teachers can have students do words sorts with words. On sentence strips, write 15 to 20 words and instruct the students to sort the words in whatever way they want. Students can sort the words according to the number of syllables, by initial sound, by ending sound, or by shared sounds (rhymes). Observe students as they sort and ask them to explain how they are sorting. The cards found in Appendix D.14 from the Concentration activity can be used; however, you can use any words that students find in their reading.

CHANGE HEN TO FOX

ACTIVITY
(GRADES 1–4)

This activity, created by Cunningham (2000), is based on *Hattie and the Fox* (1987) by Mem Fox, but it can be played with different words.

1. Instruct the students to write *hen* on the top line of their papers.
2. Then have the students change *hen* to *pen* on the next line.
3. They then keep changing words, using this sequence: *pen* to *pet* to *pit* to *sit* to *six* to *fix* to *fox*.
4. Have them discuss how only one letter was changed each time to create a new word. For example:

hen

pen

pet

pit

sit

six

fix

fox

A variation of this activity is the following. Write a word on the board (e.g., *lost*), and tell the children that they are going to change one letter at a time to create a different word (e.g., *find*). For example, write lost and directly below it write los__. Ask the children what letter to add to complete this word. Give students one word at a time so that they cannot look to the next line for the answer. Continue in this fashion until you reach the target word.

lost

los__

lo__e

l__ne

__ine

min__

__ind

The answers are lose, lone, line, mine, mind, find.

Activity Emphasizing Words Within Words

As most children begin to encode words, they start to recognize words within words; for example, *cap* is in *cape*. Later, they begin to recognize that multi-syllabic words are made up of shorter words. This is especially true of compound words; for example, *butter* + *fly* = *butterfly*. However, as you observe children read and write, you may discover that some children continue to sound out words letter-by-letter. Again, these children need some time with an adult who demonstrates the practice of recognizing smaller words within words. The following activity gives children an opportunity to see this process.

ACTIVITY **"SECRET WORDS"**

(GRADES 2–5) In Secret Words, you give the student a "secret word" (e.g., *Thanksgiving, Halloween,* or *cranberry sauce*). You then instruct the student to find as many words as possible without using a particular letter twice. (If a letter appears more than once in the word, the student may use each appearance one time.) For example:

Thanksgiving

an, at, has, gas, as, in, it, sit, thank, thanks, hang, gang, sin, sank, sink, kin

TECHNOLOGY There are many new computer programs designed to reinforce phonics skills. Effective teachers will carefully select programs that reinforce strategies that they have already introduced and practiced in small groups or shared readings. It is imperative that teachers give explicit instructions on how to use each program so that students do not waste time. Appendix A.6 lists a few of the programs that are easy to use. Each disc includes a number of different programs that focus on different skills.

Many websites also focus on reinforcing phonics skills. Some websites have auditory components while others only have visual elements. The auditory sites may be better for young children because the sound helps hold their attention.

The following sites reinforce learning the alphabet with their sounds (Duffelmeyer, 2002):

1. www.learningplanet.com/act/abcorder.htm. Reinforces the sequencing of the alphabet.
2. www.literacyhour.co.uk/kids/alph_char2.html. Reinforces matching letters with an object that begins with each letter.
3. www.enfagrow.com/language008.html. Reinforces matching upper- and lowercase letters with an object that begins with the letter.
4. http://funshool.com. "Kindergarten," "Kindergarten Games," and "Haunted Alphabet" reinforce matching lowercase with uppercase.
5. www.learningplanet.com. Offers phonic activities by grade level. Select grade level, and click on type of activity.
6. www.sesameworkshop.org/sesamestreet. "Games," "Hidden Letter," and "Big Bird Goes Camping" reinforce naming the letters of the alphabet.

CONCLUDING THOUGHTS

It is important that all teachers understand the graphophonic system that links letters and sounds. Understanding the unique sound structure of the English language will help you assess specific reading problems. You should also remember that phonics instruction must be based on what students know and that it should be systematic, explicit, and extensive. Remember to find appropriate texts and to teach phonics concepts in a meaningful context.

WORD IDENTIFICATION

A teacher is one who brings us tools and enables us to use them.

RALPH WALDO EMERSON

Scenario

When Alberto starts second grade, he is a struggling second-language reader. In the first grade, he encountered a heavy diet of phonics, which stressed letter–sound relationships in isolation. He has had very little instruction in reading words. When Mr. Youngbear asks Alberto to read a level one book from the Guided Reading box, Alberto meticulously sounds out the letters of each word without realizing when he has pronounced an entire word. He cannot pronounce sight words such as *the, one, do,* and *once.* Obviously, Alberto does not automatically recognize words.

Mr. Youngbear knows that Alberto needs to learn to recognize words by sight. He concludes that Alberto will benefit from several types of reading activity: (1) listening to simple books on tape while Mr. Youngbear points to each word, (2) reading very easy texts with few new words or texts with a repetitive structure so that he can experience success, (3) engaging in activities that focus on word patterns, and (4) working with the Dolch word list so Alberto will recognize those words automatically.

Mr. Youngbear arranges for Alberto to listen to books on CD-ROMs that highlight the words as the computer "reads" the text. He also prepares books on tape, which he records at a slow pace so that Alberto can read along with the tape as he points to each word. He places Alberto in a Guided Reading group (see Chapter 2 and the discussion later in this chapter) with two other students who need practice in whole word identification instead of "sounding out" words letter by letter. Alberto also meets with a community volunteer three days a week to work on the Dolch word list and to engage in other word recognition activities. After one semester, Alberto's reading abilities show marked progress.

INTRODUCTION

The purpose of reading is to comprehend texts for a variety of reasons, not just to read words correctly. One reads stories for entertainment, newspapers to learn about current events, menus to satisfy appetites, poetry to feed the soul, expository texts to learn about interesting topics, and instruction manuals to learn how to assemble items or operate tools.

In order to comprehend texts and enjoy reading, students should be able to instantaneously recognize a large bank of words and effortlessly analyze unknown words. In order for this **automaticity** to occur, the brain must process both visual and nonvisual information (Smith, 1997). Every time a reader identifies a letter or word, the brain is involved in a decision, "and the amount of information required to make the decision depends on the number of alternatives there are" (Smith, 1978, p. 24).

Smith's (1997) research on the brain's role in the reading process concludes that the brain is capable of identifying only four or five random letters (e.g., *wxqej*) per second. The reason for this is that when a letter is randomly presented, the brain has 26 letters from which it must choose. This means that if five to eight letters are randomly presented, it takes the brain approximately two seconds to identify the letters.

When letters are organized into a random list of words (e.g., *basket, board, sneeze, Iowa*), the brain can approach them as chunks of information, which permits a reader to identify two or more words (the equivalent of ten to a dozen letters) in one second (Smith, 1997). When the words are organized into grammatically correct sentences (e.g., *I love to read*), the brain can process four times the amount it can handle when identifying random letters. This difference occurs because readers make use of non-visual information that is already stored in the brain. Readers' prior knowledge reduces the amount of information required to identify entire words. Being able to automatically identify words and being able to comprehend texts depend "on using visual information economically and using as much non-visual information as possible" (Smith, 1978, p. 33). "Tunnel vision," a state of incomprehension when faced with a text, occurs when the brain is overloaded with visual information. Beginning readers often find themselves paralyzed by tunnel vision because they read too slowly, attempting to sound out each word letter by letter. Tunnel vision also often occurs when readers lack background knowledge or when reading materials are too difficult for them. When readers encounter too many unknown words, they pay attention to the visual aspects of reading (the letters within words), which prompts the brain to process all the letters separately.

In order to comprehend text, it is imperative that students have automatic word recognition and word analysis skills. Reading is often unpleasant for struggling readers because the task is laborious and can cause embarrassment when they must read aloud in front of peers. Because reading is a struggle and an embarrassment, they spend very little time on it and do not receive the necessary practice to become fluent. Like any other skill, word identification requires practice. It is best if students develop this skill with a teacher who can assess their reading problems, teach appropriate strategies, and provide engaging activities.

In order for reading to become pleasurable for struggling readers, they must gain the ability to automatically recognize a large bank of words. According to Pinnell (1999), word recognition includes the following elements:

- Recognizing words without conscious attention.
- Recognizing words without attending to every letter.
- Using parts of words to quickly identify new words.
- Connecting unknown words to known words (analogies).
- Connecting spelling with word meaning (homonyms, plurals, tenses, etc.).

Automatic word recognition is achieved when students read full text, not when they spend hours doing drills with isolated word lists (Clay, 1991; Gipe, 1995; Pinnell & Fountas, 1998; Taberski, 2000).

To identify words in full text, proficient readers use all four cueing systems—syntactic, semantic, pragmatic, and graphophonic—along with context clues and their receptive vocabulary. A good goal for corrective reading instruction is to have struggling readers (1) learn how to use the four cueing systems, (2) learn how to use context clues, (3) build their receptive and expressive vocabularies, and (4) increase their range of strategies for analyzing words.

Before teachers attempt to assess and assist struggling readers, however, they need to understand some basic concepts about reading.

WHAT TEACHERS NEED TO KNOW

To become proficient readers, students do not simply memorize lists of words or learn all the combinations of letter–sound relationships. Instead, they "attend to how words work and how they communicate meaning" (Pinnell & Fountas, 1998, p. 149). As proficient readers read, they simultaneously use their knowledge of the four cueing systems—syntactic, semantic, pragmatic, and graphophonic. Although these concepts were discussed in Chapter 2, I will briefly review them here and relate them to word identification.

The Four Cueing Systems

1. Syntactic system. The **syntactic** language system is often described as the system of grammar and sentence structure. The sentence structure of English is unique. For example, when attempting to translate a sentence from German to English, it is usually impossible to simply substitute English words for German words and produce a meaningful, well-formed sentence. From birth, native English speakers automatically begin to learn the flow of English syntax when they communicate with adults. When reading, most children automatically use the syntactic system to identify familiar words and learn new ones. For example, even if proficient readers do not know the word *track*, they can use syntax to help them make sense of the sentence, "The train sped down the track." They will know that any verb such as *trampled*, *tried*, or *tackled* will not be appropriate here, because the determiner *the* is not followed by a verb. Proficient readers may not be able to explain the grammatical rule, but their prior knowledge of syntax will tell them that a verb does not make sense at the end of that sentence. Struggling readers, on the other hand, do not automatically use syntax in this way.

2. Semantic system. **Semantic** refers to the meanings of words, sentences, and longer passages in language. Many words have multiple meanings. For example, *run* can be a verb, a noun, or a root word for a number of other words. In each instance, *run* has a different meaning. See Figure 7.1 for different usages

for *run*. Struggling readers may recognize *run* when it stands by itself, but they may have a problem when attempting to recognize *runner* and *runny* in a word list. However, if they read each of these words in a sentence, the context will help them identify the word. For example, most children would easily recognize *runner* in the following sentence because of the context: "As the race was about to begin, the runner waved to his dad." Also, most children would recognize *runny* in the following sentence because of the context: "The sick baby had a runny nose."

Homonyms are words that are spelled the same but have different pronunciations and meanings in different contexts. The words *minute, wind, read,* and *tear* are pronounced differently and carry different meanings in the following sentences.

> The minute hand on the clock was stuck on seven.
>
> The minute glove was too small for the giant's hand.
>
> I love to feel the soft wind on my face.
>
> Please wind the alarm clock.
>
> You need to read two chapters tonight.
>
> I read that book three times.
>
> The child's tears cascaded down her face as the balloon floated above the roof.
>
> Please do not tear any pages of the library book.

It is obvious that readers know the correct pronunciation and intended meaning of these words only when they are used in context.

3. Pragmatic system. The **pragmatic system** refers to the situational context of a word, sentence, or passage. Readers' prior knowledge and previous experiences impact the pragmatic system because all readers' experiences are different. For example, students who live in the southern United States and who have never visited the northern plains might not appreciate a description of the bone-chilling winds of a blizzard like students who live in North Dakota. In fact, a southern student may lack a whole

---

FIGURE 7.1   Multiple meanings of the word *run.*

Run! Run as fast as you can!
Mary will run for president of the Literary Club.

The run in my hose is embarrassing.
The dog run at George's Kennel is very clean.
The ski run is rough and challenging.

The baby's runny nose was disgusting.
The runner got a charley horse in his leg.
The running water sounds cool and refreshing.

range of sights, sounds, and feelings that a North Dakota student associates with a blizzard. When a student from the South reads a story set in a blizzard, she may not automatically identify words such as *blizzard, parkas,* and *toboggans* with the same ease as students in the North.

4. Graphophonic system. The **graphophonic system** refers to relationships between letters and their sounds. Refer to Chapter 6 for a detailed discussion of this cueing system.

Proficient readers use these four cueing systems automatically; however, struggling readers may not effectively use one or more of them (Rasinski & Padak, 2000).

Components of Word Identification

Automaticity is not only the ability to recognize a large bank of words by sight and to quickly decode unfamiliar words; it also includes the ability to comprehend the words in their context and thus comprehend passages. Many skills are needed in order for automaticity to function. Students need good receptive, expressive, and sight vocabularies. They need to recognize sight words instantaneously and they need the ability to use context clues when they encounter unfamiliar words. They need skill in visual analysis and blending, and they need knowledge about word structure—affixes and root words. All of this knowledge and these skills affect readers' ability to automatically identify words.

Receptive and Expressive Vocabulary

A readers' vocabulary consists of two parts—their receptive vocabulary and their expressive vocabulary. **Receptive** vocabulary is the bank of words that they can access in conversation. Readers' receptive or listening vocabulary is a result of their past experiences, conversations, and reading. Oral language in the home and community is the primary source of students' receptive vocabulary (Fountas & Pinnell, 1999b). Students' **expressive** vocabulary, often smaller than their receptive vocabulary, has two parts—one they use in speech and one they use in writing. Their oral vocabulary is usually larger than their written vocabulary.

When students encounter new words in text and attempt to identify the words, their receptive vocabulary and their expressive oral vocabulary will aid them. But if the unknown words are not part of their receptive or expressive vocabularies, they will not recognize words as they attempt to pronounce them. Too often struggling readers have limited receptive and expressive oral vocabularies. These struggling readers are often children "who live in poverty and are exposed to fewer experiences than their middle-class counterparts" (International Reading Association, 2002).

Sight Words

Sight words are words that do not conform to pronunciation rules, but appear often in simple text (e.g., *the, to, you, there, one, once*). There are many sight word lists. See Appendix B.7 for Dolch's (1948) list and Appendix B.8 for Shanker and Ekwall's (1998) list of sight word phrases. Cunningham's (2000) list of high frequency words, given in Appendix B.6, also includes many sight words.

Sight Vocabulary

Readers' **sight vocabularies** are the words that they recognize in half a second or less (Lyons, 1999; Taberski, 2000). Every readers' sight vocabulary is unique. Children learn sight words in the following three phases (Gipe, 1995):

1. They know the word in conversation, but not in print.
2. They begin to recognize the word occasionally when found in print.
3. They automatically recognize the word in print.

HIGH FREQUENCY WORDS

"One hundred words account for almost half of all the words we read and write. Ten words—*the, of, and, a, to, in, is, you, that,* and *it*—account for almost one-quarter of all the words we read and write" (Cunningham, 2000, p. 54). Many of these high frequency words are difficult for children because these words have no concrete meaning. However, students need to be able to recognize these words automatically when they read and to spell them instantaneously when they write. Displaying these words on a word wall keeps them available to students as they read and write.

Appendix B.6 features the list of high frequency words compiled by Cunningham (2000). Appendix B.7 includes the Dolch word list, a collection of high frequency words.

Context Clues

When readers come to unknown words, they use context clues—rhetorical knowledge, schema, and picture clues. **Rhetorical knowledge** is readers' knowledge about story grammar, the structure of expository text, paragraphing, and so on. **Schema** refers to readers' knowledge of the world. Readers' background knowledge (or schema) is closely related to their receptive vocabularies (Fountas & Pinnell, 1999b; International Reading Association, 2002). If the reader has background knowledge on the reading topic, unknown words will be easier to recognize. For example, if the teacher mentions that a passage is about pioneers, readers who have background knowledge about this topic will begin to think of prairies, mud houses, covered wagons, buffalo, and so on. When these readers need to "sound out" any of these words because they have never encountered them in print, their background knowledge helps them identify the words. **Picture clues,** illustrations that help readers identify unknown words, can also be a type of context clue. Proficient readers use picture clues. For example, readers may not recognize the word *iguana* in the text, but a picture may help with word recognition. To aid struggling readers, teachers often use vocabulary words that will be found in the text during a pre-reading discussion where students view and discuss the pictures.

Visual Analysis of Monosyllabic Words

When words cannot be determined from context clues, readers can use **visual analysis.** This recognition skill involves breaking syllables into smaller, known parts. In monosyllabic words, proficient readers look for parts that they know. For example, as discussed in Chapter 6, they will look for a rime within the syllable and then add the onset (e.g., *ight* + *fl* = *flight*). (See Appendix B.3 for common word families, or phonograms.)

In monosyllabic words that are not part of a word family, proficient readers are able to look at the whole word, automatically say the sound of the vowel or vowel cluster, and then add the beginning and ending consonants (e.g., *ie* + *shr* + *k* = *shriek*). Struggling readers, however, tend to mechanically sound out the word from left to right (Rasinski & Padak, 2000). This can cause problems because the sound of certain letters changes as more letters are added to a syllable. For example, with the word *knee*, readers encounter a problem if they first sound out the /k/ in *knee*, because the *k* is silent when followed by *n*.

For polysyllabic words, proficient readers understand the following basic concepts for segmenting words (Rasinski & Padak, 2000):

1. Every syllable has one vowel sound.
2. Every syllable has about three to five letters.
3. Syllables are often divided between two consonants (e.g., *hop-ping*).
4. Consonant clusters are not separated within words (e.g., *fa-ther*, not *fat-her*).
5. The final *e* is often silent.
6. The final *y* in one-syllable words is often pronounced as the long /i/ sound.
7. The final *y* in a polysyllabic word is often pronounced as a long /e/ (e.g., *merry, happy, finally*).

When attempting to pronounce unknown polysyllabic words, proficient readers will (1) find the vowel, (2) pronounce the trial syllable, (3) blend the syllables, and (4) verify the blend as a word that fits the meaning of the sentence (Rasinski & Padak, 2000). Struggling readers usually need to learn this strategy.

Blending Polysyllabic Words

Once readers recognize the smaller parts (single syllables) of words, they need to be able to quickly blend these parts to make whole words. Accurate, quick blending is necessary for pleasurable reading. Struggling readers may recognize the parts but lack the skill to quickly blend the pieces back together (Gipe, 1995). Instruction in blending should begin with word endings, such as *ed, ing, ly, er,* and *est,* since readers frequently need to recognize only the base word and the ending. Next, introducing compound words helps readers understand that longer words often consist of smaller words. Words such as *butterfly, mailbox, tablespoon,* and *teacup* are long words for children to sound out letter by letter; however, if they can quickly recognize the smaller words within the longer ones and quickly blend the smaller together, they will be able to identify these longer words automatically. After working with inflectional endings and compound words, students can work with other polysyllabic words.

Structural Analysis

As students advance in reading and writing and begin to use more polysyllabic words, it is advantageous for them to be familiar with frequently used prefixes and suffixes. Recognizing these parts helps them see the structure of words. Young readers and writers first become aware of endings that are added to words, such as *s* to make plural nouns, and *ed* and *ing* to change verb tenses. Appendix B.4 lists frequently used suffixes and prefixes with their meaning and examples. Appendix B.5 has a list of Ancient Greek word roots.

ASSESSMENT

Since reading comprehension depends on automatic word identification, it is imperative that teachers know how to assess readers' ability to identify unfamiliar words and to assess readers' sight vocabulary. Teachers should use both informal and formal assessment instruments.

Informal Assessment

As discussed above, students' receptive vocabulary, their sight vocabulary, their ability to use context clues, their ability to use visual analysis in monosyllabic words, their ability to blend, and their knowledge of word parts all affect their capacity to automatically identify words. There are informal ways teachers can assess students' abilities in each of these areas.

Checklists

At the beginning of the school year, teachers should familiarize themselves with their state's literacy standards, especially those that address word identification. To ensure that all students become competent in these standards, teachers can design a checklist to informally assess each student's growth in this area. Teachers can assess knowledge

at the beginning of the year and at the end of each quarter. Students who appear to lag behind the others should receive extra help in word identification. Students who are competent in all the areas should perform other activities when the rest of the class is focused on word identification. The partial checklist in Figure 7.2, which is based on California's first-grade Standard 1.10: Decoding and Word Recognition, was completed by Ms. Henderson after the first quarter. From her review of this checklist, she realizes that Rosa and R. J. need more time working on word identification, while Kim is competent in all the areas; therefore, Ms. Henderson plans to give him other reading materials during guided reading time. The entire checklist for this California standard is reproduced in Appendix C.28.

Assessing Receptive Vocabulary

A student's receptive vocabulary consists of words he recognizes when listening to speakers. Often the context for the conversation helps him grasp the meaning. One way teachers can informally assess a student's receptive vocabulary is by having him read a passage at his instructional level. If the reader attempts to decode a word and does not realize he has mispronounced it, the word may not be a part of his receptive vocabulary. For example, imagine that Jacob has never heard the word *signature*; when he encounters it in a text, he may pronounce it "sign-a-

---

FIGURE 7.2 Checklist for first grade, based on California's Standard 1. 10.

TEACHER Ms. Henderson   DATE 10/30/04

+ = always   X = sometimes   O = seldom/never

STANDARD   STUDENTS

STANDARD	Kourtlyn	Kim	Gillian	Quinton	R. J.	Arielle	Coy	Zachary	Rosa	Alexis	Gabrielle	Mat	Blake	Taylor	Teagan	Josh	Zeb	Tyler
1. Recognizes consonant blends.	X	+	+	X	O	X	+	+	O	X	X	+	X	X	X	O	X	X
2. Recognizes short vowel pattern: CVC	X	+	X	O	O	X	X	+	O	O	X	X	X	X	X	X	X	O
3. Recognizes long vowel patterns: CVCe and CV	X	+	X	O	O	X	X	X	O	O	O	X	O	X	X	X	X	O
4. Blends onsets with rime.	X	+	X	O	O	X	X	X	O	O	O	O	O	X	O	O	X	O

ture," with emphasis on the *sign*, with a long /i/, and never realize that he has mispronounced the word.

Assessing Sight Words

There are many word lists a teacher can use to informally assess readers' sight words. The Dolch Basic Sight Vocabulary is often used for informal assessment. It is found in Appendix B.7. Many basal readers also have graded word lists that must be mastered by the end of the school year. You can use the list as a pre-test at the beginning of the school year and as a quarterly assessment instrument throughout the year. You should decide which list is appropriate for particular struggling readers.

To use any of these lists as informal assessment tools, you can print each word on an index card, from which the student will read. To keep the cards in order of difficulty, the cards should have numbers on the back, with number one corresponding to the easiest word. You can also prepare a scoring sheet that has the list of words in order. Figure 7.3 includes a partial sample based on the Dolch list. Appendix C.29 has a complete form that can be used for any list. On the scoring sheet, you can mark all correctly pronounced words with a plus sign (+) and missed words with a minus sign (−).

To administer the word list, the student should read the list into a tape recorder as you flash the card. You should flash one or two cards per second. Once a student misses five consecutive words, you should pause the exercise. The goal is for every child to read each list that is appropriate for his grade with 90 percent accuracy (Shanker & Ekwall, 1998). Most students misread some words when they use these lists because the words are not in context. Students should be expected to master the first 110 words of the Dolch list by the end of the first grade, and all 220 words by the end of the second grade.

The following commercial informal reading inventories have graded word lists. They can be used in the same way as the Dolch list; however, they provide a scoring sheet and a list from which the students can read.

- Silvaroli, N. & Wheelock, W. (2003). *Classroom Reading Inventory* (10th ed.). Boston: McGraw-Hill.

FIGURE 7.3 Scoring sheet for a sample word list.

TEACHER *Tyler*   GRADE *2nd*

+ = yes   − = no

WORDS	BEGINNING OF YEAR	1ST QUARTER	2ND QUARTER	3RD QUARTER	4TH QUARTER
A	+				
After	−				
All	+				
Am	+				
An	+				
And	+				
Are	+				
Around	−				
As	+				
At	+				
Away	−				
Be	+				

- Shanker, J. & Ekwall, E. (2000). *Reading Inventory* (4th ed). Boston: Allyn and Bacon.
- Burns, P. & Roe, B. (2002). *Informal Reading Inventory* (6th ed.). Boston: Houghton Mifflin.

Assessing Sight Vocabulary

You can informally assess struggling readers' sight vocabulary by having them read a passage that is at their instructional level. If their sight vocabulary is weak, they will read word by word or laboriously sound out every word to the point that they won't know what word they have read by the time they get to the last sound.

You can also informally assess struggling readers' sight vocabulary by designing a personalized speed test for individual readers. To construct a personalized test, complete the following steps:

1. Write three words of equal difficulty on a line.
2. Repeat this process to make at least ten different lines. The first line should have the easiest words and the last line should have the most difficult.
3. Pronounce one of the words from the first line two times for the student.
4. Within five seconds, the student must circle the word you pronounced.
5. Repeat this process for the remaining lines.

Figure 7.4 provides a sample list for this activity.

Remember that sight vocabulary assessment must be quick and accurate. The following commercial graded word lists can also be used for sight vocabulary assessment:

1. ESA Word List (1977)
2. Basic Elementary Reading Vocabulary by Harris and Jacobson (1972)

3. DLM's Word Radar, a computer program by Chaffin, Maxwell, and Thompson (1983)

Assessing Context Clues

Students' background knowledge impacts their ability to use context clues. You can informally assess readers' background knowledge in a number of ways. The first is to ask the student to "read" the pictures in a book. While discussing the pictures, listen to the technical vocabulary the child uses while "reading" the picture. If the child does not use any specific terms and relies on words like *things, whatchamacallit,* and so on, you can assume the reader is not familiar with the topic.

You can assess a reader's ability to use context clues through a cloze test. When completing a cloze test, readers need to read for meaning as well as recognize the word that is missing. (To construct a cloze test, see the instructions in Chapter 3.) A cloze test should be administered orally so you can analyze readers' ability to fill in the blank correctly, and then ask them why they chose a particular word. If readers make wild guesses, you can infer that they are not using context clues.

The running record (also discussed in Chapter 3) is another way for you to assess if and how students use context clues. You can use it to determine if readers use picture clues or context clues within the text to help them with unknown words.

Assessing Visual Analysis

One informal way to assess readers' ability to analyze monosyllabic word parts is to give them a list of words that highlight onset and rime. Pronounce either the onset or the rime of each word, and allow five seconds for students to circle the

FIGURE 7.4   Sight vocabulary assessment.

1. the	on	of	7. read	need	end
2. when	which	with	8. answer	animal	world
3. then	them	these	9. every	earth	never
4. made	may	way	10. example	important	together
5. only	our	after	11. children	river	second
6. want	where	old	12. mountain	enough	idea

FIGURE 7.5   Words with onset and rimes.

LIST FOR READER

1. bill	6. found	11. top	16. sand	21. man
2. light	7. pup	12. see	17. hay	22. pack
3. ham	8. flat	13. hill	18. sound	23. stop
4. land	9. fan	14. might	19. cup	24. bee
5. may	10. back	15. clam	20. hat	

UNDERLINED PART PRONOUNCED

1. bill	6. found	11. top	16. sand	21. man
2. light	7. pup	12. see	17. hay	22. pack
3. ham	8. flat	13. hill	18. sound	23. stop
4. land	9. fan	14. might	19. cup	24. bee
5. may	10. back	15. clam	20. hat	

word part that you pronounced. Figure 7.5 presents a small sample list for the reader and a list of sample answers.

To informally assess readers' visual ability to analyze polysyllabic words, you should carefully observe how readers attempt to analyze unknown words. Do the readers attempt to sound out the words letter-by-letter? Do they segment the words into syllables? Do they segment the word into the correct syllables?

Assessing Blending

To assess a readers' ability to blend word parts, you should first assess auditory blending skills by saying two parts of a word and having the reader put the two sounds together. For example, you might begin with monosyllabic words by pronouncing *fl* and then *ight*. The reader should pronounce *flight*. You can proceed to two syllable words (e.g., *pic + nic = picnic*) and then progress to three- and four-syllable words.

After assessing auditory blending, you can assess students' visual blending abilities by writing the parts of words on separate cards and having the students push the cards together and pronounce the word. For example, with monosyllabic words, one card might have a *c* and another card an *at*. Students push the two cards together and pronounce *cat*. With polysyllabic words, each card displays a syllable of the word. For example, one card has *moun* and the other has *tain*. Students push the two cards together and pronounce *mountain*. See the Intervention section of this chapter for sample cards.

Assessing Structural Analysis

To informally assess readers' ability to analyze word structure, you should observe readers as they encounter words with prefixes and suffixes. Does the reader automatically pronounce the prefix and suffix as separate syllables? For example, on the word *unending*, does the reader automatically pronounce *un*, or does she attempt to sound out the *u* and then the *n*? Does the reader pronounce *ing* as one syllable?

Another informal way to assess readers' ability to recognize word parts is to give them a list of words with prefixes and suffixes (Gipe, 1995). See Figure 7.6 for an example. You should pronounce one of the parts of each word and allow five seconds for students to circle that part. You must allow no more than five seconds because word recognition must be instantaneous.

Formal Assessment

The following is a summary of diagnostic tests that include sub-tests that assess phonic skills, structural analysis, blending, visual and auditory discrimination, sight word recognition, and syllabication skills:

1. Stanford Diagnostic Reading, Third Edition (group test): Phonics, structural analysis, auditory discrimination, and auditory vocabulary.
2. Diagnostic Reading Scales (individual test): Decoding skills and word recognition.
3. Diagnostic Screening Test–Reading, Third Edition: Word analysis and word recognition.

FIGURE **7.6**   List of words with prefixes and suffixes.

LIST FOR READER

1. recalls	6. hopeless	11. friendly	16. unfriendly
2. unless	7. careful	12. quicker	17. jumpy
3. before	8. running	13. unopened	18. weakness
4. coming	9. smallest	14. unnecessary	19. reading
5. smiled	10. bigger	15. prettiest	20. teacher

UNDERLINED PART PRONOUNCED

1. <u>re</u>calls	6. hope<u>less</u>	11. friend<u>ly</u>	16. <u>un</u>friendly
2. <u>un</u>less	7. care<u>ful</u>	12. quick<u>er</u>	17. jump<u>y</u>
3. <u>be</u>fore	8. runn<u>ing</u>	13. <u>un</u>opened	18. weak<u>ness</u>
4. com<u>ing</u>	9. small<u>est</u>	14. <u>un</u>necessary	19. read<u>ing</u>
5. smil<u>ed</u>	10. bigg<u>er</u>	15. pretty<u>est</u>	20. teach<u>er</u>

4. Diagnostic Achievement Battery–2: Word analysis and word recognition.

5. Gates McKillop-Horowitz Reading Diagnostic Test, Second Edition: Word recognition, phonics, syllabication, producing letter sounds, letter naming, blending, word analysis, and use of context clues.

6. Slosson Oral Reading Test: A graded word list.

7. Gray Oral Reading Tests, Third Edition: Word recognition in context.

8. Gilmore Oral Reading Test: Word recognition in context.

9. The Durrell Analysis of Reading Difficulty, Third Edition: Word analysis in isolation and in context.

10. Diagnostic Reading Scales, Revised: Word analysis in isolation and in context.

11. Woodcock Reading Mastery Test, Revised: Word identification, word attack, and use of context clues.

12. Metropolitan Achievement Test, Seventh Edition: Word recognition.

13. Rosewell–Chall Auditory Blending Test: Blending.

14. Sipay's Diagnostic Test: Blending.

Intervention

STRATEGIES & ACTIVITIES

Word identification skills should not be taught through mechanical, isolated skills sheets (Gipe, 1995; Moustafa & Maldonado-Colon, 1999; Pinnell & Fountas, 1998; Rasinski & Padak, 2000; Taberski, 2000). Instead, skills should be taught in context—for example, while reading good literature or while writing a letter. A primary goal of teaching word identification skills is to help struggling readers gain the "systematic understanding of how words work rather than just a collection of known words" (Pinnell & Fountas, 1998, p. 78). It is fruitless to have struggling readers memorize an isolated list of words. Rather, teachers should help them learn how to think about words—for example, by looking for familiar parts within words. Many words can be identified as part of a word family, and sometimes there are familiar short words in longer words, such as *chimpanzee*, which contains *pan*, or *scare*, which contains *s + care*. Sometimes when segmenting a longer word, the result is several smaller connected words. Consider, for example, *attendance*, which segments into *at + ten + dance*. In this word and in most others like it, the smaller words must be blended together quickly to form the longer word. When teaching word identification skills, you should use writing as well as reading activities because "[w]riting experiences help children gain control of words and build into their knowledge the letter–sound association of the language" (Pinnell & Fountas, 1998, p. 72).

All the strategies and activities discussed in this section can be used in small group settings. However, it is strongly recommended that these activities be primarily used in tutoring sessions. All the instruction should take place while working with authentic children's literature and writing tasks. For most strategies and activities, I have suggested sample books to use; however, you should feel free to use texts that interest the struggling readers you are assisting.

Pinnell and Fountas (1998) contend that: "[w]ord learning, letter learning and learning how print works are related bodies of knowledge. No one area is a prerequisite to the other" (p. 72). Word identification is indeed an interaction between (1) word knowledge, (2) knowledge of letter sounds, (3) knowledge of word parts, (4) receptive vocabulary, (5) sight vocabulary, and (6) the use of context clues—a skill that often contributes to a number of different aspects of word identification.

The following activities are organized by category to help you quickly locate appropriate activities. After you assess struggling readers as they read and write, you can emphasize the specific skills that will meet their particular needs.

Small Group Activity for Teaching Word Identification Skills

In order to more effectively use your classroom time, you may want to teach concepts to small groups of students who need to develop similar skills. During these small group sessions, closely observe and assess what each child does when faced with unknown words and modify your instruction as needed.

GUIDED READING   ACTIVITY

Guided reading is an activity in which a teacher works with a small group of children who are reading at the same level and who use similar reading processes (Fountas & Pinnell, 1996). For these activities you should use leveled books that offer a minimum of new concepts to learn and take time to teach one or two new concepts in each session. The premise of guided reading is for children to experience new texts that they can read at once with minimum support. Your role is to teach students reading strategies and skills and how to use them successfully during independent reading.

The guided reading lesson follows a specific format:

1. Select a text that offers one or two new concepts. The text might be a big book that all the children in the group can clearly view.
2. Introduce the book by talking through the pictures, using the vocabulary of the text. For example, if the story is about a *humungous* bear but the children use the word *big* in the discussion, introduce the word *humungous* during further discussion.
3. After you talk through the entire text, give each child a copy of the book. They should look again at the pictures. You might ask the students to find a particular word on a particular page.
4. Next, instruct the students to quietly read the book aloud to themselves. Be sure to observe and keep watch for words that students find difficult.
5. After the reading, make a list on a whiteboard of any words that were problematic for the students. Now teach the students an appropriate word identification skill (e.g., structural analysis) and ask them to apply it to the problematic word.
6. Read the text in unison with the students.

7. Sometimes you might invite students to respond to the book to assess their comprehension. Other times you may supply writing, drama, or art extensions to complement the book. However, not every book works with such extensions.

8. Ask a student to stay so you can make a running record of his reading.

Read the scenario in the box below and examine how Mr. Francis teaches several word identification skills during a guided reading session.

A GUIDED READING SESSION

Mr. Francis is supervising a small group activity in which students quietly read aloud to themselves. As the children read *Step Inside the Rain Forest*, by Meish Goldish (1993), Mr. Francis notes that the children struggle with the word *sloth*, an unfamiliar animal, and *chimpanzee*, a longer word for this group of readers. When the children use picture clues for this word, some say, "ape," while others say, "monkey." When they have completed the story, Mr. Francis writes *sloth* on the whiteboard.

Mr. Francis: What parts do you see in this word?

Children: A *sl* and a *th*.

Mr. Francis: Good. What sound does sl make?

Children: /sl/.

Mr. Francis: Good! What sound does the th make?

Children: /th/.

Mr. Francis: Good! Do you think the o makes a short or long sound?

Carla: A short sound because there is no e at the end of the word.

Mr. Francis: Now let's blend the three parts together.

Children: /sl/ . . . /o/ . . . /th/.

Mr. Francis: A little faster now.

Children: Sloth (as Mr. Francis quickly moves his finger under the letters.)

Mr. Francis: Now turn to page 11 and let's read that page together.

Children: A sloth—it doesn't walk on the ground.

Mr. Francis: Great! We also know that *monkeys* and *apes* are incorrect words because these animals can walk on the ground. Now let's look at this word. (He writes *chimpanzee* on the board.) Again, some of you read *ape* and some of you read *monkey*. The animal on page 13 looks like a monkey or ape. But let's look at the letters of the word. What sound does monkey start with?

Children: /m/.

Mr. Francis: Correct! This word (pointing to *chimpanzee* on the board) does not begin with the /m/ sound or the letter *m*. What sound does *ape* begin with?

Carla: A long /a/ sound.

Mr. Francis: Correct! These letters (points to the ch) do not make the long /a/ sound. What word do you see in this long word?

Colin: I see *pan*. (He points to it.)

Brian: It's *chimpanzee!* A chimpanzee is like a monkey, and that has *pan* in it. Listen, chim *pan* zee.

Mr. Francis: Great job! Let's read that page together.

Children: Bats and snakes and chimpanzees.

Colin: Mr. Francis, you spelled it wrong. It has an *s* on the end.

Mr. Francis: Thanks for catching that Colin. What does that *s* mean?

Colin: That there are more than one.

Mr. Francis: Great job! Colin saw a smaller word in chimpanzee and Brian, you recalled that a chimpanzee is like a monkey. Today, boys and girls, you learned to find smaller parts in words, like in *sloth* and in *chimpanzees*. Now, let's read the entire book together.

Fountas and Pinnell's *Guided Reading: Good First Teaching for All Children* (1996), can give you more detail about how to conduct a guided reading session.

Activities Emphasizing Receptive and Expressive Vocabulary

During discussions, you may observe a child whose receptive and expressive vocabularies are very limited. The child may use general terms such as *thing* for common objects, like the *tire* or *wheel* of a car. Or the child may not know the specific names of familiar animals. When you determine that a student has a limited vocabulary, you should take time to discuss books and pictures with the child, using specific words and prompting the child to join in. The following two activities should be conducted in a tutoring session so that the tutor or teacher can adapt the activity to the child's individual needs.

WORDLESS BOOKS

ACTIVITY

(GRADES 1–5)

"Reading" a wordless book is one way to build a struggling reader's receptive vocabulary and schemata. The "reading" becomes a discussion when a teacher also comments on the pictures, using specific terms or a more advanced vocabulary than a reader has. Appendix. A.4 presents a list of wordless books that encourage this kind of discussion. For example, after viewing the first picture in the wordless book *Zoom* (1995) by Istvan Banyai, the student may say that it depicts a bird. As they turn to the second page, the teacher may agree, but say that it is a *rooster* because of the colorful crown. As they continue through the book, if the student calls the cruise ship a *boat*, the teacher can explain the difference. As they discuss the pictures, the teacher should write each specified word on an adhesive label and stick it to the appropriate page so the student can later go through the book and read these words back to the tutor.

PICTURE BOOKS

ACTIVITY

(GRADES 1–3)

Jan Brett's books have detailed pictures and borders. Often the borders are stories within the main plot or details that supplement it. Using one of Brett's books, you can help a struggling reader "read" the pictures before tackling the text. You should use specific vocabulary so the struggling reader hears potentially challenging words before he attempts to read the text. For example, while discussing the pictures in Brett's *Armadillo Rodeo* (1995), use words like *lizard, hand-tooled boots, chili pepper red boot, arena, jalapeno peppers, fiddles,* and many other words that may be unfamiliar to the student. Later as the student reads the book, he will be able to use the discussion and picture clues to help decode the unfamiliar words. Some of Jan Brett's books are listed in Figure 7.7.

FIGURE 7.7   Books by Jan Brett.

Comet's Nine Lives (1996)	*Armadillo Rodeo* (1995)
The Owl and the Pussycat (1991)	*Trouble with Trolls* (1992)
The Wild Christmas Reindeer (1990)	*Berlioz the Bear* (1991)
The Hat (1997)	*The Mitten* (1989)
Happy Birthday Duck Dear (1988)	*Beauty and the Beast* (1989)
Goldilocks and the Three Bears (1987)	*The First Dog* (1988)
Town Mouse, Country Mouse (1994)	*Gingerbread Baby* (1999)
Fritz and the Beautiful Horses (1981)	*Annie and the Wild Animals* (1985)

Activities Emphasizing Sight Words

Sight words do not follow phonetic rules, yet are found in every story. Students who do not recognize these sight words quickly fall behind the rest of the class and become struggling readers. During guided reading and other small group activities, if you notice some children who continue to struggle with sight words, such as *the*, *of*, and *once*, you should schedule some one-on-one time to work with these children. The goal should be to have each child recognize sight words automatically. If a child needs more time than others to automatically recognize sight words, you should have the child work with a tutor.

ACTIVITY

(GRADES K–1)

MATCH THE WORD

1. After reciting a poem or song with sentence strips, place them in a pocket chart.
2. Give a card with one of the sight words from the text to the child.
3. Ask the child to place the card over the correct word in the sentence strip. This may sound like it will be easy for most children; however, some will not take enough time to examine the letters within words.

This activity can also be used with big books by writing the sight word on an adhesive label and asking the child to stick it over the word in the book. Later, you can say a sight word and ask the child to point to the word in the text.

ACTIVITY

(GRADES 1–5)

DOLCH LIST BINGO

The Bingo cards in Appendix D.17 use the words from the Dolch word list. When playing Bingo, you should call out each word twice, allowing only five seconds between each word. Remember: with word identification, automaticity is the goal.

Activities Emphasizing Sight Vocabulary

As you observe children in small groups, you will often notice children who struggle with words that are not difficult for their peers to learn. These words are frequently important and necessary for understanding the topic of a particular passage. For example, when reading about natural disasters, students need to quickly and automatically recognize words such as *hurricane*, *volcano*, *tornado*, and *earthquake*. Students who do not automatically recognize these words become frustrated and often give up. These students will need one-on-one time for activities that will help them develop their sight vocabularies. The following activities should be conducted in tutoring sessions.

ACTIVITY

(GRADES 1–2)

UNSCRAMBLE THE SENTENCE

After reading a short poem, write each of the poem's lines on a separate sentence strip. For example, after reading "Perfect Children" (1997) by Brod Bagert, write the following four lines on four separate sentence strips:

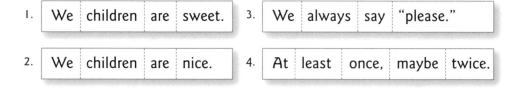

1. We children are sweet.   3. We always say "please."

2. We children are nice.   4. At least once, maybe twice.

After the student can comfortably put the four lines in the correct order and can read each sentence pointing to each word, cut up each line with one word on each piece of paper and instruct the reader to put the sentences back in the correct order.

PERSONALIZED FLASH CARDS

ACTIVITY
(GRADES 1–5)

As you and a student read books that contain vocabulary specific to the topics of the books, the student may encounter difficult words that he attempts to sound out every time the word appears in the text. You should have a stack of index cards handy to write down words that the reader needs to remember. This stack of personalized cards should never be more than 10 to 12 in number. The goal is for the reader to recognize those words quickly by sight. When these words are mastered, they should be placed in the "known" stack. It is satisfying for students to see their stack of "known" words grow.

PERSONAL WORD WALLS

ACTIVITY
(GRADES 1–5)

To help an individual struggling reader create a word bank that is meaningful to her, you can create personalized word walls on card stock or a piece of paper. The partial word list in Figure 7.8 is from Jordan's list as she reads books about birds. She adds words that are "tricky" for her as she reads different books about birds.

FIGURE 7.8   Personal word wall.

A	B bulbul	C camouflage cockatoo	D	E extinction emu
F	G ganets	H	I	J
K	L	M molting	N	O osprey
P preening plumage	Q	R	S	T
U	V	W	X	Y–Z

ACTIVITY   **UNSCRAMBLE THE WORD**

(GRADES 1–2)

1. After reading a book with the student, select some nouns from the text that the student wants to remember or that are new vocabulary for him.
2. Write out the words, using half-inch squares for each letter and cut them out.
3. Give the student the squares for one word and have the student unscramble it. Repeat for all the words.

This activity is useful for assisting tactile learners. The sample cards found in Figure 7.9 are based on *Curious George Visits the Zoo* (1985) by H. A. Rey.

FIGURE 7.9   Unscramble the letters.

e	l	e	p	h	a	n	t
g	i	r	a	f	f	e
k	a	n	g	a	r	o	o
z	o	o	k	e	e	p	e	r
m	o	n	k	e	y
b	a	l	l	o	o	n
b	a	n	a	n	a
G	e	o	r	g	e

y   o   k   n   m   e

ACTIVITY   **TECHNICAL TERMS**

(GRADES 2–5)

Many concept books have vocabulary words that are specific to the topic of the book. To familiarize a student with this specialized vocabulary, first ask the student what she knows about the topic. Then create a word-web for key terms discussed in the book. This web will aid the student as she learns to recognize the words before reading the text. The web in Figure 7.10 is the web Ms. Youngblood draws as her second grader, Ben, discusses his knowledge of the rain forest. She asks him if he has seen TV shows about the rain forest or if he has read about the rain forest at home. After Ms. Youngblood marks down the words that Ben contributes, she adds a few more words that she knows he will encounter in the text. After the discussion, she has Ben read the words in the web. This gives him an opportunity to first see these potentially difficult words in print before he reads the text.

FIGURE 7.10   Sample word web.

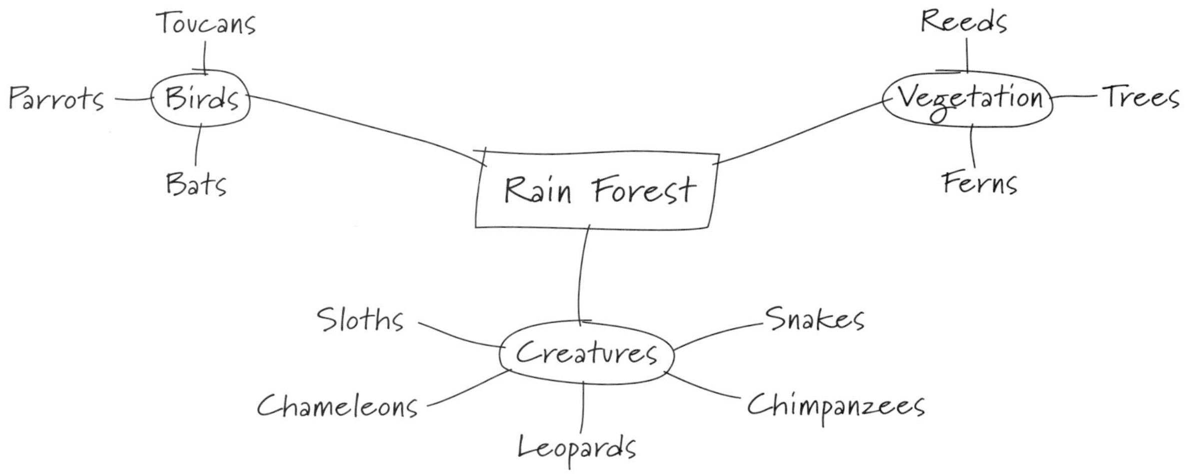

Activity Emphasizing Context Clues

While emphasizing context clues during guided reading sessions, you may observe children who still do not use the context of the text or illustrations to decode unfamiliar words. With these children, you should emphasize reading for meaning over reading words correctly.

CLOZE PASSAGES

Using books that are at the instructional level of the struggling reader, select a key word in a sentence and cover it with an adhesive label. As the child reads the passage and comes to an unknown word, instruct him to read on to the end of the sentence. Then ask him to choose a word that would make sense in the context of the sentence. If the child has no suggestions for the correct word, instruct him to look at the pictures for clues. (You should choose a book with vivid illustrations to help younger children.) If you are working with an older student and a book with no illustrations, simply instruct the student to read to the next sentence to determine the correct word. After the student selects a word, he can take off the label and check to see if the word was correct.

For a variation on this activity, photocopy a short passage at the student's instructional level. Have the student delete every fifth word or every key word and fill in the deleted words the next day. As you observe the student, look for context clues to help her select the correct word.

ACTIVITY

(GRADES 1–6)

Activities Emphasizing Visual Analysis of Monosyllabic Words

During small group reading and other activities, you may observe one or two students who continue to struggle with word families. These children often do not recognize smaller elements within monosyllabic words; if they do, they often have a difficult time quickly blending the two parts together. The following activities are intended for tutoring sessions so that struggling students can learn to automatically blend onsets with rimes.

ACTIVITY

BLENDING ONSET WITH RIME

(GRADES 1–5)   Make a set of cards with onsets and rimes (see Appendix D.18). The set should contain some two-letter rimes, some three-letter rimes, and some four-letter rimes. Slide the onset card and rime card together and have the child pronounce the two parts together. The goal is for the student to recognize the rime as one sound. Older students will usually have little trouble with rimes of two letters; however, many will need extra time to blend rimes of three or more letters. Helping a struggling reader to automatically recognize words that have onset and rime will greatly increase his sight vocabulary.

ACTIVITY

TOSS THE CUBE

(GRADES 1–5)   This activity can help a student develop the ability to create words with a given set of letters. Using three to five letter cubes (found in Appendix D.9), the student tosses the cubes and creates words from the letters. He gets one point for each word he creates. To make the activity more difficult, you can set a time limit for each toss.

Activities Emphasizing Blending Polysyllabic Words and Structural Analysis

As you observe students in small-group settings, you may notice that one student continues to sound out words letter by letter instead of breaking them into familiar parts, such as prefixes, root words, and suffixes. Struggling readers often need explicit instruction in seeing these parts within words. Working with prefixes, suffixes, and base words can be extremely helpful for a struggling student. First graders can benefit from recognizing word endings (e.g., *ing, ed, ly, er,* and *est*), while older students can work with prefixes, root words, and suffixes. You should assess what a child knows and continue to develop the skills with which she struggles.

ACTIVITY

COMPOUND WORDS

(GRADES 2–4)   After reading any book that contains a wide variety of compound words, you can create cards that display the words that make up each compound word. These cards will help students to see how many compound words they can form by putting the cards together. You can time students to make this exercise more challenging. One book that features many compound words is *The Jolly Postman* (1986) by Janet Ahlberg. Some words that relate to the postal service are found in Figure 7.11.

FIGURE 7.11   Compound words that correlate with *The Jolly Postman,* by Janet Ahlberg.

post	man	card	age	box	pal
pen	mail	box	bag	office	truck

BUILDING BLOCKS OF WORDS

Struggling readers often need explicit instruction to identify smaller parts within words. Working with prefixes, suffixes, and base words can be helpful to them. You should select books with words that have a number of prefixes and suffixes. You should first read these books with the students for enjoyment. Then you can begin to show struggling readers how the "big" words have parts (i.e., the root word) that they may already know. For example, Sam McBratney, in *Guess How Much I Love You* (1994), uses many past tense verbs and "ing" verbs: *listening, stretching, reached, swinging, laughed, touched,* and so on. Notice that all these words have endings that do not "share" letters with the base word (e.g., *listen* + *ing; swing* + *ing*). At first it is best to exclude words with double consonants and words in which the base word and the suffix ending share letters. For example, words such as *hopping* and *tumbled* should be avoided because in *hop,* the *p* is doubled to form *hopping,* and in *tumbled* the root word *(tumble)* and ending *(ed)* share the *e.*

In the building blocks activity, you should write all the base words, suffixes, and prefixes from a passage on sentence strips of different colors. For example, write all root words on blue strips, prefixes on green strips, and suffixes on orange. Then cut up the words and affixes and have the readers form as many words as possible by putting the pieces together. Figure 7.12 presents a sample list of words and affixes.

FIGURE 7.12   Root words and affixes.

ROOT WORDS

work	walk	friend	slow	clear	clean
quick	fore	behave	to	take	lead

PREFIXES

un	mis	in	be

ENDINGS

ing	ly	ed	er	s

TECHNOLOGY

Computer activities motivate many children to read. There are a number of interactive books that aid children in word identification. The Discis Series is useful for word identification because students can click the mouse once to hear the pronunciations of unknown words and click the mouse twice to hear the definition of the words. (See Appendix A.7 for a list of titles.)

Living Books also has a wide selection of interactive books that help children work with unknown words. The text is highlighted in phrases so that children can follow along. Students control the turning of each page so they do not become lost. The titles available from Living Books are listed in Appendix A.7.

Listening to a book on tape while following a printed text is also an excellent way for students to increase their ability to identify unknown words. See Chapter 9 for a thorough discussion of using books on tape.

Scholastic Publishers offers the following CD-ROMs with interactive books and strategies to increase students' word identification skills:

1. *Phonics Readers.* Includes 72 interactive books on 12 CD-ROMs.
2. *Phonics Booster.* Offers interactive books on 16 CD-ROMs.
3. *Let's Go Read 1.* 175 lively lessons build a love for reading.
4. *Let's Go Read 2.* Nine interactive stories.
5. *Dinosaur Adventure 3-D.* Learn facts about dinosaurs while solving puzzles.
6. *I Spy Spooky Mansion ("Mystery Bins").* Offers challenging riddles.

Two other CD-ROMs that include programs to increase word identification are *I Spy School Days* ("Wood Block City") and *Inspiration* ("Vocabulary Template").

When using technology, be sure to instruct students on how to operate programs so that they do not waste time. You should also continue to browse publisher websites and catalogs so that you are informed about developments in educational software.

CONCLUDING THOUGHTS

The automatic identification of words is a necessary skill for reading comprehension. Many readers struggle with sight words and others lack vocabulary to read about specified topics. To address these problems, it is vital that teachers help students see patterns in words rather than demanding that they memorize large banks of words. Recognizing onset, rime, prefixes, suffixes, and root words will help struggling readers increase their sight vocabularies. Since many words are not phonograms and do not have prefixes or suffixes, teachers also need to help students use context clues when they encounter unknown words.

VOCABULARY BUILDING

A great teacher makes hard things easy.

RALPH WALDO EMERSON

8

Scenario

Mrs. Lopez, the principal of an inner-city school, overhears some of the fourth-grade teachers in the lounge discussing the trouble that their students have reading and understanding science materials. After listening to them, she decides to remind the teachers how readers' vocabularies affect their comprehension. At the fourth-grade team meeting, Mrs. Lopez gives the teachers the following passage from her old music harmony textbook and asks them to read the passage.

> If the root of a triad remains stationary while its third and fifth rise one degree and return, a six-four chord is formed. This type differs from the appoggiatura type in that it is weak rhythmically and the sixth and fourth must enter from below in the manner of auxiliary tones. A simple analysis of one root for all three chords is always possible, the sixth and fourth being nonharmonic tones. (Piston, 1962, p. 108)

After giving the teachers time to read, she asks them to write a short summary, explaining in their own words what they have read. They cannot complete this task; they have little background knowledge about music and are not familiar with the terms *root, triad, six-four chord,* and *appoggiatura,* used in the passage. Miss Ling comments that she is not even sure what the main topic of the paragraph is. Mrs. James surmises that the paragraph's topic is music because of two words: *tone* and *rhythmically.*

Mrs. Lopez then gives the teachers the following paragraph to read:

> The French system was an extension of Franconian principles. The long, the breve, and the semibreve could each be divided into either two or three notes of the next smaller value. The division of the long was called *mood,* that of the breve *time,* and that of the semibreve *prolation;* division was *perfect* if it was triple, *imperfect* if duple. (Grout, 1964, p. 79)

Again, the teachers do not comprehend what they have read. No one knows the word *prolation.* After reading the first sentence, Mrs. James thinks the paragraph is about the French government because of the words *Franconian, system,* and *principles.* However, the word *notes* in the second sentence convinces her this paragraph must also be about music. She has no idea that it in fact has to do with rhythm, because she does not know the terms *breve* and *semibreve*—even though she does know terms such as *quarter note* and *eighth note.* Mr. White, who has a strong background in phonics instruction, thinks the paragraph has to be about marking vowels sounds in words because of the term *breve.*

Mrs. Lopez then explains the reason for the exercise. She explains to the teachers that she has heard them complain about students not being able to comprehend science texts. She reminds them that science texts are dense with new vocabulary and with common words that have multiple meanings. When students encounter many new vocabulary words and do not have background knowledge of the topic, they cannot possibly comprehend the text. She suggests that they focus on vocabulary building for the rest of the school year. She directs the teachers to assess their students' vocabularies, to develop meaningful vocabulary-building strategies to use with small groups and individuals, and to share their strategies with other teachers.

INTRODUCTION

The National Research Council (1998) and the National Reading Panel (2000b) have identified vocabulary building as one of the six multifaceted factors of effective reading instruction. The federal government is requiring school districts to document student growth in vocabulary building in order for them to receive Title I funding. Therefore, it is imperative for teachers to understand (1) how proficient readers naturally enrich their vocabulary, (2) how to assess struggling readers' vocabulary, and (3) how to build struggling readers' vocabulary. This chapter will examine these three issues.

GENERAL BACKGROUND

Research indicates that there is a strong correlation between readers' vocabulary knowledge and their reading comprehension (Blachowicz & Fisher, 2002; Cooper, 2000; Davis, 1943, 1968; Nagy & Herman, 1987). In addition, Anderson and Freebody (1981) conclude that students' knowledge of words is the single greatest predictor of their reading comprehension. Proficient readers tend to have a large working vocabulary; therefore, comprehension comes easy for them. However, students who have a limited vocabulary often struggle with reading because even if they can decode words correctly, they do not understand what they have read.

Environment affects children's vocabulary. Children who have conversations with adults who have a rich vocabulary naturally learn a wide range of words, whereas children who lack such an environment have fewer opportunities to hear and learn new words. Compare for example the different conversational environments available to the two young children in the sample sentences below:

Adult speaking to Susie: I need to inflate the balloon.

Adult speaking to Mary: I need to blow up the balloon.

Adult speaking to Susie: Watch the yellow duckling go swoosh as it submerges its head into the water.

Adult speaking to Mary: Watch the yellow ducky put its head into the water.

Adult speaking to Susie: Listen to the chirping of the cardinal.

Adult speaking to Mary: Hear the bird singing.

Adult speaking to Susie: I appreciated the daisies you gave me.

Adult speaking to Mary: I love the flower you gave me.

In a meaningful context, Susie is learning words such as *duckling, submerge, appreciate,* and *chirping,* and learning specific names for birds and flowers; in contrast, even though Mary is having conversations with adults, she is not developing an advanced vocabulary.

VOCABULARY BUILDING

Students' vocabulary includes the words that they recognize in speech and print, and understand in context. "Recognition and meaning vocabularies develop simultaneously as students learn to read and write" (Cooper, 2000, p. 228). It is estimated that the average high school senior has a vocabulary of approximately 40,000 words (Nagy & Herman, 1987). This means that from grades one through twelve, students learn approximately 2,700 to 3,000 new words a year, or seven words a day (Snow, Burns, & Griffin, 1998). The three major ways students' vocabulary increases are through life experiences in and out of school, vicarious experiences, and direct instruction, which includes activities in which teachers play with words (Blachowicz & Fisher, 2002; Rasinski & Padak, 2000).

Life Experience

Students learn the meanings of words that are used within their communities. Students from rural areas understand words such as *barns, silo, combines,* and *corncribs*; students from urban areas understand words like *skyscraper, taxi,* and *subway.* They learn these words through daily interaction in their communities. Students from different communities also learn different meanings for the same words. To rural students, an *elevator* may be a large tower used to store grain; while to the urban student an *elevator* is a boxlike enclosure that carries passengers between different floors in a building.

Children and adults constantly learn new words through new experiences. The first time in a Mexican restaurant, they learn the differences between *tacos, burritos, quesadillas,* and *tortillas.* A trip to the ocean introduces children to *low tide, high tide,* and *sand bars.* Cooking helps them understand the difference between *creaming, grating,* and *blending.* A trip with parents or an adult to a large department store introduces children to different categories of products and the various items found in each department. As mentioned earlier, students immersed in vocabulary-rich environments naturally take ownership of a broad spectrum of words.

Vicarious Experience

The second way students' vocabulary increases is through vicarious experience. Such experience might include videos, CD-ROMs, movies, television, the Internet, and books. These media take students places they have not visited in person. Educational videos and educational television channels increase students' vocabulary as technical terms are used to explain concepts. Many movies and most television shows, however, do not increase students' vocabulary because these shows often focus on everyday life issues that only reflect what students already know (Rasinski & Padak, 2000).

Reading high-quality poems and books offers the greatest opportunity to learn new words because the "authors choose vocabulary that is rich and interesting—words that create a particular mood, feel, or texture" (Rasinski & Padak, 2000, p. 132). When listening to stories and poems that are above their reading level, students' vocabulary increases because they hear new words in context and become familiar with their pronunciation and meaning (Cohen, 1968; Rasinski & Padak, 2000).

Poems have especially rich language. Jack Prelutsky (1990b) introduces readers to vivid vocabulary in many of his humorous poems. In "The Turkey Shot Out of the Oven," he uses phrases as "partly *demolished* a chair," "It *ricocheted* into a corner," "completely *obscuring* the room," "It *blanketed* every appliance," and "thought with *chagrin* as I mopped." The poem is easy for students to grasp and the italicized words in the quoted phrases add to readers' vocabularies. In another poem, "Floradora Doe" (1984), Prelutsky introduces the reader to many synonyms for *talked—recited, chatted, murmured, yammered, babbled, lectured, whispered, tittered, gossiped, prattled,* and *regaled.*

Trevor Harvey, in his poem "The Curse of the Foul-Smelling Armpit" (1998), also uses a rich vocabulary to explore the odor of the infamous armpit. In this short poem, Harvey introduces students to seven useful words—*lurks, unsuspecting, despair, frantic, foul, performance,* and *grungy*—that are easily understood in the context of the poem. Of course, poetry should not be read for the sole purpose of increasing students' vocabulary; discussing a poet's diction, however, is a crucial part of analyzing and enjoying a poem.

Authors of stories and novels also use a rich, descriptive language to describe scenes and situations to students. In the seventh chapter of *26 Fairmount Avenue*, Tomie dePaola (1999) talks about "driving on the sea of mud" and "squishing through all the muddy water." In the same chapter, he introduces the reader to the concepts of *guardian angels* and *nor'easters*. In *Beauty*, Bill Wallace (1988) carefully chooses the following words to describe a rat: "A huge, gigantic rat was hiding under the sack. He glared up at me with his beady, ratty eyes. His scaly, ratty tail was curled up behind him" (p. 83). The words *gigantic, glared, beady,* and *scaly* give readers a disturbing word picture of this creature. After reading short passages such as these, you should explain unfamiliar words and discuss how authors' word choices develop the mood of their writing and create a vivid picture in the minds of their readers.

In her books on the parts of speech, Ruth Heller also uses distinctive vocabulary to create pictures in the readers' mind. In *Many Luscious Lollipops* (1989), she introduces the reader to *star-spangled, asteroidal, mesmerizing, soggy, remarkable,* and *regal.* In *A Cache of Jewels* (1987), she introduces students to new words or words used in new ways:

> Cache of jewels (Students may be familiar with the homophone *cash.*)
>
> Batch of bread
>
> School of fish (Students may only be familiar with the *school* house.)
>
> Gam of whales
>
> Bevy of beauties
>
> Muster of peacocks (Teachers may need to explain the difference between *muster* and *mustard.*)
>
> Host of angels
>
> Kindle of kittens
>
> Pod of peas
>
> Parcel of penguins (Students may recognize the word as a package.)
>
> Coven of witches
>
> Drift of swans (Students may be familiar with *drift* used as a verb.)
>
> Brood of chicks
>
> Clutch of eggs
>
> Pride of lions (Students may be familiar with *pride* used as an adjective.)
>
> Lock of hair (Students may be familiar with "Lock the door" or "The lock on the door.")
>
> Army of ants

P. D. Edwards (1996), in *Some Smug Slug* also uses evocative vocabulary in a book that introduces young readers to alliteration. Some of the words include *sauntered, slithered, snickered, sapphire, swooshing,* shrieked, and *scurrying.* As students hear the words in context, they become familiar with their pronunciations and meanings. You can explain these words by acting them out and then inviting students to do the same so they remember the word. After sharing these book and discussing the words, you can invite the students to "Saunter and not scurry in the halls!" instead of commanding them to "Walk in the halls!" When teachers use these new words in daily conversation, students begin to take ownership of them in their own conversations. Learning new words should be an adventure for students and not a boring task!

Direct Instruction

Students' vocabulary also grows through direct instruction or word play. Direct instruction need not mean giving students a list of words to look up in the dictionary and memorize. According to Nagy (1988), Stahl (1986), and Rasinski and Padak (2000), there are five essential ingredients for effective direct instruction of vocabulary:

1. New words must be learned in meaningful context.
2. The new word must be related to previous knowledge.
3. The new word or concept must be fully understood so students can use the word in new situations.
4. Students need to use, hear, and see the new word repeatedly.
5. Teachers need to enjoy learning new words with students and make learning new words fun.

As mentioned before, vocabulary words are best learned naturally through direct experiences (Rasinski & Padak, 2000). However, much academic knowledge cannot be conveyed in a natural everyday setting. Most new concepts that children learn in school are introduced through textbooks, and each new concept includes a new set of vocabulary words. Consider a few of the terms associated with the geologic concepts of volcanoes and caves: *eruption, lava, magma, stalactite,* and *stalagmite.*

When you teach new words explicitly in the context of the topic being studied, you need to take time to have the students pronounce the new word a number of times so it flows smoothly off their tongues. Once students can pronounce the word, you can explain the word by naming a familiar synonym or by linking it to a concept the students understand. After students grasp the meaning of the new word, you should explain how the word is used in different situations.

Teachers also need to be cheerleaders for students as they pronounce new words, learn their meanings, and use them in different situations. Because words with multiple syllables are often difficult for students to pronounce, you should give them many opportunities to learn to pronounce these words fluently. I have found that having children tap out the syllables with their fingers as they pronounce new words helps them to break the words into smaller pieces.

Teachers need to give children time to play with new words in a risk-free environment. "Jazz-Man," a poem by Eleanor Fargeon in *Noisy Poems*, Bennett (1987), features a number of troublesome words—*mingle, accordion,* and *pandemonium.* This last word is difficult for some children to pronounce because they are not accustomed to five syllable words. For direct instruction, you should first work on with the pronunciation of these words by pronouncing the words and having the students repeat them, tapping their desks with each syllable. Then explain the meaning of the three words as used in the poem. *Mingle,* the easiest word of the three, means "mixed together" in this poem; however, merely giving the definition is not enough. You should also explain how this word is used in daily conversation. For example, students mingle in the halls and when they do so, they do not move in straight lines. Instead they shift around, bumping into each other, and talking over each other; the scene of mingling students may be noisy and chaotic. *Accordion,* a concrete noun, may be easier for students to understand when you point to an illustration of the instrument and explain how it is played. *Pandemonium* is somewhat harder to explain. You might first say it means noise. However, pandemonium is more than mere noise; it is chaotic noise and movement. To convey these qualities, try evoking a scene when all the children are in the gym with no teacher in sight; they are all mingling about, and the noise and movement becomes loud and boisterous. This is the beginning of *pandemonium.* Give students time to discuss the word, enjoy its sound, and use it in sentences so they can take ownership of it.

Understanding some basic language concepts can be advantageous for students as they build their vocabularies. You can give students direct instruction in all of the concepts found in Figure 8.1 and explain more about these concepts when they encounter them in texts. After students understand them, they should be encouraged to find more examples as they read. Figure 8.2 lists books that emphasize many of the concepts defined in Figure 8.1. After sharing these books with students, you can encourage students to collect further examples of these concepts and use them to write their own books. All of the direct instruction in these concepts should take place in a fun learning environment so students learn to enjoy language and vocabulary building.

VOCABULARY OF STRUGGLING READERS

Students struggling in reading often have a limited vocabulary, which may be a result of limited early language experiences. Young children who spend a

---

FIGURE 8.1 Language concepts and examples.

Synonyms: Words that mean the same or nearly the same.

  raven and *black*

Antonyms: Words that have opposite meanings.

  mingle and *separate*

Homophones: Words that sound the same but may be spelled differently and have different meanings.

  would and *wood*; *which* and *witch*

Neologisms: New words that enter our vocabulary through extensive usage or for new inventions.

  bytes, silicon

Portmanteaus: New words formed by combining two existing words and omitting some of the letters.

  breakfast + *lunch* = *brunch*; *smoke* + *fog* = *smog*

Acronyms: Words formed from initials of other words.

  NATO = North Atlantic Treaty Organization

Euphemisms: A more pleasant sounding word used in place of a word with negative connotations.

  administrative assistant instead of *secretary*

Oxymoron: Two contradictory words or ideas used together in a word or phrase.

  jumbo shrimp; *awfully good*; *plastic silverware*

Regionalisms: Words associated with particular geographic regions.

  couch or *sofa*; *pop* or *soda*; *griddle cakes* or *pancakes*

Puns: Humorous expressions that highlight the multiple meanings of a word or two words that sound alike.

  He *ran* up the flag. Rain is saved in *cloud banks.*

Onomatopoeia: Words that sound like their meanings.

  Sploosh went the fish through the water!

FIGURE **8.2**   Books emphasizing various language concepts.

VOCABULARY

Four Famished Foxes and Fosdyke by P. D. Edwards (1995). New York: Harper Collins. (Alliteration; vocabulary building)

Some Smug Slug by P. D. Edwards (1996). New York: Harper Collins. (Alliteration; vocabulary building)

A Mink, a Fink, a Skating Rink: What Is a Noun? by B. Cleary (1999). Minneapolis, MN: Carolrhoda Books, Inc. (Nouns; vocabulary building)

Hairy, Scary, Ordinary: What Is an Adjective? by B. Cleary (2000). Minneapolis, MN: Carolrhoda Books, Inc. (Adjectives; vocabulary building)

A Cache of Jewels and Other Collective Nouns by R. Heller (1987). New York: Grosset & Dunlap. (Nouns; vocabulary building)

Many Luscious Lollipops: A Book About Adjectives by R. Heller (1989). New York: Grosset & Dunlap. (Adjectives; vocabulary building)

HOMONYMS AND PUNS

The King Who Rained by R. Gwynne (1970). New York: Simon and Schuster.

A Chocolate Moose for Dinner by F. Gwynne (1976). New York: Trumpet Club.

A Little Pigeon Toad by F. Gwynne (1988). New York: Trumpet Club.

IDIOMS

In a Pickle and Other Funny Idioms by M. Terban (1983). New York: Clarion Books.

Mad as a Wet Hen! And Other Funny Idioms by M. Terban (1987). New York: Clarion Books.

Punching the Clock: Funny Action Idioms by M. Terban (1990). New York: Clarion Books.

Amelia Bedelia series by P. Parish. New York: Harper Collins. (also emphasizes homonyms and puns)

OTHER

A Word Wizard by C. Falwell (1998). New York: Clarion Books. (Anagrams)

Guppies in Tuxedos: Funny Eponyms by M. Terban (1988). New York: Clarion Books. (Eponyms)

What's a Frank Frank? Tasty Homograph Riddles by G. Maestro (1984). New York: Clarion Books. (Homographs)

What's Mite Might? Homophone Riddles to Boost Your Word Power! by G. Maestro. (1986). (Homophones)

Noisy Poems edited by J. Bennett (1987). New York: Oxford Publishing Services. (Onomatopoeia)

Opposites by M. Novick & S. Harlin (2001). San Diego, CA: Advantage. (Synonyms and antonyms)

---

great amount of time listening to and discussing stories read by an adult have an advantage over children who lack these experiences. Children who have had limited conversations with adults come to school with a limited vocabulary. It is your responsibility to help provide them with a language-rich environment and help them as they increase their vocabularies.

When students with underdeveloped language come to school, they need to be immersed in rich language experiences. These experiences include, but are not limited to, shared reading, experiments, field trips, videos, and CD-ROMs. During the field trips and after viewing videos, conversation between adults and students is important. Be sure to use the pertinent technical terms and invite students to pronounce the words with you. Lev Vygotsky's (1962) theory of the zone of proximal development stresses the importance of students interacting with someone who thoroughly understands the concept to be learned. The "zone" is the gap between what students know or can express on their own and what

they know when working and talking with an informed adult. According to Vygotsky, what students understand today when working with an adult, they will understand by themselves in the future. For this reason, it is important that during and after all the experiences and learning events listed above, students should be given ample opportunity to ask questions and discuss new concepts.

Increasing Students' Limited Vocabulary

Many studies have been conducted on how students best acquire a wide vocabulary. Beck and McKeown (1991) group this work into four basic positions on how students best acquire vocabulary: (1) through reading (Fielding, Wilson, & Anderson, 1986; Nagy & Herman, 1987), (2) through context (Jenkins, Stein, & Wysocki, 1984; Sternberg, 1987), (3) through dictionary use (Schatz & Baldwin, 1986), and (4) through direct instruction (Beck, McKeown, & Omanson, 1987; Graves,

1987; Stahl & Kapinus, 1991). Since each of these positions is supported by research, you should consider all four when you work with struggling readers.

Reading

One of your first tasks in building struggling students' vocabularies is to read to and with them and explain the definitions of new words within the text. Many authors define words in the text. They use various techniques to include a synonym or definition of the new term in the sentence. Figure 8.3 lists various examples of how authors share the meanings of unknown words with the reader. You should explain the different ways authors may define words in their texts, by using specific examples from the students' reading.

Context

Another way to teach students how to learn the meaning of words is to focus on contextual clues. Start by teaching them to read to the end of the sentence and to make a guess about what the word may mean. Sometimes they may need to read to the end of the paragraph to get the meaning of the word. Consider the word *brusque*. This word may be new to many fifth graders; however, they can get a good idea of its meaning when reading the following paragraph:

> "What's wrong with Joan?" Lynn asked.
>
> "I don't know. Why?" Deena replied.
>
> "Last night she was so brusque. When I saw her in the grocery store and asked her how she was, she replied, 'None of your business!' and stomped away."

After reading this short passage to the students, you can ask them what they think the word means. Most students will guess that it means "rude." By affirming their guesses, you will teach them that often readers learn new words from the context of the passage without using the dictionary. After sharing this sample passage, you should then repeat this procedure with examples from the material the students are currently reading. Once the students can pronounce a word and understand its meaning, you can invite them to use it in a new sentence in order to demonstrate that they understand the word. Saying the word a number of times and using the word in a new sentence gives students a sense of ownership.

Dictionary Usage

The third way students learn words is through dictionary usage. It is important that they use dictionaries that are appropriate for their age and grade level. A collegiate dictionary is daunting and inappropriate for a second grader or even a struggling fifth grader. However, many children's dictionaries are available and learning to use them can be an enjoyable experience. *Scholastic's Dictionary for Children, Macmillan Dictionary for Children,* and the *DK Merriam-Webster Children's Dictionary* have illustrations that help explain complex concepts. The print size of the Merriam-Webster dictionary is somewhat small for second and third graders, but the other two have a print size that reflects the texts that children read.

Other helpful reference books are a thesaurus and specialized dictionaries. Thesauruses help children as they learn synonyms and antonyms for words. *The Clear and Simple Thesaurus Dictionary* by Harriet Wittels and Joan Greisman (1996) is clear and concise with an appropriate print size for elementary students. *My First Phonics Book* (1996), created in association with Diane McGuinness (TK) is a helpful tool to teach students the different combinations for the vowel sounds. The clear photographs with color-coded letters make clear to students that one vowel sound can be spelled in a number of different ways. For example, the long /e/ sound is explored through the following words: *busy, bee, seal, shield, scene,* and *monkey,* among others. The discussion includes a short passage, using many of the words in context.

There are some basic components of a dictionary that you should make sure to explain to children.

FIGURE 8.3 Ways that authors define words within texts.

Definition in an appositive phrase: The *waif, a homeless child,* longed for a ten-speed bicycle.

Definition within the sentence: A *vagabond who wanders from place to place* is also called a tramp.

Synonym: Mary does not *procrastinate* because she never *postpones* her assignments.

Antonym: After the storm, the *wild* sea became *serene.*

Situation: Juan will be the *valedictorian* speaker because he *ranks first* in the senior class.

Ann is so vain; she is constantly bragging about her excellent grades and good looks.

These include guidewords, pronunciation guides, parts of speech, etymologies, orders of definitions, synonyms, and antonyms. You should teach each of these components separately and facilitate guided and independent practice sessions to ensure that students master each of these components. For example, when children use a dictionary to help them pronounce unfamiliar words, they need to be familiar with the various diacritical markings. You should begin with the known and progress to the unknown. Show students how the word *go* is marked in the dictionary and then show them that the word *so* is marked in the same manner. Then you can present entries for the words *do* and *to* and explain that even though these words also end in *o*, they are pronounced differently, and thus the diacritical markings are different. Once students understand the markings on known words, you can choose a one-syllable word that is unknown to the students and ask them to pronounce it.

To help students with definitions, you should again start with what students know and move to what they don't. Since glossaries in concept books and textbooks usually omit etymologies and provide only the definition necessary to understand that text, it may be easier for you to begin with glossaries. Once students are comfortable using glossaries, however, you should explicitly teach students how to choose the definition that fits the text, to prepare them for using dictionaries. For struggling readers, a personal dictionary for each content area may be helpful. As they are introduced to new concepts in each subject area, these readers can write down the word along with a synonym or definition in their own words.

Drawing an illustration will also help them remember the meaning of the word. The Intervention section of this chapter includes some specific activities to help struggling readers with dictionary usage.

Direct Instruction

This chapter has already discussed the importance of explicit instruction. Since CD-ROMs are often used in various subjects, especially social studies and science, it is imperative that students understand the hierarchy of words that organize most informational materials; some words are the headings, while other words fit under those headings; still others make up subheadings and individual topics. In order to teach this concept to students, it is best to begin with information that they already understand, such as departments within a department store. Figure 8.4 presents a graphic organizer that teachers can complete with students. The purpose of this exercise is to get students to understand the hierarchy of concepts that will later help them with vocabulary building in various subjects.

Accepting Students and Their Limited Vocabulary

When working with students who have underdeveloped oral language skills, you need to accept the students and their vocabularies and be patient as they encounter and learn new words. Also, you should work simultaneously to develop students' oral and aural language ability as they develop reading skills.

FIGURE 8.4 Graphic organizer to demonstrate hierarchy of word relationships.

Web of Various Departments within a Super Center

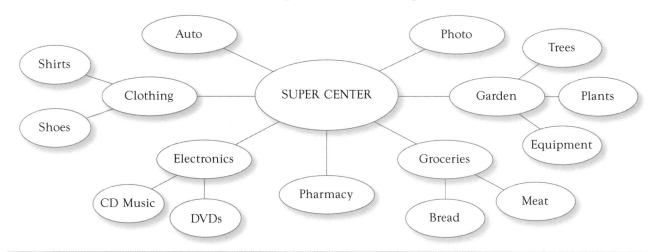

Students with weak language experiences should not be isolated from other children, but be included in small group and large group learning situations so they can hear words in meaningful contexts. However, students with underdeveloped language skills must have realistic expectations about their learning rate (Wilson & Cleland, 1989). Therefore, you also need to provide these students with special help in a risk-free environment that focuses on their strengths and successes and minimizes their weaknesses and failures. Later in this chapter you will find some strategies that can be used in these tutoring settings.

ASSESSMENT

Much of vocabulary assessment is initiated by teachers closely observing children's oral language capability in conversation and in small groups. When teachers detect students with limited vocabularies, they can use a number of assessment instruments.

Informal Assessment

You can frequently determine a pre-readers' weak vocabulary through conversation. Pre-readers with limited vocabulary often do not use specific terms in conversation. They may call any form of money—nickels, dimes, and quarters—just *money*. Sedans, SUVs, and dump trucks are all *cars*. If you detect a weak vocabulary in a student, you can perform the following assessment, starting with pictures from magazines mounted on construction paper. The pictures might be of different types of vehicles (cars, pick-ups, semi-trucks, recreational vehicles, and so on), various types of workers (firemen, police, farmer, nurse, doctor, dentist, and so on), or pictures of various kinds of animals or plants. You can prepare a checklist of the object names and then either name the object and ask the child to point to it or invite the child to first name all the different items in the category (e.g., tulips, sunflowers, roses, daises, and so on) that he knows. If the child is weak in naming specific objects, you can arrange for a tutor to take time to "talk" with him about pictures in books or about more mounted magazine pictures with specific names of the items written on them. Later, the child can go through this collection of pictures and practice reading the names.

Other informal vocabulary assessment instruments are the cloze test for older students, maze tests, zip tests, and synonym tests for younger students, and checklists, based on state standards.

Cloze tests, discussed in Chapter 3, indicate if students have the requisite vocabulary background for a particular passage. In the cloze test, the teacher deletes every fifth word or all new concept words necessary to understand a passage. Students must supply the word for each blank using only context and background knowledge. The teacher can then determine if students know specific terms related to the topic or if they merely know general ones. For example, in a passage about the jungle, the teacher might delete the word *panther*. The rest of the sentence indicates the topic is a *panther* and not a lion; however, the student's response is *lion*. The teacher concludes that the student's vocabulary lacks the technical word *panther*.

In maze tests, also discussed in Chapter 3, students are given three possible answers to fill blanks in sentences. When teachers attempt to assess students' technical vocabulary on a topic, they make one of choices for the blank the general term and one choice the specific term. The third choice is not associated with the topic. Teachers can then determine if students are familiar with the specific term. For example, a passage might be about a farm with horses and includes pictures of horses. The maze sentence reads: "Mary wanted to ride the (*animal, horse, zebra*)." The synonym cloze test is another form of maze test. A synonym is added above the deleted word and three choices are again provided for each deleted word. The synonym gives readers an excellent clue, but teachers can still assess students' technical vocabulary. The following is an example from this kind of test:

hungry

The basketball player was (*ravenous, exotic, zealous*) after the game.

The zip test, designed by Blachowicz and Fisher (2002), can be used for assessment, as well as for instruction. In the zip test, the words chosen for deletion are masked with adhesive labels. The readers attempt to supply the word and then "zip" off the label to receive immediate feedback. This permits teachers to assess students' vocabulary and students to continue reading with a sense of understanding.

Checklists, based on state standards, can assist teachers as they assess students' vocabulary growth throughout the year. You can use this type of checklist at the beginning of the year to assess what the children know and at the end of each quarter to assess which students need extra help with vocabulary. The partial checklist in Figure 8.5 is based on data from Ms. Lorenz's first-grade class. It appears from the checklist that after the first quarter most students in the class use their knowledge of individual words with compound words to predict meanings and that they have learned to use suffixes to determine word meanings. The complete checklist in Appendix C.30 is based on Florida's state standards for the first grade.

FIGURE 8.5 — Vocabulary growth checklist for first grade based on Florida's state standards.

TEACHER Ms, Lorenz   Date 10—7

+ = always   X = sometimes   O = seldom/never

STANDARD	Amy	Leigh	Marisa	Lauren	Candace	Kas	Kirby	Katie	Carly	Faith	Summer	April	Hunter	Logan	Brett	Zachary	Allie	Andy
1. Knows meaning of common words within basic categories.	+	+	X	X	X	X	X	X	X	+	X	+	+	+	+	X	+	+
2. Uses knowledge of individual words in unknown compound words to predict their meaning.	+	+	X	X	+	+	+	X	X	+	X	+	+	+	+	X	+	+
3. Uses resources/references to build word meaning (e.g., beginning dictionaries and available technology).	X	O	X	X	O	O	O	O	X	O	O	X	+	+	+	X	X	X
4. Uses knowledge of suffixes (-er, -est, -ful) to determine meaning of words.	+	+	X	X	X	+	+	X	X	X	X	X	+	+	+	X	+	+

Source: Florida Department of Education, www.firn.edu/doe/sas/fcat.htm.

Formal Assessment

Most formal vocabulary assessments are multiple-choice tests. Some tests require students to match a word with its definition. Other tests ask students to choose the word that best fits the sentence. Students are given three choices and they must select the correct word (e.g., "John took the [escalator, generator, mobile] to the third floor in the department store).

The Peabody Picture Vocabulary Test–Revised, discussed in Chapter 3, is an individual test that can be used to assess students' receptive vocabulary. The test has four pictures on a page. The teacher says the word corresponding to one of the pictures and the student must point to the correct picture. The test begins with simple noun pictures that most students know—words such as *car, ball, money,* and *mail.* The test becomes progressively more difficult through the use of words such as *attire, incisor, convergence,* and *bumptious.* Figure 8.6 lists some other formal reading tests that have vocabulary sub-tests.

FIGURE 8.6 — Formal reading tests with vocabulary sub-tests.

STANDARDIZED ACHIEVEMENT TESTS

Iowa Test of Basic Skills (Grades K–8)

Stanford Achievement Tests–Ninth Edition (Grades K–13)

Gates-Mac-Ginitie Reading Tests (Grades K–12)

Metropolitan Achievement Tests (Grades K–12)

Comprehension Tests of Basic Skills, U and V (Grades K–12)

California Achievement Tests (Grades K–9)

GROUP DIAGNOSTIC TESTS

Stanford Diagnostic Reading Test (Grades 1–12)

Iowa Silent Reading Test (Grade 6–Adult)

Gates-Mac-Ginitie Reading Tests (Grades 1–9)

Nelson-Denny Reading Tests (Grade 9–Adult)

INDIVIDUAL DIAGNOSTIC READING TESTS

Woodcock Reading Mastery Test (Grades 1–12)

Durrell Analysis of Reading Difficulties–Third Edition (Grades K–12)

Gates-McKillop-Horowitz Tests (Grades 1–12)

Intervention

As noted earlier in this chapter, learning words in isolation is rarely beneficial for students. The practice of giving students ten vocabulary words on Monday and testing them on Friday often leads to frustration and no sense of personal ownership of the words. Words learned in the context of a social studies or science unit or from stories and poems are words students will use and remember. All of the strategies explained in this section, with the exception of Troy's Super Center, should be associated with topics being studied.

Language Experience Approach (LEA)

Language experience approach (LEA) can be traced back to the late 1930s (Lamoreaux & Lee, 1943). LEA was widely used in New Zealand in the late 1960s and 1970s (Ashton-Warner, 1963; Holdaway, 1979) as an effective technique to introduce children to their oral vocabulary. In the 1970s, Roach Van Allen (1976) used it as an approach to teaching literacy in the United States. Today, LEA is a technique used in many different contexts. In LEA, reading and writing and the other language arts are viewed as interrelated and the experiences of children are used as the basis for the material that is used for reading.

For example, after a student and teacher share an experience (a science experiment; a schoolyard safari focused on environmental noise or identifying types of trees, flowers, or insects), they discuss what they have seen. Throughout the discussion, the teacher uses technical terms so the student begins to use them as well. After the discussion, the teacher serves as a scribe for the student as he creates a web about the experience. Then the student dictates sentences to the teacher about the experience. The teacher writes the text in the exact way the student dictates it. He reads the passage back to the teacher. During the reading, they discuss sentences that are awkward (grammatically incorrect) and change them. When used for vocabulary instruction, the purpose of the LEA is for a student to dictate a passage that includes words from his expanding vocabulary and then read it back to the teacher.

All of the following ideas are variations of the language experience approach and can be done with individual struggling readers. The teacher acts as the scribe for each activity, while the student reads and rereads the passage.

WORDLESS BOOKS

ACTIVITY

(GRADES 1–6)

Wordless books (see Appendix A.4 for a list) are useful for students with limited language experiences and students who are learning English. Some wordless books, *Deep in the Forest* (1976) by Brinton Turkle and *The Bear and the Fly* (1976) by Paula Winter are appropriate for younger children, while older children enjoy *Freefall* (1988), *Tuesday* (1991), *Sector 7* (1997), and *The Three Pigs* (2001) all by David Wiesner. When using wordless books, talk through the book a number of times with the student. During these discussions, you point out different aspects of the pictures, introducing new words to the student. After talking through the story a number of times, have the student dictate a story to you. Using adhesive notes, you can post the text on each page. After the dictation, it is important for the student to read and reread her story a number of times in order to learn the new vocabulary words in print.

ACTIVITY

SCIENCE EXPERIMENT

(GRADES 1–3)

After reading *The Empty Pot* (1990) by Demi, help your students plant lima beans in clear plastic cups. Each day have the children dictate notes on the new growth they observe. As you discuss the growth with them, you should be using technical terms like *soil* (instead of *dirt*), *seed* (instead of *bean*), *sprout, embryo,* and *root.* Each day the students should read back over their previous entries. Note: lima beans grow quickly so students with short attention spans see results very quickly.

ACTIVITY

LISTENING WALK

(GRADES 1–3)

After reading *The Listening Walk* (1961) by Paul Showers, take a walk on the playground or in the halls of the school with your students. As you walk, you and the children should discuss what you hear. Again, you should focus on using vivid descriptions so that the children's vocabulary is enlarged (e.g., *chatter* of voices, *squeaky* wheels, *screeching* tires, *whirling* water sprinklers, and so on). You should put each idea into a sentence so the text becomes a predictable text. For example, while in the school, you can begin each sentence with "In the school hallway, I hear _____ and _____."
Out on the playground, the sentence pattern can be as follows: "Outside my school, I hear _____ and _____.

ACTIVITY

SCHOOLYARD SAFARI

(GRADES 1–4)

In the fall or spring when there are signs of changing seasons, you and your students can go outside and write a book based on this pattern. With this activity, you should encourage vivid use of adjectives (e.g., *decomposing leaves, howling winds, multicolored hues,* or *budding blossoms*).

On the playground, I see _____, _____, and _____.

On the playground, I hear _____, _____, and _____.

On the playground, I smell _____, _____, and _____.

On the playground, I feel _____, _____, and _____.

ACTIVITY

CLOUD FORMATIONS

(GRADES 1–2)

After reading the book *It Looked Like Spilt Milk* (1947) by Charles Shaw, go outside with your students to look at the shapes of the clouds. When working with shapes, ask the children to determine if they are circular, triangular, oval, or rectangular. Then have the children write a book with the pattern that the book uses: "It looked like spilt milk. But it wasn't spilt milk, it was a _____."

ACTIVITY

OBJECT DESCRIPTIONS

(GRADES 2–3)

With this activity, give the child an object that is easy to describe. After she touches, smells, and examines the object, ask her to describe it with vivid adjectives. Some suggested objects are marshmallows, cotton balls, or Nerf balls.

CATEGORIZING: TROY'S SUPER CENTER

Categorizing words helps students associate new words with known words. To teach students how to categorize words, begin with familiar topics such as foods in a grocery store or items found in a large department store.

1. Duplicate the game board in Appendix D.19 and glue it on a file folder. Laminate it for longer usage.
2. Duplicate the cards in Appendix D.19 on card stock paper, laminate, and cut out.
3. Turn the cards face down on the table.
4. Have the student pick up a card and place it in the correct department.
5. The goal is for the student to get all cards in the correct departments.

CATEGORIZING

Older students also need practice in categorizing to connect known words to unknown words. One activity is to give main headings of areas that have been studied and ask students to name as many items as possible for each category. Figure 8.7 includes some examples of categories.

FIGURE 8.7 Categorizing.

Name as many items as possible for each category.

AIR TRANSPORTATION	WATER TRANSPORTATION	ROAD TRANSPORTATION	DOGS
airplane	ship	bike	Collie
hot air balloon	boat	car	Retriever
space ship	wave runner	truck	Labrador
helicopter	sail boat	RV	Poodle
	ocean liner	roller skates	

POETS	AUTHORS	GENRE	MINERALS
Bruce Lansky	Avi	poems	iron
Shel Silverstein	Gary Paulsen	science fiction	nickle
Brog Bagert	Anna Meyer	realistic fiction	zinc
	Richard Peck	historical fiction	copper
	Sharon Creech	plays	
	Lois Lowry	biography	
	Linda Sue Parks	autobiography	

VEGETABLES	FRUITS	CARBOHYDRATES
carrot	apple	bread
potato	orange	rice
squash	banana	pasta
pea	peach	cereal
corn	pear	

ACTIVITY

POSSIBLE SENTENCES

(GRADES 2–8)

Possible Sentences, designed by Moore and Moore (1986) is a strategy to preview new words from a story or concept book.

1. Explain six or seven new words to the students.
2. Give them an additional six or seven words that they know.
3. Ask them to write sentences, using two or more of the words from the two lists in each sentence.
4. After they read the passage you have been previewing, have students decide which of their sentences are "true" in regard to word usage.
5. Ask them to change the incorrect sentences so all information is correct.

Figure 8.8 shows an example of words to give and sentences to have students write before they read Tomie dePaola's book about clouds. Both students are applying the knowledge they know about clouds, and both will need to modify their sentences after they read the book.

FIGURE 8.8   Possible sentences based on new vocabulary.

NEW VOCABULARY WORDS	KNOWN WORDS
cumulus	clouds
stratus	rain
cirrus	weather
nimbostratus	thunder

Nathaniel's sentences: We can tell what kind of weather is coming by looking at the clouds. Cumulus and stratus clouds bring us rain. Cirrus and nimbostratus clouds bring us thunder and storms.

Anton's sentences: Some clouds do not bring bad weather, but other clouds do bring us bad weather. Cumulus clouds are just white, pretty clouds that come on sunny days. Stratus clouds look like rib cages and bring us rain. Cirrus and nimbostratus clouds are black clouds that bring us thunder and hurricanes.

ACTIVITY

ANALOGIES

(GRADES 3–8)

Standardized tests often assess students' vocabulary through analogies; therefore, it is advantageous to introduce struggling readers to analogies they will encounter in these tests. Analogies are written as *A : B : C : D* (say, "A is to B as C is to D"). Analogies display the ways that words are related. Following are six relationships that elementary students are asked to complete on standardized tests:

1. Part to whole: *Leaf* is to *tree* as *hand* is to *human.*
2. Synonym: *Black* is to *raven* as *red* is to *crimson.*
3. Antonym: *Black* is to *white* as *up* is to down.
4. Action: *Bird* is to *fly* as *fish* is to *swim.*
5. Cause and effect: *Hurricane* is to *wind* as *blizzard* is to *snow.*

6. Geography: *London* is to *England* as *Washington, D. C.* is to the *United States.*

Once students are familiar with analogies, they can write their own. Writing analogies helps students understand the words at a deeper level. Students must be able to justify each analogy by explaining the relevant relationship. Following are some examples of analogies, written by fourth graders who were studying analogies before they took standardized tests. The teacher knew that if students could write their own, they would better understand how to complete them on the test.

Cloud is to sky as dew is to _____ (grass or earth).

Seed is to apple as pit is to _____ (cherry, peach, apricot).

Barn is to cow as ____ is to bird (nest).

ORIGIN OF WORDS

ACTIVITY

(GRADES 3–6)

Exploring the origin of words with struggling readers gets them interested in new vocabulary, especially if teachers choose familiar words with interesting origins. Students and teachers may find it fascinating that candy is named after the seventeenth-century Prince Charles de Conde (pronounced con DAY), who loved sugary treats. His chef glazed bits of meats and vegetables with egg whites, sugar, and nuts so the young prince would eat the "healthy" foods. Older struggling readers may enjoy learning how the bikini swimsuit got its name, and younger children may enjoy learning how hamburgers and sandwiches got their names. *Guppies in Tuxedos: Funny Eponyms* (1988) by Marvin Terban is a book that explains the origins of many words that are familiar to all students.

Often schools are named after national or state heroes. Exploring the background of these heroes can also be fun. For instance, many schools named after heroes in the Oklahoma City area have some interesting stories—Angie Debo Elementary, Cooper Middle School, Gene Autry Elementary, Sequoyah Middle School, and Cheyenne Middle School. You can encourage students to learn about local heroines or heroes and create books about them. You might also encourage them to research the origins of words that interest them and write their own booklets. "Exploring the origin of words with students help them develop indelible memories as they link specific words with stories of the words' origin" (Rasinski & Padak, 2000, p. 141).

CROSSWORD PUZZLE

ACTIVITY

(GRADES 2–5)

Many students enjoy doing and making crossword puzzles. Crossword puzzles most often focus on definitions or synonyms; however, you can construct them using antonyms. The best crossword puzzles are those based on words found in books that students have read. Marguerite Lewis (1986) has collected a book of crossword puzzles based on Caldecott winners. Each puzzle is in the shape of the main topic of the book. For example, the puzzle for *Tuesday* (1991) by David Wiesner is in the shape of a frog.

To make crossword puzzles, select the words that are important for the reader to remember, identify shared letters among them, and assemble them in the form of a puzzle. Using large-ruled graph paper makes this task easier. Then assign numbers to the blanks and write the definitions based on the numbers in the puzzle. See Figure 8.9 for a completed crossword puzzle using the language terms from Figure 8.1 (created using PuzzleMaker.com). This puzzle is for fifth-grade students. Software is also available for creating crossword puzzles.

FIGURE 8.9 Crossword puzzle based on literary terms.

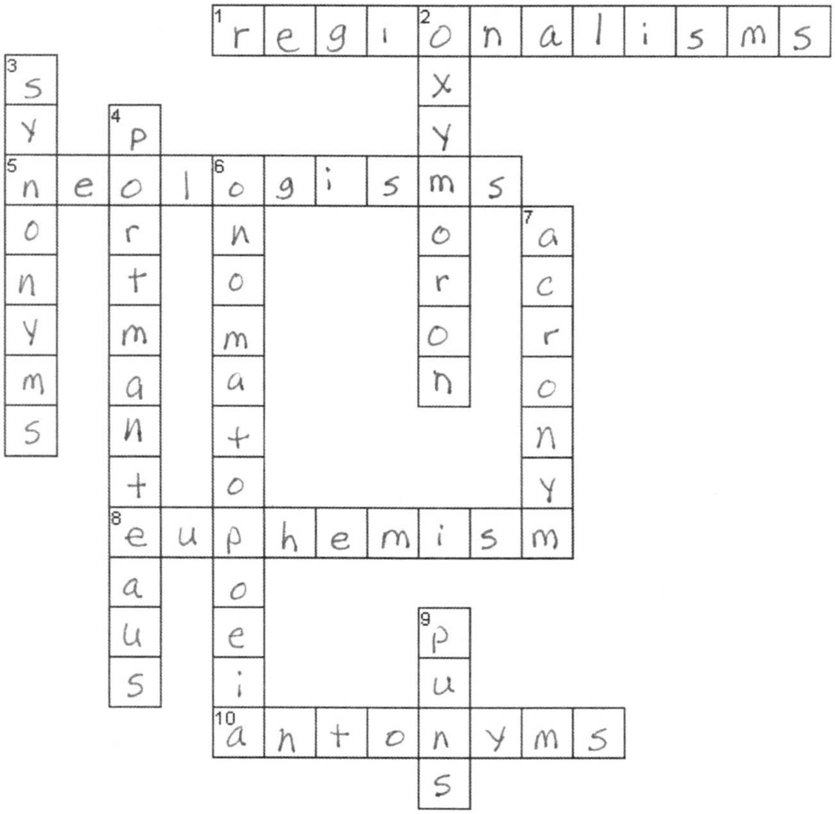
1 regionalisms
2 oxymoron
3 synonyms
4 portmanteaus
5 neologisms
6 onomatopoeia
7 acronym
8 euphemism
9 puns
10 antonyms

ACROSS

1. Words associated with particular geographic regions.
5. New words that enter our vocabulary through extensive usage or for new inventions.
8. A more pleasant sounding word used in place of a word with negative connotations.
10. Words that have opposite meanings.

DOWN

2. Two contradictory words or ideas used together in a word or phrase.
3. Words that mean the same or nearly the same.
4. New words formed by combining two existing words and omitting some of the letters.
6. Words that sound like their meaning.
7. Word formed from the initial letters of other words.
9. Humorous expressions that highlight multiple meanings of a word or two words that sound alike.

ACTIVITY

SYNONYM/DEFINITION CONCENTRATION

(GRADES 2–8)

In this activity, you should first read and discuss with students a story or informational book that includes new vocabulary. The purpose of this version of concentration is to have students match the word with its definition or its synonym.

1. During the reading, explain any vocabulary word that students do not understand.
2. After reading the book, choose 10 to 15 important words from the text and write them on square cards.

3. Create an equal number of cards with a synonym or concise definition of each word.
4. All 20 to 30 cards are turned face down.
5. Have a student turn over the cards one-by-one and match the words with the correct synonym or definition.

This activity can be used to prepare students for a test over a unit or chapter. Two or three students can engage in this activity or a teacher or tutor can watch and encourage a student as she matches the terms. Mr. Watts designed the cards in Figure 8.10 as a way for his sixth-grade students to recall the terms they learned during their unit on mythology.

FIGURE 8.10   Sample synonym/definition concentration cards.

Achilles	Amazon	Agamemnon	Atlas	Cassandra	Electra
Helen of Troy	Hercules	Jason	Muses	Odysseus	Paris
Pegasus	Penelope	Phoenix	Priam	Prometheus	Saturn
Greek warrior who could be killed only by a wound to the heel.	Greek king who led his men in the Trojan War.	Female Greek warriors who were powerfully built and ferocious.	Giant who could hold earth and sky on his shoulders.	Prophet in Troy whom no one believed.	Agamemnon's daughter, who helped kill her mother.
Daughter of Zeus and Leda.	Son of Zeus and Alcmene, who showed his strength doing the impossible.	Greek hero who found the golden fleece of a magical ram.	Nine daughters of Zeus and Mnemosyne, each representing a different art.	Greek, also called Ulysses.	He killed Achilles with an arrow.
Winged horse that flew above the earth.	Wife of Odysseus; symbol of fidelity.	Bird that could set itself on fire.	King of Troy.	Giant who stole fire from gods and gave it to humans.	Father of Jupiter.

ACTIVITY

WORDO

(GRADES 2–5)

Wordo cards are made like Bingo cards. See Appendix D.15 for a blank sample. Wordo is a good strategy to use with a small group of struggling readers so that you can check students' answers as they cover each word.

1. Write 25 to 30 words from a particular unit or book on the blackboard.
2. Ask students to write 24 randomly selected words from that list on their cards, leaving the middle space as a free space.
3. Read a sentence with the target word as a blank in the sentence.
4. Have students cover the correct word that fits the blank with a marker.

The goal is for students to get five words in a straight row, column, or diagonal line. You can vary the activity by reading the definitions of the words or their synonyms. For example, if the activity is based on literary terms (e.g., *oxymoron, onomatopoeia,* and *puns*), you can read: "Words that sound like their meaning are called _____." The students would find *onomatopoeia* on their card and cover it.

ACTIVITY

SCATTERGORY

(GRADES 2–6)

Scattergory helps students recall words that are associated with different conceptual categories. A sample of a Scattergory card is found in Appendix D.20. It is best if the card is duplicated on card stock and laminated so the cards can be reused throughout the year. To play, follow these instructions:

1. Write five to ten initial letters or consonant blends in the left column of the card.
2. Choose or have students choose categories and write them across the top row.
3. Ask students to fill in the card, working within a specified time limit.

Students should strive for the greatest number of unique words (words no other student has chosen). You can use this strategy in a tutoring situation by having the student fill in the card in a limited amount of time. It is important to remember that competition may discourage struggling readers because they rarely win in a group setting.

ACTIVITY

MULTIPLE MEANING RACE TRACK

(GRADES 2–5)

Multiple meaning race track is a strategy to highlight the multiple meanings of commonly used words. The goal of the activity is for struggling readers to give as many definitions as possible for a set of words chosen by the teacher.

1. Duplicate the racetrack in Appendix D.21 on stock card paper and laminate it.
2. Make a list of words that have multiple meanings and have been introduced to the student in various texts. See the sample list in Figure 8.11.
3. Write the words on index cards.
4. To play, have students draw cards from the deck and give as many multiple definitions as possible. Students move their game pieces one space for each correct definition. If students give an incorrect definition, they must move one space backward.
5. As on any racetrack, there are other obstacles that drivers may encounter.

| FIGURE **8.11** | Possible word list for multiple meaning race track. |

run	box	wind
chair	grate	bow
tire	hanger	frog
wing	exhaust	ring
minute		

HINK PINKS

ACTIVITY

(GRADES 2–8)

Riddles increase students' creative thinking. Hink pinks are word riddles that have two-word answers that rhyme. The two words each have one syllable. The following are hink pinks:

What is an unhappy father called? A sad dad.

What did the fish say to the bait? Squirm worm.

What is a sneaky insect called? A sly fly.

Hinky pinkies are like hink pinks; however the two words in the answer have two syllables. Some examples are the following.

What is messy writing? A sloppy copy.

What do you call a hilarious rabbit? A funny bunny.

What do you call a carpenter? A hammer slammer.

Hiniky pinikies, of course, have answers with three syllables. Examples are the following:

What do you call a soft, deluxe place of execution? Velveteen guillotine.

What do you call an evil clergyman? Sinister minister.

By folding an index card in half, students can create these riddles for classmates. They write the question on the top fold with the answer inside. Writing hink pinks encourages students to think of rhyming words and to understand syllables.

DICTIONARY: GUIDE WORDS

ACTIVITY

(GRADES 2–5)

To introduce students to the guide words printed on the top margins of dictionary pages, start with initial letters of words. Next, move to the first two letters, and then to the first three or four letters. When introducing students to guide words, give them two guide words and a list of five words that begin with the same initial letter and two words that do not begin with the initial letter of the guide words. Then proceed to activities that require students to look at the second letter. Figure 8.12 presents samples of the progression.

FIGURE 8.12 — Which words belong on the page?

Place a check on the blanks in front of the words that you would find on the dictionary page appearing between the two guide words.

dad and dog	saw and snake	juice and junk	lake and lamp
☐ dig	☐ stove	☐ Jupiter	☐ lamb
☐ do	☐ silver	☐ jump	☐ land
☐ go	☐ steal	☐ just	☐ lance
☐ bee	☐ see	☐ June	☐ lame
☐ deed	☐ swan	☐ jungle	☐ lament
☐ did	☐ scissors	☐ junior	☐ lambkin
☐ deer	☐ school	☐ jury	☐ lamprey

ACTIVITY — DICTIONARY: LOCATING THE CORRECT DEFINITION

(GRADES 3–5)

This activity helps children learn to choose the appropriate definition for a word from the multiple definitions the dictionary gives. Using a children's dictionary, write some sentences with words that have multiple meanings. Students must locate the word in the dictionary and find the correct definition. Following are some examples:

1. Father used a *saw* to cut down the tree.
2. We all *saw* the movie.
3. *Wind* the string around your finger.
4. The *wind* always blows in Oklahoma.
5. The *bow* in the little girl's hair was red.
6. Please *bow* to the queen.
7. The *bow* and arrow are gifts from my uncle.

All vocabulary-building strategies must be completed in a risk-free environment. You should make the activities enjoyable for students. At times, students can lead the activity and you can "play." By reversing roles, students are more likely to catch your enthusiasm.

TECHNOLOGY

There are many electronic books that provide word pronunciations and verbal definitions as students read the stories and poems on CD-ROM. Discis Knowledge Research's electronic books can be set to read books to the student or the computer voice can be turned off for the student to read the text from the screen. When reading the texts by themselves, students can click once for the pronunciation of an unknown word and twice for its definition. Discis books keep track of the list of words that the reader selects. These words can later be used for review. The Living Books series by Broderbund (see Appendix A.7) highlights the text as the computer "reads" the book. When readers click on various objects in the picture, the objects become animated. The animation is intended to aid students in learning the meanings of unfamiliar words. Many of the electronic books include games that aid vocabulary building, spelling, writing, and comprehension. The games make learning enjoyable for students.

CONCLUDING THOUGHTS

Because research indicates that there is a strong correlation between readers' vocabulary knowledge and their reading comprehension, it is imperative that you assess and facilitate students' vocabulary growth.

Students build their vocabulary through life's experiences, vicarious experiences, and direct instruction. Many students' vocabularies are weak because they lack life's experiences and vicarious experiences; therefore, they do not have the vocabulary necessary to comprehend grade-level texts. Work with these students in a meaningful context, focusing on building their vocabularies. As you discuss topics using content-specific terms, have students pronounce the words correctly, discuss the definitions, and use the new words until they have ownership of them.

COMPREHENSION
OF NARRATIVE TEXT

Only the curious will learn and only the resolute overcome obstacles to learning.

EUGENE S. WILSON

Scenario

During the second week of school, Mr. Garcia becomes perplexed by the behavior of his second-grade student T. J. Mr. Garcia considers T. J. to be an average reader when she reads aloud in class; however, when the class discusses stories, T. J. never contributes to the discussion even though at other times, she is very vocal and social. During guided reading, Mr. Garcia takes a running record of T. J.'s reading and finds that she makes only one error—*home* instead of *house*. When he asks her a literal question about the story, she is able to answer it; however, when he asks an inferential question, T. J. cannot respond.

During independent reading, Mr. Garcia observes T. J. reading *The Napping House* (1964) by Audrey Wood. He asks T. J. to read a page for him. She reads it with no errors. He then asks her to play the following game. He gives her sentence strips that feature the most important phrases from the book and asks her to read the phrases and arrange them in correct order. T. J. is unable to put the strips in correct order even though she can read them. When he asks T. J. why she chose that book, she replies, "Because it is easy to read, and it has a lot of words on the pages." When Mr. Garcia asks what *The Napping House* is about, T. J. replies, "About a napping house." Mr. Garcia realizes that T. J. can fluently read and decode unknown words, but she does not comprehend what she reads. The fact that she cannot put the sentence strips in order also makes him realize that she cannot sequence the events of a story.

INTRODUCTION

Comprehension is the main purpose of reading, yet many struggling readers lack this basic skill. Comprehension is an active process that requires complex, higher level thinking skills and "is based on the ability to encode and retrieve the basic building blocks (propositions) of sentences and relate the meaning within them to scenes and stories from a text" (Rose, Parks, Androes, & McMahon, 2000, p. 4). It is not easy for all readers to create meaning and to visualize scenes because of the decontextualized language found in stories. According to Beck and McKeown (2001), decontextualized language requires readers "to make sense of ideas that are about something beyond the here and now" (p. 10). Children live primarily in the present and most can comfortably use and understand language in daily conversation. However, when they begin to read, they need to learn to "use symbol systems and deal with representations of the world," skills that transcend the here and now (Donaldson, 1978, p. 89).

In order to help children enhance their vocabulary and visualize places and objects that are beyond their immediate experiences, teachers, especially in primary grades, must read to and discuss with children stories that are conceptually challenging, so that children can take "an active stance toward constructing meaning" (Beck & McKeown, 2001, p. 10). Educators agree that children need to hear stories and be given opportunities to discuss them. Most children can do this in a large or small group setting and learn from both activities. Other children, however, need to have stories read to them in a one-on-one setting. They have few opportunities at home to read and discuss stories with adults, so they may not have developed a narrative vocabulary or a sense of story grammar. Other children, including many who have attention deficit disorder (ADD) or attention deficit hyperactivity disorder (ADHD), have a difficult time focusing in a large group. Therefore, teachers need to scaffold struggling students as they begin to decode and comprehend text. Like all readers, struggling readers need to experience success as they engage with texts (Brown, 1999/2000).

Comprehension has many components and is intertwined with other reading skills—decoding, vocabulary, fluency, prior knowledge, and so on. This chapter will discuss this complex process of reading comprehension by examining (1) the relationship of comprehension to other reading skills, (2) the components of reading comprehension, (3) the characteristics of poor versus good comprehenders, (4) the developmental reading phases for reading comprehension, (5) informal and formal diagnostic and assessment instruments, and (6) strategies to aid and develop comprehension. The focus of this chapter will be on the skills and strategies needed to comprehend narrative text. Chapter 10 focuses on skills and strategies that are unique to comprehending informational text. Many of the same skills are required to comprehend both types of text.

INTERRELATIONSHIP OF COMPREHENSION TO OTHER READING SKILLS

Comprehension of narrative text is complex, just like a car is complex. Readers require fundamental skills to comprehend text just like a car requires fundamental parts in order to move down a road. Readers need decoding skills, fluency skills, and an adequate vocabulary, while a car requires four tires, an engine, a steering wheel, and a frame, among other things.

Decoding Skills

Recognizing familiar words automatically and decoding unknown words quickly are essential skills for comprehending text (Brown, 1999/2000; Richek, Caldwell, Jennings, & Lerner, 1996; Vaughn, 2000). If students spend all their energy and concentration on decoding, they have no energy left for comprehending. Chapter 7 discusses in detail how readers learn to recognize and decode words. That chapter also provides strategies to help struggling readers with decoding.

Fluency Skills

Students need to be able to recognize words effortlessly and interpret punctuation accurately in order to comprehend text. An appropriate reading rate is no less than 75 words per minute with 98 percent accuracy (Allington, 1983; Harris & Sipay, 1990; Rasinski & Padak, 2000). Readers also must be able to automatically group words into meaningful phrases so that the text is interpreted correctly. Chapter 11 discusses the components of fluency at length.

Vocabulary Skills

A large listening vocabulary is necessary for comprehension (Beck & McKeown, 2001; Oster, 2001; Vaughn, 2000). When students attempt to decode written words that are in their listening vocabulary, they will be able to more quickly recognize and grasp the meanings of these words (Beck & McKeown,

2001). When readers attempt to decode words that are not in their listening vocabulary, they may not even know if they are words. One way to increase a struggling reader's vocabulary is to discuss the topic of a story before reading it, using the new words that the reader will encounter. When introducing the new words, it is also good practice to write each word on a board and have students say it so they are more likely to recognize the word in print (Beck & McKeown, 2001). Unknown words are frequently important to the meaning of a story. Be sure to stop and discuss unknown words when you are reading aloud in order for children to understand words in context. For example, two words in *The Old Woman Who Lived in a Vinegar Bottle* (1995) by Margaret MacDonald that are important to the story's meaning are *content* and *complaining*. To make sure students understand these words it is often best to provide examples of each word since they may be easier to understand than an abstract definition. Chapter 8 discusses strategies for building struggling readers' vocabularies.

COMPONENTS OF READING COMPREHENSION

Just as a car needs more than its basic parts in order to function smoothly, readers need more than the fundamental reading skills in order to comprehend texts. Many readers can fluently call out familiar words and quickly decode unknown ones, yet just like T. J. in the opening scenario they have problems with comprehension. There are many intricate components of reading comprehension. All of these components need to be present and each component depends on the others; they all must work concurrently for comprehension to occur. These components are listed in Figure 9.1.

Comprehension Components Before Reading

Comprehension components that come into play *before* reading include *predicting* and *setting a purpose.*

Predicting

Predicting is a higher level thinking skill that requires readers to perform many different tasks simultaneously. When they predict, students draw on background knowledge, supply details, and then try to determine if their prediction was correct. Good readers make predictions automatically, while struggling readers often make no attempt to predict what will happen next in the story (Hurst, 2000; Jongsma, 1999/2000; Oster, 2001). One way to encourage struggling readers to predict is to show them the cover of the book and ask them to look at the illustration (without reading the title) to predict what may happen in the story. Predictions may include details that are not in the story, but that is fine because later it gives students an opportunity to evaluate and adjust their predictions. For example, if the teacher is about to read *The Old Woman Who Lived in a Vinegar Bottle*, the conversation may go as follows:

[Note: the cover of the book features an elderly woman with white hair pulled back in a bun, looking into a large bottle. Also on the cover is a small fairy and a chicken.]

FIGURE 9.1 Components of comprehension.

- Finding main ideas
- Predicting
- Making inferences
- Setting a purpose
- Self-monitoring
- Generating visual images
- Drawing conclusions
- Summarizing
- Retelling
- Comparing and contrasting
- Interrelating ideas

- Connecting appropriate background knowledge to new information
- Understanding characters' motives
- Sequencing events
- Self-questioning
- Analyzing text for story elements—character, plot, setting, theme, style, point of view
- Synthesizing
- Retaining information from one reading to the next
- Elaborating author's intent
- Understanding purpose

Sources: Doty, Popplewell, & Byers, (2001); Dowhower (1999); Duffy-Hester, (1999); Manning (2001); NEA Today (2001); Rose, Parks, Androes, and McMahon (2000); Vaughn (2000).

Teacher: Whom do you think this story is about?

Student: An old lady, a fairy, and a chicken.

Teacher: Why do you think the lady is old? (Attempting to also get the child to make inferences.)

Student: Because her hair is white and she has it pulled back like the old lady who lives in my building.

Teacher: Do you think she is happy?

Student: No.

Teacher: Why not?

Student: Because I think she wants a chicken.

Teacher: Do you think she will get a chicken?

Student: Yes, I think the fairy will give her one.

Teacher: Let's see if you are correct. The title of the book is *The Old Woman Who Lived in a Vinegar Bottle*.

Student: See! I was right! She is an old lady. But why would she want to live in a vinegar bottle? It must be a big bottle!

Teacher: Yes, you are right; she is an old lady. Let's find out why she lives in an old vinegar bottle, and let's see if it is a large bottle.

Predicting engages students in the reading task. The idea that the old woman wants a chicken is incorrect, but the fairy does make the old woman happy throughout the story. This is an excellent book for teachers to read while students continue to confirm predictions and make new ones. The book has repetitive text and a plot that is easy to follow: the woman constantly asks the fairy for bigger houses, but turns out to never again be content until the fairy returns her to the vinegar bottle.

If your students depend too much on the illustrations for their predictions, you should merely read the title without showing the pictures and ask readers what they think may happen in the story (Brown, 1999/2000). With younger children this may be a hard task because they enjoy the illustrations and rely on them for help with comprehension. In these discussions, you should always ask "why" questions and ask students to support their answers. Keep in mind that simply reading the title of the book *The Old Woman Who Lived in a Vinegar Bottle* while not allowing students to see the illustrations may elicit an entirely different conversation.

Teacher: This book is called *The Old Woman Who Lived in a Vinegar Bottle*. What do you think will happen in the story?

Student: A woman who lives in a vinegar bottle. (A very literal answer to a very literal question.)

Teacher: Why do you think she lives in a vinegar bottle?

Student: What's a vinegar bottle? (Good! The child recognizes her lack of prior knowledge.)

Teacher: Vinegar is a sour liquid, used to make pickles.

Student: Phew! Does it stink like pickles?

Teacher: Vinegar doesn't smell very good. So why do you think the woman lives in the vinegar bottle?

Student: Because she was old and mean and someone didn't like her so they first made her drink the vinegar and then they made her small and then they put her into the bottle so she couldn't be mean anymore.

This child has a complete, but inaccurate plot in mind. However, that is fine because as the teacher reads the story, the child will change her predictions as the story unfolds. The teacher has the child engaged in the thinking process, which is the purpose of getting the child to predict.

Predicting helps readers to interrelate ideas through the reading of a story. They begin to understand that reading is more than just reading words correctly. Predicting activities should begin using stories with simple, predictable plots in order to give students a better chance of some success with their predictions (Brown, 1999/2000). If these predictable books also have repetitive text, it is helpful because students can join in on repeated phrases and learn to recognize unfamiliar words. Appendix A.5 has a list of books with repetitive texts and predictable plots.

Setting a Purpose

Setting a purpose is an important part of reading comprehension that occurs before reading. After reading the title of a text, readers should ask themselves what type of genre the text belongs to. The primary purpose of reading narrative text is to find out who did what, when, where, and why. In both fantasy and realistic fiction, readers usually attempt to understand with whom or with what the protagonist is in conflict and how the conflict is resolved. In historical fiction, readers attempt to answer the same questions but often while learning more about the time and place in which the story is set. In a mystery, readers usually attempt to find clues in the text about how the protagonists will identify a criminal or resolve a problem.

Comprehension Components During Reading

During reading, comprehension components include *making inferences, self-monitoring, visualizing, and connecting prior knowledge to text.*

Making Inferences

According to Cooper and Kiger (2001), one of the five most significant strategies for comprehension is the ability to make inferences. Making inferences, a skill used before, during, and after reading, is the process of judging, concluding, or reasoning indirectly from the information available. In this process, readers need to use "available information and prior knowledge to construct meaning" (Cooper, 2000, p. 395). Readers need to "go beyond the literal meaning of the text to derive what is not there but is implied" (Fountas & Pinnell, 2001, p. 317). It is easy to see that inferring is also a higher level thinking skill. Proficient readers readily combine what they know with what they think is reasonable for a particular story and then draw conclusions that are not stated in the text. Struggling readers often find this task difficult (Cooper & Kiger, 2001).

Many teachers know what inferential thinking is, but find it difficult to formulate inferential questions. May (2001) suggests that we teachers need to "listen within our heads to the author and infer the messages left between the lines" (p. 114). May contends that authors "subconsciously leave empty slots for your imagination to fill in" (p. 114), and teachers need merely look for what the author omitted when they attempt to devise inferential questions.

When reading stories, readers must often make inferences about how characters feel based on how they act or what they say. At other times, readers need to make inferences about characters from what other characters say about them. Authors invite inferences because they want to show, not tell, readers about a character or a scenario and want them to use their imaginations. Katie Couric gives many opportunities for readers to imagine what kind of character Lazlo is in *The Brand New Kid* (2000). While reading this story to a struggling reader, you might ask the student how Lazlo feels when he is ignored. The story does not explicitly describe Lazlo's feeling. You also should stop reading from time to time and ask inferential questions. The reader may need to draw on personal experience to infer how Lazlo feels when being ignored. The following presents a passage from the book with some possible inferential questions:

> . . . all morning long, they kept shooting him looks.
>
> They headed to gym class, a quick softball game.
>
> When they went to pick teams, no one mentioned his name.
>
> (unpaged)

Teacher: What do you think it means to "shoot him looks"?

What kind of looks are they?

What happens earlier in the story to let you know that is how Lazlo feels?

Can you shoot me that type of look?

What does it mean when the narrator states that "no one mentioned his name"?

Do you know how it feels when no one calls your name to be on the team?

How did that make you feel?

Do you think Lazlo feels the same way?

Struggling students' inferential strategies can be strengthened by reading them books like this one and discussing the implicit aspects of characterization, setting, and plot. This will prompt them to connect their own knowledge to what they learn from the text. During discussion, you should ask probing questions that will help readers grasp characters' motives and elicit their empathy or understanding. You should always then ask students why they have particular reactions to characters or events; the "why" questions give readers a chance to practice their higher level thinking skills. More strategies for increasing readers' ability to make inferences will be discussed in the Intervention section of this chapter.

Self-Monitoring

Self-monitoring is yet another important component of reading comprehension. According to Fountas and Pinnell (2001), self-monitoring is the ability of readers to check "whether their reading sounds right, looks right, and makes sense" (p. 312). Good readers will be able to hear whether each word they read fits the syntax of the sentence. They automatically stop when it doesn't sound correct. Struggling readers, on the other hand, may pronounce words that are not real words or they may grasp at words that do not make sense in the sentence. By helping struggling readers to self-monitor these simple tasks, you can help the readers notice errors. You can stop such a student at the end of a sentence, reread the sentence the way the student read it, and ask, "Did that sound correct? Did that make sense? What word doesn't sound right or make sense?" Giving these prompts will help readers understand that what they read must match the print and must make sense. The main goal of self-monitoring is to make sure readers are making sense of what they have just read and are connecting previously read information to the passage they are reading. Therefore, you should also periodically stop students and ask them to retell what they just read. If they cannot accurately retell, ask them to reread and then retell. If students still cannot retell, read the passage again aloud and ask students to retell it. If they can then retell, this suggests that they may be spending too much energy on decoding, which is causing comprehension to break down. You can then choose an easier text for students to read, or spend more time reading stories to these struggling readers, discussing the story as it unfolds.

Sometimes during retellings, students may add information that is not in the story. In such cases, ask the child where he found the information in the story. If the student made an inference from the story's illustrations, you may conclude this reader used the entire text to comprehend. However, if he cannot locate the source of the information, attempt to find out if the student is making an inference from background experience or knowledge. The goal is to help students focus on the events of the particular story that is being read. Modeling the think-aloud strategy is one way to help students with self-monitoring.

As students begin to read longer chapter books, they need to self-monitor their comprehension from one sitting to the next. Sometimes, a day or two will pass before they get an opportunity to pick up the book and continue reading. As with the popular *Harry Potter* series, a couple of years may lapse before the author continues the story. With longer texts or text series, readers also need to relate ideas from chapter to chapter or book to book. For example, in the *Harry Potter* series, the Dursleys are introduced at the beginning of the first book, but they do not return until the second book. Readers learn some new information in the *second* book about how Harry differs from the Dursleys. Readers need to be able to interrelate all this information in order to understand the characterization and the plot of the series. Struggling readers often have trouble relating information from one chapter or book to the next.

Visualizing

Another critical skill necessary for comprehension is visualizing the imagery and events of the story as it unfolds (Beck & McKeown, 2001; Dowhower, 1999; Fountas & Pinnell, 2001; Rose, Parks, Androes, & McMahon, 2000). When visualizing, students should try to picture the scene so vividly that they can almost hear the surrounding noises and smell the scents. They should also try to imagine what each character looks like, how he or she walks or runs, and how the character speaks. Is the character's voice nasal or sweet? Husky or weak? For example, in *The Brand New Kid* (2000), the narrator describes the lunchroom in the following manner:

> As Lazlo was leaving the line with his tray
> Someone tripped him, his food it went every which way.
> The students all froze as they saw Lazlo's face
> With French fries and Ketchup all over the place.
> (unpaged)

While reading this passage from the book and without showing the pictures, you can ask the struggling readers some prompt questions that will help fill in the slots that Katie Couric leaves to the reader's imagination:

> Teacher: Who do you think tripped Lazlo?
>
> How do you think he was tripped?
>
> What was on his tray?
>
> What kind of tray was he carrying, plastic or metal?
>
> Were there any items besides French fries and ketchup on the tray?
>
> Do you think Lazlo fell to the floor or did he just stumble and drop his tray?
>
> Describe the mess on the floor.
>
> The narrator says that the students froze. What does that mean? Why did they freeze?
>
> How do you think they looked?
>
> What smells are in the cafeteria?
>
> What type of floor did the cafeteria have?

Good readers can visualize Lazlo falling or stumbling and can imagine the entire scene because good readers can visualize the details of a story (Rose, Parks, Androes, & McMahon, 2000, p. 57). Struggling readers usually have trouble with visualization (Beck & McKeown, 2001); you can help these readers develop visualization skills by asking them inferential questions.

Connecting Prior Knowledge to Texts

Another part of comprehending stories is connecting three types of background knowledge—literary background, world knowledge, and life experiences—to what you read (Fountas & Pinnell, 2001). Each of these is discussed below.

Literary knowledge. Literary knowledge includes what readers know about story elements—setting, characters, plot, climax, resolution, point of view, style, and theme. Struggling students often need help understanding these elements as they learn to become independent readers (Fountas & Pinnell, 2001; Staal, 2000). One strategy you can use to help struggling readers discover story elements is reading stories and completing story webs with them. One type of story web for young children is Staal's Story Face strategy (2000), which helps readers identify the main elements of the story. One eye on the "face" is the setting with eyelashes composed of adjectives that describe the setting. The other eye is the main character(s) with eyelashes composed of adjectives that describe these character(s). The nose is the problem. The mouth (the events) forms a smile if the story has a happy ending and forms a frown if the ending is unhappy. See Figure 9.2 and Figure 9.3 for examples.

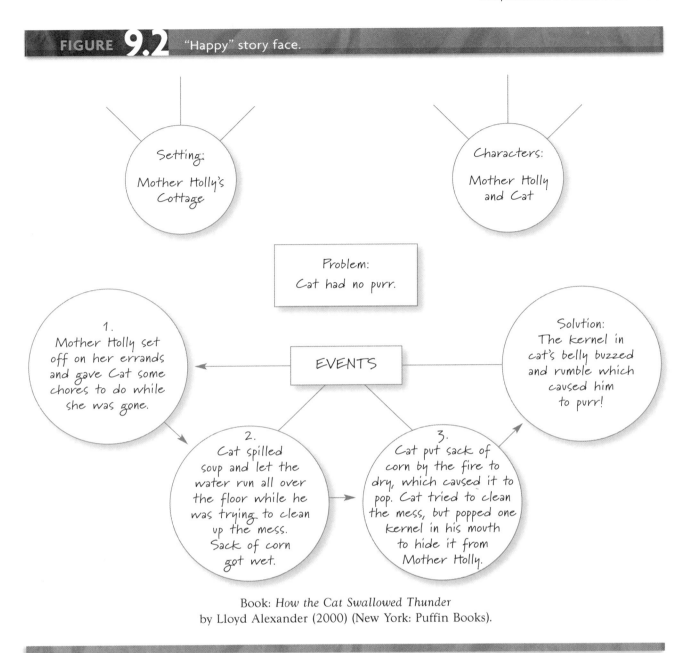

FIGURE 9.2 "Happy" story face.

Setting:
Mother Holly's Cottage

Characters:
Mother Holly and Cat

Problem:
Cat had no purr.

EVENTS

1.
Mother Holly set off on her errands and gave Cat some chores to do while she was gone.

2.
Cat spilled soup and let the water run all over the floor while he was trying to clean up the mess. Sack of corn got wet.

3.
Cat put sack of corn by the fire to dry, which caused it to pop. Cat tried to clean the mess, but popped one kernel in his mouth to hide it from Mother Holly.

Solution:
The kernel in cat's belly buzzed and rumble which caused him to purr!

Book: *How the Cat Swallowed Thunder*
by Lloyd Alexander (2000) (New York: Puffin Books).

Source: L. A. Staal (2000). The Story Face: An adaptation of story mapping that incorporates visualization and discovery learning to enhance reading and writing. Adapted from a graphic by Paula Clifford and Doug Ritsema. *The Reading Teacher, 54*(1), 26–31.

Literary knowledge also includes knowledge of the various genres and how they are similar and different from one another. For example, the fantasy genre often includes talking animals and stories that begin, "Once upon a time . . . ." Young proficient readers may not always know the names of different genres, but their previous exposure to stories helps them listen for the components of the story and recognize a fantasy, a mystery, a piece of realistic fiction, or historical fiction. Struggling readers, on the other hand, will not know to look for clues when reading a mystery; when reading historical fiction, they will often not be able to separate historical facts from fictitious details that the author added to enhance the plot. They may also find it difficult to differentiate between fantasy and realistic fiction because in the former animals and objects often take on human-like behaviors and emotions. To help readers recognize the differences between fantasy and realistic fiction, you can have them complete a Venn diagram with your assistance. The Venn diagram in Figure 9.4 provides a model.

FIGURE 9.3 "Sad" story face.

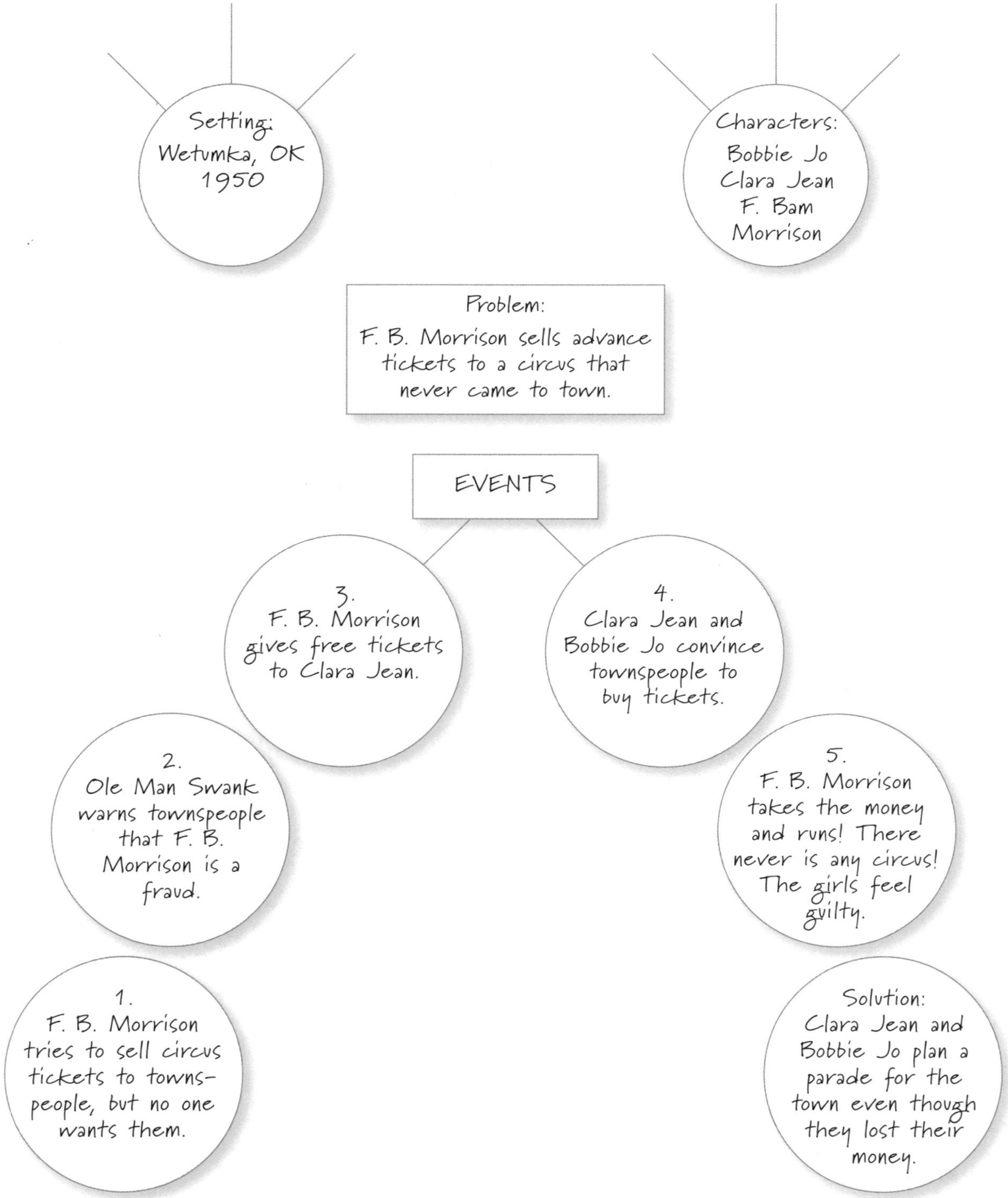

Setting:
Wetumka, OK
1950

Characters:
Bobbie Jo
Clara Jean
F. Bam
Morrison

Problem:
F. B. Morrison sells advance
tickets to a circus that
never came to town.

EVENTS

3.
F. B. Morrison
gives free tickets
to Clara Jean.

4.
Clara Jean and
Bobbie Jo convince
townspeople to
buy tickets.

2.
Ole Man Swank
warns townspeople
that F. B.
Morrison is a
fraud.

5.
F. B. Morrison
takes the money
and runs! There
never is any circus!
The girls feel
guilty.

1.
F. B. Morrison
tries to sell circus
tickets to towns-
people, but no one
wants them.

Solution:
Clara Jean and
Bobbie Jo plan a
parade for the
town even though
they lost their
money.

Book: *The Flimflam Man* by Darleen Bailey-Beard (1998)
(New York: Farrar Straus Giroux).

Source: L. A. Staal (2000). The Story Face: An adaptation of story mapping that incorporates visualization and discovery learning to enhance reading and writing. Adapted from a graphic by Paula Clifford and Doug Ritsema. *The Reading Teacher, 54*(1), 26–31.

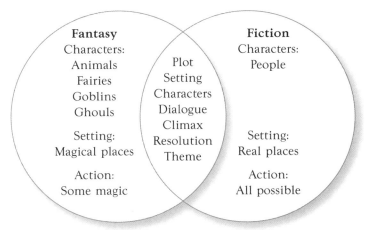

FIGURE 9.4 Venn diagram for genres.

World knowledge. The second aspect of background knowledge is readers' knowledge of the world. Settings of stories are often beyond the readers' world of experience so they may need to be introduced to some basic geography, history, or anthropology to understand the settings of stories. For example, consider the following opening sentence of a story: "Once upon a time in Antarctica, lived seven polar bears." The author assumes that readers know that Antarctica is a cold, snowy place and know something about polar bears. Readers with rich background knowledge can visualize the setting and know something about the characters from reading the first sentence. Readers with weak background knowledge will need your help to understand the setting so they can appreciate the story. In many stories, the setting plays a pivotal role in the problem. Think-alouds (discussed in the Intervention section of this chapter) help struggling readers by providing background knowledge about settings beyond their communities. For example, in the story about polar bears, you might use the think-aloud strategy by stopping after the first sentence and offering the following comments:

> Teacher: Wow! This story makes me shiver because I know Antarctica has lots of snow and ice. Does it make you cold too?
>
> I wonder if it's sunny or cloudy. What do you think?
>
> If it's sunny, the glare would hurt my eyes. Would it hurt your eyes too?
>
> I know polar bears love the cold, but I wonder if these are friendly or mean bears. Do you know if polar bears are friendly or mean?

With each statement, teachers can solicit information from readers in order to find out what they know and provide information about what they don't know. Teachers may find that a reader knows something about Antarctica and polar bears from watching some educational channel on television, but the child may not know. The think-aloud strategy also gets struggling readers engaged in the comprehension process before reading much of the story.

If the teacher had merely read the first sentence with no discussion, the struggling reader may not comprehend the events of the story because most authors assume that the reader will supply much of the background information.

Life experience. The third component of background knowledge is one's life experience. Such experience comes from family and community interactions, among other sources. All these experiences help readers construct meaning as they encounter new stories. Any reader with a family member who has suffered a stroke has a better understanding of Tomie dePaola's *Now One Foot, Now the Other* (1981). Other readers who have watched a parent struggle with depression or who have lived in a foster home may have a richer appreciation for Patricia MacLachlan's *Mama One, Mama Two* (1982).

Every reader has previous life experience; good comprehenders are able to make connections between their personal experiences and the story. For example, J. W., whose grandfather recently suffered a stroke, reads about Bob's stroke in Tomie dePaola's *Now One Foot, Now Another* (1981) and asks, "Why is Bob sick just because he cannot move his arms and legs? Why can't he talk? Why wouldn't

Bob know who Bobby was?" From these questions, J. W.'s teacher knows that he is not connecting his background knowledge to his reading because J. W. often talks about his grandpa's inability to walk and talk and his inability to recognize J. W. Poor readers do not make that connection.

On the other hand, readers may encounter comprehension problems if they rely too much on personal experiences (Beck & McKeown, 2001). Both types of reading problems—not connecting previous experiences or relying too much on such experiences—make comprehension difficult. When readers do not connect previous experiences to reading events, teachers can use text talks (Beck & McKeown, 2001). Text talks are described in the Intervention section of this chapter. When readers depend too much on previous personal experiences, teachers can ask students to locate the sentences in the text that support their comments.

Comprehension Components After Reading

Comprehension components after reading include *finding main ideas, drawing conclusions,* and *elaborating the author's intent.*

Finding Main Ideas

Finding the main idea of stories relies on students' ability to answer literal questions. Students who comprehend stories can readily relate the main ideas of a story after they read it. They readily retell who did what where and when in the correct sequence of events. In the retelling, they do not confuse their own personal experiences with those in the story; they stick to the information in the story. Unskilled readers, on the other hand, may be able to tell who did what, but not in the correct sequence of events. They may relate the climax first and then what leads up to it. Often they cannot remember where and when the story takes place. For example, Cloe, a struggling reader retelling Paula Danziger's *It's Justin Time, Amber Brown* (2001), states that Amber Brown gets a watch and a walkie-talkie for her birthday. Cloe does not relate that it is Amber's seventh birthday and that she wants the watch so that she can tell how late Justin always is when he comes over to play. Cloe also fails to relate that Justin is late the day before her birthday because he is writing a card and wrapping her gift, the walkie-talkie. Cloe only relates what gifts Amber receives. A more skilled reader would relate the story from beginning to end, summarizing the main points of the plot.

When students struggle with relating main ideas in sequence, you can construct a set of four index cards with one of these questions on each card: "Where?" "When?" Who?" and "Did what?" After reading a story, first display the "Where?" card, then the "When?" card, the "Who?" card, and finally the "Did what?" card. After using this technique for a period of time, remove the cards and ask the students to retell. Retelling events in sequence is an important skill in exploring fiction, and will also serve students later when relating scientific phenomena and historical events.

Drawing Conclusions

Drawing conclusions demonstrates students' ability to answer higher level thinking questions. The main kind of conclusion question is "Why?" The answers to these questions are not stated in the story, but students who comprehend the stories draw conclusions based on textual clues or previous experiences. Struggling readers will often have difficulty drawing conclusions because they cannot find their answer stated in the text. For example, while retelling Linda Sue Park's *A Single Shard* (2001), the proficient reader will be able to explain why Tree-ear is faithful in delivering the delicate celadon ware for Min even though it is a dangerous journey. The proficient reader reads between the lines and realizes that Tree-ear does this because Min's destiny will be determined by his delivery of the ware and because of the lessons his friend Crane-man has taught him. The struggling reader, when asked why Tree-ear is faithful to his task, may say because Min tells him to do it.

Elaborating on the Author's Intent

While discussing the story after the reading, be sure to discuss the author's intent. Did the author write the story to make readers laugh or to inspire them or to teach a lesson? Or to relate historical information or to get readers to explore another culture? It is through discussions that students learn about the author's purpose. Information revealed during discussions also may influence readers as they select another book.

SKILLED VERSUS UNSKILLED COMPREHENDERS

It is obvious that comprehension involves many higher level thinking skills that result in interpretation, analysis, and evaluation of texts. When reading a story, skilled readers have the ability "to provide sequenced explanations, logical arguments, grounded interpretations, and abstract analysis" (Jacobson, Thrope, Fisher, Lapp, Frey, & Flood, 2001, p. 2). Figure 9.5 summarizes comprehension skills used by proficient readers, and Figure 9.6 summarizes some common habits of struggling readers. It is important for teachers to be able to assess readers' strengths and weaknesses. In the next section, I will discuss some formal and informal assessments.

ASSESSMENT

Any oral assessment of comprehension is beneficial to teachers because they can observe what readers do during the reading process. Good inflection, appropriate pace, and adherence to punctuation indicate comprehension (Vaughn, 2000). Teachers

---

FIGURE 9.5 Skills of a proficient reader of narrative texts.

1. Reads for details about description of setting and character.
2. Makes inferences readily about characters' reactions and how characters feel, based on their actions.
3. Visualizes how the setting looks, smells, and feels, and imagines in detail the physical features of characters.
4. Brings in appropriate prior knowledge about periods of history or details of settings.
5. Predicts by looking at the illustrations and by evaluating the action that has taken place.
6. Summarizes in sequence the events in the plot and identifies setting and main characters.
7. Self-monitors and thus slows down or rereads a passage when having trouble understanding motive or plot.
8. Becomes engrossed in funny stories enough to laugh aloud—in sad stories enough to cry.
9. Uses many strategies to read unfamiliar words and to follow the plot.
10. Understands new vocabulary through context clues or by using the dictionary.
11. Possesses a broad vocabulary that helps elucidate the setting of the story.

12. Integrates relevant text information with background knowledge without that knowledge distorting an understanding of the text.
13. Understands metaphors and figurative language that the author uses; understands how an author employs figurative language for effect.
14. Rereads to clarify ideas when comprehension clashes with background information or previous predictions about the plot.
15. Develops valid interpretations of the theme that elucidate the author's purpose.
16. Remembers content of previous reading sessions when reading longer chapter books or books in a series.
17. Synthesizes information from similar stories. For example, if reading a number of retellings of the same fairy tale, the reader can explain how they are similar.
18. Decodes unknown words automatically by looking at patterns within one-syllable words and finding syllables in multi-syllable words.
19. Supplies necessary details from background knowledge when the author assumes readers have relevant information.
20. Draws conclusions about the mood, style, and theme that demonstrate the author's intent.

Sources: Hurst, C. O., 2000; Jitendra, A., Hoppes, M., & Xin, P., 2000; Jongsma, K. 2000; Oster, L., 2001.

FIGURE 9.6 Habits and characteristics of a poor reader.

1. Focuses exclusively on pronouncing words.
2. Remembers small, unimportant details.
3. Relies too much on picture clues.
4. Lacks appropriate background knowledge.
5. Has a limited vocabulary.

6. Doesn't recognize failures of comprehension.
7. Doesn't connect prior knowledge to text.
8. Has difficulty drawing inferences.
9. May lack decoding skills. (Some poor comprehenders have good decoding skills.)

Source: Richek, M. A., Caldwell, J., Jennings, J., & Lerner, J. W. (1996) *Reading Problems: Assessment and Teaching Strategies* (3rd ed.). Boston: Allyn & Bacon.

can also observe what readers do as they encounter unknown words. Comments made by students during reading or during retelling indicate their level of comprehension.

There are formal (standardized) comprehension tests and many types of informal tests. I recommend the informal tests in order to get a deeper understanding of readers' methods of comprehending texts.

Informal Assessment

Informal Reading Inventories

The main purpose of an informal reading inventory (IRI) is to determine students' reading level. However, IRIs can also be used to compare students' silent reading to their oral reading comprehension. First have students read a passage silently and retell the story; then have them read a grade-equivalent text orally and retell that story. Most commercial tests have questions that should be answered by the students in the retelling. You can compare the number of questions answered in the retelling after the reading of each story. After the retelling, you can ask the unanswered questions to determine if students comprehended that aspect of the story.

Miscue Analysis

Miscues are oral divergences from the written text (Goodman, Watson, & Burke, 1987). When analyzing miscues to check comprehension, ask one major question concerning each miscue: "Did the miscue disrupt meaning?" When working with a student, analyze which type of miscue most often disrupts meaning and then work with the student to eliminate that miscue. Miscues that disrupt meaning will most certainly hinder comprehension.

You should also analyze each miscue to see if it fits the syntax of the sentence prior to the miscue and if it fits the syntax or semantics of surrounding sentences. When the miscue does not fit the syntax or the semantics of adjoining sentences, it indicates that that reader is merely reading words and not reading for comprehension.

Analyzing miscues is a helpful way to understand a reader's comprehension problems. See Chapter 3 for instructions on how to administer miscue analyses and a grid to record and analyze miscues.

Retrospective Miscues Analysis

The retrospective miscue analysis (RMA) can be used for instructional purposes and for assessment

(Goodman & Marek, 1996). During the RMA session, a reader listens to an audiotape of his or her reading while following along in the text. As the student listens to the recording, the teacher asks the reader if the miscues disrupt meaning.

The "RMA seeks to empower readers to view reading miscues as repeated attempts to predict meaning and to make sense of text" (Moore & Aspegren, 2001, p. 2). You can use the RMA to analyze critically and constructively the entire reading process—in other words, to analyze what students do when they recognize their miscues (Martens, 1998; Moore & Aspegren, 2001; Goodman, K. 1996).

Running Records

Running records can also be used to assess comprehension when used for more than cueing errors. The purpose here is to analyze the errors to determine which language system—syntax (sentence sense), semantics (meaning), or graphophonic (visual)—students used (Clay, 2000). If the analysis indicates that a student uses only visual clues, the student will need instruction in developing the skills to read for meaning. You may also use running records to help determine if a student's inflection and pace hinder or aid comprehension. For example, proficient readers raise their voices when they read questions, they make a slight pause for commas, and they read at least 75 words per minute, which is considered to be a good reading rate. See Chapter 3 for instructions on how to administer and analyze running records.

Retelling

Retelling is an important indicator of reading comprehension (Allinder, 2001; Cooper, 2000; Dowhower, 1999; Fountas & Pinnell, 2001; Jitendra, Hoppes, & Xin, 2000; Rose, Parks, Androes, & McMahon, 2000). Retelling, the act of orally summarizing the most important events of the story, can be used for assessment and instruction. Retellings can help you gain insight into readers' thinking and sequencing skills and their ability to restate the main points of the story. Retellings give students opportunities to reflect and discuss the complete text (Doty, Popplewell, & Byers, 2001), not merely answer questions that cover one aspect of the story.

Think-Alouds

Jongsma (2000) suggests that think-alouds "offer excellent opportunities for teachers to assess students' developing comprehension processes" (p. 310)

because they help teachers gain insight into how students process texts. Although teachers commonly use think-alouds as a strategy to model how students *should* make sense from text (see the discussion later in this chapter), once teachers have modeled the process, think-alouds can also be used for assessment.

To use a think-aloud for assessment, check to see if students (1) predict upcoming actions, (2) visualize settings, characters, and events, (3) make inferences, and (4) self-monitor when comprehension breaks down.

Cloze Test

As discussed in Chapter 3, cloze tests can be used to determine if a passage is at a student's easy, instructional, or frustration reading level. Cloze tests are also good tools to use to diagnose and to assess reading comprehension (Gillet & Temple, 2000).

Gillet and Temple (2000) found cloze tests to be particularly worthwhile for assessing comprehension because readers need to focus on the entire meaning of the passage in order to fill in missing words. Teachers can observe students in action as they construct meaning in the cloze test. Some questions to ask yourself while observing students complete this activity include the following:

1. Does the reader give up when he or she does not know the word?
2. Does the reader make wild guesses?
3. Does the reader go back to the beginning of the sentence to fill in the blank?
4. Does the reader read to the end of a sentence before filling in the blank?
5. Does the reader read to the end of a paragraph and then come back to the blank to fill in the word?

Later, this chapter includes a discussion on how to use the cloze test to teach comprehension.

The Maze Test

The maze test is much like the cloze test, but it is designed for younger readers. Instead of a blank, three choices are given for each missing word. One word is correct, one fits the syntax of the sentence, and the third word does not fit the sentence in any way. Again, be sure to closely observe readers as they complete this test to see if students are merely guessing as they work and to observe what students do to construct meaning. Encourage the students to explain why they chose the particular word.

Figure 9.7 has a few sentences from a sample maze test. Notice how some words make sense with the preceding text but do not make sense with the text following the blank. When a maze test is designed in this manner, teachers can see if students read for comprehension and if they go back to "fix" errors.

Chapter 3 discusses how to score maze tests.

Rubrics

Rubrics, especially those based on state standards, are another way to ensure that all students are attaining the competencies needed for the criterion-referenced tests that many states use to document growth in the areas specified by the No Child Left Behind Act. The rubric in Figure 9.8 is based on Illinois State Standards for Early Elementary School English/Language Arts. Instead of comprising individual grade-level standards, these particular Illinois standards are grouped together as "early elementary," considered in most schools to be grades one through three. The rubric is based on Standard 1.C.1a, 1.C.1b, 1.C.1c, and 1.C.1d. Notice in this example that Joshua, a third grader at the end of his second quarter, can only sometimes orally retell the story and sometimes can make accurate predictions with evidence from the text. Obviously, Joshua needs some extra help in reading and interpreting stories.

FIGURE 9.7 Sample maze test.

"The Bath" from *Henry and Mudge in the Green Time* by Cynthia Rylant (1987). New York: The Trumpet Club.

On hot days Henry liked to give Mudge a bath. Henry liked it because (bath, he, she) could play with the (snake, from, water) hose and because he (could, has, cat) cool off. Mudge hated it. Mudge (could, know, knew) when he was going (for, cat, to) get a bath.

FIGURE 9.8   Rubric for narrative reading comprehension.

STUDENT *Joshua*   GRADE 3   GRADING PERIOD 1 ②3 4

LEVEL OF MASTERY

TRAIT	TARGET (5 POINTS)	ACCEPTABLE (3 POINTS)	UNACCEPTABLE (1 POINT)
1. C.1a Verify predictions	Can respond to questions that reflect higher level thinking (e.g., analyze, synthesize, infer, and evaluate). ___	Sometimes responds to questions that reflect higher level thinking (e.g., analyze, synthesize, infer, and evaluate). ___	Seldom responds to questions that reflect higher level thinking (e.g., analyze, synthesize, infer, and evaluate). _X_
	Generates questions that reflect higher level thinking (e.g., analyze, synthesize, infer, and evaluate). ___	Sometimes generates questions that reflect higher level thinking (e.g., analyze, synthesize, infer, and evaluate). ___	Seldom generates questions that reflect higher level thinking (e.g., analyze, synthesize, infer, and evaluate). _X_
	Uses evidence in text to support predictions and conclusions. ___	Sometimes uses evidence in text to support predictions and conclusions. _X_	Seldom uses evidence in text to support predictions and conclusions. ___
1. C.1b Themes and topics	Makes interpretation of text with text-based support. ___	Sometimes makes interpretation of text with text-based support. ___	Seldom makes interpretation of text with text-based support. _X_
	Identifies author's lesson, either stated or implied. ___	Sometimes identifies author's lesson, either stated or implied. ___	Seldom identifies author's lesson, either stated or implied. _X_
1. C.1c Compares reading selections	Compares/contrasts themes, topics, and story elements. ___	Sometimes compares/contrasts themes, topics, and story elements. ___	Seldom compares/contrasts themes, topics, and story elements. _X_
	Uses text information to make connections to other situations. ___	Sometimes uses text information to make connections to other situations. ___	Seldom uses text information to make connections to other situations. _X_
1. C.1d Summarization	Retells in written form the main points of the story. ___	Sometimes can retell in written form the main points of the story. ___	Seldom can retell in written form the main points of the story. _X_
	Retells orally the main points of the story. ___	Sometimes can retell orally the main points of the story. _X_	Seldom can retell orally the main points of the story. ___

TOTAL SCORE: ___13___

Scoring:

45 pts = competent in narrative comprehension (end-of-year goal)

27 pts = becoming competent in narrative comprehension (mid-year goal)

9 pts = unacceptable; needs intense instruction

Based on Illinois Early Elementary School English/Language Arts Standards 1.C.1a–1.C.1d, at www.isbe.state.il.us.

Computer Programs as Assessment Tools

Software tutorial programs can be used to assess students' current reading level and track their progress. These programs also define the level of text that students can use for independent and instructional reading. The programs save teachers time because they provide summaries that can be shared with the parents. Such software programs include the following:

1. Accelerated Reader program, distributed by Renaissance Learning.
2. Scholastic Reading Inventory program, distributed by Scholastic.
3. SuccessMaker, distributed by Computer Curriculum Corporation.
4. Launch Pad, distributed by Learning Advantage.
5. LeapTrack, distributed by Leapfrog Schoolhouse.
6. Reads, distributed by Mindplay.

In the Accelerated Reading and Scholastic Reading Inventory programs, students read a trade book and take a computer-generated quiz. The computer grades the quiz and generates a score. In most of these programs, students fill in the blank with an appropriate word (as with a cloze test) and the computer indicates if the answer is correct. Since most of the questions are literal ones, the tests measure a student's basic comprehension of the story, but do not measure if the student can make inferences.

Effective teachers administer a variety of informal assessment instruments in order to evaluate a struggling reader's skills and weaknesses. Teachers then demonstrate an appropriate strategy and permit the individual reader to practice the strategy while they monitor the event. Teachers must be knowledgeable about a variety of reading strategies in order to choose strategies appropriate for a particular reader. A number of different strategies are discussed in the last section of this chapter.

Formal Assessment

Standardized achievement tests measure the current level of students' performance in a variety of areas including reading comprehension. However, since many achievement tests are group tests, they are used mainly to evaluate groups and not individuals, and they are not designed for diagnostic purposes (Gillet & Temple, 2000). Nonetheless, teachers can look at student reading sub-test scores to get a benchmark level for how an individual student scored in comparison to his or her grade level. Some commonly used achievement tests are the current edition of the Metropolitan Achievement Test, the Comprehensive Test of Basic Skills, the Iowa Tests of Basic Skills, and the Stanford Achievement Test.

There are also standardized *diagnostic* tests, which are designed to measure what students know. These tests include a large number of sub-tests, and the items within the sub-tests are devised to measure specific skills. Some diagnostic tests are group tests while others are individual tests. One commonly used group test is the Stanford Diagnostic Reading Test, which has the following sub-tests that concern reading comprehension: auditory vocabulary, word meaning, and literal and inferential comprehension.

Individual diagnostic tests that focus only on word recognition and word analysis are the Diagnostic Screening Battery–2 and Gates-McKillop-Horowitz Reading Diagnostic Test. Since these two skills are necessary comprehension skills, teachers may use these tests if they suspect that a student lacks these skills.

Two individual oral reading tests, the Gray Oral Reading Test and the Gilmore Oral Reading Test, focus more on reading accuracy and speed than on comprehension. However, both of these tests do include comprehension questions that factor into the total reading score.

Individual diagnostic tests that include both oral and silent reading components and focus on comprehension are the Durrell Analysis of Reading Difficulty, the Diagnostic Reading Scales–Revised, and the Woodcock Reading Mastery Test–Revised. These three tests include graded word lists, graded story passages, and comprehension assessments. These tests determine reading levels, but they do not focus on analyzing miscues, which is the focus of informal reading inventories.

DEVELOPMENTAL READING STAGES FOR COMPREHENSION

In order for readers to improve comprehension, a story needs to be challenging enough to cause readers to grapple with ideas and become actively engaged in constructing meaning (Beck & McKeown, 2001). However, because these types of stories are often too difficult for the beginning and struggling readers to read by themselves, Brown (1999/2000) says, "By matching different types of text with students' development, teachers are able to work in young readers' changing zones of proximal reading development—the bridge between what they know about the reading process and what they still need to learn" (p. 292). Brown suggests that teachers should always read complex stories to children if those texts intrigue them. Once readers know about print, teachers should read predictable texts and encourage readers to chime in on words they recognize. Later, when children begin to read, they should first read decodable texts and later read less controlled texts and easy readers. This sequence is especially useful for struggling readers as they develop their comprehension skills. It is important that children be given the opportunity to retell easy, decodable texts so they can understand that reading is making sense of the story instead of merely reading words.

With each type of text, teachers should emphasize that "reading is about constructing meaning and model the kinds of comprehension strategies successful readers use" (Brown, 1999/2000, p. 293). A discussion that accompanies reading should not feature intimidating questions or quizzing, but instead informal talk about the story to help students reflect on the text's many elements (Baumann, Hooten, & White, 1999; Beck & McKeown, 2001; Gauthier, 2001; Jongsma, 1999/2000; Oster, 2001).

TEACHING COMPREHENSION STRATEGIES

Studies show that teaching comprehension strategies to students directly does enhance reading comprehension (Allinder, 2001; Baumann, Hooten, & White, 1999; Beck & McKeown, 2001; Foorman, Francis, Fletcher, Schatschneider, & Mehta, 1998; Gauthier, 2001; Jitendra, Hoppes, & Xin, 2000; Vaughn, 2000). Therefore, teachers need to know as many strategies as possible and be able to fit them to the individual needs of each struggling reader.

Before examining various activities to use with struggling readers, it is important to consider the following question: Is explicit instruction in comprehension strategies necessary? The answer to this question differs when discussing good and poor comprehenders. Swanson and DeLaPaz (1998) conclude that good comprehenders know what strategies to use even though they do not recall being explicitly taught *how* to comprehend. However, they suggest that poor comprehenders "do not *acquire* strategic reading behaviors by themselves, and that poor readers need to be taught how, where, and when to consistently carry out such procedures" (p. 209). Poor readers rarely use any strategies when comprehension breaks down. In fact, they usually fail to use the simple strategy of rereading sections of text they do not understand. This basic strategy is natural for good comprehenders.

Bos and Vaughn (1994) indicate that poor comprehenders are often good word decoders but they do not comprehend texts because they do not monitor their own comprehension or relate texts to previous knowledge. Oakhill and Patel (1991) also found that unlike good comprehenders, poor comprehenders do not make inferences or synthesize ideas from different passages; they lack strategies to assist comprehension. Many researchers (Collins, 1997; Graham, Harris, MacArthur, & Schwartz, 1997; Pressley, Woloshyn, Burkell, Cariglia-Bull, Lysynchuk, & McGoldrich et al., 1995; Sinatra, 2000; Swanson & De La Paz, 1998) agree that strategies need to be explicitly taught to poor comprehenders. Beyond this, these researchers agree that strategies need to be taught in context so readers learn to use the appropriate strategy when the need arises, and they suggest that teaching strategies as a separate part of the curriculum is ineffective.

Ciardiello (1998) found that students learn best when new material is presented in small steps. Teachers must recognize the limitations of readers' working memories. To really learn a strategy, readers need time to process the new information so it can be stored in their long-term memories. Therefore, when teaching comprehension strategies to poor comprehenders, remember the following:

- Teach in context.
- Use simple, easy-level reading material when teaching the strategy.
- Individualize! (Maybe the most important factor.)
- Choose an appropriate strategy for that material.
- Teach the strategy explicitly.
- Model the use of the strategy.
- Have the reader practice it under your supervision.
- Give appropriate feedback.
- Provide numerous opportunities for the student to practice the strategy so they can self-regulate.
- Don't present multiple strategies at one time.
- Have the student verbalize the steps of the strategy, explaining *when* it should be used.

The following section includes a number of activities to use with students who struggle with comprehension before reading, during reading, or after reading. Remember that comprehension strategies should be explicitly taught, using the techniques suggested by Ciardiello (1998).

Intervention

T he International Reading Association and the National Council of Teachers of English deem it important that all readers, including struggling readers, be able to apply a wide range of strategies for comprehension (Standards for the English Language Arts, 1996). Research suggests that learning comprehension strategies should not be taught in isolation or only for the sake of learning strategies (Baumann, Hooten, & White, 1999; Beck & McKeown, 2001; Dowhower, 1999; Fountas & Pinnell, 2001). Rather, they should be learned in context, for the sake of aiding comprehension.

In the 1960s and 1970s, the trend was to teach sub-skills through direct instruction and then to have students master each sub-skill while reading a short passage. However, research now indicates that it is more effective to teach skills to students in context, at moments when they can make an active choice to use them to aid comprehension of that particular text (Beck & McKeown, 1997; Dowhower, 1999; Fountas & Pinnell, 1996; Hamilton & Kucan, 1997). *The strategies that follow in this section should be taught in context when struggling readers need them.* Each strategy should be explicitly explained and demonstrated by the teacher, using the story that is being read.

Some of the activities presented in this section extend through all the stages of reading, while others are intended for one of the specific stages. The activities that follow are not given in any particular order. You should make sure you are familiar with many types of activities, that you understand the needs and interests of the students, and then apply the activity that best fits the need of each reader. Many of these activities can be used in large or small groups. However, it is suggested that these activities be used in a tutoring setting so they fit the needs of individual, struggling readers.

REPEATED READINGS

ACTIVITY

(GRADES 1-3)

Repeated readings both by the teacher and by the student has been shown to increase struggling readers' comprehension. Repeated readings by the teacher give struggling readers an opportunity to understand multiple layers of meaning in favorite stories. Through repeated readings and discussions, they begin to make inferences about characters' motives and how the setting affects the action. Repeated readings by students help them to focus less on decoding words and more on comprehending the story (Brown, 1999/2000; Pearson & Fielding, 1991).

READ-ALONG TAPES

ACTIVITY

(GRADES 1-6)

Ideally, you ought to be able to devote 30 minutes each day to work with each struggling reader; however, that is not reality. You should use trained tutors when possible; but if tutors are not available, you can use audiotapes, either commercial or teacher-prepared, to help struggling readers. Audiotapes permit children to hear books that are too difficult for them to read independently. They encounter new vocabulary, hear fluent reading, and get to visualize the action as the story progresses. *NEA Today* (2001) reports that audiotapes increase reading ability in students. When selecting books on tape, check the rate at which they are read to make sure the rate is appropriate for the reader. Tapes should also have a turn-of-the-page signal so the child can find his place if he loses it. Figure 9.9 lists some companies that produce read-along tapes, with examples of some of their available titles.

FIGURE 9.9   Publishers of read-along tapes, with examples of available titles.

Newbridge
P.O. Box 1270
Littleton, MA 01460
www.newbridgeonline.com
1. *Spinning a Web*
2. *Out of Space*
3. *A Butterfly Is Born*
4. *Amazing Water*
5. *Sink or Float?*
6. *An Apple a Day*

Sundance
P.O. Box 1326
Littleton, MA 01460
www.sundancepub.com
1. *Making Friends with Samson*
2. *The Fine Line*
3. *Two Hours with Tilly*
4. *Sticky Fingers*
5. *Mug Shots*
6. *Chocolate Chuckles*

Scholastic
P.O. Box 7502
Jefferson City, MO 65102
www.scholastic.com
1. *Caps for Sale*
2. *City Mouse-Country Mouse*
3. *Henny Penny*
4. *Little Rabbit's Loose Tooth*
5. *More Spaghetti, I Say!*
6. *Is Your Mama a Llama?*

Audiotape chapter books are available for older struggling readers who enjoy listening to stories that interest them but which are too difficult for independent reading. Listening to the tapes increases older students' vocabulary, comprehension, and visualization skills (Jongsma, 1999/2000). Chapter books on tape and CD are available at most local libraries and from some companies. Appendix A.8 lists Newbery medal winners and Newbery Honor books with some other well-known titles.

 **ACTIVITY**

TEACHER-MADE TAPES

(GRADES 1–3)   Marie Carbo (1996a) suggests creating read-along tapes that allow you to record the story at a pace slightly slower than normal. Then students can read along with the tape. To create read-along-tapes, do the following:

1. Select a story or passage that is at the student's instructional level.
2. Record only one short selection on one side of the tape. You should not put more than one story on one side, even if the passage is very short, so that the student can quickly find the starting point.
3. Read the story at a pace at which the reader can point to each word as he hears it and at which he can read along.
4. Be sure to include a turn-of-the-page signal with a pause long enough so that the reader has time to turn the page.

Teacher-made tapes have many advantages. You can prepare tapes that will fit a particular reader's interest, and you can read the tapes at a pace that encourages the reader to read along. Tapes can be more than a mere read-along when you give clues to readers to stop to reflect on the story by asking reflective questions. If two children listen together, they can stop the tape after each question and discuss the question together. If they disagree on an answer, they should rewind the tape and listen again so they can see who is correct.

ACTIVITY

THINK-ALOUD FOR NARRATIVE TEXT

(GRADES 1–5)   Although a think-aloud can be used for assessment, as discussed earlier in this chapter, it is also a strategy that can be used first by you to verbalize your thoughts and then by students as they read and make sense of a text. When you verbalize your thoughts while reading, you permit the students to understand the strategies you use to comprehend texts. As you read, you can comment on or question the text, bringing your "prior knowledge to bear, or making inferences or predictions" (Oster, 2001, p. 64). You then can have the students practice the strategy as you observe and scaffold readers' thought processes when necessary. Be sure to model a think-aloud using a book that is conceptually challenging to the readers. The following is an example of a teacher modeling a think-aloud, using Patricia MacLachlan's *Mama One, Mama Two* (1982). The teacher's thoughts are presented in italics and parentheses.

> Maudie heard the baby cry in the middle of the night. *(I wonder how old Maudie is and how old the baby is. I wonder if the baby is sick.)* She got up and walked through the moonlit hallway to the room. *(I wonder if she is angry that the baby woke her up.)* The baby reached out and curled his fingers around hers. *(I see the baby is a boy and that he likes Maudie.)* "Are you awake, too?" asked Katherine in the doorway. *(I wonder who Katherine is. From the picture, I think she is Maudie's mother. However, if it is Maudie's mother, she probably wouldn't be called Katherine.)* She held the baby's night bottle of milk. *(I guess the baby is hungry, not sick.)*

Later, in the story we read:

> "Tell me the story again," said Maudie, "the story about Mama One, Mama Two." *(I wonder what Maudie means. Is she talking about Katherine? Is Katherine not her real mother? Who are Mama One and Mama Two?)*

This process demonstrates to struggling readers that the teacher too is asking questions as she reads and is always attempting to find answers. After you have modeled this strategy, struggling readers should be given an opportunity to do it with a book that is on their instructional level, but they have not read previously.

TEXT-TALK

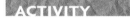

(GRADES 2–5)

In using text-talks, first introduced by Beck and McKeown (2001), the kind of text and the kind of talk used is very important. Beck and McKeown suggest that all texts should be "conceptually challenging to require grappling with ideas and taking an active stance toward constructing meaning" (p. 10) and that all talk or discussion between the teacher and reader should require the reader "to make sense of ideas that are about something beyond the here and now" (p. 10). Text-talks should be based on the following format:

1. Read a section of the story without showing the pictures.
2. Pose open-ended questions that focus on text ideas and encourage inferential thinking. The open-ended questions should encourage language development.
3. Have the child attempt to answer the questions.
4. If necessary, scaffold the child's thinking by posing more open-ended questions using the language of the book. Scaffolding is an important process as you provide information that the child has not provided.
5. Show pictures of that section of the story to encourage more discussion.
6. Repeat steps 1–5 with the each section of the story until the story is complete.

Using the language of the story during text-talks will encourage children to later use the story's vocabulary in retellings and summarizations.

RETELLINGS

(GRADES 1–5)

In a retelling, proficient readers state the main points of the story in a logical sequence. First they describe the place, time, and main characters. Next, they state the main problem and *briefly* summarize the sequence of events in chronological order; then they state the resolution. To help a struggling reader, ask for a retelling at the end of each story that is read to him and to stories that he reads to you. At first, permit students to retell the story and closely listen to the order and the events they include in the retelling. Focus on the following questions as the student retells the story: "Does the reader emphasize main points or does he focus on small details?" and "Is the retelling in the correct sequence?" If the student lacks retelling skills, use the following prompts, which will help him create a format in his mind for retelling. Using prompt cards with the questions helps the reader retell concisely and correctly in the sequence.

1. Where did the story take place?
2. When?
3. Who are the main characters?
4. What is the main problem? (Get students to state this in one sentence.)
5. How does the problem get solved?

Between questions 4 and 5, you may ask for all the main events or roadblocks in the story.

ACTIVITY

DIRECTED LISTENING–THINKING ACTIVITY (DL–TA)

(GRADES 1–3)

A directed listening–thinking activity (DL–TA) is used before and during the reading and the teacher does the reading. You may use this strategy in two ways. One way is as follows:

1. Read the title without showing the picture to the students.
2. Ask them to predict what will happen in the story.
3. Read a little of the story and have the students validate the prediction.
4. Ask the students to predict what will happen next.

These steps continue to the end of the book. The second way to use this strategy is the following:

1. Show the picture on the outside cover without reading the title.
2. Have the students predict what will happen in the story.
3. Read the title, turn to the first page, show the pictures on the first open page, and ask the students to make predictions about what will happen on that page.
4. Read that page as the students validate predictions.

These steps continue to the end of the book.

ACTIVITY

DIRECTED READING–THINKING ACTIVITY

(GRADES 1–3)

Directed reading–thinking activity (DR–TA) is a strategy used before and during reading. It differs from the DL–TA because here the students do the reading. Students look at the cover of the book, read the title, and predict what will happen in the story. Students then read to validate their predictions. This cycle continues as students read the book, with readers using chapter titles, illustrations, and so forth, to make predictions.

The DR–TA can also involve covering up the words of the book and allowing readers to make predictions about the story based solely on the pictures. Later the words are exposed and they read to validate the predictions.

SUMMARIZING

Summarizing is the act of writing out the main events of a reading selection. Again, you can practice this skill with a struggling reader by providing prompts. At first students should be permitted to write phrases only in response to the prompts. Figure 9.10 is an example of a prompt sheet.

ACTIVITY

(GRADES 1–6)

FIGURE 9.10   Prompts for writing a story summary.

Where?	Piney Creek
When?	October
Who?	Pumpkin Man, Hattie, Hattie's father
Problem?	Hattie wants to keep one pumpkin for a jack-o' lantern, but father promised 100 pumpkins to the pumpkin man.
Main Events?	Hattie tried to hide one pumpkin so her father was going to the cellar to get mother's pumpkin that she was going to use for pies.
Resolution?	Pumpkin man took the pumpkin that Hattie was hiding and carved a face in the pumpkin and gave it to Hattie.

Source: Summary based on *The Pumpkin Man from Piney Creek* by Darleen Bailey-Beard (1995). New York: Simon & Schuster.

From these prompts, the student learns how to write a summary using complete sentences and sequencing the information presented on the prompt card. You should progress from giving prompts to not giving prompts. Retellings and summaries should be completed after you have read stories to a struggling reader, and after the student reads stories independently.

EXPERIENCE–TEXT RELATIONSHIPS (ETR)

The experience–text relationship (ETR) strategy, designed by Au (1993) for use with multicultural classrooms, is used during all three stages of the reading event. During the prereading stage, ask the student questions that will relate the story's theme to her background experiences (Walker, 1996). Then connect the student's answers to the story. Following is a sequence of the strategy:

1. Explain the main idea of the story.
2. Relate the main idea to the child's life experiences.
3. Ask the reader to make predictions based on the discussion.

ACTIVITY

(GRADES 2–5)

4. Set a purpose for reading.

5. Ask the student to read a small passage to validate her predictions.

6. Have the student make more predictions and validate them until the story is complete.

7. After the story is read, connect the theme of the story to the student's background experiences.

To use this strategy, you need to know some background information about the student. For example, if you know that the struggling reader has just changed schools, Katie Couric's *The Brand New Kid* (2000) could be used for ETR. Following is a sample sequence for the discussion.

1. This story is about a boy, Lazlo, coming to a new school at the beginning of the year.

2. Have you ever moved to a new place and changed schools? How did you feel? Did you have any problems making friends?

3. Do you think Lazlo will have the same types of problems? What other types of problems do you think he could have?

4. Looking at the picture, how do you think Lazlo feels?

5. (Read a small passage to validate predictions.)

6. (More predictions are made as passages are read.)

7. Did Lazlo experience any of the same things you did when you started a new school? Did you make friends in the same manner that Lazlo did?

ACTIVITY

(GRADES 1–5)

CLOZE PASSAGES FOR MODELING COMPREHENSION STRATEGIES

Using cloze passages gives you the opportunity to model how you use language systems to comprehend text. First, prepare a passage at the reader's instructional level and demonstrate how to figure out which word fits the blank. Then explain how you attempt to see if a word sounds right, if it makes sense, and if it fits the story. Demonstrate also how you use your life experience and the text's illustrations to help find the correct word. Since pictures can help readers select the correct word, you may wish to use the book and cover every fifth word with sticky notes, which will protect the book from damage. The cloze passage should include about 200 to 300 words.

Following is a short passage from Lillian Hoban's *Arthur's Pen Pal* (1976), an I CAN READ book. Following the passage is an example of a teacher modeling how he completes the passage.

1

It was Sunday night. Mother and Father had *gone* out to dinner.

        2   3
The *baby-sitter* was watching television. Violet *was* doing her homework.

      4   5   6
She *drew* a picture of a *cow* eating grass. "Arthur," she *said*, "will you help me

    7
with my homework?

Teacher: "It was Sunday Night. Mother and Father had '*blank*.'" I am going to read to the end of the sentence to see what would make sense.

"Mother and Father had '*blank*' out to dinner."

Ah, I see it needs an action verb. Let's see what would make sense: "had went."

No, that doesn't sound good.

"Had gone." That sounds good. Let's see if that makes sense. "Mother and Father had gone out to dinner." What do you think, does that fit?

Now let's read on. "The '*blank*' was watching television." I know it has to be a noun because of the word *the*, and I know that a person can watch television.

The illustration looks like a lady. Let's see if that makes sense. "The lady was watching television." That sounds good and makes sense, but I know that when my parents went out to dinner, they got a baby-sitter for me. Would baby-sitter fit? "The baby-sitter was watching television." *Yes*, that makes sense. I think I'll keep baby-sitter because that is what I called the lady who came to take care of me when my mother and father went away. Do you think that sounds good?

Let's continue to read. "Violet '*blank*' doing her homework."

It would make sense to say, "Violet is doing her homework."

Let's begin at the beginning of the story to see if all of it makes sense.

"It was Sunday night. Mother and Father had gone out to dinner. The baby-sitter was watching television. Violet is doing" That doesn't sound right with the rest of the story. Since the author writes as if all of this happened some time ago, I think *was* would sound better. Let's try it again.

"It was Sunday night. Mother and Father had gone out to dinner. The baby-sitter was watching television. Violet was doing her homework." *Yes*, that sounds better.

"She '*blank*' a picture of a '*blank*' eating grass." The illustration looks like she is drawing a picture of a cow. Let me see if this makes sense: "She drew a picture of a cow eating grass." *Yes*, that makes sense.

"Arthur," she '*blank*,' "will you help me '*blank*' my homework?"

The question mark at the end of the sentence tells me that Violet is asking Arthur for help. Does *asked* make sense? "'Arthur,' she asked." *Yes*, that makes sense. (Notice: the correct word is *said*, but *asked* makes good sense and is grammatically correct.)

"Arthur," she asked, "will you help me '*blank*' my homework?" I think *with* would make sense. Let's see. "'Arthur,' she asked, 'will you help me with my homework?'" *Yes*, that makes sense.

Note how the teacher first reads to the end of each sentence, a good strategy to see what makes sense. Then the teacher rereads the sentence and sometimes the entire passage to see if the story makes sense. Throughout the entire process the focus is on "reading to make sense."

After the entire passage has been completed, remove the sticky notes to see if the reader has chosen the correct words. The notes should not be removed immediately because removing them does not encourage children to continue to read on for understanding.

GRAPHIC ORGANIZERS FOR NARRATIVE TEXT

ACTIVITY

(GRADES 2–5)

The general term "graphic organizer" is used to include all types of story maps, charts, webs, diagrams, or any visual representation of the story's content. Some graphic organizers chart the beginning, middle, and ending of the story. Most organizers include the setting, characters, problem, main events, and resolution. Previously in this chapter, we discussed *The Story Face* by Staal (2000). Figure 9.11 includes examples of three types of graphic organizers. When selecting one to introduce to a struggling reader, consider the age of the reader, his reading ability, and the purpose for using the strategy. For each one of these organizers, you should first model how to fill in the structure and then monitor the student as he first begins to use it.

FIGURE 9.11   Types of graphic organizers.

STORY MAP

(based on *The Wren* by P. Polacco)

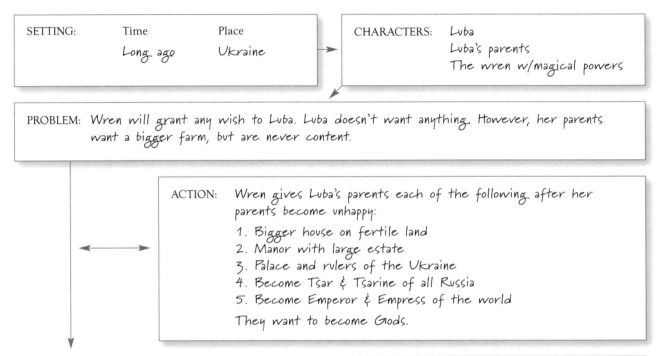

SETTING: Time   Place

Long ago   Ukraine

CHARACTERS: Luba
Luba's parents
The wren w/magical powers

PROBLEM: Wren will grant any wish to Luba. Luba doesn't want anything. However, her parents want a bigger farm, but are never content.

ACTION: Wren gives Luba's parents each of the following after her parents become unhappy:

1. Bigger house on fertile land
2. Manor with large estate
3. Palace and rulers of the Ukraine
4. Become Tsar & Tsarine of all Russia
5. Become Emperor & Empress of the world

They want to become Gods.

OUTCOME: Wren knows that Luba does not like her parents' last wish. Wren returns them to their former poor dacha on a small piece of poor land. — But they are happy!

Source: J. David Cooper, *Literacy*, Fourth Edition. Copyright © 2000 by Houghton Mifflin Company. Adapted with permission.

STORY WEB

(based on *Henny Penny*)

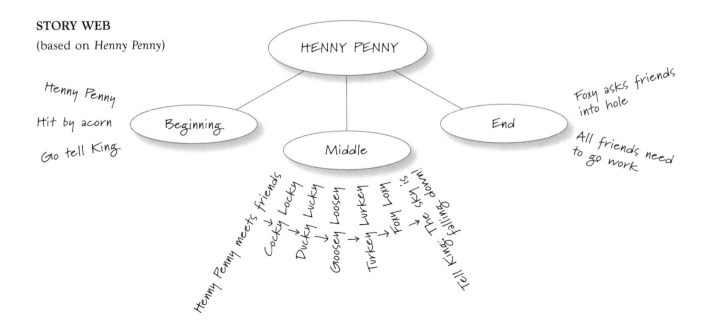

FIGURE 9.11 Continued.

MT. PLOT
(based on *The Old Woman Who Lived in a Vinegar Bottle* by M. R. MacDonald)

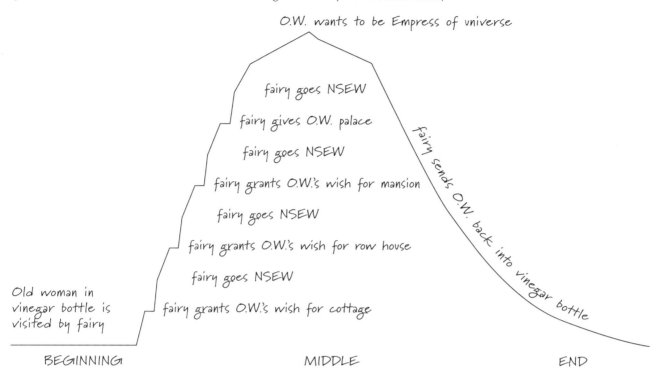

CHARACTER PERSPECTIVE CHART

ACTIVITY

(GRADES 4–6)

Many stories depict conflict between the goals of two characters. For example, in Anna Harwell Celenza's *The Farewell Symphony* (2000), Joseph Haydn and his 22 musicians have a goal to go back to their families in Austria after spending a long summer in Hungary providing music for Prince Nicholas; Prince Nicholas's conflicting goal is to remain long into the fall at his Hungarian summer palace and have the musicians provide music for all his parties. Shanahan and Shanahan (1997) introduce the Character Perspective Chart, which follows a story map from two characters' points of view. Shanahan and Shanahan suggest that this type of chart helps readers to draw inferences about the goals of each character. Figure 9.12 features a character perspective chart of *The Farewell Symphony*.

FIGURE 9.12   Character perspective chart of characters in *The Farewell Symphony*.

Haydn & Musicians	MAIN CHARACTER	Prince Nicholas
Palace in Hungary	SETTING	Palace in Hungary
Haydn and musicians want to return to Austria.	PROBLEM	Nicholas wants to stay in Hungary.
Go back to Austria	GOAL	Stay in Hungary
Musicians ask to go home	ATTEMPTS	Prince says later
Musicians beg for their families to join them.		Prince says there is no room in the palace.
Musicians say they are going home.		Prince says he will fire them if they do.
Haydn writes the Farewell Symphony to show Prince the anger of the musicians.		Prince was upset with the angry music.
Musicians play with passion.	OUTCOME	Prince is filled with compassion and permits them to go home.
Reward awaits those who are faithful.	THEME	Think of others' feelings.

Source: Adapted from T. Shanahan and S. Shanahan (1997). Character perspective charting: Helping children to develop a more complete conception of story. *The Reading Teacher, 50*(8), 668–677. Copyright © 1997 by the International Reading Association.

ACTIVITY

RETELLING WITH PUPPETS

(GRADES 1–4)   Retelling a story using simple stick or sack puppets helps readers with sequencing and recalling main points. When children act out the story, they need to draw inferences about a character's vocal quality and motives, and simple puppets help achieve this. A puppet should be created for each character, and students should manipulate all the puppets in the retelling. One enjoyable story for young children to retell with puppets is *The Little Old Woman Who Was Not Afraid of Anything* (1986) by Linda Williams. Many of students' favorite stories can be retold with the use of puppets.

ACTIVITY

"AND THIS IS THE REST OF THE STORY"

(GRADES 3–5)   To use this strategy, a teacher reads the story, stopping at a critical point, such as the climax. The student then tells the rest of the story. In order for the student's ending to be plausible, the student must have comprehended the story up to that point and must make inferences as he thinks out the ending. After he tells his ending, the teacher can read the story's ending. It is enjoyable for the student to compare his ending to the author's. Some good stories to use with this strategy are the following:

Cloudy with a Chance of Meatballs (1978) by Judi Barrett

Show and Tell (1991) by Elvina Woodruff

The Popcorn Shop (1993) by Alice Low

Vanishing Pumpkins (1996) by Tomie dePaola

Strega Nona's Magic Lessons (1982) by Tomie dePaola

RECIPROCAL QUESTIONING

In this strategy the student and teacher take turns asking each other questions. After you and the student read to a certain point in the story, instruct the student to ask you a literal question. You then ask the students a literal or inferential question. Then read another section of the story and repeat the process. Since most children ask literal questions, you can model higher-level thinking by asking inferential and evaluative questions. See Figure 9.13 for an explanation of the different kinds of questions.

FIGURE 9.13   Types of questions.

1. **Literal questions.** Literal questions can be found on the page; the purpose of a literal question is to check a reader's ability to recall information stated in the book. For example, one literal question from *Possum Magic* (1983) by Mem Fox is "What could Hush do when she was invisible?" The answer is stated in the story.

2. **Inferential questions.** The answers to inferential questions are not written verbatim in the text. In order to answer inferential questions, a student needs to read between the lines. For example, one inferential question from Patricia Polacco's *Thank you, Mr. Falker* (1998) is "Why did tears come to Mr. Falker's eyes when Trisha did learn to read?" The answer for this question is not stated directly in the story; however, there is a correct answer to the question, and a reader who comprehends the story will understand why Mr. Falker cries.

3. **Critical questions.** Critical questions require a reader to analyze and synthesize in order to give a correct answer. A critical question may require a student to gather information from a number of books or from her personal experiences.

4. **Evaluative questions.** Evaluative questions have no right or wrong answer. A reader gives his own opinions, but must provide sound reasoning. One example of an evaluative question from *Possum Magic* is "What would have happened to Hush if Grandma Poss could not make Hush visible again?" There is no correct answer; however, if a student comprehends the story and draws on his past experiences, he will have a plausible answer.

Critical and evaluative questions require a student to read past the words on the page.

WORDLESS BOOKS FOR DEVELOPING INFERENTIAL READING

While "reading" wordless books, children need to make inferences about characters, plot, and motives. They need to connect sets of pictures to make a story. Drawing inferences and connecting information to previously read information are two components of comprehension.

To use this strategy, read the title and permit the student to skim each page of the entire book. Then, have the student go back and "read" page by page. If the story is not making sense, you may ask her to go back and "read" the page again. Wordless books can be used to develop inferential reading skills when a teacher asks questions to have students add more detail to their stories. For example, concerning *Tuesday* (1991) by David Wiesner, a teacher may ask what the man who is eating the midnight snack is thinking when he sees frogs flying past the window, or why the old lady did not wake up when the frogs watched her television.

Appendix A.4 offers a list of wordless books that can be used for this strategy.

VENN DIAGRAMS FOR NARRATIVE TEXT

(GRADES 2–6) One aspect of comprehension is being able to compare and contrast information. Venn diagrams are often used to depict comparison and contrast. One effective application of this strategy involves using fairy tales that have been retold by various authors and illustrators. You and a student may read two versions of the same tale and then compare the versions by completing a Venn diagram. Figure 9.14 shows a diagram comparing Jan Brett's *The Mitten* (1989) and Alvin Tresselt's *The Mitten* (1964).

FIGURE 9.14 Venn diagram comparing two versions of *The Mitten*.

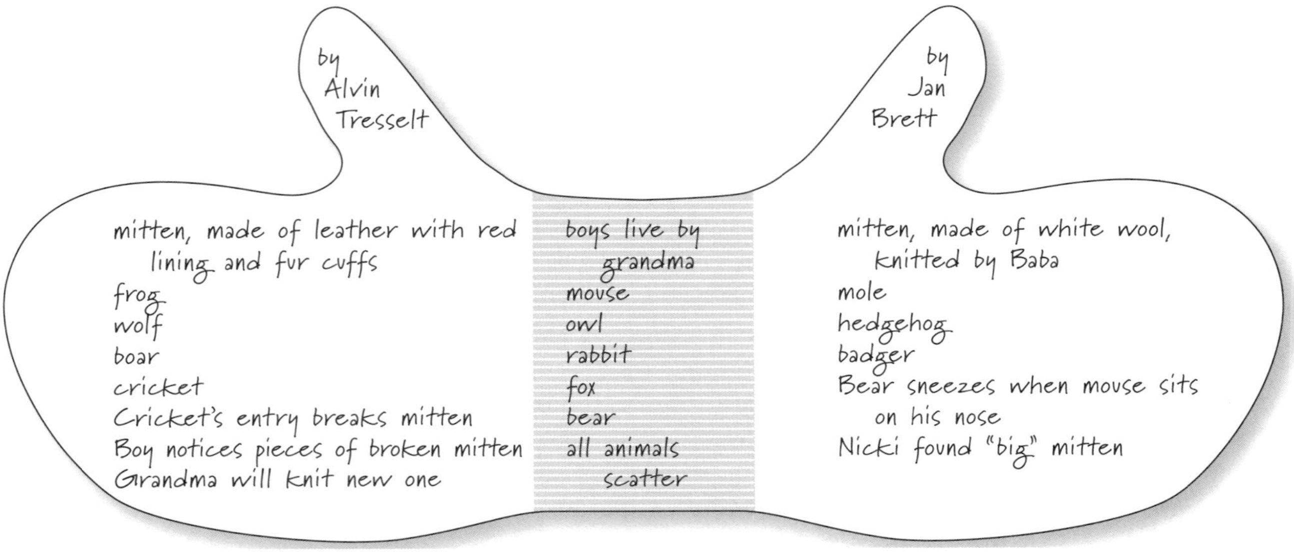

by Alvin Tresselt

mitten, made of leather with red lining and fur cuffs
frog
wolf
boar
cricket
Cricket's entry breaks mitten
Boy notices pieces of broken mitten
Grandma will knit new one

boys live by grandma
mouse
owl
rabbit
fox
bear
all animals scatter

by Jan Brett

mitten, made of white wool, knitted by Baba
mole
hedgehog
badger
Bear sneezes when mouse sits on his nose
Nicki found "big" mitten

CHARACTER SKETCH

(GRADES 3–5) A character sketch is a child's drawing of a character. This strategy encourages readers to visualize the characters. It provides graphically inclined students an opportunity to connect their artistic ability with reading.

To use this strategy, read a story to students without showing the pictures. After the reading, students can draw a picture of the characters. You then ask them to explain the drawing.

INVESTIGATOR'S REPORT

(GRADES 3–6) Manning (2001) suggests that comprehension can be increased through the study of characterization. She believes that by having children gain insights into the characters' lives, readers become more empathetic toward the characters; when students become empathetic, they demonstrate improved comprehension of the actions, feelings, and motives of the characters.

For this strategy, first read the description of the character, but do not show any pictures. In fairy tales, only one word may be used to describe the character, such as "sly

FIGURE 9.15 Investigator's report.

Completed by *Cindy*   on this date *10-15*

Character *F. Bam Morrison*   Sex *M*

Age *50*   Nationality *Caucasian*

Height *5'7"*   Weight *250*

Unique physical markings *mustache*   Tone of voice *"smooth" convincing*

Personality *Manipulative*

Close friends to call in case of an emergency *Has no friends*

Possible enemies *Bobbie Jo, Clara Jean, entire town of Wetumka, OK*

Problems the character encountered *At first townspeople would not buy circus tickets*

---

fox" or "pretty princess." In other stories the description may be longer. After you read the description, have students answer as many of the Investigator's Report questions as possible. If the story does not supply the information, readers may supply the description. Figure 9.15 is an example of the Investigator's Report based on Darleen Beard's *The Flimflam Man* (1998). You may add or delete questions in order to make the report fit the story.

ALTERNATE WRITING

ACTIVITY

(GRADES 3–6)

This strategy combines reading and writing. Alternate writing results in a story written by a teacher and a struggling reader. It helps children acquire literary knowledge such as elements of a story—setting, characters, conflict, climax, and resolution—and thus aids comprehension. Alternate writing involves the following steps:

1. With the student, agree on a topic and a title for her story.
2. Write the first sentence of the story.
3. Have the student read your sentence and then add a sentence.
4. Then, you read the first two sentences and add the third sentence. The alternate writing continues until the story is complete.
5. Discuss story elements with the student as she writes.

All good stories begin with a setting and a problem. The story needs to include roadblocks as well as a resolution. The focus throughout the writing should be on comprehension, not correct spelling.

The following is an example of an opening sentence for an alternate writing story. Note that the teacher does not name the frog. This permits the student to write a sentence about the frog's name or to begin describing the place.

Once upon a time, in a far away place, there lived a sad frog.

STORY LINES

(GRADES 3–6)

The story line is a strategy to use with struggling readers who enjoy making up their own stories. This strategy connects writing, predicting, reading, and validating. The book on which the story line is based must be new to the readers. The following is the process of the story line:

1. On a piece of paper, list 10 to 15 nouns as they appear in the story.
2. Have students write short stories, using those nouns in the given order. The story must have a beginning, middle, and end.
3. Ask students to read their stories aloud.
4. Have either you or the students read the original story and compare it to their versions.

This strategy can be used with any story. Figure 9.16 includes a list of nouns found in Tomie dePaola's *Fin M'Coul* (1981) and a student story based on *Fin M'Coul*. If you know the real story, you will recognize that this story does not follow the original plot. However, the student did include a setting, characters, a conflict, and a resolution. A student will enjoy reading the real story and comparing it to his own.

FIGURE 9.16 Creating a story line: Nouns and student story.

Giant	Earthquake	Cradle
Knitting	Charm	Bread
Causeway	Thread	Teeth
Thunderbolt	Cheese	Tea
Bread	Brass finger	

Sample Story

Once upon a time in a far away place lived a lady giant who earned her living by knitting. She lived by a causeway; her name was Thunderbolt because she could produce a thunderbolt any time she wanted to bake bread. Sometimes she baked bread so that it was hard enough to cause an earthquake. But one time, she baked soft bread and used her bread as a charm to lure a young wicked prince to her cottage. The prince was very proud and always wore red threads between his teeth although no one knew why he wore it.

The lady giant knew that this young prince loved bread with cheese more than any other food. So she took a large chunk of cheese, put a brass finger into the cheese and placed it in a cheese cradle. She baked a loaf of soft bread and invited the prince in for some bread and cheese. (She knew he would not be able to resist the offer.) As he bit into the cheese, he bit into the brass finger which caused all his teeth to fall out. Straightaway he lost all his handsome looks and could only drink lukewarm tea after that day. But after that day, he no longer was wicked; he treated all his people with respect. All the people thanked lady giant for a job well done.

C omputers fascinate many students. Often reluctant readers become interested in reading through using the computer (Sibenaller, 2001). Doty, Popplewell, and Byers (2001) found that students who read interactive CD-ROMs "obtained significantly higher scores than students who read the print version of the storybooks" (p. 3). Many CD-ROMs for younger children are interactive. The computer narrates the story as the text is highlighted. After the text is narrated, the children can click on the various characters and objects in the pictures; the talking characters and moving objects expand the story. Living Books has many titles that young children enjoy; however, with the Living Books series the computer voice cannot be turned off, so children must listen and follow along with these CD-ROMs. Most struggling readers cannot read aloud with this series because the pace is too fast for them.

Unlike Living Books, stories on CD-ROMs published by Discis Books do have the option of removing the narration; thus, students can read the story at their own pace. When they come to a word they do not know, they can click on the word and the computer will pronounce it for them. If they hold the cursor on the word, the computer will also provide the definition for the word. This type of CD-ROM becomes a useful teaching tool for struggling readers and a time-saver for busy teachers. Appendix A.7 has a list of titles from Living Books and Discis Books.

TECHNOLOGY

T he No Child Left Behind Act has named comprehension of narrative text as one of the areas of reading in which school districts must document student growth if they are to receive federal funds. Most students are able to achieve comprehension by listening to stories and by reading stories written at their instructional level. However, some students struggle with narrative comprehension.

After reviewing standardized tests scores of your students, you may become aware of the students who struggle. You may administer a number of different informal reading instruments to help you understand what causes these students to struggle. After determining the strengths and weaknesses of a student, you may choose from a number of strategies as you engage the student in authentic reading and writing tasks.

CONCLUDING THOUGHTS

COMPREHENSION OF INFORMATIONAL TEXT

Teaching means helping a child realize his potential.

ERICH FROMM

Scenario

J. J. is a third grader who loves to read stories and act them out through drama and puppet shows. She is very interested in the characters of the story; she always pretends to be one of them. When reading stories, J. J. is good at decoding unknown words and has a good reading rate.

When she begins to read informational books, she decodes the text without problems, but has difficulty summarizing what she has read. She complains to Mr. Blackright that she doesn't get the "story" because there are no characters. Mr. Blackright remembers that at the beginning of the year during share time, J. J. talked about a trip to the ocean that she had taken with her family. She told about the fish her family saw while on a boat ride. Mr. Blackright understands that J. J. thinks reading only involves stories, so he decides to wean J. J. from stories to informational text by using some nonfiction books about sea life, such as *Octopus' Den* (1997) by Deirdre Langeland, *Coral Reef Hideaway* (1998) by Doe Boyle, and *Box Turtle at Long Pond* (1989) by William George. All these books share information about sea creatures, but each author gives the creature a name so the information is presented in a story-like manner. J. J. enjoys the books because she is reading "stories" about marine life.

After reading *Octopus' Den* with J. J., Mr. Blackright asks her to tell him what she remembers about the "character" Octopus. As J. J. recalls facts, Mr. Blackright constructs a graphic organizer (found in Figure 10.1), so J. J. can remember all the interesting facts about Octopus.

After finishing the book, J. J. questions Mr. Blackright about one of the facts found in the book. "Can an octopus really shoot ink?" she asks. His response is, "Let's find out by looking up *octopus* on the Internet." They connect to the Internet and use *octopus* as a search term. Soon they find many more facts about octopi and add them to the graphic organizer.

Mr. Blackright is able to shift J. J. from narrative text to informational text by choosing a topic that interests her and by choosing books that have characters like stories do, but are based on facts like informational texts. Using the graphic organizer helps J. J. sort the facts she learns about the creature. When she questions her teacher about the information, Mr. Blackright instructs her to seek another source to confirm the information. Needless to say, J. J. soon learns to love informational texts and develops some strategies (1) to help her sort out the facts, (2) to help her remember the information, and (3) to become a critical reader.

FIGURE **10.1** Graphic organizer based on *Octopus' Den* by Deirdre Langeland.

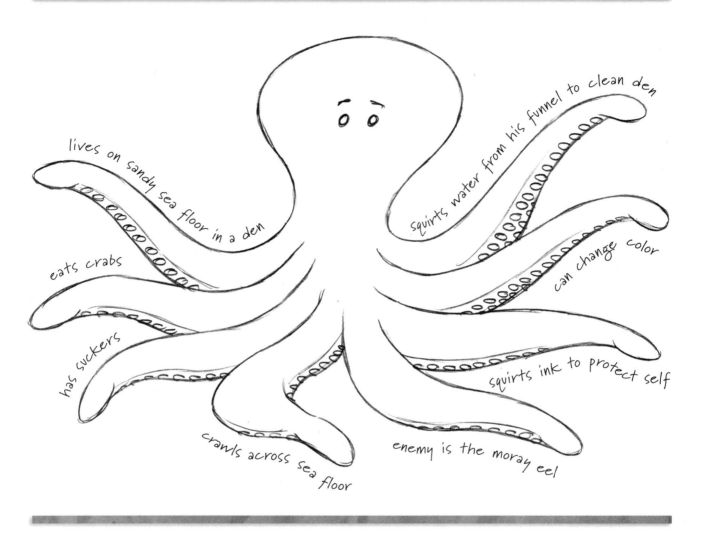

INTRODUCTION

There are many students like J. J. who read narrative text with ease and enjoyment, but who struggle with and dislike informational texts. However, since 75 to 90 percent of U. S. classrooms rely on textbooks for instruction, it is essential that students receive extensive practice reading nonfiction books and other informational sources in order to become proficient readers of expository texts (Palmer & Stewart, 1997).

Fortunately, in recent years many teachers have begun to use more sources than the assigned textbook; they supplement it with trade books and the Internet. Both are more engaging, yet can be more challenging than textbooks. They are engaging because they provide detailed information about one topic and use photographs or clear illustrations to explain the topic. They are more challenging for a number of reasons. First, trade books often include citations from primary sources, such as personal letters, newspaper articles, and diary excerpts, which may make these more challenging for poor comprehenders because primary sources sometimes introduce readers to archaic words and styles. Second, trade books and the Internet can be more challenging when students read conflicting pieces of information, because then they need to evaluate the writers' credentials. Finally, when they gather information from more that one source, readers need to synthesize the information (Afflerbach & Van Sledright, 2000).

THREE FACTORS AFFECTING THE COMPREHENSION PROCESS

Three major factors affect the comprehension process of informational text. These are (1) factors within the reader, and (2) factors within the reader's environment, and (3) factors within the text. Understanding the complexity of these factors gives teachers a better understanding of why some readers may struggle with reading in general and expository text in particular.

Factors Within Reader

Some reading skills are basic for comprehending all types of text (narrative, expository, poetry, plays, and so on). These basic skills include the following:

- The ability to recognize a large bank of sight words.
- The ability to decode unknown, one-syllable words.
- The ability to analyze words with multiple syllables.
- The ability to read at an adequate rate.
- The ability to recognize when comprehension breaks down.
- The ability to choose an appropriate strategy when comprehension breaks down.

When comprehending informational text, readers must also have the following:

- Knowledge of organizational patterns of expository text.
- Adequate background knowledge of topic being read.
- Knowledge of specific terms associated with the topic.
- Ability to analyze author's purpose and credentials.
- Ability to synthesize similar information from various sources.

Other factors that affect readers' ability to comprehend informational text are their linguistic knowledge, syntactic knowledge, semantic knowledge, decoding skills, their prior knowledge and experience, and their personal attitudes and interests.

Linguistic Knowledge

Readers' linguistic competence includes their understanding of stress, pitch, and juncture. **Stress** refers to the emphasis one word may receive over the other words in a sentence. Proficient readers know which words to stress, thus aiding comprehension (Swanson & De La Paz, 1998). In the following selection from Adler's A *Picture Book of Benjamin Franklin* (1990), proficient readers automatically stress the italicized parts that affect the meaning of the passage:

> In 1765 Benjamin went to England. He spoke at the English House of Commons *against* the Stamp Act; a tax that the American colonists felt was *un*fair.
>
> (unpaged)

Obviously, the emphasis on *against* and the *un* in *un*fair help readers understand the main point of the passage. When struggling readers read in a monotone pitch, they do not stress the important words; thus, they often miss the meaning of a passage.

Pitch refers to intonation. The end marks—period, exclamation point, and question mark—guide intonation. Notice the different message conveyed when the punctuation is changed in the following three sentences:

> Benjamin Franklin was chosen to help write the Declaration of Independence. (*Just a fact.*)
> Benjamin Franklin was chosen to help write the Declaration of Independence? (*Questioning if it really was Benjamin Franklin.*)
> Benjamin Franklin was chosen to help write the Declaration of Independence! (*Extremely excited that it was Benjamin Franklin and not some other person whom you do not trust.*)

Juncture is the pause that occurs in language. In written texts, juncture is indicated with commas. Notice the difference in meaning of the following sentences:

> Mary, Jane cannot come to the party.
> Mary Jane cannot come to the party.

In the first sentence, the speaker is telling Mary about Jane; in the second sentence, however, the speaker says that Mary Jane (one person) in unable to come the party.

Struggling readers who merely read words often do not pause for the commas; thus, they often receive the wrong message.

Syntactic Knowledge

Syntactic knowledge is also important when reading informational text. **Syntax** is the part of language that deals with word order, punctuation, and paragraphs. Word order is an important element of written language. Notice the different meaning conveyed if the first sentence below is misread as the second:

The turtle bites the head off the worm.

The worm bites the head off the turtle.

Both proficient and struggling readers' eyes move ahead of the voice when reading aloud (Smith, 1997). However, good readers recognize the obscurity of the second sentence and go back and correct the mistake; poor readers may not recognize the error and keep on reading, not realizing that their reading of the sentence does not make sense (Bos & Vaughn, 1994).

Punctuation is one way a writer makes clear the intended meaning of a passage. Notice the difference in meaning in the following two signs:

```
NO
SWIMMING ALLOWED!
```

```
NO!
SWIMMING ALLOWED!
```

The intended meaning of the author was sign number one; unfortunate readers, however, who read the sign as if it were written the second way, may find themselves in danger.

Proficient readers understand that a new paragraph signals a change in thought and that each paragraph has a main topic with supporting details. As these readers absorb new information from each paragraph, they organize and categorize the new information. They constantly make mental notes of new or expanded ideas. Good readers also check expository text features like headings and subheadings to give them clues on how the information is organized. Struggling readers lack many of these skills and strategies (Bos & Vaughn, 1994).

Semantic Knowledge

Another aspect of our language that affects readers' comprehension is **semantics.** Within a sentence, semantics refers to the common meanings of words and their combinations. For example, in this next sentence, readers who do not understand the common meaning of *hovel* will not completely understand the poor living conditions of the immigrants in South America: "The new immigrants in South America were forced to live three families to a hovel."

Struggling readers, who often do not know the multiple meanings of many common words, may struggle with this sentence: "Thomas Jefferson was asked to chair the meeting." Struggling readers may picture Thomas Jefferson sitting in a chair during the meeting while others stood.

Semantics also includes the relationships among ideas. Ambiguous pronoun usage may cause confusion for proficient readers, but ambiguous pronouns may cause the comprehension of struggling readers to completely break down. In the following passage, readers who fail to pick up on the author's assignments of gender to the raccoon and the turtle may become confused:

A young porcupine walks up to the stone. She is also looking for worms. The turtle sees her and quickly draws himself up into his shell. She turns him over, but cannot pry the shell open with her fingers. She eats the worms and wanders off.

Proficient readers use the strategy of rereading until they understand such a passage; struggling readers, however, continue to read, not realizing that they are confused (Bos & Vaughn, 1994).

Decoding Ability

Readers' ability to decode and analyze word structure also influences their ability to comprehend any type of text, narrative or expository. However, since expository text often introduces many technical terms in a short passage, readers' decoding ability helps them to pronounce terms automatically that may be part of their aural vocabularies. When they hear themselves say these words, they understand them. Struggling readers, who cannot effectively decode, do not have the benefit of hearing the word. Also when these readers spend a long time attempting to decode a word, they become discouraged because it takes so long to read each assigned passage.

Decoding skills include the knowledge of letter–sound relationships, consonant blends, consonant digraphs, vowel digraphs, and diphthongs. A skill equally important to decoding is the ability to analyze words—since many technical terms have multiple syllables. Readers who can easily break words into syllables and who know the meanings of basic prefixes, suffixes, and root words read faster and become less discouraged than readers who lack these skills. For example, the word *transferable* may be a rather long word for third-grade readers; however, if they can readily recognize the prefix (*trans*) and the suffix (*able*) and identify the meanings of each part, they can easily figure out the meaning of the entire word.

Prior Knowledge and Experience

Anders and Lloyd (1996) conclude that readers' prior knowledge "affects comprehension more than reading ability" (p. 324). Prior knowledge includes all of life's experiences—walks with adults through woods and parks, or trips to a zoo, a museum, the ocean, or other places of interest. All experiences that take children out of their immediate surroundings help them develop a broader view of the world in which they live. Through many such experiences, they are introduced to new concepts in a natural setting. This knowledge aids reading comprehension (Carr & Wixson, 1986; Richardson & Morgan, 1997). Some students come to school never having left their local community. Therefore, their background knowledge gained through first-hand experience is limited. Consider the contrast between the background of Sally, who has never been anywhere outside her own community, and that of George, who has traveled with his family to a wide variety of places in his home state, the United States, and other countries. On these trips, George has had many different first-hand experiences. Through all these experiences his vocabulary grew and his knowledge of the world increased.

When George and Sally's fifth-grade social studies class studied the Middle Ages, George had an advantage over Sally and the other students. The teacher, Mr. Black, chose Philip Steele's *I Wonder Why Castles Had Moats and Other Questions about Long Ago* (1994) as one of the books to read to the students. Mr. Black asked the students what they thought a *moat* was. Sally, who heard about castles in fairy tales and knew about queens, kings, princes, and princesses, predicted that a moat was someone who works for the royal family. Billy, who also heard stories about castles and was fascinated with the dungeons and weapons, thought a moat was a type of weapon used in the dungeons. However, George, who had visited castles, knew immediately that the moat is the water—sometimes natural, sometimes man-made—that surrounds the castle and protects its inhabitants from outside invaders. George was able to give a number of details, explaining how castles were also built on high hills and on rivers so the inhabitants of the castle could better defend it from enemies. Obviously, George was able to picture in his mind any new information about the Middle Ages more readily than the other children. George's interest in the Middle Ages was also greater than the other students' because of his experiences.

Since prior knowledge is based on all of one's personal experiences, it includes one's experience with informational text. Children who have had a parent or other adult read and discuss expository texts with them, understand that not all books tell a story. They understand that some books teach them about the world or provide important information for everyday use. As concept books are read to children, they are introduced to technical vocabulary that is unique to the particular topic. Obviously, these children have an advantage over children who have never had informational books read to them. Richardson and Morgan (1997) suggest that students with a broad background and understanding of the world will have an easier time comprehending texts than students with a more limited background.

Interests and Attitudes

A positive attitude toward learning and reading is one key to being a successful lifelong learner. A positive attitude, of course, may often originate in the home. There are many factors in the home that may cause children to have a negative attitude toward learning and reading. Parents who cannot read obviously cannot read to their children. Other parents who had bad experiences in school often express negative opinions of school and teachers. Children often embrace the negative attitudes of their parents. Teachers need to work with these negative attitudes and firmly grasp the fact that these children can achieve academic success. Sometimes the key to success is finding a subject that really interests the child.

Teachers must capitalize on the interests of struggling readers. Remember that not all children are interested in the same topics that interest the teacher and that it's okay for children to be passionate about a topic that makes the teacher squirm. If children are exclusively interested in snakes and bugs, the teacher needs to find books on those topics and read them with the children. To encourage expository reading, teachers need to elicit the interests of students by finding out what they do in their spare time and what they would like to do when they become adults.

Richardson and Morgan (1997) argue that poor readers need encouragement and a positive support system. You can offer encouragement and support not only by helping students find books and Internet sites on topics that really interest them, but also by making sure these sources are at their easy reading level so that students are not discouraged by overly difficult texts. The Assessment section of this chapter contains an Interest Inventory that will aid you in learning more about your students' interests.

It is clear that many factors affect readers' comprehension of informational texts. Figure 10.2 lists some characteristics of skilled and unskilled expository readers.

FIGURE 10.2   Characteristics of skilled and unskilled readers of informational texts.

SKILLED READERS

1. Know purpose for reading (e.g., to find comparisons, understand details).
2. Know if their purpose in reading was fulfilled.
3. Recognize large bank of words automatically.
4. Analyze technical words with ease.
5. Possess background knowledge of many topics and make use of it when reading.
6. Have advanced vocabulary about many topics.
7. Make inferences about information in the passage.
8. Use fix-up strategies when comprehension breaks down.
9. Are flexible in the use of strategies.
10. Paint mental pictures of the topic.
11. Recognize organizational structure of text (e.g., cause/effect, comparison/contract, sequence, definition).
12. Build relationships between larger units of text (e.g., relate information among chapters or books).
13. Know where to go for more information if passage is not clear (e.g., go to Internet, databases, or other books).
14. Use appropriate graphic organizers to summarize and to remember text.

UNSKILLED READERS

1. Are often poor decoders.
2. Give up when passage is not clear.
3. Lack word analysis skills.
4. Have limited background knowledge.
5. Do not relate limited background knowledge to the passage.
6. Have limited vocabulary.
7. Cannot monitor comprehension.
8. Cannot make inferences.
9. Do not create mental pictures of the passage's topic.
10. Do not recognize organizational structures of text.
11. Do not build relationships between larger units of text.
12. Have poor summarizing skills.
13. Do not acquire strategic strategies; need to be taught how, when, and where to consistently use appropriate comprehension strategies.

Sources: Anders & Lloyd (1996); Bos & Vaughn (1994); Gipe (1995); Kletzien (1991); Oakhill & Patel (1991); Richardson & Morgan (1997); Swanson & De La Paz (1998); Symons & Pressley (1993); Winn, Graham, & Prock (1993).

Factors Within the Environment

Home

Of the three environments most students inhabit—home, community, and school—the home most affects reading comprehension and is the foundation upon which attitudes toward reading are built. Richardson and Morgan (1997) argue that children who are good comprehenders have parents who read and discuss many different types of texts with their children, and have books, magazines, and other informational materials available in their home. They also view and discuss videos and educational TV programs with their children. They make good use of the community's library by checking out informational videos, CD-ROMs, and trade books, and by using the Internet in the library if they do not have access at home. Many parents model the love of learning new things by reading, viewing, and discussing complicated ideas and facts with their children; these children have a great source of prior knowledge from which to draw when reading informational texts.

Unfortunately, not all children come from language-rich home environments. Many homes have no access to books or magazines. Their parents do not take them to the library to check out books or to participate in educational programs. These parents do not recognize the importance of reading skills for their children, nor do they read for enjoyment themselves. Many poor comprehenders also have poor oral skills because they do not have adults with whom they converse. These children have parents who talk *to* them, but not *with* them. They do not discuss educational TV programs together, do not read together, and do not take nature walks together. Chapter 14 will address in detail the correlation between home experiences and reading comprehension.

Community

The second childhood environment that affects reading comprehension is that of the community. Consider, for example, two contrasting communities—Educationwise and Noread. The leaders of the little town of Educationwise love to learn new things and want the children in their community to learn about the world in which they live. After all, their wheat crops are exported to all parts of the world! Educationwise's community library is a great source of information because the community leaders understand the importance of providing funds for the library. This library has a vast selection of books, videos, and computer programs. There are many computers with free access to the Internet. This library also has many Saturday and after-school programs, such as story time, and focused studies on particular topics, authors, and genres. The Educationwise Public Library also provides classes that teach a range of crafts and other disciplines from different cultures. Some programs provide summer day camps in nature parks and other places of interest. The library staff welcomes children and young people and encourages them to "hang out" in the library and see what is happening inside. The children from Educationwise, who have access to such a library, have the opportunity to develop a rich vocabulary and a broad background of knowledge on many topics.

A second community in the same state as Educationwise is Noread. Noread has town leaders who do not see the importance of widening their children's horizons. This town's library, a very small, dilapidated building, houses outdated books. It has no computers or videos. It provides no Saturday or after-school programs or summer day camps to explore nature. In fact, it does nothing to entice children to come and explore the few books that are there. The children from Noread have few opportunities for outside enrichment in the community. The community leaders of Noread do not understand that the community's resources affect children's reading, their academic achievement, and life success.

A community can provide many resources that support the public schools and children's learning. All of these resources enrich children's background knowledge and encourage them to read more about the topics that interest them.

School

The third influential childhood environment is the school, and the most important aspect of the school environment is the classroom. The teacher is the most important element of the classroom, who can ensure that learning occurs. Successful classrooms have the following features:

1. Teachers who model a love of reading and learning new things.
2. Teachers who expect all children to succeed.
3. Teachers who accept all children as they are and do not assign blame for a student's lack of skills.
4. Teachers who encourage risk-taking, which happens when there is:
   - Little emphasis on grades.
   - No ridicule from other students.
   - Appropriate praise for good attempts.
   - Tolerance for mistakes.
   - Appropriate and timely feedback, given in a constructive and caring manner.
5. Teachers who ask higher-level thinking questions in addition to literal questions with correct answers.
6. Teachers who provide materials for all reading levels.

Effective, positive teachers provide a wide variety of learning materials. Besides many informational texts on a variety of topics, their classrooms contain computers and computer programs that appeal to a variety of interests, not just programs that enhance skills. There are science stations where experiments take place. Tables hold old appliances (with electrical cords cut off) that students can disassemble and then reassemble to understand how the appliance works. These teachers understand that hands-on experiences enhance the background knowledge that students use to comprehend informational texts. They also understand that many struggling readers first need hands-on experiences to entice them to read about the topic.

Factors Within Text

Although 75 to 90 percent of classrooms still rely exclusively on textbooks (Palmer & Stewart, 1997), there is a shift in recent years by many classroom teachers to supplement textbooks with quality nonfiction trade books, computer programs, and the Internet. These instructors realize that reading informational texts requires more than decoding skills and literal comprehension. Using a variety of reading materials requires students to (1) synthesize information, (2) analyze authors' credentials, and (3) apply critical thinking skills when confronted with conflicting information. These skills are higher-level thinking skills, which struggling readers are often not expected to use. Too often struggling readers are only asked to perform lower-level thinking tasks because teachers are convinced that these students are incapable of higher-level thinking. However, struggling readers are capable of higher-level thinking; they only need the opportunity to develop the skills. One way to develop these skills is to help the readers understand the organizational structure of expository texts and to help them develop an extensive technical vocabulary on specific topics. In this section, I will examine the following issues: (1) the organizational structure of expository text, (2) the use of technical vocabulary, (3) the characteristics of well-written texts, and (4) the use of readability formulas.

Organizational Structure of Expository Text

Expository text may be difficult for some students who have little difficulty with narrative text because the organizational structure of the former differs from that of the latter. In reading fictional stories, children become familiar with settings, characters, and plots, and focus on conflicts that need to be resolved. Since the organizational structure of expository texts omits many elements of a fictional narrative, students need to develop a new schema to grasp how the information is organized in expository texts. There are eight commonly used organizational patterns in expository texts: chronology or sequence, description or enumeration, listing, classification or hierarchy, comparison/contrast, cause/effect, problem/solution, and persuasion.

Chronology or sequence. A text that presents information in a chronological or sequential pattern features events that happen in a particular order, and the order is important to understanding the information presented. In chronological texts, the information is often organized around dates. Most of the time, the dates are explicitly stated; sometimes, however, the author gives only the number of years between events. With this type of text, students need to make inferences to attach dates to the events. David Adler, in *A Picture Book of Benjamin Franklin* (1990), includes dates and phrases that represent the passage of time. Following are some examples:

> Benjamin Franklin *was born* in Boston, Massachusetts on *January 17, 1706.*
> Benjamin *began school* when he was *eight years old.*
> When Benjamin *was ten,* he began to *work in his father's soap-and-candle shop.*
> When he was *twelve,* his father put Benjamin to *work in a print shop.*
> (unpaged)

From this information, the student can infer the following facts:

> 1706 – Benjamin Franklin was born.
> 1714 – He began school.
> 1716 – He quit school and began working in soap-and-candle shop.
> 1718 – He began working in print shop.

If the information in a text is sequential, the author will often use signal words such as *first, second, next, then, finally, at the same time,* and *meanwhile.* Teachers need to help struggling readers find these words so they can understand the sequence of the events.

Description or enumeration. If the organizational structure of the text is description, the author explains or describes in detail an event, an object, or a phenomenon so the reader can better understand it. Notice in the following examples how Seymour Simon describes the sperm whale in *Whales* (1989).

> The sperm whale is the only giant among the toothed whales. It is the animal that comes to mind when most people think of a whale. A sperm whale has a huge, squarish head, small eyes, and a thin lower jaw. All the fist-sized teeth, about fifty of them, are in the lower jaw. The male grows to sixty feet long and weighs as much as fifty tons. The female is smaller, reaching only forty feet and weighing less than twenty tons.
>
> (unpaged)

As with so many effective descriptions, Simon paints a picture with words. It is the readers' responsibility to transform those words into a mental picture. In this example, readers need to be able to draw a mental picture of a square head with a thin lower jaw and small eyes in order to understand what a sperm whale looks like. The readers also need to picture teeth that are the size of human fists. Proficient readers can do this without assistance. They may use a specific strategy, such as slowing down or rereading the passage, in order to create the picture in their minds (Bos & Vaughn, 1994). Struggling readers often just read the words without picturing these images. Teachers need to help struggling readers paint these mental pictures. Later in the chapter, I will discuss some strategies for this kind of visualization.

In the following example, from *I Wonder Why Castles Had Moats and Other Questions About Long Ago,* the author paints a picture so that readers can imagine the events and images of a Japanese *No* play.

No are Japanese plays in which actors wear masks and move very slowly, telling story-poems through mime and dance.

(p. 27)

As discussed earlier in the chapter, background knowledge is very important for comprehension of expository texts. It is clear here that readers will benefit from background knowledge about mime and story-poems in attempting to learn about *No* plays. Writers who use description and enumeration expect readers to bring the necessary background knowledge to the reading event because it is cumbersome for writers to explain every concept or term in detail. Teachers may need to demonstrate *mime* and read a *story-poem* in order for struggling readers to understand the author's description of *No*.

In enumeration, an author states a concept and then elaborates on it. In the text *Frogs* (1996), written for young readers, Carolyn MacLulich explains how a frog makes a croaking sound:

Male frogs make a croaking sound. They puff up the vocal sac under their chin, which makes the sound louder.

(p. 13)

Texts for older readers have more detailed descriptions. Notice how Seymour Simon enumerates the process by which the mother whale feeds her calf:

The mother squirts milk into the young calf's open mouth forty times a day. The milk is rich in fat and energy. Each feeding is very brief, because the baby must surface for air. But in a few seconds, the baby drinks two or three gallons of milk. In one day, a baby whale drinks more than 100 gallons of milk and may gain as much as 200 pounds.

(unpaged)

Listing. In this third type of organizational structure, authors may merely list all the things that fall into a particular category. In *Frogs* (1996), Carolyn MacLulich lists all the things frogs eat: "Frogs eat insects, spiders and worms. Some frogs eat larger animals, such as lizards, mice or even other frogs" (p. 12).

In the emergent reader book *Who Lives in the Rainforest?* (1998), Susan Canizares lists the inhabitants of a rainforest. Each type of creature is pictured on its own page with a simple two-word phrase. The text begins with the question "Who lives in the rainforest?" The following are some of the answers to this question:

Iguanas do.

Snakes too.

Jaguars do.

Pumas too.

This simple list with the colorful photographs of each creature intrigues even the emergent reader to find more information about rainforest creatures.

Classification or hierarchy. Scientific texts often use classification to show relationships among concepts. Notice how Mary Cerullo explains the categorical relationships among dolphins, whales, and humans in *Dolphins: What They Can Teach Us* (1999).

Dolphins are small, toothed whales. They belong to the group known as cetaceans (from the Latin word *cetus*, meaning large sea animals), which includes all whales, dolphins, and porpoises ... Dolphins and humans have a lot in common, we are both mammals.

(pp. 4–5)

This text requires higher levels of thinking because readers need to see the main classification with the families under it. Struggling readers will need help to understand how whales, dolphins, porpoises, and humans are related to each other. Later in this chapter, I will present various types of graphic organizers to sort this kind of information.

Comparison/contrast. In a comparison/contrast text, authors explain a concept by showing how one event, subject, or object is similar to or different from another. Comparison/contrast helps young readers better understand concepts when authors directly present the similarities and differences between the two items. Sandra Markle, in *Outside and Inside Sharks* (1996), explains how sharks differ from fish:

Look at the reef shark and the soldier fish. They are both fish. They both need oxygen, a gas in air and water, to live. And they both have special body parts called gills that carry oxygen from the water into their bodies. But there are differences between sharks and other fish. A shark's gills are in separate pouches with slits opening to the inside and outside of its body. The soldier fish, and other fish like it, have gills grouped in one chamber .... A shark's tail usually has a top part that is longer than the bottom. Other fish usually have tails with two equal parts. But the biggest difference between sharks and other fish is on the inside.

(p. 5)

In passages that compare and contrast concepts, authors use signal words such as *alike, different, similarly, on the other hand, but, in contrast, in the same way, meanwhile, either/or,* and *unlike.* Teachers often need to point these words out to struggling readers so they can better comprehend these passages.

Cause/effect. Cause/effect passages are often found in science texts to explain what causes natural phenomena. For example, Jenny Wood, in *Caves: Facts and Stories and Activities* (1990), explains how caves form.

> The process of making a cave takes thousands of years. It starts when surface water trickles down through tiny cracks in the rock. The water contains a gas called carbon dioxide which is absorbed from the air and this forms a mild acid that eats away the limestone. As it travels underground, the water continues to eat away some of the rock, forming passages and caves.
>
> (p. 4)

In *Volcano: The Eruption and Healing of Mount St. Helens* (1986), Patricia Lauber explains what causes a volcano to erupt.

> Beneath the crust is a region called the mantle. It is made of rock that is very hot. Rock of the mantle can flow, like thick tar. The crust floats on the mantle . . . . The plates are in motion, moving a few inches each year . . . . There are places where plates pull away from each other. Here molten rock wells up and sometimes volcanoes erupt.
>
> (pp. 51–52)

Notice that in both of these passages, readers need to be able to mentally picture the action as it happens. As mentioned before, struggling readers often cannot paint mental pictures as they read; therefore, they have great difficulty with cause/effect texts. It is helpful for these readers to know that authors use signal words to indicate relationships between effects and causes. These words include *because, hence, therefore, as a result,* and *this led to.*

Problem/solution. Another organizational structure commonly found in expository texts is problem/solution. Often the explanation of a problem will expand for a number of pages before the solution is stated. In *Children of the Dust Bowl: The True Story of the School at Weedpatch Camp* (1992), Jerry Stanley devotes the first chapter to naming all the problems the Oakies endured during the 1930s before he offers a possible solution to the Oakies'

problem—moving to California. With this text, it is useful for teachers and students to make a list of all the problems that Oklahoma faced during the 1930s. In this way, the students will better understand why much of the state's poorer population migrated to California. The text explores the following problems in detail:

- Small farms
- No irrigation
- No reservoirs or canals
- No rain
- Crops shriveled
- Great Depression
- Wheat prices low
- Dust storms
- Bankruptcy
- Foreclosures on mortgages; evictions from homes

Finally, the text offers what many Oklahomans perceived to be a solution to the problem by describing how many loaded their possessions on trucks and moved to California, seeking a better life for their families.

Persuasion. Persuasion is a type of writing designed to change readers' minds or thinking. Teachers will usually need to specifically point out to struggling readers how authors attempt to persuade them to change their thinking. For instance, some authors attempt to change readers' thinking about environmental issues such as offshore oil drilling, the harm of logging, and the need to protect wildlife. Authors will attempt to persuade readers by using striking adverbs, adjectives, and other powerful word choices, or by offering a personal assessment of the topic that he or she is describing. Notice Todd Wilkinson's persuasive technique in *Bison for Kids* (1994). The underlined words are examples of subtle persuasion; the last sentence, however, is not subtle, it is emphatic.

> What happened after that is a <u>sad</u> story. People killed millions of buffalo for food and hides. Settlers <u>slaughtered</u> them to make room on the Great Plains for cattle. One of the most famous bison hunters was William "Buffalo Bill" Cody, who delivered mail for the Pony Express and shot bison to feed railroad workers. He killed thousands of bison. As a result of the <u>over hunting,</u> only a few hundred wild buffalo were left in the United Stated at the end of the 1800s. <u>Bison needed to be protected fast!</u>
>
> (pp. 15–16, emphasis added)

Sometimes, authors use more forceful techniques to persuade readers to accept their point-of-view. Teachers need to point out these techniques to their students.

Propaganda is a persuasive technique that often involves distortion of facts or manipulation of readers. Because propaganda is so prevalent in advertisements, readers need to understand the propaganda techniques that writers use. Listed below are seven propaganda techniques accompanied by brief descriptions.

- *Name calling*: denouncing one product or person to promote another.
- *Card stacking*: giving one side of the story or telling half-truths. Note: advertisements for medications now are required to list negative side effects as they list the benefits.
- *Plain folk*: using ordinary people to promote a product.
- *Glittering generalities*: stating a list of positive attributes without giving any specific details.
- *Testimonial*: using a popular person to promote a product that he or she uses.
- *Transfer*: using a popular person to promote a product that is not associated with his or her job or ability.
- *Bandwagon*: an attempt to convince consumers that "Everyone is doing it, so you should do it too."

Technical Vocabulary

In addition to the frequently unfamiliar organizational patterns, the technical vocabulary used in expository texts may be overwhelming for struggling readers. "Students' comprehension is greatly influenced by their vocabulary knowledge" (Richardson & Morgan, 1997, p. 215). According to Bruner (1966), first-hand experiences are the best way to understand technical terms. Some of these experiences include field trips, experiments, and demonstrations. Vicarious experiences, such as educational videos and computer programs, are also effective means to understanding technical vocabulary. However, first-hand and vicarious experiences are not always available. Good authors understand this and use writing techniques to help readers understand technical terms.

Sometimes authors will first give a definition and then state the vocabulary word. For example, in *Bison for Kids*, Wilkinson explains *wisents* in this manner: "Huge ancestors of the modern bison, know as the wisent (VEE-SENT), roamed far and wide" (p. 12). Notice how Wilkinson even indicates how the word is pronounced by using parentheses and capital letters. Seymour Simon uses the same technique in *Whales* by setting off the technical term in commas:

"A whale's nostril, called a blowhole, is at the top of its head. A whale breathes through its blowhole."

(unpaged)

Another technique of some authors is to introduce a term and then define it, setting the definition off in commas: "Dolphins are remarkable mimics, copying others' behavior and sounds" (Cerullo, 1999, p. 18). Others provide definitions by setting them off with a dash: "This humpback whale is breaching—jumping almost clear out of the water and then crashing down in a huge spray of foam" (Simon, 1989, unpaged).

Other authors use a mix of techniques. In the following example, Philip Steele (1994) uses a sentence to describe one term, an appositive phrase to describe another, and a participial phrase to explain the last term: "Minarets are the tall slender towers on mosques, the building where Muslims pray to God. They, too, point to heaven. At the top of the minaret is a balcony, where a man called a muezzin stands to call people to prayer" (Steele, 1994, p. 13).

Like many authors, Wood (1990) uses boldface to draw attention to new words and then states definitions immediately after: "Another group of scientists who are interested in caves are **geologists.** Geologists study caves, rocks, soil, mountains, rivers, oceans, and other parts of the Earth" (p. 23). Watt (1993) uses boldface to indicate that the word is included in the glossary at the back of the book.

Teachers must explicitly teach struggling readers about the techniques that authors use to define new words because struggling readers do not necessarily recognize these aids by themselves (Swanson & De La Paz, 1998).

ANALYSIS OF INFORMATIONAL TRADE BOOKS AND TEXTBOOKS

When analyzing texts, there are a number of elements to consider: eye appeal, text features, author's writing style, assumptions about readers' background knowledge, and various other elements.

Eye Appeal

When examining a text, teachers should do the same thing students do when first given a book—thumb through it to see if it looks interesting. Visual appeal is an important characteristic of informational texts; attractive books can entice students to read them (Palmer & Stewart, 1997). The following are traits of an appealing text:

- Appropriate size of text for grade level

- Generous margins (white spaces) on a page
- Attractive, up-to-date photographs, representing both genders and different ethnicities
- Charts that are easy to read
- Pages with the appropriate amount of text *with* pictures, graphs, and so on (Pages filled with text scare young readers!)
- Many subheadings so no passage is too long

Text Features

Good textbooks have specialized features that aid reader comprehension: a table of contents, a glossary, questions at the beginning and end of each chapter, and highlighted vocabulary words. Teachers should examine these features to see if they will be useful to readers.

The table of contents should give an overview of the text and depict the relationships among the various topics. The table of contents represents the progression of topics through the text. For example, a table of contents for a history book should indicate if the text is organized chronologically or by topic. Figure 10.3 shows a table of contents for one chapter of a science textbook. Notice how all the subheadings support the main topic of the

chapter: Changes in the Earth's Surface. Notice also how each "Lesson" topic is presented in the form of a question. From these questions, good readers will be able to readily infer that volcanoes, earthquakes, and wind are some causes for changes in the earth's surface. Teachers may need to read a table of contents with struggling readers so they learn how to make inferences about its terms and headings. Asking the struggling student questions about these items also will activate his or her background knowledge.

Many textbooks and trade books have a glossary and an index. The glossary permits readers to understand the definitions of words as they are used in the reading selections. The index helps readers locate the pages that include discussion about particular concepts or vocabulary words. A good informational book highlights new vocabulary terms in some fashion. Some textbooks define new terms in the margin using colored ink. Others may use italics or boldface type to highlight the word and use embedded text to define it, as demonstrated in the Technical Vocabulary section of this chapter. See Figure 10.4 for an example from the same science textbook.

Good textbooks that are designed for elementary and middle school grades include some thought

FIGURE **10.3**   Sample table of contents.

Unit C   Earth Science

Source: Pages C5, C8, and C13 from *Scott Foresman Science* Grade 3 © 2000 by Addison-Wesley Educational Publishers Inc. Reprinted by permission of Pearson Education, Inc.

FIGURE 10.4 Sample definition of terms.

How Volcanoes Form

Hot, melted rock and gases are bursting out of the volcano in the picture. A **volcano** is a special type of mountain with an opening, or vent, at its top. Thousands of years ago, this volcano did not exist. So what happened to form this volcano?

Glossary

volcano (vol kā´ nō), a type of mountain that has an opening at the top through which lava, ash, or other types of volcanic rock flows

Glossary

Source: Pages C5, C8, and C13 from *Scott Foresman Science* Grade 3 © 2000 by Addison-Wesley Educational Publishers Inc. Reprinted by permission of Pearson Education, Inc.

questions at the beginning and end of each chapter. These questions should be literal, inferential, or critical/evaluative (see Chapter 9). For example, in *Bison for Kids*, a literal question would be, "What are wisents?" The answer is stated in the text, which provides a definition of wisents. An inferential question from *Bison for Kids* would be "Why was it not possible for bison and cattle to live on the Great Plains together?" A critical/evaluative question for *Bison for*

Kids would be "Was it wrong for settlers to kill bison for food and hides? Explain you answer."

Figure 10.5 has an example from the same science textbook that presents main questions with supporting questions under each main heading. Figure 10.6 provides an example of the questions often found at the end of a chapter. Take time to evaluate the questions in a text. Are all three types of questions represented?

FIGURE 10.5 Pre-reading questions.

INQUIRING ABOUT
Changes in the Earth's Surface

LESSON 1
How Do Volcanoes and Earthquakes Change the Earth?

LESSON 2
What Landforms Are on the Earth's Surface?

LESSON 3
How Do Water and Wind Change the Earth's Surface?

LESSON 4
How Can Living Things Affect the Earth's Surface?

How do volcanoes form?

How do volcanoes change the earth?

How do earthquakes change the earth?

How do scientists study volcanoes and earthquakes?

How can you be safe during earthquakes?

Where are some landforms?

What are some kinds of landforms?

How does weathering change rocks?

How does erosion change the earth?

How do plants and animals change the earth?

How do people change the earth?

Copy the chapter graphic organizer onto your own paper. This organizer shows you what the whole chapter is all about. As you read the lessons and do the activities, look for answers to the questions and write them on your organizer.

Source: Pages C5, C8, and C13 from *Scott Foresman Science* Grade 3 © 2000 by Addison-Wesley Educational Publishers Inc. Reprinted by permission of Pearson Education, Inc.

FIGURE 10.6   End of chapter questions.

LESSON 1 REVIEW

1. How does a volcano erupt?
2. How do volcanoes change the earth?
3. How do earthquakes change the earth?
4. How do scientists study earthquakes and volcanoes?

5. What are some ways to stay safe during an earthquake?
6. **Main Idea**
   Read the material on page C10. What is the main idea of this material?

Source: Pages C5, C8, and C13 from *Scott Foresman Science* Grade 3 © 2000 by Addison-Wesley Educational Publishers Inc. Reprinted by permission of Pearson Education, Inc.

Writing Style

Writing style includes such aspects of writing as presentation of facts, grammatical structure, sentence length, tense, mood, and voice. These aspects affect the readability of a text. Palmer and Stewart (1997) found that many textbooks are cold and clinical and present facts in an encyclopedic manner. They call this type of textbook "a parade of facts." This type of writing is often not engaging and difficult to comprehend because the reader must process too many facts at once.

Textbooks may also have poor grammatical structure, with problems such as the ambiguous use of pronouns. For example, in the following sentence it is difficult to determine what the writer means: "Remove the plastic lids from the cans and throw them away." From this sentence, it is not clear if one should throw the lids or cans away.

Other times a text can be composed of short simple sentences that show no relationship among the ideas. Notice the short, choppy sentences used in *Sam the Sea Cow*.

> One manatee turns to face Sam.
> He puts his snout right up to Sam's.
> They rub noses.
> They rub whiskers.
> The manatees begin to twist and roll.
> They pop up and down.
> They play follow-the-leader.
> They swim off together.
> (Jacobs, 1979, pp. 42–43)

With this style, it may be difficult to understand that the description indicates that the manatees become friends and swim off together.

Some texts have so many embedded phrases that it is difficult for struggling readers to identify the main idea. Examine the following short paragraph and note how many ideas the brain needs to process.

The bones of whale's skull form huge upper and lower jaws. Each tooth in this sperm whale's jaw weighs more than half a pound. Whales have external ears, very little hair, and no sweat glands. A thick layer of fatty tissue beneath their skin, called blubber, helps insulate them against the cold water and also stores energy. Whales were once hunted mostly for their blubber, which was boiled down to whale oil aboard the whaling ships and used as fuel in oil lamps.

(Simon, 1989, unpaged)

Texts in the passive voice are more difficult to comprehend than those in the active voice. Notice how the following two sentences convey the same message. But in the second sentence, the active voice makes comprehension easier for readers because the action is more vivid and direct.

> The fish was safely reeled in by two sailors, struggling not to fall out of the heaving boat.

> Two sailors, struggling not to fall out of the heaving boat, safely reeled in the fish.

Author's Assumption of Readers' Background Knowledge

Authors tend to choose words that will best describe an event, an action or a phenomenon; however, unfamiliar vocabulary may make the passage difficult for struggling readers. You must be able to detect words that may cause problems for readers with a limited vocabulary. In reading the following passage, struggling readers may not create the appropriate mental picture of the swimming dolphins because they do not know the words *proportioned* and *penetrate*.

> You have to watch a dolphin swim for a few seconds to see that it is perfectly proportioned to penetrate the wave.

> (Cerullo, 1999, p. 10)

In reading the next passage, struggling readers' comprehension may break down because they cannot pronounce *Cetaceans* and *cetus*; they may not understand that *Latin* is a language like Spanish and English and that *Cetaceans* is a name of a classification. Teachers should explain these facts to struggling readers.

> They [dolphins] belong to the group known as Cetaceans (from the Latin word *cetus*, meaning large sea animal), which includes all whales, dolphins, and porpoises.
>
> (Cerullo, 1999, p. 4)

Authors may also assume that readers have sufficient general background knowledge to fully comprehend the text and visualize its images. In the following passage, readers need to know the location of several different countries in order to understand what is meant by the word *Ring* in the phrase *Ring of Fire*.

> Some of these volcanoes are on the ocean floor. Others are on land. Most of the land volcanoes circle the Pacific Ocean. They run from South America to Alaska to Japan, Indonesia, and New Zealand. Together they are known as the Ring of Fire.
>
> (Lauber, 1986, p. 51)

Some authors do not provide a sufficient number of illustrations, graphs, charts, or photographs to explain the text. The paragraph above would be easier to comprehend if the author had included a picture of that area of the world and illustrated the circle or ring of volcanoes. Many trade books do use illustrations and/or photographs to help explain the information presented in the text. Figure 10.7 features a list of books that use clear illustrations and/or photographs.

Authors can aid readers' comprehension by organizing materials in a cohesive manner, using clear diagrams and charts, and composing well-found sentences. Figure 10.8 presents a concise list of characteristics of considerate textbook styles versus inconsiderate ones. As you critique textbooks, you may want to add to the list. In addition, you can use the checklist provided in Appendix D.4 for textbook evaluation.

FIGURE 10.7 Informational books with clear illustrations or photographs.

Children of the Dust Bowl: The True Story of the School at Weedpatch Camp by Jerry Stanley (1992). New York: Trumpet Club Special Edition.

Who Lives in the Rainforest? by Susan Canizares and Mary Reid (1998). New York: Scholastic.

Frogs by Carolyn MacLulich (1996). New York: Scholastic.

Bison for Kids by Michael Francis (1997). Minnetonka, MN: NorthWord.

Octopus' Den by Deirdre Langeland (1997). New York: Scholastic.

A Picture Book of Benjamin Franklin by David Adler (1990). New York: Trumpet Club Special Edition.

Coral Reef Hideaway: A Story of a Clown Anemonefish by Doe Boyle (1995). New York: Scholastic.

Sam the Sea Cow by Francine Jacobs (1979). New York: Trumpet Club.

Caves: Facts, Stories, Activities by Jenny Wood (1990). New York: Scholastic.

Whales by Seymour Simon (1989). New York: Scholastic.

Outside and Inside Sharks by Sandra Markle (1996). New York: Aladdin Paperbacks.

Dolphins: What They Can Teach Us by Mary Cerullo (1999). New York: Scholastic.

I Wonder Why Castles Had Moats and Other Questions About Long Ago by Philip Steele (1994). New York: Kingfisher Books.

Earthquakes and Volcanoes by Fiona Watt (1993). New York: Scholastic.

The Really Hairy Scary Spider and Other Creatures with Lots of Legs by Theresa Greenway (1996). New York: A DK Publishing Book.

Polar Wildlife by Kamini Khanduri (1992). New York: Scholastic.

Sarah Morton's Day: A Day in the Life of a Pilgrim Girl by Kate Waters (1989). New York: Scholastic.

Rainforest Wildlife by Antonia Cunningham (1993). New York: Scholastic.

Frogs by Susan Canizares (1998). New York: Scholastic.

What Comes in a Shell? by Susan Canizares (1998). New York: Scholastic.

Elephants by Anthony Fredricks (1999). Minnetonka, MN: NorthWord.

FIGURE 10.8   Considerate and inconsiderate textbook styles.

CONSIDERATE

1. Organization of text's structure is clear to reader
2. Concepts are logically, clearly explained
3. Main ideas are explicitly stated
4. Subtopics relate and support main idea
5. Appropriate signal words are used for each type of text (e.g., sequence = *first, second*)
6. Clear pronoun/antecedent agreement
7. Necessary background information is provided
8. Definition of new terms is clearly stated
9. New concepts are clearly and concisely explained
10. Visual aids complement text

INCONSIDERATE

1. No logical text structure
2. Ungrammatical sentence structure
3. Sentence length is long
4. Lack of pictorial aids
5. No use of subordinating conjunctions to show relationships
6. Ambiguous pronouns
7. Assumption of advanced background knowledge
8. New vocabulary is not defined
9. Information presented in encyclopedic fashion
10. Pages of text without visual aids

Sources: Ambruster, B. (1996), Considerate text. In D. Lapp, J. Flood, & N. Farman (Eds.), *Content Area Reading and Learning: Instructional Strategies* (2nd ed.), pp. 47–58. Boston: Allyn & Bacon; Olson, M. W. & Gee, T. (1991), Content reading instruction in the primary grades: Perceptions and strategies, *The Reading Teacher, 45,* 298–307; Palmer, R. & Stewart, R. (1997), Nonfiction tradebooks in content area instruction: Realistic and potential, *Journal of Adolescent and Adult Literacy, 40*(8), 630–642; Richardson, J. & Morgan, R. (1997), *Reading to Learn in the Content Areas* (3rd ed.), Belmont, CA: Wadsworth Publishing Co.

Readability Formulas

Readability formulas are often used to *approximate* the reading level of texts. The formulas are based on examining the number of syllables and the sentence length within passages. (See Chapter 2 for a description of the Fry Readability Formula, 1977.) The assumption is that shorter words and shorter sentences are easier to comprehend. However, teachers must also look at the vocabulary used in the passage because new readers are often familiar with many four- and five-syllable words, while remaining ignorant about many single syllable words. Compare the words *hippopotamus* and *rhinoceros* to the words *brusque* and *crux*. According to a readability formula, *hippopotamus* and *rhinoceros* would make the passage's reading level higher than the passage with the one-syllable words. However, educators know that children are familiar with the two animals but may never have heard the other two words in conversation. Teachers must also understand that concrete words such as *butterfly* and *astronaut* are easier to understand than abstract words such as *transformation* and *prejudice*. A *butterfly* and *astronaut* can be seen and felt, while one cannot see or touch a *transformation* or a *prejudice*. Obviously, readability formulas should not be the sole determinant of the readability of a textbook or trade book, but they can provide an *approximate* reading level when used with a checklist like the one found in Appendix D.4.

ASSESSMENT

Reading expository text takes all the skills that are needed to read narrative texts. It is necessary that a reader has a large bank of words that she recognizes on sight. It is also important that she has good decoding skills as she encounters technical terms. For decoding, she needs to know letter–sound relationships, digraphs, diphthongs, consonant blends, and syllabication. If she is struggling with decoding, the teacher should determine what aspect of decoding is troublesome for her. (Refer back to Chapters 6 and 7 for ways to assess a reader's decoding and word analysis skills.) After assessment, teachers need to assist the readers as they build the necessary skills to master expository texts.

Informal Assessment

Rubrics

Designing rubrics based on state standards can help teachers as they monitor individual student growth in comprehending expository text. The partial rubric in Figure 10.9 is based on Colorado's standards for the fourth grade. Notice that Wade, at the end of the second quarter, sometimes uses effective strategies to comprehend expository text and sometimes can identify supporting details and main ideas; however, he cannot summarize long text pas-

FIGURE 10.9 Rubric for reading comprehension based on fourth-grade reading standard for Colorado.

FOURTH GRADE

STUDENT _Wade_ TOTAL SCORE _11_ GRADING PERIOD 1 ②3 4

LEVEL OF MASTERY

TRAIT	TARGET (5 POINTS)	ACCEPTABLE (3 POINTS)	UNACCEPTABLE (1 POINT)
Uses full range of strategies (skims, scans, self-monitors)	Always uses appropriate strategies to comprehend texts (skims, scans, self-monitors). ___	Sometimes uses appropriate strategies to comprehend texts (skims, scans, self-monitors). _X_	Seldom uses appropriate strategies to comprehend texts (skims, scans, self-monitors). ___
Identifies main ideas with supporting details	Always identifies main ideas with supporting details. ___	Sometimes identifies main ideas with supporting details. _X_	Seldom identifies main ideas with supporting details. ___
Summarizes long expository texts	Always summarizes long expository texts. ___	Sometimes summarizes long expository texts. ___	Seldom summarizes long expository texts. _X_
Draws inferences	Always draws inferences using contextual clues. ___	Sometimes draws inferences using contextual clues. ___`	Seldom draws inferences using contextual clues. _X_
Sets purpose	Always sets purpose for reading. ___	Sometimes sets purpose for reading. ___	Seldom sets purpose for reading. _X_
Use text features	Always uses text features (bold print, subheadings, etc.) ___	Sometimes uses text features (bold print, subheadings, etc.) ___	Seldom uses text features (bold print, subheadings, etc.) _X_
Sequential order	Always identifies sequential order in expository text. ___	Sometimes identifies sequential order in expository text. ___	Seldom identifies sequential order in expository text. _X_

Source: Based on Colorado's State Standards for Fourth Grade.

sages or draw inferences. His teacher is somewhat concerned about his progress since most of his classmates can summarize longer texts and draw inferences. Wade's teacher discusses his progress with his mother and they decide that Wade will benefit from weekly tutoring sessions with a paraprofessional.

Running Records and Miscue Analysis

Using informational texts for running records and miscues analyses will help you determine which cueing systems the students use while reading informational passages. A reader may use the same systems she does for narrative or she may approach informational text in a different way. For example, she may use more visual clues such as dividing words into parts instead of using semantic clues such as relying on background information. Chapter 3 discusses how to administer, score, and analyze both of these assessment instruments. Many commercial miscue analyses have one informational passage for each grade level.

Often teachers find that the majority of the students can read a book or passage; one or two students, however, appear to struggle with the text. There are two other ways to assess if a text is at the easy level, the instruction level, or the frustration level for a particular student: the cloze test and the maze. Each of these assessments helps determine the appropriateness of a particular book for a particular student.

Cloze Procedure

The cloze procedure can be used to determine if an expository passage is appropriate for a particular reader. Many struggling students cannot read what their classmates can. A teacher can easily determine the reading level—easy, instructional, or frustration—for a particular passage. The cloze procedure is especially helpful in finding out (1) if the reader has the background knowledge for the passage, (2) if she is using syntax to determine unknown vocabulary words, and (3) if she is using her structural analysis skills to understand technical vocabulary (e.g., the *logy* in *geology* indicates that geology is the study of something). When administering a cloze test with struggling readers, be sure to observe the reader as she completes the task in order to determine what language clues she uses. See Chapter 3 to review how to prepare and administer the cloze procedure.

Figure 10.10 features a sample cloze procedure taken from Lisa deMauro's *Bats* (1990). A student who scores 50 percent or better can read the passage independently; a reader who scores 30–49 percent can read the passage with assistance, while a reader who scores below 30 percent would find this passage frustrating. When using the cloze procedure, do not be concerned about the grade level of the book; the focus should be on whether the student can read the book.

When assessing the cloze procedure, ask the following questions to determine what reading strategies the child uses:

FIGURE 10.10 Cloze procedure using *Bats* by Lisa deMauro.

The facts about vampire bats are a lot less frightening than the stories. Vampires are rare. There __1__ only three kinds of __2__ bats out of almost __3__ kinds of bat worldwide. __4__ vampire bats are found __5__ Mexico, and the Central and __6__. The most famous one, __7__ common vampire bat, is __8__ small, shy animal covered __9__ reddish brown or gray-brown __10__. Its head and body __11__ about three inches long __12__ it weighs a little __13__ than an ounce—about __14__ same as a small __15__ of potato chips. It __16__ a small, pushed-in snout; __17__, pointed ears; and a __18__ in its lower lip. __19__ also has long, triangular-shaped __20__ teeth and very long __21__ that help in its __22__ ability to walk.

The __23__ vampire most often preys __24__ large hoofed animals, such __25__ cattle and horses. Sometimes __26__ will attack goats or __27__. It rarely attacks people, __28__ if it does, it __29__ bites the big toe! __30__ two other types of __31__ seem to prefer birds. __32__ vampires are able to __33__, they probably don't need __34__ when they are hunting __35__ prey. Vampires seem to __36__ sight and smell to __37__ them find their way.

__38__ it has located its __39__, the bat flies up __40__ the sleeping animal and __41__ silently, often on an __42__ back. Sometimes it lands __43__ few feet away and __44__ over to the animal. __45__ it neatly slices off __46__ small piece of skin __47__ its razor-sharp teeth. The __48__ is quick and painless. __49__ sleeping victim usually isn't __50__ of what's going on. (Even people who are bitten by vampires generally don't realize it until morning when they notice the blood.)

(pp. 45–46)

ANSWERS:

1. are	2. vampire	3. 1,000	4. All	5. in	6. South America
7. the	8. a	9. with	10. fur	11. are	12. and
13. more	14. the	15. bag	16. has	17. short	18. notch
19. It	20. incisor	21. thumbs	22. unique	23. common	24. on
25. as	26. it	27. pigs	28. but	29. usually	30. The
31. vampire	32. Although	33. echolocate	34. to	35. large	36. use
37. help	38. When	39. target	40. to	41. lands	42. animal's
43. a	44. creeps	45. Then	46. a	47. using	48. cut
49. The	50. aware				

Source: Excerpt from DeMauro, L. (1990). *Bats.* New York: Parachute Press. Reprinted with permission.

1. Does the answer fit the sentence grammatically? For example, with the first blank, a proficient reader would know that a verb is needed. A reader may first suggest "is" as her response, but if she has a good understanding of grammar, she will go back and offer "are" as the correct response. When the student gives the correct answer, you know the student is using her syntax knowledge.

2. Does the answer fit the content of the passage? If it does, it means the student is using her background knowledge about bats. If it does not make sense, it may indicate that the reader does not have sufficient background knowledge on the topic. For example, for blank 20, a student needs background on different types of teeth to correctly use "incisor" as a response.

Maze Technique

The maze technique, which closely resembles the cloze procedure, is more suitable for younger children than the cloze procedure because it gives readers three choices for each blank. The instructions for preparing and assessing the maze technique are found in Chapter 3. Figure 10.11 is a sample from Francine Jacobs's *Sam the Sea Cow* (1979).

Little research has been done on the maze test and its scoring. Usually the following criteria are used.

Easy reading level = 85–100%

Instructional reading level = 60–85%

Frustrating reading level = 59% and below

Using the maze technique, you can determine if the reading level of a book is appropriate for a particular student and also assess what cueing systems the student uses when she approaches an unfamiliar word. For example, in the second blank, "fast" does not fit the sentence. When a student is only reading words and not for meaning, she will not hesitate with this incorrect response; this indicates that she is not using syntax clues. You can also determine if the student uses her phonological knowledge as she reads the passage. For example, in the first blank if she responds with "went," she is looking at the initial letter of the first choice, which

---

FIGURE 10.11 The maze technique.

Spring comes to southern Florida. A huge, gray animal (*walks, moves, farm*)[1.] slowly down a river (*over, fast, toward*)[2.] the sea. It is (*a an, the*)[3.] shy, harmless manatee. On (*her, their, black*)[4.] broad back, the manatee (*jumps, carries, river*)[5.] a brand-new calf, just (*born, freed, heavy*)[6.] He is three feet (*high, long, pass*)[7.] and weighs forty pounds. (*Her, The, His*)[8.] name will be Sam. (*Across, An, The*)[9.] manatee rises so her (*calf's, daughter's, over*)[10.] head is above the (*lake, water, float*)[11.] Shoo-of! The calf breathes (*in, from, water*)[12.] Aah-shoo! He breathes out. (*Since, All, Even*)[13.] though a manatee lives (*across, in, after*)[14.] the water, it breathes (*water, after, air*)[15.] just like you and (*me, him, too*)[16.]

Minutes go by. Sam (*stays, arrests, home*)[17.] on his mother's back. (*The, She, He*)[18.] ducks him. Blub! Blub! (*Shoo, Blub, So*)[19.]! He bubbles. Sam must (*tie, hold, from*)[20.] his breath. His mother (*ties, lifts, across*)[21.] him into the air (*over, again, here*)[22.] Shoof-of! He snorts, happy (*from, for, house*)[23.] a breath. His mother (*swims, ducks, chances*)[24.] him once more. They (*cross, practice, through*)[25.] this way until Sam (*swims, breathes, changes*)[26.] in the air and (*toward, breathes, holds*)[27.] his breath underwater.

(pp. 7–11)

ANSWERS:

1. moves	2. toward	3. a	4. her	5. carries	6. born
7. long	8. His	9. The	10. calf's	11. water	12. in
13. Even	14. in	15. air	16. me	17. stays	18. She
19. Blub	20. hold	21. lifts	22. again	23. for	24. ducks
25. practice	26. breathes	27. holds			

Source: Excerpt from Jacobs, F. (1979). *Sam the Sea Cow.* New York: Walker & Co. Printed by arrangement with Walker & Co.

is "walks," without reading all the letters in the word. Assuming that the response is not a guess, you can also determine if the student has the necessary background knowledge on manatees. In the sentence, "He is three feet (*high, long, pass*) . . . ," a reader may need to use background knowledge about manatees (i.e., that they do not stand upright on land, but swim in the water).

Assessing Reading Interests

It is important when working one-on-one with a struggling student that you attempt to get the child "hooked on reading." Often the student may enjoy stories but dislikes reading informational books. Choosing a topic that interests the student is essential. It is often advantageous for a student to choose the topic. In order to select a book of interest, first make sure the book is on the reader's instructional reading level. If a student is a reluctant, struggling reader, you may prefer to choose a book that is on her easy reading level so that she experiences success. You can learn about a student's interests by developing an interest inventory that gives students prompts to get them thinking about personal interests. Figure 10.12 is an example of a partially completed interest inventory that will help a teacher select appropriate informational texts. Appendix C.10 has a blank inventory.

Assessing Background Knowledge

It is important for teachers to assess students' background knowledge in order to determine if they are comprehending informational material. One way to assess this aspect of reading is to give students a list of major concepts from a passage, and ask them what they know about each concept. Another way to assess background knowledge is by using a K-W-L chart, which is explained in the Intervention section of this chapter.

Vocabulary Assessment

Knowing a vocabulary word is more than being able to recite its definition. Knowing a word is being able to use the word and explain it to others. Informational books are dense with technical terms. The goal is to encourage students to "own" a word so they can use the specific term instead of the phrase, "this thing." According to Dale, O'Rourke, and Bamman (1971), there are four levels of knowing a word:

> I've never seen or heard the word before.
> I've heard it, but don't know what it means.
> I recognize the word in context.
> I know and can use it.

Dale et al. (1971) suggest four methods a teacher can use when assessing readers' vocabulary knowledge:

FIGURE 10.12   Sample interest inventory.

NAME: Matt   AGE: 10   DATE:

THINGS THAT INTEREST ME

All of these questions are about your interests! You can list more than one thing for each question.

1. What is your favorite topic to study in science? *torandos and earthquakes*

2. What topic in science that you have not studied do you wish you could study? *How space ships get up in space*

3. What sport would you like to read about? *Football*

4. Who is your favorite athlete? *I don't have one*

5. What would you like to learn about him/her? *X*

6. Do you watch any discovery shows on TV? If so, are they about animals, earthquakes, hurricanes, rocks, different places in other parts of the world, space? *earthquakes and torandos*

1. Ask students to give the definition orally or in writing.
2. Have students complete a multiple-choice exercise.
3. Have them complete a matching exercise.
4. Ask students to check words in a list that they know.

For the first method of assessment, you would choose a list of words from a passage that you think may be new to readers. The readers then explain the terms in their own words. You can readily determine on what level readers know the word. Since readers can resort to guessing on multiple-choice and matching exercises, I do not recommend these two methods.

In the fourth method, students are merely letting teachers know if they know or do not know the meaning of the word. If this is done as a pre-reading task, you should take the time to explain the words that are needed to comprehend the passage. If this exercise is done as a post-reading task, you can evaluate how well readers comprehend the concepts.

Having readers look up unknown words before they read the passage is nonproductive (Weaver, 2002). However, it is beneficial for readers to have teachers explain the many ways a writer defines new, technical words within the passage. (See the Technical Vocabulary section of this chapter for discussion.)

Assessing Readers' Growth

The most accurate assessment of students' growth in reading expository text is watchful observations of students over a long period of time in a variety of settings—one-on-one tutoring, independent reading, and large and small group participation. The assessments must include all types of informational reading materials—textbooks, trade books, computer programs, age-appropriate Internet sites, magazines, and instructions (e.g., for board games, science experiments, arts and crafts projects).

When struggling readers do not recognize their own miscues, they just continue to plod along. The goal for every reader is to become self-monitoring. One way to assess readers' self-monitoring growth is to have a child read a passage of expository text into a tape recorder; later, play it back and have the student identify his own errors. Teachers should be silent observers, checking to see if the child finds the errors. The goal is for the child to recognize reading miscues as he makes them.

Many students are critical of themselves and have poor self-concepts. You may find that it is detrimental for these students to find their *own* errors. In that case, you can first tape a passage that is at the reader's level and include some deliberate miscues. Then the students can listen to the teacher-made recording while following the script, listening for your errors. When you make the recording, be sure to read a little slower than normal and very distinctly, so students can hear the errors. You should closely observe students during this activity, and then discuss the miscues that were heard on the tape. After students are comfortable with this procedure, they can then tape their own readings.

To record struggling students' reading growth throughout the school year, you can use the tapes and a checklist similar to the one found in Appendix C.32. Remember to date the checklist so there is a record of when the readers accomplished each task. The checklist can also help you write short-term goals for readers if it is used once a week or every other week.

Formal Assessment

Two types of standardized tests that assess students' reading comprehension are achievement tests and criterion-referenced tests. Many of the reading sub-tests that measure comprehension have informational passages as well as stories. As you will recall from Chapter 3, achievement tests measure the current level of students' performance in a variety of areas, including reading. There are three different types of standardized achievement tests—reading readiness, norm-referenced, and criterion-referenced. Only norm-referenced and criterion-referenced tests have comprehension sub-tests with informational passages. The following is a list of norm-referenced and criterion-referenced tests with comprehension sub-tests.

STANDARDIZED NORM-REFERENCED ACHIEVEMENT TESTS

1. Iowa Test of Basic Skills (Grades K–8)
2. Stanford Achievement Tests (Grades K–13)
3. Gates-Mac-Ginitie Reading Tests (Grades K–12)
4. Metropolitan Achievement Tests–Reading (Grades K–12)
5. Comprehension Test of Basic Skills, U and V (Grades K–12)
6. California Achievement Tests–Reading (Grades K–9)

STANDARDIZED CRITERION-REFERENCED TESTS

1. Comprehensive Test of Basic Skills–Reading, Expanded Edition (Grades K–12)
2. Phonics Criterion Test (Grades 1–3)
3. Prescriptive Reading Performance Test (Grades 1–12)

Also recall that the No Child Left Behind Act has prompted state departments of education to design criterion-referenced tests that are aligned with their state standards (also called benchmarks or competencies in some states).

Intervention

**STRATEGIES
& ACTIVITIES**

s discussed in Chapter 9, it is important to instruct students explicitly in comprehension strategies. Following are activities that will help students develop comprehension strategies for expository text.

ACTIVITY

(GRADES 2–5)

SCIENCE EXPERIMENTS, CRAFTS, AND MATH GAMES

One way to show struggling readers the importance of reading expository text accurately and interpreting it correctly is to have them read about and perform simple science experiments, craft and art projects, or math games. A teacher can refer to an Interest Inventory (see Appendix C.10) to see which area interests the children most. Often struggling readers are tactile and kinesthetic learners and doing experiments, crafts, and games meets their needs to move around and use their hands. Reading the directions emphasizes the importance of being able to read accurately and to comprehend what they read. A teacher should permit the students to do the experiment, craft, or game just as they understand it from reading the directions, so they learn by experience the importance of reading directions correctly. Materials used should be inexpensive and safe so there is no great loss if the children misinterpret the directions. Science experiments are also wonderful ways to incorporate writing as the children can make predictions and keep a log of changes throughout the experiments. Read the vignettes in the box on page 227 to learn about some factual reports of experiences college tutors had when working with tutees. All the names are fictitious.

An excellent book to use for science experiments is Janice Van Cleave's *200 Gooey, Slippery, Slimy, Weird and Fun Experiments* (1993). Florence Tempo's *Origami Magic* (1993) is a great book to use for origami. For the struggling reader who has a love for math, there are math learning games and math mysteries that children need to carefully read in order to solve the mystery or play the game. Two good books that incorporate reading with math are Marcia Miller's *Quick and Easy Learning Games: Math* (1996) and Mark Illingworth's *Real-life Math Problem Solving* (1996). Other helpful books are found in Figure 10.13.

FIGURE 10.13 Science, math, and art books that can be used to emphasize the importance of comprehension.

Van Cleave, J. (1993). *Gooey, Slippery, Slimy, Weird & Fun Experiments*. New York: John Wiley & Sons.

Churchill, R., Loeschnig, L., & Mandell, M. (1998). *365 More Simple Science Experiments with Everyday Materials*. New York: Black Dog & Leventhal Publishers.

Wiese, J. (1995). *Rocket Science: 50 Flying, Floating, Flipping, Spinning Gadgets Kids Create Themselves*. New York: John Wiley & Sons.

Wiese, J. (1996). *Detective Science: 40 Crime-solving Case-breaking Crook-catching Activities for Kids*. New York: Scholastic.

World Book (1995). *Clever Kids Science: Ages 8–10*. Chicago, IL: World Book.

Smith, A. (Ed.). (1996). *The Usborne Big Book of Experiments*. New York: Scholastic.

Miller, M. (1996). *Quick-and-Easy-Learning Games: Math*. New York: Scholastic.

Knapp, Z. (1995). *Super Math Tricks: Solve Every Challenging Math Problem and Become a Super Sleuth Detective!* Los Angles, CA: Lowell House Juvenile.

Illingworth, M. (1996). *Real-Life Math Problem Solving: 40 Exciting, Classroom-tested Problems with Annotated Solutions*. New York: Scholastic.

Watt, F. (1999). *The Usborne Book of Art*. New York: Scholastic.

Tempo, F. (1993). *Origami Magic*. New York: Scholastic.

Urton, A. (1992). *50 Nifty Origami Crafts*. Los Angeles, CA: Lowell House Juvenile.

ACTIVE LEARNING

Vignette #1

As part of a course requirement, Mary, an elementary education major, was assigned to work with Joe, a third grader, twice a week. Each tutoring session was 50 minutes long. After being encouraged to use science experiments with Joe, Mary found a recipe to make Slime. Mary was convinced Joe would love to get his hands onto the experiment because he loved science and loved working with his hands. Mary made sure the steps for the recipe were written a little below Joe's reading level to ensure success.

Excited, Joe carefully read and followed each step. However, he misread the amount of water that he had to add. Mary remembered from the discussion in her college class that it was important for the child to do the experiment based on his interpretation of the instructions if he was to learn the importance of reading instructions carefully. Therefore, Mary let Joe proceed. Needless to say, Joe's Slime did not come out with the desired consistency.

However, desirable learning did occur. On his own, Joe said, "Wow! I must have read something wrong! Let's reread the directions." He did reread them. As he got to the step for adding water he realized he had not read the amount accurately. He said, "Man, I'm not ready to be a rocket scientist if I make a mistake on something so simple!" Joe was not discouraged. He made a plea: "I promise to read the directions better if you let me do this again." Of course, Mary did. The small amount of wasted white school glue and borax powder was worth the learning experience.

Vignette #2

Bob, an elementary education major, was assigned to work with George, a very active third-grade reader. George could not sit still for any length of time. In fact, in the middle of a paragraph he would stand up as he continued to read. Because he was so active, George often omitted words, or even lines, which made his comprehension very poor. Bob also noticed that George's fingers were in constant motion as he read and that George's drawings were very detailed and advanced for a third grader. George indicated on an Interest Inventory that he loved art. Bob decided to try some origami with George.

Wanting George to be successful, Bob wrote the directions for constructing the origami frog at George's easy reading level. George carefully read and reread the directions as he meticulously followed each step. The frog was neatly constructed, and it did jump! After making the frog, George asked, "Where did you get these directions? I want to do more of these." Bob showed George the book. George picked up another piece of paper, read the directions *from the book* (which Bob thought were too difficult for George to read) and made a box that could be inflated. Throughout the semester, George wanted to do origami during every session. He did not care that he had to read the instructions in order to correctly construct each object.

Bob also used George's interest to help his writing skills. George did not like to write. However, when Bob invited George to write in his own words some of the instructions for his favorite origami structures so he could share them with friends, George readily agreed. Through the writing experience, George learned the importance of writing directions clearly so others could understand them.

Activities for Teaching Comprehension Strategies

The following section is divided into four parts: (1) strategies to use before, during, and after reading; (2) strategies to use before reading; (3) strategies to use during reading; and (4) strategies to use after reading. As you work with a struggling reader, attempt to teach more than one strategy so the child learns more than one way to aid her reading and comprehension of expository text. But remember: a reader should master one strategy before she is introduced to the next.

Strategies to Use Before, During, and After Reading

GRAPHIC ORGANIZERS FOR EXPOSITORY TEXT

ACTIVITY

(GRADES 2–5)

"Mapping is thinking: constructing and creating the organizational design of ideas, selecting the information that is relevant and sorting this into its proper place, relating all facts to the whole and relating facts to other facts, and finally responding with personal reaction to the material" (Hanf, 1971, p. 229). Graphic organizers map how ideas are connected in the expository text. Heubach (1995) found that graphic organizers helped poor readers comprehend the material, which improved their attitude about informational books. Of course, educators know that when the readers' attitudes improve, they will spend more hours reading.

As discussed earlier in this chapter, expository text is usually organized in one of the following patterns: chronological or sequential, enumeration or description, listing, classification, comparison/contrast, cause/effect, problem/solution, and persuasion. Graphic organizers are used to show how the information within a particular passage is related. Each expository pattern has a different type of graphic organizer. Mosenthal (1994) found that direct instruction in text organizational patterns before, during, and after reading improves comprehension and aids contextual understanding.

It is important to note that all graphic organizers should be concise, should clearly depict relationships, and should not be cluttered. At first, you should construct the correct type of organizer and model how to map the information. Later you can construct the organizer and have the student map the information. Graphic organizers can be used as a pre-reading strategy to see what a student already knows about the topic. During reading, the information can be filled in as the reader learns new facts. After reading, the child can use it for recalling the information. Figures 10.14 through 10.22 show graphic organizers that can be used for each organizational pattern.

- *Chronology and sequence.* The timeline in Figure 10.14 is based on David Adler's *A Picture Book of Benjamin Franklin* (1990). The graphic organizer in Figure 10.15 depicts the butterfly's cycle.
- *Description and enumeration.* Figure 10.16 is based on William George's *Box Turtle at Long Pond* (1989).
- *Classification.* A graphic organizer used to show classification should clearly indicate the hierarchy of various categories. Figure 10.17 depicts the three levels of government.
- *Comparison/contrast.* Various organizers may be used to show comparisons and differences between two entities. Figures 10.18 and 10.19 show two different types.
- *Cause/effect.* Figure 10.20 depicts the acts of nature that cause a volcano. The information is taken from Fiona Watt's *Earthquakes and Volcanoes* (1993).
- *Problem/solution.* The problem/solution graphic organizer in Figure 10.21 is based on Jerry Stanley's *Children of the Dust Bowl* (1992).
- *Persuasion.* A teacher can use any advertisement from a magazine or newspaper to show how corporations persuade consumers to buy their products. The advertisement for Tums shown in Figure 10.22 is an example of card stacking.

FIGURE 10.14 Graphic organizer: timeline.

Born in Boston	Went to school	Worked in soap and candle shop	Worked in brother's print shop	Opened own print shop	Got married	Published *Poor Richard's Almanac*	Represented colonies in England	Represented colonies in France	Helped write peace treaty	Delegate to Constitutional Convention	Died in Philadelphia
1706	1714–1716	1716–1718	1718–1723	1728	1730	1732–1758	1765–1775	1776–1785	1782	1787	1790

Timeline based on Adler, D. (1990). *A Picture Book of Benjamin Franklin.* New York: Trumpet Club.

FIGURE 10.15   Graphic organizer: sequence.

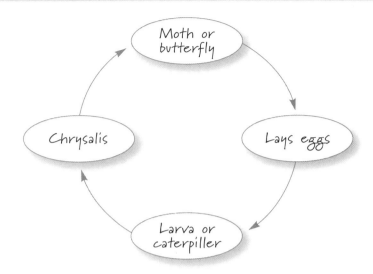

FIGURE 10.16   Graphic organizer: description or enumeration.

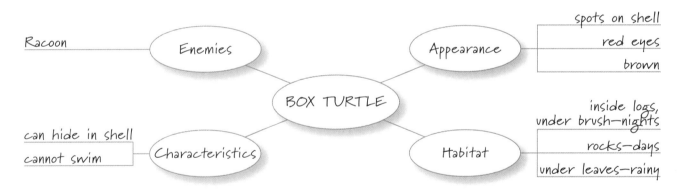

Organizer based on George, W. (1989). *Box Turtle at Long Pond.* New York: Trumpet Club.

FIGURE 10.17   Graphic organizer: classification.

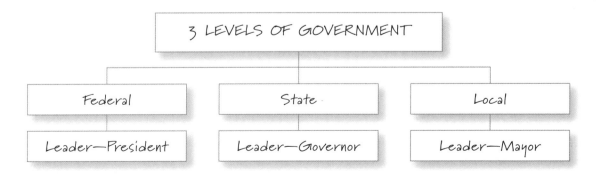

FIGURE 10.18 Graphic organizer: comparison/contrast (Venn diagram).

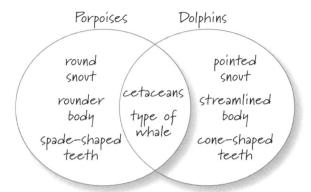

Porpoises   Dolphins

round snout

rounder body

spade-shaped teeth

cetaceans type of whale

pointed snout

streamlined body

cone-shaped teeth

Organizer based on Cerullo, M. (1999). *Dolphins: What They Can Teach Us.* New York: Scholastic.

FIGURE 10.19 Graphic organizer: comparison/contrast.

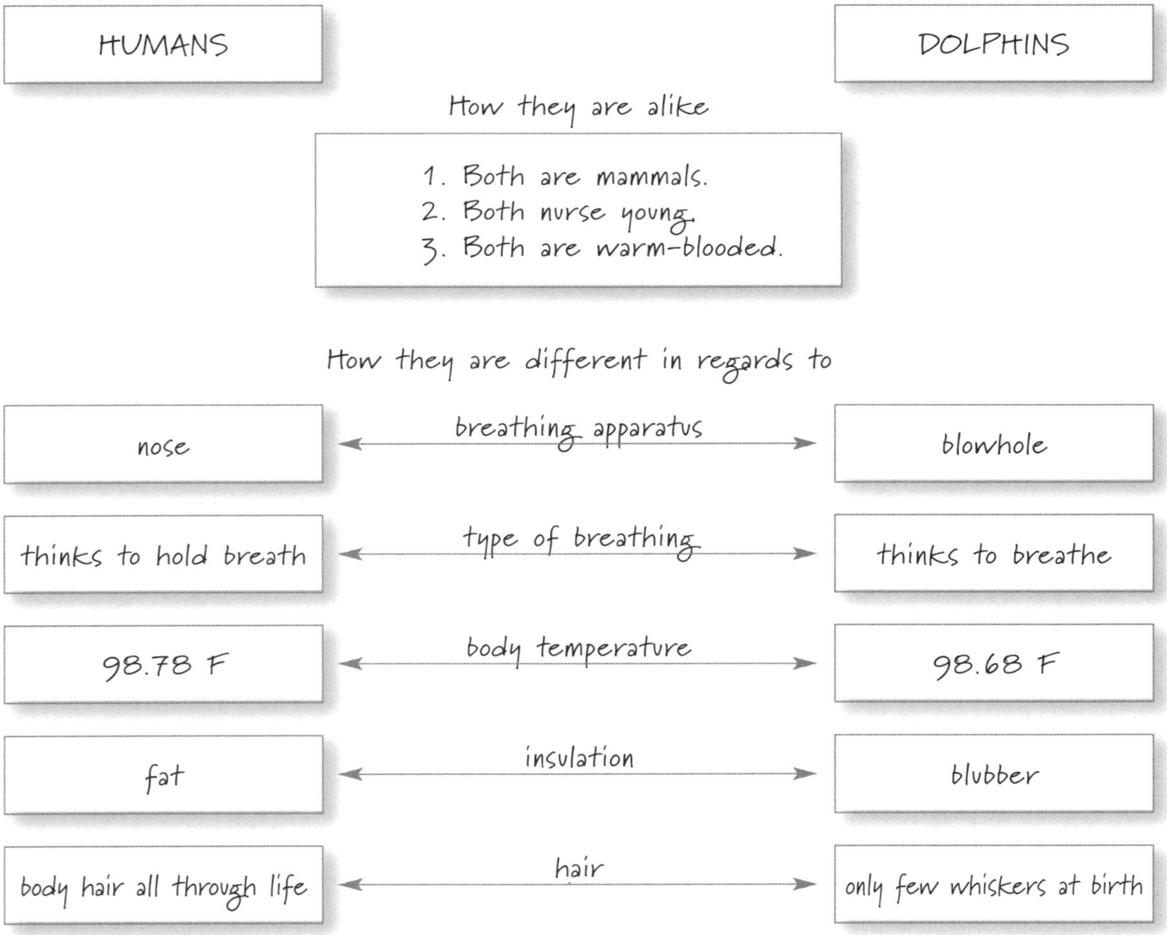

HUMANS

DOLPHINS

How they are alike

1. Both are mammals.
2. Both nurse young.
3. Both are warm-blooded.

How they are different in regards to

HUMANS		DOLPHINS
nose	breathing apparatus	blowhole
thinks to hold breath	type of breathing	thinks to breathe
98.78 F	body temperature	98.68 F
fat	insulation	blubber
body hair all through life	hair	only few whiskers at birth

Organizer based on Cerullo, M. (1999). *Dolphins: What They Can Teach Us.* New York: Scholastic.

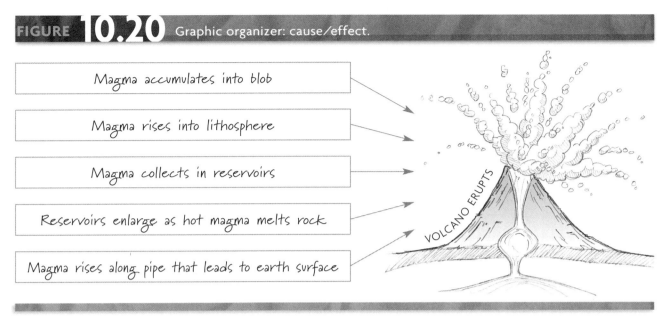

FIGURE 10.20 Graphic organizer: cause/effect.

Magma accumulates into blob

Magma rises into lithosphere

Magma collects in reservoirs

Reservoirs enlarge as hot magma melts rock

Magma rises along pipe that leads to earth surface

VOLCANO ERUPTS

Organizer based on Watt, F. (1993). *Earthquakes and Volcanoes.* New York: Scholastic.

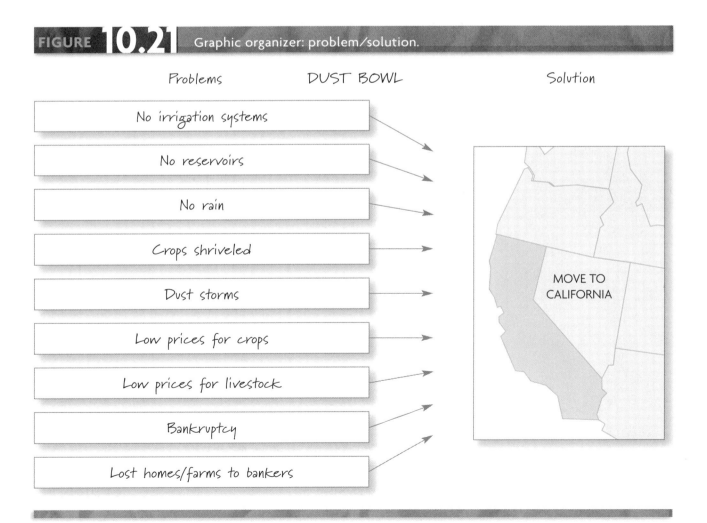

FIGURE 10.21 Graphic organizer: problem/solution.

Problems   DUST BOWL   Solution

No irrigation systems

No reservoirs

No rain

Crops shriveled

Dust storms

Low prices for crops

Low prices for livestock

Bankruptcy

Lost homes/farms to bankers

MOVE TO CALIFORNIA

Organizer based on Stanley, J. (1992). *Children of the Dust Bowl: The True Story of the School at Weedpatch Camp.* New York: Trumpet Club Special Edition.

FIGURE 10.22   Graphic organizer: persuasion.

card stacking/glittering generalities

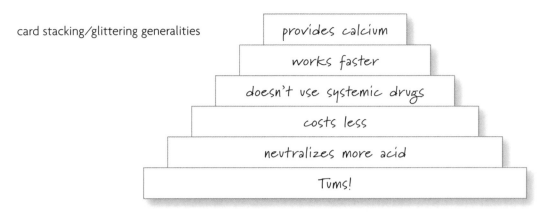

provides calcium

works faster

doesn't use systemic drugs

costs less

neutralizes more acid

Tums!

ACTIVITY   K-W-L

(GRADES 2–6)

The K-W-L method, developed by Donna Ogle (1986) as an aid to help students become active readers of expository text, is often used in classrooms, but it is also a useful strategy for a teacher to use with a struggling reader.

1. To construct a K-W-L chart, divide a piece of paper into three columns as in Figure 10.23. Label the first column **K,** which stands for WHAT I KNOW ABOUT THE TOPIC. Label the second column **W,** which stands for WHAT I WANT TO LEARN. The third column, labeled **L,** stands for WHAT I LEARNED.

2. Write the topic across the top of the chart and ask the student to dictate everything she knows about the topic. It is suggested that you take the role of scribe so the student does not withhold information because she does not know how to spell words. During the discussion, find out where and when the student learned the information. It is interesting to learn, for example, if a struggling reader has learned about bats, sharks, or whales from viewing educational programs on TV or from listening to books read by an adult.

3. Using the second column, ask the student to dictate to you everything she wants to learn about the topic. From this step, you may find that although the text matches the student's reading level, it may not be appropriate because the text holds no new information for the reader. The chosen text would then be boring to the reader. In such cases, find more appropriate materials for the reader at her instructional level.

4. After reading the passage, have the child again dictate to you what she did learn. (Later, have the student write, permitting her to use inventive spelling or look up the words that she does not know how to spell.)

5. You and the reader may now go back to the first column to see if all the background knowledge is accurate. Then they can go back to the second column to see if the student learned everything that she wanted to learn. If not all learning objectives were reached, you and the student may want to seek another source on the same topic.

K-W-L is a helpful strategy to use with a struggling reader because it permits a teacher to see what background knowledge the child has. K-W-L also gets a student actively involved in the reading process by encouraging him to think about what he would like to learn. Finally, K-W-L indicates to a teacher if the student has comprehended the material.

FIGURE 10.23 Comprehension strategy K-W-L on caves.

K	W	L
1. Caves are hollowed into rock.	1. Do they all have bats in them?	1. Some caves are made from red-hot flowing lava.
2. There are many different kinds.	2. Do they all have snakes in them?	2. Stalactites hang down from ceiling.
3. They have water in them.	3. What are the things that hang down called?	3. Stalagmites build up from floor.
4. They are dark inside.	4. Can you breathe in them?	4. Geologists study caves.
5. You can get trapped in them.		5. All caves are cold and damp.
6. They have many tunnels.		6. Bears hibernate in caves.
		7. Some caves have bats.

Chart based on Wood, J. (1990). *Caves: Facts, Stories, and Activities.* New York: Scholastic.

Strategies to Use Before Reading

The purposes of before-reading strategies are to activate prior knowledge and to generate interest in the topic of the reading material. These strategies are especially beneficial for struggling readers because they usually need to be more actively engaged in the reading process. Again you should use the strategy that will be most beneficial to the particular reader. Once a reader uses a particular strategy by herself, another strategy can be introduced so she has more than one strategy to activate prior knowledge.

SURVEY OF TEXT FEATURES

ACTIVITY

(GRADES 1–5)

With this strategy, you help a student examine the features of a textbook to predict what he will learn. (Some trade books have the same features.) First, encourage the child to look for the text features that are aids for the reader. Read with the student the table of contents and ask him to predict what he thinks he will learn from reading the selected passage. You should also attempt to activate prior knowledge by asking the student if he knows anything else about the topic. If there is a glossary or index, you can assist the student to understand how helpful these two sections of the text are. While reading, if he cannot figure out the definition of the term from context clues, he simply needs to check the glossary or look in the index to see where else that topic is discussed in the text.

Next, turn to a selected chapter and help the student read the captions of the pictures. Again, the purpose is to generate interest and activate prior knowledge. Sometimes by talking about the picture, you can introduce vocabulary that will be a part of the reading material. A student will then have heard the terms in context before reading the passage. After previewing the pictures, read chapter headings and subheadings to help the reader predict how they are related to one another. Last, read with the student any questions that are found in the front of the chapter. If there are none, then the student should read the questions found at the end of the chapter. Reading the questions will help the student to focus on the main points of the chapter as he reads. The reading of all the text features will help a struggling reader to become familiar with vocabulary and the topic before he attempts to read.

ACTIVITY   **GUIDED READING STRATEGY**

(GRADES 2–5)   Bean and Pardi (1979) developed the guided reading strategy (GRS) for struggling readers. This strategy uses text features and includes steps to encourage a struggling reader to remember the topics that were discussed. These are the steps for the GRS:

1. Together with the student, read chapter titles, subheadings, and vocabulary lists found at the beginning or end of the chapter as well as graphs, maps, picture captions, and chapter questions.
2. Close the book and have the reader dictate everything she remembers to you, who records what she says.
3. Have the student open the text to check if the information is correct and what is missing. Update the list.
4. Discuss the information with the student.
5. Together, organize the information into a graphic organizer.
6. Have the student silently read the entire passage.
7. Give the student a ten-item quiz on the material.
8. A week later, give the student another ten-item pop quiz.
9. Discuss the results of the quiz with the student.

ACTIVITY   **EXPECTATION GRID**

(GRADES 2–5)   The expectation grid combines reading with writing. A teacher and a struggling reader preview the chapter title, headings, subheadings, pictures, and graphs. Then they decide what the main topics are and draw a diagram like the one found in Figure 10.24. The details are added as the student reads the passage.

FIGURE 10.24   Sample expectation grid.

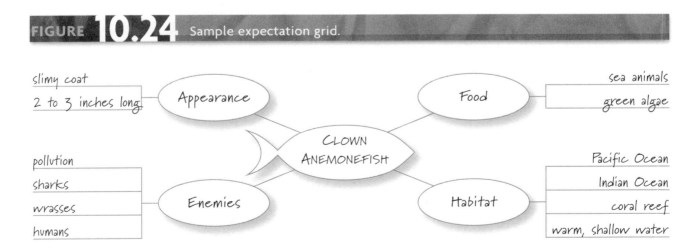

Bold information is completed after reading headings. The other information is completed as child reads passage.

Grid based on Boyle, D. (1998). *Coral Reef Hideaway*. New York: Scholastic.

PRE-READING PLAN (PReP)

Pre-reading plan is a questioning strategy also used to activate prior knowledge and to develop a student's interest in the topic (Anthony & Raphael, 1996). The following is an example of a discussion between teacher and student before they read *Caves: Facts, Stories, Activities*:

> Teacher (asking general questions about caves): Have you ever heard of stalactites and stalagmites?
>
> Child: I think so.
>
> Teacher: What do you think they are?
>
> Child: I think they are the icicles that are in caves.
>
> Teacher: Do you know anything else about them?
>
> Child: I think the stalagmites hang from the cave and the other ones come out of the floor of the cave.
>
> Teacher: Where did you learn all that?
>
> Child: I saw a show on TV about going down into a cave. It was really cold and dark in it.
>
> Teacher: That sounds interesting. I think the stalagmites come out of the cave's floor and the stalactites hang from the ceiling. But let's read and find out for sure which is correct.
>
> Child: I think you are right. I remember the man hit his head on a stalactite and it was hanging from the ceiling.

PReP is especially helpful to correct a student's misconceptions about a particular topic.

INFERENCE TRAINING

Often a struggling reader does not connect book knowledge with everyday experiences and thus learning seems irrelevant. Inference training stresses the importance of a student relating the information to her personal life (Anthony & Raphael, 1996). Following is an example of a teacher and a student engaging in inference training:

> Teacher: Today we are going to read about hurricanes. Do you know anything about a hurricane?
>
> Student: No.
>
> Teacher: Have you ever heard of a tornado?
>
> Student: Oh yes! My grandpa's house blew away in a tornado!
>
> Teacher: What caused his house to blow away?
>
> Student: Really strong wind!
>
> Teacher: Well, a hurricane is somewhat like a tornado. Both have strong winds and both are natural disasters, meaning that nature causes them and not humans. Today we are going to read about the Andrew hurricane. Look at the pictures and tell me where do you think it took place.
>
> Student: Some place by an ocean and where there is this kind of tree (pointing to a picture of a palm tree).
>
> Teacher: That's correct. Do you know what this tree is called?
>
> Student: No.

Teacher: A palm tree.

Student: Oh, I think they are in places where it is hot all year long.

Teacher: Yes, they are. Where do you think the Andrew hurricane was?

Student: I think it was in Texas because it is hot there all the time and I think it is on the ocean.

Teacher: It is hot in Texas most of the year, but we will have to read and see if Andrew was a hurricane in Texas. When do you think Andrew happened?

Student: I think it was in the 1800s; long before there were weather people.

Teacher: That is an interesting observation; we'll have to read about it and see if that is true. Do you think it was an bad one?

Student: It looks like everything was destroyed and some people were killed (as she looks at the pictures).

The student reads the passage to the teacher, affirming or changing predictions as they read. The student will learn that many aspects of her predictions were incorrect, but she was correct about some people dying.

After reading the passage, the teacher relates the information to the student's personal experience. Students from the Midwest can distinguish hurricanes from tornadoes by looking at the endurance of the storms, the wind speeds, and the rainfall.

Strategies to Use During Reading

The during-reading strategies should emphasize that reading is an active process. As comprehension breaks down, good readers stop, reread, or try to figure out what the author is attempting to explain. Again, you should be working on these strategies one-on-one with struggling readers with the goal to help them monitor their comprehension as they read.

ACTIVITY

(GRADES 2–5)

THINK-ALOUD FOR EXPOSITORY TEXT

The purpose of the think-aloud strategy is for a teacher to model to students what proficient readers do to make sense of a text (Davey, 1983). In this strategy, you should choose a passage that has new vocabulary and unfamiliar information, and then perform the following steps:

1. Read the title or heading of the passage and make predictions about the topic. "I think this will be about _____" or "I think I will learn_____" or "This subheading tells me I will also learn_____."
2. Describe the images that come to mind as you read the passage. For example, "I can almost feel (or hear or see or smell) _____."
3. Give analogies that relate the material to your personal life. "I (saw/heard/tasted/felt) _____ that is very similar to (*topic of passage*)."
4. Verbalize passages or phrases that you don't understand. This helps the student understand that proficient readers do not need to know everything to succeed.
5. Demonstrate the strategy you use to understand the passage (e.g., rereading, looking at a diagram or picture, looking up a word in the glossary, or reading ahead to see if the concept is explained).

Figure 10.25 is an example of a think-aloud using the section "Running Rivers" (pp. 30–31) in John Farndon's book *All About Planet Earth* (2000).

After you model a think-aloud, have the student do a think-aloud while you are observing. The think-aloud should become a regular habit for struggling readers.

FIGURE 10.25   Think-aloud based on John Farndon's *All About Planet Earth*.

1. The title "Running Rivers" tells me I will maybe learn why rivers run, where they come from, and where they go.

2. I could almost hear the noise of the "Thundering Water."

3. It reminds me of noise at Niagara Falls. I could not even hear my sister talking to me when we went to Niagara Falls even though we were standing right by each other. It also smelled like rain water as it roared over the ledge.

4. I still don't understand why a river winds. I would think that the closer it got to the sea, it would just go straight. I wonder if I can find out some more information about why rivers wind instead of going straight.

5. This diagram helps me better understand the three reaches of a river and how it becomes broader. I am surprised that many rivers don't become so broad in the lower reaches that they become lakes.

Based on Farndon, J. (2000). *All About Planet Earth.* New York: Anness Publishing.

TEXT CODING

ACTIVITY

(GRADES 3–6)

Text coding is another strategy that forces readers to monitor comprehension as they read. The purpose of text coding is to help readers recognize (1) unknown information, (2) newly learned information, and (3) passages they do not understand. To demonstrate this strategy, duplicate a passage of a text so you can write on the copy. Or to avoid duplicating passages or defacing books, sticky notes with the appropriate symbols can be placed in the margins. You then should have the student do the following:

1. If the information in the sentence is known, put a (+) in the margin or above the sentence.

2. If the information in the sentence is new, put a (!) in the margin or above the sentence.

3. If the information is not clear, put a (?) in the margin or above the sentence.

4. At the end of the reading, write out any remaining questions about the material and attempt to find the answers even if you must reread or seek another source.

See Figure 10.26 for an example of this process.

FIGURE 10.26   Sample of text coding.

(+)   (!)
Not all caves are hollowed out of limestone rock. **Lava** tube caves, for example, are formed by red-hot
(!)
lava flowing from a volcano. As the lava streams down the sides of the volcano, its outer surface cools
(?)   (?)
and hardens into rock. Underneath, the lava remains liquid and continues to flow. Eventually it drains
(!)
away, leaving a hollow tube. These often have very smooth sides and a regular shape. They are usually
(?)
near the surface and may have many openings in their roofs.

QUESTIONS   First (?) Where does it go? Does it ever rest and become hard?
Second (?) Why doesn't the tube cave in?
Third (?) What is near the surface? The surface of what? How big are the roofs?
Can you see sunlight through the roofs?

Source: Extracted material from Wood, J. (1990). *Caves.* New York: Scholastic.

CHECKLIST

With the checklist strategy, students see reading as an active process, constantly analyzing what is being read. You can model the process for students using the following steps:

1. Prepare statements about a passage that are either true or false.
2. Together with students read the statements before beginning to read the passage.
3. As you read, place a (+) before each true statement.
4. At the end of the reading, go back and reword the false statements so they become true. If necessary, you and the students should reread the material.

Figure 10.27 is a checklist that a teacher and student completed while reading "Into the Bat Cave" from Jenny Wood's *Caves* (1990).

FIGURE **10.27**   Checklist for *Caves* by Jenny Wood.

+   1. Bats live in colonies.
+   2. Bats live in caves.
−   3. They sleep during the night.
−   4. Bats are almost deaf.
−   5. Bats have excellent eyesight.
+   6. Echolocation is continuous high-pitched sounds.
+   7. Glowworms are found in New Zealand caves.
+   8. A glowworm's rear end gives off light.
−   9. Glowworms trap flying insects in their mouths.

CORRECTION OF FALSE STATEMENTS

3. Bats sleep during the day.
4. Bats have excellent hearing.
5. Bats are almost blind.
9. Glowworms trap insects with sticky threads that they have spun.

REQUEST

ReQuest is a good strategy for struggling readers because the teacher and students reverse roles. The students ask you the questions, and you provide the answers. The following steps are used with ReQuest:

1. Together with students, silently read a paragraph.
2. Have the students ask you a question that can be answered after reading the passage. It is the students' responsibility to clearly state the question. If it is not clearly stated, you should say, "I don't understand the question."
3. If the question cannot be answered from the material read, ask students to help you find the answer.

This strategy is especially enjoyable for students if you occasionally give an incorrect response. You, of course, are checking the students' comprehension through this strategy. Using this strategy, students learn to formulate good questions and begin to understand that for some questions the answers are right there in the book, while other questions demand readers to "read between the lines." Ciardiello (1998) found that when students formulate questions, they internalize new information and use higher-level thinking skills.

Strategies to Use After Reading

The main purposes of after-reading strategies are (1) to help readers locate answers to questions, (2) to help readers summarize the main ideas of passages, and (3) to give students tools to remember the material.

ANSWERING QUESTIONS

ACTIVITY

(GRADES 3–6)

Answering questions is a metacognitive strategy; it is a strategy to help struggling readers become aware of *how* they know (Swanson & De La Paz, 1998). When struggling readers answer questions after reading a passage, be sure to ask *where* they found the answer. Was the answer in the book? Or did they have to think and search? Or was the answer in their head? Students need to realize that some answers are stated in the text, while some answers are implicit. With these questions, readers need to search and connect the information in the book with the knowledge they have in their heads.

SCANNING

ACTIVITY

(GRADES 3–5)

It is important to provide opportunities for students to practice scanning while they find answers to textual questions. Too often, struggling readers will begin looking for an answer by reading from the beginning of the passage. This is very time consuming and unnecessary. Struggling readers need to be taught to check headings to see if the answer can be located in a particular section. If the question asks for a date, students should be taught to scan the page for numerals, such as 1776 or 2002. If the question asks for a name, the students should be taught to scan the page for the capital letters of proper nouns. Struggling readers need to remember that definitions can often be located by boldface or italic text. These dates, names, and definitions are easy for the eye to locate when scanning the printed page. You can demonstrate to struggling readers what to do when looking for dates, names, and definitions. Then they should practice the strategy with you.

PARAGRAPH FRAMES

ACTIVITY

(GRADES 2–4)

Paragraph frames are especially helpful with sequential information and are an excellent way to correlate reading, writing, and illustrating skills. After reading a sequential passage, the students write a short paragraph using signal words such as *first, second, next, then,* and *finally.* After writing the paragraph, the students illustrate the steps. In order to illustrate the sequence, the students need to have visualized the steps in their minds, a task that struggling readers often find difficult. The combination of writing and illustrating will also help struggling readers remember the material. Figure 10.28 presents a sample frame.

FIGURE 10.28   Paragraph frames of how a gardener grows flowers.

First, the gardener needs to prepare the ground by hoeing the soil. Second, the gardener digs one-inch-wide rows across the garden. Third, the gardener plants the seeds one inch apart. Next, the gardener gently covers the seeds. Then, he waters the garden. Finally, he enjoys the flowers.

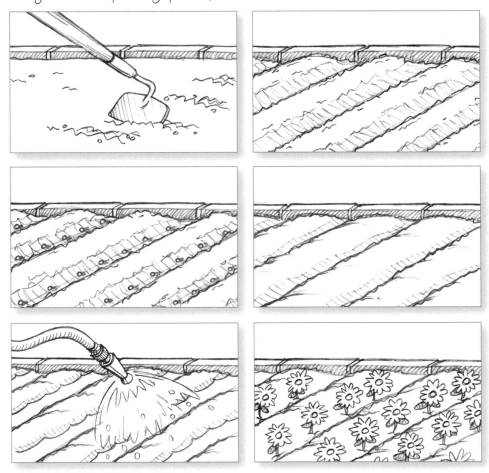

LEARNING LOGS

(GRADES 2–6)   Using learning logs is another after-reading strategy that connects reading and writing. With learning logs, students recall what they have read and then articulate it in a concise summary. Learning logs are associated with all types of informational texts—textbooks, trade books, computer programs, magazines, and so on. After you have read and discussed a text with students, they should close all reading materials and write about what they have learned. Students write about the content and any new strategy they have learned. You should carefully analyze what the students have written, attempting to see if they recalled the main ideas or unimportant details. Determine if the students can explain concepts in logical order. You can also determine if the readers understood the new strategy. Figure 10.29 presents an example of a learning log entry and its analysis by the teacher. This student has just read *Octopus' Den* (1997) by Deirdre Langeland. Figure 10.30 is a science log of a second-grade student.

FIGURE **10.29**   Learning log entry and analysis.

March 1: Octopus

An octopus eats crabs and glass. He has funny eyes. He squirts ink. He eats snakes and apples. I learned how to draw a circle with lines.

Teacher Analysis

The following information is incorrect. The octopus does not eat glass or snakes. The text states: "When he is sure it is safe, Octopus snakes an arm toward the piece of glass and snatches it back to the safety of the rock. For a moment he investigates it, the suckers on his arms tasting [not eating] the new object and feeling its shiny-smooth surface."

The last statement in the log is also incorrect. The text states: "The tiny opening is the size of an apple." The octopus does not eat apples.

Obviously, this reader reads concrete words and paints mental pictures of those objects, which causes the reader to see the octopus eating snakes and apples. It is apparent that the reader is not aware that these words have multiple meanings and uses.

(From the last statement, the teacher also realizes that the child does not know the term *graphic organizer*.)

FIGURE **10.30**   Sample science log, second grade.

Science
Lesson
(what I'v larned this year)

Scientists think there might be a tenth planet Because something keeps messing up uranus and neptunes orbet. Scientists are determine to know if there is, a tenth planet, however we will not know till they discover more.

India

ACTIVITY **HERRINGBONE**

(GRADES 3–6)   The Herringbone strategy makes a skeleton summary of the text, highlighting answers to the following questions: Who? Did what? When? Where? How? Why? (Tierney, Readence, & Dishner, 1990). Figure 10.31 has a sample of a herringbone, based on Jerry Stanley's *Children of the Dust Bowl.*

FIGURE 10.31   Sample herringbone.

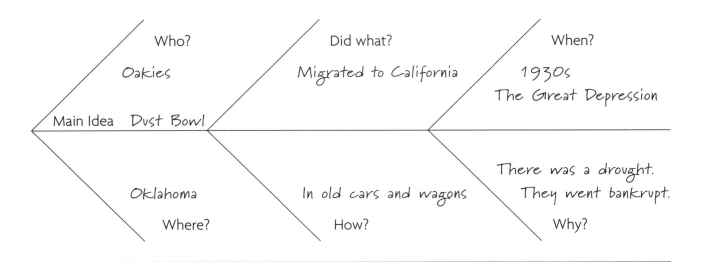

TECHNOLOGY   The Internet is an excellent means to get reluctant readers interested in learning facts about their favorite topics, authors, and so on. Teachers need to take the time to teach students how to use Internet search engines and how to follow links that might elaborate on the topic that they are researching. Since the Internet offers a vast amount of information on each particular topic from a variety of sources, you can teach students how to use graphic organizers to chart their Internet research.

There are many educational CD-ROMs designed to encourage problem solving and comprehension skills. Appendix A.7 lists programs available from Scholastic.

CONCLUDING THOUGHTS   In this chapter, you have been introduced to assessment inventories and a number of reading strategies that readers can use to aid their comprehension of expository text. It is the responsibility of teachers to explicitly teach such strategies to struggling readers. To be reflective in their teaching, teachers must also analyze which strategies are best for each particular reader.

FLUENCY

A teacher who is attempting to teach without inspiring the pupil with a desire to learn is hammering on cold iron.

HORACE MANN

Scenario

ne . . . win . . . ter . . . morn . . . ing . . . Lip . . . lap . . . (long pause)
woke . . . up . . . and . . . look . . . ed . . . out . . . his . . . (long pause)
win . . . dow . . . The . . . (long pause) first . . . snow . . . fall . . . had . . .
(long pause) cov . . . ered . . . his . . . yard . . . with . . . a . . . (long pause)
blank . . . et . . . of . . . (long pause) spark . . . ling . . . white.
(London, 1994, p. 1)

Mrs. Ling is listening as Katie reads the first page of *Liplap's Wish* (1994) by Jonathan London, with an expressionless tone and a slow rate. Katie is pronouncing each syllable correctly; her reading, however, indicates that she is not comprehending the story. After she reads five pages, Katie turns to Mrs. Ling and remarks, "I'm tired. Will you read the rest of the story?" Later that day, Mrs. Ling listens patiently to Ronald's attempt to read *Henry and Mudge in the Green Time* (1987) by Cynthia Rylant.

I-l-n-n . . . t-t-the . . . s . . . s . . sum . . mer . . . summer . . . Hen . . Henry and h . . his b . . big d-d-dog M . . . Mudge l . . . l . . . liked . . . to . . . go . . . on . . . p . . . pi . . . pic . . . picn . . n . . .

Mrs. Ling: *picnics.*

At the end of a couple of pages, Mrs. Ling informs Ronald he can stop reading because it is time to go to music.

Mrs. Ling realizes that sitting with these two children as they attempt to pronounce each word

correctly is a waste of her time and theirs. Katie needs help with reading phrases, reading with expression, and increasing her speed. Ronald needs help in all those areas, but also needs help in recognizing words automatically. Mrs. Ling's goal for both students is to develop their fluency. Mrs. Ling decides to work with the two students together, using the poem "I Liked Growing," by Karla Kuskin, found in *Ready . . . Set . . . Read!* (1990) by Joanna Cole and Stephanie Calmenson. She chooses this short poem because of its easy vocabulary and short sentences.

Mrs. Ling decides to read the poem first, modeling the phrasing, rate, and expression. She then invites the two students to echo read with her. She reads the first sentence and Katie and Ronald echo it back, using the same intonation and rate. Later, she has the two students read it in unison, and then they practice reading it to each other, maintaining the same rate and expression.

INTRODUCTION

Fluency, the ability to read with the intended interpretation of the author, is a critical but often-neglected component of reading instruction (Allington, 2001; Anderson, 1981). Often children's and adults' reading ability is measured by their fluency—but what does fluency entail? Listeners know that fluent readers read at a good pace. They attend to the punctuation in sentences; their voices rise for questions marks, pause for commas, and increase in volume for exclamation marks. Fluent readers recognize words automatically and quickly decode unknown words. They also slow down when needed. Audiences enjoy listening to fluent readers because they use expression to interpret the text as they read; when struggling readers read in a slow, staggering, monotone voice, however, audiences have a difficult time listening to and comprehending the text. Dysfluency is not only a problem for the audience though; it also causes comprehension problems for the reader.

Dysfluency causes readers to become self-conscious of their reading and they soon learn to avoid reading in public. Readers who are not fluent also read less because it takes them longer to read a passage than it takes proficient readers (Mastropieri, Leinart, & Scruggs, 1999). Because reading takes so much time, they become discouraged and avoid reading altogether.

Comprehension is the main purpose for all reading, and fluency is important for comprehension. According to the National Research Council Report, one of the five necessary elements for effective early reading is fluency in all types of text (Snow, Burns, & Griffin, 1998). In this chapter, a variety of studies on fluency and the components of fluency will be discussed along with the different definitions of fluency. Then I will present various instruments used to assess fluency. Finally, I will explain a number of strategies that have proven to be effective with individual struggling readers and small groups.

Reciprocal Theory

Researchers and educators understand the connection between fluency and comprehension. Reciprocal theory suggests the relationship between fluency and comprehension is reciprocal rather than unidirectional. Correctional studies conducted on fluency and comprehension indicate that when fluency increases, comprehension increases and vice-versa (Allinder, 2001; Dowhower, 1991; Fuchs & Fuchs, 1992; Lipson & Lang, 1991; Pinnell et al., 1995; Tyler & Chard, 2000; Vaughn, 2000). The reciprocal theory claims that as the reader is able to comprehend more material, her fluency increases, because the brain does not need to slow down to process the print. And when the reader can read fluently, her brain is free to focus on comprehension.

Reading is like any skill; the more a student practices it, the easier it becomes. When a task is easy, the student spends more time at the task, which in turn makes the student perform better. For example, pianists know that it takes time and practice to perfect the sub-skills of playing the piano. One of the first essential sub-skills is knowing the notes on the staff and being able to match these notes with the keys of the piano. Other sub-skills include fingering, playing the correct rhythm, and playing with expression. A beginning pianist is slow and methodical when attempting to play the correct keys on a very simple piece. It takes all the pianist's effort to merely depress the correct keys. However, as the pianist becomes proficient, playing correct notes and using correct fingering become automatic and the pianist can concentrate on playing with expression or interpreting the music as the composer intended it to be played. When playing becomes a pleasant experience, the pianist practices even more and becomes better. Reading is like playing the piano. Once readers master the sub-skills of reading, they can devote their reading energies to comprehending the material; when they comprehend more thoroughly, their fluency also increases.

What Is Fluency?

There are a number of definitions of fluency. Each definition emphasizes a different component of fluency.
Fluency is . . .

"rapid reading, phrased so that the reader reproduces the author's intended syntax (grammatical structure) while constructing meaning" (Fountas & Pinnell, 2001, p. 315).

"the process of automatically, accurately and rapidly recognizing words" (Cooper & Kiger, 2001, p. 165).

"the ability to read orally in a smooth and effortless manner" (Allinder, 2001, p. 48).

"the appropriate grouping or chunking of words into phrases that are characterized by correct intonation, stress and pauses" (Vaughn, 2000, p. 326).

"the ability to project the natural pitch, stress and juncture of the spoken word on written text, automatically and at a natural rate" (Richards, 2000, p. 534).

"the ability to read smoothly, easily and readily with freedom from word recognition problems and dealing with words and larger language units with quickness" (Rasinski & Padak, 1994, p. 158).

"the accuracy of word recognition and reading speed" (Samuels, 1979/1997, p. 377).

From the definitions above, we may conclude that fluency has four major components that must come together in order for the reader to reproduce the author's intended meaning. The four main components are automaticity, rate, prosody (phrasing), and expression. All four components must be present if the result is to be fluent reading. In order for students to become fluent readers, teachers need to help them develop these four components. The majority of readers who have been assessed as having reading difficulties lack one or more components of fluency (Wolf, Miller, & Donnelly, 2000). Furthermore, to develop automaticity, readers need to master four sub-skills: (1) phonological, (2) word identification, (3) word analysis, and (4) semantic. Allington (2001) and Fountas and Pinnell (1996) describe the traits of fluent readers versus disfluent readers. They are summarized in Figure 11.1.

COMPONENTS OF FLUENCY

Rate

A slow rate is one of the most common indicators of inefficient reading (Rasinski, 2000). Reading researchers have varying opinions about what constitutes an appropriate reading rate. According to the NAEP's 1992 report, 15 percent of all fourth graders read at a rate of 74 or fewer words per minute (Pinnell et al., 1995). Students reading at this rate are focusing too much on "sounding out words." They take long pauses before unknown words and are confused by new vocabulary. Students reading at this rate are not sufficiently aware of syntax or phrasing. They often ignore punctuation and thus it is difficult for these readers to keep track of ideas developed in the passage.

Samuels (1979/1997) suggests a goal of 85 words per minute (WPM) for all readers. Allington (1983) suggests 75 WPM with 98 percent accuracy. Rasinski and Padak (2000) and Harris and Sipay (1990) suggest different rates for different grades. Figure 11.2 presents the two slightly different recommended rates of Rasinski and Padak and Harris and Sipay. In both lists, the target rate increases with the grade level. Harris and Sipay established the rates for younger children through oral reading, and the rates for older students through silent reading. Harris and Sipay found that in younger students, the oral and silent rates do not vary; in older students, however, the gap between oral and silent reading is substantial. Rasinski and Padak established their target rates through oral reading alone.

Slow reading affects the amount of reading students can accomplish. For example, students who read at a rate of 74 WPM take twice as long to read a 500-word passage as most proficient readers. It takes slow readers about seven minutes to read a 500-word passage, while proficient readers, often reading at 140 WPM, can read it in three and one-half minutes. Because it takes the disfluent readers more time to read, they read less material than flu-

---

FIGURE 11.1   Traits of fluent readers versus disfluent readers.

FLUENT READERS

1. Use knowledge of language to keep reading.
2. Use an appropriate reading rate.
3. Slow down to solve problems.
4. Have automatic word recognition.
5. Have automatic word analysis skills.
6. Use intonation to convey meaning.
7. Adhere to punctuation cues.
8. Use knowledge of story structure and expository text to keep reading.
9. Reproduce the natural phrasing of the text.

DISFLUENT READERS

1. Lack knowledge of language skills.
2. Read word-by-word.
3. Think fast reading is good reading.
4. Have a poor bank of sight words.
5. Lack word analysis skills.
6. Lack expression.
7. Omit punctuation.
8. Lack prior knowledge of story structure and expository text structure.
9. Lack the ability to phrase text appropriately.

Sources: R. L. Allington (2001). *What Really Matters for Struggling Readers: Designing Research-based Programs.* New York: Longman. I. D. Fountas & G. S. Pinnell (1996). *Guided Reading: Good First Teaching for All Children.* Portsmouth, NH: Heinemann.

FIGURE 11.2 Target reading rates.

HARRIS AND SIPAY		RASINSKI AND PADAK	
Grades	WPM	Grades	WPM
1	60–90	1	80
2	85–120	2	90
3	115–140	3	110
4	140–170	4	140
5	170–195	5	160
6	195–220	6	180
7	215–245		
8	235–270		
9	250–270		
12	250–300		

Sources: A. J. Harris & E. R. Sipay (1990). *How to Increase Reading Ability* (8th ed.). New York: Longman. T. Rasinski & N. Padak (2000). *Effective Reading Strategies: Teaching Children Who Find Reading Difficult* (2nd ed.). Upper Saddle River, NJ: Merrill.

ent readers. Fluent readers read more in any given time, which in turn leads to greater fluency. "Fluency and reading volume are cause and consequence of one another" (Rasinski, 2000, p. 147).

Oral reading rate is calculated by counting how many words the student reads in 60 seconds. To find the most accurate rate for an individual student, have the student read at least three timed passages on the same easy reading level, and then average the reading rates. The silent reading rate is calculated by multiplying the total number of words read by 60 and then dividing that number by the total number of seconds it takes the student to read the passage.

$$\frac{\text{Silent reading: Number of words read} \times 60}{\text{Number of seconds to read}} = \text{WPM}$$

Teachers working with struggling readers, who typically read at a snail's pace, need to establish short-term, attainable goals. The reading material must be at the easy reading level or (later) at the instructional level. Readers must remember that comprehension is the purpose for reading; therefore, a fast reading rate can never substitute for comprehension. Teachers must help struggling readers understand that proficient readers slow down when the passage is difficult to comprehend and speed up when the text is easy to comprehend.

Automaticity

Rate and fluency depend on automaticity, which is "the ability to engage and coordinate a number of complex sub-skills and strategies with little cogni-

tive effort" (Allington, 2001). One of the reading theories associated with fluency and its importance to comprehension is the automaticity theory of S. J. Samuels (1979/1997). Samuels' automaticity theory has two emphases: (1) accuracy of word recognition and interpretation of punctuation and (2) reading rate. Samuels argues that readers who recognize words effortlessly can devote all their mental energies to comprehension, while struggling readers who struggle with decoding words and interpreting punctuation have fewer cognitive resources available to process meaning. It is obvious that readers who struggle with word recognition are spending much of their mental ability on remembering letter–sound relationships or on breaking words into smaller chunks. If the reader needs to slow down to "sound out" a word, the rate decreases drastically.

Recognizing Common Words

One of the sub-skills of automaticity is the ability to recognize common words, often referred to as "sight words," that appear in almost all texts (see Chapter 7). Many of the sight words are irregular and cannot be sounded out according to phonics rules. For example *have, done, live,* and *come* would all have long vowel sounds if they followed the silent e rule. Some other sight words that do not follow phonics rules are *two, play, laugh, said, do,* and *buy.* In the opening scenario to this chapter, Katie's passage from *Liplap's Wish* had a total of 24 words. Eleven of those words (almost half of them) were sight words. Ronald's passage had a total of 14 words; 8 were sight words. Ronald's reading would have been more fluent if he had mastered the basic sight words of Dolch's list. Chapter 7 has more information on sight words and some strategies to develop a reader's bank of sight words.

Associating Letter/Letter Combinations with Their Sounds

A second sub-skill of automaticity is the ability to associate letters or letter combinations (e.g., /sh/, /wr/, /oi/) with their sounds. For example, fluent readers recognize the /sh/ in *shake* as one sound, while too often disfluent readers will attempt to sound out the word *shake* letter by letter: /s/ + /h/ + /a/ + /k/ + /e/. This sub-skill includes familiarity with the various sounds the vowels make and when the various vowel sounds are used. The proficient reader quickly recognizes that adding an *e* to *cap* makes the *a* a long sound and changes the word to *cape*. Proficient readers quickly recognize the subtle differences between the two vowel sounds of the words *pin* and *pen*. They understand and recognize vowel digraphs, diphthongs, and consonant clusters (see Chapter 6).

Recognizing Chunks/Syllables Within Words

A third sub-skill of automaticity is the ability to quickly analyze unknown words by recognizing chunks, or syllables, within words, such as onset and rime, prefixes, suffixes, and root words. When readers recognize onset and rime, they quickly combine two sounds instead of sounding out three or more sounds. For example *hat* = /h/ + /at/ for readers who recognize onset and rime, while disfluent readers sound out the three letters: /h/ + /a/ + /t/. Readers who see the syllables within unknown words also cut down on reading time. For example, readers who recognize *transportation* as *trans + por + ta + tion* have a faster reading rate than readers who attempt to sound out every letter (*t + r + a + n + s + p + o + r + t + a + t + i + o + n*). With a polysyllabic word such as *transportation*, it takes readers such a long time to sound out each letter that they often forget the beginning sound by the time they get to the last letter. It is very difficult to remember the sounds of 14 letters and then blend them back together. In fact, with the word *transportation*, readers produce the wrong sounds if they sound out the individual letters of the last syllable. They need to recognize *tion* as /shun/ instead of /t/ + /i/ + /o/ + /n/. For more information on prefixes, suffixes, root words, and blending, see Chapter 7.

Recognizing the Meanings of Words

A fourth sub-skill of automaticity is the ability to recognize the main meaning of words as well as the multiple meanings of these words. Readers who know the meaning of *crimp* read on when they encounter it in this sentence: "Fisherman Joe's job was to crimp the fish as Fisherman Mike tossed them to him." Some readers may be able to pronounce *crimp*, but do not know its meaning. They will begin to slow down their reading rate when they read the word because their comprehension breaks down.

Knowing multiple meanings of common words is also a part of this sub-skill. Take for example, the multiple meanings of *frog*. When students read, "Mother has a frog in her throat," they must realize that Mother is hoarse, but does not have a green creature in her throat. If they do not realize that Mother has a sore throat, comprehension breaks down, which also hinders the reading rate. Chapter 8 has more information on building readers' vocabularies.

Automaticity results only if readers (1) quickly recognize the common "sight words," (2) quickly attach letter sounds to letters, (3) quickly decode unknown words, (4) can quickly identify the meanings of a large bank of words, and (5) quickly recognize multiple meanings of words. When students have mastered these five sub-skills, their mental energies can be devoted to comprehending the text instead of identifying words. Each of these sub-skills is discussed in greater detail elsewhere in this text.

Phrasing or Prosody

Another component of fluency is a reader's ability to recognize phrases instead of seeing each word in isolation. Some readers recognize words quickly and have a good understanding of multiple meanings, but are cautious readers who read words instead of grouping words into phrases. Recognition of phrases, also called **prosody,** greatly increases readers' fluency. Consider the following two readings of the same sentence. The first reader reads the sentence word by word, as Katie in Mrs. Ling's class does.

> The . . . little . . . girl . . . with . . . the . . . pink . . . bow . . . was . . . playing . . . with . . . her . . . new . . . doll.

The second reader automatically recognizes prepositional and other phrases and reads the sentence as follows:

The little girl

with the pink bow

was playing

with her new doll.

Reading word-by-word may be a result of poor instruction given to struggling readers. Struggling readers often spend more time reading orally than proficient readers who mostly read silently—which is faster than oral reading (Allington, 2001). Struggling readers are also interrupted more often and more quickly than proficient readers when reading aloud (Allington, 2001). Struggling readers are "taught" to stop when they do not know a word, which, of course, slows down their reading process. The teacher or a classmate usually gives these struggling readers the unknown words instead of sharing strategies for figuring them out.

Other teachers have the habit of affirming each time struggling readers read a word correctly. Their students learn to wait for confirmation after each word (Allington, 2001). Consider the different length of time it takes two different students to read the following two sentences:

Student #1: The

Teacher: un-hunh.

Student #1: elephant

Teacher: Yes.

Student #1: was

Teacher: un-hunh.

Student #1: the

Teacher: un-hunh.

Student #1: first

Teacher: Good.

Student #1: animal

Teacher: Right!

Student #1: in

Teacher: un-hunh.

Student #1: the

Teacher: mm-hmm.

Student #1: parade.

Teacher: Good. Read on.

Student #2: The elephant was the first animal in the parade.

Teachers need to be conscious of their actions when working with struggling readers. Instead of giving students unknown words, teachers should teach students to skip the unknown word, read to the end of the sentence, and then go back to see what word makes sense in the blank. The student then confirms that the word is correct by checking to see if her choice matches the spelling of the word in the text.

Students who read words instead of phrases need to be taught to parse phrases correctly. Teachers can conduct a number of activities to help phrasing. First, they can give students texts that are written at their easy reading level and that are composed of natural phrases. For younger students, teachers can use many of Dr. Seuss's books, which are formatted in short, readable phrases. For example, the following page of *I Can Read With My Eyes Shut!* (1978) features phrases written in a natural, conversational form:

If you read with your eyes shut

you're likely to find

that the place where we're going

is far, far behind.

(unpaged)

The first page of *Oh, The Thinks You Can Think!* (1975) is written and formatted in the same manner:

You can

think up

some birds.

That's what you can do.

You can think about yellow

or think about blue.

(unpaged)

Teaching students to group words in phrases increases their rate of reading and helps them to comprehend connected thoughts.

For older students, teachers can choose short poems that are written in a natural style. Notice how each line of the Bill Dobbs's poem "Big Mary," in Lansky (1998), found in Figure 11.3, is a natural phrase. Later, teachers can mark texts with arches to represent phrases, or put phrases within slash marks. See Figure 11.4 for an example. Teachers can then model the phrasing and have students echo the phrases back to them. After some practice with echo reading, students should practice reading the text with the marked phrases on their own until they become comfortable (see the Intervention activity on echo reading later in this chapter). The marked phrases can become longer after students learn to read the short ones.

Understanding Punctuation

Punctuation marks help writers convey their message. Students who read fluently understand and

FIGURE 11.3 Poem with natural phrasing.

BIG MARY

Mary had a little lamb,
a little toast,
a little jam,
a little pizza
and some cake,
some French fries
and a chocolate shake,
a little burger
on a bun.
And that's why Mary
weighs a ton.

Source: Copyright © 1998 by Bill Dodds. Reprinted from *Miles of Smiles* with permission from Meadowbrook Press.

FIGURE 11.4 Sample poem with marked phrases.

"Momma's sewing machine / clanked all week long. / Sometimes I woke up / and heard the Singer / before the morning sawmill whistle blew. / And sometimes / I fell asleep at night / listening to the rhythm / of the foot pedal / hitting the floor. But tonight was Friday / and we were going / to the picture show./ So Momma tucked the machine away / in a corner / like a broom / waiting to be used again."

Source: K. Willis Holt (1998). *Mister and Me.* New York: G. P. Putnam's Sons, p. 1.

respond to the punctuation marks. Notice how punctuation changes the message of the following sentences:

Woman without her man is nothing!

Woman: without her, man is nothing.

Slow children playing.

Slow! Children playing.

Many struggling readers do not read commas or end marks (Fountas & Pinnell, 1996). Without observing these punctuation marks, their comprehension breaks down. Notice the differences between the following two sentences. The first reader omits the commas and believes that the author is asking for two kinds of juice. The second reader understands that the author is referring to three kinds of juice.

Reader #1: Please give me cranberry apple and orange juice.

Reader #2: Please give me cranberry, apple, and orange juice.

When readers omit periods, comprehension and reading rate also quickly deteriorate. Once comprehension breaks down, the student reads words and not complete thoughts. The following passage is from Jan Brett's *Daisy Comes Home* (2002). The punctuation has been dropped to indicate how it might sound to a reader who omits punctuation.

Dawn broke over the Gui Mountains as the basket drifted along the river branches brushed against it fish swam silently by and birds flew overhead suddenly Daisy felt a thump.

(unpaged)

How difficult was it to grasp the meaning of the passage? Did you have to read the passage twice to comprehend what was happening?

When fluent readers encounter ellipses, they understand that ellipses indicate a form of pause for emphasis—they tell the reader to pause before reading on. Consider the sentence from *The Old Woman Who Lived in a Vinegar Bottle* (1995) by Margaret MacDonald: "There sat the old woman . . . complaining." The ellipses tell the reader that the author intends a pause between the words *woman* and *complaining* to emphasize the action, complaining.

Parentheses indicate less important material, which may suggest that readers pause and read the words in parentheses with a lowered voice. Notice in the following sentence how the author uses parentheses to help readers understand the term *readers theatre*. The phrase is set off with a pause after *theatre* and the phase is read in a lowered voice.

> Readers theatre [pause, and with lowered voice] (conveying drama through vocal expression rather than acting) [pause and return to natural voice] is a great activity to develop fluency.

Explain to readers the purpose of punctuation marks and model the pauses and vocal inflections when "reading" them. For many beginning and older students, echo reading and unison reading are good strategies to help develop awareness of punctuation marks.

Expression

Expressive reading is another component of fluency. Reading with expression is about making written words sound like speech. Many young children enjoy hearing the deep, low voice of Papa Bear, the medium-size voice of Mama Bear, and the high, squeaky voice of Baby Bear in "Goldilocks and the Three Bears." Older children enjoy hearing the mysterious voice of a storyteller who knows ghost stories. An expressive voice makes a story come alive! Fluent readers distinguish the various voices in dialogue and are able to "project the natural pitch, stress and juncture of the spoken word" (Richards, 2000, p. 534). Disfluent readers do not distinguish different voices in dialogue; instead they read every word in the same tone without expression. Note that expressionless, monotonous readers often read words correctly, but may not be comprehending the passage. Any reader who reads: "Ouch! You got my finger pinched in the door!" in a monotone voice does not comprehend the passage.

When fluent readers express the tone and message of a passage, they emphasize important words, slow down for suspenseful passages, and change volume to convey the mood. Readers who read with expression indicate that they comprehend the intended message of the author. Read the following passage from *Daisy Come Home* (2002) by Jan Brett two different ways: one in a monotone voice and one with the intended expression, responding to the exclamation marks, the italics, and the two speakers. Notice the difference in the meaning between the two readings.

> The fisherman ran after them, furious. "Stop!" he yelled at Mei Mei. "That's *my* hen!"
> "Finders keepers!" Mei Mei called over her shoulder.

To teach expressive reading, first model this skill and then assist struggling readers through echo reading and unison reading. Readers' comprehension, rate, prosody, and expression increase when teachers model through "teacher-directed lessons in which children spend maximum amount of time engaged in reading connected text" (Stahl & Kuhn, 2002, p. 582).

Selecting appropriate material for expressive reading is crucial. During the teacher-directed lessons, the material should be at the instructional level of the student, and during individual practice reading time, the material should be at the reader's easy level. The passages should be complete stories or chapters from a chapter book. When modeling, be sure to select materials that have lots of expressive dialogue or suspenseful narration.

Linda Williams's *The Little Old Lady Who Was Not Afraid of Anything* (1986) has excellent passages to model expression for younger children. The beginning of the story presents the peaceful setting of the Little Old Lady leisurely walking through the forest at night, when "Suddenly she stopped!" (Long pause) "Right in the middle of the path were *two big shoes*. And the shoes went CLOMP! CLOMP!" When you model this short passage, you should use appropriate expression and then discuss with the students what you did with your voice to make the story interesting. Then invite students to read it with you, using the same expression. When the students can imitate your reading, the students should practice it individually.

With older students, take passages from chapter books that have extensive dialogue. It is good to work with dialogue because most struggling readers can imagine the voices of different people. First, model reading the passage with appropriate expression and then invite students to read it in unison with you. If the passage has dialogue with two characters, you can assign the two characters' parts to two groups of students while you read the explanatory words and narrative.

Figure 11.5 features a short selection from Karen Hesse's (1998) *Just Juice*. The passage has been divided into three parts—for the teacher, Group 1, and Group 2. This selection, like all selections used for beginning expressive instruction, does not have difficult vocabulary. This particular selection needs to be read with expression in order to convey first the encouragement and then the despair of the father (Group 2), and first the fear and then the kindness and encouragement of Juice (Group 1).

ASSESSMENT

Teachers need to be able to recognize which of the sub-skills is causing problems for a struggling reader's fluency. Teachers use both informal and formal assessment instruments to diagnose fluency. Following are some formal and informal assessments. I contend that listening to students and using the informal assessment instruments are most helpful in diagnosing fluency problems. However, many school districts require the use of formal assessment instruments if the student is to receive help from any program that is federally funded.

Informal Assessment

Teachers can informally assess fluency through observation and anecdotal records. It is easy to detect disfluent reading by watching and listening to a reader. Disfluent readers often point to each word; as discussed earlier, they tend to read word-by-word, read at a snail's pace, and lack intonation. Disfluent readers often reread words and phrases and do not recognize when they mispronounce words. They often mumble because they lack confidence to articulate.

Checklists

The checklist found in Appendix C.33 shows four stages of reading fluency. If the checklist is used throughout the school year, the progression from one stage to the next should be evident. The Fluency Checklist for Narrative Text found in Appendix C.34 is simple enough for students in grades two

FIGURE 11.5 Selection for expressive instruction from Karen Hesse's *Just Juice.*

TEACHER:	I hang out at the door to Pa's shop awhile, then hop over the timber frame and come in.
GROUP 1 (Juice):	"You think, Ma had trouble with the truck?"
TEACHER:	I ask.
GROUP 1:	"You think she got stuck in the mud?"
TEACHER:	Pa takes his cap off and rubs his head.
GROUP 2 (Pa):	"I don't think so, honey. She'll be back soon. Don't worry."
TEACHER:	But I am worried.
GROUP 1:	"Were they mean to you at the town offices, Pa, when you were there?"
GROUP 2:	"They were nice enough. But they thought I was some stupid because of not reading those letters. I guess they were right, too. I am stupid."
GROUP 1:	"You're not stupid, Pa. No more than I am. Miss Hamble says some of us are wired up different inside our brains. You and me, we just have a different kind of wiring. You know?"

(pp. 129–130)

Source: Excerpt from K. Hesse (1998). *Just Juice.* New York: Scholastic.

through eight to use as they assess their own reading on the audiotape.

Running Records and Miscue Analysis

Running records and miscue analyses, both discussed in detail in Chapter 3, are also used to analyze fluency. The purpose of both of these informal reading assessments is for teachers to examine the graphophonic, semantic, and syntactic clues the reader uses. The teacher calculates what type of errors or miscues the reader most often makes. Mispronunciations indicate that readers lack graphophonic knowledge or word analysis skills. Substitutions for words indicate that readers lack the basic vocabulary needed for that text. Students who do not read punctuation or read in a monotone voice are most often disfluent readers. By administering the running record and miscue analysis, teachers can decide which specific fluency skill the reader lacks and then teach strategies that will aid the reader.

Retrospective Miscue Analysis

The retrospective miscue analysis, discussed in Chapter 3, helps a student assess her own fluency. As they listen to their reading, the teacher can have the student time the reading to check the rate. If the rate is very slow, the student can practice reading the passage and record it again to see if the rate has improved. While listening to the audiotape, the student should also be taught to analyze her expression and phrasing. The Fluency Checklist for Narrative Text found in Appendix C.34 is simple enough for students in grades 2 through 8 to use to assess their own reading on the audiotape.

Rubrics

Rubrics, particularly those based on state standards, are yet another useful way for teachers to assess a student's fluency and rate. Most states agree with the National Reading Panel that fluency is an important component of reading and that fluency includes many other reading skills—word analysis, vocabulary, and automaticity—although many states have only a few standards that specifically relate to fluency. For example, Illinois has two benchmark indicators for fluency. The two benchmarks are reflected in the rubric in Figure 11.6.

Formal Assessment

Diagnostic tests, which are norm-referenced and standardized, are given to students who show signs of reading difficulty. There are a number of diagnostic tests that measure fluency by calculating rate and/or accuracy. They include the following:

1. Stanford Diagnostic Reading Test. Levels four and beyond measure rate.
2. Gates-McKillop-Horowitz Reading Diagnostic Test. This test, for grades one–six, assesses oral reading fluency of story passages without evaluating comprehension. One part of the test includes students' recognition of whole words when flashed in isolation.
3. Gray Oral Reading Tests. This test focuses on oral accuracy and speed, and results in an oral reading quotient.
4. Gilmore Oral Reading Test. This test measures reading rate separately from comprehension.

FIGURE 11.6 Rubric for reading comprehension based on Standard 1.B.1d for early elementary school English/Language Arts, state of Illinois.

STUDENT: _Jake_   GRADING PERIOD ①2 3 4   TOTAL SCORE 4

LEVEL OF MASTERY

TRAIT	TARGET (5 POINTS)	ACCEPTABLE (3 POINTS)	UNACCEPTABLE (1 POINT)
Fluency and Accuracy	Always reads with rhythm, volume, and flow that sounds like everyday speech. ___	Sometimes reads with rhythm, volume, and flow that sounds like everyday speech. ___	Seldom reads with rhythm, volume, and flow that sounds like everyday speech. _X_
	Reads orally age-appropriate text at instructional level with 90% accuracy. ___	Sometimes reads orally age-appropriate text at instructional level with 90% accuracy. _X_	Seldom reads orally age-appropriate text at instructional level with 90% accuracy. ___

5. The Durrell Analysis of Reading Difficulty. This test assesses oral fluency by counting the oral reading miscues. Rate is not measured.

6. Diagnostic Reading Scales. This test assesses oral fluency by counting the oral miscues. Rate is also measured.

7. Woodcock Reading Mastery Test. The three sub-skills of fluency that are measured in this test are word identification, word attack, and passage comprehension. Rate is not measured.

8. Testing of Reading Fluency (TORF). The student is timed as he reads for one minute. The teacher calculates the number of correct words read in the one minute. The average of three readings gives the student's score.

The focus of the formal assessments is rate and accuracy. Informal assessment of individual students helps the teacher focus on all four components of fluency: rate, automaticity, prosody, and expression.

GOOD VERSUS POOR INSTRUCTION

As mentioned earlier in this chapter, the type of instruction given to struggling readers may be a source of their disfluent reading. Often teachers give a different type of instruction to fluent readers than they do to disfluent readers. Although this is not intentional, teachers' lack of expertise in working with struggling readers may be the cause of the discrepancy (Allington, 2001). Figure 11.7 compares characteristics of instruction typical for fluent readers to the instruction typically directed to disfluent readers.

In order for teachers to avoid poor instructional practices, it is imperative that they understand what reading researchers have discovered regarding specific types of instruction and the kinds of materials to use with struggling readers. Figure 11.8 lists some research findings related to fluent reading. From the research studies cited, one can conclude that there are seven principles that should guide fluency instruction (Rasinski & Padak, 1994).

1. Students need to hear fluent reading.

2. Students need to have direct instruction in fluency with feedback.

3. Students need support while reading. Support can be unison reading or reading along with an audiotape or CD-ROM.

4. Students need opportunities to repeat readings. However, all repeated readings need a purpose or goal! Some benefits of repeated readings are (a) readers increase rate and accuracy, (b) readers better understand phrasing, and (c) readers increase their comprehension.

5. Students need specific instruction to learn phrasing skills.

6. Students need easy reading to practice fluency.

7. Students need time to work on increasing their reading rate and fluency.

FIGURE 11.7 Instruction given to fluent and disfluent readers.

INSTRUCTION OF FLUENT READERS

1. Given materials that are easy or on their instructional reading level.

2. Given time to read silently.

3. Are expected to self-monitor.

4. Taught strategies to see groups of letters within words.

5. Are expected to self-correct; only interrupted at end of sentence.

6. Asked to cross-check when they misread.

INSTRUCTION OF DISFLUENT READERS

1. Given materials that are too difficult.

2. Asked to read orally, which slows down rate.

3. Interrupted more often.

4. Encouraged to sound out words letter by letter.

5. Interrupted when error is made.

6. Given words with no strategies.

Source: Adapted from R. L. Allington (2001). *What Really Matters for Struggling Readers: Designing Research-based Programs.* New York: Longman.

FIGURE 11.8   Research related to fluent reading.

FINDINGS	STUDIES
1. "Guided repeated oral reading and repeated reading provide students with practice that substantially improves word recognition, fluency, and—to a lesser extent—reading comprehension" (National Reading Panel, pp. 3–20).	The National Reading Panel (2000a); Samuels (1979/1997); Dowhower (1989); Duffy-Hester (1999); Fox & Wright (1997); Fuchs, Fuchs, Mathes, & Simon (1997); Sindelar, Monda, & O'Shea (1990); Young, Bowers, & MacKinnon (1996); Kuhn (2000); Allington (2001)
2. Assisted reading at the appropriate rate increases word recognition and fluency.	Carbo (1978, 1998); Richards (2000); Stahl & Kuhn (2002); Stahl, Heubach, & Cramond (1997); Mastropieri, Leinart, & Scruggs (1999); Matthew (1997); Morris & Nelson (1992); Sippola (1997); Taylor, Hanson, Justice-Swanson, & Watts (1997); Koskinen, Blum, Bisson, Phillips, Creamer, & Baker (1999)
3. Fluency affects comprehension.	Allington (1983, 2001); Anderson (1981); Duffy-Hester (1999); Rasinski & Padak (1994, 2000); Rasinski, Padak, Linck, & Sturtevant (1994); Vaughn (2000); Reutzel & Hollingsworth (1993); Young, Bowers, & MacKinnon (1996)
4. Dyad reading increases fluency.	Oliver, Wilcox, & Eldredge (2000); Vaughn (2000); Topping & Ehly (1998); Fuchs, Fuchs, Mathes, & Simmon (1997)
5. Cross-age tutoring is an effective strategy to increase fluency of both readers.	Taylor, Hanson, Justice-Swanson, & Watts (1997); Fox & Wright (1997)
6. Readers theatre exercises improve fluency.	Martinez, Roser, & Strecker, (1998/1999); Gill (2000); Ivey & Broaddus (2000); Koskinen, Blum, Bison, Phillips, Creamer, & Baker (1999); Larkin (2001)
7. Choral reading improves fluency.	Hadaway, Vardell, & Young (2001)
8. Prosodic instruction improves fluency.	Allington (2001); Anderson (1981); Bray, Kehle, Spackman, & Hintze (1998); Dowhower (1991); Schreiber (1991); Young, Bowers, & MacKinnon (1996)
9. Guided Reading is an effective instructional practice to increase fluency.	Fountas & Pinnell (1996); Fawson & Reutzel (2000)
10. Specific instruction in fluency is beneficial for readers in all grade levels.	Allinder (2001); Reutzel & Hollingsworth (1993)
11. Instruction focused on semantic and syntactic cues helps readers with the interpretation of author's intended meaning.	Allington, (2001); Gill (2000); Moore & Aspegren (2001)
12. Instruction in morphological strategies (e.g., recognizing affixes and root words) aids automaticity.	Kane (1999)
13. Instruction in self-monitoring (analyzing one's own rate, accuracy, and expression) increases fluency.	Moore & Aspegren (2001); Goodman & Marek (1996)
14. Readers' rate effects comprehension.	Rasinski & Padak (2000); Harris & Sipay (1990); Samuels (1979/1997); Allington (1983)

Intervention

Direct instruction in fluency can be accomplished in various settings. Some strategies are best practiced in a tutoring setting, while other strategies are best practiced in small groups because the students can benefit from peer interaction. The following strategies are divided into two categories—strategies to use in tutoring settings and strategies best used in small groups and practiced with peers. The suggested grade levels are given in parentheses after the name of the strategy. All fluency strategies should be taught, using whole texts that interest the student.

Strategies for Tutoring Settings

The following strategies, designed for use in tutoring sessions, permit the teacher to focus on the unique needs of the disfluent reader.

ECHO READING

ACTIVITY

(GRADES K–4)

Echo reading involves a teacher reading a short phrase or sentence and the student echoing the phrase back, using the same rate and intonation that the teacher used. It is important that the teacher interpret the passage with the author's intended meaning. To introduce echo reading, you should choose a short poem or other short passage that presents natural phrases on single lines. For example, Nancy White Carlstrom's *Guess Who's Coming, Jesse Bear* (1998) for younger students and Karen Hesse's *Come On, Rain!* (1999) for older students both use poetry to tell their stories. To echo-read these books, you read a line, emphasizing the underlined words, and the student echoes it, using your rate and intonation. The back slashes indicate where you should stop and have the reader echo.

Guess Who's Coming, Jesse Bear

Wednesday /

I <u>count</u> and <u>look</u> and then <u>sit</u> down. /

She <u>knows</u> she <u>never</u> will be <u>found.</u> /

At <u>hiding</u> Sara is the <u>best.</u> /

It gives us <u>both</u> a little rest. /

(Unpaged)

Come On, Rain!

"Is there <u>thunder</u>?" Mamma asks. /

"No <u>thunder,</u>" I say. /

"Is there <u>lightning</u>?" Mamma asks. /

"No <u>lightning,</u>" Jackie-Joyce says. /

"You <u>stay</u> where I can <u>find</u> you," Mamma says. /

"<u>We will,</u>" I say. /

"<u>Go</u> on then," Mamma says, /

<u>lifting</u> the glass to her lips to take a <u>sip.</u> /

(unpaged)

Echo reading can be enjoyable for both you and the students when you practice small segments of passages that you both enjoy.

 **ACTIVITY**

(GRADES 1–5)

IMPRESS READING

Impress reading is a type of unison reading that involves both teacher and student. The passage used should be at the instructional level of the student. When you and the student begin reading the passage, yours should be the dominant voice. As the student becomes more familiar with the vocabulary and the style of the passage, you can make your voice softer and allow the student's voice to become dominant.

ACTIVITY

(GRADES 1–5)

PREVIEW-PAUSE-PROMPT-PRAISE (PPPP STRATEGY)

The preview-pause-prompt-praise (PPPP) strategy, developed by Keith Topping (1998), can be used by teachers, reading specialists, adult volunteers, and trained paraprofessionals.

1. During the *preview* segment, ask the reader to predict what will happen in the story, based on the title and book cover.
2. Begin reading in unison with the student until she taps the desk to indicate that she wishes to read by herself.
3. When the student makes an error, *pause* three seconds or wait until the student gets to the end of the sentence.
4. If the student does not self-correct in three seconds or by the end of the sentence, give two *prompts:* (a) "Let's read that again" and (2) if the student still does not self-correct, tell her the word.
5. Then, begin again to read with the student until the student taps.
6. If the student does self-correct after three seconds, *praise* the student and read again with the student until she taps the desk.
7. After the passage is complete, discuss the story and talk about favorite parts with the student.

This strategy focuses on fluency because the teacher reads along with the student, and it focuses on comprehension by emphasizing predictions before reading and discussion afterward.

ACTIVITY

(GRADES 2–5)

ORAL RECITATION LESSON (ORL)

Oral recitation lesson (ORL), developed by Reutzel and Hollingsworth (1993), was designed to be used in a classroom setting with second graders. However, this strategy can be modified to work with any struggling reader who lacks comprehension and prosody skills. The materials should be at the instructional level of the student. Passages with repeated refrains, cumulative episodes, rhyming patterns, or poetry are good to use for this strategy. The ORL has two major components: the first is direct instruction by the teacher; the second component is indirect instruction. The following are the steps for the direct instruction:

1. Read and discuss the story with the student while doing a story map (see Chapter 9).
2. Ask the student to write a summary using the story map.
3. Model expressive reading.
4. Have the student practice by reading chorally with you.

The indirect instruction occurs when the student practices the short passage in a "soft reading voice" while you check progress in accuracy and fluency. After the student has "polished" the passage, he can perform it for a small group or for the class.

CARBO RECORDED BOOK METHOD

Research indicates that children benefit from assisted reading. Reading along with audio-tapes increases a reader's fluency, word identification, and comprehension (Allington, 2001; Carbo, 1998; Koskinen, Blum, Bison, Phillips, Creamer, & Baker, 1999; Sippola, 1988; Slaughter, 1993). However, too often commercial read-along tapes proceed too quickly through a text for most struggling readers to read along with the tape. The Carbo Recorded Book Method is a technique for using teacher-produced audiotapes. The teacher selects interesting reading material that is at or a little above the reader's reading level. The passage is record-ed (1) at a slow pace, (2) in short, natural phrases, and (3) with excellent expression.

The purpose of this method is to produce audio texts recorded at a rate that permits the disfluent reader to read along with the tape. After reading along with them at school, the audiotapes can be sent home with the children so they can practice at home and to involve their parents in the learning process. See Chapter 9 for a discussion of teacher-made tapes.

TAPE, CHECK, CHART

Tape, Check, Chart, designed by Allington (2001), is a type of repeated reading that read-ers can use independently to improve their accuracy. The student reads from a photo-copy of a passage, which is either a story or a poem, and performs the following steps:

1. The student reads the passage into a tape recorder.
2. While following the text, the student listens to the tape and marks each word read in error with a *black* pen.
3. Without rewinding the tape, the student reads the same passage into the tape again.
4. While following the text, the student listens to a second reading and checks each error with a *green* pen.
5. Without rewinding the tape, the student reads the same passage into the tape.
6. While following the text, the student listens to the third reading and checks each error with a *blue* pen.
7. Using the chart found in Appendix D.22, the student tallies the number of errors for each reading. Figure 11.9 is a partially completed example of Amy's reading of *Secret Soup* (1989) by Jenny Hessell. The little book has 51 words.

The goal is to have students make fewer errors with each repeated reading. You can check the accuracy by listening to the three recordings. If the child misses some of the errors, lis-ten to the tape with the student, stopping the tape when an unmarked error is made, and asking the student to listen closely to the tape as she follows the text. The chart and tape can be sent home in order for the parents or guardians to listen to it with the student.

FIGURE 11.9 Tape, check, chart.

STUDENT Amy

Story	1st reading errors	2nd reading errors	3rd reading errors	Teacher's comments
1. Secret Soup	⊬⊬⊬ // 8	⊬⊬⊬ 5	/ / / 3	Had difficult time w/mushroom and lunch

Teacher Overall Comments:

ACTIVITY

(GRADES 2–8)

TAPE, TIME, CHART

Tape, Time, Chart, also designed by Allington (2001), is much like Tape, Check, Chart; now, however, the goal is to increase the rate at which a passage is read. Readers can choose any reading material that is at their independent reading level. For this activity, the passage does not need to be photocopied because students do not mark the text. The technique involves the following steps:

1. The student reads onto a tape and notes on the chart the time it takes to read the passage. The chart is found in Appendix D.23. Figure 11.10 is a partially completed example for Amy's reading of *Secret Soup*. With this reading, she is attempting to increase her reading rate.

2. The student reads the same passage the second and third time, also recording, timing, and charting. The goal is to improve the rate at which the passage is read.

The teacher reviews the tapes to cross-check for accuracy and improved rates. These charts and tapes can also be sent home so parents or guardians can examine them for improvement.

FIGURE 11.10   Tape, time, chart.

STUDENT   *Amy*

Story	1st reading time	2nd reading time	3rd reading time	Teacher's comments
1. Secret Soup	85 seconds	78 seconds	65 seconds	Amy needs to use expression w/dialogue

Teacher Overall Comments:

ACTIVITY

(GRADES 1–5)

FLASHCARDS

Flashcards, based on some of the key words found in the passage, give students opportunities to practice sight word recognition, a sub-skill of automaticity. When preparing the flashcards, placing the key word in a short sentence is beneficial to the students because they can see the word in context (Nicholson, 1998). However, it is best if the sentence on the flashcard is not the sentence from the book, but rather one that relates to their life experience. For example, the words *worried* and *proud* appear multiple times in *A Fine, Fine School* (2001) by Sharon Creech. Examples of cards with these words in sentences are the following:

I was <u>worried</u> I would get an F.

I was <u>proud</u> of my new book.

The goal is to have the students recognize the underlined word immediately and read the sentence fluently in one phrase.

Strategies to Use with Small Groups

Many fluency strategies are designed for use with a small group because as small groups practice reading together, they encourage and support each other's fluency. The teacher should teach the following strategies to a small group and then give that group ample time to practice the strategy. The small groups need to be taught to support each other in order for students to create a safe reading environment.

FLUENCY DEVELOPMENT LESSON (FDL)

One strategy to use with a small group is the fluency development lesson (FDL), designed by Rasinski, Padak, Linck, and Sturtevant (1994), who found that using this strategy three to four times a week resulted in nearly all students developing fluent reading. The lesson is 10 to 15 minutes in length. You should choose short passages of 50 to 185 words that are at the students' instructional level. Then complete the following steps:

1. Give a copy of the passage to each student.
2. Read the passage while the students follow along.
3. Discuss story content and the quality of your reading (e.g., reasons for pausing or changing rate).
4. With small groups of students, read the passage chorally (in unison) or antiphonally (you read a phrase or sentence, and the students echo the phrase or sentence).
5. Group the students in pairs and have each student read the passage three times to his or her partner.
6. Ask individuals or small groups to volunteer to perform the passage for the class.
7. Have students take the passage home and read it to their parents. Appendix D.24 can be sent home with the student in order for the parents to log the child's fluency. Figure 11.11 is a partially completed example.

FIGURE 11.11   Sample fluency log.

Books I Can Read By _____ Jeff W. _____

TITLE	AUTHOR	PARENTS' COMMENTS	START DATE	NUMBER OF TIMES READ
1. Fox on Stage (250 words)	James Marshall	We worked on expression. But book was too long.	9/8	1
2. Get-up Machine (115 words)	Sunshine Book	I read a phrase and he repeated it (1st time). 2nd time he read by himself.	9/10	2
3. Henry, Mudge, & the long weekend (250 words)	Cynthia Rylant	He loved the book and wanted to practice it w/expression.	9/12	4
4. How to Make Salsa (192 words)	Book Shop	Information book was more difficult to get expression. He read words.	9/15	1
5.				

ACTIVITY

SUPPORTED-READING STRATEGY

(GRADES 2–3)   Morris and Nelson (1992) found that the following supported-reading strategy increased second graders' reading ability when used three days a week for six months. In this strategy, instructional-level reading material is used in a three-day cycle. The focus is first on comprehending the story and then on expression.

1. Day 1
   a. Read and discuss story elements (setting, characterization, plot, climax, resolution, theme, style, point of view) with students.
   b. Together with students echo read segments of the passage, focusing on expression.
2. Day 2
   a. Have students read in pairs with each student reading alternate pages.
   b. Have the pairs then practice a short passage of their choice, focusing on expression.
   c. In each pair, partners read the passage to each other, critiquing each other's expression. The fluency checklist, used for retrospective miscue analysis and found in Appendix C.34, can be used by the partners.
3. Day 3
   a. Ask individuals to read to you while you check for accuracy and expression.

ACTIVITY

DYAD READING

(GRADES 2–3)   Another type of paired reading exercise that focuses on fluency is dyad reading. Dyad reading is unison reading with a buddy. The buddies share the same copy of text. One reader is usually somewhat stronger than the other. Dyad reading is most effective when the reading material is two grade levels above the instruction level of the reader (Oliver, Wilcox, & Eldredge, 2000). It is the responsibility of the lead reader to set the pace and point to each word while the buddies read.

Repeated Readings

Many of the strategies already discussed include some type of repeated readings. Studies show that repeated readings increase students' fluency (Allington, 2001; Dowhower, 1987; Gill, 2000; Hedrick & Pearish, 1999; Koskinen, Blum, Bisson, Phillips, Creamer, & Baker, 1999; Larkin, Ivey, & Broaddeus, 2000; Samuels, 1979/1997; Sindelar, Monda & O'Shea, 1990; Young, Bowers, & MacKinnon, 1996) and accuracy (Samuels, 1979/1997). Some studies indicate that the repeated reading strategy is more effective than practicing rapid word recognition on flashcards and more effective than listening repeatedly to audiotapes (Herman, 1985; O'Shea, Sindelar, & O'Shea, 1987; Rashotte & Torgeson, 1985; Samuels, Schermer, & Reinking, 1992). However, in order for repeated readings to be effective, they need to have a clear purpose (e.g., to increase rate, to increase accuracy, to improve phrasing, to increase comprehension). Repeated readings can be performed with an individual reader or with a small group of readers. The following two strategies, readers theatre and choral reading, also provide specific purposes for repeated readings and are effective for any grade.

ACTIVITY

READERS THEATRE

(GRADES 1–12)   Readers theatre, the presentation of prose that is expressively read aloud by a group, is similar to a play; however, the participants convey the message through vocal expression alone rather than through full acting. Readers theatre is an activity that provides a purpose for repeated readings. There are seven positive aspects of readers theatre activities (Giorgis, & Johnson, 2002; Martinez, Roser, & Strecker, 1998/1999):

1. Because readers theatre is practiced and performed in a cooperative setting, students learn fluency from one another and are encouraged by peers to interpret the lines accurately.
2. A script has short assigned segments instead of long passages; thus, the length of the passage that students are assigned to read rarely discourages them.
3. Students need to comprehend the script in order to convey the message of the author through vocal expression.
4. Students practice their vocal expression, which develops their reading fluency.
5. Readers theatre builds readers' confidence.
6. This activity brings literature to life.
7. Students of differing abilities participate in the same group.

Readers theatre is appropriate for all ages (Larkin, Ivey, & Broaddus, 2000). Teachers can assign parts with longer segments to more proficient readers and shorter segments to struggling readers. In order for readers theatre to aid in the development of fluency, time should be scheduled for the group to discuss how they want to interpret the script. Then students should be given ample time to practice their lines by themselves and then with the group. Blocks of time each day over a period of a couple of days should be set aside for the group to work on expression and fluency. All readers theatre activities should result in performances. The performance can be for other classmates, other classes, or parents.

Books that include action and dialogue make excellent material for readers theatre. A different reader can read each character's part, while the action is read by narrators. When writing a script, be sure to keep the narrator's part short by dividing long passages among three or four readers. Figure 11.12 has a short sample of *The Little Red Hen Makes a Pizza* retold by Philemon Sturges (1999).

FIGURE 11.12 Sample of readers theatre.

CHARACTERS:	Little Red Hen	Duck	Dog	Cat
	Narrator 1	Narrator 2	Narrator 3	

NARRATOR 1:   Hi! My name is _____, and I am a narrator.

NARRATOR 2:   Hi! My name is _____, and I am also a narrator.

NARRATOR 3:   Hi! My name is _____, and I am also a narrator.

LITTLE RED HEN: Hi! My name is _____, and I am Little Red Hen.

DUCK: Hi! My name is _____, and I am Duck.

DOG: Hi! My name is _____, and I am Dog.

CAT: Hi! My name is _____, and I am Cat.

NARRATOR 1:   Little Red Hen had eaten the last slice of her tasty loaf of bread. She had sipped a cup of chickweed tea and had taken her nap.

NARRATOR 2:   Now she was hungry again.

NARRATOR 3:   She scratched through her cupboard and spied a can of tomato sauce.

LITTLE RED HEN: Why don't I make a lovely little pizza?

NARRATOR 1:   She rummaged through her pan drawer.

NARRATOR 2:   There were bread pans, cake pans, muffin pans, frying pans . . .

(continued)

FIGURE **11.12** Continued.

NARRATOR 3:	. . . but there was not one single pizza pan.
LITTLE RED HEN:	Cluck! I need a pizza pan!
NARRATOR 1:	She stuck her head out the window.
LITTLE RED HEN:	Good morning, my friends! Does anyone have a pizza pan I may borrow?
DUCK:	Not I!
DOG:	Not I!
CAT:	Not I!
LITTLE RED HEN:	Very well, then. I will fetch one myself.
NARRATOR 1:	Little Red Hen went to the hardware store and bought a pizza pan . . .
NARRATOR 2:	. . . a large mixing bowl, a pizza slicer . . .
NARRATOR 3:	. . . and a bunch of other stuff!

Source: Excerpt from P. Sturges (1999). *The Little Red Hen Makes a Pizza.* New York: Puffin Books.

All readers theatre materials must be manageable and interesting for all readers. *Twenty-Five Just-Right Plays for Emergent Readers* (1998) by Carol Pugliano-Martin is excellent for grades kindergarten through first grade. Aaron Shepherd's website (www.aaronshep.com/rt/index.html) offers readers theatre scripts that are appropriate for all ages, from emergent readers to high school students. Teachers can write scripts from students' favorite books, like the one found in Figure 11.12. Later, students can write their own scripts, using favorite books or making up their own stories. Some books that can be used for readers theatre are listed in Figure 11.13.

FIGURE **11.13** Books for use in readers theatre.

EASY BOOKS

Eastman, P. D. (1960). *Are You My Mother?* New York: Random House.

Eastman, P. D. (1968). *The Best Nest.* New York: Random House.

Fox, M. (1987). *Hattie and the Fox.* New York: Bradbury.

Lopshire, R. (1960). *Put Me in the Zoo.* New York: Random House.

McBratney, S. (1994). *Guess How Much I Love You.* New York: Scholastic.

Oppenheim, J. (1989). *"Not Now!" Said the Cow.* New York: Bryon Priess Book.

Power, J. (1988). *Henny Penny.* New York: Checkerboard Press.

Sadler, M. (1983). *It's Not Easy Being a Bunny.* New York: Random House.

AVERAGE BOOKS

Brown, M. (1991). *Arthur Meets the President.* Boston: Little Brown.

Hall, D. (1994). *I Am the Dog, I Am the Cat.* New York: Dial.

Johnson, A. (1989). *Tell Me a Story, Mama.* New York: Orchard.

Stevens, J. (1995). *Tops and Bottoms.* San Diego, CA: Harcourt Brace.

Wood, A. (1964). *The Napping House.* San Diego, CA: Harcourt Brace Jovanovich.

CHALLENGING BOOKS

Beard, D. B. (1995). *The Pumpkin Man from Piney Creek.* New York: Simon & Schuster.

Ehlert, L. (1992). *Moon Rope/Un lazo a la luna.* San Diego, CA: Harcourt Brace Jovanovich.

Karlin, B. (1992). *Cinderella.* Boston: Little Brown.

Kimmel, E. A. (1994). *Anansi and the Talking Melon.* New York: Holiday House.

Regan, D. C. (1997). *Dear Dr. Sillybear.* New York: Henry Holt.

CHORAL READING

Like readers theatre, choral reading is a group activity. Choral reading selections, however, do not transform texts into scripts. The purpose of choral reading is to read the selection with the interpretation intended by the author or poet. The poem or other text is divided among a number of readers. Each reader is responsible for using vocal expression to communicate the meaning of the selection to the listeners. Poems are often used for choral reading because poems come alive when they are read aloud. When conducting a choral reading, you can use the following format:

1. Read the poem to the students.
2. In a second reading, have the students echo read, using your rate and expression.
3. Together with the students, read the selection in unison.
4. Discuss the meaning of the selection, noting rhyming words, word patterns, and word meanings.
5. With the help of students, arrange the selection as a choral reading.

Figures 11.14 and 11.15 have examples of poems arranged as choral readings.

If you are new to choral reading, you may wish to begin this activity by using poems that are written for two or more voices. Paul Fleischman has written two poetry books for two voices. They are the Caldecott winner *Joyful Noise* (1988), which features poems about insects, and *I Am Phoenix* (1985), which features poems about birds. His newest book, *Big Talk: Poems for 4 Voices* (2000), is uniquely formatted, using four different colors to depict the four voices. The poems can be read with four individual voices or four groups. Theoni Pappas's unique poetry book *Math Talk* (1991) is written for two voices. *Math Talk* presents poems about easy mathematical concepts such as numbers, circles, and fractions as well as more advanced concepts, such as radicals, tessellations, and infinity.

ACTIVITY

(GRADES K–12)

FIGURE 11.14   Example of choral reading.

The First Two Verses of "SPAGHETTI, SPAGHETTI!" by Jack Prelutsky

ALL VOICES:	Spaghetti! Spaghetti!
VOICE 1:	You're WONDERFUL (draws out the word) stuff,
VOICE 2:	I LOVE (draws out the /ah/ sound) you, spaghetti.
VOICE 3:	I can't get enough.
VOICE 4:	You're covered (voice rises and falls as if covering) with sauce,
VOICE 5:	and you're sprinkled (staccato voice) with cheese (draws out the /e/ sound)
ALL VOICES:	Spaghetti! Spaghetti!
	Oh, give me some more, please (in a plaintive voice).
ALL VOICES:	Spaghetti! Spaghetti!
VOICE 1:	Piled (draws out the long /i/) high (voice moves up in pitch) in a mound,
VOICE 2:	you wiggle (makes hand wiggle) you wriggle (makes body wiggle),
VOICE 3:	you squiggle (shaky voice) around.
VOICE 4:	There's slurpy (draws out the /slur/) spaghetti
VOICE 5:	all over my plate,
ALL VOICES:	Spaghetti! Spaghetti!
	I think you are GREAT! (emphasize *great*)

FIGURE 11.15 Example of choral reading.

The First Verse of "The Sleepover" by Betsy Franco

VOICE 1:	My dad approved an overnight. I promised (emphasizes word) we would sleep—
VOICE 2:	that after ten (emphasizes word) o'clock at night
VOICE 3:	he wouldn't hear a peep. (voice soft and with staccato)
VOICE 1:	My friends came over to the house, they brought their sleeping (emphasizes word) stuff.
VOICE 2:	We played full-contact football . . .
VOICE 3:	. . . till it got a little *rough*. (emphasizes word)

Source: © Betsy Franco. Reprinted with permission of the author.

Some poems suitable for choral reading are the following:

Sara Holbrook's "Copycat" and "The Dog Ate My Homework."
Douglas Florian's "Delicious Wishes," "School Cafeteria," and "Twins."
Carol Diggory Shields' "Clock-watching."
Janet Wong's "Face it."
Karla Kuskin's "The Question."

Websites that focus on poetry and have poems that are suitable for choral reading include the following:

www.wings.buffalo.edu/epc.
www.pw.org.
www.poetrymagazine.com
http://potatohill.com.

Books that do not feature action explained by narrators also make good choral reading selections. Books, such as *Mama, Do You Love Me?* (1991) by Barbara Joosse, that have a question and answer format are excellent for two groups or for two voices. Small groups give younger, struggling students the support they need to build confidence. Struggling readers should be pleased with more proficient readers. Here is a short example of choral reading using *Mama, Do You Love Me?*

GROUP 1:	Mama, do you love me?
GROUP 2:	Yes, I do, Dear One.
GROUP 1:	How much?
GROUP 2:	I love you more than the raven loves his treasure, more than the dog loves its tail, more than the whale loves his spout.

(unpaged)

Knots on a Counting Rope (1987), by Bill Martin, Jr. and John Archanbault, is suitable for older readers because no action is directly described in the book; the entire story is a conversation between a grandfather and grandson. These two voices can be read by two groups, reading in unison, or by two individuals. The following is a short example:

VOICE 1:	(a low pitch, slow pace) Once there was a boy child.
VOICE 2:	(a higher pitch, faster pace) No, Grandfather.
	Start at the beginning.
	Start where the storm

Was crying (draw out word) my name.

VOICE 1:   (low pitch) You know the story, Boy.

Tell it . . .

(unpaged)

Zin! Zin! Zin! A Violin (1995) by Lloyd Moss can also be divided into a number of voices, with each voice here playing the part of a different instrument. This book features poems that represent different instruments. No action is narrated in the book. The poem for each instrument gives students an opportunity to develop expression and fluency. Phrases like "soaring high and moving in with Zin! Zin! Zin!" invite readers to change the pitch of their voices with each *Zin!* The evocation of the low trombone's "mournful moan" encourages the reader to draw out these words in a soft, low voice. Later, the same reader might raise and lower the pitch of his voice when "high notes go low." To choral read this text, first model the change of pitch, volume, and rate for each instrument and invite the students to echo read. Demonstrate how varying the rate, pitch, and volume helps you interpret the meaning of the selection.

Like all repeated readings, choral readings must be practiced in an environment that is enjoyable and relaxing. The materials for choral reading must be (1) engaging and inviting for students to use expressive voices, (2) manageable at the instructional level of the students, and (3) short enough so that students can repeat their readings a number of times during one reading session. Poems and books are good sources.

Choral readings increase fluency and comprehension because there is a clear purpose for the repeated readings. The short-term purpose is having fun with language and the long-term purpose is performance. Choral readings also encourage cooperation in small groups. Members of the groups should be reminded to help each other with fluency so the product is entertaining for the audience and instructive for the performers.

TECHNOLOGY

To build fluency, students can listen to books on CD-ROMs. Students can listen to the stories as the computer reads them or students can read along with the computer. The Living Books and Discis Books series have a wide variety of such books. Appendix A.7 lists titles in both series.

CONCLUDING THOUGHTS

Fluency is an important aspect of reading. Research indicates that there is a correlation between comprehension and fluency. Fluency has four major components—rate, automaticity, prosody, and expression. Teachers can use fluency-enhancing strategies that are designed for individuals or for small groups. Teachers need to model the strategy and then provide ample time for the individual or group to practice it. Many of these strategies result in a performance for peers, other classes, or for parents.

WRITING

Scenario

I t is the third week of school during Writing Workshop when Mr. West notices that Trevor, one of his third-grade students, has again drifted to reading his novel instead of writing. Mr. West asks Trevor if he will join him at the conference table with his writing folder. Mr. West asks Trevor to show him his folder. Mr. West is not surprised to see a short start to a story, a short paragraph about tornadoes, and one line of a poem. Mr. West asks Trevor to tell him about his writing and Trevor replies, "I hate to write!" Mr. West asks him why he hates writing. Trevor has many reasons: he never knows what to write, it is hard, he would rather read, and he has a hard time spelling all those words. Mr. West explains to Trevor that his goal is to help Trevor with his writing. He says that he first needs some information from Trevor. He asks Trevor to fill out the Self-Interest Inventory (discussed in Chapter 3).

Later, Mr. West gives Trevor the Writing Attitude Survey (also discussed in Chapter 3) and the Bear, Invernizzi, Templeton, and Johnston (2000) Spelling Inventory List (found in Appendix C.40). Mr. West, who enjoys writing and word play, hopes that Trevor, who clearly loves to read, will grow to also enjoy writing. Mr. West knows he needs to assess Trevor's interests, attitudes, and spelling ability, and then "share the pen" with Trevor to engage him in functional writing activities.

INTRODUCTION

The Secretary of Education's Reading Leadership Academy suggests that reading and writing "depend on fluent understanding and use of language at many levels. Each enhances the other" (Learning First Alliance, 2000, p. 21). Recent research also supports the conclusion that reading and writing enhance one another (Bear, Invernizzi, Templeton, & Johnston, 2000; Fountas & Pinnell, 2001; Hughes & Searle, 2000; McCarrier, Pinnell, & Fountas, 2000; Pinnell, 1999; Turbill, 2000). During the last decade, much has been written about the reading–writing connection and the impact that each process has on the other. Constance Weaver (2002) argues that "Reading will not flourish without writing" (p. 276).

Many teachers have embraced reading–writing workshops and have connected reading and writing by encouraging students to write reflections about passages that they read. Effective teachers understand, however, that good writing does not "just happen" because students read and reflect. The two processes are as "separate as they are same" (Johnston, 2000/2001, p. 377). Learning one skill does not guarantee that a student will automatically learn the other.

In this chapter, discussion will focus on (1) the similarities and differences between reading and writing, (2) the developmental writing stages, (3) tips for helping struggling writers during the five steps of the writing process, and (4) various assessments and strategies for writing.

THE READING–WRITING CONNECTION

Similarities in Reading and Writing Cognitive Processes

Reading and writing are complex cognitive developmental processes that occur before, during, and after each distinct reading or writing task (Graham & Harris, 1997; Hughes & Searle, 2000; Pinnell, 1999; Rymer & Williams, 2000; Shanahan, 1997; Tompkins, 2002; Weaver, 2002). When students read and write, they also use cognitive processes such as gathering ideas, questioning, and hypothesizing. As readers, students gather their background knowledge and connect it to the new information they are processing. As writers, they gather (synthesize) their thoughts as they articulate a message on paper. Readers question the author in order to better understand the passage, and writers question

whether their thoughts are clearly articulated. Readers need to hypothesize as they read. A substantial part of comprehension involves inferring what the author implied in a passage or predicting what is coming next in a passage. Writers also hypothesize about what their audience will know regarding the topic of their work.

Reading and writing depend on the same cognitive systems—semantic, syntactic, graphophonic, and pragmatic. Earlier chapters discussed these systems as they relate to reading. Their relationship to writing will be presented later in this chapter.

Similarities in the Goals of Reading and Writing

Reading and writing not only share many of the same cognitive processes, they also share many of the same goals. Pinnell (1999) compiled the following list of seven goals for students as they read and write:

Goal #1: To have students recognize or write words without conscious awareness.

Goal #2: To have students read and write words without focusing on every letter.

Goal #3: To connect unknown words to known words.

Goal #4: To focus on chunks of words.

Goal #5: To use root words to help determine meaning.

Goal #6: To connect spelling with meaning (e.g., homophones).

Goal #7: To focus on the main purpose of reading and writing, which is to communicate meaning.

Differences between Reading and Writing

There are two big differences between reading and writing. First, when students read, they need to decode words; when they write, they need to encode words. As students write, they must pay close attention to the internal details of words as they spell them. Many struggling writers merely sample words as they read; they do not pay close attention to letter patterns (Fountas & Pinnell, 2001). The second difference between reading and writing is that readers need to gather information and comprehend what others have written, while writers are challenged to use their knowledge of print to express their ideas on paper (Hughes & Searle, 2000).

Because writers need to generate ideas and articulate them clearly, writing is more difficult for some students. Most teachers encounter students who are proficient and active readers, but are poor writers. One might assume that because reading introduces students to new and interesting words and demonstrates how words are spelled (Rymer & Williams, 2000; Turbill, 2000) that all good readers would be good writers. Writing, however, does not develop naturally; it needs to be nurtured (Graham & Harris, 1997). Even though meaningful reading and discussion of texts provides an optimum environment for students to learn how to write (Pinnell & Fountas, 1998), as with any skill, teachers need to demonstrate writing and guide the students as they practice it (Calkins, 1994; Graham & Harris, 1997; Graves, 1983; Pinnell & Fountas, 1998; Smith & Elley, 1997; Weaver, 2002).

WRITING INSTRUCTION

The current trend in U. S. schools is to provide students blocks of time to write on topics of their choice and to give them peer and teacher feedback while they write (Wolf & Wolf, 2002). Nevertheless, many students still struggle with writing. Many of these students equate writing with spelling words correctly. Effective teachers understand that writing is more than spelling words correctly, and they work with struggling writers to help them understand that the main task of writing is composing. Writing is being able to articulate ideas, opinions, information, and creative thoughts in print.

In this section, the emphasis will be on how teachers can aid struggling writers as they learn to express themselves in print. First, I will discuss the language systems that cause writers problems. Then, I will review the developmental writing stages and the writing process.

Components of Writing

As they write, students struggle with five aspects of language—graphic, semantic, graphophonic, syntactic, and pragmatic (which relates to audience) (Zecker, 1999). (Note that the graphic component is a language system that is unique to the writing process.)

Graphic. The **graphic** aspect of writing in English involves knowledge about how to form the 26 letters of the alphabet. Students need to learn to form letters correctly and write legibly in order for others to understand their writing. Some emergent and even older students struggle with letter formation, along with the directionality and the spacing of letters and words.

Semantic. The English language is symbolic. Words, made up of letters, come to represent objects, actions, and abstract ideas. Very young children sometimes think that big objects call for big words. They make large scribbles for *cow* because it is a big animal and make small scribbles for *ant* because it is small. As they learn letters, they may string many letters together for the word *horse*, and only a few letters for the word *mosquito* because of the physical size of each creature (Zecker, 1999). For young children, it is quite a complex concept to understand that letters form words, which represent ideas.

During writing, students should clarify word meanings, expand ideas, and rewrite if the meaning is not clear (Tompkins, 2002). Writers must understand that many words have multiple meanings. For example, *run* can be used as a noun or verb and has multiple meanings (e.g., I have a run in my hose. Please run in the race with me. The ski run was a challenge for the best skier.). Students need to understand how suffixes can make a word into a different part of speech. By adding an ending to *run*, it can become an adjective (e.g., the baby's nose is runny). Knowing the meanings of affixes and root words and understanding homonyms, synonyms, and antonyms aids students' writing ability. Writers examine the meanings of words to ensure that their intended meaning for a passage is clearly conveyed.

Graphophonic. Students need to learn letter–sound relationships and how one sound may be written in a number of ways (e.g., the long /a/ sound can be written as *a*, *ey*, *ay*, and *ei*). Learning all the possible letter–sound relationships is a complex cognitive process. They sound out the word for encoding by learning about patterns within words and learning how to break multisyllabic words into smaller parts (Bear, Invernizzi, Templeton, & Johnston, 2000; Fountas & Pinnell, 2001; Fresch, 2000; Fresch & Wheaton, 1997; Hughes & Searle, 2000; Johnston, 2000/2001). Struggling writers often have trouble with irregular spellings; therefore, they need explicit instruction in common word patters (Cunningham, 2000; Heald-Taylor, 1998; Hughes & Searle, 2000; Pinnell & Fountas, 1998; Rosencrans, 1998).

Syntactic. Writers need to understand a great deal about how to write a good sentence. They must learn how to be concise and how to organize ideas into paragraphs. They need to understand how to organize a composition or story so that it is easy and enjoyable for the reader and how to organize expository material in the appropriate text structure (e.g., cause and effect, enumeration, etc.). They need to understand the different forms of the different genres. Many writers struggle with these tasks and need practice with immediate feedback from teachers (Smith & Warwick, 1997).

Audience. Writers need to understand the audience for whom they are writing. As they think of their audience, they need to estimate the audience's background knowledge. Writers understand that some information will be supplied by the readers, while other information needs to be explicitly and concisely explained. They must also decide if the passage needs to be formal or informal. For example, writing a letter to the president of the United States requires more formal language than writing a note to friends. Audience is too often forgotten; thus student writing often lacks a clear purpose.

Writing Stages

Zecker (1999) describes seven stages of emergent writing. All children pass through these stages, but at different rates and at different ages. Some young children are given "writing" utensils early in life and are given early instruction on how to form letters. These children have an advantage over children who are not given these opportunities before they enter school. Zecker found that children who are taught to listen to sounds within words and are taught to connect sounds with letters will also advance through the stages faster than children who have not had such opportunities.

The seven stages of the emergent writer are listed and described in Figure 12.1. Figure 12.2 presents a sample of each stage.

Since writing is a skill, it can be developed. Therefore, teachers need to understand everything they can about the writing stages and how to aid struggling writers as they attempt to develop better skills. Writing activities should be designed to be developmentally appropriate for particular students. A number of different activities are provided in the last part of this chapter. The following paragraphs describe activities appropriate for the drawing, invented spelling, and conventional stages of writing.

Activities Appropriate for the Drawing Stage

When students are in the drawing stage, teachers can ask students to "read" their stories aloud and then write a short caption for the student, preferably a sentence, under the picture. Teachers can then read the sentence to the student, pointing to each word as they read it.

Activities Appropriate for the Invented Spelling Stage

When students are in the invented spelling stage, teachers can begin to write interactively with them. Interactive writing is a writing event in which teachers and students "share the pen" (Clay, 1993; Fountas & Pinnell, 1999b, 2001; McCarrier, Pinnell, & Fountas, 2000; Weaver, 2002). Interactive writing is based on Vygotsky's (1978) theory of the zone of proximal development, which states that what students can do with an adult today, they can do independently in the future. In interactive writing, the teacher asks a student what he or she would like to write. The teacher writes most of the sentence, but invites the student to listen to the beginning sounds of the words and to write letters that he or she knows. As the student writes, the teacher emphasizes the letter–sound relationships. As the student learns more letter–sound relationships, he or she writes more, and the teacher adds the few unknown words.

FIGURE 12.1   Zecker's seven stages of emergent writing.

1. Drawings: Pictures that represent the word; child can tell stories that fit pictures.

2. Scribbles: The lines and marks do not resemble the forms of any letters; no directionality to the writing.

3. Letter-like forms: Lines and marks resemble letters.

4. Letter strings: "Words" have repeated patterns or include letters that the child knows. Letters do not correspond to any text.

5. Copying: The child copies from environmental print.

6. Invented spelling: The child begins to connect letters to some of the sounds heard in words. (In Chapter 13, I will explain the various stages of inventive spelling.)

7. Conventional: Students spell most words correctly and use the correct format for each genre.

Source: Zecker, L. (1999). Different texts, different emergent writing forms. *Language Arts, 76*(6), 483–490.

FIGURE 12.2 Graphic examples of writing stages.

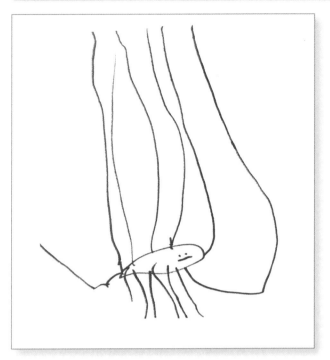

Stage 1: Sydney's spider that bites. Age 2

Stage 2: Grey's scribbles. Age 2

Stage 3: Sydney's bugs. Age 3

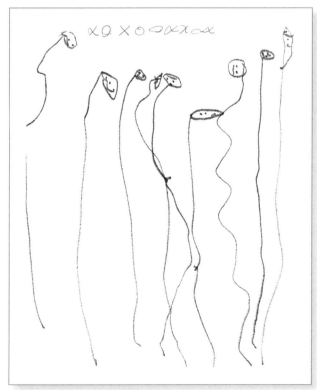

Stage 4: Sydney's snakes. Age 3

FIGURE **12.2**   Continued.

Stage 5: Grey copying from Hide-and-Find. Age 5

Stage 6: Grey's scorpion. Age 5

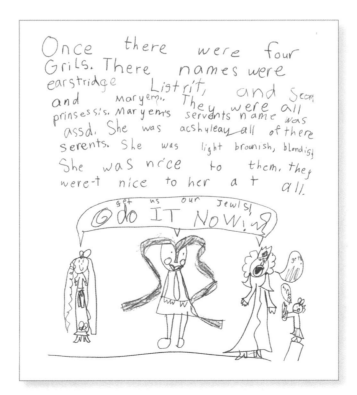

Stage 7: India's story of the Four Princesses. Age 7

Most children have success when interactive writing is conducted in small groups. However, other children need one-on-one interactive writing sessions with teachers. It is important that teachers get students to generate the ideas for the writing exercise. Young children need to understand that the focus of writing is composing, not spelling words or filling in blanks. Interactive writing is also an appropriate strategy to use with older struggling writers because the writing task is shared (Fountas & Pinnell, 2001).

Activities Appropriate for the Conventional Stage

As struggling students progress to the conventional writing stage, teachers can use the Reading Recovery method with sound boxes (Clay, 1993). In Reading Recovery, students write a "story" (usually only one or two sentences) on the bottom section of a double folded slip of paper. The top section of the paper is reserved for students to try out possible spellings of unknown words. For example, Billy, who has visited with his grandpa over the weekend, wants to write: "My grandpa said his dog Bo was ornery when it got out of the backyard." Billy notes how his grandpa

said *ornery*, and he likes that word. Billy wants to write the sentence above. Ms. Grimes, his teacher, knows the sentence will challenge Billy because he does not know how to spell *ornery* or *grandpa*. Ms. Grimes aids Billy as he writes his "story." Their writing task is explained in Figure 12.3. Notice that on the top half of the paper, Ms. Grimes draws the sound boxes for *grandpa* and *ornery*. She asks Billy what sounds he hears. Billy has learned how to draw out the sounds of words as he listens for each letter sound. The numbers under each box indicate the order in which Billy hears the sounds. When Billy gets to the word *ornery*, Billy gives an *e* for the final *y*, so the teacher asks Billy what other letters can stand for the long /e/ sound at the end of words. With the teacher's prompting, Billy spells the word *ornery* correctly.

In this case, Billy is willing to put much effort into his "story" because he has a personal interest in it. Notice all the strategies Billy used to write his sentence. When Billy came to the two new words, Ms. Grimes taught him to draw a line and continue to write the words he did know so he would not lose his train of thought. When spelling *his*, he used his previous knowledge of patterns within words. When

---

FIGURE 12.3 Billy's writing task.

"My grandpa said his dog Bo was ornery when it got out of the backyard."

1. Billy knows *my* and writes it correctly.
2. Billy does not know *grandpa*, so Ms. Grimes suggests they draw a blank line and come back to it later.
3. When Billy attempts to write *said*, he quickly refers back to the book they have just read because he knows that *said* was in the story.
4. Billy sounds out *his* and knows that it is an /h/ sound before *is*.
5. Billy has no problem with *dog*.
6. Billy correctly sounds out *Bo*, but does not capitalize it. But with Ms. Grime's question, "What do you do with the first letter of names?" Billy quickly made the *b* a capital letter.
7. Billy has no problem with *was*.
8. When he gets to the word *ornery*, Ms. Grimes again suggests that he draw a long line and come back to that word.

9. When Billy comes to the word *when*, he consults his personal word wall and finds *when* on it.
10. Billy has no problems with "he got out of the."
11. Billy writes *backyard* as two words. Ms. Grimes explains that *backyard* is a compound word and was one big word. Billy is pleased with the big word he now writes correctly.
12. After the sentence is complete, they return to the word *grandpa*. Ms. Grimes draws the sound boxes and helps Billy spell it correctly.
13. Then they return to Billy's new word and use the sound boxes to spell it correctly. By drawing out the sounds as he says the word, Billy is able to hear the sounds and spell *ornery* correctly. He decides to add that "fun" word to his wordlist. He also decides to add *grandpa* because he says he will be writing more stories about grandpa.

spelling *said*, he went to a book where he had read the word. When he spelled *when*, he went to his personal word wall. It is obvious that Ms. Grimes has taught Billy strategies he can use when he writes independently. Ms. Grimes also understands that Billy still needs prompting so he does not become discouraged.

Activities that connect reading and writing are also appropriate during the conventional stage of writing. As students clarify and question their writing content, they become more critical readers and better writers (Atwell, 1987). Teachers should explore and evaluate texts with students so they understand how published authors write. Students can be encouraged to use some of the same techniques that their favorite authors use. Some reading–writing ideas for the conventional writing stage are found in Figure 12.4. All of these tasks should

first be completed with a teacher, and then students should be encouraged to engage in these tasks during writing workshop.

Skilled Versus Unskilled Writers

When working with struggling writers, it is important for teachers to understand the difference between skilled and unskilled writers. Figure 12.5 lists the characteristics of skilled and unskilled writers.

The Writing Process

As students progress to the conventional stage of writing, many teachers adopt the writing process designed by Donald Graves (1990, 1991, 1994) and

---

FIGURE 12.4 General ideas to connect reading and writing.

1. Read poems that follow a pattern (e.g., acrostic, diamante, cinquain, haiku, or tanka) and write a poem based on that pattern.
2. Write a play based on a short favorite scene in a story or a fable. The plot is already organized for the student.
3. Write text for wordless books.
4. Use graphic organizers to summarize information from expository texts. (This makes it more difficult for students to plagiarize when they write summaries.)

FIGURE 12.5 Characteristics of skilled and unskilled writers.

SKILLED WRITERS

1. Find out more about the topic than is needed.
2. Delete information when needed.
3. Evaluate passages for clarity.
4. Write with audience in mind.
5. Search for more information when needed.
6. Spend time planning.
7. Have an inner voice.
8. Organize material.
9. Include details and elaborate.
10. Spend a substantial amount of time on composition.
11. Self-edit.
12. Are concerned about content.
13. Proofread their own work.

UNSKILLED WRITERS

1. Write only what they know.
2. Do not plan.
3. Do not reflect on what they have written.
4. Have no idea of audience.
5. Lack organization.
6. Very seldom delete material.
7. Lack detail and elaboration.
8. Spend a short amount of time on composition.
9. Struggle with mechanics.
10. Emphasize form instead of content.
11. Lack knowledge of the writing process.
12. Do not research topics.
13. Do not proofread.

Sources: Harris, 1997; Hughes & Searle, 2000; Turbill, 2000.

practiced by many researchers (Atwell, 1987; Calkins, 1994; Hansen, 1987). Consider six essential elements when planning a writing workshop: (1) schedule regular, sustained writing sessions, (2) give students choices, (3) give teacher and peer feedback, (4) establish a structure, (5) build a cooperative learning community, and (6) provide mini-lessons for direct, explicit instruction. The underlying premise of the writing workshop is that all writers need regular, sustained times for writing. Student writers need to be able to choose their topics and the genres. Traditionally, teachers often assigned class-wide topics in which students may have little interest. Students need structure, which for many writers includes the same predictable environment at the same time of day. Writing workshops also emphasize the importance of community. Teachers need to provide a supportive environment, where students feel free to share their thoughts with peers without being ridiculed. Sharing ideas with an audience that extends beyond the teacher is an important aspect of writing. Teachers also need to share their expertise with students in mini-lessons. The writing process is used in writing workshops. Graves (1990) argues that accomplished authors go through five steps as they produce manuscripts. Each step does not take the same amount of time. The steps of the writing process are described in Figure 12.6

Just because you schedule time for writing does not ensure that all students will develop good writing skills. You must assist struggling writers and teach them how to complete each of the five steps of the process (Graham & Harris, 1997). It is best if this help is provided in a tutoring session or in a very small group. See the end of this chapter for intervention activities.

Pre-writing Stage

During the pre-writing stage, teachers need to teach struggling writers how to gather information. If writing a story, ask students what kind of characters they want to write about. If students have no ideas, brainstorm with students on all the possible characters they could have in a story. Referring back to some favorite stories may be helpful. For example, if Sally really loves Norman Bridwell's *Clifford the Big Red Dog* series, a teacher can suggest that she use Clifford or another dog as a character. With the help of the teacher, Sally then brainstorms a list of all the possible things Clifford could do or the problems Clifford could encounter. Then the teacher and Sally construct a plot step by step. All this planning takes place before Sally begins to write. When writing stories and other compositions, struggling writers need to understand that brainstorming is an important part of writing. Pre-writing is a time to make a plan.

If students do not have a good sense of plot, you may use wordless books, such as *Carl's Afternoon in the Park* (1991) by Alexander Day. This book and the others listed in Appendix A.4 have no words after the first page, but present a clear sequence of events that thrill most children. Ask students what is happening on each page, and write the students' thoughts on sticky notes. During this pre-writing, you can also share note-taking responsibilities with the students. When working with wordless books, it is best to work with one child at a time since children often have different ideas about the story lines of wordless books.

If students are going to write an expository text, teachers need to help them find a topic that really interests them. When the topic interests them, stu-

---

FIGURE 12.6 The writing process.

Prewriting:	Students read for ideas, gather ideas, reflect on possible topics, web ideas, and think.
Drafting:	Students write without worrying about correct mechanics.
Revising:	Students examine the context of the composition, making sure the organization is correct and details are clearly explained. If needed, students gather more information to add to the composition. During this step, students may conference with peers and/or teacher to receive feedback about the clarity of the piece.
Editing:	Students check the composition for correct spelling, capitalization, punctuation, paragraphing, and format.
Publishing:	Students share their work with an intended audience, which goes beyond the teacher.

dents take ownership of their writing (Graham & Harris, 1997). Teachers also need to help students find topics that give them a chance to learn. Struggling writers often think they need to know everything about a topic if they are going to write about it; however, if they know too much about a topic, they have no need to research it. They need to learn that the first part of writing expository text is researching the topic. Once a topic is chosen, pose questions to help students consider multiple aspects of the topic. The questions should be based on what students want to learn. Creating a graphic organizer based on the questions will give students organization and focus. Once they pose the questions, they read different sources to answer only those questions. Figure 12.7 is a graphic organizer based on information about bats. Graphic organizers also keep students from copying (plagiarizing) complete paragraphs from books because they must write phrases instead of complete sentences on the organizer.

Another aspect of pre-writing is defining an intended audience. Teachers need to help struggling writers understand the importance of knowing their audience before they write. Students should choose the format for their composition based on the audience.

Drafting

The first-draft stage of the writing process may be difficult for students because they often think form is more important than content (Graham & Harris, 1997). Teachers must assure students not to worry about spelling and other mechanics during this stage. At first, teachers may need to do interactive writing with the student just to keep them from getting dis-

couraged. By sharing the pen, students get more text written in a shorter amount of time. Teachers need lots of patience as they work with struggling writers. They need to sit with these children and ask probing questions to keep the process moving.

Revising

Struggling writers typically do not like to revise; they prefer to write it once and do not like to delete or add information. Teachers need to pose questions to help the students understand when and what needs elaboration. During this stage, it is important to get students to understand that doing further research is often necessary. Deleting text is often more painful for struggling writers than adding it because it took them so much time to get the words down the first time. Again, posing the correct questions will help the student to understand the importance of cutting material.

Editing

It is best to get students to self-edit (Hughes & Searle, 2000; Turbill, 2000). Providing a wall chart with an editing or proofing checklist is helpful and makes students responsible. Figure 12.8 is a checklist that writers can use to evaluate their work or to have a peer evaluate it. Items that students check are based on the rules that have been taught during mini-lessons. The main categories are (1) capitalization rules, (2) punctuation rules, (3) paragraphing, and (4) spelling. At first, you may need to go through the checklist with struggling writers and then observe them as they fill it out. It is important to teach struggling writers to become independent proofreaders.

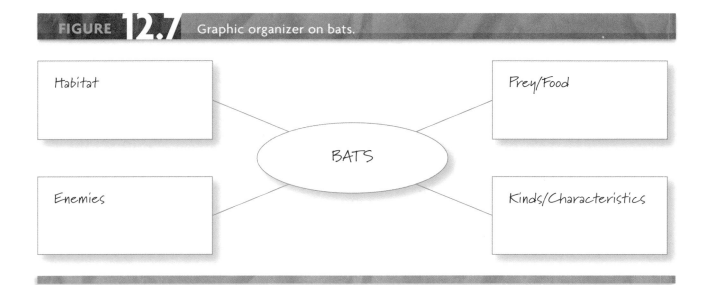

FIGURE 12.7 Graphic organizer on bats.

Habitat

Prey/Food

BATS

Enemies

Kinds/Characteristics

FIGURE 12.8 Checklist for proofreading (second grade).

Student _____   Date _____

Title _____

CAPITALIZATION:

_____ First words of all sentences

_____ Proper nouns (names of people and places, titles of books, musical works, etc.)

_____ Proper adjectives

PUNCTUATION:

_____ All sentences end with a period, question mark, or exclamation point.

_____ Commas

_____ Quotation marks around dialogue (what characters say)

PARAGRAPHING:

_____ Each new idea begins a new paragraph

_____ Indented for each new paragraph

_____ Only one idea in a paragraph

_____ Ideas well developed in paragraph

_____ In dialogue, each time a speaker changes, there is a new paragraph

SPELLING:

_____ Check every word closely

_____ Use word wall when in doubt

_____ Check spelling in another book

_____ Use dictionary

Student's Signature _____

Classmate's Signature _____

Publishing

All students, even struggling writers, need to see their writing in print and share it with an audience that goes beyond the classroom teacher. Giving students special stationary cards to write thank you notes to the cafeteria workers or to parents who sponsored a skating party or to senior citizens for supervising a field trip helps students realize that their writing must be correct and neat. They know that someone is going to read their note.

You can also publish classroom poetry books. Each student can contribute a poem for which they have received peer and teacher feedback. They should check to make sure all the mechanics are correct and then neatly rewrite or type their poem so it can be added to the class book.

You may do the same thing with informational books. Each student can research one or two aspects of a topic and then write a passage about what they have learned. They can use illustrations and diagrams to explain the concept. When students contribute one page to a book, the task is not daunting for any student. All the classroom books become a part of the classroom library and can be read often by the teacher or classmates. At the end of the year, if there is one class book for every student, you may attach a number to each book and hold a lottery to determine who gets to keep which book.

Evaluating Writing Instruction

If you desire to be an effective writing instructor, evaluate your own performance in five different areas (Barr, Blachowicz, Katz, & Kaufman, 2002). The five areas are (1) classroom environment, (2) instruction, (3), class schedule, (4) professional role model, and (5) professional growth.

1. *Classroom environment.* When evaluating their classroom environment, periodically check to make sure all materials (pens, pencils, paper, pencil sharpener, folders, staplers, paper clips) are available. The classroom also needs to be a print-rich environment. There should be an abundance of posters for class word walls, personal word walls, dictionaries, personal dictionaries, and thesauruses, and posted rules on mechanics and standard usage. To build a genuine classroom community, provide a risk-free environment. Students must be accepting of each others' work. Students need to be taught first how to state specific aspects of their peers' writing that they like and then to offer some constructive suggestions for improvement. Comments should begin

with phrases such as "I like how you . . . ." When they offer suggestions, they should begin with phrases such as "Have you thought about . . . ." Model these two steps in one-on-one conferences so students learn to imitate them.

2. *Instruction.* Instruction includes whole-class instruction, small-group instruction, and individual instruction. **Whole-class instruction** can occur during mini-lessons that begin the writing workshop time. The mini-lesson should be approximately five to seven minutes (Atwell, 1987; Hansen, 1987) and should teach a skill or concept that the entire class needs to know. The mini-lesson is for group learning and should not be preparation for a worksheet that the students must complete. The concept shared in the mini-lesson should be one that students will be able to use later in their individual writing. **Small group instruction** is best conducted in guided writing groups when you can focus on one area in which the small group is weak (Fountas & Pinnell, 2001). This instruction is explicit, with you modeling the skill, guiding the students in group practice, and then supervising the group as they practice the skill independently. **Individual instruction** should occur at the "teachable moment." When a student is writing and you are conferencing with the student, attempt to convey a concept or skill that the student needs at that moment. Teachers need to evaluate themselves, making sure that they engage in all three types of instruction.

3. *Class schedule.* Check your class schedule to make sure all students have a sustained, regular time to work on writing. The length of time must be developmentally appropriate for the student's age. Time must be given for a mini-lesson, self-selected writing, guided writing, conferencing, and the author chair (from which students share writing with classmates).

4. *Professional role model.* As a teacher, you are a professional role model. You should model writing for your students. You should share your own writing with students so your students see their teachers as writers. When you comment on the word choice of authors or how an author described something, students become more conscious of how professional authors write. You should also demonstrate a think-aloud on spelling of words, both known and unknown, and engage the students in word play.

5. *Professional growth.* Professional growth includes reading books and professional journals on writing research, attending workshops and conferences, conducting workshops, writing collaborative-

ly with other professionals, and sharing personal writing successes with colleagues.

ASSESSMENT

Informal Assessment

Portfolios

The authentic way to assess student writing is by having students compose a passage based on a topic that interests them, and the authentic way to document students' writing growth is through the use of portfolios. The writing portfolio includes writing attitude surveys, writing self-assessment surveys, spelling inventories completed periodically throughout the year, and samples of the student's work with scoring rubrics. Some rubrics, used throughout the year, document growth; other rubrics are designed for a particular type of composition. Since I believe that the best way to assess writing growth is through students' compositions, the focus of the next two sections is on developing rubrics, which is a form of informal assessment.

Assessing the Writing Process with Rubrics

When using the five steps of the writing process, it is important that teachers assess students' process as well as their product. Using rubrics forces teachers to look at many aspects of the process. In designing a rubric for the writing process, all five steps of the writing process must be considered, and rubrics must also be appropriate for the developmental stage of the students. The best rubrics are those designed by teachers for their own classrooms because they know the developmental stage of their students and what standards the state requires for each grade level. Appendix C.36 is an example of a rubric for assessing the writing process in the primary grades and Appendix C.37 is an example of a rubric for assessing third graders. Both may be used as springboards for teachers who have never developed scoring rubrics. Both are designed so they can be used over the entire year. As the year progresses, children's scores should improve. When you use a rubric that documents growth, you can quickly detect in which areas each student needs to improve.

Assessing Writing Products with Rubrics

Rubrics for writing products need to be designed for each assignment. Narrative and expository writing are very different from each other; scoring rubrics should reflect these differences. The developmental writing stage of the students must also be considered; no teacher expects the same quality of writing from a first grader as she would expect from a fourth grader.

Two sample rubrics are included in Appendices C.38 and C.39. One is for fourth-grade story writing, the second one is for a fourth-grade research report. Figure 12.9 contains a rubric for a sixth-grade research project. This rubric states the expected performance for three levels of mastery. The rubrics in Appendices C.38 and C.39 give ratings of Excellent to Poor with a number assigned to each rating (e.g., excellent corresponds to five points).

Another way to design rubrics is to weigh each component of the writing product differently. For example, in the rubric for stories, you may choose to assign five possible points for characterization, five points for setting, but only two for character motivation. You might make this decision because you and your students have examined vivid literary descriptions of characters and settings and you want your students to create similar descriptions. You may have mentioned the motives of characters in class but did not emphasize examples in literature or you may not have told students that they had to include descriptions of the characters' motives. To design a rubric with different values for each component of the story you can list the possible points after each component, as in the example below.

COMPONENT	POINTS
1. Description of setting (5 points)	____
2. Description of characters (5 points)	____
3. Motives of characters (2 points)	____

The sample sixth-grade research rubric found in Figure 12.9 is based on Oklahoma's State standards that focus on conducting and writing a research report. Mr. Harmon, who designed the rubric for the first quarter, did not use the state's standards as the sole measure for assessing the research paper. In the first quarter, he realized that no student would be competent in all the standards that came under the heading of "research." Therefore, he created a rubric based on the criterion set for the first research paper of the school year. He required students to use at least three different techniques to find sources. His students already knew how to use the card catalog, but he introduced them to the new databases in the library and reviewed how to use the Internet. For the first paper, he required five sources, including one primary source, and he taught them how to use direct quotations and citations in the exposition. He encouraged his students to carefully read and analyze each source. He did not teach them how to synthesize the information, which was another part of the standards on research; he planned to teach them how to synthesize the next semester. Notice the emphasis he puts on correct spelling.

Attitude Surveys

When using the writing process, teachers need to assess more than the product; they also need to assess students' attitudes toward writing, how they perceive themselves as writers, and their views on the writing process and the written product. Many times students' attitudes toward writing is the greatest obstacle to their success. Appendices C.12 and C.15 include a writing attitude survey for younger students and one for older students. Another excellent survey that has been tested for reliability and validity is the Writer-Self-Perception Scale (WSPS), designed by Bottomley, Henk, and Melnick (1998).

The WSPS measures the affective elements related to writing. The four categories of self-perception assessed are the following:

1. General progress, students' perception of past and present performance
2. Observational comparison, perception of how student compares him/herself to others
3. Social feedback, perception others have of students' work
4. Physiological state, internal feelings of students while they write

The scale is designed for students in grades four through six.

The WSPS is made up of 38 statements that are written simply for easy reading. One of the statements is general ("I think I am a good writer") and each of the other 37 statements represents one of the five categories. The responses are based on the five-level Likert scale: "Strongly Agree," "Agree," "Undecided," "Disagree," and "Strongly Disagree." Some samples of the statements follow:

- "I write better than other kids in my class." [observational comparison]
- "I need less help to write well than I used to." [general performance growth]
- "I choose the words I use in my writing more carefully now." [specific performance improvement]
- "My teacher thinks my writing is fine." [social feedback]
- "When I write, I feel calm." [physiological]

Each of the five areas on the WSPS has a different number of questions; the scoring guide indicates which statements belong in each category. A

FIGURE 12.9 Assessment rubric for first quarter research project, sixth grade.

STUDENT: _Char_   DATE: _November 11_

TOPIC: _Weather balloons_   TOTAL SCORE: _28_

LEVEL OF MASTERY

TRAIT	TARGET (5 POINTS)	ACCEPTABLE (3 POINTS)	UNACCEPTABLE (1 POINT)
1. Accessing information	Selected the best sources for the topic. ___	Selected some good sources for the topic. _X_	Did not select appropriate sources for the topic. ___
2. Sources used	Used 3 sources (card catalog, computer database, Internet) to research topic. ___	Used 2 of the 3 sources (card catalog, computer database, Internet) to research topic. _X_	Used only one source (card catalog, computer database, Internet) to research topic. ___
3. Authors used	Used as least 1 primary & 4 secondary sources to gather information. _X_	Used only 1 primary & 3 secondary sources. ___	Used 3 or less sources to gather information. ___
4. Note taking	Used at least 3 strategies to aid comprehension of difficult material. ___	Relied on 1 or 2 strategies to aid comprehension of difficult material. _X_	Used no organizational strategies to aid comprehension of difficult material. ___
5. Use of reference features	Used 2 or more reference features of printed text, such as citations, endnotes, & bibliographies to locate relevant information about topic. _X_	Used at least 1 reference feature of printed text, such as citations, endnotes, & bibliographies to locate relevant information about topic. ___	Used no reference features of printed text, such as citations, endnotes, or bibliographies to locate relevant information about topic. ___
6. Analysis	Determined the appropriateness of an information source for the topic. ___	Determined the appropriateness of some of the information sources for the topic. _X_	Did not determine the appropriateness of any information source for the topic. ___
7. Citations	No more than 2 citation errors. ___	3 or 4 citation errors. ___	More than 4 citation errors. _X_
8. Paragraphs	1 topic per paragraph & logically organized. ___	1 topic per paragraph but not logically organized. _X_	More than 1 topic per paragraph. ___
9. Capitalization	No capitalization errors. ___	1 or 2 capitalization errors. ___	More than 3 capitalization errors. _X_
10. Punctuation	No punctuation errors. ___	1 or 2 punctuation errors. ___	More than 3 punctuation errors. _X_

NOTE: THERE WILL BE ONE POINT TAKEN OFF FOR EVERY SPELLING ERROR! (Start by using your spell check!)

TEACHER'S COMMENTS:

You used some good sources and included interesting information.
Concentrate on details such as spelling and punctuation, too!

score in any category that is "slightly below, equal to or slightly greater than the mean indicates a normal range" (Bottomley & Henk, 1998, p. 294). If the score is lower than this range, there is cause for concern; any score higher than the normal range indicates that the student has a positive self-perception of his writing.

The WSPS was tested for validity and reliability with 964 students in grades 4, 5, and 6. Correlation among the five scales ranged from .51 to .76, showing significant relationships and scale distinctiveness. Strong reliability characteristics were also demonstrated. The WSPS with scoring sheet and the directions for administering, scoring, and interpreting is provided in Appendix C.17. It may be photocopied for classroom use.

Self-Assessment Instruments

Fountas & Pinnell (2001) designed a self-assessment writing and spelling instrument for grades 3–6. It is published in its entirety in *Guided Readers and Writers Grades 3–6: Teaching Comprehension, Genre, and Content Literacy*, Appendix 53. This self-assessment asks the students about their writing habits; for example, what kind of writing they have completed and what is their favorite piece. It also asks them what they can do well as a writer and how they have improved throughout the grading period. The last questions have the students reflect on the mechanical aspects of writing and ask what conventions they use very well.

Formal Assessment

Standardized tests, such as the Iowa Test of Basic Skills, Comprehensive Test of Basic Skills, California Achievement Test, and Metropolitan Achievement Test, have sub-tests for language (which usually means grammar). In each of these sub-tests, students are asked to find the segment of the sentence that has some type of a mechanical error. The error can be a punctuation error, capitalization error, or a usage error. This type of testing assesses the student's ability to edit a product, not her ability to write. However, since writing is now generally viewed as a meaning-making process, educators realize they must assess the process as well as the product.

Many state departments of education also recognize the weakness of these standardized tests to assess students' ability to write; therefore, they have created standardized rubrics to assess students' writing. In many states, teachers are aware of the benchmarks on the rubric and teach their students how to write in order to score well on the rubric. Some educators believe that these students' papers now rigidly conform to the rubric, which can make their "writing become more uniform and much less interesting (Strickland, Bodino, Buchan, Jones, Nelson, & Rosen, 2001, p. 1).

Intervention

The strategies in this section focus on connecting reading and writing. Many struggling writers do not enjoy writing because, like Trevor in the opening scenario of this chapter, they do not know what to write about, they see writing as a big task, and they struggle with spelling. Teachers working with struggling writers need to begin with small tasks that connect reading to writing. Interactive writing activities make writing tasks smaller and less intimidating for students and give teachers opportunities to model writing strategies.

STRATEGIES & ACTIVITIES

GUIDED WRITING

Guided writing is based on the same format as guided reading (Fountas & Pinnell, 2001). A teacher works with a small group of students who have the same writing needs. The instructor teaches a concept or skill and then guides students as they apply it. The lesson is based on the needs of the group. For example, the teacher may work with one group of students who struggle with certain homophones, while another group may need help with quotation marks. Some concepts taught in guided writing are listed in

ACTIVITY

(GRADES 1–6)

Figure 12.10. Guided writing differs from the traditional method of "teach and drill" because it does not follow a script or predetermined sequence. The teacher teaches what the students need to know when they need to use the skill. However, the sequence of a guided writing lesson does follow the format of traditional teaching. The teacher

1. teaches the concept.
2. demonstrates how to use it.
3. guides students as they practice the concept/skill.
4. expects students to use the concept/skill in independent writing.

It is a good practice for students to keep a personal record of conventions learned in guided writing sessions so they can refer to them when they work independently (Calkins, 1994). Figure 12.11 is a log sheet for students to record writing conventions they learned in guided writing. Guided writing also helps a teacher manage class time because she works with small groups instead of individual students.

FIGURE 12.10 Concepts to teach in guided writing.

1. Capitalization rules
2. Punctuation rules
3. Vivid noun choice and usage
4. Vivid adjective choice and usage
5. Vivid verb choice and usage
6. Character description (appearance, speech, dress, actions)
7. Pronoun–antecedent agreement
8. Subject–verb agreement
9. Creating clues for mysteries
10. Back flashes
11. Creating good topic sentences
12. Adding and sequencing details
13. Transition words

FIGURE 12.11 Sample log sheet for writing conventions.

Skills _____Marcie_____ learned in Guided Writing

SKILL	DATE
1. Don't put "and" between all ideas.	9–7
2. Instead of short sentences, use comma with "and."	9–12
3. Begin new paragraph with new idea.	9–15
4. Use "return" key to begin new paragraph.	9–16
5. Make stories become real with quotations.	9–23
6. Use verbs other than "said" in dialogue.	9–30

MT. PLOT

(GRADES 1–3)

Responding to stories by creating story maps is one way to connect reading and writing. It also gives a topic to students who have "nothing to write about." Some story maps are described in Chapter 9. Mt. Plot is a story map that records main events of a story with distinct roadblocks (see Appendix D.25 for a blank example). The plot obstacles are written going up the side of the mountain, the climax is written at the peak, with the resolution going down the other side of the mountain.

PARODIES

(GRADES 1–2)

Books with repetitive text give students a springboard for writing. Give students the basic formula for the sentences and ask them to fill in the blanks with their ideas.

It Looked Like Spilt Milk (1947) by Charles Shaw is a good choice for a parody for young students. First, give students a blue piece of construction paper with a drop of white poster paint. Using a straw, the children can blow the white paint around to create an image. On the bottom of the page, write: "It looked like a _____, but it wasn't a _____. Students fill in the blank, based on the image.

For a parody of I Went Walking (1989) by Sue Williams, write the first phrase: "I went walking. What did I see? I saw a _____ looking at me." Students can first draw a picture and then fill in the blank with a word. Encourage students to copy the phrase and add more pages to the story.

For a parody of Brown Bear, Brown Bear, What Do You See? (1983) by Bill Martin, you can also write the formula phrase the first time: "Brown Bear, Brown Bear, what do you see? I see a _____ looking at me." Students can complete the first page with a picture and a word and should go on to write more pages for the story. Having students draw a cover for the story on a piece of construction paper gives them the successful feeling of writing a book!

Older students, after reading stories like The True Story of the Three Little Pigs (1995) by John Scieszka can write their own "true stories" of any fairy tale character. They can write the true story of the wolf who visited Little Red Riding Hood or the true story of the Giant in Jack and the Beanstalk.

SEQUELS

(GRADES 2–6)

After reading many books, you can help a student predict what might happen "after the story." Stories like Nana Hannah's Piano (1996) by Barbara Bottner invite a sequel with an ending such as, "I'm trying out for the Little League soon. I have a new piano teacher who lives next door and likes potato dumplings." You can ask the student to predict how well the team will play, to describe the new piano teacher, and to explain why the teacher likes potato dumplings. Show and Tell (1991) by Elvira Woodruff suggests a sequel with an illustration of a twisted fork on the final page. An older student may be able to write a sequel to Demi's The Empty Pot (1990) by explaining what happens when Ping becomes the new emperor. Books like Eloise and Madeline invite students to imagine more adventures for these two characters.

ACROSTIC POEMS

(GRADES 1–4)

Acrostic poems are formed by writing a single word or short phrase vertically and using its letters to start the horizontal lines of the poem. Following is an example of an alphabet acrostic poem on spring.

Sailing kites on a warm afternoon

Planting young flowers

Raking old, dead leaves

Irises bobbing their purple faces in the breeze

Narcissus swaying to the rhythm of the woodlands

Getting out of school for an entire week!

After reading and discussing an acrostic poem, such as the one above, you and your students can create your own poems.

ACTIVITY

CINQUAIN POEMS

(GRADES 2–5) A cinquain is a five-line poem that follows a grammatical formula. The formula is somewhat flexible and two versions of it follow. The first formula is easier for young students because they do not need to worry about counting syllables.

FORMULA #1

Line 1: a one-word subject

Line 2: two adjectives describing the subject

Line 3: three verbs that describe actions of the subject

Line 4: four words expressing a feeling or observation about the subject

Line 5: one word that renames the subject

FORMULA #2

Line 1: a one-word subject with two syllables

Line 2: four syllables describing the subject

Line 3: six syllables describing an action

Line 4: eight syllables expressing a feeling or an observation about the subject

Line 5: two syllables describing or renaming the subject

AN EXAMPLE OF FORMULA #1	AN EXAMPLE OF FORMULA #2
Connie	Novels
Humorous, kind	Thin, thick, old, new
Biking, swimming, running	Inviting me to read
Always there for me	They carry me to new places.
Friend	Best friends

ACTIVITY

DIAMANTE

(GRADES 2–5) A diamante is a seven-line poem that follows a formula and is written in the shape of a diamond. This poem helps students focus on parts of speech and antonyms. The formula is as follows:

Line 1: one noun subject

Line 2: two adjectives describing the subject on line one

Line 3: three particles (ending in *ing*) that tell about the subject

Line 4: four nouns; the first two nouns relate to the subject in first line; the third and fourth nouns relate to the antonym in line seven

Line 5: three particles (ending in *ing*) that tell about the antonym in line seven

Line 6: two adjectives describing the antonym in line seven

Line 7: an "antonym" of line one (The term *antonym* is used loosely in this case. In many cases a noun does not have a true antonym and the poem will use a word that, in students' minds, contrasts with the noun in line one.)

EXAMPLE: Pizza

Delicious, spicy

Bubbling, steaming, tantalizing

Cheese, mushrooms—scraps, litter

Molding, rotting, decaying

Smelly, yucky

Garbage

RESPONSE JOURNALS

Response journals are used to increase the depth of readers' responses. When writing entries, you can encourage students (1) to relate a story to personal experiences, (2) to explain how a text is similar to other books by the same author or by other authors, (3) to explain how a book is similar to a movie, and (4) to describe favorite passages. For struggling writers, it is beneficial for the response journal to be written in the form of a letter to the teacher. This gives you the opportunity to model good responses through your letters back to the student.

ACTIVITY

(GRADES 1–5)

FRIENDLY LETTERS

In this strategy, students learn the correct format for friendly letters and learn to write with a particular audience in mind. For example, after reading *Yours Truly, Goldilocks* (1998) by Alma Flora Ada, students can write a letter to one of their favorite fairy tale characters. Figure 12.12 is a sample of a third grader's response to Pig One, Pig Two, and Pig Three's invitation to a house-warming party. The writer has been told that Goldilocks, Baby Bear, Little Red Riding Hood, and Peter Rabbit will all be attending.

ACTIVITY

(GRADES 2–3)

FIGURE 12.12   Response to the three little pigs' invitation.

April 10, 2004

Dear Little Pigs,

I was so happy to get your invitation to your house-warming party for Goldilocks.
She is one of my very best friends. And I have always wanted to meet Little Red Riding Hood and Peter Rabbit.
I have met Baby Bear. He is so sweet.
Please let me know if you would like me to take some pork chops to barbeque.
Or don't you eat pork? If you want me to take some lettuce and carrots,
I can buy some from my neighbor Mr. MacGregor.
Have a great day! Thanks for inviting me.

Love, your friend,

Betsy

If this task is daunting for a student, you can use the interactive approach by sharing the pen with him as he writes his letter.

ACTIVITY

SCHOOLYARD EXPLORATION

(GRADES 2–4)   After going outside and observing the schoolyard, students can make a Schoolyard Safari booklet. Each page is devoted to one of four sensory abilities—to hear, smell, feel, and see. (You should not include taste since it can be dangerous for students to taste things in nature.) With this activity, you can first have the students brainstorm and create a web with all their ideas for each sense. From these ideas, students can decide what to write on each page. A sample web and ideas for booklet pages are shown in Figure 12.13.

FIGURE 12.13   Sample web and ideas for booklet pages.

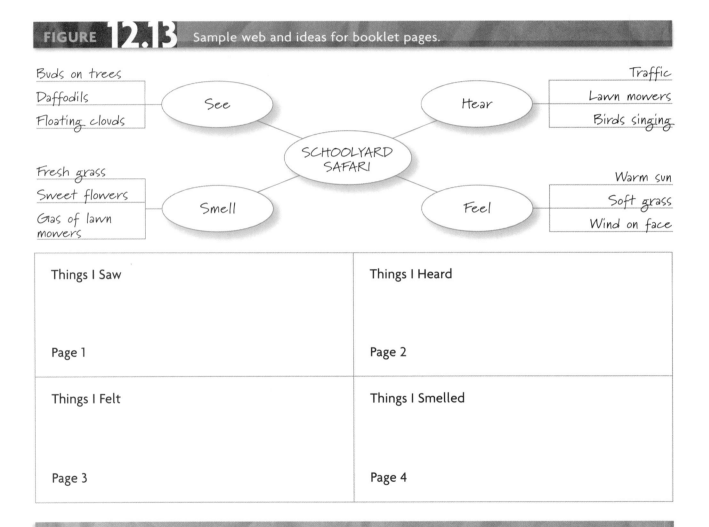

Things I Saw	Things I Heard
Page 1	Page 2
Things I Felt	Things I Smelled
Page 3	Page 4

ACTIVITY

WORDLESS BOOKS

(GRADES 2–5)   Often struggling writers cannot think of a plot for a story. Wordless books aid students because the story line is already suggested. Students can easily progress through all the steps of the writing process. First, they can "read" the pictures with you and discuss the story line. Next, they can use notes to jot down possible ideas for each page. Then, using sticky notes of different colors, they can write the first draft on each page. After that, students should reread their story and make revisions, adding or deleting when necessary. Then, have students edit each page with a different color pen, attending to grammar, punctuation, capitalization, and spelling. For the last step, have students rewrite the final draft on yet another set of sticky notes and share the story with their classmates. Appendix A.4 lists a number of wordless books. It is important that you select a book that is appropriate for the particular student.

NOUN STORIES

ACTIVITY

(GRADES 3–5)

Before reading a book with students, choose seven to ten nouns from the book. Write the nouns in a column, in the sequence that they are found in the book, but do not give the title to the book. Have students write a story using the nouns in that sequence. By using these nouns, students have a springboard for a story. After students share their stories, you can read the book to them so that they can compare their stories to the original. Following are nouns from Darleen Bailey-Beard's *Twister* (1999).

Swing	Hail
Wheelbarrow	Candle
Guacamole	Cellar
Raindrops	Cobwebs
Lightning	Sunshine
Thunder	

Word Processors

TECHNOLOGY

To many students and adults, word processors are to writing as calculators are to math. Word processors with spell check and grammar check have helped many frustrated writers. However, these tools are not magical; students still need to decide on a writing topic or story line, articulate ideas, have a good idea about the grammar and spelling of words and sentences, and be able to recognize the correct spelling from a given list.

It is imperative that young children first learn adequate keyboarding skills. Then they can be taught how to use word processors correctly. The following is a list of software that is useful for writers.

DEVELOPING KEYBOARD SKILLS

- Kid Keys (DOS, Macintosh)
- Mario Teaches Typing (Macintosh, Windows)
- Mavis Beacon Teaches Typing (Macintosh, Windows)
- Ultra Key (Macintosh, Windows)

WORD PROCESSORS

- ClarisWorks (Macintosh, Windows)
- Apple Works (Macintosh, Windows)
- Microsoft Creative Writer (Macintosh, Windows)
- Microsoft Word (Macintosh, Windows)
- Storybook Weaver (DOS, Macintosh, Windows)
- Storybook Weaver Deluxe (Macintosh, Windows)

- The Amazing Writing Machine (Macintosh, Windows)
- Ultimate Writing and Creativity Center (Macintosh, Windows)
- Writer's Toolkit (Macintosh)

Most sophisticated word processing programs have the capability to work in 'outline view.' This allows students to create headings for main ideas with supporting information and to move the information around in order to achieve a satisfactory structure. *The Amazing Writing Machine* (available for Macintosh and Windows) is a program that permits students to create outlines and concept maps. Many struggling writers often omit the pre-writing stage. Teaching students to use this feature will save them time as they write and revise.

Word processors are especially useful to students in the revising stage when they know how to use the 'copy and paste' feature. (This feature is preferable to "cut and paste," because there is no chance that a wrong key will be pressed and the student loses part of the composition.)

Word processors give encouragement to students who have messy handwriting. This does not excuse students from practicing penmanship; when students are composing, however, the focus should be on the content of the passage, not on neat handwriting. The two tasks should be approached separately. When teachers want students to practice penmanship, students should be permitted to copy favorite poems or environmental print in the classroom.

Using Computers for Authentic Writing Tasks

 **ACTIVITY**

(GRADE 2–ADULT)

EMAIL

The Internet has become a quick way to communicate with colleagues, friends, and family. Sending an email is one form of authentic writing. A teacher can set up pen pals for students with children in other elementary schools within the district, within the state, in other states, or in other countries. Struggling writers may need assistance in learning how to send emails. Still, most reluctant writers enjoy this opportunity for authentic writing because they can use the computer.

ACTIVITY

(GRADES 1–8)

CONNECTING WITH CHILDREN'S BOOK AUTHORS

Many authors of children's literature and young adult books have websites that provide information about their life and works. Many of these authors include age-appropriate writing activities and/or word puzzles for their readers. Some authors sponsor writing contests, while others ask children for feedback on their latest books. Some authors will correspond with children through email, while others give students the opportunity to subscribe to their electronic newsletter. Jan Brett's website offers electronic postcards that feature her art. Students can choose a postcard, write a message, and send it to anyone in the world. These authors frequently update their sites so they stay fresh and exciting for children to visit. Be sure to periodically check them so you can share the new ideas with students and make sure the URLs still work. The following is a list of sites of popular children's authors:

Avi, www.avi-writer.com

Judy Blume, www.judyblume.com

Jan Brett, www.janbrett.com

Betsy Byars, www.betsybyars.com

Eric Carle, www.eric-carle.com

Tomie dePaola, www.tomie.com

Mem Fox, www.memfox.net

Jean Craighead George, www.jeancraigheadgeorge.com

Gail Gibbons, www.gailgibbons.com

Dan Gutman, www.dangutman.com

Virginia Hamilton, www.virginiahamilton.com

Phyllis Reynolds Naylor, www.simonsays.com/alice

Katherine Paterson, www.terabithia.com

Gary Paulsen, www.garypaulsen.com

Patricia Polacco, www.patriciapolacco.com

J. K. Rowling, www.scholastic.com/harrypotter/index.htm

Louis Sachar, www.cbcbooks.org/html/louissachar.html

Jon Scieszka and Lane Smith, www.kidsreads.com/series/series_warp-author.asp

Jerry Spinelli, www.carr.lib.md.us/authco/spinelli-j.htm

Audrey Wood, www.audreywood.com

Anyone who uses the web knows that websites often change or disappear. It is good to remember that most authors can also be located by going to a search engine such as www.yahoo.com and using the name as the search term.

PUBLISHING ON THE WEB

ACTIVITY

(GRADES 2–12)

There are a number of websites that publish students' work. The websites listed below invite students to submit their work for others to read. Publishing poetry or stories for the world to read is exciting for young writers.

Cyberkids, www.cyberkids.com/index.html

Scholastic, http://teacher.scholastic.com/writewit/index.htm

Young Writer's Club, www.cs.bilkent.edu.tr/~david/derya/ywc.html

KidsView, www.eduplace.com/kids/rdg/chall.html (This site invites students to write book reviews of books that Houghton Mifflin publishes online.)

Student Publishing Center, www.sesd.sk.ca/publish/

CONCLUDING THOUGHTS

Students must become fluent writers as well as fluent readers. Legislators emphasized the importance of writing competence when they included it as one objective of the No Child Left Behind Act. As with reading, some students need special attention to develop the skills and confidence to express themselves. By administering writing attitude surveys and self-assessments, teachers can better understand why particular students may not enjoy writing.

Students learn to write by writing completing texts. Some students may need mentoring as they go through the five steps of the writing process. When students understand this process, they know that before they write they need to gather information. When they begin to write a passage, they know they must focus on getting their ideas down on paper and postpone work on revisions and mechanics. Developing writers need to feel good about their work by "publishing" their final copy and sharing it with an audience.

SPELLING

The road to success is often under construction.

JIM MILLER

Scenario

t the beginning of the school year, Ms. Jackson is amazed by her first graders' wide range of spelling abilities. A few students are like Kris, who has no grasp of letter–sound relationships. The students no longer scribble, but most of their stories are conveyed in pictures or with random letters for words. Occasionally they even use numbers for letters. The majority of the students in her class write short sentences or captions under their pictures by writing the initial sound of each word. For example, Marie's target sentence, "I have a new baby," is written like this: "Ihanube." Dameon is one student who always wants every word to be spelled correctly, and will not write a word if he cannot spell it. If he can't find a desired word in a book, on the word wall, or on posters around the room, he will stop writing until Ms. Jackson tells him how to spell it.

Ms. Jackson knows she has a challenge in this wide range of spelling abilities. She wants every child to enjoy writing and to learn how to spell words correctly. She decides to set up "guided spelling" sessions. The main purpose of these sessions is to mentor students as they progress from one spelling stage to another. While she gives the students ample time throughout the day to compose their stories, poems, and other assignments, this time is exclusively for spelling. She groups her students according to their current spelling abilities. For the few students who had no concept of letter–sound relationships,

she introduces one letter sound each day. The children practice listening to the sound, saying the sound, and thinking of words that begin with that sound. As the students call out words, Ms. Jackson writes them on a flip chart. The children read the words and then take turns pointing to those Ms. Jackson reads from the list. Ms. Jackson then selects three or four words from the list that have only three or four letters (e.g., for "C" day, she chooses *Cat, Can, Cal* [one of the students in the group], and *Call*), writes them on a clean sheet of paper, and asks the students to copy these words in their notebooks.

For the students who used initial letters to spell the entire words, Ms. Jackson works with magnetic letters and sound boxes. She starts the year with word families (e.g., *all, at,* and *an* families) and helps the students see patterns in these groups of words. For example, with the "an" family, she spells out "an" with magnetic letters and invites students to find a letter that can go in front of the "an" to make a new word. At first, Ms. Jackson offers only magnetic letters that form a word; later she adds some letters that cannot form a word. After the students create a list of words, Ms. Jackson writes them on a whiteboard and has the students copy them into their "personal dictionaries." At other times, Ms. Jackson selects a word for this group that will be introduced in the science lesson and asks the children how they think it is spelled. For example, one morning before they are scheduled to go outside and look for some cocoons, she chooses the word "cocoon" and asks the students to help her spell it. She creates five sound boxes (see Figure 13.1) and asks the students what sounds they hear. With the first sound, some students say /c/ and others say /k/. Ms. Jackson quickly draws another five sound boxes to illustrate how children can find out the correct spelling when a sound can be spelled with two different letters. (Figure 13.1 shows the process of spelling the word.) She makes one box for the /oo/ sound and explains that sometimes one sound is spelled with two letters. When they finally have the word spelled two ways—one with /c/ and the other with /k/, she takes out the science sheet that they will be using and shows them the correct spelling. The students then add "cocoon" to their "personal dictionaries."

Ms. Jackson works with Dameon during independent writing time. She also introduces him to sound boxes so that he can begin listening to individual sounds in words. Once he has a pretty good idea of how a word is spelled, he can check the spelling by looking it up in the Merriam-Webster Children's Dictionary.

FIGURE 13.1   Sound boxes for *cocoon*.

Ms. Jackson has to demonstrate how the /oo/ sound is spelled with the two o's. Some students think the /oo/ sound is spelled /yu/, but they quickly decide that does not look correct. After looking up the word on the science sheet, they find that *cocoon* is the correct spelling. In this lesson, Ms. Jackson encourages students to "make educated" guesses but to check a source if they are not completely certain about a spelling.

INTRODUCTION

Although spelling is secondary to composing (Hughes & Searle, 2000), it is an important skill for effective writing (Turbill, 2000). As noted in previous chapters, effective readers may be poor spellers. Merely reading words does not ensure that students can spell them (Hughes & Searle, 2000; Turbill, 2000). Assigning a list of spelling words one day of the week and testing them a couple of days later does not ensure that students use, much less correctly spell, those words in their writing (Fresch, 2000; Gentry, 1987; Heald-Taylor, 1998; Hughes & Searle, 2000; Pinnell & Fountas, 1998). Assigning writing projects does not ensure good spelling either (Turbill, 2000). Hughes and Searle (2000) suggest that students begin to spell correctly when they "care about what they are writing and about how their ideas are received by readers" (p. 204). Good spellers see "the link between spelling and the role of the audience" (p. 205). Hughes and Searle argue that good spellers are skilled, avid readers and committed writers who have found their writing voice. Good spellers' writing is personal. They learn how to spell interesting words when they encounter them in reading and when they desire to use them in their writing.

SPELLING INSTRUCTION

Good spelling instruction is "teaching children how to spell, not what to spell" (Rosencrans, 1998, book title). The traditional technique for "teaching" spelling was to assign a list of words from a commercial publishing company on Monday and test the students on Friday. The students were expected to memorize the words by writing them a number of times. No thought was given to the individual needs of students; there was one list for all. Most often these lists were not connected to other relevant subject areas. With this technique, good spellers were not challenged because they already knew the words and poor spellers memorized the words only for the test (Fresch, 2000; Gentry, 1987; Hughes & Searle, 2000; Rymer & Williams, 2000). Such assigned lists fail to impact students' writing (Fresch, 2000; Gentry, 1987; Rymer & Williams, 2000). The worksheets that typically accompany such lists focus on parts of speech, definitions, using the word correctly in the sentence, or on mnemonic rules such as "when two vowels go walking, the first one does the talking." Since only 46 percent of English words are spelled phonetically (Heald-Taylor, 1998), it is not beneficial to have students memorize rules and a few words that fit the rule. Instead, students need to be taught to look for patterns within words (Bear, Invernizzi, Templeton, & Johnston, 2000; Fresch, 2000; Fresch & Wheaton, 1997; Rosencrans, 1998).

Abandoning commercial spelling lists does not mean that teachers must take a laissez-faire attitude toward spelling. Rather, teachers need to intervene and use direct, explicit spelling instruction when students need it (Sipe, 2001). Teachers need to adopt the attitude of an active participant in the "co-construction" process, based on Vygotsky's (1978) theory of the zone of proximal development. Teachers must assist students as they progress from what they know about spelling to what they do not know. This active teaching and active learning compliment one another. The first steps to becoming an active participant is for teachers to develop background knowledge about (1) the developmental stages of spelling, (2) the complexities of English spelling, and (3) the orthographic patterns of words.

DEVELOPMENTAL STAGES OF SPELLING

Researchers agree there are developmental stages of spelling, but differ on the number of stages and the names for each stage. In Chapter 12, Zecker's (1999) seven stages of emergent writers were discussed. Bear, Invernizzi, Templeton, and Johnston (2000), Gentry and Gillet (1993), Rosencrans (1998), and Ferroli and Shanahan (1987) all identify five stages of spelling but disagree about their contents. Fresch and Wheaton (1997) and Bear and Templeton (1998) identify six stages, while Sipe (2001) identifies seven. The different developmental stages are listed and explained in Figure 13.2. The various stages are not substantially different from each other; they do overlap. Some researchers break down spelling stages into smaller units than other researchers do. The different lists are not intended to confuse you, but to provide all the relevant information so as you observe your students' spelling, you can use this information to better understand struggling spellers.

Instructional Practices for Each Spelling Stage

For the following discussion I will rely on Bear, Invernizzi, Templeton, and Johnston's (2000) spelling stages. Most stages are closely related and it should be easy to connect strategies with the names of the stages of different researchers.

Emergent Spelling Stage

Children in this stage need to be given ample opportunity to "write" and need adults to respond to their writing by asking the child to "read" them their story, poem, or other creation.

In order for children to develop from the prephonetic to phonetic stage, they need to begin to represent their thoughts with words, and in order to use words, they need "to move toward using letters of the alphabet" (Buchanan, 1989, p. 15). Some strategies teachers can use are labeling items around the classroom and calling attention to the labels. Teachers can draw attention to students' name cards on their desks and ask them to find other names or

---

FIGURE **13.2**   Developmental spelling stages.

BEAR, INVERNIZZI, TEMPLETON, AND JOHNSTON'S STAGES

1. Emergent: Scribbles or letter-like shapes; conventional left-to-right direction.
2. Alphabetic: Uses beginning and ending consonants and consonant blends; vowels in every word.
3. Within Word Pattern: Long vowels spelled correctly; confuse long vowel digraphs.
4. Syllables and Affixes: Uses inflectional endings correctly (double consonant with short vowel sounds); prefixes and suffixes spelled correctly.
5. Derivational Relations: Most polysyllabic words spelled correctly; unaccented vowels in derived words spelled correctly.

BEAR AND TEMPLETON'S STAGES

1. Prephonemic: Scribbles
2. Semiphonemic: Single letter for entire word (b = baby)
3. Letter Name: Use initial, ending, and medial consonant sounds ("wuntz" = once)
4. Within Word Pattern: Most sounds are in words ("seet" or "sete" = seat)
5. Syllable Juncture: Polysyllabic words (hopping and hoping)
6. Derivational: Understands root words with affixes

GENTRY AND GILLET'S STAGES

(see Figure 13.3 for sample work from the following stages)

1. Precommunicative: Random letters; scribbles; drawings; no knowledge of letter–sound relationships.
2. Semiphonetic: Realizes letters represent sounds in words; uses initial letter and ending letters of words; writes left to right; may or may not have spacing.
3. Phonetic: Hears most consonants in words.
4. Transitional: Includes vowels in each syllable; begins to use knowledge of affixes and inflectional endings.
5. Conventional: Most words spelled correctly.

FERROLI AND SHANAHAN'S STAGES

1. Preliterate: No letter–sound relationships.
2. Initial Consonant: Initial letter is correct.
3. Consonant Frame: Initial and ending consonant sounds are present.
4. Phonetic: Initial, medial, and final sounds are present.
5. Transitional: Words are spelled as they sound ("wuntz" for once).

ROSENCRANS'S STAGES

1. Pre-phonetic: Drawings of sticks and shapes; no letter–sound relationships.
2. Phonetic: Letter–name strategy (e.g., r = are); only initial and final sounds; similar sounds may be substituted (e.g., "sete" = city).
3. Graphophonic: Uses sound–symbol cues; uses phonic rules for letter sounds.
4. Ortho-phonic: Uses knowledge of sound–letter sequence (qwd is not a possible answer).
5. Morpho-phonic: Understands affixes, derivations, and structural units.

FRESCH AND WHEATON'S STAGES

1. Preliterate/Prephonetic: Scribble; aware that words are print.
2. Preliterate/Phonetic: Learns alphabet; strings letters together to spell words.
3. Letter Name: Uses environmental print as aid; learns some sight words; exchanges short vowel sounds for closest long vowel sounds; spells words as they sound (e.g., r for are).
4. Within Word: Develops sight words; use short vowels correctly; confuses long vowel digraphs (boat is "bote"); uses d for all past tense words; knows every word has vowel; internalizes rules (silent e); overgeneralizes rules.
5. Syllable Juncture: Correctly doubles consonants before inflectional endings; struggles with schwa sound.
6. Derivational Constancy: Understands relationship of words, derivations, and multiple meanings.

SIPE'S STAGES

1. Scribbles: Scribble.
2. Letter-like shapes: Mostly scribble with some letters and numbers randomly included.
3. Sequence of Letters: Understands words are more than one letter, but letters are random.
4. Encode Words with Initial Consonants: Initial consonant represents the entire word.
5. Encode Words with Initial and Ending Consonants: Both initial and ending consonants are present.
6. Encode Words with Medial Sounds: Adds the medial sound.
7. Conventional Forms: Most words are spelled correctly.

FIGURE 13.3   Graphic examples of spelling stages.

Precommunication:
"Grey is king on his birthday" (age 4).

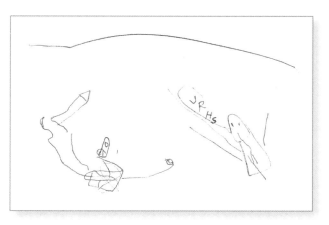

Semiphonetic:
"You are hurting us!" Grey's drawing (age 5).

Phonetic:
"Destroy" (Grey's man, age 5).

Transitional Stage: "God Loves You"
(Grey's feeling after Bible school, age 6).

Transitional Stage:
Half Man, Half Bat (Grey's batman, age 6).

Conventional:
"India's Friend" (story, age 7).

words that begin with the same letter, or to find the longest name and shortest names in the class. Teachers can also demonstrate these writing lessons by (1) writing short captions under student's pictures, (2) spelling out the letters of each word, (3) saying each word aloud, (4) reading the caption, and finally (5) asking the child to point to each word as he reads the caption. After sharing a big book with a group, the teacher can play "I spy" by asking students to point to a particular letter or word on the page. Spellers in this stage need lots of time to examine letters and hear letter sounds.

Alphabetic Spelling Stage

Students in this stage are aware of the initial sounds of words. At the early alphabetic stage, students often think there are always as many letters in a word as there are syllables. Thus they spell *baby* as "bb" and *horse* as "h." As the students move through this stage, they begin to write the main sounds within a word. Thus *baby* becomes "babe." At this stage, students need plenty of demonstrations and chances to listen to the sounds within words.

One strategy for this stage is interactive writing. During the Morning Message, the teacher can spell out the words aloud as she writes them; when students come to a familiar word, the teacher can ask for a student who knows the beginning letter of that word to come and write it. If the teacher always begins the Morning Message with "Good Morning, boys and girls," she can invite students to write the familiar letters they know.

Within Word Pattern Spelling Stage

During this stage, a teacher must help students discover patterns within words. A teacher can begin with three-letter phonograms (word families). A teacher can write the rime of a phonogram on a flip chart and ask students to provide the onsets to create as many words as possible. The teacher can also copy poems word by word onto flip charts that identify word families and ask students to name the word family for each word.

While doing this activity, the teacher can also ask students to find rhyming words (words that share the same sound but not the same letters) and identify some pairs of words that rhyme. In the following passage from *Guess Who's Coming, Jesse Bear* (1998) by Nancy White Carlstrom, the teacher can draw attention to the rhyme of *whale* and *tail* and to the different spellings of their rhyming words.

Saturday

Sara swims like a shark,

Or should I say a whale?
She says she'll nibble on a fish
And tries to grab my tail.
(unpaged)

Whenever students are writing, they need to be encouraged to spell by putting down the letters they think might be in a word and then checking the sounds of the word. When they ask if a word is correct, you can direct them to a page in a book or you can have them use sound boxes.

Syllable and Affixes Spelling Stage

At this stage, a teacher's goal is to help students see chunks within words so that they learn to listen for these groups of letters and spell them. It is far easier than attempting to listen for the single letters of multi-syllabic words.

Teachers can use big books to show how many words end in *ing* or *ed*. After reading a book together, the teacher can play "I spy" and ask the students to point to words that end with an *ing* or *ed*. While working with these two endings, the teacher can call out a verb and ask students on their individual papers to make that verb and the *ing* and *ed* verbs. Later, teachers can challenge students to find other prefixes and suffixes.

Also during this stage, teachers can design an exercise using one-inch cards with prefixes in green, root words in red, and suffixes in blue; and then challenge the students to push three cards together (one of each color) to make words. This exercise is especially helpful for tactile learners.

Derivational Relations Spelling Stage

Since students are now spelling most words correctly, the teacher should encourage students to check each other's papers for spelling errors. In this stage, students can apply simple spelling rules, such as when to double consonants before adding an *ing*. (See Appendix B.9, Generalizations About Word Spellings.) The rules can be written on a chart that is posted in the classroom. Students should be encouraged to check the rules when they have questions about spelling. After working with multisyllabic words, students should be taught the correct way to hyphenate words. When hyphenating words, students should explain what rule they applied when they hyphenated each word.

During this stage, students should learn how to use the spell-check features on word processors. At this stage, they should be able to recognize the word they are spelling out of a number of other possible options.

PATTERNS OF ENGLISH SPELLING

Orthographic Patterns of Words

Researchers suggest that good spellers understand **orthography**—letters and their sequence in words (Fresch, 2000; Hughes & Searle, 2000; Pinnell & Fountas, 1998; Rymer & Williams, 2000; Turbill, 2000). Therefore, the purpose of explicit spelling instruction is to expand students' "knowledge of the principles of English orthography and broaden the range of strategies they use to spell unknown words" (Rymer & Williams, 2000, p. 242).

You should aim to make all students word solvers. Word solvers have orthographic categories in their heads (Fountas & Pinnell, 2001). They know different spellings for the same sound and understand how words are organized. They easily identify patterns within words and learn to make connections among words instead of memorizing whole words. Word solvers learn unknown words:

- through sound (phonemic strategy)
- through vision (visual strategy)
- through meaning (morphemic strategy)
- through analogies (linking strategy)
- through inquiry (dictionary usage) (Fountas & Pinnell, 2001; Heald-Taylor, 1998; Zecker, 1999)

Being a word solver "is not so much about learning individual words as it is about learning how written language is organized—how written language 'works.'" (Fountas & Pinnell, 2001, p. 369).

In order for teachers to teach English orthography, they need to understand some generalizations about word patterns. Appendix B.9 lists common generalizations that teachers need to understand in order to aid students as they learn to spell unknown words. Appendix B.10 presents more generalizations about words. These generalizations are not intended as rules that students should memorize. Instead, point out these generalizations to resolve specific problems as they work with students. Students need to learn to recognize word patterns, not memorize the rules!

As noted earlier, teaching students to see patterns in words or showing them how words are put together is more beneficial than having them memorize word lists. Understanding *visual* connections such as consonant blends, digraphs, and diphthongs aid young students as they learn word patterns. Making lists of words that follow certain word patterns can be fun for children. They can keep the lists in a booklet so they have them as a reference when they write independently. Appendix B.10 lists common word patterns with a few examples. Stu-

dents should be encouraged to see how many words they can add to each list.

You should help students learn word patterns that have consonant blends (e.g., *tr, gr, fl*), vowel digraphs (e.g., *oa, ie*), diphthongs (e.g., *oi* [*oil*], *au* [*taught*]), and controlled-*r* sounds. When students are in the later writing stages, you can help students focus on patterns in words that are based on meaning. Focusing on prefixes, suffixes, inflectional endings, and homonyms aids students in learning patterns in words as they spell. Direct instruction helps students to understand how words change when they become different parts of speech (e.g., *musical* to *musician*). Students can also have fun as they discover how accents change with different forms of words (e.g., MUS-ic, but not MUS-ic-ian).

Complex Patterns of English Spelling

Learning to spell is a complex, developmental process (Heald-Taylor, 1998; Johnston, 2001a; Pinnell & Fountas, 1998; Rymer & Williams, 2000), and teachers need to understand the complexities of English spelling in order to assist students as they master it. In order to show the complexities of English spelling, George Bernard Shaw, the English playwright, spelled the word *fish* "phonetically" as *ghoti*. The *gh* came from the sound in *rough*, the *o* from its sound in *women*, and the *ti* from its sound in *nation* (cited in Johnston, 2001a). However, Johnston points out that (1) *gh* never calls for an /f/ sound at the beginning of a word, and (2) the *ti* for the /sh/ sound occurs only in the medial position of words. Appendix B.11 lists other complex patterns of English spelling. It is advantageous for teachers to understand these patterns as they aid students with their spelling. By including these complex patterns, I am not however, suggesting that students memorize these patterns. Rather, I believe that if teachers are aware of these patterns, they can better assist their students.

GOOD VERSUS POOR SPELLERS

There are distinctive differences between good and poor spellers. When good spellers proofread their work, they recognize their spelling errors and correct them without seeking outside help (Hughes & Searle, 2000; Turbill, 2000). When they encounter a word they do not know how to spell, they "generate sensible written alternatives that can be compared in order to select the one that makes the most sense and 'looks right'" (Hughes & Searle, 2000, p. 205). Good spellers understand the writing process (Turbill, 2000); they understand that during the first draft, there should be little concern for conventions. The purpose of editing, however, is to focus on mechanics, which includes spelling. As you work with struggling spellers, it is helpful to understand what good spellers can do. By recognizing what good spellers do naturally, you can attempt to help poor spellers do the same things. Figure 13.4 lists traits of good and poor spellers.

ASSESSMENT

Informal Assessment

With spelling, as with other skills, teachers need to understand what students already know and give them tasks that will develop their ability and knowledge. Informal spelling instruments such as inventories and checklists are effective ways to determine students' spelling skills so that appropriate instruction can be planned.

Spelling Inventories

A number of researchers have designed developmental spelling tasks that help teachers assess what children know about spelling (Bear, Invernizzi, Templeton, & Johnston, 2000; Henderson, 1990). The inventories are alike in that they feature lists that progress from easy words (with CVC and CVCe pat-

terns) to more difficult (multi-syllable words) and are intended as individual tests. It is beneficial for teachers to observe students as they spell the words; often the process will help teachers understand what students can and cannot do when they write words. The purpose of each inventory is to have students spell the dictated words so teachers can analyze what students already know about spelling. When the inventories are administered throughout the year, teachers track the progress of their students. Any of these inventories are helpful for teachers to identify students that need individual help. All three lists are included in Appendices C.40–41 so teachers can select the one that best fits their students' needs. The first two inventories (in Appendix C.40) are from Bear, Invernizzi, Templeton, and Johnston (2000), and the third inventory (in Appendix C.41) is from Henderson (cited in Fresch & Wheaton, 1997).

All three inventories can be administered using the same directions. The teacher says a word from the list once or twice and uses it in a sentence. To set the student's mind at ease, the student is told that these are words that he is not expected to know, but he is to write them the way he thinks the words are spelled. Most sets of words are presented in groups of five. When a student misses three out of five, the teacher stops the test. Teachers need to remember that these are not tests to compare children's abilities; they are inventories to assess what a student knows about constructing words.

FIGURE 13.4 Traits of good and poor spellers.

GOOD SPELLERS	POOR SPELLERS
1. Pay attention to internal details of words.	1. Attempt to learn whole spelling of each word.
2. Are excellent, avid readers.	2. May be good or poor readers.
3. Are committed writers who find their voice.	3. Do not have their own writing voice.
4. Learn to spell new words when they want them in their writing.	4. Use words they know.
5. Self-monitor.	5. Do not understand self-monitoring.
6. Correct their own errors.	6. Get someone else to correct errors.
7. Quickly recognize their own errors.	7. Do not recognize their own errors.
8. Self-edit.	8. Attempt to memorize words.
9. Learn orthographic patterns within words.	9. Do not see orthographic patterns in words.
10. Learn different spellings for the same sounds.	10. Do not know different spellings for same sound.
11. Slow down when a word looks wrong.	11. Believe spelling is arbitrary.
12. Use a wide range of strategies.	12. Know no strategies.
	13. Sample only parts of words when they read.

Sources: Hughes, M. & Searle, D. (2000). Spelling and "the second 'R.'" *Language Arts, 77*(3), 201–208. Turbill, J. (2000). Developing a spelling conscience. *Language Arts, 77*(3), 209–217. Fresch, M. (2000). What we learned about Josh: Sorting out word sorting. *Language Arts, 77*(3), 232–240.

A student's spelling stage can be determined by how many words he spells correctly. For example, using the two inventories in Appendix C.40, the following criteria apply (Bear, Invernizzi, Templeton, & Johnston, 2000):

SPELLED CORRECTLY	STAGE OF DEVELOPMENT
0	Emergent
1–5	Alphabetic
5–10	Within Word Pattern
10–15	Syllables and Affixes
15–25	Derivational Relations

To assess the spelling stage of students, teachers can use the following guidelines:

1. In the emergent stage, students will first write the initial sound, then add the ending sound.
2. In the alphabetic stage, students correctly spell short vowel sounds and later digraphs and blends.
3. In the within-word-pattern stage, students can spell long vowels (including the silent *e* when the word has the CVCe pattern) and vowels that are controlled by *r*.
4. In the syllable/affixes stage, students add inflectional endings, prefixes, and suffixes. They also know when to double the consonant if they add *ed* or *ing*.
5. In the derivational stage, students are able to spell unknown words by listening for the root words and adding the correct prefixes and suffixes.

Once teachers understand the spelling stages, they can develop their own inventories. They can also determine a student's spelling stage by recording and analyzing the spelling of words from a student's independent writing tasks. The template demonstrated in Figure 13.5 is for recording and analyzing these words. The first step is to record the words

FIGURE 13.5 Samples of recording students' spelling.

STUDENT **Jon** GRADE **K**

Word	Precommunicative	Semiphonetic	Phonetic	Transitional	Conventional
1. lady	(scribble)				
2. once	abc				

STUDENT **Krystal** GRADE **1**

Word	Precommunicative	Semiphonetic	Phonetic	Transitional	Conventional
1. lady		ld			
2. once		wn			

STUDENT **Mary B.** GRADE **2**

Word	Precommunicative	Semiphonetic	Phonetic	Transitional	Conventional
1. lady			lade		
2. once			wunz		

STUDENT **Kim** GRADE **3**

Word	Precommunicative	Semiphonetic	Phonetic	Transitional	Conventional
1. popping				poping	
2. caught				cought	

STUDENT **Cooper** GRADE **5**

Word	Precommunicative	Semiphonetic	Phonetic	Transitional	Conventional
1. popping					popping
2. caught					caught

exactly as the students spell them. List the words in the column that corresponds to the appropriate spelling stage. (See Figure 13.2 for descriptions of how words might be spelled in each stage.) Then assess how the child spelled each word in a five-word set to determine the child's spelling stage. Appendix C.42 has a blank form to use to record and analyze students' spelling. The developmental stages are based on Gentry and Gillet's (1993) classification.

Checklist Based on State Standards

Many states, such as Texas, have now added standards that are specific to students' spelling ability. A checklist is one way a teacher can monitor which students in her class need extra help. She can group students with similar needs and help them with specific problems. The partial checklist in Figure 13.6 indicates that at the end of the second quarter, Phil, Kim, Heather, and Marc need help with inflections, prefixes, and suf-

fixes. Most students need to learn how to use resources such as dictionaries and spell checks on word processors. A blank checklist is available in Appendix C.43.

Formal Assessment

Standardized tests, such as the Iowa Test of Basic Skills, Comprehensive Test of Basic Skills, California Achievement Test, and Metropolitan Achievement Test have sub-tests for spelling. In some of these sub-tests, students are asked to select the correctly spelled word from a list of four or five words. Teachers need to remember that this type of testing assesses the students' ability to edit, not to spell words. However, since editing is an important step in the writing process, teachers understand that they must assess the process as well as the product. In other sub-tests, students may need to select the correct letter combination that is missing in a word. This type of test assesses students' knowledge of word patterns.

FIGURE 13.6 Checklist for spelling standards.

TEACHER *Mr. Green*   QUARTER 1 ② 3 4

+ = always   X = sometimes   O = seldom/never

STANDARD   STUDENTS

ACCURATE SPELLING:	April	Colby	Candace	Phil	Cole	Sara	Ivan	Kim	Mike	Heather	Jamie	Steven	Marc	Evette	Evonne	Jon	Cy	Alonzo
Closed, open syllables	+	+	X	X	+	+	+	+	X	+	+	X	X	+	+	X	X	+
Consonant before *le*	X	+	X	X	+	X	X	X	X	X	+	X	X	+	+	X	+	X
Qu patterns	+	+	X	+	+	+	+	+	+	+	+	+	+	+	+	+	+	+
N before *v*	+	+	X	X	+	+	X	+	X	X	+	X	X	+	+	X	+	X
M before *b*	+	+	X	X	+	+	X	X	X	O	+	X	X	+	X	X	X	X
M before *p*	+	+	X	X	+	+	X	X	X	O	+	X	X	+	X	X	+	X
Change *z* to *c* with *es*	+	+	X	X	X	+	+	X	X	X	+	X	X	+	X	X	X	+
Root words	+	+	+	+	+	+	+	+	+	X	+	X	X	+	+	X	X	+
Tense inflections	X	X	X	O	X	+	+	O	X	O	+	X	O	+	+	X	X	X
Number inflections	X	X	X	O	X	+	X	O	X	O	X	X	O	+	+	O	X	X
Suffixes *-able* & *-less*	X	+	O	O	X	X	O	X	O	O	+	O	O	X	+	O	X	O
Prefixes *re-* & *un-*	X	+	X	O	+	+	X	X	+	O	+	X	O	+	+	+	X	X
Use resources to find correct spelling	O	O	O	O	O	O	X	O	X	O	X	O	O	X	O	O	X	O
Accurate spelling in final draft																		

Intervention

he first activities in this section focus on working with word patterns. These strategies are best taught in tutoring sessions so that the teacher can observe the child as she makes sense of patterns in words.

MAGNETIC LETTERS

ACTIVITY

(GRADES 1–2)

Working with magnetic letters helps students who are tactile learners and students who do not like to erase because it is messy. If students are really weak with spelling, you can pre-select letters and put them in a pile. First you and the student should work with word families (onset and rimes) that have the CVC pattern (e.g., *at, ap, am, an,* and *up* families).

1. Pronounce the word
2. Have the student pronounce the word and then both pronounce it slowly, drawing out the sounds.
3. Ask the student to spell the word.
4. Give another word from the same word family.
5. For the second word, ask the student to find all three letters from the pile; she should not merely change the first letter, because it is important that she sees four or five words with the same pattern.

Much time should be given to manipulating the letters to spell new words. It is beneficial for the student to copy all the words written with magnetic letters on a personal word wall (a sheet of paper with the rime written at the top of the page and words listed from the bottom). An example of the *at* family is given below.

"at" family
cat
bat
fat
sat
mat
gnat
flat

This same activity can be performed with word stamps. For students in grades 3–5, this activity can be done on small dry erase boards. Many older students also need practice with listening to the sounds within words and seeing patterns. Older students can work with the *ight* (*light, sight*), the *ound* (*found, sound*), and *own* (*clown, frown*) families.

FOAM BOARD LETTERS

ACTIVITY

(GRADES 1–5)

You can make letter tiles from foam-board sheets, which can be purchased in school supply or art supply stores. (See samples of tiles in Appendix D.18.) For this activity:

1. Cut the foam board into one-half-inch squares.
2. Using a permanent marker, write one letter on a square.
3. Have students spell word family words or unscramble the letters to make other words with these squares.

For example, after reading a book about the jungle, select animal names (*lion, tiger, elephant, kangaroo*), scramble the letters for each word and have the student put the letters in correct order. These same foam board letters can be used to play Scrabble, a game most children already know. Students who perceive themselves to be poor spellers benefit from playing this game with the teacher; mistakes are usually less embarrassing for the student than those made while playing with peers.

ACTIVITY

(GRADES 1–5)

WORD SEARCHES

The goal in a word search is to find as many words as possible, by reading up, down, backward, and diagonally. Again, you should make word searches based on stories the child has read or on words that trouble her. Figure 13.7 shows an example of a word search based on Mem Fox's *Possum Magic* (1983).

FIGURE 13.7   Word search based on *Possum Magic*.

WORDS TO FIND IN *POSSUM MAGIC* WORD SEARCH

Australia	magic	Lamington	koala	scones
Grandma	tail	invisible	see	adventure
stop	poss	sea	dingoes	his
possums	ate	hush	Pavlova	

A	L	A	O	K	A	T	E	I	N
I	G	R	A	N	D	M	A	N	E
L	I	S	H	A	E	Z	G	V	A
A	T	T	U	E	M	C	I	I	V
R	P	O	S	S	U	M	S	S	O
T	E	P	H	I	S	X	S	I	L
S	E	O	G	N	I	D	O	B	V
U	S	E	N	O	C	S	P	L	A
A	D	V	E	N	T	U	R	E	P
A	N	O	T	G	N	I	M	A	L

ANAGRAMS

(GRADES 2–4)

Finding words in other words or rearranging letters from one word to form a new word is fun for most children, especially if done in a risk-free environment with a teacher. After reading *Word Wizard* (1998) by Cathryn Falwell, you can write the child's first and last name and have the student make as many words out of her name as possible.

VARIATION: ANAGRAMS WITH ALPHABET CEREAL

(GRADES 1–3)

Anagrams made with alphabet cereal is a tasty way to play with words. You spell one word for the student, and by adding, deleting, or rearranging one letter at a time, the student creates new words. Manipulating and eating the letters can make spelling an enjoyable chore!

WHEEL-OF-FORTUNE

(GRADES 3–5)

Following the model of the television game show Wheel-of-Fortune, think of a phrase with which the student is familiar and that includes words that might give the student trouble. Or, using Fred Gwynne's books, *The King Who Rained* (1988), *A Chocolate Moose for Dinner* (1988), or *A Little Pigeon Toad* (1999), you can work with homonyms, stressing the correct spelling of the words in the "Wheel-of-Fortune" blanks. You write out the blanks, and the student must guess the letters. Figure 13.8 presents two examples from Gwynne's books.

FIGURE 13.8 Wheel-of-Fortune based on Fred Gwynne's books.

_ _ _ _ _ _ _   _ _ _ _   _   _ _   _   _ _ _ _ _ _   _ _ _ _ .

(Mother says I am a little dear.)

_ _ _   _ _ _ _   _ _ _   _ _ _ _ _ _ _ .

(The king who reigned.)

MNEMONICS, MEMORY AIDS

(GRADES 3–6)

Mnemonic strategies are unique ways to remember difficult or unusual words. For example, the sentence "George Ellen's old grandfather rode a pig home yesterday" spells GEOGRAPHY. Also, it is easy to remember the difference between *dessert* and *desert* because children want two desserts (two *s*'s). The *c* and *s* are not confusing in *license* when one remembers that a *car* always needs to *stop* at a stop sign. (The *c* comes before the *s* in the sentence.) *Attendance* creates a command: "At ten dance!" And *capacity* is the command to "Cap a city!" You should teach students how to create mnemonics and when to use them.

TECHNOLOGY

Computers

Word processors are a great tool for encouraging students to check their manuscripts for spelling errors. Teachers should take the time to demonstrate how the spell-check feature works on the word processing programs that are available to their students. Students should practice using them while the teacher is observing them so that the teacher can be sure they are using them correctly. Once students have been taught how to use spell check, encourage them to type the final drafts of their work and require that all spelling be correct.

The Internet

A number of websites feature word searches, puzzles, and other spelling activities. One good website that focuses on building spelling skills is available at www.mindfun.com/wordscramble/htm. The following websites offer word searches and other word puzzles that focus on the spelling of words:

www.qualint.com/wsdownload.html This site allows teachers to create word searches.

www.eduplace.com/kids/games/wwf/ This site has weekly word find puzzles on a variety of subjects.

www.thepotters.com/puzzles/kids.html This site has kid's puzzles on cities, states, holidays, letters, sports, movies, aviation, Arthur, and other topics for children.

www.e-funsoft.com/hangman/index.htm This site features a "hangman" game, where children need to fill in letters to guess the phrases. It is similar to the TV game Wheel-of-Fortune.

www.wordsearchmaker.com This site permits the user to make word search puzzles.

www.edHelper.com On this site teachers and students can enter word lists and have the site build word puzzles based on them.

CONCLUDING THOUGHTS

Spelling is an important skill that is critical for students' writing. When working with spelling skills, teachers need to understand the developmental spelling stage of students and provide strategies that will help them reach the next stage. In each developmental stage, strategies should focus on identifying patterns within words so that students can learn to spell groups of letters within words.

TEACHERS AND CAREGIVERS
AS PARTNERS

*Act as if it
were impossible
to fail.*

DOROTHEA BROUDE

Scenario

It is the end of May and Mr. Blackhawk has just completed his first year of teaching. He is reflecting on the trials and triumphs of the year. He decides to begin on a positive note and to list his triumphs first. He is pleased with the list of accomplishments. Then he begins to list his trials. At the top of his list he writes: PARENTS. He was told as an undergraduate that teachers are responsible for working with parents and making them a part of their children's education. He never expected, however, the wide range of the parents' personalities and their unpredictable reactions. In general, he has encountered five approaches from this year's parents and caregivers: (1) those who are concerned and want to do anything and everything to aid their child, (2) those who appear not to care in the least about their child's education or education in general; they seem to not want to be "bothered" with school, (3) those who refuse to believe that their child has any problem with school, (4) those who cannot help their child because of a language barrier; he realizes that many of these parents really do care about their child's progress, and (5) those parents who seem to blame him for everything; these parents seem to be always at school, frequently interrupting his class.

Mr. Blackhawk decides his top priority for the summer is to research professional journals and books on working with and understanding parents. He remembers glancing through one *Educational Leadership* issue on this topic in the faculty lounge. He decides that reading that issue will be a good starting point. He returns to the faculty lounge and finds the magazine. It is the May 1998 issue on *Engaging Parents and the Community in School*. He decides to begin with the article, "Turning Parents from Critics to Allies" by Charlene Giannetti and Margaret Sagarese (pp. 40–42).

INTRODUCTION

Parental involvement is an important ingredient in children's education. There have been initiatives at the local and national levels to promote parental involvement. The Goals 2000: Educate America Act states: "Every school will promote partnerships that will increase parental involvement and participation in promoting social, emotional, and academic growth of children." The National PTA has developed national standards for parental involvement programs. The standards charge both the school and parents with specific responsibilities. The school is responsible for (1) scheduling regular communication between home and school, (2) supporting parenting skills, and (3) involving parents in major decisions, while the parents are responsible for (1) assisting in their child's learning, (2) volunteering at school, and (3) collaborating with their community to provide resources to the schools. Many local districts have also initiated school literacy programs in response to the No Child Left Behind Act and subsequent legislation. These programs challenge students to read books at home and to have their caregivers document that they have read them. The purpose is not only to have children read at home, but also to make literacy a family affair.

Parental involvement encompasses two basic categories: involvement at school and involvement at home. The involvement at school includes activities such as attending scheduled family–teacher conferences, attending PTA or PTO meetings, holding positions on local school boards, being part of decision-making committees, chaperoning class field trips, and volunteering on a regular basis in the classroom, on the playground, or in the library. Involvement at home includes such activities as providing breakfast for one's children, monitoring their homework, reading and writing with them, and making sure they get the proper amount of rest. Studies have shown that parental involvement at home impacts students' learning more than parental engagement at school (Finn, 1998; Wang, Haertel, & Walberg, 1993). However, both affect students' grades, test scores, and attitudes (Sheldon, 2002).

This chapter will focus on (1) the benefits of parental involvement, (2) who are the engaged parents, (3) parents' expectations of teachers, (4) the importance of teachers understanding students' home life, (5) techniques for communicating with parents, (6) parental involvement that makes a difference, (7) strategies for communicating with disengaged or hostile parents, and (8) technology and parental involvement. Teachers must remember that not all students in their classroom will be living with their biological parents. Instead of using the word "parent" in all of their communications with the home, teachers should also address children's "caregivers." All references to *parents* in this chapter should be taken to also refer to *caregivers*.

BENEFITS OF PARENTAL INVOLVEMENT

Students benefit in a number of ways—academically, physically, socially, and emotionally—if their parents or caregivers are actively involved in their education. Studies indicate that students who are more successful academically have parents who are involved in their schooling (Henderson, 1988; Love, 1996; National PTA, 1998; Rasinski & Padak, 2000; Sheldon, 2002). This is true of students from across the socio-economic spectrum and from both majority and minority groups (Ho, 2002). Their improved academic success is reflected in the daily grades and test scores. Students who have parents who value learning and monitor homework also have a more positive attitude toward learning. Students whose parents discuss school with them also earn higher grades (Keith, 1991).

Children who have academically-involved parents also enjoy better physical well-being (Finn, 1998). Involved parents care for their child's physical growth by making sure the child eats well-balanced meals. They avoid sugary snacks and provide regular meals. Involved parents who qualify for free or reduced breakfast at school make sure the child is at school in time to eat breakfast. Involved parents monitor their child's sleep habits. They make sure the child gets plenty of rest. They also understand the importance of regular physical exercise; they play outside with their children and make sure there is ample time for physical activity. Involved parents monitor the number of hours their child sits in front of the television and the shows that their child watches. They often watch and discuss shows together.

Students who have involved parents are socially well-adjusted (Finn, 1998). Parents model the importance of social interaction when they are involved with PTA or PTO, school-wide projects, or class field trips. Through their parents' involvement, students learn the importance of contributing to society by helping others.

Students also benefit emotionally from parental involvement in school (Finn, 1998). When there is communication between the school and parent, the student knows that two sets of people who are significant in her life are caring for her. When parents and teachers have common goals for a child, there will not be a conflict between home and school expectations. Children benefit from that stability.

Parental involvement not only improves students' performance, but it also improves parents' perception of school effectiveness (Henderson, 1988; Ho, 2002). Parental involvement gives them ownership in the school. When parents become personally involved in a school project, they work hard for it to be a success. When the project is successful, they take pride in their work; however, if the project is not as successful as expected, they understand the factors that kept it from being a "complete success" and are not as critical as uninvolved parents.

Students whose parents are not involved frequently have poor developmental patterns. They often have parents who are "authoritarian in their interactions with their children, who fail to provide guidance or structure in the family setting and who fail to provide the emotional support needed when the child encounters problems" (Steinberg, 1996, p. 23).

ENGAGED PARENTS

Parents become engaged when they believe that (1) they can affect their child's education, (2) they are important in their child's development, (3) their school wants their help, (4) they feel comfortable helping at school, and (5) they can be successful in helping with their child's learning (Hoover-Dempsey & Sandler, 1997). As stated above, there are two types of parental engagement: engagement at school and engagement at home. Parents who are engaged with a child's education at home may not always be engaged at school. For example, in 1996, the National Center for Education Statistics estimated that in two-parent families, only 15 percent of fathers and 41 percent of mothers volunteered in their child's school, while in single-parent families, only 23 percent of fathers and 29 percent of mothers volunteered (NCES, 1998). Who are the parents that are involved in their children's school? Statistically, they are more likely to be mothers who do not have full-time jobs outside the home (Eccles & Harold, 1993), Caucasian parents, parents with higher education and higher incomes, families with two parents, and parents who have ties with other parents from their child's school (Ho, 2002; Sheldon, 2002). However, social-economic status, formal education, and racial background alone do not explain why parents become involved. Parents are inclined to become involved at school *when they feel welcomed and needed by teachers and administrators* (Hoover-Dempsey & Sandler, 1997). Hoover-Dempsey and

Sandler found that 12 percent of parents they surveyed were never invited to be involved at school and never became involved.

Who are the parents who are involved in children's education at home? Caucasian and non-Caucasian mothers have similar levels of parental involvement at home. Parents who have more ties with other adults—such as relatives or parents from other schools—are more involved than parents who are isolated. Urban parents have lower involvement at home than do rural or suburban parents (Sheldon, 2002). Sheldon found that when parents are connected to at least one or two parents from the same school, they become more involved in their children's education at school *and* at home. The social interactions give parents the opportunity to discuss mutual concerns and to offer advice. If parental involvement increases a child's learning, it is important that teachers and administrators work at connecting parents and understanding parents' needs.

PARENTS' EXPECTATIONS OF TEACHERS

If a primary goal of schools is to get parents involved, schools need to learn how to communicate with parents. They need to listen to parents and respond appropriately. One concern of most parents is: "Who is the person teaching my child?" They know that their child spends six to seven hours a day with this person, and this person greatly influences their child's perception of learning. They know that teachers can turn a child on to learning or can make learning a miserable experience. Administrators and teachers need to understand what traits parents look for in teachers. Dorothy Rich (1998) found that parents across the United States desire three basic attributes in their child's teachers: (1) teachers who know and care about teaching, (2) teachers who know and care about *their* child, and (3) teachers who know and care about communicating with them. Parents expect teachers to know, care, and communicate!

Rich (1998) compiled a list of other traits parents desire in their child's teachers. Parents believe that effective teachers:

1. Enjoy teaching and believe in what they do.
2. Set attainable, high goals for all individual students.
3. Know the subject matter.
4. Provide a safe and engaging environment.
5. Assign meaningful homework.
6. Understand how a child learns.

7. Treat students with respect.

8. Establish clear learning goals.

9. Practice fair, consistent discipline.

10. Contact parents promptly with individual concerns.

11. Provide helpful information during conferences.

12. Honestly tell parents how their child is doing in class.

13. Provide a variety of tools to report progress.

14. Promptly respond to parents' telephone calls.

15. Provide clear information about class expectations.

16. Cooperate with parents to help their children.

Boers (2002) found that parents also desire the following traits in their children's teachers:

1. Enthusiastic, energetic, happy, positive.

2. Competent, well-read, confident, research-based.

3. Personal, respectful, communicative, welcoming.

4. Student-centered, differentiating, homework-efficient, work-responsive.

5. Well-planned, honest, holistic.

Parents appear to have fair expectations of teachers. It is wise for administrators and teachers to review these lists and strive to ensure that every teacher's goal is to be the kind of teacher that parents will want to cooperate with in their child's education, both at home and at school. It is the building principal's responsibility to put policies in place that help teachers communicate with parents in a timely fashion and encourage parental involvement.

Both Rich (1998) and Boers (2002) found that parents want teachers who communicate with them. In the following section, I discuss various ways to communicate with parents.

THE IMPORTANCE OF TEACHERS UNDER-STANDING THEIR STUDENTS' HOME LIFE

It is imperative that teachers understand the homes from which their students come. Many teachers work in cultural environments that differ from their own backgrounds. Different cultures sometimes emphasize different value systems and different ways of communicating. Listed are some areas that teachers must consider.

- Some families value cooperation; therefore, their children may readily share answers with someone who does not know the answer.

- Some parents instruct children to lower their eyes when they are being reprimanded; their children may never look into the eyes of teachers when they are being reprimanded.

- Some parents would never ask a child a question if the parent already knows the answer. These children may not respond to questions if they think the teacher knows the answer.

- In some families, a child brings disgrace to the family if they do some task incorrectly. These children may not respond in class or hand in work unless they know the answers are correct.

- In some families, men do not expect a woman to tell them what do to, and their children may not accept instruction from a woman.

Teachers must also be careful not to make assumptions about a child based on the child's neighborhood. Often teachers teach in communities where the average socioeconomic status differs from their own. Following are some situations to consider.

- Not all poor children who live in the inner city come from homes affected by crime and drugs.

- Not all suburban middle-class children come from homes that are free from crime and drugs.

- Some working parents are often on business trips and have little time to spend with their children.

- Some parents who live in poverty work two or three jobs to keep food on the table. When they are home, they frequently have no energy to read and write with their child.

- Some students may live with two dads or two moms.

- Some parents who live in poverty move from apartment to apartment because of evictions. These children may attend two or three different schools a year.

- Some children live in ethnically blended families.

- Some children live with an aging grandparent, another relative, or in a foster home.

- Some children live in homes where domestic employees do everything for them. They may lack some essential practical skills.

- Some children (regardless of their class or neighborhood) live with abusive parents.

- Some children are locked out of their homes at night so a parent can engage in prostitution or drugs.

- Some parents overemphasize the importance of being popular or thin.

- Some parents who do not speak English love their children very much and desire them to succeed.
- Some professional parents will not accept the thought that their child has difficulty learning.

All of these and many others are situations that teachers must consider when working with children. Their home life affects their ability to concentrate on reading and writing.

WAYS TO COMMUNICATE WITH PARENTS

It is imperative that teachers communicate with parents so they feel connected to the school and understand that their involvement greatly influences their children's learning (Ames, DeStefano, Watkins, & Sheldon, 1995; Cooper, 2000). There are a number of ways teachers can communicate with all parents—introductory letters, newsletters, bulletin boards, parents' nooks, good news calls, happy grams, portfolios with personal notes, greeting parents in the morning or after school, and family–teacher conferences (Cooper & Kiger, 2001; Love, 1996).

Introductory Letters

Introductory letters from new or first-year teachers are very important to parents. Parents are often wary of a first-year teacher or teachers who are new to the community or building. Introductory letters give parents a brief description of a teacher's past experiences and hobbies. Sharing this information makes the teacher sound like a "professional human being." The letter should also include a brief description of the educational goals for the class, any school-wide initiatives for the year, a description of any new national or state standards, and a brief statement of their teaching philosophy. The letter can also include a list of materials that would be useful for the class throughout the year, such as empty plastic containers, old appliances for students to disassemble, materials for science experiences, or old magazines. The letter must also include important lists of materials the students are required to have for class, a telephone number and email address with the best times to contact the teacher, and reminders about upcoming events. The letter should conclude with an invitation for parents to become involved at school and name some specific opportunities, such as reading with children, playing literacy games with children, typing the classroom's newsletter, and so on. Figure 14.1 presents a sample letter of introduction from a fourth-grade teacher.

Newsletters

Regular newsletters include general information about school-wide activities and special projects taking place in the classroom. The teacher should emphasize what topics the class is studying in all subjects and what book(s) the class is reading together. This gives parents an opportunity to talk about these topics and books and maybe even research the topic on the Internet or in the public library with their child. Other items to include in the newsletter are the following:

1. Class poems and stories.
2. A plea for parental help or materials for an upcoming class project.
3. "Hats Off To . . ." column, which recognizes and thanks all volunteers.
4. Recommended books to read with the students.
5. Upcoming educational television programs.
6. Upcoming community events, such as those held at a local library or museum.
7. Word puzzles, such as crossword puzzles or word searches, designed by the teacher.

It is very important in a newsletter not to use jargon that parents do not understand and not to talk down to parents! Teachers always must have a good proofreader edit the newsletter; parents are quick to criticize teachers who make spelling or grammar errors. Figure 14.2 presents a sample newsletter.

Bulletin Boards

A bulletin board with notices of upcoming school events, such as school pictures, field trips, and so on, should be placed where all parents see it when they enter the building. Important school policies, such as what happens during a tornado watch, a snowstorm, or a hurricane should also be posted on the board. Upcoming community events can also be posted. The bulletin board should be colorful and neat. Old notices should be removed and no personal advertising should be posted.

Parents' Nook

A parents' nook is a special corner of the school that has books, magazines, and pamphlets that parents may borrow. The nook should include a checkout list so parents can sign out the materials. Two suggested books are Jim Trelease's *The Read-Aloud Handbook* (2001) and Margaret Read MacDonald's *The Parent's Guide to Storytelling: How to Make Up New Stories and Retell Old Favorites* (2001). The school librar-

FIGURE **14.1** Sample letter of introduction.

August 2005

Dear Parents and Caregivers:

I am excited to be a new member of this community and to become a partner in your child's learning! This summer I moved to Littletown from Chicago, where I also taught fourth grade. I already have enjoyed Littletown's new library and the Children's Summer Theatre program. Besides reading and going to plays, I love to take long walks and bike rides.

You may be familiar with recent federal legislation, which focuses on every child becoming a successful reader. That is my goal, too. I love to read and want all of my students to enjoy reading materials that interest them. In order to ensure that no student at Littletown Elementary is left behind, we are embracing a new reading program this year called Soaring High with Reading. The school's goal is to have each child read at least 100 pages each week at home. Our school is encouraging parents and caregivers to listen to their child read when possible and to discuss the material with them. At Open House I will further explain this new program and answer any questions you may have.

Littletown Elementary's Open House is Tuesday, September 2, 2005, at 7 P.M. I am eager to meet each one of you and to personally encourage you to become involved at school if you can. At Open House I will have sign-up sheets for different activities—reading with students, playing word games with students, binding their books, organizing our classroom library, recording our "Soaring High with Reading" pages, and many other activities.

Meanwhile, please save your plastic containers, old scraps of fabric, and any broken appliances. Our class will be needing all these materials for art and science projects.

I am looking forward to meeting you at Open House on September 2. Meanwhile, if you need to talk with me, you can email me at bwagner@littletownschools.edu or call me at school between 8:00 and 8:20 any weekday morning.

Sincerely,

Beth Wagner

---

ian can post an annotated bibliography of new books in the school library or a recommended reading list for each grade level. The nook can also serve as the school's lost and found area, and a place for parents to exchange games, toys, or books.

Telephone Calls

Teachers are known to contact parents when there is a problem with their child. However, teachers often fail to call parents with a good report. It may be about a task with which the child struggled, but now has mastered, or about some kind act the child did for another student. Telephone calls that "emphasize the positive [are] a simple but powerful means of gaining parents' support and conveying the message that the teacher cares" (Love, 1996, p. 441).

Happy Grams

Another way you can communicate good behavior to parents is through happy grams. Happy grams

FIGURE **14.2** Sample of monthly newsletter.

FOURTH-GRADE MONTHLY NEWSLETTER

November 2, 2005

CONGRATULATIONS

In the month of October, our class read an average of 106 pages a week! That is higher than our goal. We thank you for encouraging us at home, giving us quiet time to read, and for discussing these great books with us. We hear that you are turning off the TV and reading along! Keep up the good work!

Poem of the Month

(A cinquain poem)
—BY ANTOINE G.

Halloween
Spooky, scary
Creaking, rustling, pretending
Goblins at the door.
Trick-or-Treat!

FIELD TRIP

On Friday, November 14, our class is going to see the play, *You're a Good Man, Charlie Brown*, at 12:00 P.M. at Littletown's Community Hall. The buses will leave at 11:30 A.M. and return at the end of the school day. Our class needs five or six adults who will come with us. Your ticket, like the students' tickets, is free! Please call or email me if you can help us! When you see any of Littletown's Art Council members, thank them for giving us this opportunity! They are providing the free tickets.

---

include words of praise, comments about kind acts, and reports of accomplishments. Happy grams must be honest and genuine. Parents appreciate hearing good news, and students are sure to give these notes to parents. You can design your own happy gram or use the design in Figure 14.3. Happy grams can be photocopied on bright yellow card stock paper.

Portfolios with Personal Notes

Weekly portfolios with personal notes attached to children's work papers are another means of communicating with parents. The portfolio can include graded work from all the subject areas. The notes can give tips on how parents can help children mas-

FIGURE **14.3** Sample happy gram.

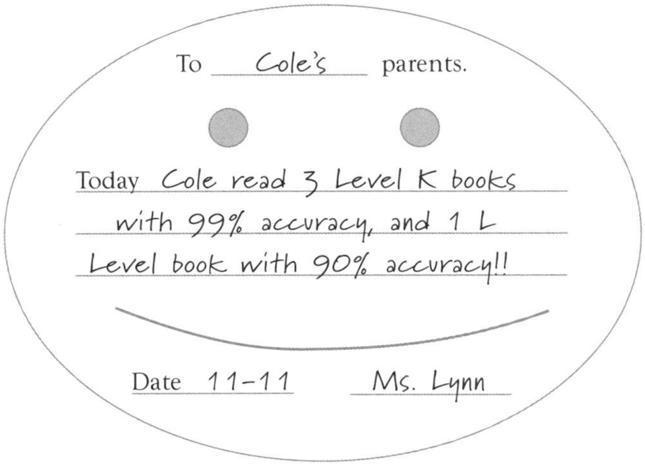

To ___Cole's___ parents.

Today Cole read 3 Level K books with 99% accuracy, and 1 L Level book with 90% accuracy!!

Date ___11–11___   ___Ms. Lynn___

ter a skill that still needs to be mastered, or the note can encourage parents to ask their children to explain a concept that they have learned. These personal notes make parents a part of their children's education. It is important for teachers to include personal comments on every student's paper. Some teachers include a form that parents must sign, indicating that they have read the note. A sample of a return form is presented below in Figure 14.4.

Daily Welcome

Parents appreciate seeing friendly faces at the school door when they drop their child off at school or pick her up in the afternoon. Just a brief, "How are you? Have a great day!" gives parents the assurance that their child is in caring hands. Many children ride the bus to school. Teachers should take turns greeting the children as they come off the bus. This greeting should be more than a duty; it should be a time to make children feel welcome and for connecting with parents. Parents appreciate knowing that their child is arriving in a friendly, caring atmosphere.

Family–Teacher Conference

Family–teacher conferences are important opportunities for teachers, parents, and children to exchange information about the children's education. There are a number of things you must consider when planning for the conference:

1. Schedule a time that is good for parents. Many working parents cannot come during the school day. Ask them for times and days when they will be able to come. Some parents who have a number of chil-

FIGURE 14.4 Sample return form.

DATE: _____

DEAR _____

Thanks for reviewing and discussing the enclosed papers with your child. I am interested in your comments and questions. Please sign the form and return it with your child on Monday.

Thanks again for letting me share in your child's education!

Sincerely,

- -

I reviewed and discussed _____ (child's name) work that you placed in the portfolio.

_____ I have no comments or questions.

_____ I have these comments, questions, or concerns:

SIGNATURE: _____

dren in the same building appreciate being able to schedule times around siblings' conferences.

2. Find out if the parents can read and/or speak English. It is important that teachers communicate clearly with these parents about the time and place of the conference. If necessary, you may need to schedule an interpreter for the conference.

3. Be aware of who is coming to the conference. Not all children live with their biological parents. Children may live in a foster home, with grandparents, or with some other relative. Also, be sensitive if there has been a recent death in the family, a divorce, or another difficult event.

4. Be sensitive of parents who live in poverty. They may not have transportation to the school and may not have a working telephone. Be understanding and do not pressure the caregivers so that they feel guilty or hostile. Be creative and attempt to let those caregivers know that they are an important part of their child's education.

5. Prepare for the conference by gathering samples of children's reading, writing, and other work. It is a good practice for you to record a student's reading on a tape recorder. The parents can listen to the tape during the conference, and they can discuss the student's strengths and weaknesses.

6. Involve students. Have students help select the work they want their parents to view. Discussing concerns about children when they are present reassures them that both parents and the teacher care about their progress.

7. Arrange a clean, comfortable place for the conference. Do not sit behind the teacher's desk! The desk becomes a wall between the parents and the teacher. Also remember that student desks are not comfortable for most adults. A round table with adult-size chairs is the best setting. The room should also be clean with no extra clutter.

8. Use a timer if you have conferences that run back-to-back. It is impolite to keep the next set of parents waiting.

9. Begin on a positive note. All parents like to hear something positive about their child. This is also a time when you can help negative parents understand that their child can do things well.

10. Have some goals. Know what you want to accomplish during each conference. A few written notes can keep the conversation on track.

11. Listen to parents' concerns and questions. Parents may also have goals they want to accomplish

in the conference. It is important that you understand how parents perceive their children.

12. Don't become defensive when parents question your instructional approach or classroom policies. Many parents think they know what should be done in the classroom and disagree with how a teacher conducts her class. Give the parents plenty of time to air their concerns. If appropriate, tell them that you will consider their criticisms and suggestions.

13. Never talk about another student. Often highly competitive parents want to compare their child to classmates. Avoid mentioning the other children. Some parents may also complain about other children. Listen to what they say and reassure them that you will give their child a safe and effective learning environment.

14. Do not use jargon that parents do not understand. The purpose of the conference is to inform the parents about their child's progress, not impress them with your knowledge.

15. End the conference with specific goals. The goals should be attainable for the child and should be goals that the parents can help the child attain. Always thank parents for coming. It is important that parents go away with valuable information and a positive feeling about the child's classroom.

Communicating with parents is an important way to get and keep them interested and involved in their children's education.

PARENTAL INVOLVEMENT THAT MAKES A DIFFERENCE

General Suggestions to Share with Parents

Parental engagement at home is more important than engagement at school (Finn, 1998; Wang, Haertel, & Walberg, 1993). Teachers are often asked by parents what they can do at home to help their children. There are many general suggestions teachers can offer, and you may want to compile a list to share with parents. First, effective parental home involvement includes having a distinct style of interacting with the child. Parents need to ask about their children's day: "What did you learn?" "What problems did you have in your subjects?" "What fun things did you do with your friends?" and "What problems did you have with classmates?" Parents need to listen attentively and give encouragement. Second, parents need to provide an emotionally supportive home environment. Children should feel safe discussing anything with their parents without fear that their parents will become angry and stop listening. Third, parents need to provide reassurance when children encounter failure. When their children are having a difficult time with reading, writing, or spelling in school, parents should help them as they attempt to gain competence in the skill. Parents should encourage their children to practice without pressure or ridicule. Parents need to help children understand that in order to be skillful in any task, one needs to practice.

Boers (2002) collected a list of traits that teachers desire parents to have. He found that teachers hope to encounter the following kinds of parents:

1. Parents who initiate communication about their child's learning style, personality, family arrangements, extracurricular activities, and perceived school problems.
2. Parents who monitor homework at home.
3. Parents who create a time and place for homework and work with their child's basic reading and writing skills.
4. Parents who value learning by allowing time for homework.
5. Parents who get involved by coming to family–teacher conferences, open houses, and other school-wide activities.
6. Parents who discuss school matters with their child at home.
7. Parents who establish good student behavior by teaching respect, courtesy, patience, and clean language.
8. Parents who do not cover for their child.
9. Parents who respect teachers by encouraging them.
10. Parents who emphasize reading. They read with their child, to their child, and model reading for their child.
11. Parents who respond to notes promptly.
12. Parents who recognize health factors by monitoring their child's eating and sleeping habits and by making sure the child comes to school clean.

Administrators can tactfully list such "Good Parenting Tips" in a school-wide newsletter that is sent home to all parents at the beginning of the year. Parents need to understand that when they perform these acts at home, they have a positive impact on their child's education.

When administrators and teachers encourage parents to become involved in their child's education in the home, there are some factors teachers must remember. First, poor families may have few books in the home and may not have transportation to go to the public library. Second, parents may lack literacy skills and may be embarrassed to read to their children. These same parents may not know how to engage children in a story or provide help with writing assignments (Finn, 1998). Third, some parents may not speak English. These parents may desire to help their children, but cannot read or write English. Fourth, full-time working parents may not have the time or energy to devote to their children's homework (Eccles & Harold, 1993). Fifth, some families are involved in so many community activities and extracurricular activities that there may be little time for homework at home (Rasinski & Padak, 2000). Sixth, some parents, although they are the exception, may not value education and may not care if their children do poorly (Giannetti & Sagarese, 1998).

As a teacher, you must accomodate all of these challenges as you attempt to get parents involved in their child's education. First, for parents who cannot read or are poor readers, you can send a tape recorder home with taped stories that you have prepared. Children and parents can listen together and discuss the story. Wordless books are also great resources for these families as well as for families where the parents do not speak English. The parents and the child can discuss the illustrations and make up their own story. For writing, word searches can get parents who lack writing or spelling skills involved in the study of words. Solving sentence puzzles (a sentence that is written on a sentence strip and then cut up into individual words) is another fun activity for home. You can write the sentence on the plastic bag of pieces so children can self-correct the puzzle. For working parents, you should particularly avoid assigning busy work to complete at home. The tasks should not be time-consuming and should be meaningful.

Literacy Involvement at Home

The No Child Left Behind Act of 2002 reform effort suggests ten ways parents can help their children be good readers:

1. Read to your elementary age children daily.
2. Let your children see you reading for pleasure or information.
3. Talk with your children about what they read.
4. Take your children to the library and help them check out books.
5. Provide a quiet time each evening for homework.
6. Encourage early attempts to write and spell.
7. Answer their questions about letters and sounds.

8. Help children look for spelling patterns in print in their environment.

9. Have conversations about books.

10. Let your children see you use reading and writing in daily activities such as cooking and shopping.

You can include these ten suggestions in a newsletter, or design a bookmark with these ten suggestions and give one to each parent at the first open house of the school year. The following section discusses different national literacy activities in which many school districts participate.

Just Read

Just Read is a national reform effort to get children to read books independently (Wolf, 1998). Again the home is an essential element in the success of the Just Read program. In this program, students log the books that they read by recording the titles and the number of books read each week. Parents sign the logs and send them to school with their child. The school records the number of books read each week by all the students and displays the results of the students' reading efforts at the entrance to the building. This process involves and encourages both parents and students.

In the classroom, you can build a book chain based on the books read by the class. The chain is made up of certificates that the parents sign, documenting that the student read the book at home. Figure 14.5 is a sample of such a certificate.

Pizza Hut Book

The Pizza Hut Book is a school-wide reading initiative to get children to read independently at home. Again, the parents are responsible for monitoring and documenting the books the children read. When children meet the goal that is established by the teacher, they receive a certificate for a free pizza.

Reading Aloud to Children

Just Read and Pizza Hut Book projects are for independent reading. However, you should stress the importance of parents reading to their children and offer parents suggestions for reading, such as the following:

1. Parents should read aloud everyday to their child.

2. They should select a comfortable place in which they will not be disturbed. (The room with the family television is usually not a good place.)

3. The book should be one that both the parent and child enjoy.

FIGURE 14.5   Certificate for Just Read initiative.

CERTIFICATE OF BOOK READ

This certifies that _____

read _____ (name of book)

by _____ (author).

The book had _____ pages.

Date: _____

_____
Parent's signature

4. The parent should read the book with expression so it is entertaining for the child.

5. There should be time for discussion; however, this discussion should not be a "test."

Rasinski and Padak (2000) suggest that when parents read to their children, they use the following format:

1. First, the parent reads a passage to the child (or they both listen to a tape) and then they discuss the story.

2. Parent and child read the passage in unison (or child reads along with tape).

3. Parent listens as the child reads the passage.

4. Parent and child choose one or two words from the passage and write them on an index card. They use these cards to play different word games such as concentration or word sorts. They can sort words according to syllables, word patterns, or by root words.

To help parents who have a limited number of books in the home and do not have access to the public library, you can supply the books by putting them in a plastic or canvas bag and sending them home with students. For parents who cannot read or do not read English, you can include a tape recorder with books on tape.

Traveling Tales

Another literacy activity that parents can do with their child at home is Traveling Tales. Ray Reutzel and Parker Fawson (1990) designed Traveling Tales to promote writing at home. Teachers introduce and explain the process of Traveling Tales to the parents at Opening Night at the beginning of the year. Parents are given a list of instructions so they can recall how to conduct the activity. The teacher puts together a backpack or old briefcase of writing materials that travels from one student to the next. Each child receives the backpack for two nights. Figure 14.6 lists materials that should be included in the backpack.

In the Traveling Tales program, parents are encouraged to write a story with their child, using the all the steps of the writing process, as follows:

1. The parent and child brainstorm ideas for a topic for a poem, skit, puppet play, recipe, or story.

2. They decide on the intended audience and begin to write the first draft. While drafting, they focus on content and not on mechanics.

3. They read the passage and decide how they want to revise it. They are encouraged to add information, delete unnecessary material, to rearrange the material so it is easier for the reader to understand, and to look at word choice.

4. They read the second draft carefully to check for spelling and the other issues of writing mechanics. The final copy must be neat, clear, and accessible.

5. After the activity is completed, parents are invited to come to school and share the result with the class.

FIGURE 14.6   Materials for Traveling Tales backpack.

Instructions and ideas	Stapler with staples
Unlined paper	Brass fasteners
Lined paper	Card stock paper
Various colors of construction paper	Hole punch
Drawing paper	Yarn
Poster paper	Wallpaper for book covers
Crayons	Glue sticks
Watercolors	Tape
Water-based markers	Ruler
Colored pencils	Letter stencils
Pencils	Paperclips
Felt-tip pens	Sticky notes
Plastic scissors	Examples of other books made by students

Source: Reutzel, D. R. & Fawson, P. C. (1990). Traveling tales: Connecting parents and children through writing. *The Reading Teacher, 22,* 222–227.

Word Study

Teachers can encourage word study by making word puzzles, sending them home and having the parents complete them with their children. Other game-like activities are listed in Chapter 5 (Phonemic Awareness), Chapter 7 (Word Identification), and Chapter 8 (Vocabulary Building). After you have introduced these activities to students, you can send them home with the children so they can play them with their parents. Children can have the satisfaction of teaching their parents a new game! All of these activities reinforce literacy skills.

Interactive Books

If you know that there is a computer at home, you can permit the child to take home CD-ROMs of interactive books. If the family has access to the Internet, you can share website URLs. (Some websites are listed at the end of this chapter.) All home-involvement activities should be fun so that the time is enjoyable for both parents and children.

Parental Involvement at School

Parental involvement at home may impact children's learning more than parental involvement at school (Finn, 1998; Wang, Haertel, & Walberg, 1993); however, parental engagement at school also has a positive correlation with children's reading and writing achievement, test scores, and report card grades (Keith, Keith, Quirk, Sperduto, Santillo, & Killings, 1998; Sheldon, 2002). Therefore, it is important that teachers encourage parents to be involved at school. Some parents prefer to do clerical work when they volunteer, while other parents want to work with the children. There are usually jobs for both types of workers. The clerical jobs that teachers give parents should not be any type of job that gives them access to other students' grades and files. Some appropriate clerical jobs include the following:

1. Type the class newsletters or other general letters that go home to all parents (keyboarding skills are required).
2. Hang individual certificates to make the class book chain.
3. Change bulletin boards.
4. Photocopy certificates, happy grams, and newsletters.
5. Organize the classroom library.
6. Repair books and games.
7. Make posters announcing new class projects.
8. Assist students with bookbinding.

9. Maintain records for any school-wide reading program (e.g., Just Read or Pizza Hut Book).

If parents prefer to work with children, there are many activities they can do:

1. Listen to a child read.
2. Read to a child.
3. Assist a group of students as they prepare a puppet show.
4. Assist a group of students as they practice a readers theatre script.
5. Assist a student with editing the final copy of his composition.
6. Assist a student as she reads a passage into a tape recorder.
7. Participate in one of the activities (e.g., word, Scrabble, and so on) that reinforces a particular skill. (Each chapter lists a number of them.)
8. Assist a student as she researches a topic.
9. Assist a student with spelling words.
10. Read with a group of advanced readers while the teacher works with the struggling readers.

If you have a difficult time finding parents to volunteer at school, remember that retired members of the community are a great "untapped resource" (Halford, 1998). Many older adults are enthusiastic when they are asked to help in the classroom. When they are involved, they are less critical and more supportive of the local school. This support may extend to the voting booth when school bond issues are on the ballot.

If the school is located near a university that has a teacher education program, you can call the education department and ask for volunteers. Many pre-service teachers enjoy working with children and appreciate getting experience before they student-teach.

WORKING WITH DIFFICULT PARENTS

Teachers would be living in utopia if all parents were involved in their child's education and fully supported their schools. There are three types of parental approaches that pose challenges for both seasoned and beginning teachers. They are (1) parents who seem not to value education, (2) parents who are highly critical of everything the teacher does, and (3) parents who will not accept that their child is struggling in reading or writing. The first group of parents may appear to avoid responsibility for any part of their children's education. These parents may seem not to care if their child learns to read and write or if their child is in school at all.

The parents in the second group may seem to be always at school, demanding the teacher's attention. They may often come at inappropriate times—times when the teacher is engaged with class instruction. In the eyes of these parents, the teacher is almost always at fault. These parents may blame the teacher for their child doing poorly. Parents in the third group are often highly educated and have high expectations for their child. They may not accept that their child has a difficult time with something as basic as reading and writing. All three groups of parents present different types of challenges.

Each of these parents is worthy of the teacher's respect. A teacher needs to remember the child when dealing with these parents. Every child deserves a fair education, and no child should be left behind.

Parents Who Do Not Seem to Value Education

For the children of these parents, it is important that you provide as much extra help as possible in school because these children are unlikely to receive any help at home. Pairing these children with an older, caring adult (either retired or a university student) or with a buddy from a middle school may help them see the importance of learning to read and write. You should send home happy grams as often as possible so the parents come to see education in a more positive light. If the class does puppet shows or readers theatre presentations for parents, be sure to call these parents and encourage them to see their child in the performance. When it is time for family–teacher conferences, you should also call these parents, encouraging them to see the good work their child has completed. These parents need help changing their attitude about education; a positive teacher, doing positive work can be what changes these parents' perceptions.

Parents Who Seem Highly Critical

These parents present a totally different problem; they are negative and attempt to control the teacher and the class. Giannetti and Sagarese (1998) have some suggestions on how to transform these adversaries into educational partners:

1. Roll out the welcome mat when it is appropriate. When these parents come at inappropriate times, get your calendar and ask them when they can come back at a time when you can give them all your attention.
2. Let them know you are an expert at what you do.
3. Show these parents a positive portrait of their children. Let them know that you too think their child has great potential, but be honest!

4. Convey some long-term goals that you know you share with the parents. Plan with the parents some short-term goals that will help the child attain the long-term goals.
5. Reassure the parent that their child will be in a physically and emotionally safe environment.
6. Be consistent.
7. Do not at any time make negative comments about other children. They will think you say negative things about their child to other parents.
8. Listen! Listen! Listen! They will eventually run out of steam!
9. Do not turn any conversation into a shouting match!
10. Ask the parents what they suggest you do with "the situation."

Parents Who Seem Not to Accept Their Child's Academic Difficulties

These parents frequently care a great deal for their child, involve him in many extracurricular activities, and have high goals for the child. With these parents, you can use some of the same tactics that you use with the aggressive parent:

1. Share with the parents the things that the child can do well. Be positive about the child. Let them know that you too think their child has great potential.
2. Be friendly, warm, consistent, and honest.
3. Never compare their child to another child in the class.
4. Never talk about another child.
5. Share honestly the concepts and skills with which their child struggles. Have examples of the child's work on hand to share with the parents. Your goal is to get the parents to understand that there are some skills that are difficult for their child. Convey to them that their goal is your goal: that their child be successful in school.
6. Let the parents know that with extra help from them and with extra help in class, the child will succeed.
7. With the parents, set long-term goals.
8. Also set short-term goals so that parents can see progress.
9. Send progress reports regularly to the parents.

It is a fair expectation of all parents that their child's teacher care about their child and provide a safe learning environment in which every child can succeed.

Technology Nights

Many parents understand that computers are essential tools in the 21st century. Through different events, schools can share with parents what they are doing with computers. One event that can connect parents to the school is to have a technology night at the school (DuPont, 1998). It can be a one-night event in which parents come to school to see what their child can do on the computer. The children are the teachers for the evening with the classroom teacher monitoring the activities. You can present a sample of each child's writing, and have the child demonstrate to his parents how he uses the word processor for revisions. For parents who lack computer skills such a demonstration may be impressive. Parents who work daily on a computer will appreciate that their child is learning how to use this important tool.

On a technology night, a younger child can demonstrate how she reads along with the computer. Using one of the many interactive books on CD-ROM, the child can share how the computer helps her pronounce unknown words and how the computer gives her the definitions of words she does not know.

Technology Classes for Parents

Some schools are in neighborhoods where most parents do not have a computer at home. These schools can sponsor a technology class for parents on a Saturday morning or some other time when most parents can attend. It is important for the instructor to know which computer programs are available to the parents in the public library so they can introduce parents to those programs first. Then parents can go with their child to the library and use the computer together.

Technology in the Home

If a teacher works in a neighborhood where most households have computers in the home, it is often helpful to parents for the teacher to share educational websites with parents. Many authors of children's literature have websites with many different types of activities. The activities are age-appropriate for the author's readers. Many of these authors have free newsletters that they email to interested parties and their websites explain how to subscribe and unsubscribe. Chapter 12 includes a list of authors' websites.

Other educational websites are designed for home use. One such site is www.afterschool.gov. This site has links to other enriching websites that help reinforce skills and provide information about the world (Henkel, 2002). Pacific Bell's site (www.kn.pacbell.com) also has links to many different types of educational materials. All the links at Pacific Bell's site are annotated so parents can determine which ones are age-appropriate for their child.

Three websites provide rich reading material for students who enjoy nature. The sites are

1. www.AllAboutNature.com/biomes/pond/pondlife.shtml
2. www.naturegrid.org.ul/pondexplorer/pondcross.html
3. www.Yahooligans.com This site includes information on specific animal's adaptations to marine life.

The following sites focus on poetry. Some include poems to read, while others help children write poems.

1. www.gigglepoetry.com/poetryclass.cfm
2. www.members.aol.com/bats4kids/magnet/magpoem1.htm

3. http://rhyme.lycos.com
4. www.poetry4kids.com/index.html
5. http://teacher.scholastic.com/writewit/poetry/index.htm
6. www.night.net/tucker/

Encourage parents to explore these websites with their child. It gives them an opportunity to read, write, and learn together in an enjoyable setting. Parents should be encouraged to share websites that they have found to be appropriate for students in your class. You should always check out these websites before you print them in the newsletter. Be sure to also publicly thank and recognize the parents who suggested the sites.

CONCLUDING THOUGHTS

Working with parents can be the most challenging piece of the teaching puzzle. However, there are great benefits for children when parents become involved in their children's education at school and at home. Parents can be very helpful to teachers by offering ideas and resources. It is important to remember that parents and teachers share a common goal: they want the child to succeed in school and to remain a lifelong learner.

A

RESOURCES

A.1 COMMERCIAL INFORMAL READING INVENTORIES

Bader, L. A. (1997). *Bader Reading and Language Inventory* (3rd ed.). Upper Saddle River, NJ: Prentice Hall.

Burns, P. & Roe, B. (1992). *Informal Reading Inventory* (4th ed.). Boston: Houghton Mifflin.

Ekwall, H. & Shanker, J. (1993). *Ekwall–Shanker Reading Inventory* (3rd ed.). Boston: Allyn & Bacon.

Flynt, E. & Cooter, R. (1997). *Flynt–Cooter Reading Inventory for the Classroom* (3rd ed.). Upper Saddle River, NJ: Prentice Hall.

Manzo, A., Manzo, U., & McKenna, M. (1994). *Informal Reading–Thinking Inventory*. New York: Harcourt Brace College Publishers.

Silvaroli, N. (1996). *Classroom Reading Inventory* (8th ed.). Dubuque, IA: Brown and Benchmark.

A.2 ALPHABET BOOKS

The following alphabet books are by Jerry Pallotta and Fred Stillwell. All are published by Charlesbridge Press.

The Airplane Book

Albertina and Arriba

The Bird Alphabet Book

The Boat Alphabet Book

The Butterfly Alphabet Book

Children from Australia to Zimbabwe

Crayon Count

The Desert Alphabet Book

The Dinosaur Alphabet Book

The Flower Alphabet Book

The Freshwater Alphabet Book

The Frog Alphabet Book

The Furry Animal Alphabet Book

Going Lobstering

The Icky Bug Alphabet Book

The Jet Alphabet Book

The Ocean Alphabet Book

The Spice Alphabet Book

The Underwater Alphabet Book

The Vegetable Alphabet Book

The Yucky Reptile Alphabet Book

The following is a partial list of the 672 alphabet books found at www.amazon.com, using the search term: alphabet books.

Parading with Piglets: An ABC Pop-Up by B. Akerberge-Hansen (1996). Peterborough, New York: National Geographic.

Birding Montana: A Falcon Guide by T. McEneaney (1993). Guildford, CT: Falcon.

ABC I Like Me by N. Carlson (1999). New York: Puffin.

The Graphic Alphabet by D. Pelletier (1996). New York: Orchard Books.

Z is for Zamboni: A Hockey Alphabet by M. Napier (2002). Chelsea, MI: Sleeping Bear Press.

Navajo ABC: A Dine Alphabet Book by L. Tapahonso and E. Schick (1999). B+ Bound.

Black and White Rabbit's ABC by A. Baker (1999). Boston: Larousse Kingfisher Chambers.

Mr. Paint Pig's ABC's by R. Scarry (2002). New York: Random House.

The Alphabet Book by P. Eastman (2000). New York: Random House.

Animal ABC by P. Steward (1999). Mineola, New York: Dover.

Chicka Chicka Boom Boom by J. Archambualt (2000). New York: Aladdin Library.

Dr. Seuss's ABC (I Can Read by Myself) by Dr. Seuss (1963). New York: Random House.

Journey Around Boston from A to Z by M. Zschock (2001). Beverly, MA: Commonwealth Editions.

Barney's ABC, 123 and More by G. Davis and D. McKee (1999). Lyrick Publishers.

Journey Around New York from A to Z by M. Zschock (2002). Beverly, MA: Commonwealth Editions.

Alphabet Theme-A-Saurus: The Great Big Book of Letter Recognition by J. E. McKinnon and G. Bittinger (1991). Everett, WA: Warren Publishing House.

Alpha Bugs: A Pop-Up Book by D. Carter (1994). New York: Little Simon.

Journey Around Cape Cod and the Islands from A to Z by M. Zschock (2001). Beverly, MA: Commonwealth Editions.

ABCs of Wisconsin by D. Hillestad-Butler (2000). Black Earth, WI: Trails Books.

A Is for Appalachia by L. Hager-Pack (2002). Louisville, KY: Harmony House.

The Alphabet Tree by L. Lionni (1990). New York: Knopf.

A Walk in the Rainforest by K. Pratt (1992). Nevada City, CA: Dawn.

Anno's Alphabet: An Adventure in Imagination by M. Anno (1987). New York: HarperCollins.

My Whole Food ABC's by D. Richard (1997). Bloomingdale, IL: Vital Health Publishing.

The Amazing Alphabet Maze Book by P. Baldus (2002). Los Angeles: Price Stern Sloan.

ABC Book (Books of Wonder) by C. B. Falls and P. Glassman (2002). New York: Morrow Junior.

The Amazing I Spy ABC by K. Laidlaw (1996). New York: Dial Books for Young Readers.

A Mountain Alphabet by M. Ruurs and A. Kiss (1996). Toronto, Canada: Tundra Books.

The Secret Code by D. Meachen-Rau (1998). San Francisco: Children's Press.

Robert Crowther's Most Amazing Hide-And-Seek Alphabet Book by R. Crowther (1999). Cambridge, MA: Candlewick Press.

The Alphabet Mouse Books by M. Felix (1994). Creative Editions.

A Swim Through the Sea by K. Pratt (1994). Dawn Publishing.

Animalia by G. Base (1987). New York: Abrams Books for Young Readers.

A.3 POETRY COLLECTIONS AND MOTHER GOOSE BOOKS

A Hippopotamusn't by J. P. Lewis (1990). New York: Trumpet Club.

A Light in the Attic by S. Silverstein (1981). New York: HarperCollins.

A Pizza the Size of the Sun by J. Prelutsky (1994). New York: Greenwillow Books.

Falling Up by S. Silverstein (1996). New York: HarperCollins.

I Can Draw a Weeposaur and Other Dinosaurs by E. Greenfield (2001). New York: Greenwillow Books.

If Pigs Could Fly . . . and Other Deep Thoughts by B. Lansky (2000). New York: Meadowbrook.

Miles of Smiles: Kids Pick the Funniest Poems, Book #3 edited by B. Lansky (1998). New York: Meadowbrook.

My Tooth Ith Loothe: Funny Poems to Read Instead of Doing Your Homework by G. Ulrich (1995). New York: Bantam Doubleday Dell Books.

Noisy Poems collected by J. Bennett (1987). Oxford, New York: Oxford University Press.

Ready . . . Set . . . Read! Compiled by J. Cole and S. Calmenson (1990). New York: Doubleday.

Side by Side: Poems to Read Together collected by L. Bennett Hopkins (Not dated). New York: Trumpet Club Special Edition.

Sing a Song of Popcorn selected by B. Schenk de Regniers, E. Moore, M. Michaels White, and J. Carr (1988). New York: Scholastic.

Something Big Has Been Here by J. Prelutsky (1990). New York: Greenwillow Books.

Spooky Riddles by Marc Brown (1983). New York: Random House.

Sylvia Longs' Mother Goose collected and illustrated by S. Long (1999). San Francisco, CA: Chronicle Books.

The Book of Pigericks by A. Lobel (1983). New York: Harper & Row.

The New Kid on the Block by J. Prelutsky (1984). New York: Greenwillow Books.

The Random House Book of Poetry for Children: A Treasury of 572 Poems for Today's Children selected by J. Prelutsky (1983). New York: Random House.

The Real Mother Goose collected and illustrated by B. Fisher Wright (1916). New York: Checkerboard Press.

The 20th Century Children's Poetry Treasury selected by J. Prelutsky (1999). New York: Alfred A. Knopf.

Tomie dePaola's Book of Poems collected by T. dePaola (1988). New York: Putnam's Sons.

Treasury of Poetry selected by A. Hedley (2000). Bath, UK: Parragon Publishing.

Where the Sidewalk Ends by S. Silverstein (1974). New York: HarperCollins.

Zoo Doings: Animal Poems by J. Prelutsky (1983). New York: Trumpet Club.

A.4 WORDLESS BOOKS

A Boy, A Dog, and A Frog by M. Mayer (1967). New York: Dial.

Ah-Choo! by M. Mayer (1976). New York: Dial.

Amanda and the Mysterious Carpet by F. Krahn (1985). New York: Clarion Books.

Ben's Dream by C. Van Allsburg (1982). Boston: Houghton Mifflin.

Carl's Afternoon in the Park by A. Day (1991). New York: Green Tiger.

Clown by Q. Blake (1996). New York: Holt.

Deep in the Forest by B. Turkle (1976). New York: Dutton.

Do You Want to Be My Friend? by E. Carle (1971). New York: Putnam.

Free Fall by D. Wiesner (1988). New York: Clarion.

Frog Goes to Dinner by M. Mayer (1974). New York: Dial.

Frog on His Own by M. Mayer (1973). New York: Dial.

Frog, Where Are You? by M. Mayer (1969). New York: Dial.

Good Dog, Carl by A. Day (1985). New York: Farrar, Straus & Giroux.

Junglewalk by N. Tafuri (1988). New York: William Morrow.

Mouse Around by P. Schories (1991). New York: Farrar, Straus & Giroux.

Noah's Ark by P. Spier (1977). New York: Doubleday.

Pancakes for Breakfast by T. dePaola (1978). New York: Harcourt Brace.

ReZoom by I. Banyai (1995).

Sector 7 by D. Wiesner (1997). New York: Clarion.

The Bear and the Fly by P. Winter (1976). New York: Crown.

The Grey Lady & the Strawberry Snatcher by M. Bang (1980). New York: Four Winds.

The Hunter and the Animals by T. dePaola (1981). New York: Holiday.

The Patchwork Farmer by C. Brown (1989). New York: Greenwillow.

The Snowman by R. Briggs (1978). New York: Random House.

The Swan by V. Mayo (1994). Haupauge, NY: Barron's Educational Series.

The Three Pigs by D. Wiesner (2001). New York: Clarion.

The Yellow Umbrella by H. Drescher (1987). New York: Atheneum.

Tuesday by D. Wiesner (1991). New York: Clarion.

Where's My Monkey? by D. Schubert (no date). New York: Dial.

Zoom by I. Banyai (1995). New York: Puffin.

A.5 BOOKS WITH RHYME, PHONOGRAMS, ALLITERATION, AND OTHER LANGUAGE PLAY

"Not Now" Said the Cow by J. Oppenheim (1989). New York: Bantam Little Rooster Books.

A B C by Dr. Seuss (1963). New York: Beginner Books.

A Fly Went By (In *The Big Blue Book of Beginner Books*) by M. McClintock (1994). New York: Random House.

A Giraffe and a Half by S. Silverstein (1964). New York: HarperCollins.

A Hippopotamusn't by J. P. Lewis (1990). New York: Trumpet Club.

A Summery Saturday Morning by M. Mahy (1998). New York: Puffin.

Alphabears: An ABC Book by K. Hague (1984). New York: Henry Holt.

Bears in Pairs by N. Yektai (1987). New York: McClanahan.

Carrot/Parrot by J. Martin (1991). New York: Trumpet Club.

Daisy-Head Mayzie by Dr. Seuss (1994). New York: Beginner Books.

Four Famished Foxes and Fosdyke by P. D. Edwards (1995). New York: HarperCollins.

Fox in Socks by Dr. Seuss (1963). New York: Beginner Books.

Frog Went A-Courting by J. Langstaff (1966). San Diego, CA: Voyager Books.

Going to Sleep on the Farm by W. C. Lewison (1992). New York: Trumpet Club.

Good-Night Moon by M. W. Brown (1947). New York: Harper & Row.

Green Eggs and Ham by Dr. Seuss (1960). New York: Beginner Books.

Guess How Much I Love You by S. McBratney (1994). New York: Scholastic.

I Know an Old Lady Who Swallowed a Fly retold by N. Westcott (1980). Boston: Little Brown.

I Know an Old Woman Who Swallowed a Pie by A. Jackson (1997). New York: Scholastic.

I Read With My Eyes Shut by Dr. Seuss (1978). New York: Beginner Books.

If You Were My Bunny by K. McMullan (1996). New York: Scholastic.

In the Haunted House by E. Bunting (1990). New York: Trumpet Club.

Is Your Mama a Llama? by D. Guarino (1989). New York: Scholastic.

It's the Bear by J. Alborough (1994). New York: Scholastic.

Jamberry by B. Degen (1983). New York: Harper-Collins.

Jesse Bear, What Will You Wear? by N. W. Carlstrom (1986). New York: Aladdin Paperbacks.

Miss Spider's New Car (Board Book) by D. Kirk (1999). New York: Scholastic.

Mitten/Kitten by J. Martin (1991). New York: Trumpet Club.

Oh, the Things You Can Count by Dr. Seuss (1995). New York: Scholastic.

Oh, the Places You'll Go by Dr. Seuss (1990). New York: Beginner Books.

Oh, the Thinks You Can Think by Dr. Seuss (1975). New York: Beginner Books.

One Fish Two Fish Red Fish Blue Fish by Dr. Seuss (1960). New York: Beginner Books.

One Green Frog by Y. Hooker (1981). New York: Grosset and Dunlap.

Pigs Aplenty, Pigs Galore! by D. McPhail (1993). New York: Scholastic.

Put Me in the Zoo by R. Lopshire (1960). New York: Random House.

Rachel Fister's Blister by A. MacDonald (1990). Boston: Houghton Mifflin.

Ready . . . Set . . . Read! compiled by J. Cole and S. Calmenson (1990). New York: Doubleday.

Sheep in a Jeep by N. Shaw (1986). New York: Houghton Mifflin.

Sheep Out to Eat by N. Shaw (1992). New York: Trumpet Club.

So Many Bunnies by R. Walton (1998). New York: Lothrop Lee & Shepard Books.

Some Smug Slug by P. D. Edwards (1996). New York: HarperCollins.

The Book of Pigericks by A. Lobel (1987). New York: HarperCollins.

The Brand New Kid by K. Couric (2000). New York: Doubleday.

The Cat in the Hat by Dr. Seuss (1957). New York: Beginner Books.

The Cat in the Hat Comes Back by Dr. Seuss (1958). New York: Beginner Books.

The Itsy Bitsy Spider retold by I. Trapani (1993). New York: Scholastic.

The Roly-Poly Spider by J. Sardegna (1994). New York: Scholastic.

There's a Bug in My Mug by K. Salisburg (1997). New York: McClanahan.

There's a Wocket in My Pocket by Dr. Seuss (1974). New York: Beginner Books.

This Old Man retold by P. Adams (1974). Singapore International Ltd: Child's Play.

Today I Feel Silly and Other Moods That Make My Day by J. L. Curtis (1998). New York: Harper-Collins.

Twinkle, Twinkle, Little Star illustrated by S. Long (2001). New York: Scholastic.

When the Fly Flew In . . . by L. W. Peters. (1994). New York: Trumpet Club.

Who Is the Beast? by K. Baker (1993). New York: Trumpet Club.

Zin! Zin! Zin! A Violin by L. Moss (1995). New York: Scholastic.

A.6 COMPUTER PROGRAMS FOR DEVELOPING VARIOUS SKILLS

IDENTIFYING UPPERCASE AND LOWERCASE LETTERS OF THE ALPHABET

1. *I Spy Junior* (riddle section)
2. *Kidspiration* (reading and writing section)

PHONEMIC AWARENESS

1. *Kidspiration* ("Initial Me" permits students to place first initial and last letter of name in two boxes and then identify symbols with those beginning sounds.)
2. *I Spy School Days* ("Wood Block City" and "Chalkboard" use riddles to promote listening to the sounds in rhyming words.)

PHONICS

1. *Kidspiration* ("Alphabet Examples" has activities to match beginning sounds with letters.)

2. *I Spy School Days* ("Code Breaker" has activities to match beginning and ending sounds with letters.)

WORD IDENTIFICATION

1. Books on CD-ROMs (See Appendix A.7.)
2. *I Spy School Days* ("Wood Block City" helps students to develop visual discrimination of words and to increase visual memory.)
3. *Inspiration* ("Vocabulary Template" permits students to build words with root word, prefixes, and suffixes.)
4. *I Spy Spooky Mansion* ("Mystery Bins" promotes logical and creative thinking skills in developing strategies to identify words.)

VOCABULARY BUILDING

1. *Kidspiration* (Students can create personal dictionaries.)
2. *Stories and More: Animal Friends* ("Gunnywolf" and "Trek Map" focus on vocabulary building.)
3. *I Spy School Days* ("Code Breaker" and "Chalkboard" have activities to assist vocabulary building.)
4. *Inspiration* ("Vocabulary Template" has synonyms, antonyms, and homonyms; this template also gives students an opportunity to create personal dictionaries.)
5. *I Spy School Days* ("Make Your Own I Spy" gives students an opportunity to write riddles using synonyms, antonyms, and homonyms.)

WRITING

1. *Kidspiration* (Students can create graphic web for main topic and supporting details; "Duckling Journey" is a template for creating personal stories.)
2. *Stories and More: Animal Friends* ("My Thoughts" gives opportunity for student to retell story and write personal reflections.)
3. *Stories and More: Time and Place* ("Galimoto" is a pen pal activity.)

COMPREHENSION

1. CD-ROMs of books (See Appendix A.7.)
2. *Stories and More: Animal Friends* ("My Thoughts" permits students to retell the story and write personal connections.)
3. *I Spy Junior* ("Puppet Maker," "The Gunnywolf," and "Owl and the Moon" develop listening skills in sequencing.)
4. *Kidspiration* ("Duckling's Journey" permits students to write their own story.)
5. *Stories and More: Time and Place* ("House on Maple Street" has sequencing activities. The "Thinking About" part of each story is an activity that focuses on reinforcing the content of the story. All stories in this program have activities for students to make predictions, based on clues.)

A.7 STORY BOOKS ON CD-ROMs

LIVING BOOKS SERIES

101 Dalmatians

An American Tail

Ariel's Story Studio

Arthur's Birthday

Arthur's Computer Adventure

Arthur's Teacher Trouble

Berenstein Bears Collection

Dr. Seuss' The Cat in the Hat

Dr. Seuss' Green Eggs and Ham

D. W.: The Picky Eater

Harry and the Haunted House

Imo and the King

Just Grandma and Me

Just Me and My Day

Just Me and My Grandpa

Just Me and My Mom

Lion King

Little Golden Books, Sailor Dog

Little Monster at School

Mike Mulligan and His Steam Shovel

Pocahontas

Ruff's Bone

Stellaluna

The New Kid on the Block

The Tortoise and the Hare

Winnie the Pooh
Winnie the Pooh and Tigger Too

DISCIS BOOKS

A Long Hard Day on the Ranch
A Promise Is a Promise
Aesop's Fables
Anansi
Cinderella
Heather Hits Her First Home Run
Johnny Appleseed

Moving Gives Me a Stomach Ache
Mud Puddle
Northern Lights: The Soccer Trails
Paul Bunyan
Pecos Bill
Scary Poems for Rotten Kids
Somebody Catch My Homework
The Paper Bag Princess
The Tale of Benjamin Bunny
The Tale of Peter Rabbit
Thomas' Snowsuit

A.8 CHAPTER BOOKS ON TAPE*

A Year Down Yonder by R. Peck
Bud, Not Buddy by C. P. Curtis
Out of the Dust by K. Hesse
From the Mixed-up Files of Mrs. Basil E. Frankweiler
    by E. L. Konigsburg
A Wrinkle in Time by M. L'Engle
The Giver by L. Lowry
Shiloh by P. R. Naylor
Island of the Blue Dolphins by S. O'Dell
Missing May by C. Rylant
Holes by L. Sachar
Brian's Return by G. Paulsen
Joey Pigza Loses Control by J. Gantos
Call It Courage by A. Sperry
Charlotte's Web by E. B. White

The Cricket in Times Square by G. Selden
Ella Enchanted by G. Carson Levine
The Fledgling by J. Langton
Hatchet by G. Paulsen
A Long Way from Chicago by R. Peck
Ramona Quimby, Age 8 by B. Cleary
The Sign of the Beaver by E. George Speare
The Watsons Go to Birmingham–1963 by C. P. Curtis
Bloomability by S. Creech
The Boxcar Children by G. C. Warner
Bunnicula: A Rabbit Tale of Mystery by D. Howe
The Amber Brown Collection I & II by P. Danziger

*Available by Bantam Books.

A.9 COMPUTER PROGRAMS THAT PROMOTE COMPREHENSION AND PROBLEM SOLVING

(All available from Scholastic Publishing.)

Oregon Trail, 5th ed. (Upper Elementary)
Road Adventures USA (Upper Elementary)
*Playhouse Disney's the Book of Pooh: A Story Without
    a Tail* (Ages 3–6)
Scooby Doo! Showdown in Ghost Town (Ages 5–10)
Zobooma Foo: Animal Kids (Ages 3–8)
I Spy Junior (Ages 3–6)
Reader Rabbit First Grade: Capers on Cloud Nine

*Reader Rabbit Second Grade: Mis-cheese-ious
    Dreamship Adventure*
I Spy Spooky Mansions (Ages 6–10)
My First Amazing World Explorer/USA (Ages 6–10)
Carmen San Diego (Ages 8–10)
Castle Explorer (Age 10–Adult)
I Spy Treasure Hunt (Ages 6–10)
Jump Start Animal Adventure (Ages 6–10)

APPENDIX B

LISTS AND GUIDES

B.1 VOWEL DIPHTHONGS, DIGRAPHS, AND VARIANTS WITH EXAMPLES AND UTILITY OF EACH

VOWELS	EXAMPLES	UTILITY
aw	*law*	100%
oy	*boy*	98%
oi	*oil*	98%
ay	*day*	96%
ew	*dew*	95%
au	*haul*	94%
oa	*road*	94%
ee	*fleet*	86%
ai	*rain*	74%
oo	*moon*	59%
oo	*foot*	36%
ey	*key* (long /e/)	58%
ey	*they* (long /a/)	20%
ea	*leaf* (long /e/)	51%
ea	*bread* (short /e/)	26%
ie	*chief* (long /e/)	51%
ie	*lie* (long /i/)	17%
ie	*ancient* (schwa)	15%
ow	*know* (long /o/)	50%
ow	*now* (/ou/)	48%
ei	*eight* (long /a/)	40%
ei	*receive* (long /e/)	26%
ei	*foreign* (short /i/)	13%
ei	*seismic* (long /i/)	11%

B.2 CONSONANT PRONUNCIATION GUIDE

Letter	Formation	Counterpart	Other Spellings	Other Sounds	Voiced	Voiceless
B Bat Cab	Lips are lightly pressed together. A puff of breath opens the lips to create sound.	P	silent in final position (*comb, lamb*)		+	
C Soft as in Cent	Edge of tongue touches toward top of mouth near upper teeth. Hissing sound comes when breath strikes teeth.	Z		/K/	+	
C Hard as in Cut	Back part of tongue is raised. Breath erupts through mouth.	/g	k	/s/		+
D Dog Bed	Front of tongue is in back of upper front teeth. Jaws are slightly open.	T			+	
F Fun Leaf	Lower lip is under upper teeth. Breath moves out between teeth and lower lips to create sound.	V	gh (*laugh*) ph (*phone*) lf (*half*) ft (*often*)	/v/ of		+
G Gate Dog	Back part of tongue is raised and pressed against lower part of front teeth.	/K/	gh (*ghost*) gue (*plague*) x (*excite*)	/j/ (*gym*) silent (*gnat*) ng (*sing*) gh = f (*rough*)	+	
H Hat	It is made with a simple breath.		silent (*heir*) (*ghost*) (*rhyme*) (*exhaust*)			+
J Jeep	Lips are slightly rounded, stick out. Teeth are together with tongue pressed against them.	ch	d (*educate*) di (*soldier*) dg (*bridge*) de (*grandeur*)		+	
K Keep Book	Back part of tongue is raised. Breath erupts through the mouth.	/g/	ck (*sock*) c (*cat*) q (*queen*) k (*except*)	silent when followed by n (*know*)		+
L Leaf Bail	Front of the tongue behind the upper front teeth while allowing vibrating breath to emerge.	None	None	None	+	
M Milk Drum	Lips are lightly pressed together. Lips vibrate when breath passes through sinuses.		mb (*lamb*) lm (*calm*) mn (*column*)		+	

Letter	Formation	Counterpart	Other Spellings	Other Sounds	Voiced	Voiceless
N Nut Run	Tongue is pressed tightly against upper teeth. Breath passes through sinuses.		gn (*gnat*) kn (*knee*) pn (*pneumonia*) mn (*mnemonic*)		+	
P Pet Soup	Lips are closed and pressed together. Sound comes when breath quickly passes through lips.	B	ph (*diphtera*)	silent when followed by n, s, t ph = /f/		+
Q Queen Bouquet	Back part of tongue is raised. Breath erupts through mouth.	/g/	always followed by u, except in *Iraq*	/kw/ (*quite*) /k/ (*bouquet*)		+
R Run Four	Tip of tongue is raised toward the top of mouth with jaw slightly open.		wr (*wren*) rhy (*rhythm*) rps (*corps*)		+	
S Sun Bus	Edges of tongue touch the jaws near the sockets of upper teeth. Hissing sound comes when breath strikes teeth.		c (*city*) ps (*psychology*) z (*waltz*)	/z/ (*dogs*) /sh/ (*sugar*) /zh/ (*pleasure*)		+.
T Ten Tent	Mouth is slightly open. Tongue is pressed against inside of upper palate.	D	th (*thyme*) bt (*debt*) ed (*talked*) ght (*light*) tw (*two*) pt (*receipt*)	silent after f & s (*often, listen*) silent with quet (*bouquet*) ch (*natural*) sh (*question*)		+
V Van Five	Lower lip is slightly under the upper teeth.	F	f (*of*) ph (*Stephen*) lv (*half*)		+	
W We	Lips closed, but not pressed together. Vibrating the vocal chords produces sound.	Wh	ju (*marijuana*) ou (*Ouija*)	silent in *wr*	+	
Y Yo-yo	With teeth separated, sides of tongue are pressed against upper teeth.		i (*onion*) e (*azalea*) j (*hallelujah*)	/i/ (*fly*) /e/ (*happy*) ay (*day*) /i/ (*lymph*)	+	
Z Zip Quiz	Edges of tongue touch the jaws near sockets of the teeth.	S	s (*does*) ss (*scissors*) x (*xylophone*) sc (*discern*) cz (*czar*) si (*business*) sp (*raspberry*)	/s/ (*pretzel*)	+	

B.3 MOST COMMON WORD FAMILIES

AT	AN	AM	ALL	AND	AD
bat	ban	dam	ball	band	bad
cat	can	ham	call	hand	dad
hat	Dan	jam	fall	land	had
mat	fan	ram	hall	sand	lad
pat	man	clam	mall	brand	mad
rat	pan	cram	tall	grand	sad
sat	ran	gram	wall	stand	sad
brat	tan	slam	small	strand	glad
chat	van	swam	stall		
flat	clan	yam			
that	plan	wham			
	scan				
	than				

AG	AP	AB	AR	ART
bag	cap	cab	bar	cart
rag	lap	dab	car	dart
sag	map	jab	far	mart
wag	nap	nab	jar	part
brag	rap	lab	star	tart
flag	tap	tab		start
drag	clap	crab		chart
shag	flap	stab		smart
snag	slap	grab		
tag	trap	slab		
	snap			
	wrap			
	strap			

ACK	ASH	ANK	ELL	ET	ED
back	bash	bank	bell	bet	bed
jack	cash	sank	cell	get	fed
lack	dash	tank	fell	jet	led
rack	gash	yank	sell	let	red
sack	hash	blank	tell	met	bled
tack	mash	crank	well	net	fled
black	rash	drank	shell	pet	shed
crack	sash	plank	smell	set	sled
quack	crash	prank	spell	vet	shred
shack	clash	spank	swell	wet	
snack	flash	thank	dwell	yet	
stack	smash				
track	slash				
	trash				

EN	EG	EST	ECK	IT	IG
Ben	beg	best	deck	bit	big
den	peg	nest	neck	fit	dig
hen	leg	pest	peck	hit	fig
men	keg	rest	check	kit	pig
pen		test	speck	lit	rig
then		vest	wreck	pit	wig
when		west		sit	
wren				quit	
				skit	
				spit	

IN	ILL	IP	ING	INK	ICK
bin	bill	dip	king	link	kick
fin	dill	hip	ping	mink	lick
pin	fill	lip	ring	pink	pick
tin	kill	nip	sing	rink	sick
win	mill	rip	wing	sink	tick
chin	pill	sip	bring	wink	brick
grin	will	tip	cling	blink	chick
thin	chill	zip	fling	clink	flick
twin	drill	chip	sling	drink	quick
shin	grill	clip	sting	stink	stick
skin	skill	drip	thing	think	thick
spin	spill	flip	wring	shrink	trick
	still	ship	spring		
		skip	string		
		slip			
		trip			
		whip			

OT	OP	OG	OB	OCK	ONG
cot	cop	bog	cob	dock	bong
dot	hop	dog	gob	lock	gong
got	mop	fog	job	rock	long
hot	pop	hog	mob	sock	song
jot	top	jog	rob	tock	strong
lot	drop	log	sob	block	throng
not	flop	clog	blob	flock	
pot	shop	frog	glob	frock	
blot	slop		snob	shock	
knot	stop			smock	
plot					
shot					
slot					
spot					

UT	UB	UG	UM	UN	UNG
but	cub	bug	bum	bun	hung
cut	hub	dub	gum	fun	lung
gut	rub	hug	hum	gun	rung
hut	tub	jug	chum	run	sung
nut	club	mug	drum	sun	slung
rut	grub	rug	plum	spun	strung
shut	stub	tug	scum	stun	sprung
		drug			wrung
		slug			
		snug			
		plug			

UCK	UMP	UP	UFF
buck	bump	cup	buff
duck	dump	pup	cuff
luck	hump		huff
suck	jump		muff
tuck	lump		puff
yuck	pump		fluff
cluck	plump		
pluck	stump		
stuck	thump		
truck			

B.4 FREQUENTLY USED SUFFIXES AND PREFIXES

SUFFIXES	COMMON MEANING	EXAMPLE
s, es	plural	*boys, churches*
ed	past tense	*walked*
ing	verb form/present participle	*smiling*
ly	characteristic of	*quickly*
er, or	person connected with	*printer, editor*
ion, tion	act, process	*transportation*
ation, ition	process of, condition of, result of	*action*
ible, able	can be done	*edible*
al, ial	having characteristics of	*denial*
y	characterized by	*discovery*
ness	state of, condition of	*happiness*
ity, ty	state of	*responsibility*
ment	action or process	*management*
ic	having characteristics of	*heroic*
ous, eous	possessing the qualities of	*courageous*
ious	full of	*glorious*
en	made of	*forgotten*
er	comparative	*happier*
ive, ative, itive	adjective form of noun	*expensive*
ful	full of	*playful*
less	without	*helpless*
est	superlative	*homliest*

PREFIXES	COMMON MEANING	EXAMPLE
un	not, opposite	*unhappy*
re	again	*redo*
in, im, ir, ill	not	*impossible*
dis	not, opposite of	*disagree*
en, em	cause to	*encourage*
non	not	*nonliving*
in, im	in or into	*invade*
over	too much	*overzealous*
mis	wrongly	*mislead*
sub	under	*submerge*
pre	before	*prelude*
inter	between, among	*interstate*
fore	before	*foreground*
de	opposite of	*decompose*
trans	across	*transport*
super	above	*supercede*
semi	half	*semicircle*
anti	against	*antisocial*
mid	middle	*midway*
under	too little	*underweight*

B.5 GREEK WORD ROOTS WITH DEFINITIONS AND EXAMPLES

aer: air; *aerial*

agog: leader; *synagogue*

angel: messenger; *angelic*

aster/astr: star; *asteroid*

auto: self; *autograph*

bio: life; *biology*

chron: time; *chronicle*

chlor: greenish-yellow; *chlorine*

derm: skin; *epidermis*

eco: house; *ecology*

gram: thing written; *telegram*

graph: writing; *autograph*

hydr: water; *hydrant*

hyper: over, above, beyond; *hypermedia*

hypo: below, beneath; *hypodermis*

logo: word, reason; *logic*

meter/metr: measure; *metric*

micro: small; *microscope*

mono: one, single; *monotone*

od/hod: road, way; *episode*

phe/phem: to speak; *blaspheme*

phil: love; *philanthropy*

phon: sound; *telephone*

photo/phos: light; *photograph*

pol/polis: city, state; *police*

scope: instrument for viewing; *microscope*

techn: art, skill, craft; *technical*

therm: heat; *thermometer*

zoo: animal; *zoology*

Source: Words their way: Word study for phonics, vocabulary, and spelling instruction (3rd ed.). by Bear/Invernizzi/Templeton/Johnston, © 2004. Reprinted by permission of Pearson Education, Inc., Upper Saddle River, NJ.

B.6 HIGH FREQUENCY WORD LIST

about	don't	it	phone	they're
after	down	it's	play	thing
all	drink	joke	presents	this
am	each	jump	pretty	those
an	eat	junk	question	time
and	family	kick	rain	to
animal	father	know	ride	too
are	favorite	like	right	trip
as	first	line	run	truck
at	fly	little	said	two
be	for	long	sale	up
because	friend	look	saw	us
been	from	made	school	use
best	fun	mail	see	very
big	get	make	she	want
black	girl	many	sister	was
boy	give	me	slow	way
brother	go	more	skate	we
bug	good	mother	small	went
but	green	my	snap	were
by	gym	name	so	what
call	had	new	some	when
can	has	nice	sports	where
can't	have	night	stop	which
car	he	no	street	who
caught	her	not	talk	why
children	here	now	teacher	will
city	him	of	tell	with
clock	his	off	than	won
coat	house	old	thank	won't
come	how	on	that	would
could	hurt	one	the	write
crash	I	or	their	you
day	if	other	them	your
did	in	out	then	zoo
didn't	into	over	there	
do	is	people	they	

Source: From Patricia Cunningham, *Phonics They Use,* © 2000. Published by Allyn and Bacon, Boston, MA. Copyright © 2000 by Pearson Education. Reprinted by permission of the publisher.

APPENDIX B

B.7 **DOLCH WORD LISTS**

EASIER 110			HARDER 110		
a	go	over	about	hurt	small
after	going	play	again	just	start
all	good	put	always	keep	take
am	green	ran	any	kind	tell
an	had	red	ask	laugh	thank
and	has	ride	ate	let	that
are	have	round	because	light	their
around	he	run	been	live	them
as	help	said	before	long	then
at	her	saw	best	many	there
away	here	see	better	much	these
be	him	she	both	must	they
big	his	so	bring	myself	think
black	I	some	buy	never	those
blue	if	soon	clean	new	today
brown	in	stop	could	now	together
but	into	ten	cut	off	try
by	is	the	does	once	upon
call	it	this	done	only	us
came	its	three	draw	open	use
can	jump	to	drink	or	very
carry	know	too	eight	our	walk
cold	like	two	every	own	want
come	little	under	fall	pick	warm
did	look	up	far	please	wish
do	made	was	five	pull	were
down	may	went	found	read	when
eat	me	what	four	right	where
fast	my	who	full	say	which
find	no	will	gave	seven	white
fly	not	with	goes	shall	why
for	of	yellow	got	show	wish
from	old	yes	grow	sing	work
funny	on	you	hold	sit	would
get	one	your	hot	six	write
give	out		how	sleep	

Source: (1936). Basic Sight Vocabulary, *Elementary School Journal, 36,* 456–560. Published by the University of Chicago Press, Copyright © 1936 by University of Chicago. All rights reserved. Reprinted by permission of the publisher.

B.8 SIGHT WORD PHRASES BY SHANKER AND EKWALL (1998)

LIST 1	LIST 2	LIST 3
he had to	look at him	look at me
she said that	as little	can you
to the	at all	a little one
you and I	I have a	you will see
but they said	have some	what is that
on a	there is	my cat
for his	down there	I will get
of that	then we have	when did he
that was in	to go	like this
it was	to be there	get them
	look up	so you will see
	look at her	I could
	we go out	we were
	I am	would not
		yes, I do

LIST 4	LIST 5	LIST 6
a big ride	I take every	ran away
went into	the four green	let me help
if I ask	they don't want	going to sleep
come over with	right around	five yellow ducks
they went	a good jump	the old turtle
I am very	a pretty rabbit	by their mother
there are blue	I know how	call after six
a long book	where can I	the brown rabbit
an apple	the duck got	I am well
your red book	it is about	will think
its name	don't put any	will make
they came just now	take from	you saw
	too little	here it is

APPENDIX B

LIST 7	LIST 8	LIST 9
we eat	black and white	open and find
two may walk	start a new	Jill ate the
on or off	must try once	those are done
before seven	don't keep much	is funny
today is cold	it does go	buy us three
play by myself	always drink milk	this is only
don't stop	will bring ten	gave a warm
it is round	lad goes	soon we ate
who is eight	write and tell	had a full
have never been	work is first	run and hold
can fly again	can give it	made a big
		it is better
		our duck

LIST 10	LIST 11
sit with both	wash in hot
you use it	because it is
carry a small	grow best
the cut hurt	once upon
the fast car	sing and laugh
then the light	please thank
which will fall	we draw these
pull it in	shall we show
had found	the wish is
under her	we clean
be kind	they live
pick it up	too far
Bill can read	all together
my own bed	many turtles
why is it	
I can say	

Source: Locating and Correcting Reading Difficulties (7th ed.) by Ekwall/Shankar, © 1998. Reprinted by permission of Pearson Education, Inc., Upper Saddle River, NJ.

B.9 GENERALIZATIONS ABOUT WORD SPELLINGS

1. Every syllable has a vowel sound.
2. Blends and digraphs always stay together (e.g., *fa-ther*, not *fat-her*).
3. Syllables ending with a vowel have a long sound. Pattern = CV
4. Syllables ending with a consonant have short vowel sounds. Pattern = CVC
5. Inflectional endings are usually separate syllables (e.g., *play-ing*).
6. Prefixes are usually separate syllables (e.g., *re-turn*).
7. The consonant before a final *le* is part of the last syllable (e.g., *dou-ble, a-ble*).
8. When words end in silent *e*, the *e* is dropped before adding the ending (e.g., *giving, having, hoping*).
9. With most words, ending is added to root word (e.g., *walked, smiles*).
10. When words end in y, change y to *i*, unless the ending is *ing* (e.g., *married, marrying*).
11. When words end in single vowel and consonant, double the final consonant before adding an ending that begins with a vowel (*sit, sitting; hop, hopping*).
12. The letter *q* is followed by *u* (exception: *Iraq*).
13. The final *e* remains on root word when suffix begins with a consonant (e.g., *lately*).
14. When singular noun ends with consonant y, the y is changed to *i* to form plural (e.g., *babies*).
15. When singular noun ends with vowel y, only the *s* is added to form plural (e.g., *boys*).
16. The letter *i* before *e* except after *c* or when digraph sounds like the long /a/ sound (e.g., *receive, eight*).
17. In one-syllable words with the pattern CVCe (*cape*), the vowel is long.
18. In one-syllable words with the pattern CVVC (*road*), one vowel is *usually* long.
19. In one-syllable words with the patterns CVC (*hop*) or CCVCC (*chick*), the vowel is short.
20. In two-syllable words with pattern CVC-CV (*rabbit*), the vowel is short in the first syllable.

Sources: Bear, D., Invernizzi, M., Templeton, F., Johnston, F. (2000). *Words their way: Word study for phonics, vocabulary and spelling instruction.* Upper Saddle River, NJ: Merrill.

Fountas, I. & Pinnell, G. S. (2001). *Guided readers and writers: Grades 3–6: Teaching comprehension, genre and content literacy.* Portsmouth, NH: Heinemann.

Heald-Taylor, B. G. (1998). Three paradigms of spelling instruction in grades 3–6. *The Reading Teacher, 51*(5), 404–413.

B.10 COMMON WORD PATTERNS

1. "oo" as in *cook* (one syllable): *book, look*
2. "oo" as in *cook* (multi-syllable): *cookie, cookbook*
3. "oo" as in *moon* (one syllable): *noon, broom*
4. "oo" as in *moon* (multi-syllable): *mushroom, noontime*
5. "ea" as long /e/ (one syllable): *tea, sea*
6. "ea" as long /e/ (multi-syllable): *really, easy*
7. "ck" as in /k/ (one syllable): *black, truck*
8. "ck" as in /k/ (multi-syllable): *drumstick, chicken*
9. "a"-consonant-"e" (one syllable): *face, cake*
10. "a"-consonant-"e" (multi-syllable): *unsafe, escape*
11. "i"-consonant-"e" (one syllable): *hike, write*
12. "i"-consonant-"e" (multi-syllable): *bedtime, clockwise*
13. "o"-consonant-"e" (one syllable): *bone, froze*
14. "o"-consonant-"e" (multi-syllable): *backbone, flagpole*
15. "e"-consonant-"e" (one syllable): *these, gene*
16. "e"-consonant-"e" (multi-syllable): *athlete, concrete*
17. "u"-consonant-"e" (one syllable): *cute, flute*
18. "u"-consonant-"e" (multi-syllable): *excuse, intrude*
19. Words ending in "ful": *bashful, wishful*
20. Words ending in "ment": *basement, statement*
21. Words ending in "est": *quickest, richest*
22. Words ending in "less": *endless, jobless*
23. Words ending in "ness": *gladness, illness*
24. Words ending in "y" with long /i/ sound: *by, sky*
25. Multi-syllable words ending in "y" with long /e/ sound: *bunny, funny*
26. Words with prefix "un": *unwise, unsafe*
27. Words with prefix "mis": *misfit, misspell*
28. Words with prefix "sub": *subject, subtract*
29. Words with prefix "in": *invite, inside*
30. Words with prefix "trans": *transform, translucent*
31. Words with prefix "re": *recall, reprint*
32. "ow" as long /o/: *blow, slow*
33. "ow" as in "cow": *how, now*
34. Words ending in "ch": *peach, teach*
35. Words ending in "tch": *batch, patch*
36. Words ending in "tion": *action, vacation*
37. Words ending in "sion": *explosion, television*
38. Words with "ough" ending: *rough, though, through*

B.11 **COMPLEX PATTERNS OF ENGLISH SPELLING**

1. "gh" in *sigh, light, night,* etc. serves as a marker for the long /i/ sound.

2. "h" marks alternative sound for *t, c, s,* and *p* (*think, chip, shy,* and *phase,* which are all digraphs).

3. double consonants mark short vowels (*hill, pass, butter, silly*).

4. "ck" at end of word makes vowel short (*truck, clock*).

5. "tch" at end of word makes vowel short (*match, itch*).

6. "ch" at end of word makes vowel short when there is only one vowel (*rich, such*); when the word has a vowel digraph, the vowel is long (*teach, coach*).

7. "ge" at the end of a word makes the "soft" *g* sound (*orange, ledge, ridge, sponge*).

8. "ge" within a word makes the "soft" *g* sound (*dungeon, pigeon, angel*).

9. "ce" at the end of a word gives *c* the /s/ sound (*prince, dance*).

10. "c" at the end of word calls for the /k/ sound (*magic, picnic*).

11. "c" followed by *e, i, y* makes a "soft" *c* (*city, cent, cycle*).

12. "c" followed by *a, o, u* makes a /k/ sound (*cat, cot, cut*).

13. initial "g" followed by *a, o, u* makes a "hard" *g* (*gate, goat, gut*).

14. initial "g" followed by *y* makes a "soft" *g* (*gym*).

15. initial "g" followed by *i* or *e* is often inconsistent (*give, get, giant, gem*).

16. the "k" in "kn" at the beginning of words is silent (*know, knee*).

17. the "g" in "gn" at beginning of words is silent (*gnaw, gnat*).

18. When long /u/ sound is at end of a word, it is spelled "oo" (*zoo*), "ew" (*few*), or "ue" (*blue*). The one is exception is *you.*

Source: Johnston, Francine R. (Dec 2000/Jan 2001). Spelling exceptions: Problems or possibilities? *The Reading Teacher,* 54(4), 372–378. Reprinted with permission of Francine R. Johnston and the International Reading Association. All rights reserved.

ASSESSMENT DEVICES

These devices are discussed in Chapter 3, Assessment.

C.1 **MISCUE ANALYSIS GRID**

TEXT	Substitution	Mispronun- ciation	Insertion	Omission	Repeats	Self- correction	Syntax acceptable	Meaning disrupted
TOTAL MISCUES:								

Notes:

C.2 **RUNNING RECORD FORM**

Student: _____ Date: _____

Teacher: _____ Reading Level: _____

Story: _____

Number of Errors: _____ Percentage: _____

Running Words: _____ Level for Student: Easy, Instructional, Frustration

Comments:

TEXT	ANALYSIS			
	Number		System Used	
	E	SC	E	SC
PAGE				

C.3 **SAMPLE LITERACY CHECKLIST**

Teacher: _____   Date: _____

+ = always   x = sometimes   o = seldom/never

STANDARD   STUDENTS

1. Reads and comprehends fiction suitable for grade level.

2. Reads and comprehends non-fiction suitable for grade level.

3. Uses prereading strategies to preview and make predictions.

4. Uses picture clues and graphic organizers as prereading strategies.

5. Asks questions to aid comprehension of fiction and nonfiction.

6. Makes inferences about events, characters, and ideas in fiction.

7. Connects knowledge and experience to story.

8. Supports interpretations with examples from text.

9. Retells story in sequence.

10. Produces oral and written summaries of main ideas and supporting details.

11. Identifies cause/effect relationships.

12. Makes comparisons and draws conclusions based on reading.

13. Describes character traits, changes, and relationships.

14. Integrates the use of semantics, syntax, and graphophonics to grasp meaning.

Standards from the Oklahoma State Department of Education (revised 2002). *A Core Curriculum for Our Children's Future: Priority Academic Student Skills (PASS)*. Oklahoma City, OK: Oklahoma State Department of Education.

C.4 **CHECKLIST FOR OBSERVATIONS OF PROGRESS TOWARD STANDARDS**

Name: Grade: Date:

STANDARDS	CONTEXT	DATE OBSERVED	CONTEXT	DATE OBSERVED	CONTEXT	DATE OBSERVED
1. Reads a wide range of print and nonprint texts						
2. Reads a wide range of literature (many time periods, many genres)						
3. Applies a wide range of strategies to comprehend, interpret, evaluate, and appreciate texts						
4. Adjusts use of spoken, written, and visual language to communicate effectively						
5. Employs a wide range of strategies for writing and different writing process elements to communicate effectively						
6. Applies knowledge of language structure, conventions, media techniques, figurative language, and genre to create, critique, and discuss print/nonprint texts						
7. Conducts research by generating ideas and questions, and by posing problems						
8. Uses a variety of technological and informational resources to gather/synthesize information and create/communicate knowledge						

STANDARDS	CONTEXT	DATE OBSERVED	CONTEXT	DATE OBSERVED	CONTEXT	DATE OBSERVED
9. Understands and respects diversity in language use, dialects, and cultures						
10. If SLL, makes use of native language to develop English competency						
11. Participates in a variety of literacy communities						
12. Uses spoken, written, and visual language to accomplish own purposes						

*The standards used in this checklist are the NCTE/IRA Standards for the English Language Arts. Any state standards could be used and the checklist can be made grade-level specific as well.

Source: Cecil, N. and Gipe, J. (2003). *Literacy in the Intermediate Grades.* Scottsdale, AZ: Holcomb Hathaway. Used with permission.

APPENDIX C

C.5 OBSERVATIONAL CHECKLIST OF LITERACY HABITS: EARLY EMERGENT LITERACY STAGE

Student: _____   Grade: _____

Teacher: _____

− = Behavior not observed   + = Behavior observed   X = Progressing

	DATES				
EARLY EMERGENT LITERACY STAGE:					
1. Shows pleasure in read-alouds.					
2. Can retell stories in sequence.					
3. Uses book language in retellings.					
4. Likes to make up stories.					
5. Holds books correctly.					
6. Recognizes environmental print (e.g., cereals, cookies).					
7. Pretends to read.					
8. Scribbles messages.					
9. Writes some letters correctly.					
10. Has phonemic awareness.					

C.6 OBSERVATIONAL CHECKLIST OF LITERACY HABITS: EMERGENT LITERACY STAGE

Student: Grade:

Teacher:

− = Behavior not observed   + = Behavior observed   x = Progressing

	DATES				
EMERGENT LITERACY STAGE:					
1. "Reads" top to bottom of page.					
2. "Reads" front to back of book.					
3. "Reads" left to right.					
4. Recognizes nonstandard English.					
5. Enjoys jokes.					
6. Enjoys alliteration.					
7. Hears rhyming words.					
8. Knows difference between words and letters.					
9. Matches words with voice when reading.					
10. Knows, title, author, and illustrator of books.					
11. Recognizes letters in random order.					
12. Matches uppercase with lowercase letters.					
13. Recognizes name in print.					
14. Can write most letters.					
15. Uses phonemic awareness when writing.					
16. Can name initial and ending letter sounds of words.					
17. Shows interest in writing stories, notes, etc.					

Source: Adapted from J. David Cooper and Nancy Kiger. *Literacy Assessment: Helping Teachers Plan Instruction.* Copyright © 2001 by Houghton Mifflin Company. Adapted with permission.

APPENDIX C

C.7 OBSERVATIONAL CHECKLIST OF LITERACY HABITS: BEGINNING READING AND WRITING STAGE

Student: _____ Grade: _____

Teacher: _____

− = Behavior not observed   + = Behavior observed   x = Progressing

	DATES				
BEGINNING READING AND WRITING STAGE:					
1. Self-corrects nonstandard English.					
2. Can paraphrase what others say.					
3. Can summarize a story.					
4. Participates in discussion.					
5. Enjoys nonsense and silly poems.					
6. Recognizes all letters in random order.					
7. Recognizes many sight words.					
8. Uses phonics to pronounce new words.					
9. Understands concepts of onset and rime.					
10. Reads own writing.					
11. Chooses to write independently.					
12. Word-by-word reading.					
13. Sounds out words instead of guessing.					
14. Lip-voicing movements in silent reading.					
15. Finger-points at every word.					
16. Uses spelling that reflects phonics knowledge.					
17. Uses word processing when writing.					
18. Uses all five steps of writing process.					
19. Adequate reading rate.					
20. Adequate vocabulary knowledge.					

APPENDIX C

C.8 OBSERVATIONAL CHECKLIST OF LITERACY HABITS: NEARLY FLUENT STAGE

Student: _____   Grade: _____

Teacher: _____

− = Behavior not observed   + = Behavior observed   x = Progressing

NEARLY FLUENT LITERACY STAGE:	DATES				
1. Uses oral standard English.					
2. Uses new vocabulary words correctly.					
3. Listens and questions speaker.					
4. Appreciates symbolic language.					
5. Uses structural analysis to determine unknown words.					
6. Uses context clues.					
7. Reads with 90% accuracy in grade-level materials.					
8. Self-corrects.					
9. Understands stories read to him/her that are above his/her grade level.					
10. Reads/comprehends a variety of genres.					
11. Prefers to read silently.					
12. Aware of own purpose for reading.					
13. Understands expository text structures.					
14. Beginning to synthesize information from a variety of sources.					
15. Can interpret simple graphs.					
16. Can locate information on a CD-ROM.					
17. Writes good stories.					
18. Writes good paragraphs.					
19. Uses word processing tools to revise and edit work.					
20. Uses five steps of writing process.					
21. Uses vivid language when writing.					

APPENDIX C

Source: Adapted from J. David Cooper and Nancy Kiger. *Literacy Assessment: Helping Teachers Plan Instruction.* Copyright © 2001 by Houghton Mifflin Company. Adapted with permission.

C.9 OBSERVATIONAL CHECKLIST OF LITERACY HABITS: FLUENT READING AND WRITING STAGE

Student: _____   Grade: _____

Teacher: _____

− = Behavior not observed   + = Behavior observed   x = Progressing

FLUENT READING AND WRITING STAGE:	DATES				
1. Enjoys readers theatre.					
2. Enjoys giving speeches in front of class.					
3. Understands the elements of stories.					
4. Understands differences in genres.					
5. Uses effective strategies when reading.					
6. Can self-correct when reading.					
7. Enjoys reading during free time.					
8. Knows where to locate information.					
9. Uses writing to persuade.					
10. Can edit classmates' work.					
11. Can edit own writing.					
12. Self-checks spelling and grammar.					
13. Revises own work when necessary.					
14. Recognizes authors' style and techniques in writing.					
15. Attempts to copy a writer's style.					

Source: Adapted from J. David Cooper and Nancy Kiger. *Literacy Assessment: Helping Teachers Plan Instruction.* Copyright © 2001 by Houghton Mifflin Company. Adapted with permission.

APPENDIX C

C.10 INTEREST INVENTORY

Name: _____ Grade: _____ Date: _____

Write more than one item for each category if more than one item interests you. Explain why for each response. For example, why do you enjoy football?

1. My favorite foods are _____

2. My favorite eating places are _____

3. My favorite snacks are _____

4. My favorite TV shows are _____

5. My favorite TV characters are _____

6. My favorite movies are _____

7. My favorite actors are _____

8. My favorite actresses are _____

9. The best book I ever read is _____

10. My favorite music group is _____

11. My favorite song is _____

12. My favorite sport is _____

13. My favorite school subject is _____

14. I know I am very good at _____

15. When I am alone, I like to _____

16. My favorite thing to do with my friends is _____

17. My least favorite thing to do is _____

18. My favorite thing to do on Saturday and Sunday is _____

19. The thing I fear most is _____

20. If I had a million dollars, I would _____

C.11 READING ATTITUDE SURVEY FOR PRIMARY STUDENTS

Name: _____   Grade: _____   Date: _____

1. How I feel when the teacher reads to me.

2. How I feel when classmates read in class.

3. How I feel when asked to read aloud in class.

4. How I feel when asked to read aloud just for my teacher.

5. How I feel when I read stories to my family.

6. How I feel when I read to myself.

7. How I feel during "Drop Everything and Read."

8. How I feel about reading mystery stories.

9. How I feel about listening to my teacher read mystery stories.

10. How I feel about reading funny stories.

11. How I feel about listening to my teacher read funny stories.

12. How I feel about reading scary stories.

13. How I feel about listening to my teacher read scary stories.

14. How I feel about reading poetry.

15. How I feel about listening to my teacher read poetry.

16. How I feel about reading informational books about sports.

17. How I feel about reading informational books about spiders, snakes, and other creatures.

18. How I feel about reading informational books on places to visit.

19. How I feel about reading stories on the computer.

20. How I feel about finding information on the computer.

See C.13, "Scoring Sheet for Attitude Surveys."

APPENDIX C

C.12 WRITING ATTITUDE SURVEY FOR PRIMARY STUDENTS

Name: _____ Grade: _____ Date: _____

Pre-test or Post-test (Circle one)

1. How I feel when asked to write a story.

2. How I feel when asked to write riddles.

3. How I feel when asked to write about my favorite sport or pet.

4. How I feel when asked to write to my favorite author.

5. How I feel when asked to write a poem.

6. How I feel when asked to write about myself.

7. How I feel when asked to write a thank you note.

8. How I feel when asked to write in front of my classmates.

9. How I feel when I write on a dry-erase board.

10. How I feel when I write on the computer.

11. How I feel when I write *with* classmates.

12. How I feel when I write with my teacher.

13. How I feel about writing science reports.

14. How I feel when asked to check for mistakes in my writing.

15. How I feel about my spelling ability.

16. How I feel when asked to change something in my writing.

17. How I feel when my story or poem or article is posted for my classmates to read.

18. How I feel when my teacher reads my poem, story, or article to the class.

19. How I feel if I did not have to write in school.

20. How I feel if I had more time to write in school.

See C.13, "Scoring Sheet for Attitude Surveys."

C.13 **SCORING SHEET FOR ATTITUDE SURVEYS**

Student: _____ Grade: _____ Pre-test Date: _____

Teacher: _____ Post-test Date: _____

Scoring Guide:

Happy character = 4 points

"Somewhat" happy character = 3 points

Neutral character = 2 points

Unhappy character = 1 point

ITEMS: PRE-TEST

1. _____   2. _____   3. _____   4. _____   5. _____   6. _____

7. _____   8. _____   9. _____   10. _____   11. _____   12. _____

13. _____   14. _____   15. _____   16. _____   17. _____   18. _____

19. _____   20. _____   TOTAL: _____

Comments:

ITEMS: POST-TEST

1. _____   2. _____   3. _____   4. _____   5. _____   6. _____

7. _____   8. _____   9. _____   10. _____   11. _____   12. _____

13. _____   14. _____   15. _____   16. _____   17. _____   18. _____

19. _____   20. _____   TOTAL: _____

Comments:

C.14 READING ATTITUDE SURVEY FOR OLDER STUDENTS

Student: _____   Grade: _____   Date: _____

Pre-test or Post-test (Circle one)

Respond to the statement by circling SL for Strongly Like, L for Like, O for Okay, DL for Dislike, and SD for Strongly Dislike.

1.	Completing research on the Internet.	SL	L	O	DL	SD
2.	Reading my science text.	SL	L	O	DL	SD
3.	Reading my history text.	SL	L	O	DL	SD
4.	Reading informational CD-ROMs.	SL	L	O	DL	SD
5.	Reading informational books for a report.	SL	L	O	DL	SD
6.	Reading realistic fiction.	SL	L	O	DL	SD
7.	Reading historical fiction.	SL	L	O	DL	SD
8.	Reading poetry.	SL	L	O	DL	SD
9.	Reading a funny book.	SL	L	O	DL	SD
10.	Reading the comics in a newspaper.	SL	L	O	DL	SD
11.	Reading the sports section of a newspaper.	SL	L	O	DL	SD
12.	Reading a sports magazine.	SL	L	O	DL	SD
13.	Reading *People* magazine.	SL	L	O	DL	SD
14.	Reading a fashion magazine.	SL	L	O	DL	SD
15.	Reading *Newsweek* or *Time* magazine.	SL	L	O	DL	SD
16.	Listening to classmates read.	SL	L	O	DL	SD
17.	Listening to my teacher read.	SL	L	O	DL	SD
18.	Reading in front of my peers.	SL	L	O	DL	SD
19.	Reading on the weekend.	SL	L	O	DL	SD
20.	Learning to become a better reader.	SL	L	O	DL	SD

Answer the following questions. Be honest in your responses.

1. Do you consider yourself a good reader? Explain.

_____

2. Do you like to help other classmates with their reading problems? Explain.

_____

3. What is the hardest thing for you to do in reading?

_____

4. What do you do best as a reader?

_____

APPENDIX C

C.15 WRITING ATTITUDE SURVEY FOR OLDER STUDENTS

Student: _____ Grade: _____ Date: _____

Pre-test or Post-test (Circle one)

Respond to the statement by circling SL for Strongly Like, L for Like, O for Okay, DL for Dislike, and SD for Strongly Dislike.

Name: _____ Date: _____

1.	Writing a story for class.	SL	L	O	DL	SD
2.	Writing about my science project.	SL	L	O	DL	SD
3.	Writing a history or other report.	SL	L	O	DL	SD
4.	Writing poetry.	SL	L	O	DL	SD
5.	Writing lyrics for a song.	SL	L	O	DL	SD
6.	Writing letters and notes to friends.	SL	L	O	DL	SD
7.	Writing in a personal diary or journal.	SL	L	O	DL	SD
8.	Writing in a dialogue journal with your teacher.	SL	L	O	DL	SD
9.	Writing a script for a play or readers theater.	SL	L	O	DL	SD
10.	Writing jokes or other funny material.	SL	L	O	DL	SD
11.	Writing scary stories or mysteries.	SL	L	O	DL	SD
12.	Pre-writing in writing workshop.	SL	L	O	DL	SD
13.	Writing my first draft in writing workshop.	SL	L	O	DL	SD
14.	Revising and editing in writing workshop.	SL	L	O	DL	SD
15.	Having other classmates read my story or report.	SL	L	O	DL	SD
16.	Helping classmates edit their work.	SL	L	O	DL	SD
17.	Having other classmates edit my work.	SL	L	O	DL	SD
18.	Using a word processor for writing.	SL	L	O	DL	SD
19.	Using paper and pen or pencil for writing.	SL	L	O	DL	SD
20.	Writing in my spare time.	SL	L	O	DL	SD
21.	Writing emails to friends.	SL	L	O	DL	SD
22.	Writing information for web pages.	SL	L	O	DL	SD

Answer the following questions honestly.

1. I think I am a (good or not-so-good) writer because

_____

2. I wish I could write like my favorite author because

_____

3. The hardest thing for me to do in writing is

_____

C.16 **READER SELF-PERCEPTION SCALE**

Listed below are statements about reading. Please read each statement carefully. Then circle the letters that show how much you agree or disagree with the statement. Use the following:

SA = Strongly Agree
A = Agree
U = Undecided
D = Disagree
SD = Strongly Disagree

Example: **I think pizza with pepperoni is best.**   SA   A   U   D   SD

If you are *really positive* that pepperoni pizza is best, circle SA (Strongly Agree).
If you *think* that it is good but maybe not great, circle A (Agree).
If you *can't decide* whether or not it is best, circle U (Undecided).
If you *think* that pepperoni pizza is not all that good, circle D (Disagree).
If you are *really positive* that pepperoni pizza is not very good, circle SD (Strongly Disagree).

[GPR]	1. I think I am a good reader.	SA	A	U	D	SD
[SF]	2. I can tell that my teacher likes to listen to me read.	SA	A	U	D	SD
[SF]	3. My teacher thinks that my reading is fine.	SA	A	U	D	SD
[OC]	4. I read faster than other kids.	SA	A	U	D	SD
[PS]	5. I like to real aloud.	SA	A	U	D	SD
[OC]	6. When I read, I can figure out words better than other kids.	SA	A	U	D	SD
[SF]	7. My classmates like to listen to me read.	SA	A	U	D	SD
[PS]	8. I feel good inside when I read.	SA	A	U	D	SD
[SF]	9. My classmates think that I read pretty well.	SA	A	U	D	SD
[PR]	10. When I read, I don't have to try as hard as I used to.	SA	A	U	D	SD
[OC]	11. I seem to know more words than other kids when I read.	SA	A	U	D	SD
[SF]	12. People in my family think I am a good reader.	SA	A	U	D	SD
[PR]	13. I am getting better at reading.	SA	A	U	D	SD
[OC]	14. I understand what I read as well as other kids do.	SA	A	U	D	SD
[PR]	15. When I read, I need less help than I used to.	SA	A	U	D	SD
[PS]	16. Reading makes me feel happy inside.	SA	A	U	D	SD
[SF]	17. My teacher thinks I am a good reader.	SA	A	U	D	SD
[PR]	18. Reading is easier for me than it used to be.	SA	A	U	D	SD
[PR]	19. I read faster than I could before.	SA	A	U	D	SD
[OC]	20. I read better than other kids in my class.	SA	A	U	D	SD
[PS]	21. I feel calm when I read.	SA	A	U	D	SD
[OC]	22. I read more than other kids.	SA	A	U	D	SD
[PR]	23. I understand what I read better than I could before.	SA	A	U	D	SD
[PR]	24. I can figure out words better than I could before.	SA	A	U	D	SD
[PS]	25. I feel comfortable when I read.	SA	A	U	D	SD

APPENDIX C

[PS]	26.	I think reading is relaxing.	SA	A	U	D	SD
[PR]	27.	I read better now than I could before.	SA	A	U	D	SD
[PR]	28.	When I read, I recognize more words than I used to.	SA	A	U	D	SD
[PS]	29.	Reading makes me feel good.	SA	A	U	D	SD
[SF]	30.	Other kids think I'm a good reader.	SA	A	U	D	SD
[SF]	31.	People in my family think I read pretty well.	SA	A	U	D	SD
[PS]	32.	I enjoy reading.	SA	A	U	D	SD
[SF]	33.	People in my family like to listen to me read.	SA	A	U	D	SD

Source: Henk, William A., & Melnick, Steven A. (March 1995). The reader self-perception scale (RSPS): A new tool for measuring how children feel about themselves as readers. *The Reading Teacher, 48*(6), 470–482. Reprinted with permission of William A. Henk and the International Reading Association. All rights reserved.

The Reader Self-Perception Scale Scoring Sheet

Student name: _____

Teacher: _____ Grade: _____ Date: _____

Scoring key:

    5 = Strongly Agree (SA)
    4 = Agree (A)
    3 = Undecided (U)
    2 = Disagree (D)
    1 = Strongly Disagree (SD)

SCALES

General Perception (GPR)	Progress (PR)	Observational Comparison (OC)	Social Feedback (SF)	Physiological States (PS)
1. _____	10. _____	4. _____	2. _____	5. _____
	13. _____	6. _____	3. _____	8. _____
	15. _____	11. _____	7. _____	16. _____
	18. _____	14. _____	9. _____	21. _____
	19. _____	20. _____	12. _____	25. _____
	23. _____	22. _____	17. _____	26. _____
	24. _____		30. _____	29. _____
	27. _____		31. _____	32. _____
	28. _____		33. _____	

Raw score	_____ of 45	_____ of 30	_____ of 45	_____ of 40

Score interpretation	PR	OC	SF	PS
High	44+	26+	38+	37+
Average	39	21	33	31
Low	34	16	27	25

C.17 WRITER SELF-PERCEPTION SCALE

Listed below are statements about writing. Please read each statement carefully. Then circle the letters that show how much you agree or disagree with the statement. Use the following scale:

SA = Strongly Agree
A = Agree
U = Undecided
D = Disagree
SD = Strongly Disagree

Example: **I think Batman is the greatest super hero.**   SA   A   U   D   SD

If you are *really positive* that Batman is the greatest, circle SA (Strongly Agree).
If you *think* that Batman is good but maybe not great, circle A (Agree).
If you *can't decide* whether or not Batman is the greatest, circle U (Undecided).
If you *think* that Batman is not all that great, circle D (Disagree).
If you are *really positive* that Batman is not the greatest, circle SD (Strongly Disagree).

[OC]	1.	I write better than other kids in my class.	SA	A	U	D	SD
[PS]	2.	I like how writing makes me feel inside.	SA	A	U	D	SD
[GPR]	3.	Writing is easier for me than it used to be.	SA	A	U	D	SD
[OC]	4.	When I write, my organization is better than the other kids in my class.	SA	A	U	D	SD
[SF]	5.	People in my family think I am a good writer.	SA	A	U	D	SD
[GPR]	6.	I am getting better at writing.	SA	A	U	D	SD
[PS]	7.	When I write, I feel calm.	SA	A	U	D	SD
[OC]	8.	My writing is more interesting than my classmates' writing.	SA	A	U	D	SD
[SF]	9.	My teacher thinks my writing is fine.	SA	A	U	D	SD
[SF]	10.	Other kids think I am a good writer.	SA	A	U	D	SD
[OC]	11.	My sentences and paragraphs fit together as well as my classmates' sentences and paragraphs.	SA	A	U	D	SD
[GPR]	12.	I need less help to write well than I used to.	SA	A	U	D	SD
[SF]	13.	People in my family think I write pretty well.	SA	A	U	D	SD
[GPR]	14.	I write better now than I could before.	SA	A	U	D	SD
[GEN]	15.	I think I am a good writer.	SA	A	U	D	SD
[OC]	16.	I put my sentences in a better order than the other kids.	SA	A	U	D	SD
[GPR]	17.	My writing has improved.	SA	A	U	D	SD
[GPR]	18.	My writing is better than before.	SA	A	U	D	SD
[GPR]	19.	It's easier to write well now than it used to be.	SA	A	U	D	SD
[GPR]	20.	The organization of my writing has really improved.	SA	A	U	D	SD
[OC]	21.	The sentences I use in my writing stick to the topic more than the ones the other kids use.	SA	A	U	D	SD

APPENDIX C

[SPR]	22.	The words I use in my writing are better than the ones I used before.	SA	A	U	D	SD
[OC]	23.	I write more often than other kids.	SA	A	U	D	SD
[PS]	24.	I am relaxed when I write.	SA	A	U	D	SD
[SPR]	25.	My descriptions are more interesting than before.	SA	A	U	D	SD
[OC]	26.	The words I use in my writing are better than the ones other kids use.	SA	A	U	D	SD
[PS]	27.	I feel comfortable when I write.	SA	A	U	D	SD
[SF]	28.	My teacher thinks I am a good writer.	SA	A	U	D	SD
[SPR]	29.	My sentences stick to the topic better now.	SA	A	U	D	SD
[OC]	30.	My writing seems to be more clear than my classmates' writing.	SA	A	U	D	SD
[SPR]	31.	When I write, the sentences and paragraphs fit together better than they used to.	SA	A	U	D	SD
[PS]	32.	Writing makes me feel good.	SA	A	U	D	SD
[SF]	33.	I can tell that my teacher thinks my writing is fine.	SA	A	U	D	SD
[SPR]	34.	The order of my sentences makes better sense now.	SA	A	U	D	SD
[PS]	35.	I enjoy writing.	SA	A	U	D	SD
[SPR]	36.	My writing is more clear than it used to be.	SA	A	U	D	SD
[SF]	37.	My classmates would say I write well.	SA	A	U	D	SD
[SPR]	38.	I choose the words I use in my writing more carefully now.	SA	A	U	D	SD

Source: Bottomley, Diane M., Henk, William A., & Melnick, Steven A. (Dec 1997/Jan 1998). Assessing children's views about themselves as writers using the Writer Self-Perception Scale. *The Reading Teacher, 51*(4), 286–291. Reprinted with permission of Diane M. Bottomley and the International Reading Association. All rights reserved.

Writer Self-Perception Scale Scoring Sheet

Student name: _____

Teacher: _____ Grade: _____ Date: _____

Scoring key:

  5 = Strongly Agree (SA)
  4 = Agree (A)
  3 = Undecided (U)
  2 = Disagree (D)
  1 = Strongly Disagree (SD)

SCALES

General Progress (GPR)	Specific Progress (PR)	Observational Comparison (OC)	Social Feedback (SF)	Physiological States (PS)
3. _____	22. _____	1. _____	5. _____	2. _____
6. _____	25. _____	4. _____	9. _____	7. _____
12. _____	29. _____	8. _____	10. _____	24. _____
14. _____	31. _____	11. _____	13. _____	27. _____
17. _____	34. _____	16. _____	28. _____	32. _____
18. _____	36. _____	21. _____	33. _____	35. _____
19. _____	38. _____	23. _____	37. _____	
20. _____		26. _____		
		30. _____		

RAW SCORES

_____ of 40	_____ of 35	_____ of 45	_____ of 35	_____ of 30

Score interpretation	GPR	SPR	OC	SF	PS
High	39+	34+	37+	32+	28+
Average	35	29	30	27	22
Low	30	24	23	22	16

APPENDIX C

C.18 **READING LOG FOR PRIMARY STUDENTS**

Books I Have Read

Name: _____ Grade: _____

Circle the face that best shows how you feel about the book.

BOOK	AUTHOR/ILLUSTRATOR	COMMENTS
		☺ ☻ ☹
		☺ ☻ ☹
		☺ ☻ ☹
		☺ ☻ ☹
		☺ ☻ ☹
		☺ ☻ ☹
		☺ ☻ ☹
		☺ ☻ ☹
		☺ ☻ ☹
		☺ ☻ ☹
		☺ ☻ ☹
		☺ ☻ ☹
		☺ ☻ ☹
		☺ ☻ ☹
		☺ ☻ ☹

C.19 **READING LOG FOR INTERMEDIATE STUDENTS**

Books I Have Read

Name: _____   Grade: _____   Quarter: 1 2 3 4

BOOK	AUTHOR	GENRE	DATE STARTED/ ENDED	COMMENTS

My favorite book I read this quarter was _____

because _____

C.20 READING REFLECTION LOG

My Thoughts about My Reading

Name: _____ Grade: _____ Quarter: 1   2   3   4

1. The informational books I read were about

    _____

    _____

    _____

2. The novels I read were mostly: realistic, historical, biographies, autobiographies, mysteries, science fiction, fantasy, folktales.

3. My favorite author is _____

    _____

4. The best book I read was _____

    _____

5. When I dislike a book, I _____

    _____

6. My favorite place to read is _____

    _____

7. My reading habits at home are _____

    _____

8. I do not enjoy reading books about _____

    _____

9. The book I recommended to my friends was _____

    _____

10. After I read a book, I like to _____

    _____

C.21 **QUICK PHONEMIC AWARENESS ASSESSMENT DEVICE**

A high correlation exists between the ability to recognize spoken words as a sequence of individual sounds and reading achievement. Explicit instruction can increase the phonemic awareness of children. To assist in determining the level of phonemic awareness of each child in your class, the following assessment items may be utilized. **Use as many samples as necessary to determine mastery.**

Assessment 1. Isolation of beginning sounds. Ask the child what the first sound of selected words is.

> "What is the first sound in dog?"

Assessment 2. Deletion of initial sound. Read a word and ask the child to say it without the first sound.

> "Say the word cat. Say cat without the /k/."

Assessment 3. Segmentation of phonemes. Ask the child to say the separate sounds of the word being read.

> "What are the two sounds in the word go?"

Assessment 4. Blending of phonemes. Slowly read the individual sounds of a word and ask the child to tell what the word is.

> "What word am I saying? /d/ /o/ /g/"

Assessment 5. Phoneme manipulation. Read a word and ask the child to replace the initial sound with another. Have the child say the new word.

> "In the word fan, the first sound is a /f/. If you replace the /f/ with an /m/, how would you say the new word?"

Source: Cecil, N. L. (2003). *Striking a Balance: Best Practices for Early Literacy,* 2nd Ed. Scottsdale, AZ: Holcomb Hathaway. Used with permission.

C.22 PRE-ASSESSMENT FOR PHONEMIC AWARENESS

Name: _____   Date: _____

NOTE: The teacher will check "Yes" if the child can do the task, and "No" if the child cannot do the task. It is good to give one example to the child so they fully understand the task they are asked to perform. Examples are provided here.

Syllabicating Words

Practice: "Words have different syllables. Some words have one syllable such as *hand* (clap once). *Mitten* has two syllables: mit- (clap once) tin (clap once). *Celebrate* has three syllables: cel- (clap once) e (clap once) brate (clap once). Clap and tell me how many syllables *table* has (   ). How about *shop* (   ) and *wandering* (   )."

	YES	NO
1. Clap each time you hear a syllable in the following word:		
Sally	☐	☐
Bob	☐	☐
Kimberly	☐	☐
Mary	☐	☐
John	☐	☐

TOTAL CORRECT ____

Distinguishing Initial Sounds

Practice: "Many words begin with the same sound. *Pig* and *penny* both begin with the /p/ sound. Tell me two words that begin with the same sound as *wind* (   ), *tent* (   ), and *jump* (   )."

	YES	NO
2. Name two other words that begin with the same sound as the word:		
cat	☐	☐
Sally	☐	☐
bed	☐	☐
milk	☐	☐
fat	☐	☐

TOTAL CORRECT ____

Distinguishing Rime and Rhyme

Practice: "Rhyming words sound the same at the end. I can rhyme three words: *sad, bad, glad.* Tell me a word that rhymes with *pin* (   ), *round* (   ), and *cup* (   )."

	YES	NO
3. Tell me if the two words rhyme.		
sand – hand	☐	☐
big – pig	☐	☐
rule – milk	☐	☐
fair – farm	☐	☐
bat – hat	☐	☐

TOTAL CORRECT ____

Distinguishing Oddity

Practice: "Sometimes in a group of three words, two words will begin with the same sound, but the other word will begin with a different sound. For example, with the three words *fox, fur,* and *tree, tree* does not begin with the same sound as *fox* and *fur.* Tell me which word begins with a different sound: *juice, milk, mom* (   ), *wind, weather, sun* (   ), *big, funny, fat* (   )."

4. Tell me which word does not begin with the same sound as the other two words:		
hat – man – hot	☐	☐
leg – lips – nose	☐	☐
man – money – nose	☐	☐
dog – tag – time	☐	☐
big – pull – push	☐	☐

TOTAL CORRECT ____

Blending Onset with Rime

Practice: "Many one-syllable words have two parts that can be blended together. For example, I can put a /b/ sound in front of *ug* and get *bug.* I want you to put an /m/ sound in front of /at/ and say the new word (   ); now put /s/ in front of /and/ (   ); now put /m/ in front of /eat/ (   )."

5. I am going to give you two parts of a word. I want you to blend the two parts together to make a word:		
/s/ + *at*	☐	☐
/k/ + *ake*	☐	☐
/b/ + *ug*	☐	☐
/j/ + *ump*	☐	☐
/n/ + *ight*	☐	☐

TOTAL CORRECT ____

Blending Letter Sounds

Practice: "Words are made up of individual sounds. For example, if I put /m/ + /u/ + /g/ together, I get *mug*. I want you to put these three sounds together: /f/ + /u/ + /n/ (   ). Now add /b/ + /u/ + /g/ (   ). Now add /s/ + /i/ + /t/ (   )."

YES   NO

6. I am going to give you three sounds. I want you to blend the sounds together and say the word:

   /c/ + /u/ + /t/   ☐ ☐
   /f/ + /a/ + /n/   ☐ ☐
   /b/ + /i/ + /g/   ☐ ☐
   /h/ + /o/ + /t/   ☐ ☐
   /l/ + /e/ + /g/   ☐ ☐

TOTAL CORRECT   ____

Segmenting Sounds in Words

Practice: "I can hear sounds in words. For example, when I say *bit*, I hear /b/ + /i/ + /t/. Tell me what sounds do you hear in *cat* (   ), in *fan* (   ), and in *ham* (   )."

7. I want you to tell me what three sounds you hear in each word:

   sad (/s/ + /a/ + /d/)   ☐ ☐
   pop   ☐ ☐
   bun   ☐ ☐
   him   ☐ ☐
   hen   ☐ ☐

TOTAL CORRECT   ____

Manipulating Initial Sounds in Words

Practice: "I can change a sound in a word to make a new word. For example, in the word *land*, I can change the /l/ to /s/ and get *sand*. Tell me what new word you get when you change one letter for another. In the word *round*, change the /r/ to /s/ (   ). In the word *light*, change the /l/ to /n/ (   ). In *frown*, change the /fr/ to /cl/ (   )."

8. I am going to say a word; then I will ask you to change one sound to make a new word:

   fan – change /f/ to /m/   ☐ ☐
   hut – change /h/ to /c/   ☐ ☐
   right – change /r/ to /n/   ☐ ☐
   meat – change /m/ to /n/   ☐ ☐
   fat – change /f/ to /b/   ☐ ☐

TOTAL CORRECT   ____

Deleting Initial Sounds of Words

Practice: "With some words, I can take off the initial sound and get a new word. For example if I take /b/ off of *beat*, I get *eat*. Tell me what word you get when you take /m/ off of *man* (   ); /f/ off of *fit* (   )."

	YES	NO

9. I am going to say a word; then I will ask you to take off a sound and give me the new word:

	YES	NO
late – take off the /l/	☐	☐
sand – take off the /s/	☐	☐
ham – take off the /h/	☐	☐
fat – take off the /f/	☐	☐
land – take off the /l/	☐	☐

TOTAL CORRECT ____

Manipulating Sounds in Words

Practice: "I can get a new word if I replace one sound for a different sound in a word. For example, in the word *bat*, if I change the /b/ to /c/, I have *cat*. Tell me what word you get when you change the /b/ in *bug* to /r/ (   ); the /s/ in *sack* to /b/(   ), the /l/ in *land* to /s/ (   )."

10. I am going to say a word; then I will ask you to change one sound in the word. Tell me both words:

	YES	NO
right – change /r/ to /f/	☐	☐
found – change /f/ to /s/	☐	☐
map – change /m/ to /l/	☐	☐
bake – change /b/ to /m/	☐	☐
hop – change /h/ to /t/	☐	☐

TOTAL CORRECT ____

GRAND TOTAL CORRECT ____

It is important to look at each section to determine strengths and weaknesses because each question is a different task. In each section, five correct responses indicate that the child has mastered the skill. Three or four correct responses indicate that the child is developing the skill and only one or two correct responses indicate that the child has difficulty with the task.

GENERAL COMMENTS:

APPENDIX C

C.23 POST-ASSESSMENT FOR PHONEMIC AWARENESS

Name: _____   Date: _____

NOTE: The teacher will check "Yes" if the child can do the task, and "No" if the child cannot do the task. It is good to give one example to the child so they fully understand the task they are asked to perform. Examples are provided here.

Syllabicating Words

Practice: "Words have different syllables. Some words have one syllable such as *hand* (clap once). *Mitten* has two syllables: mit- (clap once) tin (clap once). *Celebrate* has three syllables: cel- (clap once) e (clap once) brate (clap once). Clap and tell me how many syllables *table* has (   ). How about *shop* (   ) and *wandering* (   )."

	YES	NO
1. Clap each time you hear a syllable in the following words:		
Peter	☐	☐
Jane	☐	☐
Nathaniel	☐	☐
Joe	☐	☐
Molly	☐	☐

TOTAL CORRECT ____

Distinguishing Initial Sounds

Practice: "Many words begin with the same sound. *Pig* and *penny* both begin with the /p/ sound. Tell me two words that begin with the same sound as *wind* (   ), *tent* (   ), and *jump* (   )."

2. Name two other words that begin with the same sound as the word:

	YES	NO
coat	☐	☐
snake	☐	☐
banana	☐	☐
money	☐	☐
fish	☐	☐

TOTAL CORRECT ____

Distinguishing Rime and Rhyme

Practice: "Rhyming words sound the same at the end. I can rhyme three words: *sad, bad, glad.* Tell me a word that rhymes with *pin* (   ), *round* (   ), and *cup* (   )."

	YES	NO
3. Tell me if the two words rhyme.		
clock – block	☐	☐
fan – man	☐	☐
drink – doughnut	☐	☐
zoo – child	☐	☐
light – night	☐	☐

TOTAL CORRECT ____

Distinguishing Oddity

Practice: "Sometimes in a group of three words, two words will begin with the same sound, but the other word will begin with a different sound. For example, with the three words *fox, fur,* and *tree, tree* does not begin with the same sound as *fox* and *fur.* Tell me which word begins with a different sound: *juice, milk, mom* (   ), *wind, weather, sun* (   ), *big, funny, fat* (   )."

4. Tell me which word does not begin with the same sound as the other two words:

milk – man – nuts	☐	☐
lamp – hut – house	☐	☐
clock – meat – mouse	☐	☐
snake – goat – smile	☐	☐
sun – fun – friend	☐	☐

TOTAL CORRECT ____

Blending Onset with Rime

Practice: "Many one-syllable words have two parts that can be blended together. For example, I can put a /b/ sound in front of *ug* and get *bug.* I want you to put an /m/ sound in front of /at/ and say the new word (   ); now put /s/ in front of /and/ (   ); now put /m/ in front of /eat/ (   )."

5. I am going to give you two parts of a word. I want you to blend the two parts together to make a word:

/f/ + *un*	☐	☐
/l/ + *ight*	☐	☐
/r/ + *ug*	☐	☐
/s/ + *and*	☐	☐
/b/ + *ump*	☐	☐

TOTAL CORRECT ____

Blending Letter Sounds

Practice: "Words are made up of individual sounds. For example, if I put /m/ + /u/ + /g/ together, I get *mug*. I want you to put these three sounds together: /f/ + /u/ + /n/ (   ). Now add /b/ + /u/ + /g/ (   ). Now add /s/ + /i/ + /t/ (   )."

                                                                    YES   NO

6. I am going to give you three sounds. I want you to blend the sounds together and say the word:

    /f/ + /a/ + /t/   ☐   ☐
    /r/ + /u/ + /g/   ☐   ☐
    /p/ + /i/ + /g/   ☐   ☐
    /p/ + /o/ + /t/   ☐   ☐
    /m/ + /a/ + /n/   ☐   ☐

                                                    TOTAL CORRECT ____

Segmenting Sounds in Words

Practice: "I can hear sounds in words. For example, when I say *bit*, I hear /b/ + /i/ + /t/. Tell me what sounds do you hear in *cat* (   ), in *fan* (   ), and in *ham* (   )."

7. I want you to tell me what three sounds you hear in each word:

    pen = /p/ + /e/ + /n/   ☐   ☐
    Dad   ☐   ☐
    top   ☐   ☐
    sun   ☐   ☐
    fin   ☐   ☐

                                                    TOTAL CORRECT ____

Manipulating Initial Sounds in Words

Practice: "I can change a sound in a word to make a new word. For example, in the word *land*, I can change the /l/ to /s/ and get *sand*. Tell me what new word you get when you change one letter for another. In the word *round*, change the /r/ to /s/ (   ). In the word *light*, change the /l/ to /n/ (   ). In *frown*, change the /fr/ to /cl/ (   )."

8. I am going to say a word; then I will ask you to change one sound to make a new word:

    man – change /m/ to /f/   ☐   ☐
    cut – change /c/ to /h/   ☐   ☐
    might – change /m/ to /s/   ☐   ☐
    cake – change /c/ to /b/   ☐   ☐
    hat – change /h/ to /f/   ☐   ☐

                                                    TOTAL CORRECT ____

Deleting Initial Sounds of Words

Practice: "With some words, I can take off the initial sound and get a new word. For example if I take /b/ off of *beat*, I get *eat*. Tell me what word you get when you take /m/ off of *man* (   ); /f/ off of *fit* (   )."

	YES	NO

9. I am going to say a word; then I will ask you to take off a sound and give me the new word:

	YES	NO
fan – take off /f/	☐	☐
band – take off /b/	☐	☐
meat – take off /m/	☐	☐
Sam – take off /s/	☐	☐
rat – take off /r/	☐	☐

TOTAL CORRECT ____

Manipulating Sounds in Words

Practice: "I can get a new word if I replace one sound for a different sound in a word. For example, in the word *bat*, if I change the /b/ to /c/, I have *cat*. Tell me what word you get when you change the /b/ in *bug* to /r/ (   ); the /s/ in *sack* to /b/(   ), the /l/ in *land* to /s/ (   )."

10. I am going to say a word; then I will ask you to change one sound in the word. Tell me both words:

	YES	NO
sight – change /s/ to /m/	☐	☐
round – change /r/ to /f/	☐	☐
big – change /b/ to /p/	☐	☐
make – change /m/ to /c/	☐	☐
land – change /l/ to /b/	☐	☐

TOTAL CORRECT ____

GRAND TOTAL CORRECT ____

It is important to look at each section to determine strengths and weaknesses because each question is a different task. In each section, five correct responses indicate that the child has mastered the skill. Three or four correct responses indicate that the child is developing the skill and only one or two correct responses indicate that the child has difficulty with the task.

GENERAL COMMENTS:

C.24 **CHECKLIST FOR PHONEMIC AWARENESS FOR PRIMARY GRADES**

(Based on the Seven Dimensions)

Teacher: _____ Date: _____

+ = always   x = sometimes   o = seldom/never

DIMENSION	STUDENTS																
1. Ability to hear syllables within words																	
2. Ability to hear initial sounds or recognize alliteration																	
3. Ability to hear rhyming words																	
4. Ability to distinguish oddity																	
5. Ability to blend words orally																	
6. Ability to segment words:																	
• Drop beginning sound																	
• Drop ending sound																	
7. Ability to manipulate sounds orally to create new words																	

C.25 CHECKLIST OF KNOWN LETTER NAMES AND SOUNDS

Student: _____   Date: _____

LETTER	UPPERCASE NAME	LOWERCASE NAME	SCRIPT NAME	SOUND	WORD WITH INITIAL SOUND	WORD WITH ENDING SOUND
K						
N						
E						
J						
A						
T						
B						
S						
I						
M						
O						
D						
C						
Y						
G						
V						
Z						
P						
F						

Photocopy and enlarge these cards for use with children.

Master Card of Letters

K	N	E	J	A	T
B	S	I	M	R	H
L	W	X	Q	O	D
C	Y	G	V	Z	P
U	F				

k	n	e	j	a	t
b	s	I	m	r	h
l	w	x	q	o	d
c	y	g	v	z	p
u	f				

Master Card of Script Letters

C.26 **PHONICS MASTERY SURVEY**

Instructions: Before administering this survey, reproduce letters and words on 3 × 5-inch cards in large, lowercase letters, so the child can see them with ease. This survey should be administered to one child at a time. Use a separate sheet to document each child's progress. In the first section, stop if the child makes more than ten errors. For every other section, stop when child makes five or more errors. When sounds are incorrect, write the sound the child makes above the word.

1. **Consonant Sounds**

Show the child one card at a time, featuring lowercase consonant letters. Ask the child to tell you what sound the letter makes. On the assessment sheet, circle the letter if an incorrect sound is given. Write the incorrect sound the child gives on top of the letter.

p   b   m   w   f   v   t   s   d   r   j   h   z   n   l   y   k   c   g

If the child is not able to identify at least ten sounds, terminate this assessment.

2. **Rhyming Words**

Ask the child to read the following words and to say three words that rhyme with each of them. Nonsense words are acceptable.

1. be _____
2. go _____
3. say _____
4. do _____
5. make _____
6. will _____
7. get _____
8. blink _____
9. tan _____
10. bug _____

3. **CVC Words**

Ask the child to read the following short-vowel, CVC nonsense words. There are four examples of each short vowel sound. Indicate which vowel sounds were read correctly and which were not.

1. nid _____	11. wat _____
2. gat _____	12. vin _____
3. bul _____	13. lom _____
4. rup _____	14. hap _____
5. sen _____	15. yub _____
6. nat _____	16. pem _____
7. det _____	17. dom _____
8. rit _____	18. kud _____
9. nup _____	19. wom _____
10. nop _____	20. zet _____

4. Consonant Blends

Ask the child to read the following words that contain beginning or ending consonant blends (or both). Indicate any blends the child says incorrectly.

1. blithe _____	11. trink _____
2. clog _____	12. brind _____
3. plush _____	13. scup _____
4. flounce _____	14. stint _____
5. frisk _____	15. smeat _____
6. dwelt _____	16. spole _____
7. skig _____	17. gluck _____
8. crass _____	18. brame _____
9. trek _____	19. dredge _____
10. swap _____	20. lasp _____

5. Consonant Digraphs

Have the child read the following words containing consonant digraphs. Indicate any digraphs the child says incorrectly.

1. shan _____	11. scord _____
2. thort _____	12. squean _____
3. phrat _____	13. sling _____
4. chib _____	14. sprill _____
5. phant _____	15. strug _____
6. yeth _____	16. splom _____
7. rosh _____	17. shred _____
8. lotch _____	18. squim _____
9. gresh _____	19. throbe _____
10. chass _____	

6. Long Vowel Sounds

Have the child read the following nonsense words that contain long vowel sounds. There are four examples of each long vowel sound. Indicate which vowels are read correctly and which are not.

1. stope _____
2. kade _____
3. fede _____
4. gride _____
5. blude _____
6. kroan _____
7. jaike _____
8. theade _____
9. smight _____
10. dreud _____

11. ploan _____
12. tayne _____
13. sheed _____
14. vied _____
15. trewd _____
16. whade _____
17. strean _____
18. blipe _____
19. roke _____
20. krume _____

7. Other Vowel Sounds

Have the child read the following words that contain variant vowel sounds. Indicate vowel sounds the child reads incorrectly.

1. nook (oo) _____
2. krouse (ou, ow) _____
3. sar (ar) _____
4. moil (oi) _____
5. noy (oy) _____
6. thirl (ir, er, ur) _____
7. floom (oo) _____

8. gorn (or) _____
9. chaw (aw, au) _____
10. zout (ou) _____
11. larm (ar) _____
12. groil (oi) _____
13. nirl (ir, er, ur) _____
_____

8. Number of Word Parts (Syllables)

Ask the child to read the following words and count the number of word parts or syllables in each word. (Correct answers are in parentheses.)

1. retention (3) _____
2. ride (1) _____
3. panic (2) _____
4. carnival (3) _____
5. monster (2) _____

6. contaminate (4) _____
7. computer (3) _____
8. antagonist (4) _____
9. guess (1) _____
10. consider (3) _____

Source: Cecil, N. L. (2003). *Striking a Balance: Best Practices for Early Literacy,* 2nd Ed. Scottsdale, AZ: Holcomb Hathaway.

APPENDIX C

C.27 CHECKLIST FOR LETTER–SOUND RELATIONSHIPS, FIRST GRADE

Teacher: _____ Period   1   2   3   4

+ = always   X = sometimes   O = seldom/never

SUB-STANDARD	STUDENTS																			
1. Names and identifies each letter																			
2. Understands that written words are composed of letters that represent sounds																			
3. Identifies letter–sound relationships for all consonants																			
4. Identifies letter–sound relationships for short vowels																			
5. Identifies letter–sound relationships for r-controlled vowels																			
6. Identifies letter–sound relationships for consonant blends																			
7. Identifies letter–sound relationships for consonant digraphs																			
8. Identifies letter–sound relationships for vowel digraphs																			
9. Identifies letter–sound relationships for vowel diphthongs																			
10. Blends onset with rime																			

Source: Adapted from the Texas Education Agency, (1997). *TEKS for English Language Arts and Reading.* Austin, TX: State Department of Education., pp. B-29–D-30.

C.28 DECODING AND WORD RECOGNITION CHECKLIST

Based on California's Standard 1.10

Teacher: _____   Date: _____

+ = always   x = sometimes   o = seldom/never

STANDARD	STUDENTS																
1. Recognizes consonant blends																	
2. Recognizes short vowel pattern: CVC																	
3. Recognizes long vowel patterns: CVCe and CV																	
4. Blends onsets with rime																	
5. Recognizes common irregular sight words																	
6. Uses knowledge of vowel digraphs to read words																	
7. Uses knowledge of r-controlled vowels to read words																	
8. Reads compound words																	
9. Reads contractions																	
10. Recognizes inflectional endings when reading words																	
11. Finds root words in order to recognize words																	
12. Reads common word families																	
13. Reads in manner that sounds like natural speech																	

Source: Based on California's State Standard: First Grade, Standard 1.10.

APPENDIX C

C.29 SCORING SHEET FOR WORD LIST

Student: _____   Grade: _____

+ = yes   − = no

WORDS	BEGINNING OF YEAR	1ST QUARTER	2ND QUARTER	3RD QUARTER	4TH QUARTER

C.30 **VOCABULARY GROWTH CHECKLIST**

FOR FIRST GRADE, BASED ON FLORIDA'S STATE STANDARDS

Teacher: _____ Date: _____

+ = always   X = sometimes   O = seldom/never

STANDARD	STUDENTS																				
1. Knows meaning of common words within basic categories																					
2. Uses knowledge of individual words in unknown compound words to predict their meanings																					
3. Uses reference resources to learn word meanings (e.g., beginning dictionaries and available technology)																					
4. Uses knowledge of suffixes (-er, -est, -ful) to determine meanings of words																					
5. Develops vocabulary by listening to and discussing both familiar and conceptually challenging selections read aloud																					

APPENDIX C

C.31 INTEREST INVENTORY FOR INFORMATIONAL TEXTS

THINGS THAT INTEREST ME

All of these questions are about your interests! You can list more than one thing for each question.

Name: _____ Date: _____

1. What is your favorite subject in school?

   _____

2. What subject that is not offered in school do you wish you could study?

   _____

3. What is your favorite sport?

   _____

4. What is your favorite TV program?

   _____

5. Who is your favorite athlete?

   _____

6. Who is your favorite actor/actress?

   _____

7. On Saturday, what is your favorite thing to do?

   _____

8. What type of music do you like?

   _____

9. What do you want to be when you grow up?

   _____

10. What is your favorite book?

    _____

11. If you could hop on a magic carpet, where in the world would you like to go?

    _____

12. If you could live in "another time," what time would it be? In the future? In the past?

    _____

13. What subject would you like to read about when we are working together?

    _____

C.32 **OBSERVATION CHECKLIST OF STUDENT'S EXPOSITORY READING**

Student: _____   Grade: _____

BEHAVIOR	Most of the time	Sometimes	Seldom	Never
BEFORE READING				
1. Determines purpose for reading	☐	☐	☐	☐
2. Predicts by reading headings	☐	☐	☐	☐
3. Skims to get overview of passage	☐	☐	☐	☐
4. Checks how long the passage is	☐	☐	☐	☐
5. Relates prior knowledge to passage	☐	☐	☐	☐
DURING READING				
1. Does not omit unknown words	☐	☐	☐	☐
2. Attempts to pronounce new words	☐	☐	☐	☐
3. Decodes new words easily	☐	☐	☐	☐
4. Does not use finger or other object to keep place	☐	☐	☐	☐
5. Does not insert words	☐	☐	☐	☐
6. Reads punctuation correctly	☐	☐	☐	☐
7. Rereads if comprehension breaks down	☐	☐	☐	☐
8. Connects reading material to prior knowledge	☐	☐	☐	☐
9. Reads figures, pictures, etc.	☐	☐	☐	☐
10. Looks up unknown words in glossary	☐	☐	☐	☐
11. Does not mouth words when reading silently	☐	☐	☐	☐
12. Does not have difficult time staying on task during silent reading	☐	☐	☐	☐
AFTER READING				
1. Summarizes in logical order	☐	☐	☐	☐
2. Retells main points	☐	☐	☐	☐
3. Retells information not found in text	☐	☐	☐	☐
4. Relates information to prior knowledge	☐	☐	☐	☐
5. Interprets text correctly	☐	☐	☐	☐
6. Makes inferences	☐	☐	☐	☐
7. Shows signs of critical thinking	☐	☐	☐	☐
8. Asks questions about material	☐	☐	☐	☐
9. Desires to know more about topic	☐	☐	☐	☐

COMMENTS

C.33 FLUENCY CHECKLIST

Name: _____   Grade: _____

Evaluator: _____

CHARACTERISTIC	DATE	DATE	DATE	DATE
STAGE 1				
Rate: Word-by-word reading with many pauses				
Prosody: No phrasing				
Prosody: Omits punctuation				
Automaticity: Sounds out letter by letter; ignores chunks in words				
Expression: Lacks expression				
STAGE 2				
Rate: Some two- or three-word phrases with many pauses				
Prosody: Aware of some end marks (periods, question marks)				
Automaticity: Begins to recognize chunks within monosyllabic words (onsets & rimes)				
Expression: Lacks expression				
STAGE 3				
Rate: Appropriate most of the time				
Prosody: Attentive to end marks and commas				
Automaticity: Recognizes chunks within words and inflectional endings				
Expression: Beginning to recognize dialogue				
STAGE 4				
Rate: Varies speed with difficulty of text				
Prosody: Attentive to all punctuation, good phrasing				
Automaticity: Recognizes syllables				
Expression: Appropriate for dialogue and mood				

C.34 FLUENCY CHECKLIST FOR NARRATIVE TEXT

Name: _____   Date: _____

Story: _____   Number of Words: _____

Time it took to read: _____   WPM: _____

TRAIT	YES	NO
1. Stopped for periods	☐	☐
2. Raised voice for question marks	☐	☐
3. Read with excitement for exclamation marks	☐	☐
4. Made slight pause for commas	☐	☐
5. Read phrases correctly	☐	☐
6. Changed voice for different characters (watched quotation marks)	☐	☐
7. Changed volume for different moods	☐	☐
8. Changed rate for different moods	☐	☐
9. Paused for ellipses	☐	☐
10. Emphasized italic words	☐	☐

C.35 **FLUENCY LOG**

Books I Have Read

Name: _____ Grade: _____

TITLE	AUTHOR	PARENTS' COMMENTS	DATE BEGAN	NUMBER OF TIMES READ
1.				
2.				
3.				
4.				
5.				
6.				

C.36 RUBRIC FOR ASSESSING THE WRITING PROCESS OF WRITERS IN PRIMARY GRADES

Name: _____   Grade: _____

Scores: Consistently present = 5, Sometimes present = 3, Not present = 0

COMPETENCY		DATES/SCORES			
PREWRITING	DATES:				
1. Generates own writing ideas.					
2. Reflects on idea before writing.					
3. Self-starter.					
4. Shares ideas with others.					
5. Draws before writing.					
DRAFTING					
1. Writes without worry about mechanics.					
2. Writes in various formats.					
3. Forms letters correctly.					
4. Uses invented spelling.					
5. Shows awareness of letter–sound relationships.					
6. Generates many ideas.					
7. Stories have beginning, middle, and end.					
8. Writes independently.					
9. Completes a passage.					
REVISING					
1. Rereads passage.					
2. Adds to passage.					
3. Deletes sections.					
4. Reads passage to peers.					
5. Reads ideas to others.					
6. Listens to others read.					

EDITING

1. Looks at spelling patterns.				
2. Checks and corrects letter formation.				
3. Self-edits.				
4. Rewrites passage to make "clean" copy.				
5. Seeks help from teacher.				
6. Seeks help from peers.				
7. Helps peers with their editing.				

PUBLISHING

1. Willing to share in author's chair.				
2. Willing to share written copy with others.				
3. Enjoys listening to others' stories.				
TOTAL:				

TEACHER'S COMMENTS:

From *Literacy Assessment and Intervention for the Elementary Classroom*, by Beverly DeVries. Copyright @2004 by Holcomb Hathaway, Publishers, Scottsdale, AZ.

C.37 RUBRIC FOR ASSESSING THE WRITING PROCESS OF THIRD GRADERS

Student: _____

Teacher: _____

Scores: 0 = Never   1 = Seldom   2 = Sometimes   3 = Usually   4 = Always

STRATEGY		DATES/SCORES			
PREWRITING	DATES:				
1. Researches books, magazines, or _____ (other).					
2. Brainstorms ideas on graphic organizers.					
3. Shares ideas with classmate(s).					
4. Makes notes.					
5. Plans for a particular audience.					
6. Makes good use of time.					
7. Has correct supplies.					
8. Records ideas through writing/drawing.					
9. Plans purpose.					
DRAFTING					
1. Uses plans and resources.					
2. Writes without deleting.					
3. Takes risk with new genre.					
4. Knows audience.					
5. Writes without worry about mechanics.					
6. Stays on task.					
REVISING					
1. Deletes material.					
2. Conducts more research.					
3. Reorganizes material.					
4. Seeks comments from peers.					
5. Seeks comments from teacher.					
6. Is willing to rewrite.					
7. Focuses on good word choice.					

APPENDIX C

EDITING				
1. Self-checks spelling.				
2. Self-checks punctuation.				
3. Self-checks usage.				
4. Self-checks legibility.				
PUBLISHING				
1. Puts text in neat, final form.				
2. Shares with class.				
3. Shares with wider community.				
TOTAL:				

TEACHER'S COMMENTS:

C.38 RUBRIC FOR WRITING STORIES

Name: _____   Date: _____

Scores: Excellent = 5   Fair = 3   Poor = 0

COMPETENCY	EXCELLENT	FAIR	POOR
1. Setting description	☐	☐	☐
2. Character description	☐	☐	☐
3. Actions of characters	☐	☐	☐
4. Dialogue of characters	☐	☐	☐
5. Motives of characters	☐	☐	☐
6. Story starter	☐	☐	☐
7. Plot with roadblocks	☐	☐	☐
8. Climax to plot	☐	☐	☐
9. Resolution to plot	☐	☐	☐
10. Choice of adjectives	☐	☐	☐
11. Choice of verbs	☐	☐	☐
12. Choice of nouns	☐	☐	☐
13. Use of figurative speech	☐	☐	☐
14. Quotation marks	☐	☐	☐
15. Spelling	☐	☐	☐
16. Punctuation	☐	☐	☐
17. Paragraphing	☐	☐	☐
18. Standard usage	☐	☐	☐
19. Presentation	☐	☐	☐

TEACHER'S COMMENTS:

APPENDIX C

C.39 **RUBRIC FOR RESEARCH PAPER**

Name: _____ Date: _____

Scores: Yes = 5 points   Somewhat = 3 points   No = 0 points

COMPETENCY	YES	SOMEWHAT	NO
1. Used books to get information.	☐	☐	☐
2. Used video to get information.	☐	☐	☐
3. Used CD-ROM to get information.	☐	☐	☐
4. Interviewed others for information.	☐	☐	☐
5. Wrote interesting introduction.	☐	☐	☐
6. Developed ideas with explanations, details, or examples.	☐	☐	☐
7. Organized information within paragraphs.	☐	☐	☐
8. Good organization within report.	☐	☐	☐
9. Used descriptive language, specific nouns.	☐	☐	☐
10. Included new, interesting information.	☐	☐	☐
11. Used writing conventions such as:			
Capitalization	☐	☐	☐
Correct usage	☐	☐	☐
Correct spelling	☐	☐	☐
Indents paragraphs	☐	☐	☐
Correct paragraphing	☐	☐	☐
12. Wrote complete sentences.	☐	☐	☐
13. Summarized ideas at end.	☐	☐	☐
14. Included references in correct format.	☐	☐	☐
15. Presented in neat format.	☐	☐	☐

TOTAL _____

TEACHER'S COMMENTS:

C.40 BEAR, INVERNIZZI, TEMPLETON, & JOHNSTON QUALITATIVE SPELLING INVENTORY

ONE

SET #1

| 1. bed | 2. ship | 3. when | 4. lump | 5. float |

SET #2

| 1. train | 2. place | 3. drive | 4. bright | 5. shopping |

SET #3

| 1. spoil | 2. serving | 3. chewed | 4. carries | 5. marched |

SET #4

| 1. shower | 2. cattle | 3. favor | 4. ripen | 5. cellar |

SET #5

| 1. pleasure | 2. fortunate | 3. confident | 4. civilize | 5. opposition |

TWO

SET #1

| 1. net | 2. trip | 3. crime | 4. dump | 5. then |

SET #2

| 1. chain | 2. forest | 3. trail | 4. soap | 5. reaches |

SET #3

| 1. preparing | 2. popping | 3. cattle | 4. caught | 5. inspection |

SET #4

| 1. comparing | 2. topping | 3. battle | 4. fought | 5. intention |

SET #5

| 1. rupture | 2. stellar | 3. treasure | 4. confident | 5. tempest |

Source: Words their way: Word study for phonics, vocabulary, and spelling instruction (3rd ed.). by Bear/Invernizzi/ Templeton/Johnston, © 2004. Reprinted by permission of Pearson Education, Inc., Upper Saddle River, NJ.

C.41 HENDERSON'S WORD LIST AS CITED IN FRESCH & WHEATON

SET #1

| 1. send | 2. gift | 3. rule | 4. trust | 5. soap |

SET #2

| 1. batter | 2. knee | 3. mind | 4. scream | 5. sight |

SET #3

| 1. chain | 2. count | 3. knock | 4. caught | 5. noise |

SET #4

| 1. careful | 2. stepping | 3. chasing | 4. straw | 5. nerve |

SET #5

| 1. thirsty | 2. baseball | 3. circus | 4. handle | 5. sudden |

Source: Fresch, M. J. & Wheaton, A. (1997). Sort, search, and discover: Spelling in the child-centered classroom. *The Reading Teacher, 51*(1), 20–31. Copyright by the International Reading Association. All rights reserved.

C.42 **RECORDING AND ANALYZING SPELLING**

Student: _____   Grade: _____

Word	Precommunicative	Semiphonetic	Phonetic	Transitional	Conventional
1.					
2.					
3.					
4.					
5.					
6.					
7.					
8.					
9.					
10.					

TEACHER'S COMMENTS:

C.43 **CHECKLIST FOR SPELLING, FIFTH GRADE**

Teacher: _____ Period 1 2 3 4 _____

+ = always   x = sometimes   o = seldom/never

STANDARD	STUDENTS																
Accurate Spelling:																	
Closed, open syllables																	
Consonant before *le*																	
qu patterns																	
n before *v*																	
m before *b*																	
m before *p*																	
Change *z* to *c* with *es*																	
Root words																	
Tense inflections																	
Number inflections																	
Suffixes *-able* & *-less*																	
Prefixes *re-* & *un-*																	
Uses resources to find correct spelling																	
Accurate spelling in final draft																	

APPENDIX D

INSTRUCTIONAL MATERIALS

These materials are discussed, and directions given, in the indicated chapters.

D.1 **LESSON PLAN FOR TUTORS**

Tutor: _____   Date: _____

Tutee: _____   Grade: _____

Easy Reading Objective:

Rereading of Last Session's Book Objective:

Word Study Objective:

Writing Objective:

Reading of Instructional Materials Objective:

LESSON PLAN	PLANNED ACTIVITY	TIME	REFLECTION

D.2 LOG SHEET OF STRATEGIES

STRATEGIES TAUGHT TO _____ **BY** _____

DURING EASY READ

DURING WRITING

DURING WORD STUDY

DURING NEW BOOK

D.3 **LOG SHEET OF BOOKS READ**

BOOKS READ DURING TUTORING

Tutor: Tutee:

BOOKS READ BY TUTOR	DATE	BOOKS READ BY TUTEE	DATE

D.4 **TEXTBOOK AND TRADEBOOK EVALUATION CHECKLIST**

Rate the statements below, using the following rating system:

5 = Excellent
4 = Good
3 = Adequate
2 = Poor
1 = Unacceptable
NA = Not applicable

Further comments may be written in the space provided.

Book Title: _____

Publisher: _____

Copyright date: _____

FORMAT – Eye Appeal

_____ A. Photographs

_____ B. Photographs that include different races and both sexes

_____ C. Colorful charts and diagrams

_____ D. White spaces on page

_____ E. No two side-by-side pages of ALL text

_____ F. Appropriate size of text for grade level

_____ G. Appropriate text font for grade level

FORMAT – STRUCTURE

_____ A. Detailed Table of Contents

_____ B. Glossary

_____ C. Index

_____ D. Main headings in larger type

_____ E. Subheadings in different font/size

_____ F. New vocabulary in boldface or italics

_____ G. Definitions of new vocabulary in margins

_____ H. Appropriate captions under photographs and illustrations

_____ I. Important facts repeated in illustrations and diagrams

_____ J. Important facts highlighted in separate boxes

_____ K. Pre-chapter questions—literal, inferential, and critical

_____ L. Pre-chapter organizers

_____ M. End-of-chapter questions—literal, inferential, and critical

TEXT

_____ A. Readability appropriate for intended grade

_____ B. New vocabulary explained adequately

_____ C. Appropriate assumption of reader's vocabulary

APPENDIX D

_____ D. Appropriate assumption of reader's background knowledge

_____ E. Information logically presented

_____ F. Important new information restated through visual aids

_____ G. Clear explanation of new concepts

_____ H. Text is not so oversimplified that relationships among ideas is not clear

_____ I. Appropriate in-depth presentation of information

_____ J. Information presented in a non-encyclopedic manner

_____ K. Sentence structure grammatically correct

_____ L. Appropriate use of conjunctions so relationships among ideas are clear

_____ M. Good pronoun usage

_____ N. Active voice

EXTENSION OF INFORMATION

_____ A. Lists of books where students can get more information

_____ B. Lists of websites where students can get more information

_____ C. Suggestions for outside projects

_____ D. In science texts, good description of appropriate step-by-step experiments

STRENGTHS OF BOOK:

_____

_____

_____

_____

WEAKNESSES OF BOOK:

_____

_____

_____

_____

Recommended for use by _____ (Child's name).

by _____ (Teacher's name).

D.5 DIRECTIONS FOR CREATING GAME BOARDS AND PICTURE/WORD CARDS

To assemble:

- Create a front title page.
- Glue the title on the front of a colored file folder.
- Copy the game board from appendix or create your own. Decorate and add color to game board. Glue the game board inside the file folder.
- Reproduce the pictures for the various activities on colorful stock card paper. Laminate and cut them out so that they can be stacked in a deck.
- Using the directions given in the chapter Intervention sections earlier, copy or create a sheet of directions. Glue the directions and an envelope to store playing pieces on the back of the folder.

D.6 **HOW MANY SYLLABLES IN THE ZOO? GAME BOARD AND PICTURE CARDS**

  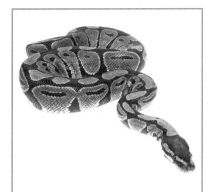

D.7 REMEMBER THE BEGINNING SOUND PICTURE CARDS

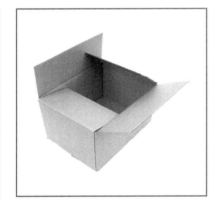

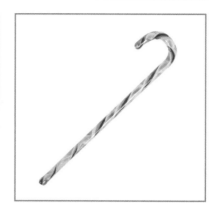

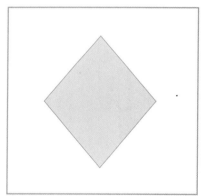

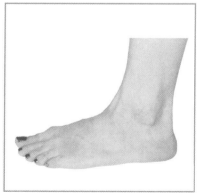

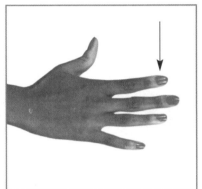

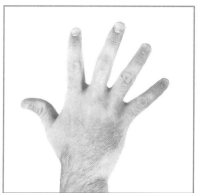

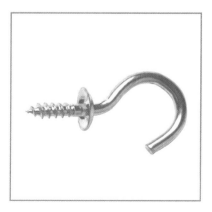

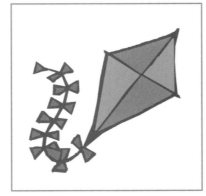

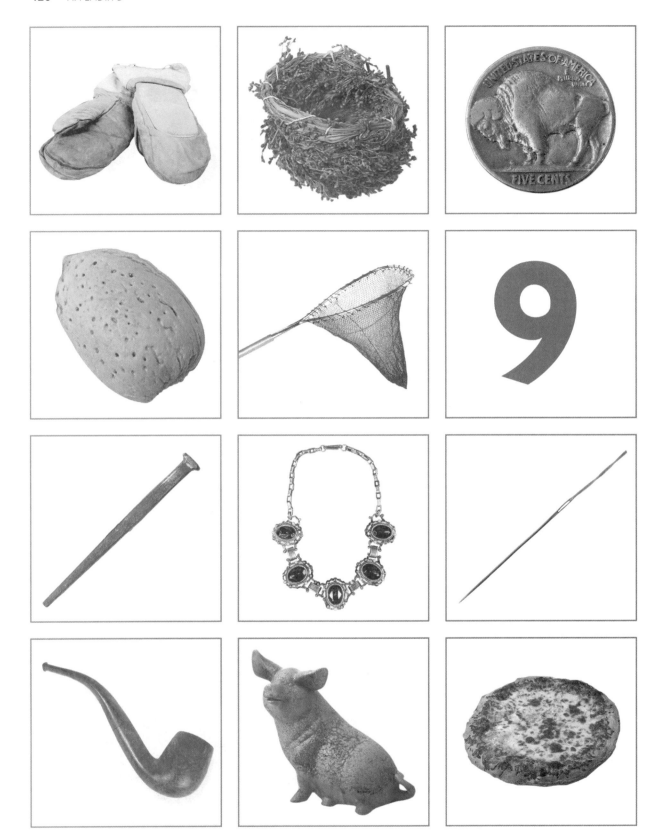

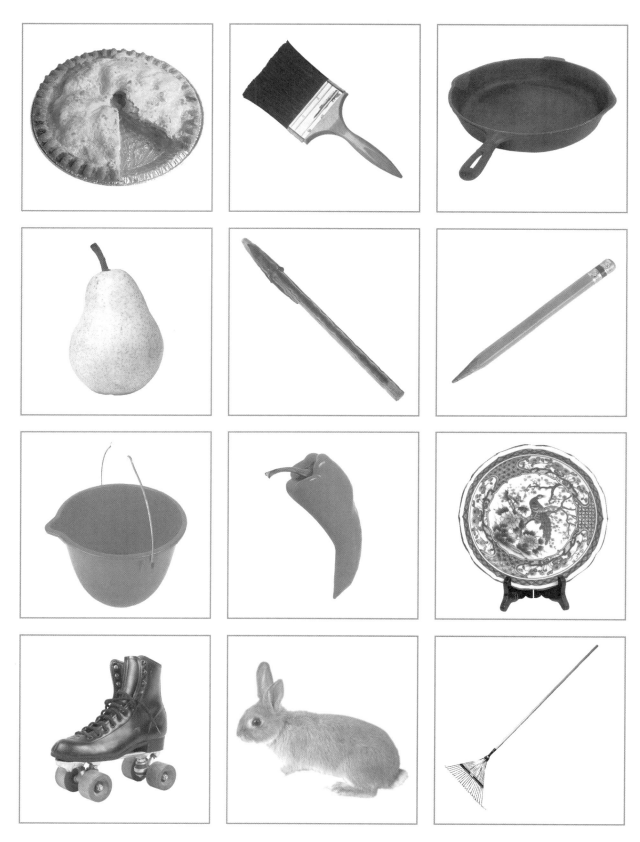

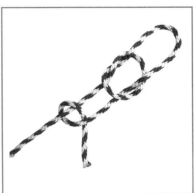

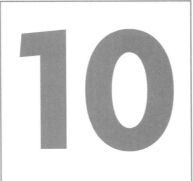

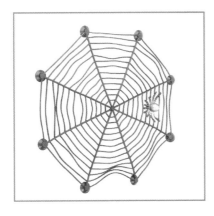

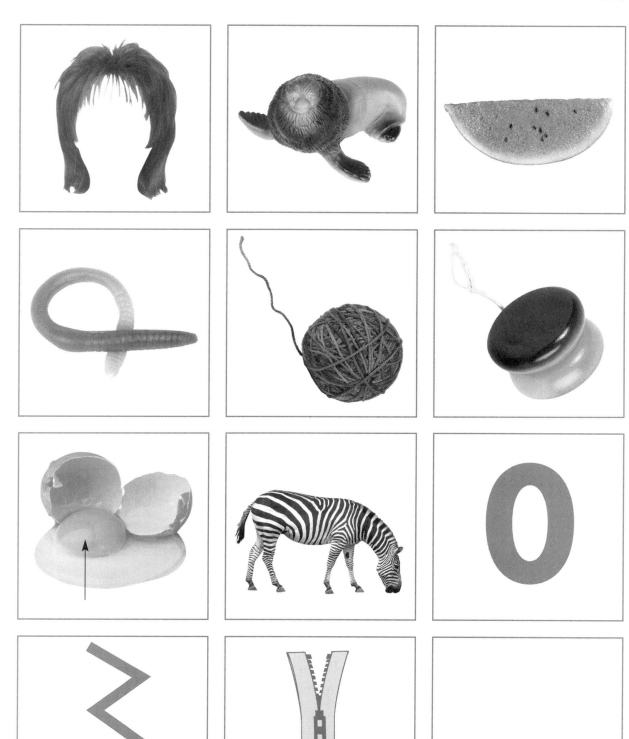

D.8 INITIAL SOUND PICTURE BINGO CARDS

Initial Sound Bingo

Initial Sound Bingo

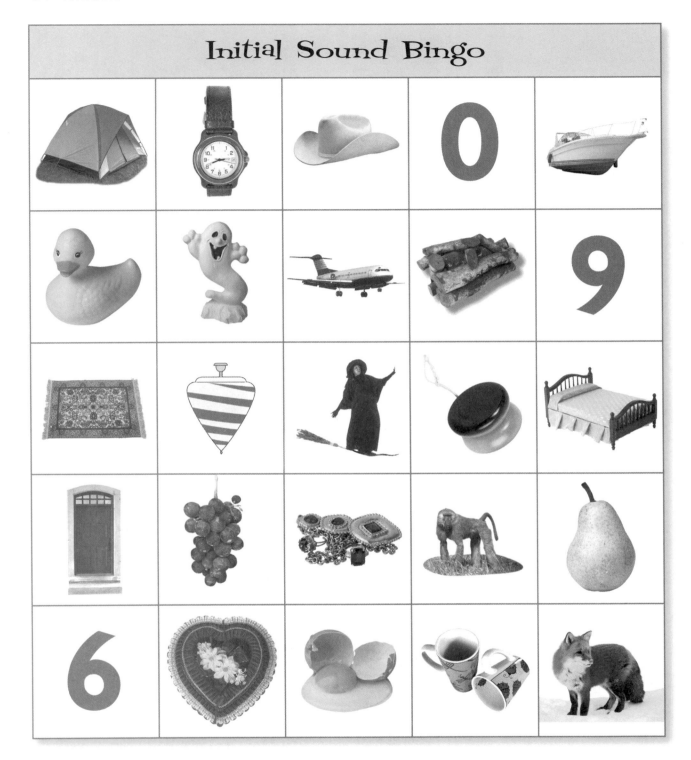

Initial Sound Bingo

Initial Sound Bingo

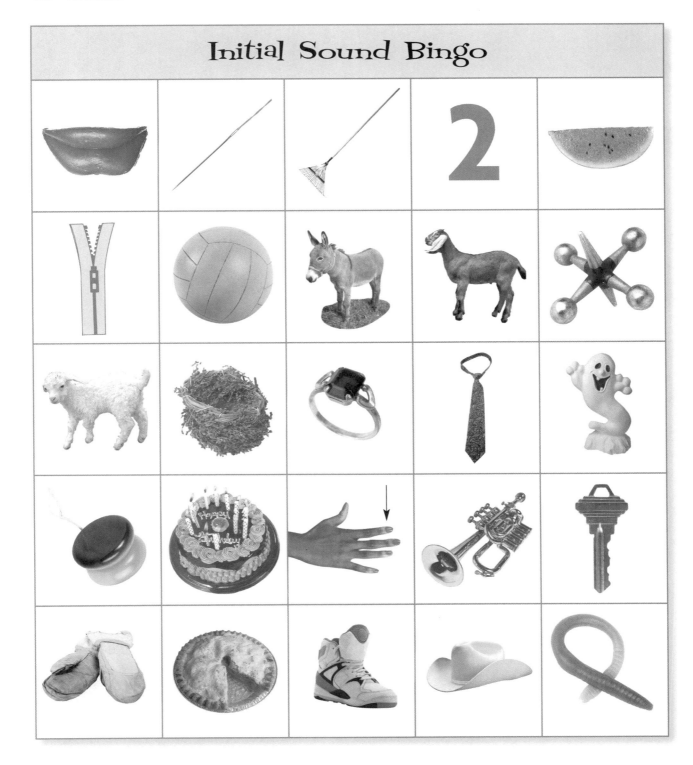

Initial Sound Bingo

Initial Sound Bingo

Initial Sound Bingo

Initial Sound Bingo

Initial Sound Bingo

D.9 TOSS THE CUBE ART

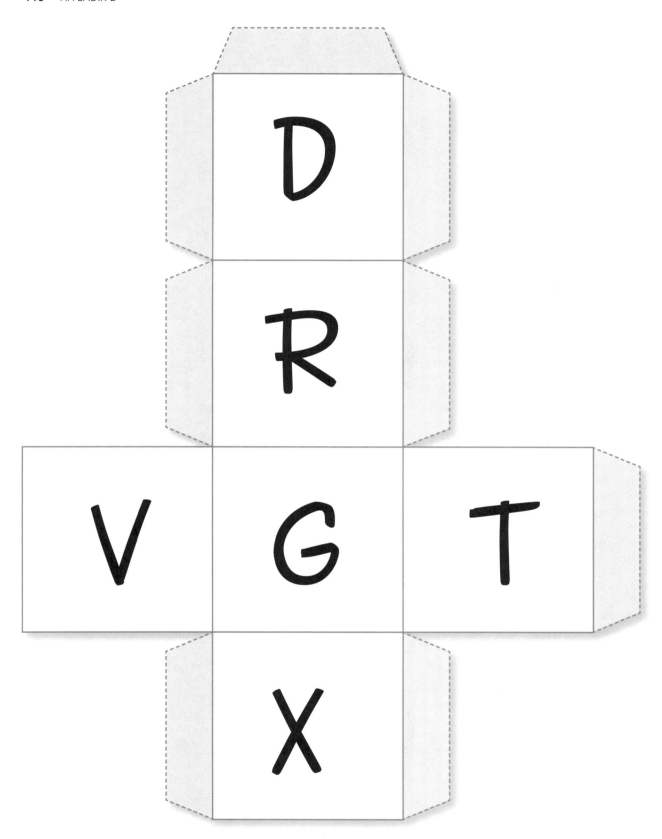

N

P

S   B   K

C

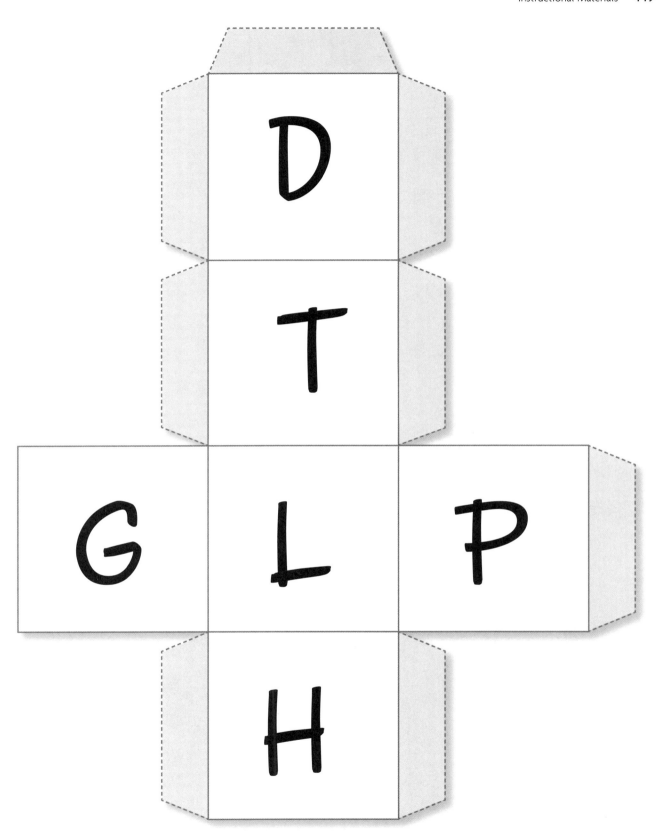

D.10 **GO FISH PICTURE CARDS**

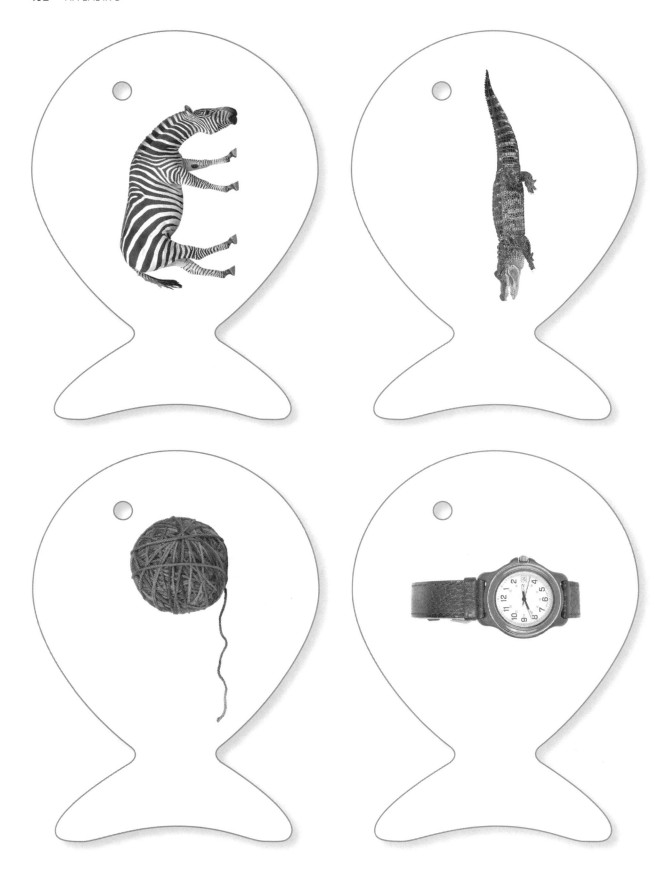

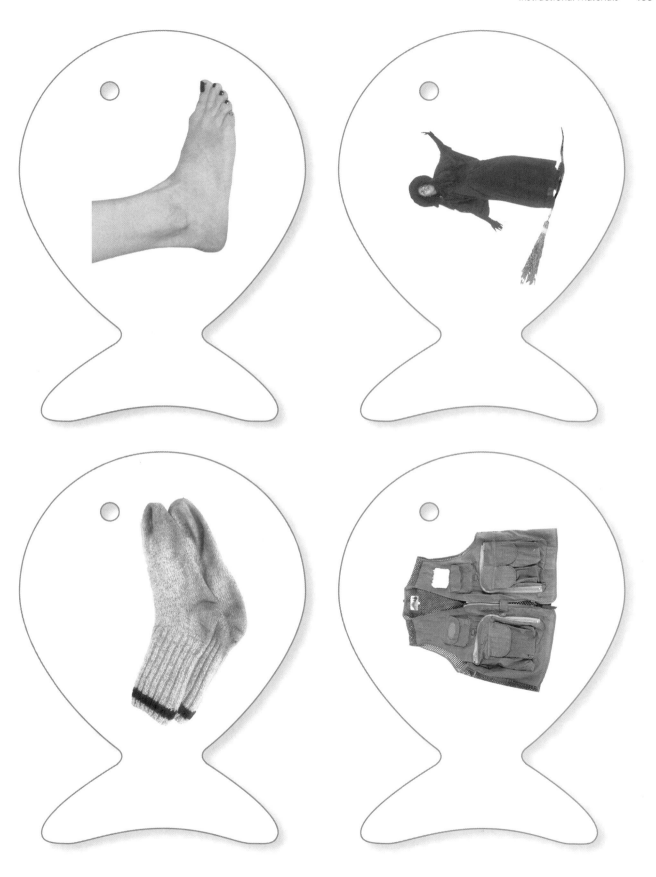

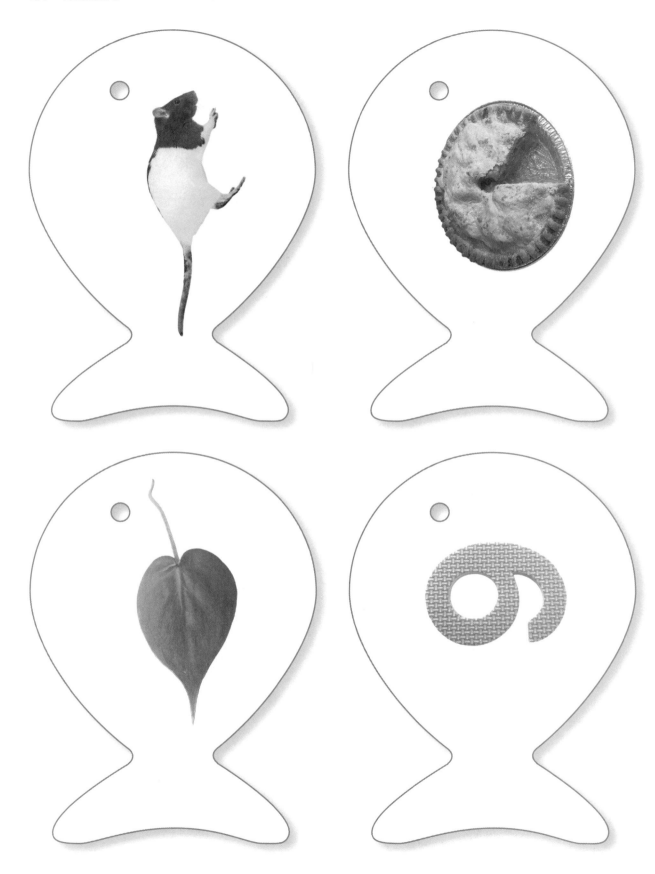

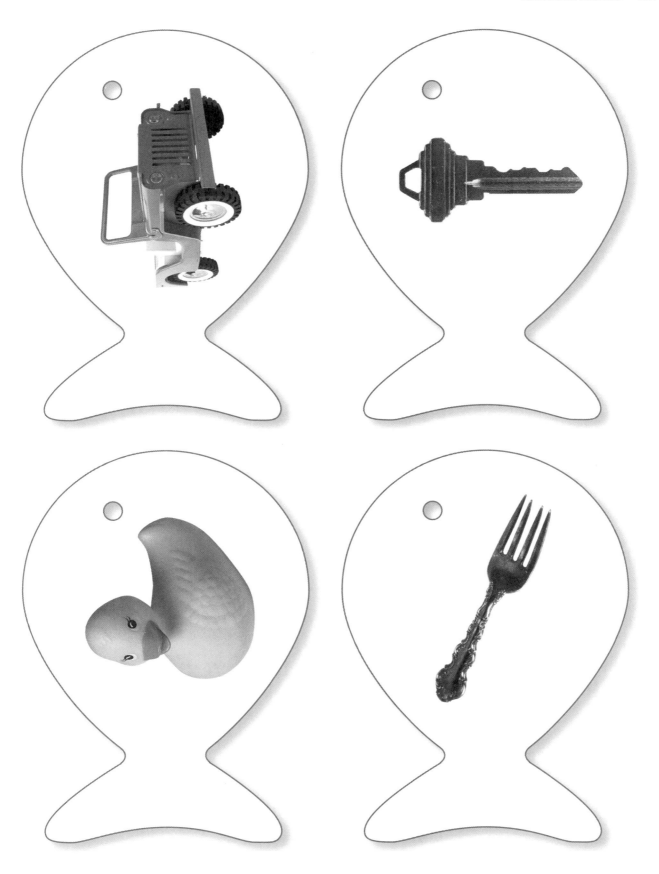

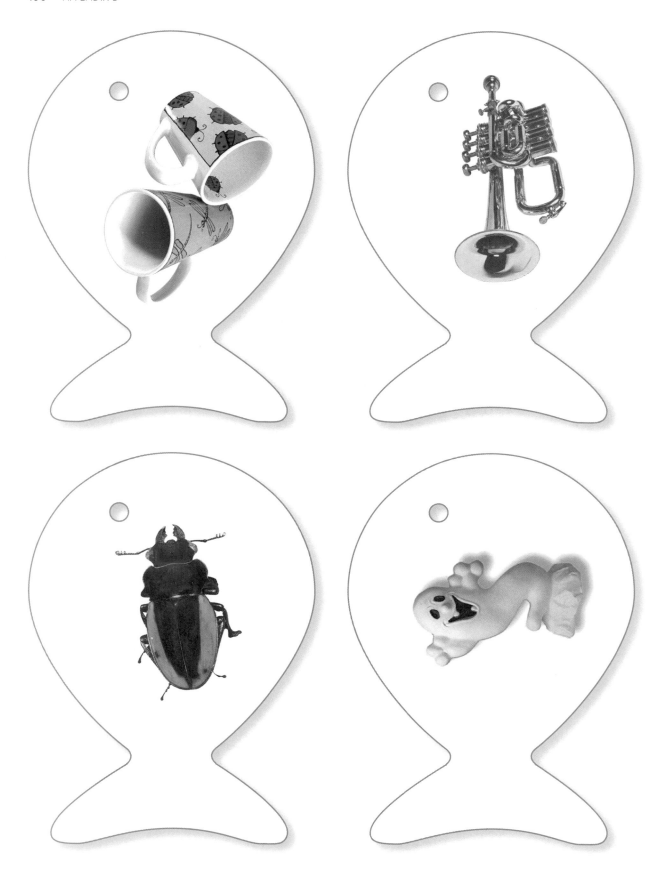

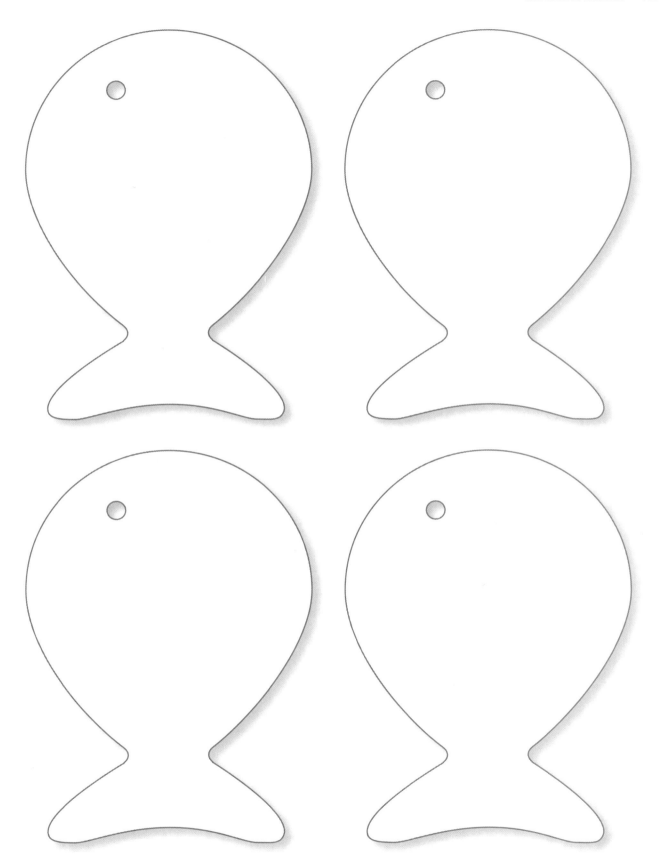

D.11 **HUMPTY DUMPTY GAME BOARD AND PICTURE CARDS**

Folder title (place on outside of folder)

Humpty

Dumpty

Sat on a Wall

Humpty

Dumpty

Had a Great Fall!

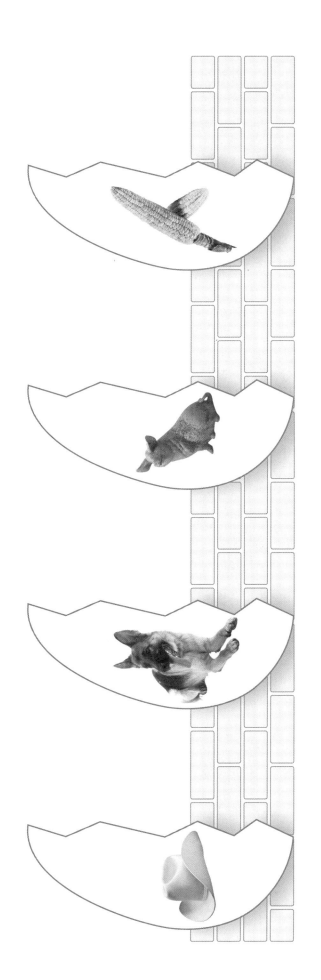

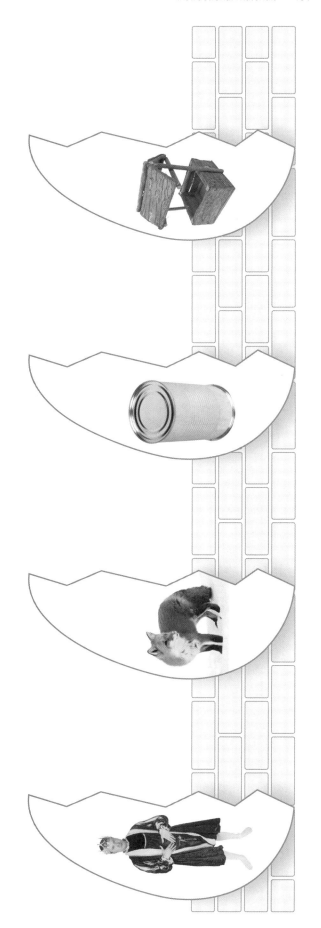

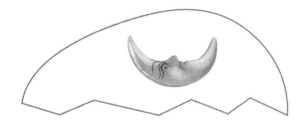

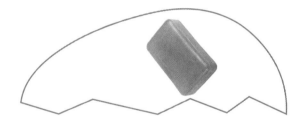

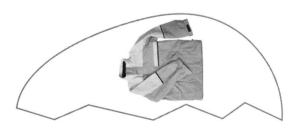

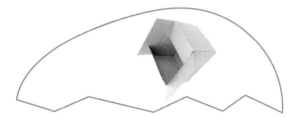

D.12 LISTEN FOR THE INITIAL CONSONANT BLEND SOUND GAME BOARD AND PICTURE CARDS

tw	sc	cr	tr
qu	st	pr	sk
gr	sw	tr	sc
br	sp	dr	br
fr	sk	sm	fr

sm	sk	fr	sc
dr	sp	br	tr
tr	sw	gr	st
pr	st	qu	sk
cr	sc	tw	cr

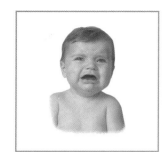

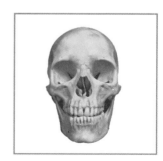

20
12

?

 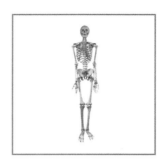 

D.13 **WORD DOMINOS**

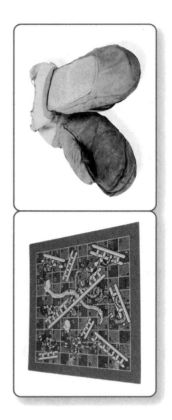

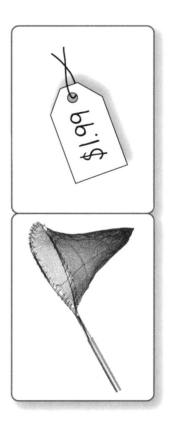

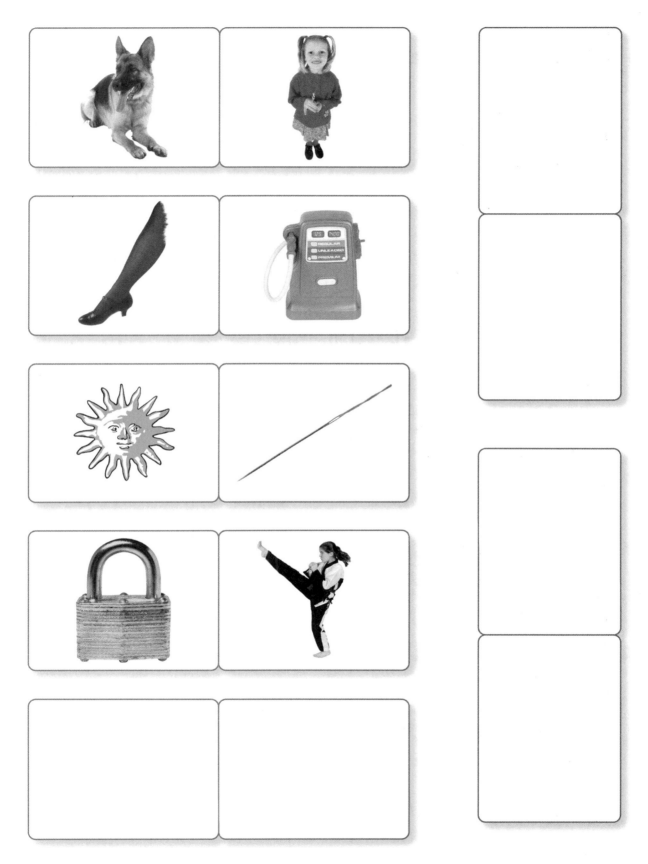

D.14 **CONCENTRATION WORD CARDS***

*Game pieces on this page are based on *Sheep Out to Eat* by Nancy Shaw (1992).

Eat	Seat	Sheep	Keep
Cake	Mistake	Smash	Crash
Slurp	Burp	Mop	Slop
Custard	Mustard	Bites	Appetites
Fill	Hill	Ear	Hear

Cat	Sat	Seen	Green
Arm	Farm	Hand	Sand
Ham	Sam	Goat	Coat
Where	There	Game	Shame
Let	Net	Feed	Seed

Llama	Mama	Dad	Glad
Pup	Up	Night	Might
Moon	Soon	Look	Book
Lock	Sock	Hog	Frog
Pack	Sack	Bake	Take

Sound	Found	Red	Bed
Fish	Wish	Box	Fox
Shut	Hut	Tall	Fall
Way	Day	Sing	Thing
Mess	Less	Stop	Top

D.15 SHORT VOWEL BINGO GAME CARD

B	I	N	G	O
		Free		

D.16 LISTEN TO THE VOWEL SOUND GAME BOARD AND GAME PIECES

ĭ	ŭ	ĭ	a
e	ū	o	ā
ē	o	ō	e
a	ō	u	ē
ā	ĭ	ū	ĭ

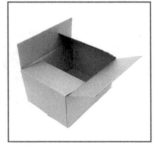

D.17 DOLCH LIST BINGO WORD CARDS

B	I	N	G	O
a	after	all	am	an
and	are	around	as	at
away	be	big	black	blue
brown	but	by	call	came
can	carry	cold	come	did

B	I	N	G	O
go	going	good	green	had
has	have	he	help	her
here	him	his	hurt	I
if	in	into	is	it
its	jump	know	like	little

B	I	N	G	O
look	over	play	put	ran
red	ride	round	run	said
saw	see	she	so	some
soon	stop	ten	the	this
three	to	too	two	under

B	I	N	G	O
up	about	again	any	ask
ate	because	been	before	best
better	both	bring	buy	clean
could	cut	does	done	draw
drink	eight	every	fall	far

B	I	N	G	O
hurt	just	keep	kind	laugh
let	light	live	long	many
much	must	myself	never	new
now	off	once	only	open
or	our	own	pick	please

B	I	N	G	O
small	start	take	tell	thank
that	their	them	then	there
these	they	think	those	today
together	try	upon	us	use
very	walk	want	warm	wish

D.18 ONSET AND RIME CARDS

C	B	F	H
M	P	S	at
B	C	D	F
M	N	P	R
V	an	B	H

S	St	L	and
Br	F	Fl	L
M	N	R	S
Fr	ight	B	F
H	M	P	R
S	ound		

D.19 CATEGORIZING GAME BOARD AND CARDS FOR TROY'S SUPER CENTER

TROY'S SUPER CENTER

GROCERIES

PHARMACY

ELECTRONICS

GARDEN CENTER

SCHOOL SUPPLIES

CLOTHING

TOYS

Carrots	Ice Cream	Orange Juice	Bread
Peanut Butter	Bananas	Milk	Meat
Cereal	Crackers	Potato Chips	Pop
Music CDs	Televisions	Tape Recorder	Videos
Computer	Camera	Puzzles	Dolls

Games	Flowers	Garden Hose	Rake
Seeds	Aspirin	Cough Drops	Bandages
Shorts	Socks	Belts	Sweaters
Jeans	Shoes	Pencils	Paper
Staples	Notebooks	Crayons	Markers

D.20 **SCATTERGORY GAME CARD**

CATEGORIES

INITIAL LETTER OR CONSONANT BLEND				
T				
R				
St				
L				
Br				
D				

D.21 **MULTIPLE MEANING RACE TRACK BOARD**

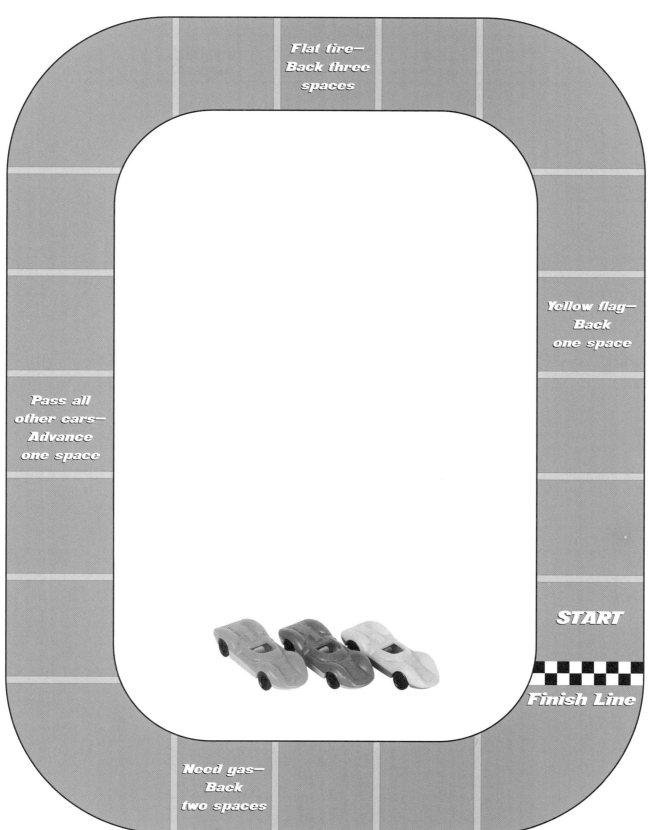

D.22 TAPE, CHECK, CHART

Name: _____   Grade: _____

STORY	1ST READING ERRORS	2ND READING ERRORS	3RD READING ERRORS	TEACHER COMMENTS
1.				
2.				
3.				
4.				
5.				
6.				
7.				
8.				
9.				
10.				

TEACHER'S OVERALL COMMENTS:

D.23 **TAPE, TIME, CHART**

Name: _____ Grade: _____

STORY	1ST READING TIME	2ND READING TIME	3RD READING TIME	TEACHER COMMENTS
1.				
2.				
3.				
4.				
5.				
6.				
7.				
8.				
9.				
10.				

TEACHER'S COMMENTS:

D.24 **FLUENCY LOG**

Books I Can Read

BY _____

TITLE	AUTHOR	PARENTS' COMMENTS	DATE	NUMBER OF TIMES READ
1.				
2.				
3.				
4.				
5.				
6.				
7.				

D.25 **MT. PLOT**

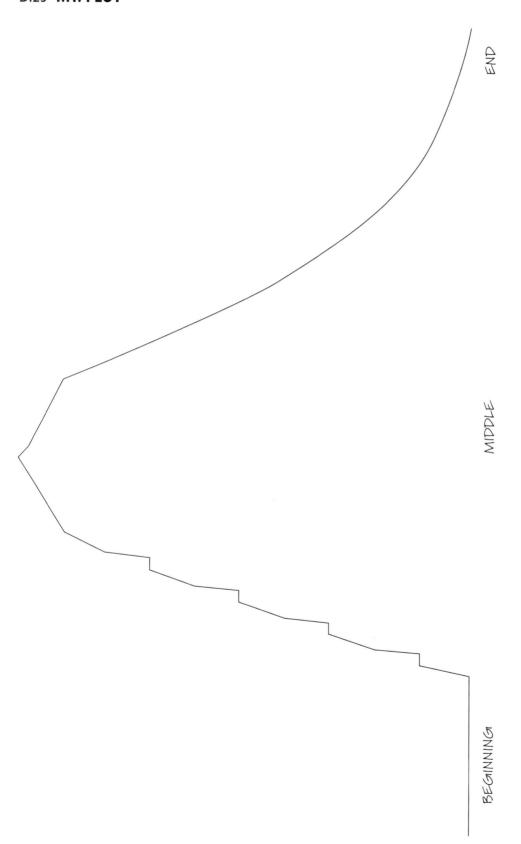

REFERENCES

Ada, A. F. (1998). *Yours truly, Goldilocks.* New York: Atheneum Books.

Adams, M. J. (1990). *Beginning to read: Thinking and learning about print.* Cambridge, MA: MIT Press.

Adler, D. (1990). *A picture book of Benjamin Franklin.* New York: A Trumpet Club Special Edition.

Afflerbach, P. & VanSledright, B. (2001). Hath! Doth! What? Middle graders reading innovative history text. *Journal of Adolescent & Adult Literacy, 44* (8), 696–708.

Ahlberg, J. (1986). *The jolly postman.* New York: Scholastic.

Alborough, J. (1994). *It's the bear.* New York: Scholastic.

Alexander, J. (1998). Reading skill and context facilitation: A classic study. *Journal of Educational Research, 91* (5), 314–319.

Allington, R. (2002). What I've learned about effective reading instruction: From a decade of studying exemplary elementary classroom teachers. *Phi Delta Kappan, 83* (10), 740–747.

Allington, R. (2001), *What really matters for struggling readers: Designing research-based programs.* New York: Longman.

Allinder, R. (2001). Improving fluency in at-risk readers and students with learning disabilities. *Remedial and Special Education, 22* (1), 48–56.

Allington, R. L. (1983). Fluency: The neglected goal. *The Reading Teacher, 36,* 556–561.

Allinder, R., Fuchs, L., & Fuchs, D. (1998). Curriculum-based measurement. In H. B. Vance (Ed.), *Psychological assessment of children: Best practice for school and clinical settings* (2nd ed.), pp. 106–132. New York: Wiley.

Allington, R., Johnston, P., & Day, J. (2002). Exemplary fourth-grade teachers. *Language Arts, 79* (6), 462–466.

Allington, R. & Walmsley, S. (Eds.) (1995). *No quick fix: Rethinking literacy programs in America's elementary schools.* New York: Teachers College Press.

Ambruster, B. (1996). Considerate text. In D. Lapp, J. Flood, & N. Farnan (Eds.), *Content area reading and learning: Instructional strategies* (2nd ed.), pp. 47–58. Boston: Allyn and Bacon.

Ames, C., DeStefano, L., Watkins, T., & Sheldon, S. (1995). Teachers' school-to-home communications and parent involvement: The role of parent perceptions and beliefs. (Report NO. CFC28). Baltimore, MD: Center of Families, Communities, Schools and Student Learning.

Anders, P. & Lloyd, C. (1996). The significance of prior knowledge in the learning of new content-specific ideas. In D. Lapp, J. Flood, & N. Farnan (Eds.), *Content area reading and learning: Instructional strategies* (2nd ed.), pp. 323–338. Boston: Allyn and Bacon.

Anderson, R. (1981). The missing ingredient: Fluent oral reading. *The Elementary School Journal, 81,* 173–177.

Anderson, R. C. & Freebody, P. (1981). Vocabulary knowledge. In J. Guthrie (Ed.), *Comprehension and teaching: Research review,* pp. 77–117. Newark, DE: International Reading Association.

Anthony, H. & Raphael, T. (1996). Using questioning strategies to promote students' active comprehension of content area material. In D. Lapp, J. Flood, & N. Farnan (Eds.), *Content area reading and learning: Instructional strategies* (2nd ed.), pp. 307–322. Boston: Allyn and Bacon.

Ashton-Warner, S. (1963). *Teacher.* New York: Simon & Schuster.

Askew, B. J. (1999). Helping young readers learn how to problem solve words while reading. In I. C. Fountas & G. S. Pinnell (Eds.), *Voices on word matters: Learning about phonics and spelling in the literacy classroom,* pp. 143–154. Portsmouth, NH: Heinemann.

Asselin, M. (2001). Literacy and technology. *Teacher Librarian, 28* (3), 49.

Atwell, N. (1987). *In the middle.* Portsmouth, NH: Heinemann.

Au, K. (1993). *Literacy instruction in multicultural settings.* Fort Worth, TX: Harcourt Brace Jovanovich.

Bagert, B. (1997). *The gooch machine: Poems for children to perform.* Honesdale, PA: Boyds Mills Press.

Bailey-Beard, D. (1999). *Twister.* New York: Farrar, Straus, & Giroux.

Baker, K. (1990). *Who is the beast?* New York: Trumpet Club.

Barr, R., Blachowicz, C., Katz, C., & Kaufman, B. (2002). *Reading diagnosis for teachers: An instructional approach.* (4th ed.). Boston: Allyn & Bacon.

Barry, A. (1998). The evolution of reading tests and other forms of educational assessment. *Clearing House, 71* (4), 231–236.

Baumann, J., Hooten, H., & White, P. (1999). Teaching comprehension through literature: A teacher-research project to develop fifth graders' reading strategies and motivation. *The Reading Teacher, 53* (1), 38–51.

Beall, P. C. & Nipp, S. H. (1979). *Wee sing: Children's songs and fingerplays.* New York: Price Stern Sloan.

Bean, T. W. & Pardi, R. (1979). A field test of a guided reading strategy. *Journal of Reading, 23,* 144–147.

Bear, D., Invernizzi, M., Templeton, S., & Johnston, F. (2004). *Words their way: Word study for phonics, vocabulary, and spelling instruction* (3rd ed.). Upper Saddle River, NJ: Pearson, Merrill, Prentice Hall.

Bear, D., Invernizzi, M., Templeton, S., & Johnston, F. (2000). *Words their way: Word study for phonics, vocabulary and spelling instruction* (2nd ed.). Upper Saddle River, NJ: Merrill.

Bear, D. & Templeton, S. (1998). Exploration in developmental spelling: Foundations for learning and teaching phonics, spelling and vocabulary. *The Reading Teacher, 52* (3), 222–242.

Beck, I. & McKeown, M. (2001). Text talk: Capturing the benefits of read-aloud experiences for younger children. *The Reading Teacher, 55* (1), 10–21.

Beck, I. L. & McKeown, M. G. (1991). Developing questions that promote comprehension: The story map. *Language Arts, 58,* 913–918.

Beck, I., McKeown, M., & Omanson, R. (1987). The effects and uses of diverse vocabulary instructional techniques. In M. G. McKeown & M. E. Curtis, (Eds.), *The nature of vocabulary acquisition.* Hillsdale, NJ: Lawrence Erlbaum.

Bemelmans, L. (1986). *Madeline and the gypsies.* New York: Viking.

Bennett, J. (Ed.) (1987). *Noisy poems.* Oxford, New York: Oxford University Press.

Blachowicz, C. & Fisher, P. (2002). *Teaching vocabulary in all classrooms* (2nd ed.). Upper Saddle River, NJ: Merrill.

Blevins, W. (2001). *Teaching phonics and word study in the intermediate grades.* New York: Scholastic.

Blevins, W. (1998). *Phonics from A to Z: A practical guide.* New York: Scholastic.

Blevins, W. (1997). *Phonemic awareness activities for early reading success.* New York: Scholastic.

Boers, D. (2002). What teachers need of parents. *Education Digest 67* (8), 37–41.

Bond, L. (1996). Norm- and criterion-referenced testing. *Practical assessment, research and evaluation, 5* (2). 4 pages.

Booth, D. (1999). Language delights and word play: The foundation for literacy learning. In I. C. Fountas & G. S. Pinnell (Eds.), *Voices on word matters: Learning about phonics and spelling in the literacy classroom,* pp. 91–102. Portsmouth, NH: Heinemann.

Bos, C. S. & Vaughn, S. (1994). *Strategies for teaching students with learning and behavior problems.* Boston: Allyn and Bacon.

Bottner, B. (1996). *Nana Hannah's piano.* Boston: Houghton Mifflin.

Bottomley, D., Henk, W., & Melnick, S. (1998). Assessing children's views about themselves as writers using the Writer Self-Perception Scale. *The Reading Teacher, 51* (4), 286–296.

Boyle, D. (1998). *Coral reef hideaway: The story of a clown anemonefish.* New York: Scholastic.

Bray, M., Kehle, T., Spackman, V., & Hintze, J. (1998). An intervention program to increase reading fluency. *Special Services in the Schools, 14,* 105–125.

Brett, J. (1995). *Armadillo rodeo.* New York: G. P. Putnam's Sons.

Brett, J. (1991). *Berlioz the bear.* New York: G. P. Putnam's Sons.

Brett, J. (1989). *The Mitten.* New York: G. P. Putnam's Sons.

Brophy, J. & Alleman, J. (1992/93). Elementary social studies textbooks. *Publishing Research Quarterly, 8* (4) 12–23.

Brown, K. (1999/2000). What kind of text—For whom and when? Textual scaffolding for beginning readers. *The Reading Teacher, 53* (4), 292–308.

Bryne, B. & Fielding-Barnsley, R. (1991). Evaluation of a program to teach phonemic awareness to young children: A 2- and 3-year follow-up and a new preschool trial. *Journal of Educational Psychology, 87,* 488–503.

Buchanan, E. (1989). *Spelling for whole language classrooms.* Winnipeg: Whole Language Consultants.

Bulter, F. (1999). Reading partners: Students can help each other read. *Education and Treatment of Children, 22* (4), 415–427.

Bunting, E. (1990). *In the haunted house.* New York: Trumpet Club Special Edition.

Buros Institute (2002). *Reading.* 3 pages. Available at: http://www.unl.edu/buros/index13.html [2003, October 5].

Calkins, L., Montgomery, K., Santman, D., & Falk, B. (1998). *A teacher's guide to standardized reading tests.* Portsmouth, NH: Heinemann.

Calkins, L. M. (1994). *The art of teaching writing* (rev. edition). Portsmouth, NH: Heinemann.

Canizares, S. & Reid, M. (1998). *Who lives in the rainforest?* New York: Scholastic.

Carbo, M. (1998). *Reading styles: High rapid reading gains with diverse learners.* Syosset, NY: National Reading Styles Institute.

Carbo, M. (1997). Four key questions to evaluate reading programs. *Education Digest, 62* (5), 4 pages.

Carbo, M. (1996a). Recorded books raise reading skills. *Education Digest, 61* (9), 4 pages.

Carbo, M. (1996b). Selecting the 'right' reading method. *Teaching PreK–8, 27* (1), 3 pages.

Carbo, M. (1996c). Whole language or phonics? Use both! *Education Digest, 61* (6), 4 pages.

Carbo, M. (1987). *Reading Styles Inventory.* Syosset, NY: National Reading Styles Institute.

Carbo, M. (1983). Research in learning styles and reading: Implications for exceptional children. *Exceptional Children, 49,* 486–494.

Carbo, M. (1978). Teaching reading with talking books. *The Reading Teacher, 32,* 267–273.

Carbo, M. & Cole, R. (1995). Nurture love of reading and test scores. *Education Digest, 61* (4), 3 pages.

Carbo, M., Dunn, R., & Dunn, K. (1986). *Teaching students to read through individual learning styles.* Englewood Cliffs, NJ: Prentice Hall.

Carlstrom, N. (1998). *Guess Who's Coming, Jesse Bear.* New York: Aladdin Paperbacks.

Carlstrom, N. (1986). *Jesse Bear, what will you wear?* New York: Aladdin Paperbacks.

Carr, E. & Wixson, K. (1986). Guidelines for evaluating vocabulary instruction. *Journal of Reading, 29,* 588–595.

Cauley, L. B. (1992). *Clap your hands.* New York: Scholastic.

Celenza, A. H. (2000). *The farewell symphony.* Watertown, WA: Charlesbridge Publishing.

Cerullo, M. (1999). *Dolphins: What they can teach us.* New York: Scholastic.

Chall, J. S. (1983). *Learning to read: The great debate* (rev. ed.). New York: McGraw-Hill.

Chambers, B., Abrami, P., McWhaw, K., & Therrien, M. (2001). Developing a computer-assisted tutoring program to help children at risk learn to read.

Educational Research and Evaluation, 7 (2–3), 223–239.

Ciardiello, A. (1998). Did you ask a good question today? Alternative cognitive and metacognitive strategies. *Journal of Adolescent & Adult Literacy, 42* (3), 210–220.

Clay, M. (2000). *Running records for classroom teachers.* Portsmouth, NH: Heinemann.

Clay, M. (1993). *Reading Recovery: A guidebook for teachers in training.* Portsmouth, NH: Heinemann.

Clay, M. (1991). *Becoming literate: The construction of inner control.* Portsmouth, NH: Heinemann.

Clay, M. (1985). *The early detection of reading difficulties* (3rd ed.). Portsmouth, NH: Heinemann.

Cohen, D. (1968). The effect of literature on vocabulary and reading achievement. *Elementary English, 45,* 209–213, 217.

Cohen, J. (1986). Theoretical considerations of peer tutoring. *Psychology in the School, 23,* 175–186.

Cohn-Vargas, B. & Grose, K. (1998). A partnership for literacy. *Educational Leadership, 55* (8), 45–48.

Cole, J. (Ed.). (1989). *Anna Banana: 101 jump-rope rhymes.* New York: A Beech Tree Paperback Book.

Cole, J. & Calmenson, S. (Eds.) (1990). *Ready . . . Set . . . Read!* New York: Doubleday.

Collins, J. L. (1997). *Strategies for struggling writers.* New York: Guilford.

Cooper, J. D. (2000). *Literacy: Helping children construct meaning* (4th ed.). Boston: Houghton Mifflin.

Cooper, J. D. & Kiger, N. (2001). *Literacy assessment: Helping teachers plan instruction.* Boston: Houghton Mifflin.

Cooper, J. D. & Kiger, N. (2000). *Instructor's resource manual and assessment guide* (4th ed.). Boston: Houghton Mifflin.

Crawford, D. & Carnine, D. (2000). Comparing the effects of textbooks in eight-grade U. S. history: Does conceptual organization help? *Education & Treatment of Children, 23* (4), 387–423.

Cunningham, A. (1990). Explicit versus implicit instruction in phonemic awareness. *Journal of Experimental Child Psychology, 50,* 429–444.

Cunningham, J., Cunningham, P., Hoffman, J., & Yopp, H. (1998). *Phonemic awareness and the teaching of reading: A position statement from the Board of Directors of the International Reading Association.* Newark, DE: International Reading Association.

Cunningham, P. (2001). *Phonics they use: Words for reading and writing* (3rd ed.). New York: Longman.

Cunningham, P. (2000). *Phonics they use: Words for reading and writing.* New York: Addison-Wesley.

Cunningham, P. & Allington, R. (2003). *Classrooms that work: They can all read and write* (3rd ed.). Boston: Allyn & Bacon.

Dahl, K. & Scharer, P. (2000). Phonics teaching and learning in whole language classrooms: New evidence from research. *The Reading Teacher, 53* (7), 584–594.

Dale, E., O'Rourke, J., & Bamman, H. (1971). *Techniques of teaching vocabulary.* Palo Alto, CA: Field Educational Publication.

Daneman, M. & Ellis, M. (1995). Memory for expository text: The effects of verbal and pictorial enhancements. *Educational Psychology, 15* (2), 115–127.

Daniels, H., Zemelman, S., & Bizar, M. (1999). Whole language works: Sixty years of research. *Educational Leadership, 57* (2), 32–41.

Danziger, P. (2001). *A is for Amber: It's Justin time, Amber Brown.* New York: G. P. Putnam's Sons.

Darling-Hammond, L. (1999). *Teacher quality and student achievement: A review of state policy evidence.* Seattle: Center for Teaching Policy, University of Washington.

Davey, B. (1983). Think aloud: Modeling the cognitive processes of reading comprehension. *Journal of Reading, 27,* 44–47.

Davidson, A. (1991). *Birds of a feather.* Auckland, New Zealand: Shortland Publications.

Davis, F. B. (1968). Research in comprehension in reading. *Reading Research Quarterly, 3,* 499–544.

Davis, F. B. (1943). Fundamental factors of comprehension in reading. *Psychometrika, 9,* 185–197.

dePaola, T. (1999). *26 Fairmount Avenue.* New York: G. P. Putnam's Sons.

dePaola, T. (1997). *Strega Nona.* New York: G. P. Putnam's Sons.

DeFord, D. E. (1985). Validating the construct of theoretical orientation in reading instruction. *Reading Research Quarterly, 20,* 351–367.

DeMauro, L. (1990). *Bats.* New York: Trumpet Club.

Demi. (1990). *The empty pot.* New York: Trumpet Club.

Dolby Laboratories (1997). *Children's Favorites.* Redway, CA: Music and Little People.

Dolch, E.W. (1948). *Problems in reading.* New York: The Garrard Press.

Donahue, P., Voelkl, K., Campbell, J., & Mazzeo, J. (1999). National assessment of educational progress: 1998 reading report card for the nation and the states. Princeton, NJ: Educational Testing Service.

Donaldson, M. (1978). *Children's minds.* Glasgow, Scotland: Fontana/Collins.

Dorhout, J. (2002). *Reading: Multi-media resources.* Waterloo, IA: Technology Center, Waterloo Community Schools.

Doty, D., Popplewell, S., & Byers, G. (2001). Interactive CD-ROM storybooks and young readers' reading. *Journal of Research on Computing in Education, 33* (4), 374–385.

Dowhower, S. (1999). Supporting a strategic stance in the classroom: A comprehension framework for helping teachers help students to be strategic. *The Reading Teacher, 52* (7), 672–688.

Dowhower, S. (1991). Speaking of prosody: Fluency's unattended bedfellow. *Theory Into Practice, 30,* 165–175.

Dowhower, S. (1989). Effects of repeated reading on second-grade transitional readers' fluency and comprehension. *Reading Research Quarterly, 22,* 389–406.

Dowhower, S. (1987). Effects of repeated readings on second-grade transitional readers' fluency and comprehension. *Reading Research Quarterly, 22* (2), 180–202.

Downes, T. & Fatouros, C. (1996). *Learning in an electron world: Computers and the language arts classroom.* Portsmouth, NH: Heinemann.

Duffelmeyer, F. (2002). Alphabet activities on the internet. *The Reading Teacher, 55* (7), 631–635.

Duffy, G. (1997). Powerful models or powerful teachers? An argument for teachers as entrepreneurs. In S. Stahl & D. Hayes (Eds.), *Instructional models in reading,* pp. 331–365. Mahwah, NJ: Erlbaum.

Duffy, G. & Hoffman, J. (1999). In pursuit of an illusion: The flawed search for a perfect method. *The Reading Teacher, 53* (1), 10–16.

Duffy-Hester, A. (1999). Teaching struggling readers in elementary school classrooms: A review of classroom reading programs and principles for instruction. *The Reading Teacher, 52* (5), 480–495.

Dunn, R., Denig, S., & Lovelace, M. K. (2001). Two sides of the same coin or different strokes for different folks? *Teacher Librarian, 28* (3), 9 pages.

DuPont, A., (1998). Technology night. *Educational Leadership, 55* (8), 74–75.

Eccles, J. & Harold, R. (1993). Parent–school involvement during the early adolescent years. *Teachers College Record, 94,* 560–587.

Ehri, L. (1994). Development of the ability to read words: Update. In R. Ruddell, M. R. Ruddell, & H. Singer (Eds.), *Theoretical models and processes of reading,* pp. 323–358. Newark, DE: International Reading Association.

Ehri, L. C., Numes, S. R., Willows, D. M., Schuster, B. V., Yaghoub-zadeh, Z., & Shanahan, T. (2001).

Phonemic awareness instruction helps children learn to read: Evidence from the National Reading Panel's meta-analysis. *Reading Research Quarterly, 36* (3), 250–287.

Ekwall, E. (1986). *Teacher's handbook on diagnosis and remediation in reading.* Boston: Allyn & Bacon.

Eldredge, J. L. (1999). *Phonics for teachers: Self-instruction, methods and activities.* Upper Saddle River, NJ: Merrill.

Elkonin, D. B. (1973). U.S.S.R. In J. Downing (Ed.), *Comparative reading.* New York: Macmillan.

Falwell, C. (1998). *Word wizard.* New York: Clarion Books.

Fargeon, E. (1987). Jazz-man. In J. Bennett (Ed.), *Noisy poems.* Oxford, New York: Oxford University Press.

Farndon, J. (2000). *All about planet earth.* New York: Anness Publishing.

Fawson, R. & Reutzel, D. R. (2000). But I only have a basal: Implementing guided reading in the early grades. *The Reading Teacher, 54* (1), 84–97.

Ferroli, L. & Shanahan, T. (1987). Kindergarten spelling: Explaining its relation to first grade reading. In J. E. Readence and R. S. Baldwin (Eds.), *Research in literacy: Merging perspectives* (36th yearbook of the National Reading Conference). Rochester, NY: National Reading Conference.

Fiderer, A. (1999). *40 rubrics and checklists to assess reading and writing.* New York: Scholastic.

Fielding, L. G., Wilson, P. T., & Anderson, R. C. (1986). A new focus on free reading: The role of trade books in reading instruction. In T. E. Raphael (Ed.), *Contexts of school-based literacy,* pp. 149–160. New York: Random House.

Finn, J. (1998). Parental engagement that makes a difference. *Educational Leadership, 55* (8), 20–24.

Fisher, D. (2001). Cross-age tutoring: Alternatives to the reading resource room for struggling adolescent readers. *Journal of Instructional Psychology, 28* (4), 234–241.

Fleischman, P. (2000). *Big talk: Poems for four voices.* Cambridge, MA: Candlewick Press.

Fleischman, P. (1988). *Joyful noise: Poems for two voices.* New York: Harper & Row.

Fleischman, P. (1985). *I am phoenix: Poems for two voices.* New York: Harper Trophy.

Foorman, B., Francis, D., Fletcher, J., Schatschneider, C., & Mehta, P. (1998). The role of instruction in learning to read: Preventing reading failure in at-risk children. *Journal of Educational Psychology, 90,* 37–58.

Foorman, B., Novy, D., Francis, D., & Liberman, D. (1991). How letter-sound instruction mediates progress in first-grade reading and spelling. *Journal of Education Psychology, 83,* 456–469.

Fountas, I. & Pinnell, G. S. (2001). *Guiding readers and writers, grades 3–6: Teaching comprehension, genre, and content literacy.* Portsmouth, NH: Heinemann.

Fountas, I. C. & Pinnell, G. S. (1999a). *Matching books to readers: Using leveled books in guided reading, K–3.* Portsmouth, NH: Heinemann.

Fountas, I. C. & Pinnell, G. S. (Eds.) (1999b). *Voices on word matters: Learning about phonics and spelling in the literacy classroom.* Portsmouth, NH: Heinemann.

Fountas, I. C. & Pinnell, G. S. (1996). *Guided reading: Good first teaching for all children.* Portsmouth, NH: Heinemann.

Fox, B. & Wright, M. (1997). Connecting school and home literacy experiences through cross-age reading. *The Reading Teacher, 50* (5), 396–403.

Fox, M. (1989). *Shoes for grandpa.* New York: Scholastic.

Fox, M. (1983). *Possum magic.* San Diego, CA: Gulliver Books.

Fresch, M. J. (2000). What we learned from Josh: Sorting out word sorting. *Language Arts, 77* (3), 232–240.

Fresch, M. J. & Wheaton, A. (1997). Sort, search, and discover: Spelling in the child-centered classroom. *The Reading Teacher, 51* (1), 20–31.

Fry, E. (2002). Readability versus leveling. *The Reading Teacher, 56* (3), 286–291.

Fry, E. (1987). Picture nouns for reading vocabulary improvement. *The Reading Teacher, 41* (2), 187.

Fry, E. (1977). Fry's readability graph: Clarifications, validity, and extension to level 17. *Journal of Reading, 21,* 242–252.

Fuchs, D. & Fuchs, L. (1992). Identifying a measure for monitoring student reading progress. *School Psychology Review, 21* (1), 45–58.

Fuchs, D., Fuchs, L., Mathes, R., & Simmon, D. (1997). Peer-assisted learning strategies: Making classrooms more responsive to diversity. *American Educational Research Journal, 34* (1), 174–206.

Gadt-Johnson, C. & Price, G. (2000). Comparing students with high and low preferences for tactile learning. *Education, 120* (3), 5 pages.

Galin, J. R. & Latchaw, J. (1998). *The dialogic classroom: Teachers integrating computer technology, pedagogy and research.* Urbana, IL: National Council of Teachers of English.

Gardner, H. (1993). *Multiple intelligences: The theory into practice.* New York: Basic Books.

Gardner, H. (1983). *Frames of mind: The theory of multiple intelligences.* New York: Basic Books.

Gauthier, L. (2001). Coop-Dis-Q: A reading comprehension strategy. *Intervention in School & Clinic, 36* (4), 217–221.

Gentry, J. (1987). *Spell . . . is a four-letter word.* Portsmouth, NH: Heinemann.

Gentry, J. R. & Gillet, J. W. (1993). *Teaching kids to spell.* Portsmouth, NH: Heinemann.

George, W. (1989). *Box turtle at Long Pond.* New York: A Trumpet Club Special Edition.

Giannetti, C. & Sagarese, M. (1998). Turning parents from critics to allies. *Educational Leadership, 55* (8), 40–42.

Gill, S. (2000). Reading with Amy: Teaching and learning through reading conferences. *The Reading Teacher, 53* (6), 500–509.

Gillet, J. W. & Temple, C. (2000). *Understand reading problems: Assessment and instruction* (5th ed.). New York: Longman.

Giorgis, C. & Johnson, N. (2002). Multiple perspectives. *The Reading Teacher, 55* (5), 486–494.

Gipe, J. (1995). *Corrective reading techniques for classroom teachers* (3rd ed.). Scottsdale, AZ: Gorsuch Scarisbrick.

Glazer, T. (1973). *Eye Winker, Tom Tinker, Chin Chopper.* New York: Doubleday.

Goldish, M. (1993). *Step inside the rain forest.* New York: MacMillan.

Goodman, K. (1996). *Ken Goodman: On reading.* Portsmouth, NH: Heinemann.

Goodman, K. (1969). Analysis of reading miscues: Applied psycholinguistics. *Reading Research Quarterly, 5* (1), 652–658.

Goodman, Y. (1996). *Notes from a kidwatcher: Selected writings of Yetta M. Goodman.* Portsmouth, NH: Heinemann.

Goodman, Y. (1972/1997). Reading diagnosis—qualitative or quantitative? *The Reading Teacher, 50* (7), 534–538.

Goodman, Y. & Burke, C. L. (1972). *Reading miscue inventory: Procedures for diagnosis and evaluation.* New York: MacMillan.

Goodman, Y. & Marek, A. (1996). *Retrospective miscue analysis: Revaluing readers and reading.* Katonah, NY: Richard C. Owen.

Goodman, Y., Watson, D., & Burke, C. (1996). *Reading strategies: Focus on comprehension* (2nd ed.). Katonah, NY: Richard C. Owen.

Goodman, Y., Watson, D., & Burke, C. (1987). *Reading miscue inventory: Alternative procedures.* Katonah, NY: Richard C. Owen.

Goyen, J. (1992). Diagnosis of reading: Is there a case? *Educational Psychology, 12* (3/4), 13 pages.

Graham, S. & Harris, K. (1997). It can be taught, but it does not develop naturally: Myths and realities in writing instruction. *School Psychology Review, 26* (3), 414–425.

Graham, S., Harris, K. R., MacArthur, C., & Schwartz, S. (1997). Writing instruction. In B. Y. L. Wong (Ed.), *Learning about disabilities.* New York: Academic Press.

Graves, D. (1994). *A fresh look at writing.* Portsmouth, NH: Heinemann.

Graves, D. (1991). *Build a literate class.* Portsmouth, NH: Heinemann.

Graves, D. (1990, July 27). The process-writing model. Paper presented at OKTAWL Conference, Norman, OK.

Graves, M. F. (1987). The roles of instruction in fostering vocabulary development. In M. G. McKeown & M. E. Curtis (Eds.), *The nature of vocabulary acquisition,* pp. 165–184. Hillsdale, NJ: Lawrence Erlbaum.

Grout (1964). A history of Western music. New York: W. W. Norton.

Guarino, D. (1989). *Is your mama a llama?* New York: Scholastic.

Gunning, T. G. (2000). *Phonological awareness and primary phonics.* Boston: Allyn & Bacon.

Hadaway, N., Vardell, S., & Young, T. (2001). Scaffolding oral language development through poetry for students learning English. *The Reading Teacher, 54* (5), 796–806.

Hague, K. (1984). *Alphabears: An ABC book.* New York: Henry Holt.

Halford, J. M. (1998). For significant support, turn to seniors. *Educational Leadership, 55* (8), 40–42.

Hall, D. P. & Cunningham, P. M. (1999). Multilevel word study: word charts, word walls and word sorts. In I. C. Fountas & G. S. Pinnell (Eds.), *Voices on word matters: Learning about phonics and spelling in the literacy classroom,* pp. 114–130. Portsmouth, NH: Heinemann.

Hall, K. (1995). *A bad, bad, day.* New York: Scholastic.

Hamilton, R. & Kucan, L. (1997). *Questioning the author: An approach for enhancing student engagement with text.* Newark, DE: International Reading Association.

Hanf, M. B. (1971). Mapping: A technique for translating reading into thinking. *Journal of Reading, 14,* 225–230, 270.

Hansen, J. (1987). *When writers read.* Portsmouth, NH: Heinemann.

Harris, A. J. & Sipay, E. R. (1990). *How to increase reading ability* (8th ed.). New York: Longman.

Harris, T. & Hodges, R. (Eds.). (1995). *The literacy dictionary: The vocabulary of reading and writing.* Newark, DE: International Reading Association.

Harvey, T. (1998). The curse of the foul-smelling armpit. In B. Lansky (Ed.), *Miles of smiles: Kids pick the funniest poems, Book #3,* pp. 66–67. New York: Meadowbrook Press.

Hawisher, G. & Selfe, C. (1999). Reflections on research in computers and composition studies at the century end. In J. Hancock (Ed.), *Teaching literacy using information technology,* pp. 31–47. Newark, DE: International Reading Association.

Heald-Taylor, B. G. (1998). Three paradigms of spelling instruction in grades 3 to 6. *The Reading Teacher, 51* (5), 404–412.

Hedrick, W. & Pearish, A. (1999). Good reading instruction more important than who provides the instruction or where it takes place. *The Reading Teacher, 52* (7), 716–726.

Heller, R. (1989). *Many luscious lollipops.* New York: Grosset & Dunlap.

Heller, R. (1987). *A cache of jewels.* New York: Grosset & Dunlap.

Henderson, A. (1988). Parents are a school's best friend. *Phi Delta Kappan, 70,* 148–153.

Henderson, E. H. (1990). *Teaching spelling* (2nd ed.). Boston: Houghton Mifflin.

Henk, W. A. & Melnick, S. A. (1995). The Reader-Self Perception Scale (RSPS): A new tool for measuring how children feel about themselves as readers. *The Reading Teacher, 48,* 470–482.

Henkel, J. (2002). Finding activities for kids after school. *FDA Consumer, 36* (3), 33.

Herman, P. (1985). The effects of repeated readings on reading rate, pauses, and word recognition accuracy. *Reading Research Quarterly, 20* (3), 553–565.

Herman, P. A., Anderson, R. C., Pearson, P. D., & Nagy, W. E. (1987). Incidental acquisition of word meaning from expositions with varied text features. *Reading Research Quarterly, 22,* 263–284.

Hesse, K. (1999). *Come on, rain!* New York: Scholastic.

Hesse, K. (1998). *Just juice.* New York: Scholastic.

Hessell, J. (1989). *Secret soup.* Crystal Lake, IL: Rigby.

Heubach, K. (December, 1995). Integrating literature into fourth-grade social studies curriculum: The effects on student learning and attitude. Paper presented at the meeting of National Reading Conference, New Orleans, LA.

Hiebert, E., (1999). Text matters in learning to read. *The Reading Teacher, 52* (6), 552–566.

Higgins, N. & Hess, L. (1999). Using electronic books to promote vocabulary development. *Journal of Research on Computing in Education, 31* (4), 425–431.

Ho, E. S. & Williams, J. (1996). Effects of parental involvement of eighth grade achievement. *Sociology of Education, 69* (2), 126–141.

Ho, B. (2002). Application of participatory action research to family school intervention. *School Psychology Review, 31* (1), 106–122.

Holdaway, D. (1979). *The foundations of literacy.* Sydney, Australia: Ashton Scholastic.

Holt, K. W. (1998). *Mister and me.* New York: G. P. Putnam's Sons.

Hooker, Y. (1981). *One green frog.* New York: Grosset & Dunlap.

Hoover-Dempsey, D. & Sandler, H. (1997). Why do parents become involved in their children's education? *Review of Education Research, 67,* 3–42.

Hughes, M. & Searle, D. (2000). Spelling and "the second 'R.'" *Language Arts, 77* (3), 203–208.

Hurd, E. T. (1970). *Johnny Lion's bad day.* New York: Trumpet Club.

Hurst, C. (2000). Guided reading can strengthen comprehension skills. *Teaching PreK-8, 31* (2), 70–72.

Illingworth, M. (1996). *Real-life math problem solving.* New York: Scholastic.

International Reading Association (2003). *International Reading Association's summary of the (U. S.) National Reading Panel Report.* [Online]. Available at: http://www.reading.org/advocacy/nrp/chapter2.html. [2003, October 5].

International Reading Association (2002). Educators meet to discuss early childhood literacy issues. *Reading Today, 20* (1), 1.

International Reading Association (2000). All about assessment. *Reading Today, 18* (2), 34.

International Reading Association & The National Association for the Education of Young Children (1998). Learning to read and write: Developmentally appropriate practices for young children. *Young Children, 53* (4), 30–46.

International Reading Association and The National Council of Teachers of English (1996). *Standards for the English language arts.* Newark, DE: International Reading Association & Urbana, IL: National Council of Teachers of English.

Invernizzi, M., Rosemary, C., Juel, C., & Richard, H. (1997). At-risk readers and community volunteers: A three-year perspective. *Scientific Studies of Reading, 1* (3), 279–300.

Ivey, G. & Broaddus, K. (2000). Tailoring the fit: Reading instruction and middle school readers. *The Reading Teacher, 54* (1), 68–78.

Jackman, H. (1999). *Sing me a story! Tell me a song!* Thousand Oaks, CA: Corwin Press.

Jacobs, F. (1979). *Sam the sea cow.* New York: A Trumpet Club Special Edition.

Jacobson, J., Thrope, L., Fisher, D., Lapp, D., Frey, N., & Flood, J. (2001). Cross-age tutoring: A literacy improvement approach for struggling adolescent readers. *Journal of Adolescent & Adult Literacy, 44* (6), 528–537.

Jenkins, J. R., Stein, M., & Wysocki, K. (1984). Learning vocabulary through reading. *American Education Research Journal, 21,* 767–788.

Jitendra, A., Hoppes, M., & Xin, Y. P. (2000). Enhancing main idea comprehension for students with learning problems: The role of a summarization strategy and self-monitoring instruction. *Journal of Special Education, 34* (3), 127–140.

Johnston, F. (2001a). Spelling exceptions: Problems or possibilities? *The Reading Teacher, 54* (4), 372–378.

Johnston, F. (2001b). The utility of phonics generalizations: Let's take another look at Clymer's conclusions. *The Reading Teacher, 55* (2), 132–143.

Johnston, F., Invernizzi, M., & Juel, C. (1998). *Book buddies: Guidelines for volunteer tutors of emergent readers.* New York: The Guilford Press.

Jongsma, K. (2000). Teaching—aids & devices—book review. *The Reading Teacher, 54* (1), 80–83.

Jongsma, K. (1999/2000). Vocabulary and comprehension strategy development. *The Reading Teacher, 53* (4), 310–313.

Joosse, B. (1991). *Mama, do you love me?* New York: Scholastic.

Joyce, I. (1967). *Never talk to strangers.* New York: Scholastic.

Kalan, R. (1981). *Jump, frog, jump!* New York: Greenwillow Books.

Kane, S. (1999). Teaching decoding strategies without destroying story. *The Reading Teacher, 52* (7), 770–772.

Kear, D., Coffman, G., McKenna, M., & Ambrosio, A. (2000). Measuring attitude toward writing: A new tool for teachers. *The Reading Teacher, 54* (1), 10–23.

Keith, T. (1991). Parent involvement and achievement in high school. *Advances in Reading/Language Research, 5* (1), 125–141.

Keith, T. Z., Keith, P. B., Quirk, K. J., Sperduto, J., Santillo, S., & Killings, S. (1998). Longitudinal effects of parent involvement on high school grades: Similarities and differences across gender and ethnic groups. *Journal of School Psychology, 36,* 335–363.

King, S. (1996). Classroom materials. *Roeper Review, 18* (4), 303.

Kirk, D. (1999). *Miss Spider's new car.* New York: Scholastic Press. (Board book)

Kletzien, S. B. (1991). Strategy use by good and poor comprehenders reading expository text of differing levels. *Reading Research Quarterly, 26,* 67–86.

Koskinen, P., Blum, I., Bisson, S., Phillips, S., Creamer, T., & Baker, T. (1999). Shared reading, books, and audiotapes: Supporting diverse students in school and at home. *The Reading Teacher, 52* (5), 430–444.

Krashen, S. (1993). *The power of reading.* Englewood, CO: Libraries Unlimited.

Kreuger, E. & Braun, B. (1998/1999). Books and buddies: Peers tutoring peers. *The Reading Teacher, 52* (4), 410–415.

Kuhn, M. (2000). The effects of repeated readings and non-repeated readings on comprehension. Unpublished doctoral dissertation, University of Georgia, Athens.

Labbo, L. & Teale, W. (1990). Cross-age reading: A strategy for helping poor readers. *The Reading Teacher, 43,* 362–369.

Langeland, D. (1997). *Octopus' den.* New York: Scholastic.

Lansky, B. (2000). *If pigs could fly . . . and other deep thoughts.* New York: Meadowbrook Press.

Lansky, B. (Ed.). (1998). *Miles of smiles: Kids pick the funniest poems, book #3.* New York: Meadowbrook Press.

Lapp, D., Flood, J., & Farnan, N. (1996). *Content area reading and learning: Instructional strategies* (2nd ed.). Boston: Allyn and Bacon.

Larkin, R. B. (2001). Can we act it out? *The Reading Teacher, 54* (5), 478–481.

Lauber, P. (1986). *Volcano: The eruption and healing of Mount St. Helens.* New York: Bradbury Press.

Learning First Alliance. (2000). *Every child reading: A professional development guide.* Baltimore, MD: Association for Supervision and Curriculum Development.

Lipson, M. & Lang, L. (1991). Not as easy as it seems: Some unresolved questions about fluency. *Theory Into Practice, 30,* 218–227.

London, J. (1994). *Liplap's wish.* New York: Scholastic.

Los Angeles County Office of Education. (2001). Yopp-Singer test of phonemic segmentation. [Online]. Available at: http://teams.lacoe.edu/reading/assessments/yopp.html [2003, October 5].

Love, F. (1996). Communication with parents: What beginning teachers can do. *College Student Journal, 30* (4), 440–445.

Lyons, C. A. (1999). Letter learning in the early literacy classroom. In I. C. Fountas & G. S. Pinnell (Eds.), *Voices on word matters: Learning about phonics and spelling in the literacy classroom*, pp. 57–66. Portsmouth, NH: Heinemann.

MacDonald, M. R. (2001). *The parent's guide to storytelling: How to make up new stories and retell old favorites*. Little Rock, AR: August House.

MacLulich, C. (1996). *Frogs*. New York: Scholastic.

Maheady, L., Harper, G. F., & Mallette, B. (1991). Peer-mediated instruction: A review of potential application for special education. *Reading, Writing and Learning Disabilities, 7*, 75–103.

Manning, M. (2001). Characterization. *Teaching PreK–8, 31* (8), 84–87.

Markle, S. (1996). *Outside and inside sharks*. New York: Aladdin Paperbacks.

Martens, P. (1998). Using retrospective miscue analysis to inquire: Learning from Michael. *The Reading Teacher, 52* (2), 176–180.

Martin, B., Jr. & Archambault, J. (1987). *Knots on a counting rope*. New York: Trumpet Club.

Martin, B., Jr. (1983). *Brown bear, brown bear, what do you see?* New York: Henry Holt.

Martin, J. (1991a). *Carrot/parrot*. New York: Trumpet Club Special Edition.

Martin, J. (1991b). *Mitten/kitten*. New York: Trumpet Club Special Edition.

Martinez, M., Roser, N., & Strecker, S. (1998/1999). "I never thought I could be a star": A readers theatre ticket to fluency. *The Reading Teacher, 52* (4), 326–334.

Maslow, A. (1987). *Motivation and personality* (3rd ed.). New York: Harper & Row.

Mastropieri, M., Leinart, A., & Scruggs, T. (1999). Strategies to increase reading fluency. *Intervention in School and Clinic, 34* (5), 278–285.

Matthew, K. (1997). A comparison of influence of interactive CD-ROM storybooks. *Journal of Research on Computing in Education, 29* (3), 262–276.

May, F. (2001). *Unraveling the seven myths of reading: Assessment and intervention practices for counteracting their effects*. Boston: Allyn and Bacon.

McBratney, S. (1994). *Guess how much I love you*. New York: Scholastic.

McCarrier, A., Pinnell, G. S., & Fountas, I. C. (2000). *Interactive writing: How language and literacy come together, K–2*. Portsmouth, NH: Heinemann.

McCormick, S. (1999). *Instructing students who have literacy problems* (3rd ed.). Upper Saddle River, NJ: Merrill.

McGill-Franzen, A. (2000). Policy and instruction: What is the relationship? In M. Kamil et al., (Eds.), *Handbook of reading research (Vol. III)*, pp. 891–908. Mahwah, NJ: Erlbaum.

McGuinness, D. (1999). *My first phonics book*. New York: Dorling Kindersley.

McKenna M. C. & Kear, D. J. (1990). Measuring attitude toward reading: A new tool for teachers. *The Reading Teacher, 43*, 626–639.

McKeown, M. & Curtis, M. E. (Eds.). (1987). *The nature of vocabulary acquisition*, pp. 165–184. Hillsdale, NJ: Lawrence Erlbaum.

McPhail, D. (1993). *Pigs aplenty, pigs galore!* New York: Scholastic.

Meyer, B., Marsiske, M., & Willis, S. (1993). Test processing variables predict the readability of everyday document read by older adults. *Reading Research Quarterly, 28* (3), 235–249.

Miller, M. (1996). *Quick and easy learning games: Math*. New York: Scholastic.

Miller, W. (2000). *Strategies for developing emergent literacy*. Boston: McGraw Hill.

Miller. W. (1988). *Reading teacher's complete diagnosis and correction manual*. New York: Center for Applied Research in Education.

Moats, L. (1995). *Spelling, development, disability, and instruction*. Baltimore: York Press.

Moore, D. W. & Moore, S. A. (1986). Possible sentences. In E. K. Dishner, T. W. Bean, J. E. Readence, & D. W. Moore (Eds.), *Reading in the content areas*, pp. 174–178. Dubuque, IA: Kendall Hunt.

Moore, R. & Aspegren, C. (2001). Reflective conversations between two learners: Retrospective miscue analysis. *Journal of Adolescent & Adult Literacy, 44* (6), 492–504. [Online]. Available at:

Moore, R. & Brantingham, K. L. (2003). Nathan: A case study in reader response and retrospective miscue analysis. *The Reading Teacher, 56* (5), 466–474.

Morris, D. (1999). *The Howard Street Tutoring manual: Teaching at-risk readers in the primary grades*. New York: Guildford Press.

Morris, D. (1993). A selective history of the Howard Street Tutoring Program (1979–1989). (ERIC Document Reproduction Service NO. 355-473).

Morris, D. & Nelson, L. (1992). Supported oral reading with low-achieving second graders. *Reading Research and Instruction, 31*, 49–63.

Morris, D., Shaw, B., & Perney, J. (1990). Helping low readers in grades 2 and 3: An after-school volunteer tutoring program. *The Elementary School Journal, 91*, 132–150.

Morrow, L. M. (1997). *Literacy in the early years: Helping children read and write.* Boston: Allyn & Bacon.

Mosenthal, J. (1994). Text structure. In A. Purves, L. Papa, & J. Jordan (Eds.), *Encyclopedia of English studies and languages arts,* pp. 1201–1203. New York: Scholastic.

Moss, L. (1995). *Zin! Zin! Zin! A violin.* New York: Scholastic.

Moustafa, M. (1996). Reconceptualizing phonics instruction in a balanced approach to reading. Unpublished manuscript. San Jose State University.

Moustafa, M. & Maldonado-Colon, E. (1999). Whole-to-parts phonics instruction: Building on what children know to help them know more. *The Reading Teacher, 52* (5). 448–456.

Muller, C. & Kerbow, D. (1993). Parent involvement in the home, school and community. In B. Schneider & J. S. Coleman (Eds.), *Parents, their children, and schools,* pp. 13–42. Boulder, CO: Westview.

Murphy, S. (1995). Revisioning reading assessment: Remembering to learn from the legacy of reading tests. *Clearing House, 68 (4),* 5 pages.

Nagy, W. E. (1988). *Teaching vocabulary to improve reading comprehension.* Urbana, IL: National Council of Teachers of English.

Nagy, W. E. & Herman, P. A. (1987). Breadth and depth of vocabulary knowledge: Implications for acquisition and instruction. In M. G. McKeown & M. E. Curtis (Eds.), *The nature of vocabulary acquisition,* pp. 19–35. Hillsdale, NJ: Lawrence Erlbaum.

Nagy, W. E., Herman, P. A., & Anderson, R. C. (1985). Learning words for context. *Reading Research Quarterly, 20,* 233–253.

National Center for Education Statistics (1998). Statistical analysis report: Fathers' involvement in their children's schools.

National Center for Education Statistics (1996). National Assessment of educational progress facts: Listening to children read aloud: Oral fluency, 1 (1). (Publication No. NCES 95-762).

National Institute of Child Health and Human Development. (2000). *Report of the National Reading Panel: Teaching children to read.* Washington, DC: National Institute for Literacy.

National Institute for Literacy (2000). *Report of national reading panel: Teaching children to read.* Washington, DC: U. S. Department of Health and Human Services.

National PTA (1998). *1998 parent involvement policy.* Chicago, IL: National PTA.

National Reading Panel (2000a). Report of the subgroups. Washington, DC: National Institute of Child Health and Human Development. [Online]. Available at: http://www.nationalreadingpanel.org/Publications/subgroups.htm. [2001, September 30].

National Reading Panel. (2000b). *Teaching children to read: An evidence-based assessment of the scientific research literature on reading and its implications for reading instruction.* Washington, DC: National Institute for Literacy.

National Research Council (1998). *Preventing reading difficulty in young children.* Washington, DC: National Academy of Sciences.

NEA Today (2001). How to increase reading skills through recorded books. *NEA Today, 19* (5), p. 27.

Nicholson, T. (1998). The flashcard strikes back. *The Reading Teacher, 51* (2), 188–192.

Nunnery, J., Ross, S., Smith, L., Slavin, R., Hunter, P., & Stubbs, J. (1999). An assessment of Success for All program component configuration effects on the reading achievement of at-risk first grade students. Baltimore, MD: Center for Research on the Education of Students Placed at Risk, John Hopkins University.

Oakhill, J. & Patel, S. (1991). Can imagery training help children who have comprehension problems? *Journal of Research in Reading, 14,* 106–115.

Ogle, D. M. (1986). K-W-L: A teaching model that develops active reading of expository text. *The Reading Teacher, 39* (7), 564–570.

Oklahoma State Department of Education (2002). *A core curriculum for our children's future: Priority academic student skills (PASS).* Oklahoma City, OK: Oklahoma State Department of Education.

Oliver, K., Wilcox, B., & Eldredge, J. L. (2000). Effect of difficulty levels on second-grade delayed readers using dyad reading. *Journal of Education Research, 94* (2), 113–120.

Olson, M. & Gee, T. (1991). Content reading instruction in the primary grades: Perceptions and strategies. *The Reading Teacher, 45,* 298–307.

Opie, I. (Ed.). (1996). *My very first Mother Goose.* Cambridge, MA: Candlewick Press.

Oppenheim, J. (1989). *"Not now!" said the cow.* New York: Byron Press Book.

O'Shea, L., Sindelar, P., & O'Shea, D. (1987). The effects of repeated reading and attentional cues on the reading fluency and comprehension of learning disabled readers. *Learning Disabilities Research, 2* (1), 103–109.

Oster, L. (2001). Using the think-aloud for reading instruction. *The Reading Teacher, 55* (1), 64–70.

Palmer, R. & Stewart, R. (1997). Nonfiction trade books in content area instruction: Realities and potential. *Journal of Adolescent & Adult Literacy,* 40 (8) 630–642.

Pappas, T. (1991). *Math talk: Mathematical ideas in poems for two voices.* San Carlos, CA: Wide World Publishing/Tetra.

Park, L. S. (2001). *A single shard.* New York: Clarion Books.

Pearson, P. D. & Fielding, L. (1991). Comprehension instruction. In R. Barr, M. Kamil, P. Mosenthal, & P. D. Pearson (Eds.), *Handbook of reading research* (Vol. 2), pp. 815–860. New York: Longman.

Peart, N. & Campbell, F. (1999). At-risk students' perceptions of teacher effectiveness. *Journal for a Just & Caring Education, 5* (3), 269–285.

Peck, R. (2000). *A year down yonder.* New York: Dial Books for Young Readers.

Piaget, J. & Inhelder, B. (1969). *The psychology of the child* (H. Weaver, Trans.). New York: Basic Books.

Pikulski, J. J. & Tobin, A. W. (1982). The cloze procedure as an informal assessment technique. In J. J. Pikulski & T. Shanahan (Eds.), *Approaches to the informal evaluation of reading,* pp. 42–62. Newark, DE: International Reading Association.

Pinnell, G. S. (1999). Word solving: Investigating the properties of words. In I. C. Fountas & G. S. Pinnell (Eds.), *Voices on word matters: Learning about phonics and spelling in the literacy classroom,* pp. 3–12. Portsmouth, NH: Heinemann.

Pinnell, G. S. (1989). Reading Recovery: Helping at-risk children learn to read. *The Elementary School Journal, 90,* 161–183.

Pinnell, G. S. & Fountas, I. C. (1998). *Word matters: Teaching phonics and spelling in the reading/writing classroom.* Portsmouth, NH: Heinemann.

Pinnell, G. S., Pikulski, J. J., Wixson, K. K., Campbell, J. R., Gough, R. B., & Beatty, A. S. (1995). *Listening to children read aloud: Data from NAEP's integrated reading performance record (IRPR) at grade 4.* Report No. 23-Fr-04. Prepared by Educational Testing Center for Education Statistics, Office of Educational Research and Improvement, U. S. Department of Education.

Piston, W. (1962). *Harmony* (3rd ed.). New York: W. W. Norton.

Polacco, R. (1987). *Meteor!* New York: Philomel Books.

Prelutsky, J. (Ed.). (1999). *20th century children's poetry treasury.* New York: Alfred A. Knopf.

Prelutsky, J. (1990a). *Beneath a blue umbrella.* New York: Greenwillow Books.

Prelutsky, J. (1990b). *Something big has been here.* New York: Greenwillow Books.

Prelutsky, J. (1984). *The new kid on the block.* New York: Greenwillow Books.

Prelutsky, J. (1983). *Zoo doings: Animal poems.* New York: Trumpet Club Special Edition.

Pressley, M. & Woloshyn, V. (Eds.). (1995). *Cognitive strategy instruction that really improves children's academic performance* (2nd ed.). Cambridge, MA: Brookline.

Pugliano-Martin, C. (1998). *25 just-right plays for emergent readers.* New York: Scholastic.

Rafferty, C. (1999). Literacy in the information age. *Educational Leadership, 57* (2), 22–25.

Rankin-Erickson, J. & Pressley, M. (2000). A survey of instructional practices of special education teachers nominated as effective teachers of literacy. *Learning Disabilities Research & Practice, 15* (4), 20 pages.

Ransom, K., Santa, C. M., Williams, C., & Farstrup, A. (1999). *Using multiple methods of beginning reading instruction: A position statement of the International Reading Association.* Newark, DE: International Reading Association.

Rashotte, C. & Torgeson, J. (1985). Repeated readings and reading fluency in learning disabled children. *Reading Research Quarterly, 20* (2), 180–202.

Rasinski, T. (2000). Speed does matter in reading. *The Reading Teacher, 54* (2), 146–151.

Rasinski, T. & Padak, N. (2000). *Effective reading strategies: Teaching children who find reading difficult* (2nd ed.). Upper Saddle River, NJ: Merrill.

Rasinski, T., Padak, N. (1994). Effects of fluency development on urban second-grade readers. *Journal of Educational Research, 87* (3) 158–165.

Readence, J. & Moore, D. W. (Eds.). (1989). *Reading in the content areas,* pp. 174–178. Dubuque, IA: Kendall-Hunt.

Reutzel, D. R., & Fawson, P. C., (1990). Traveling tales: Connecting parents and children through writing. *The Reading Teacher, 44,* 545–554.

Reutzel, D., Hollingsworth, P. (1993). Effects of fluency training on second graders' reading comprehension. *Journal of Educational Research, 86,* 325–331.

Reutzel, D., Hollingsworth, P., & Eldredge, J. (1994). Oral reading instruction: The impact on student reading development. *Reading Research Quarterly, 29,* 40–62.

Rey, H. A. (1985). *Curious George visits the zoo.* Boston: Houghton Mifflin.

Rich, D. (1998). What parents want from teachers. *Educational Leadership, 55* (8), 37–39.

Richards, M. (2000). Be a good detective: Solve the case of oral reading fluency. *The Reading Teacher, 53* (7), 534–539.

Richardson, J. & Morgan, R. (1997). *Reading to learn in the content areas* (3rd ed.). Belmont, CA: Wadsworth.

Richek, M. A., Caldwell, J. S., Jennings, J. H., & Lerner, J. W. (1996). *Reading problems: Assessment and teaching strategies* (3rd ed.). Boston: Allyn and Bacon.

Rose, D., Parks, M., Androes, K., & McMahon, S. (2000). Imagery-based learning: Improving elementary students' reading comprehension with drama techniques. *Journal of Educational Research, 94* (1), 55–64.

Rosencrans, G. (1998). *The spelling book: Teaching children how to spell, not what to spell.* Newark, DE: International Reading Association.

Routman, R. (1991). *Invitation: Changing as teachers and learners.* Portsmouth, NH: Heinemann.

Ruddell, R. (1964). A study of cloze comprehension technique in relation to structurally controlled reading material. Proceedings of the International Reading Association 9, pp. 298–303.

Rylant, C. (1987). *Henry and Mudge in the green time.* New York: Trumpet Club.

Rymer, R. & Williams, C. (2000). "Wasn't that a spelling word?": Spelling instruction and young children's writing. *Language Arts, 77* (3), 241–249.

Samuels, S., Schermer, N., & Reinking, D. (1992). Reading fluency and techniques for making decoding automatic. In S. Samuels & A. Farstrup (Eds.), *What research says about reading instruction* (2nd ed.), pp. 124–144. Newark, DE: International Reading Association.

Samuels, S. J. (1979/1997). The method of repeated readings. *The Reading Teacher, 50* (5), 376–381.

Sardegna, J. (1994). *The roly-poly spider.* New York: Scholastic.

Savage, H. (2001). *Sound it out: Phonics in a balanced reading program.* Boston: McGraw Hill.

Schatz, E. K. & Baldwin, R. S. (1986). Context clues are unreliable predictors of word meanings. *Reading Research Quarterly, 21,* 439–453.

Schmidt, R., Rozendal, M., & Greenman, G. (2002). Reading instruction in the inclusion classroom. *Remedial and Special Education, 23* (3), 11 pages.

Schneider, R. (1993). *That's not all!* Grand Haven, MI: School Zone.

Schnur, S. (1999). *Spring: An alphabet acrostic.* New York: Clarion.

Schreiber, P. (1991). Understanding prosody's role in reading acquisition. *Theory into Practice, 20,* 158–164.

Schulman, M. B. & Payne, C. D. (2000). *Guided reading: Making it work.* New York: Scholastic.

Seuss, Dr. (1957). *The cat in the hat.* New York: Random House.

Seuss, Dr. (1960). *Green eggs and ham.* New York: Random House.

Shanahan, T. (1997). Reading–writing relationships, thematic units, inquiry learning . . . In pursuit of effective integrated literacy instruction. *The Reading Teacher, 51* (1), 12–19.

Shanahan, T. & Shanahan, S. (1997). Character perspective charting: Helping children to develop a more complete conception of story. *The Reading Teacher, 50* (8), 668–677.

Shanker, J. & Ekwall, E. (2000). *Ekwall/Shanker reading inventory* (4th ed.). Boston: Allyn and Bacon.

Shanker, J. L. & Ekwall, E. E. (1998). *Locating and correcting reading difficulties* (7th ed.). Upper Saddle River, NJ: Merrill.

Shaw, C. (1947). *It looked like spilt milk.* New York: Harper Festival.

Shaw, N. (1992). *Sheep out to eat.* New York: A Trumpet Club Special Edition.

Sheldon, S. (2002). Parents' social networks and beliefs as predictors of parent involvement. *The Elementary School Journal, 102* (4), 301–316.

Shower, P. (1961). *The listening walk.* New York: Harper Trophy.

Sibenaller, K. (2001). Reading assessment tools and tangible improvement. *Median and Methods, 37* (5), 6–8.

Simon, S. (1989). *Whales.* New York: Scholastic.

Sinatra, R. (2000). Teaching learners to think, read, and write more effectively in content subjects. *Clearing House, 73* (5), 266–274.

Sindelar, P., Monda, L., & O'Shea, L. (1990). Effects of repeated readings on instructional and mastery-level readers. *Journal of Educational Research, 83,* 220–226.

Sipe, L. (2001). Invention, convention, and intervention: Invented spelling and the teacher's role. *The Reading Teacher, 55* (3), 264–273.

Sippola, A. (1997). Language master redux. *The Reading Teacher, 51* (3), 271–272.

Slavin, R. E., Madden, N. A., Dolan, L. J., Wasik, B. A., Rose, S. M. Smith, L. J., & Dianda, M. (1996). Success for All: A summary of research. *Journal of Education for Students Placed at Risk, 1* (1), 41–76.

Smith, F. (1999). Why systematic phonics and phonemic awareness instruction constitutes an education hazard. *Language Arts, 77* (2), 150–155.

Smith, F. (1997). *Reading without nonsense* (3rd ed.). New York: Teachers College Press.

Smith, F. (1978). *Reading without nonsense.* New York: Teachers College Press.

Smith, J. & Elley, W. (1997). *How children learn to write.* Katonah, NY: Richard C. Owen.

Smith, N. B. (1965). *American reading instruction.* Newark, DE: International Reading Association.

Snow, C., Burns, M., & Griffin, P. (Eds.). (1998). *Preventing reading difficulties in young children*. Washington, DC: National Academy Press.

Staal, L. (2000). The story face: An adaptation of story mapping that incorporates visualization and discovery learning to enhance reading and writing. *The Reading Teacher, 54* (1), 26–31.

Stahl, S. A. (1986). Three principles of effective vocabulary instruction. *Journal of Reading, 29*, 662–671.

Stahl, S. A. & Fairbanker, M. M. (1986). The effects of vocabulary instruction: A model-based meta-analysis. *Review of Educational Research, 56* (1), 72–110.

Stahl, S. A. & Kapinus, B. A. (1991). Possible sentences: Predicting word meanings to teach content area vocabulary. *The Reading Teacher, 45* (1), 36–43.

Stahl, S. & Kuhn, M. (2002). Center for improvement of early reading achievement. *The Reading Teacher, 55* (6), 582–584.

Stahl, S. & Kuhn, M. (1995). Does whole language or instruction matched to learning styles help children learn to read? *School Psychology Review, 24* (3), 12 pages.

Stahl, S., Heubach, K., & Cramond, B. (1997). *Fluency-oriented reading instruction* (Research Report No. 79). Athens, GA: National Reading Research Center.

Stanley, J. (1992). *Children of the Dust Bowl: The true story of the school at Weedpatch Camp*. New York: A Trumpet Club Special Edition.

Stanovich, K. E. (1991). Word recognition: Changing perspectives. In R. Barr, M. L. Kamil, P. Mosenthal, & P. D. Pearson (Eds.), *Handbook of reading research*, vol. 2, pp. 418–452. Hillsdale, NJ: Erlbaum.

Steinberg, L. (1996). *Beyond the classroom*. New York: Simon & Schuster.

Steele, P. (1994). *I wonder why castles had moats and other questions about long ago*. New York: Kingfisher Books.

Sternberg, R. J. (1987). Most vocabulary is learned from context. In M. G. McKeown & M. E. Curtis (Eds.), *The nature of vocabulary acquisition*, pp. 89–105. Hillsdale, NJ: Lawrence Erlbaum.

Stowe, C. (1996). *Spelling smart!: A ready-to-use activities program for students with spelling difficulties*. West Nyack, NY: The Center for Applied Research in Education.

Sturges, P. (1999). *The Little Red Hen makes a pizza*. New York: Puffin Books.

Sullivan, P. (1998). The PTA's National Standards. *Educational Leadership, 55* (8), 43–44.

Swanson, P. & De La Paz, S. (1998). Teaching effective comprehension strategies to students. *Intervention in School & Clinic, 33* (4), 209–219.

Symons, S. (1993). Prior knowledge affects text search success and extraction of information. *Reading Research Quarterly, 28* (3), 250–259.

Symons, S. & Pressley, M. (1993). Prior knowledge affects text search success and extraction of information. *Reading Research Quarterly, 28* (3), 250–259.

Taberski, S. (2000). *On solid ground*. Portsmouth, NH: Heinemann.

Taylor, B., Pressley, M., & Pearson, D. (2000). Research-supported characteristics of teachers and schools that promote reading achievement. Ann Arbor, MI: Center for the Improvement of Early Reading Achievement (CIERA).

Taylor, B., Hanson, B., Justice-Swanson, K., & Watts, S. (1997). Helping struggling readers: Linking small-group intervention with cross-age tutoring. *The Reading Teacher, 51* (3), 196–209.

Taylor, R. (1996). Adolescents' perceptions of kinship support and family management practices. *Child Development, 21* (3), 687–695.

Tempo, F. (1993). *Origami magic*. New York: Scholastic.

Terban, M. (1988). *Guppies in tuxedos*. New York: Clarion Books.

Texas Education Agency (1997). *TEKS for English Language Arts and Reading*. Austin, TX: Texas State Education Department.

Thompson, R.A. (1971). *Summarizing research pertaining to individualized reading*. Arlington, VA: ERIC Document Reproduction Service (ERIC Document Reproduction Service No. ED 065 836).

Thrope, L. & Wood, D. (2000). Cross-age tutoring for young adolescents. *The Clearing House, 73*, 239–242.

Tierney, R. J., Readence, J. E., & Dishner, E. K. (1990). *Reading strategies and practices: A compendium* (3rd. ed.). Boston: Allyn & Bacon.

Tindal, G. & Marston, D. (1990). *Classroom-based assessment: Evaluating instructional outcomes*. Columbus, OH: Merrill.

Tompkins, G. (2002). *Language arts: Content and teaching strategies*. Upper Saddle River, NJ: Merrill.

Topping, K. & Ehly, S. (1998). *Peer assisted learning*. Mahwah, NJ: Lawrence Erlbaum.

Trelease, J. (2001). *The read-aloud handbook*. New York: Penguin Books.

Trelease, J. (1996). Have your read to your kids today? *Instructor* (May–June), 56–60.

Turbill, J. (2000). Developing a spelling conscience. *Language Arts, 77* (3), 209–217.

Turkle, B. (1976). *Deep in the forest*. New York: Dutton.

Tyler, B. & Chard, D. (2000). Using readers theatre to foster fluency in struggling readers: A twist on the repeated reading strategy. *Reading and Writing Quarterly, 16* (2), 162–169.

U. S. Department of Education (1998). *National assessment of educational progress: 1998 reading report card.* Washington, DC: Government Printing Office.

Ulrich, G. (1995). *My tooth ith loothe: Funny poems to read instead of doing your homework.* South Holland, IL: A Yearling Book.

University of Iowa (1999). Iowa testing programs: Interpreting test scores. [Online]. Available at: http://www.uiowa.edu/~itp/ed-interpret.htm [2003, October 5].

Van Allen, R. (1976). *Language experiences in education.* Boston: Houghton Mifflin.

Van Cleave, J. (1993). *200 gooey, slippery, slimy, weird and fun experiments.* New York: John Wiley.

Vaughn, S. (2000). Fluency and comprehension interventions for third-grade students. *Remedial and Special Education, 21* (6).

Vellutino, R. (1991). Introduction to three studies on reading acquisition: Convergent findings on theoretical foundations of code-oriented versus whole-language approaches to reading instruction. *Journal of Educational Psychology, 83* (4), 437–444.

Vygotsky, L. (1978). *Mind in society: The development of higher psychological processes.* Cambridge, MA: Harvard University Press.

Vygotsky, L. (1962). *Thought and language* (E. Hanfmann & G. Vaka, Eds. & Trans). Cambridge, MA: MIT Press.

Wagner, R. & Torgesen, J. (1987). The nature of phonological processing and its causal role in the acquisition of reading skills. *Psychological Bulletin, 101,* 192.

Wagstaff, J. (1997/1998). Building practical knowledge of letter–sound correspondences: A beginner's word wall and beyond. *The Reading Teacher, 51* (4), 298–304.

Walker, B. (2000). *Diagnostic teaching of reading: Techniques for instruction and assessment.* Upper Saddle River, NJ: Merrill.

Walker, B. (1996). *Diagnostic teaching of reading* (3rd ed.). Englewood Cliffs, NJ: Merrill.

Wallace, B. (1988). *Beauty.* New York: A Minstrel Book.

Wang, M. C., Haertel, G. D., & Walberg, H. J. (1993). Toward a knowledge base for school learning. *Review of Educational Research, 63* (3), 249–295.

Wasik, B. (1999). Reading coaches: An alternative to reading tutors. *The Reading Teacher, 52* (6), 653–657.

Wasik, B. (1998). Using volunteers as reading tutors: Guidelines for successful practices. *The Reading Teacher, 51* (7), 562–571.

Wasik, B. (1997). Volunteer tutoring programs. *Phi Delta Kappan, 79* (4), 282–288.

Watt, F. (1993). *Earthquakes and volcanoes.* New York: Scholastic.

Weaver, C. (2002). *Reading process and practice* (3rd ed.). Portsmouth, NH: Heinemann.

Weaver, C. (1994a). Phonics in whole language classrooms. *ERIC DIGEST.*

Weaver, C. (1994b). *Reading process and practices: From socio-psycholinguistics to whole language* (2nd ed.). Portsmouth, NH: Heinemann.

Weaver, C., Gillmeister-Krause,. L., & Vento-Zogby, G. (1996). *Creating support for effective literacy education.* Portsmouth, NH: Heinemann.

Wiesner, D. (2001). *The three pigs.* New York: Clarion Books.

Wiesner, D. (1997). *Sector 7.* New York: Clarion Books.

Wiesner, D. (1991). *Tuesday.* New York: Clarion Books.

Wiesner, D. (1988). *Freefall.* New York: Clarion Books.

Wiley, B. J. (1999). Interactive writing: The how and why of teaching and learning letters, sounds and words. In I. C. Fountas & G. S. Pinnell (Eds.), *Voices on word matters: Learning about phonics and spelling in the literacy classroom,* pp. 25–36. Portsmouth, NH: Heinemann.

Wilkinson, T. (1994). *Bison for kids.* Minnetonka, MN: NorthWord.

Wilson, R. M. & Cleland, C. J. (1989). *Diagnostic and remedial reading for classroom and clinic.* Columbus, OH: Merrill.

Winn, P., Graham, L., & Prock, L. (1993). A model of poor readers' text-based inferencing: Effects of explanatory feedback. *Reading Research Quarterly, 28* (1), 52–64.

Winter, P. (1976). *The bear and the fly.* New York: Crown.

Wittels, H. & Greisman, J. (1996). *The clear and simple thesaurus dictionary* (Revised). New York: Grosset & Dunlap.

Wolf, J. (1998). Just read. *Educational Leadership, 55* (8), 61–63.

Wolf, M., Miller, L., & Donnelly, K. (2000). Retrieval automaticity, vocabulary elaboration, orthography (RAVE-O): A comprehensive, fluency-based reading intervention program. *Journal of Learning Disabilities, 33* (4), 375–387.

Wood, A. (1964). *The napping house.* San Diego: Harcourt Brace Jovanovich.

Wood, J. (1990). *Caves: Facts and Stories and Activities.* New York: Scholastic.

Woodruff, E. (1991). *Show and tell.* New York: A Trumpet Club Special Edition.

Wray, D. & Medwell, J. (2001). The teaching practices of effective teachers of literacy. *Education Review, 52* (1), 10 pages.

Wray, D., Medwell, J., Fox, R., & Poulson, L. (2000). The teaching of practices of effective teachers of literacy. *Educational Review, 52* (1), 75–85.

Yellin, D., Blake, M., & DeVries, B. (2004). *Integrating the language arts* (3rd ed.). Scottsdale, AZ: Holcomb Hathaway.

Yopp, H. K. & Yopp, R. H. (2000). Supporting phonemic awareness development in the classroom. *The Reading Teacher, 54* (2), 130–143.

Young, A., Bowers, E., & MacKinnon, G. (1996). Effects of prosodic modeling and repeated reading on poor readers' fluency and comprehension. *Applied Psycholinguistics, 17,* 59–84.

Zecker, L. B. (1999). Different texts, different emergent writing forms. *Language Arts, 76* (6), 483–490.

AUTHOR INDEX

SUBJECT INDEX